W9-AUX-748

1967

1967

*Israel, the War, and
the Year That Transformed
the Middle East*

TOM SEGEV

TRANSLATED BY JESSICA COHEN

METROPOLITAN BOOKS

HENRY HOLT AND COMPANY | NEW YORK

m

Metropolitan Books
Henry Holt and Company, LLC
Publishers since 1866
175 Fifth Avenue
New York, New York 10010
www.henryholt.com

Metropolitan Books® and m® are registered
trademarks of Henry Holt and Company, LLC.

Originally published in Israel in 2005 under the title
1967: Vehaaretz shinta et paneiha by Keter Publishers, Jerusalem.

Library of Congress Cataloging-in-Publication Data
Segev, Tom, 1945–
    1967 : Israel, the war, and the year that transformed the
Middle East / Tom Segev; translated by Jessica Cohen.—1st American ed.
        p.   cm.
    Includes bibliographical references and index.
    ISBN-13: 978-0-8050-7057-6
    ISBN-10: 0-8050-7057-5
    1. Israel-Arab War, 1967.   2. Israel—Politics and
government—20th century.   I. Title.   II. Title: Nineteen hundred sixty seven.
III. Title: Nineteen sixty seven.
DS127.S4413 2007
956.04'6—dc22   2006047043

Henry Holt books are available for special promotions and
premiums. For details contact: Director, Special Markets.

First U.S. Edition 2007

Designed by Kelly Too

Printed in the United States of America
1   3   5   7   9   10   8   6   4   2

For Itai, at twenty-five

CONTENTS

PART IV: THEY THOUGHT THEY HAD WON

1967

June 5, 1967, borders

Areas occupied
by Israel after
June 10, 1967

LEBANON

SYRIA

ISRAEL

JORDAN

Suez
Canal

E G Y P T

S I N A I

Eilat

SAUDI
ARABIA

Sharm el-
Sheikh

Straits of Tiran

WEST
BANK

Border of
Israeli-annexed
East Jerusalem

J E R U S A L E M

Mt.
Scopus
Old City

N

Litani River

LEBANON

Banias

DMZ

Dishon

Kuneitra

GOLAN
HEIGHTS

Kibbutz
Yehiam

Haifa

Lake
Tiberias

DMZ

Afula

Jordan River

Jenin

Tul Karem

Netanya

Kfar
Saba

Nablus

Kalkilya

W E S T

B A N K

Tel Aviv

Ramallah

Rishon
Lezion

Jericho

Latrun

JERUSALEM

Bethlehem

GUSH ETZION

Hebron

J O R D A N

Mediterranean

Samua

GAZA
STRIP

Gaza

Khan Younis

Beersheba

Dead
Sea

Rafiah

I S R A E L

El-Arish

Dimona

S I N A I

June 5, 1967, borders

No-Man's-Land

Areas occupied by Israel
after June 10, 1967

Sea

Kms.

0

30

Miles

30

© A. Karl / J. Kemp, 2007

HEROES

1. YEHIAM

On June 5, 1966, in the evening hours, Yosef Weitz lit two candles in memory of his son, Yehiam, on the twentieth anniversary of his death. Weitz, who was seventy-six at the time, was the head forester for the Jewish National Fund (JNF), one of the Zionist movement's institutions, concerned with the acquisition of public land. He had lived in the land of Israel for close to sixty years, during which time the JNF had planted millions of trees. Weitz had come from Russia at the age of eighteen; he began his life in Palestine as an agricultural laborer and was promoted over the years until he became one of the directors of the JNF. He was also involved in planning new communities and was considered a founding father of the Israeli state. In his old age, he wrote children's stories. Sitting by the memorial candles, Weitz looked through old letters from his son; his Yehiam, he wrote in his diary, gazed down at him from a photograph on the wall, smiling sadly.

Yehiam received his name in the midst of a flurry of war and hope. He was born in October 1918 in one of the first Zionist agricultural settlements, Yavnel, in the Lower Galilee. The army of the British general Edmund Allenby was in the final stages of occupying Turkish-ruled Palestine; his mounted soldiers reached the Yavnel area on the night of Yehiam's birth. Eight days later, on the day of Yehiam's circumcision and naming, Yosef Weitz first heard about the statement issued by the British foreign secretary, Lord Arthur James Balfour, proclaiming support for the Zionist movement's aspirations to build a "national home" in Palestine, a Jewish state. The Balfour Declaration had been issued some ten months earlier, but the Lower Galilee was still under Turkish rule at the time and had no contact with the British-occupied areas.

Weitz and his neighbors were ecstatic when they learned of the declaration; as they gathered for the bris, a "vision of imminent salvation" beat in their hearts. "Their shining eyes and joyous exclamations voiced a blessing—that the Jewish people shall live in their land," wrote Weitz. When the mohel asked for the name of the newborn, one of the guests shouted out, "Yehiam! Yehiam!"—a Hebrew construct meaning "Long live the nation." And that was how the boy got his name. It was "a token of the covenant the English had made with the Hebrew nation, that it would be resurrected in its own land," in Weitz's words. He could not have conceived of a more patriotic name; it had never been given before.

Yehiam grew up in Jerusalem. His father was one of the founders of a comfortable, remote neighborhood in the western part of town, Beit Hakerem: stone houses with red tiled roofs were surrounded by the greenery of pine trees and cypresses. Daffodils and cyclamens blossomed in the gardens, and Yosef Weitz had a cherry tree. The residents of the neighborhood raised their children as loyal Zionists and pioneering leaders, in the spirit of European culture, in preparation for life in the long-awaited "national home."

Yehiam studied at the Hebrew Gymnasium, as did most of the children of Jerusalem's founding elite. He was a good student, who once complained that his teachers were not adequately preparing their students to serve the homeland. He grew into a handsome, charismatic young man, and he joined Hashomer Hatzair, the socialist youth movement, to train himself for a working life on a kibbutz, as was customary among many young people. When the Arab revolt against the British and the Zionists erupted in 1936, Yehiam "joined the ranks," as his father wrote—meaning the Hagana, the largest military organization of the Jewish community in Palestine. "He seems to be gaining serenity," his father wrote; "has he found himself?" It seemed he had not: Yehiam soon left to study chemistry and botany at the University of London. "I'm falling in love with London," he wrote to his parents. But when the Second World War broke out he came home and soon enlisted again, this time in the Palmah, the Hagana's quasi-standing army.

After the war, Yehiam was trained to carry out anti-British operations. British immigration policy, intended to gain favor with the Arabs, prevented victims of Nazi persecution from settling in Palestine. On the night of June 16, 1946, Palmah units, striking a blow at British control, attacked eleven bridges, destroying ten of them, during the Night of the Bridges. Yehiam was killed near Ahziv, in the north. His father read about the operation in the newspaper the next day and a few hours later was called to the hospital in Haifa. He asked to see his son's body. "I pulled back the edge of the sheet and saw his curls and his forehead. His thick hair was wild and alive and his brow was smooth and thoughtful. Here was Yehiam, forever silenced."[1]

He was buried just as he had lived, as the son of his father, a prominent figure in a very small society: almost everyone knew everyone and many were related. "Jewish Jerusalem in their thousands yesterday accompanied Yehiam, the son of Yosef Weitz, to his final resting place," reported the daily newspaper *Davar*. The national flag was draped over the body. Thirteen men had been killed with Yehiam that night, but their bodies had been shattered, thus his funeral stood for theirs, too. The public was called to take part: in Haifa, where the funeral procession began, all work came to a halt, transportation stood still, schools were closed. In Jerusalem the procession could hardly make its way through the crowds. Yehiam was buried on the Mount of Olives.

Weitz poured his pain into his diary. "The beloved son is gone! One cannot accept it—is he truly gone? He lives on in every corner of the house; he springs next to every tree and every plant; he is reflected in every book, every line, even at this very moment. . . . I hear his voice, hear his final *shalom*, uttered in a hurry as he left the house. He enters every thought and interrupts it. I find it hard to write, I lament him, and Rema, too." Rema Samsonov was Yehiam's wife. She came from a family that had lived in the small town of Hadera for many years and later gained fame as a soprano vocalist. "Two young people, tall and upright, beautiful, kind. I had such high hopes for them."

WEITZ BLAMED HIMSELF. "WHY DID I NOT GO WITH HIM? . . . IF I HAD BEEN WITH HIM perhaps he would not have been harmed?" He had a "burning passion" to know exactly how Yehiam was killed, how and where he was hit, what had happened in his final moments, what he had said at the end. Friends reported his son's last words, and yes, they contained a heroic element of sacrifice for the homeland: "I am lost. . . . Go on with the operation," or "I am finished—you continue," and also, "Take care of Rema." His father seemed hurt: "No words of farewell for his grieving parents?" But perhaps Yehiam no longer had the strength.

Describing how he dealt with his pain, Weitz wrote, "My soul is torn in two, the collective and the individual." He found comfort in the mass participation in his mourning, the public aspect seeming to place a screen, at least at first, between him and his true, private pain; he felt that his task was to fulfill the public role of a bereaved father. "In Haifa and in Jerusalem, the whole nation accompanied us," he wrote in his diary, "and throngs of people from every walk of life rushed to my home for condolence visits. They say he is the nation's sacrifice."

Yehiam's death indeed took on a national and historical dimension. One of the newspapers wrote: "We are not fostering a cult of sacrifice, but every sacrifice like Yehiam Weitz is precious to us sevenfold. Not only because of the way he lived, but because of the way his life was lost." Among those who paid consolation was the most senior Zionist leader in Palestine at the time, Moshe Shertok, who would later become Moshe Sharett, Israel's first foreign minister and second prime minister. He told Weitz that Yehiam had followed the true path and had fulfilled "a sacred duty." Weitz embraced Shertok's words. "I said it too: we must have strength in the face of the evil goyim, both Arab and British. And Yehiam chose that path. He believed in it. He was devoted to it. He is admired by all." The father was aware of the irony of his son dying in an anti-British operation—he, of all people, who had been born with the Balfour Declaration and had grown up as the "national home" was being built with such great hope, under the auspices of the empire.

At the funeral, Weitz approached Shertok, although in "whispers," with the most difficult question a bereaved father can ask a national leader: "Was the operation necessary? And what was the point of it?" Shertok, whose eyes, according to Weitz, were "kind and comforting," replied with the answer Weitz felt he needed to hear: Yes, the operation on the bridges was necessary, for it brought us closer to our goal. "The heart of stone was touched with tender drops," Weitz recalled. He tormented himself with the same question every year, always reminding himself that his son had not been killed in vain. Working the land and being willing to die for it were, to him, values that reinforced the Jews' right to Eretz Israel, the land of Israel. He came to see a unity between his dead son and the land of Israel—all of it. "I go to wander in the country," he once wrote, "and as I breathe the air of the entirety of my land from border to border, and that of the people who live in it and embrace it, my people, I hear a comforting voice that says: Yes, it was necessary and it shall be rewarded. The son, and all the other sons, are here, in the sea and the land, in the mountains and valleys, in the fields and gardens, in the shrubs and trees. They are part of the nation and part of the land and when the two grow and become one, great and strong, then will their memory be celebrated by every generation. The memory of all the sons."

And so Yehiam became a national myth, an emblem of his generation, his image rooted in the country's soil and in the Jewish struggle for independence. The author S. Yizhar, his cousin, described him as "a tree in its glory."[2] The myth took hold rapidly. Yehiam was described as a member of a generation that breathed the country's "free air," that had learned to love it, build it, and fight for it: "This generation produced the finest pioneers, conquerors and defenders of the wilderness; a freeborn and upright generation—the Diaspora and its ways were foreign to it." Moshe Dayan, who was three years older than Yehiam; Yigal Allon, who was the same age; and Yitzhak Rabin, four years younger, all belonged to the same generation, as did many of the figures who led Israeli society and molded its culture. Yehiam Weitz was supposed to symbolize the "New Hebrew," whom Zionist leaders hoped to create in Palestine. He was the opposite of the "Old Jew," the Diaspora Jew, who was viewed with contempt. In Yehiam, they saw "a new man."*

Three months after the Night of the Bridges, Yosef Weitz traveled to the Arab village of a'Zib, north of Acre, and from a distance observed the place where Yehiam had been killed. "I could not go right there and prostrate myself and search for the drops of his blood which the earth had soaked up," he wrote. Looking east, he saw the remnants of Qala'at Djedin, or the Heroes' Fortress, an impressively tall stone tower built by the Crusaders that had become a stronghold of the Galilee ruler Daher el'Omar. The sun was setting, the tower "glimmered and lit up the entire area, all the way to Haifa." And then Weitz knew; he swore that this would be where Yehiam's monument would rise. A new Jewish pioneering settlement had to be built here, in this place, for defense, for forestation, and for agriculture. "The fortress shall be renewed and it shall be ours," he wrote, "and above it shall fly the name of Yehiam, a token of innocence and dedication and sacrifice, and by its side an eternal flame shall send light into the distance." This endeavor, Weitz told his wife, Ruhama, would be their solace. Thus Kibbutz Yehiam was founded.

---

*In Yehiam's letters, published posthumously, he defined himself as a Zionist and a socialist, in the spirit of his father. He intended, like many of his generation, to continue on the path his parents had paved. One critic praised the "age-old Jewish sorrow" reflected in his letters, which pointed up the identity conflict between the Diaspora Jew and the New Hebrew that remained at the center of Israeli public discourse for many years after Yehiam's death. Letters written by soldiers who fell in Israel's wars were often published, as much to immortalize the writers as to convey an admirable educational message.[3]

• • •

JUST BEFORE THE FIFTH ANNIVERSARY OF THEIR SON'S DEATH, YOSEF AND RUHAMA
Weitz published a notice asking families with sons named after Yehiam to
come to the planting of a memorial grove near Ma'ale Hahamisha, a kibbutz on the way to Jerusalem, whose name refers to five settlers killed by
Arabs. They received dozens of responses, including one from Lincoln,
Nebraska.[4] It was a lively gathering, as some two dozen excited, neatly
combed toddlers, one in a sailor suit, crowded around the first Yehiam's
mother and father and had their photograph taken as a souvenir. These
were the children of the Zionist dream. Many were the first generation of
Israelis born in the country; few of their parents had been born in Palestine. Most came from Eastern Europe. Two fathers were from Turkey, one
mother from Germany. There was a lawyer and a housewife, a plumber
and a secretary, a mechanical engineer, a driver, and a storekeeper. The father of one Yehiam was a government employee; another's parents had
founded a moshav, a collective village, in the Galilee, where they farmed
the land. Some served as army officers in the Israel Defense Forces (IDF).
Most, identifying with the Israeli establishment, read *Davar*, the newspaper that voiced the positions of the social democratic party in power, Mapai, led by David Ben-Gurion. The little Yehiams would soon be reading
Davar Le-Yeladim, the children's weekly section of the newspaper. Their
parents could safely anticipate happiness and prosperity for their children. They could also reasonably hope that these boys' lives would be better than their own, in an environment that was Hebrew, secular, and safe:
they would no longer be persecuted. The children all knew they were
named after a hero, and some would grow up with a sense that their
name had burdened them with a patriotic duty.[5]

WHILE THE YEHIAMS WERE STILL IN THEIR CRADLES, THEIR NAME HAD ALREADY BEEN
dragged into a major patriotic dispute. On November 29, 1947, the United
Nations General Assembly proposed its plan to partition Palestine into
two states, one Jewish and one Arab. Most of the Jews living in Palestine
at the time agreed with the assembly's decision, often enthusiastically,
but there were those who opposed it because they wanted the state to
control the whole of Eretz Israel. The opposition published a manifesto
that proclaimed, "We will have a state—but with no Yehiam." According
to the partition plan, Kibbutz Yehiam, founded in accordance with Yosef
Weitz's vision, would have fallen within the terrritory to be part of the

Arab state. *Ha'aretz* observed that the tomb of King David, on Mount Zion in Jerusalem, would also be left outside the state borders, so that Yehiam would be in good company. Jerusalem, in the partition map, was destined to be a separate entity, under international rule.[6]

At the end of 1947, war broke out. It resulted in the establishment of the State of Israel, and its territory included Yehiam as well as West Jerusalem and other areas not intended for it under the partition plan. Yosef Weitz believed that the success of the Zionist enterprise necessitated the removal of the Arab population from Palestine. During and after the war, he was involved in deporting Arabs from territories conquered by the IDF, preventing refugees from returning, and forcibly transferring Arabs within the state. In the 1950s he was instrumental in attempts to encourage Israeli Arabs to leave the country. He continued to believe in the "transfer" of Arabs until the end of his days.[7]

THE TERMS OF THE CEASE-FIRE WERE SET IN 1949, AND THE BORDERS WERE MARKED ON the map with a green line. The West Bank of the Jordan River and East Jerusalem soon came under the control of the Hashemite Kingdom of Jordan. The Mount of Olives was also outside the territory of Israel, and Yosef Weitz could no longer visit his son's grave. The Gaza Strip was transferred to Egyptian control.

Many Israelis refused to give up the original Zionist dream, hoping for the day when Israel would embrace both sides of the Jordan. Some Israeli politicians, including Ben-Gurion, as well as some IDF generals did not rule out military action to expand the state over the Green Line. But for the most part, Israelis did not seriously consider the possibility that the borders would change, and Israel repeatedly declared that it wanted peace based on the existing situation.[8] Nonetheless, Israelis generally believed they had not seen their final war. "Sadly, almost from an inherent inclination, Israelis waited for the next war as for the predictable visit of a wearisome mother-in-law," wrote Amos Elon.[9] While they were not necessarily expecting a fresh round of fighting in the foreseeable future, most thought the Arabs had not abandoned their goal of destroying Israel and that Israelis could offer nothing to induce them to recognize the state and make peace. Until the beginning of 1966, Israelis believed that time was on their side, and assumed that as the country grew stronger, the Arabs would adapt to reality.

When Israelis used the term "Arabs," they were mainly referring to Egyptians, Jordanians, Syrians, Lebanese, and Iraqis—not to the Palestinians. Ever since they had fled and been deported during Israel's War of Independence, the Palestinians had ceased being considered an enemy force and were mentioned only as a diplomatic nuisance: refugees whose affair came up for discussion once a year at the UN. Terrorist attacks were mostly attributed to the Arab states, not to the Palestinian national struggle. The 1949 armistice between Israel and its neighbors was violated by numerous acts of terrorism and border incidents, and in 1956 Israel and Egypt engaged in a "second round" of combat, known as the Sinai Campaign.

Most of the Yehiams were in elementary school during the Sinai Campaign, and they were too young to remember the War of Independence. It was not until 1964 that they began to join the army, part of the country's first enlisted generation. Army service was something they took for granted, part of a routine that most Israelis felt both committed to and powerless to change. "I was at the end of eleventh grade, and all I cared about back then was where I would serve in the army," one of the Yehiams recollected.[10] Their war came in 1967.

2. ABIE

In the mid-1960s Israel was emerging as one of the more impressive success stories of the twentieth century, and most Israelis had good reason to be proud of their country and believe in its future. Many lapped up the progressive spirit of the sixties, perceptible primarily in Tel Aviv. Most cars driving downtown on Dizengoff Street were European and American models, but one out of every four new cars was assembled in Israel.[11] The models bore Hebrew names—Carmel, Gilboa, Sussita—and there was even the Sabra, a fanciful sports car. One model assembled in Israel was the Contessa, a family car manufactured by the Japanese company Hino. Its design was reminiscent of American cars, but the engine was in the rear. "How come you don't have a Contessa?" asked the advertisements, as if it were a social duty to own one.[12]

The U.S. ambassador described the local automotive industry as "one of Israel's miracles." Whether harmless fantasy or a megalomaniac adventure, however, the industry was short-lived. But while it lasted it was yet another manifestation of the Israeli dream, born in Tel Aviv, "the first Hebrew city," around a plaza with a fountain, wooden benches, and palm trees.[13]

Dizengoff was more than a street: it was a cultural and social ideal that even enriched the Hebrew language with a new verb, "to Dizengoff," coined by the popular weekly magazine *Ha'olam Hazeh*. When people said they were going to Dizengoff, they meant they were going out to see and be seen in an innovative, secular, urban milieu, while longing for

London and New York. Buyers of luxury items found expensive boutiques and shoe shops that displayed the latest fashions from Milan and Paris. The sidewalks were dotted with café tables where authors and poets, journalists and actors, and other doyens of local culture took care of business. They did not have far to go—work was close by: downtown Tel Aviv was the center of Israel's cultural activity. Theaters and concert halls, museums and newspapers, they were all here. This was where the newest movies were screened and subversive ideas were bandied about.

Tel Aviv gave off a Mediterranean ease, but many of the coffeehouse habitués, immigrants who had come to the city in the 1920s, were from Eastern Europe and often still spoke in Russian, Polish, and Yiddish. The thirties had seen the arrival of refugees from Central Europe, many of whom still spoke German. These were the people who populated Dizengoff Street by day. But as evening fell, the crowd changed and the cafés filled up with a younger clientele, many born in Israel. Café Roval was the place to see attractive young women and *gvarvarim*—another term coined by *Ha'olam Hazeh*—meaning the swaggering young men who acted twice their age. They drove Vespas and Lambrettas made in Italy. Actor and film director Uri Zohar set a few scenes from his film *A Hole in the Moon* in Café Roval. It was a satirical film, one of the first to poke fun at the Zionist ethos. The iconic Café Kassit was the place for argument and subversion. Here journalist Amos Kenan and the sculptor Yigal Tumarkin signed a letter to Prime Minister Levi Eshkol informing him that they had decided to break the law and enter prohibited military zones to identify with the struggle of the Israeli Arabs, who had been living under various restrictions since 1948.[14] This was a civil rights cause, not unlike the campaign against racial discrimination in the United States. Not far from Café Kassit was an eatery owned by a man everyone knew as Abie. Popular among politicians and IDF generals, Abie's place was called the California, and it served the first Israeli hamburger.

Abie Nathan was a well-liked man, and rightly so, because he sought to do good. Most people did not take him seriously—this, too, with good reason. They liked him because he was naïve and seemed loath to grow up. Originally from Iran, he was the son of an affluent textile merchant who observed Jewish traditions and spoke English at home. At the age of six, Abie was sent to a Catholic school in Bombay, where the rest of the family eventually moved. He was brought up as an uncompromising Zionist. Among other things, he was taught a Hebrew song with words by Ze'ev (Vladimir) Jabotinsky, the right-wing Revisionist leader whose political movement believed that the biblical land of Israel promised to the Jews stretched fully to the Euphrates. "The River Jordan has two banks," so went the words of the song. "This one is ours, the other one too." No one ever bothered to explain the meaning of the words to young Abie.[15]

After graduating from high school, Abie had trouble deciding whether to be a lawyer or an actor. He eventually settled on becoming a pilot and joined the Indian air force. After moving to Palestine, he became one of the first pilots in the Israeli air force, in 1948, and during the War of Independence bombed several Arab villages. Walking in one village, Sa'asa, in the north of Israel, he found the place abandoned and most of the houses destroyed. Among the ruins Abie saw scorched corpses. "I was overcome by a deep depression," he later recounted. "More and more I began to be troubled by what war does to people."[16] He had also taken part in the air attacks on the Faluja pocket, an Egyptian stronghold near Kibbutz Negba in southern Israel. One Egyptian officer who survived that attack was Gamal Abdel Nasser, who went on to become president of Egypt.

When the war was over, Abie first found work as a pilot with the Israeli airline, El Al, and then he opened the California. A handsome man, oozing with charm, he married, had a daughter, divorced, and cultivated his image as a wealthy and generous playboy who believed in a better world. He often donated money to good causes.

Abie was a new kind of hero, completely different from Yehiam Weitz. At some point over the years, between the time of the Jerusalem-bred warrior who epitomized the national epic and the moment of the amiable Tel Aviv celebrity who symbolized the good life, Israel had changed to become a country quite different from the vision of its founders.

In the early 1960s, the Israeli air force had launched the slogan "The best join the air force." The slogan was controversial, but caught on.[17] Abie's history as a pilot in the War of Independence awarded him a place among "the best." His ownership of a private airplane, even if it was leased, was seen as an exciting innovation. Set against the labor values of the first Zionists, the socialist economy they instituted, and the national ideology they nurtured—glorifying the kibbutz farmer and scorning the urban entrepreneur—Abie emerged as one of the first agents of an American culture that had begun to penetrate Israel. Surrounded by glamorous women, he was a daring man breaking free from the shackles of convention, although not a real revolutionary. As a forty-year-old child he also found a real purpose in life: to make peace. His friends convinced him to run for the Knesset in the November 1965 elections and during his campaign he pledged to fly to Egypt and hold peace talks with Nasser.

• • •

ON THE ELECTION BALLOT, EACH POLITICAL PARTY IS REPRESENTED BY TWO OR THREE Hebrew letters; Abie's letters were nun-samekh, which happen to spell the Hebrew word for "miracle." He received only 2,135 votes, but his non-parliamentary popularity was unharmed by his defeat.[18] On the contrary, his failure in politics only burnished his image as one of "the best." Abie's fantasy of flying to see Nasser persisted, although he never said, and most likely had no idea, what he would tell the president of Egypt when they met—perhaps he thought the encounter itself would have the power to change history. He promoted the idea frequently, and wrote to prominent figures around the world asking for their support. One of them, the under-secretary general of the UN, Ralph Bunche, tried to explain with the utmost gravity why there was no chance that Nasser would respond to the initiative. Minister Yigal Allon came to the California to try to pre-vent the escapade, but by the time Allon had finished his meal, according to Abie, he was promising to go along on the flight.[19]

It is hard to pinpoint exactly when the flight ceased being a Dizengoff-style gimmick and became a real operation. By talking up the idea, Abie had put his integrity and courage on the line. He felt he had to prove to his friends, and perhaps to himself, that he was true to his word, for the sake of peace. In February 1966, he published a call for the public to sign a petition of support. Many Israelis responded, excited by Abie's promise to hop over the borders of little Israel and sally directly into the regions of peace. They wanted Abie's flight to happen much as the British, almost a century earlier, had wanted Phileas Fogg to successfully go around the world in eighty days. Perhaps they felt the "sorrow of distances" that writer Amos Oz had identified among the kibbutz youth, a sorrow experi-enced by people who felt shut in. "Their hearts long for other places that are not specific, but they are distant."[20] One way or another, the mass support deepened Abie's commitment. He consulted his attorney, signed a will, and invited journalists to view crates that were full, he said, of pages bearing tens of thousands of signatures. When he had counted one hundred thousand, he decided it was time.[21]

ON THE MORNING OF FEBRUARY 28, 1966, ABIE WAS AWOKEN BY HIS PHONE RINGING. Zvi Elgat, a reporter for *Maariv*, was on the line. An hour later, Elgat came to drive Abie to a little airfield in the small town of Herzliya, as they had agreed the night before while sitting at the bar at the California. On the way, they picked up a photographer from the newspaper. They told the airfield employees that Abie was there to have his picture taken next to a plane he had leased from a fertilization company. It was a single-engine Stearman built in 1927, the year Abie was born, with an open cockpit. The name *Peace 1* had been painted on the white plane in Hebrew, English, and Arabic.

Abie, wearing a flight suit, sat down behind the controls, looked directly at the camera, and started up the engine. "For a second, perhaps an infinite moment, my heart stopped beating," Elgat wrote the next day. "I had a feeling that maybe, after all, it was just a dream. I went up to him and shouted. My voice was drowned out by the propeller. I came closer. 'Abie, are you flying?' He nodded. I knew. I was proud of him. Abie had done it! I will never know who was more excited—Abie or myself. I only know that I had time to ask him, 'Abie, are you scared?' He was pale, wearing a helmet, and he signaled one word: 'No!' Then he took off. For a moment I refused to believe it."

Elgat was the only reporter who had accompanied Abie, but by the time his scoop was published, news had come from an American press agency in Cairo that the plane had crashed and Abie Nathan was dead. The popular restaurateur became an instant national hero. "I will sue anyone who says that the man was only doing it for publicity," Elgat swore.[22] The news of Abie's death sent the country into mourning. The Hebrew dailies *Maariv* and *Yediot Aharonot* came out with special editions; the radio interrupted normal broadcasting. Throngs of people gathered outside the California, many weeping as if they had lost a friend and a hope. Abie's close friends, many of whom were artists and media people, squeezed into the restaurant and spoke in whispers. Suddenly one of them, a gallery owner, raised his voice: "I am his best friend, but I didn't sign the petition. It shouldn't have been signed. You sent him to die in Egypt. You killed him!" There was a terrible silence. And then Haim Hefer, the songwriter, made his way through the crowds and shouted, "He's alive! He's alive!" There had been an announcement on the radio.

The Associated Press, which had initially reported Abie's death, had made a mistake. After taking off, Abie had made a sharp turn toward the ocean and flown as low as he could, to avoid being picked up by Israeli Air Force radar. When he flew over Tel Aviv he was almost touching the rooftops; as he passed over the sea he was sprayed with foam from the waves. The air force detected him and alerted planes to escort him back, but he refused and kept going.[23] And then they lost him. He did not have a radio, nor enough fuel to reach Cairo. He got as far as Port Said, at the northern end of the Suez Canal, where he landed safely, introduced himself to the astonished airport employees, and asked to be taken to Nasser. The Egyptians did not harm him. They took him to the local governor, gave him a hearty meal, allowed him to spend the night, and even drove him into town to buy some pajamas. Then they took him back to the airport. At night he played cards with the guards and won. The next day they told him to go home.

When the news that he was alive reached the restaurant, people hugged and kissed one another, tears of joy mingling with champagne. Someone out on the sidewalk said a prayer of thanks. Word traveled quickly, and there were reports of spontaneous gestures of celebration all around the country. Soldiers in Kiryat Gat bought a bottle of cognac and asked passersby to raise a toast. The next day, thousands of people came to greet Abie at the airfield, and the runway had to be cleared so he could land. His fans hugged him almost to death.[24] It was a decisively Israeli moment: nothing characterized Israelis more than these sudden transitions between paralyzing depression and intoxicating joy, between the depths of despair and the joy of salvation. That was also the story of 1967.

THE SIX-DAY WAR WAS A CULMINATION OF EVENTS THAT HAD BEGUN SEVERAL YEARS earlier. Starting in the mid-1960s, Fatah, the Palestinian National Liberation Movement, began attacking military and civilian targets in Israel, seeing these actions as a direct continuation of the Palestinian defeat in 1948. Despite the Israelis' disregard of the Palestinians as an enemy force, the war that broke out in June 1967 was, in fact, another round in the conflict between the two peoples. Many of the terrorists who infiltrated Israel prior to June 1967 came from Syrian territory, which led to an increase in friction on the northern border. On April 7, the Israeli air force shot down six Syrian air force planes in response to such infiltrations. Further warnings and threats voiced in Israel just before Independence Day in May created the impression that Israel was close to attacking Syria, which had a defense pact with Egypt. In mid-May, the Egyptians decided to intervene and began deploying troops to the Sinai Desert.

The most concise description of this development can be found in the government minutes from May 16, 1967, in a statement by Prime Minister Levi Eshkol: "In light of information and requests reaching Egypt from Syria regarding Israel's intentions to take extensive actions against Syria, in light of Israeli declarations and warnings over the last few days, and in light of the difficult situation in which Egypt has found itself following April 7, Egypt decided that it cannot sit by idly given the current state of affairs." In Eshkol's judgment, Egypt intended to deter Israel from carrying out its threats against Syria.[25] The tension on the Egyptian front quickly spread to the Jordanian and Syrian fronts. While war with Egypt was the outcome of Israel's demoralization and a sense of helplessness, the fighting with Jordan and Syria expressed a surge of power and messianic passion.

The events that led to the war, as well as its course and consequences, have been widely researched and analyzed, but to understand why it broke out in the first place, it is not enough to know the diplomatic and military background. What is needed is deep knowledge of the Israelis themselves. In 1966, they had been struck by an emotional, political, and moral earthquake. There were just over 2.3 million Jews and a few more than 300,000 Arabs in the country. Beginning in 1966, more and more Israelis had started to lose faith in themselves and sink into depression. The doubt was everywhere, and it led to despair. "What to do, people, what to do?" lamented the songwriter Haim Hefer. "Nothing goes right and there's not a drop of good luck . . . / Everything is depressing and everybody sad / Things aren't working out and no one knows why."[26]

The year saw a dreadful economic recession and a sharp drop in immigration. Tens of thousands left Israel permanently. Israel's Ashkenazi-European culture was threatened by the influx of Mizrahim, Jewish immigrants from Arab countries, resulting in social tension and resentment. These developments led to a deep and painful identity crisis, and the Zionist vision seemed to have run its course. "We are a pathetic people," said one Mapai leader, and many concluded that, as one newspaper put it, "the project had failed."[27]

In the months leading up to the war there was a widespread feeling that the state's most basic values of sacrifice and national unity had lost their heft and meaning, yet there was nothing to replace them. Drawing again and again on the basic tenets of Zionism, people argued a lot, and often these were not merely political arguments between "left" and "right," but rather fundamental examinations of the Israeli dream itself. Many felt that the society was falling apart. Against this background, an editor at *Maariv* explained the need felt by so many to love Abie Nathan and embrace him as a hero: "You took us away, at least for one day, from the terrible routine that eats away at us."[28]

The crisis prior to the Six-Day War found Israelis utterly downcast. "I am filled with fear," wrote the minister of agriculture, Haim Gvati, in his diary.[29] Israel, he felt, was about to be tested as it had not been since the War of Independence. "Everyone understands this is a battle to the death." In the prime minister's office, Gvati heard that the Soviet Union had apparently decided "to go all the way, no longer hesitant to destroy Israel." There was no basis for this report in fact, but primed for annihilation, Israelis let no rumor go unheeded. Soldiers home for the weekend spoke of dejection and low morale in the army. "There are rumors that we are not prepared for war . . . there is no faith that we can stand up to our enemies," the minister wrote. This fear had no basis in reality, either. But war appeared inevitable. As Gvati participated in a cabinet meeting, IDF Chief of Staff Yitzhak Rabin interrupted to report that four Soviet-made Egyptian planes had infiltrated Israeli airspace. The planes had been driven out, but two of them had apparently had time to photograph the nuclear reactor at Dimona.[30]

Prepared for an apocalypse, many Israelis pondered the Holocaust. "How could this be?" a woman from Ramatayim wrote to a former classmate living in Los Angeles. "Not twenty-five years have gone by since World War II and it's happening again?"[31] A report to President Lyndon Johnson said that Ephraim Evron, an Israeli diplomat in Washington, had come to ask for U.S. support "with tears in his eyes."[32]

When war finally broke out, Minister Gvati spent the first few hours in a bomb shelter, together with his neighbors. The next day, the whole thing was virtually over. "It was the greatest day in our lives, perhaps in all the history of the Jewish people," he wrote.[33] Most Israelis believed that the IDF had saved them from destruction. Many described the victory as a miracle, as if they had been sprung from hell and borne up to the summit of salvation. It was "the hand of God," declared *Yediot Aharonot* in an editorial.[34] The sense of total doom all but disappeared; history was about to begin again. Two popular jokes drive home this reversal of mood. According to the first, told before the war, a sign hangs near the boarding gate at Lod Airport asking the last one out of the country to turn off the lights. In the second, after the war, two officers are talking about how to spend their day. "Let's conquer Cairo," one proposes. The other replies, "But what will we do after lunch?"[35]

SOME MONTHS BEFORE THE WAR, MOSHE DAYAN HAD VISITED VIETNAM. "THE AMERIcans are winning everything here—except the war," he wrote when he returned.[36] Not long after June 1967, the opposite could have been said of the Israelis: their only achievement was actually winning the war. Nothing was gained by occupying the territories captured in the war. But swept away by fear and subsequently by the intoxication of victory, their emotions often propelled them to act against their national interests, a pattern of behavior the Israelis often attributed to the Arabs, prompting the British ambassador to write in amazement to his superiors in London: "It is remarkable how often the Israelis can behave in a manner more Arab than the Arabs."[37] There was indeed no justification for the panic that preceded the war, nor for the euphoria that took hold after it, which is what makes the story of Israel in 1967 so difficult to comprehend.

PART I

BETWEEN RISHON LEZION AND MANHATTAN

In the second half of the 1930s, a young man by the name of Gabriel Stern came to Jerusalem from Germany. He took courses in Middle Eastern studies at the Hebrew University and devoted himself to bringing about reconciliation between Jews and Arabs. During the War of Independence in 1948 he was stationed at a guard post in the Italian Hospital, in Jerusalem's Musrara neighborhood. One day he suddenly found himself face-to-face with a man in uniform who was aiming a gun at him, finger on the trigger. The enemy. The man was standing at the end of a long, dimly lit corridor. Stern did not know how he had gotten there. He felt at that moment that his life was on the line: one of them would open fire and live. The other would die. Stern pulled the trigger. The bullet went straight into the figure—and shattered it into a thousand fragments of glass: it was a large mirror. Stern had shot at himself. He never shot at anyone again.

CHAPTER 1

SUSSITA DAYS

1. ISRAELIS I: "GETTING ALONG PRETTY WELL"

On Thursday, May 18, 1967, Yehoshua Bar-Dayan came home from work and took his Sussita for an oil change. Bar-Dayan, thirty-five, worked for the Citrus Fruit Marketing Council in Rishon Lezion. To get the oil changed, he had to go to Rehovot, and he took his two-year-old son, Yariv, with him. On the way to the garage, Bar-Dayan noticed there weren't many trucks on the roads, which was unusual. The IDF had begun calling up reservists because of sudden tensions along the border with Egypt. "I have a feeling I will be called up tonight," Bar-Dayan wrote in the diary he started writing the next day.[1] He hoped he wouldn't be called, but in his gut he knew it would happen that night.

His wife, Gila, a kindergarten teacher, was busy with the usual Thursday errands, including a visit to the hairdresser. The couple went to sleep at eleven-thirty that night. Bar-Dayan had trouble falling asleep, and at midnight the phone rang: it was Uzi Avrahami, an army friend. "Be ready in ten minutes," he said. Bar-Dayan wrote of that night in his diary, "Gili was trembling. I comforted her, but I was also trembling." He drove the Sussita to Uzi's and over the next few hours they used army-issued address lists to go from door to door and call up fellow soldiers, drivers, and vehicle crews for reserve duty. The same scene repeated itself at each of their stops: they would walk up the steps and ring the doorbell. Frightened wives would get their husbands out of bed and prepare backpacks for them. The men would go into their children's bedrooms and kiss the children; sometimes there would be elderly parents to kiss as well. They would say good-bye to their wives and set off for the staging area. Unlike the other men, Bar-Dayan got to return home again after rounding up the reservists. He was back just before dawn and slept for two hours. Gili had prepared his gear. Uzi came to pick him up at six-thirty. It was Friday, May 19. The atmosphere in the country had been tense, and now everyone was suddenly talking of war.

A year and a half earlier, things had looked very different. Yehoshua Bar-Dayan, known to friends and family as Shuka, was an optimistic and contented man. Rishon Lezion, with a population of almost 36,000, preserved something of its original character as one of the first Zionist agricultural settlements in Palestine. Letters written by residents to friends and relatives overseas depicted a lifestyle common among Israelis. Nine out of every ten lived in towns, one out of three in cities like Tel Aviv, Haifa, or Jerusalem.[2] At the beginning of 1966, letters sent by Israelis expressed satisfaction and a fundamental faith in their future. They saw themselves as part of the Western world and shaped their expectations of life and the country accordingly. They traveled abroad often, and they bought televisions; although there were no Israeli broadcasts yet, they expected there would be soon. Since the end of the 1956 Sinai Campaign, they had lived with a sense of security, believing that life was only getting better and would continue to do so. In the mid-sixties, it did indeed seem that Israel was chalking up immense accomplishments, in practically every arena of life. The standard of living had improved greatly since the establishment of the state and was now approaching that of several European countries, with soaring production levels, a surplus of jobs, and a continuous increase in salaries and prices. In the early sixties the economy experienced extremely high real growth rates of 10 to 12 percent a year.[3] An upswing was apparent in all Israeli cities, generating hope and pride. The architecture reached for the stars, just like in America.

Beersheba's first fourteen-story residential building was constructed. In Kiryat Eliezer, a suburb of Haifa, the tallest residential building sprang up, twenty stories high. In Ramat Gan they were about to finish constructing the twenty-seven-floor Diamond Exchange. In Tel Aviv the tallest building in Israel opened, a thirty-four-floor skyscraper. From the Shalom Observatory at the top, one could look north and see the outskirts of Haifa, or south to glimpse the periphery of Jerusalem. In the south of the country, "the most planned city in the world" was rising out of the sand: Arad. New public-use buildings were opening all over the country. In October, the cornerstone for Beit Hatefutsot, the Museum of the Jewish Diaspora, was laid in Tel Aviv. A few months prior to that, the

Israel Museum had opened in Jerusalem. On the hilltop across the way, the new Knesset building opened in August 1966. According to *Yediot Aharonot*, the ceremony was the most magnificent the country had ever seen. The "shrine of the Knesset," as it was described, was built with funds donated to the state by the British branch of the Rothschild family. Institutes of higher education were also developing rapidly. "A university is born in the Negev," reported *Maariv* from Beersheba. The University of Haifa announced it was moving up "Phase A" of its establishment, and planned an eighteen-story high-rise building. Tel Aviv University opened a law school.

Israelis could read their newspapers with a sense of pride. *Maariv* reported that Israel would be involved in the French space program, which was setting up a satellite communications system. *Ha'aretz* quoted a prominent scientist, Ernst David Bergman, who asserted that there was reason to expect an Israeli space program. An international survey comparing achievement levels in mathematics among students in a dozen countries ranked Israelis first; U.S. students came last. That same year, Israel won the Asian championship in basketball. "We're getting along pretty well," one government minister said, aptly describing the local frame of mind.[4] In Rishon Lezion, a young couple ordered a rocking chair for the living room of their apartment on Weizmann Street.

Life had been kind to the young couple, David and Rina: like their neighbors, Yehoshua and Gila Bar-Dayan, they had a cute little baby who made them very happy. One evening, Rina wrote a letter to her older sister, Edna, in New York as she sat with David on their balcony. As she wrote, she was tossing a matchbox to him and he kept throwing it back to her, and so they amused themselves, she mentioned in the letter. The baby was sleeping. It was almost midnight. She was in her twenties, and she was preparing for a teaching certification exam, taking a break from her studies to write the letter. As usual, she was using a postage-paid airmail letter issued by the post office; it was easier and cheaper than a normal letter with an envelope. The rocking chair would come with an ottoman, she wrote, and the upholstery would match the colors of the room nicely. They were planning to order a matching lampshade, and if things went well financially they would also buy a lovely rug.[5]

In 1966, the average working Jewish family lived on an income of 700 liras a month. An electrical engineer and his wife, who made almost twice that much, could live very well. "My net monthly salary is about 850 liras, and as a teacher, Zippora makes about 400 Israeli liras a month," wrote one young man, Yehuda Yost, to friends in Los Angeles. "With these salaries we can live well—we have a phone, we bought furniture for the apartment, we're paying back debts, and of course we have to live, too." They owned a car, a secondhand British Hillman.[6] In that regard they were in the upper brackets: only one in ten Israeli families owned their own car, but the numbers were rapidly increasing.[7]*

Rina and her husband had decided it was time for her to learn how to drive. In the meantime they continued to make improvements in the apartment: they installed wood paneling on the wall opposite the front door and along the hallway from the kitchen. It was Finnish pine, with lots of dark knots, Rina wrote. "It's really lovely. You sit in the living room and the wall gives it a warm, homey feeling." She put the philodendron next to that wall. In November 1966, they were informed that they would be getting a telephone. The Postal Ministry, which oversaw the telephone network, had already sent them a bill for 650 liras. "The whole thing came as a complete surprise, because we only ordered the phone last November, and in Israel you usually wait about two or three years (usually three) to get it," they wrote to New York. Now they would only have to wait a few months at most.† The telephone arrived just before Passover, with a six-digit number, and was awarded a detailed description in the next letter to Manhattan: "It's ivory white and for now it sits in the study, where it fits in nicely with the Formica tabletop." They added an extension outlet in the hallway. Soon they would buy a large copper tray for the telephone; it would perch on wooden legs against the new wood-paneled wall in the entryway.‡

David worked hard every day. Like Yehoshua Bar-Dayan, he was an expert on citrus fruit marketing. He had a degree from the University of California and had served as a regiment commander in the IDF's artillery corps. Several times a year, he was called up for reserve duty. His wife cleaned the house, cooked, and took care of the baby. "Every day I find

---

*An Israeli-made four-speed Contessa cost approximately 10,000 liras, while a VW Beetle cost close to 15,000. In Tel Aviv one could get hold of the latest Mercedes, BMW, and Volvo models, as well as a variety of American cars.[8]

†Telephones were installed in three out of every ten apartments at the time, and nearly 60,000 people were waiting for lines. In another reflection of the improved economy, the Postal Ministry kept lessening the waiting time.

‡Many telephone owners placed them in the entryway to their apartments because neighbors would often come by to make calls. Hana Bavli, the Israeli doyenne of European etiquette, responded to a reader of *Ha'aretz* who wanted to know how to handle a neighbor who came over and made long phone calls. "One can offer to refuse payment for the call, and this hint will usually suffice," Bavli wrote. "But if she does not understand, one can politely inform her that one is waiting for an outside call."[9]

something important to tidy or buy and I never knew there could be so many chores," she wrote, assuring her sister that she was not at all bored. Sometimes she took the baby to the Weizmann Institute swimming pool. "It's a big, clean, beautiful pool, and the people who go there are very 'select.' They are employees of the Institute, or people from outside who buy an annual membership for the large sum of a few hundred liras." Once she wrote to her sister about a new pair of black shoes. "A combination of suede and patent leather. They're the latest fashion, with a very wide heel, closed backs and squared in front." Her sister sent her "adorable" pants and a sweater for the baby, and a lace slip that arrived just in time: "I have an appointment with the seamstress tomorrow."

Once or twice a week Rina would pop in to see her parents, who lived nearby on Sokolov Street. Her mother was a teacher who had come to Israel in the mid-thirties from Bialystok, Poland. Her father, an accountant, was from the Ukraine. They had been among the founders of a kibbutz and had moved with their younger son to Rishon Lezion after twenty years. "A pleasant family atmosphere," their daughter wrote to her sister. "We all sit around in the kitchen. Father eats cauliflower with butter and Mother peels potatoes at the sink."* They had a gas stove for cooking and, as did nine out of ten Israeli families, an electric refrigerator. They used kerosene stoves to heat their apartment, like most Israelis. The kerosene peddlers would make their rounds of the neighborhoods, ringing bells as they went. Some of them still used horse-drawn carts; others came with motorized vehicles. The Friedman company of Jerusalem sold a kerosene heater that was considered a dramatic improvement in home convenience; it bore an English name, Fireside. Rina's parents did not have a telephone. Lunch was the family's main meal. Rina had gone to visit her parents because she was "exempt from cooking" that day, as she wrote: her husband would be home late from work.

2. WOMEN: "SHOULD THE BOY SEW HIS OWN BUTTONS?"

A woman's role in the home was taken for granted. "Your husband deserves to be spoiled by you, at least a little," *Ha'aretz* advised its female readers. The piece went on, "He is, after all, the man around whom your life revolves. Let him feel that you value his efforts for the family." In the spirit of optimism of the time, the newspaper recommended: "Be satisfied

---

*As part of the continual improvement in convenience, toward the end of 1966 milk in Israel began to be sold in plastic bags, instead of glass bottles.[10]

with your life and do not hesitate to admit it." There was also a list of practical suggestions:

- Before your husband comes home, air the house to get rid of cooking odors, except those that are pleasant. Make sure you leave time to freshen up and rest before he gets home.
- When your husband arrives, muster all your intuitive energies to observe his mood. If he seems irritable and tense, let the meal wait and give him time to freshen up. Or better yet—take preventative measures: decorate the table with a vase of flowers, turn on the radio, play some soft music and smile when he walks in.
- When your husband is home from work, you will make him very happy by sitting at the table with him, even if you have already eaten earlier with the children. Half a man's enjoyment of a good meal is the pleasant company of his wife after a day's work.
- A drawn-out and laborious process of clearing the dishes off the table and washing them might ruin the comfortable atmosphere you have managed to create. Let the meal go on for as long as he wishes, and finish it off with a cup of coffee, served in the living room and not at a table full of dishes. You will have time to wash them later.

In order for a wife to look "cute, as any man would wish," the paper suggested that its female readers have their hair done regularly, not just for special events. "Make sure your hair is always expertly cut and softly combed. A handsome, neat hairstyle can serve as a source of pride and satisfaction for your husband." The paper went on to caution that no man wants to run his fingers through a stiff, prickly hairdo that makes excessive use of hairspray—this was one of the "womanly sins" that most men find difficult to forgive. Other transgressions were lipstick marks on a woman's teeth or beyond her lips, a bra strap peeking through the sleeve of her dress, or dandruff on her shoulders after brushing her hair.

An impressive appearance was not sufficient, however. "A woman capable of providing her husband with interesting conversation even after twenty years of marriage, who tells him of the events of her day with humor, keeps up with worldly affairs by listening to the radio and reading newspapers, and debates current affairs with him will enchant him even after many years of living together," promised *Ha'aretz*. A husband would also be happy for his wife to engage in a hobby of some sort, such as flower arranging, gardening, or painting. "Do not be too concerned about the results," the newspaper suggested, "the enjoyment comes mainly from the activity itself."

Still, women were supposed to be wary of too much independence: "When you are planning to purchase a new item for your home, discuss it with your husband. Not only because it is his money and his home, but because he may be able to offer some good advice." If a woman bought a new appliance, she would do well to follow the manual. "Men tend to lose their patience with women who break every object they touch," wrote *Ha'aretz*, and offered one final piece of advice: "Having to watch a woman while she cleans the house makes a man just as uncomfortable as if he had seen her with rollers in her hair and cream on her face. Try to plan your work so that most of it is done while your husband is not at home."[11]

One reader asked the newspaper if she should make her son mend his own clothing: "Should the boy sew his own buttons?" The response was that a boy must not be compelled to perform activities that might impede the development of his masculinity, such as sewing buttons. A girl should obviously do so, wrote one of the paper's advisors, Tamar Hareli, since girls are naturally inclined to stay at home, while boys are supposed to branch out and play at Tarzan, cowboys, sailors, soldiers, and such things. She continued with a caution: a boy whose father figure is weak and submissive, while his mother is controlling and dictating, could suffer damage. He might acquire the characteristic tendencies of women—in taste, in style, in sex, and more. "This will distort his social, moral, emotional and perhaps also mental development." And so Hareli decreed that, for the good of the child, a mother must "restrain herself" and leave her husband in a position of respect in the family. Hareli was also concerned by the state of things in schools. "Feminization sometimes enters into the educational content, which is unjustifiable," she wrote. She insisted that, at the very least, informal education during after-school hours should provide young boys with masculine role models.*

Rina, the mother from Weizmann Street, dressed her baby in his first winter outfit. He had two pairs of flannel jeans, one from his grandparents and the other from his parents. "Each pair has impressively large cuffs, as it should be with jeans," she wrote proudly. "He looks like a man." Her sister, meanwhile, was trying to find work in New York. She

---

*There were almost three times as many female as male teachers in elementary schools. By contrast, in secondary schools there were more male teachers than female.[12]

had left intending only a visit, but now she wanted to stay. Her younger brother viewed the trip as "a good investment," so long as she did come back; he believed she would.

MORE THAN A HUNDRED THOUSAND ISRAELIS WENT ABROAD IN 1966. MOST OPTED FOR relatively cheap trips, taking boats to Europe and from there traveling by bus or charter flights. The trips usually lasted about a month and encompassed six or seven countries. One out of every two Israelis who traveled abroad went to Switzerland. Such a trip cost between 1,600 and 1,700 liras, and was a formative Israeli experience.[13]

When they got to Europe, many Israelis liked to seek out other Israelis. Most of them had not traveled outside of Israel the previous year and knew they would not do so the next. Before leaving Israel, a typical tourist would fill his notebook with telephone numbers of distant relatives, forgotten acquaintances, and the forgotten acquaintances of forgotten acquaintances, according to the journalist Yoel Marcus. As soon as the tourist got to his hotel, he would quickly phone everyone to let them know he was in Paris and to ask, "What is there to do here?" He lacked self-confidence and suffered from an inexplicable fear that he was not behaving properly or that he would get lost. And so he would look for a "clean, cheap" hotel near the Israeli embassy: the proximity to Israeli territory gave him confidence. He would visit the embassy for no real reason, just to ask how things were going at home. Upon hearing Hebrew speakers on the street, he would go up to them unhesitatingly and ask, "Are you also Israelis?" And then, "What are you doing here?"

Israeli tourists took lots of pictures. The rolls of Kodak film came with yellow fabric bags in which they were sent back to be developed. Several weeks later, the returned traveler would organize a slide-show evening. "We are greeted by a pleasant dimness," wrote the journalist Tamar Avidar of one such evening. "The crowd is already sitting comfortably on couches, armchairs and rugs, and Yael prods Haim, '*Nu*, start already, it's nine-thirty and we have three thousand slides.' At eleven-thirty a few people try to escape, claiming they've got the children at home. But then tea or coffee and cake are served, and more slides are shown. At twelve-forty-five someone snores lightly and everyone laughs and the lights come on. The guests sense this is their moment to flee and the hosts promise that next time they'll start earlier."[14]

But Israelis did not travel overseas only to be photographed at the foot of the Eiffel Tower or Big Ben. The clichéd perception of Israel as "a small country surrounded by enemies" represented the reality and reflected a feeling of claustrophobia. The author Moshe Shamir expressed the sentiment in his novel *Hagvul* ("The Border"), published in 1966. An article about Israeli industrialists attempting to set up factories abroad was entitled "Is Israel Too Small?" The newspapers invested a fair amount of patriotic fervor in demanding that the entry-visa requirements for European countries be canceled. *Ha'aretz* printed the daily departure and arrival schedules for Lod Airport, and often reported the comings and goings of public figures. President Zalman Shazar's visits to South America and the United States were covered in the lead headlines as if they bore true political significance.

Foreign travel deepened Israelis' sense that they belonged to the world at large; each homecoming seemed to persuade them that they were living in Israel out of choice, not as refugees with nowhere else to go. This also meant that few things irritated them more than the travel tax they were required to pay. They were vexed not only by the payment itself, but primarily by the feeling that their freedom to come and go as they wished was being restricted.[15]

When writing to his sister in New York about daily life, Uri from Sokolov Street in Rishon Lezion described Israel as "provincial." America aroused his curiosity. He asked his sister for pictures from New York and wanted to know what the buildings and shops looked like. He also asked about American television, having heard all about "commercials" and that there was a show called *Candid Camera*. He also took an interest in the news: Were there programs on television that showed the Vietnam War? His family did not own a television.

3. TELEVISION: "A CERTAIN SYMBOLISM"

By 1966, the number of Israelis watching TV had reached some fifty thousand. They sometimes picked up black-and-white broadcasts from Cairo and Beirut, and the lucky ones could get pictures from Cyprus, but often all they saw was "snow." Television manufacturers took out large advertisements in the newspapers, and *Ha'aretz* gave its readers guidance on how to purchase the appliance. At this stage, the paper wrote, it was important that the television be designed as an attractive piece of furniture, "appropriate for the apartment and pleasing to look at even when it is not turned on."[16]

Secret talks on starting local television broadcasts had begun in the early sixties, and various government committees were examining the national benefit to be gained by broadcasts, primarily educational programming.

The assumption was that local programming would accelerate the formation of a common identity for the immigrants from various countries living in Israel. Television was supposed to expand the use of Hebrew, help people get to know the country, and bring them information "about developments in government." Above all, Israeli television would stop the country's citizens from watching broadcasts from Arab countries.[17]

In January 1966, an experimental broadcast went out. The first image seen on the screen was a fly hovering over still photographs from various places around Israel, as Suppé's "Light Cavalry" played in the background. The broadcast continued for about thirty minutes, and when it ended viewers saw a HAWK missile battery and heard Tchaikovsky's "1812 Overture." The experiment drew general admiration. In Tel Aviv, people crowded around appliance stores to watch the marvel in the display windows, another innovation that promised to bring them closer to the world, and the world closer to them.[18]

Three months later, Prime Minister Levi Eshkol pushed the button that activated the first educational program, a twenty-five-minute math class for the ninth grade.[19] Educational television was established with donations from the French Rothschilds. And thus, reported Ha'aretz, television won its place in Zionist history: "There is something symbolic in the fact that the family that helped lay the foundations for agricultural Jewish settlement in Palestine and placed picks and hoes in the hands of youths . . . is now helping to assure more excellent education for the offspring of the first settlers and for those who came to Israel after."[20] Some months later, an agreement was signed with CBS in America to launch a general-interest TV channel. It was the triumph of common sense over common nonsense, asserted Ha'aretz, since common sense dictated that Israeli television be Israeli and not Arab.*

At home in Rishon Lezion, Uri and his family listened to the radio. He liked Two's Company, a popular quiz show. His parents liked the Friday night concerts. They were enthusiastic consumers of culture, and often wrote to their daughter about plays they had seen.

CULTURALLY, ISRAELI CITIES RESEMBLED OTHER MAJOR CITIES IN THE REST OF THE WORLD. On an ordinary January evening in 1967, theatergoers in Tel Aviv could

---

*An IDF officer, First Lieutenant Herzl Bodinger, wrote to the prime minister that the benefits Israel would gain by broadcasting in black and white would be insufficient: in order for it to have a clear advantage, color broadcasts must be instituted immediately.[21] In the meantime, the government assigned an IDF general, Elad Peled, to oversee the matter.

choose among *Nathan the Wise, Who's Afraid of Virginia Woolf?, The Maids, Hedda Gabler, Othello,* and *Richard III,* all in Hebrew, as well as about a dozen other plays, including some written by Israeli playwrights. One newspaper devoted a lead story to the vibrant spirit of Israeli theater and to a series of fine productions that included *Little Malcolm and His Struggle Against the Eunuchs* and the musical *Man of La Mancha.* The producer and impresario Giora Godik imported several successful Broadway musicals and produced them in Hebrew, becoming a primary force in Israel's emulation of American culture. These and similar plays, wrote *Ha'aretz,* were well received by a new type of audience that was young, curious, alert, and picky.[22]

It was the Israel Philharmonic Orchestra's thirtieth season. Since its opening concert in December 1936, conducted by Arturo Toscanini, the Philharmonic had become one of the Zionist movement's prominent cultural undertakings. Much like the Hebrew University and the *Hebrew Encyclopedia,* the orchestra embodied the effort to mold a European society in Palestine. A subscription to the Philharmonic was a status symbol, not only because of the cost and the orchestra's caliber, but mainly because of how difficult it was to obtain. A subscription was an asset, for which people waited for years and which they aspired to hand down to their children; at least one couple bestowed one on their daughter as a dowry upon her marriage.

Among Israel's guests during those months were the musicians David Oistrakh, Otto Klemperer, Mstislav Rostropovich, and Artur Rubinstein; the writers Günther Grass and John Steinbeck; the historian Barbara Tuchman; and the sculptor Henry Moore. Marlene Dietrich and Alfred Hitchcock also popped over, as did luminaries from practically every field of the arts and humanities. S. Y. Agnon became the first Israeli to receive the Nobel Prize in Literature. With twenty-four daily newspapers, fifteen of them in Hebrew, Israelis were exposed to some "virulent and destructive brainwashing," wrote a British embassy staff worker. But, he said, in some publications the level of Israeli journalism exceeded that of most daily newspapers in Britain.

There were innovations in leisure activities, too. The new Cinerama auditorium in Tel Aviv boasted that its films were projected on the largest screen in the world. Movies were the most popular form of entertainment, and new ones were shown almost simultaneously with their release abroad. Most Israelis went to the movies almost every week. Many wrote to their friends abroad about the films they saw. One of Rina's letters to New York praised *The Spy Who Came in from the Cold*—the plot was too complicated and hard to follow, but Father had explained it. *The Russians Are Coming, the Russians Are Coming* was also enjoyed, as was Israel's own *Three Days and a Child,* by director Uri Zohar.*

In 1966 about a million and a half tickets were sold for five Israeli movies, including *Moishe Ventilator,* a parody of spy movies. The film included cameo appearances by Shaike Levi, Yisrael "Poli" Poliakov, and Gavri Banai, who constituted Israel's most famous comedy troupe, Hagashash Hahiver. The trio came into being at the end of 1963, after finishing their service in one of the military entertainment troupes, which were popular at the time. In April 1966, they opened their second show of songs and sketches. Their biggest hit was "The Telephone Song," about the trials of using public payphones. No one did more than the Gashashim, as they became known, to develop a specifically Israeli brand of humor, and no one could make Israelis laugh quite the way they could. Another popular form of entertainment, identified primarily with the author and interviewer Dan Ben-Amotz, involved interviews with public figures conducted in hotels and public auditoriums.

The British Wimpy hamburger chain opened more and more branches in Israel; the food was not noted for its quality, but together with a soft drink called Sunfresh, it seemed to make Israel part of the big wide world. An eatery called Pam Pam advertised itself as "a household name among gourmands in Paris, Nice, Milan, Capetown, Montreal, Tahiti, and everywhere around the world." All of its features had non-Hebrew names: the Grill Bar, Milk Bar, Bistro, Conditoria, and Quick Bar, emblems of the good life abroad. Several *Ha'aretz* readers were also contending with culinary problems: "The selection of wines on the Israeli market is large and varied and it is difficult to make sense of the maze of names."[23]

AT SUMMER'S END, 1966, THE LETTERS FROM RISHON LEZION REPORTED AN IMPORTANT change: Uri had started high school. He had successfully faced one of the traumatic experiences inflicted upon Israeli students, the "Survey Exam," which determined who among the eighth-grade graduates would go on to the more prestigious academic schools, who would get only a vocational or agricultural education, and who would leave school and look for

---

*Films had to be approved by the censor before being screened. Most passed, but an Italian film about the slave trade was disqualified so as not to insult the Ivory Coast and Dahomey: Prime Minister Eshkol was scheduled to visit Africa soon.

work. Educators and politicians were still involved in a debate over reforms that were supposed to institute a junior high school system, but in
the meantime the state offered eight years of free education to all children through age fourteen. High school tuition was between seventy and
eighty liras a month, and the Survey Exam also determined which students were eligible for a subsidy. The exam was therefore a central event
in the life of every student and his or her family, and was described as
"the great god of education." Essays written about the exam by students
in Jerusalem reflect extreme anxiety.

Eight out of every ten eighth-grade graduates went on to study at a secondary school, but only half graduated.[24] Uri excelled at his studies, particularly math and English. His letters were written with humor and
vivacity. Together with his absent sister's boyfriend, a student at the Hebrew University who had remained in Israel while his girlfriend traveled,
he would fill out forms for the soccer lottery, the Totto. The two also solved
the crosswords and other puzzles that appeared in *Maariv*, and they once
won a book for submitting the correct answer to a math question. Like
many other students, Uri liked to read Ephraim Kishon, another founding
father of Israeli humor. He also enjoyed taking photographs. Once he
went with his sister's boyfriend to the annual flower show in Holon.

The two young men, Uri and his sister Edna's boyfriend, often wrote
letters to New York about the political state—"the situation," as it was
called in Hebrew—repeating scraps of information picked up from the radio and newspapers, as did Rina. There was nothing new to report, she
wrote, "except for a warm exchange of greetings once in a while on the
Syrian border, everything is all right." The exchanges were of bullets. But
there was one piece of good news: "Yesterday an important visitor arrived
in Israel. An Iraqi pilot who defected with his plane. He is a Christian. He
claims he is tired of the long war against the Kurds. Because of his religion
he has no chance of promotion, so Israel seems to be the solution to all
his problems." This sort of report occupied a paragraph or two in many
letters Israelis sent to friends and family abroad; they were always keen to
hear the news. "The situation" was part of their existence and often affected their mood. The reports frequently took on an ironic, noncommit-
tal tone.[25]

Uri also wrote to his sister about the Iraqi pilot and his MiG, as did her
boyfriend, and they were both very proud, as if about a personal accomplishment. The brother was impressed by the plane's three-million-lira
value and the country's sudden windfall. "Everyone in the country will
get one lira and the rest will go to the JNF," he wrote. He also wrote about

the exchange of fire between Israel and Syria: "Things are getting lively on the northern border." The boyfriend mentioned that the United States, France, and Britain wanted to inspect the plane, but Israel "of course" would not allow that, for political reasons. "There's enough trouble with Russia as it is," he explained knowledgeably.* Like most Israelis, he did not think there was any reason to expect war, not right at the moment. The heads of state were up to their ears in domestic troubles, making it unlikely that they would entangle the country in war, "an adventure that would not ultimately resolve anything," as he wrote. Not soon, anyway.

He wrote enthusiastically about Ionesco's *Hunger and Thirst,* which he saw at the Ohel Theater. The avant-garde play concerned a man detached from reality, who leaves everything and goes off to wander in search of perfect happiness. But, as the boyfriend wrote, it turns out there is no such thing as perfect happiness. He wanted his girlfriend to come back. They were planning to build their lives in Israel, and the idea of settling in another country never entered his mind.

4. PARENTS: "HOPEFULLY WE WON'T HAVE A DROUGHT"

The parents wanted their daughter Edna to come home, too. From the first they had been opposed to her trip. They would have preferred that she continue on the path they had charted for her—work, directly after university—instead of "losing a year" in America. They usually sent joint letters, written at the end of their day. At eleven P.M. they listened to the last news broadcast on Kol Israel radio. Over and over they reminded their daughter to keep in touch with the aunts and uncles in America. The packages she sent irritated her father, offending his Israeli ego. "We lack nothing here," he scolded her, and besides, the shipping and customs fees made the gifts far too expensive. He called her *tochter*—the Yiddish word for "daughter"—as if doubting the power of Hebrew to accurately express the depth of his feeling.

He also wrote about "the situation" often. Even the weather could prompt him to think in terms of the collective: "There has been some rain, and if it continues, hopefully we won't have a drought." In one

---

*He was wrong: Israel acquiesced to the American request and handed over the MiG for inspection. Most Israelis did not know that the arrival of the Soviet-manufactured MiG-21 had been organized by the Mossad, which was responsible for Israel's covert operations abroad. The plane was the first MiG of its type obtained by any country in the Western bloc, and the Mossad gave it a symbolic name: 007.[26]

letter he wrote of the achievements of the neo-Nazi party in Bavaria, Germany: "The world has learned nothing, least of all the Germans." He believed that Jews belonged in Israel. Then he told her angrily about a remark attributed to Dr. Nahum Goldman, the president of the World Zionist Organization. Supposedly Goldman had said that the State of Israel had been established prematurely. The mother was also angered by things she heard on the news. The former commander of UN observers in the Middle East, General Carl von Horn, of Sweden, published his memoirs, in which he said that Israel used female IDF soldiers to seduce male UN personnel for spying purposes.[27] "Mother is upset just like everyone is, and she takes it personally," Uri wrote to his sister. Like so many others, they read *Davar* and identified completely with the state.

The summer of 1966 was marked by the father's illness: he suffered from high blood pressure and was hospitalized for several months. His membership in the Histadrut health fund assured him, as it did most working Israelis, reasonably good medical treatment at no extra cost. His job was secure and the office treated him fairly, at some point even sending him work to do at home. His baby grandson gave him much joy and was the main protagonist of his letters. "*A ganzer mensch*" ("a real mensch"), he wrote in Yiddish, because the boy could already sit at the table with everyone and eat grown-up food—Mother's fish and a bit of tzimmes.

In January the mother went to Jerusalem to stand in for her daughter at the graduation ceremony at the Hebrew University. The daughter had studied Hebrew literature and the Bible and was planning to be a teacher when she got back from America. It was one of the most important days in the mother's life. She bought a new coat for the occasion, "which passed muster with Father," she wrote, and brown suede shoes, so she would look elegant. "We made up our minds and that's what we did," she said proudly.

Graduation from the Hebrew University was not a given. Out of the approximately 1,700 undergraduates who completed their degrees that year, only a third were women.[28] The ceremony was impressive. The mother had some disapproving comments on the miniskirts she saw, but she came home full of excitement. The father explained the deeper roots of this enthusiasm to his daughter: "You seem to have fulfilled a dream of hers. She dreamed of university and ended up on a kibbutz, and now she is thrilled with your accomplishment." The mother confirmed this, and said she was "counting the months" until her daughter came home.

Just before summer, the boyfriend wrote that they needed to make a big decision: it was time to buy an apartment in a new development for young couples. The apartment on offer had three mid-sized rooms, a small hallway, a bathroom, a separate toilet, and a kitchen. Its area was 635 square feet.

At least six out of every ten Israeli families lived in their own apartments, and almost no one wanted to rent. Renting might have been more economical, but apartment ownership was the prevailing aspiration—it was expected, much like education, health care, job security, and a pension. There was probably a historical aspect to this ambition: owning an apartment promised the same permanence and security that ownership of land was supposed to ensure the entire Jewish people.

A survey conducted by the Ministry of Housing found that most Israelis hoped to move from their current apartments into more spacious homes. One of every four young couples fulfilled this hope within the first four years of marriage. Many said they hoped to move once more, to an even larger apartment. Most said, optimistically, that this wish would come true. The survey also found that almost 75 percent of the cost of an apartment came from savings and parental assistance, the rest from mortgages and bank loans. The ministry suggested to citizens that they start saving early in a "Bar Mitzvah savings plan," to ensure that their children too would one day be able to live in their own homes. In northern Tel Aviv, a new one-and-a-half-bedroom apartment sold for 34,000 to 39,000 liras, an average of about $12,000.[29]* In places like Rishon Lezion, such an apartment could be bought for around 26,000 liras. The asking price for a new single-family house—known in Hebrew as a *villa*—in the upscale suburb of Savyon was 99,780 liras, twice as much as the biggest prize in the national weekly Mifal Hapayis lottery.[30]

The apartment under discussion in the correspondence with Manhattan was in Jerusalem, opposite a subsidized housing development on Emek Refaim Street, not far from the swimming pool and near the railroad crossing. The price was 23,000 to 24,000 liras, depending on the floor. The down payment was only 9,000 liras; the rest would be covered by a fixed-rate mortgage. It was a reasonable offer.

Advertisements for apartments praised not only the construction quality, but also the caliber of the neighbors. One promotional piece featured Edna and Binyamin Suttendorf, a young couple living in the Rimon

---

*The official exchange rate in 1966 was 3 liras to the dollar. The black market rate in April 1967 hovered at around 3.5 liras to the dollar.

neighborhood near Tel Aviv. She studied architectural drawing in the evenings and taught during the day, the developer said in its ad, while he studied economics and journalism and worked at the university library. Their parents liked the neighborhood because they knew the apartment would keep its value, and the couple decided to settle in Rimon because of the other young couples who lived there. These sort of people, who seemed to enjoy life and have faith in the future, also starred in a series of ads for Ascot cigarettes, named for the British racecourse. In January 1966, one such advertisement featured a photograph taken at the entry to a Picasso exhibition in the Tel Aviv Museum.*

Yehoshua and Gili Bar-Dayan lived in their own apartment in Rishon Lezion. They were the kind of Israelis sometimes described as "the salt of the earth." He was a child of the inner Zionist circles in Palestine, one of the first Israeli generations that could say that their country was good to them. His grandfather Alexander Alexandrowitz Abraham Sussman, from Odessa, was a well-known agronomist and a founder of Bilu, one of the earliest Zionist organizations. In October 1899 he had come to observe the situation in Palestine with the noted Zionist writer Ahad Ha'am, and in 1924 settled in Nahalat Yehuda, a moshav not far from Rishon Lezion.[32] Out on the moshav, Grandfather Sussman had cows and an orchard and a vineyard. He often socialized with his neighbor and friend from Kfar Malal, Shmuel Sheinerman—Ariel Sharon's father. The three palm trees he planted have survived him by decades, and are the tallest in Israel. His wife was an aunt of Moshe Shertok (Sharett), a familial connection that placed Bar-Dayan at the heart of the political and military establishment that led the Jewish population to independence. His uncle Ezra was a well-known poet and his mother, Devorah, was a doctor. Dr. Devorah Sussman, an ardent feminist, kept her maiden name after marrying Ben-Zion Borodianski, who later changed his name to Bar-Dayan; he was also a physician. During the twenties, Devorah Sussman rode a donkey around the Jezreel Valley to get from one kibbutz to another and treat her patients. On Kibbutz Degania, one of the children she cared for was Devorah and Shmuel Dayan's little son, Moshe. The Sussman–Bar-Dayan family later lived in the town of Afula, where their son Yehoshua was born, and then moved to Kfar Saba, not far from Tel Aviv, where Dr. Bar-Dayan was given a horse and carriage. The couple spoke Russian with each other, Hebrew with Shuka and his two brothers.

*A pack of Ascots cost 82 *aguras;* there were cheaper cigarettes, but there were also more expensive ones. Silon cost 50 *aguras,* Time cost 1.25 liras.[31]

When he graduated and finished his army service, Yehoshua Bar-Dayan settled not far from the border with the Gaza Strip, on Kibbutz Erez, where he tended the orchard and beehives. The kibbutz sent him to visit Brother Adam, a German-born Benedictine monk who lived in Devonshire and was a world-renowned authority on beekeeping. After eight years on Kibbutz Erez, Bar-Dayan moved to Tel Aviv. He took part in the first training course for certified tour guides and later found permanent work in the Citrus Fruit Marketing Council. The council sent him to London, where he met another Israeli living there at the time, Gila Samsonov, who came from a well-known family of citrus growers in Rishon Lezion. Her aunt Rema was Yehiam Weitz's widow and a well-known soprano. When Bar-Dayan returned home, he asked Gila Samsonov to go with him. They named their first son Yariv.[33] Gili and Shuka planned to have more children. He liked his job, which gave him an annual bonus and a Sussita. The couple had faith in their future.

And then everything seemed to fall apart.

5. RECESSION: "AN ILL WIND IS BLOWING"

It started at the beginning of 1966. A new buzzword took over life in Israel: *mitun,* or recession. The term referred to a slowdown in economic activity, reflected in the transition from excessive demand to paralysis and cutbacks, from a surplus of jobs to unemployment. The shift had not begun abruptly: its origins were in 1965, but the election campaign had concealed it. Before the election, thousands of Israelis had received salary raises, most of which would be swallowed up in the wave of price increases the country experienced soon after. By one count, a family that spent approximately 735 liras a month in 1966 would have needed at least 85 more liras to maintain the same lifestyle in 1967. But the public seemed to become aware of the recession as if a sudden catastrophe had occurred. Letters sent to friends and relatives overseas reflected a sense that Israelis were going through something extremely dramatic. Many of the letter writers were not directly affected, but they feared the country was losing its ability to offer citizens the good life many had grown accustomed to—and that many more were hoping to achieve.

Economists spoke of a curbing of economic growth and explained that the primary cause was a slowdown in population growth, from 4 percent in 1964 to zero in 1966. This had happened mainly as a result of decreased immigration, as well as a drop in the birthrate. Low population growth rate affected the demand for housing. The slump in construction spread to related industries and resulted in decreased demand for a variety of products and services. Many businesses went bankrupt.

The second factor depressing economic activity was a drop in investments: a 30 percent decline in construction, 20 percent in industry. At the same time, foreign investment plummeted by 40 percent in 1964 and another 15 percent in 1966. The growth in means of payment—cash and checking account deposits held by the public—also dropped, and this trend, in turn, further reduced demand, as did the 8 percent rise in prices in 1966. Only once in the preceding decade had there been a sharper increase in prices: in 1962, when the lira was devalued. Then two years later (in 1964) there was a 17 percent decrease in the reparations awarded by Germany to victims of Nazi persecution. Anticipating a further devaluation of the lira, people deposited their German marks in the bank and left them there, thereby further constraining economic activity. The mid-sixties also saw the completion of several large projects that had fueled economic activity: the National Water Carrier, the Port of Ashdod, and development work at the Dead Sea Industries. The government failed to initiate new projects, depicting the recession as the result of a deliberate policy intended to reduce spending and increase production, particularly for export.[34] Israelis were asked to exercise restraint.

In February 1966, Prime Minister Eshkol attempted to explain that the recession was necessary because life in Israel was too good. Nowhere in the world, he said on a radio broadcast, was there a country whose quality of life had grown as rapidly as Israel's had during the past five years. His speech was a reprimand: "We dress far better today, we eat far better," he asserted. "One family trades in their apartment for a bigger one, the other buys new furniture. . . ." Apartments were full of new electrical appliances, he added. "One man buys a moped, the other a car." But, as Eshkol would have it, all this spending was funded not by Israeli labor but by capital recruited abroad. The Jews of the world were giving money, as were the United States, West Germany, and private investors. The funds served for development; development led to prosperity. But the prosperity, claimed Eshkol, had created "a frenzy of grab-and-eat, grab-and-drink." The people were, in his words, living in "a fools' paradise."

Eshkol took the opportunity to denounce workers' groups demanding salary raises that he described as inordinate, and he commended a group of professors who had initiated a "concession movement," agreeing to waive compensation owed to them for previous years' pay. Eshkol also quoted a letter from a disabled ex-serviceman named Avraham Shapira, who declared he was giving back to the Ministry of Defense 600 of the

621 liras he had received as benefit payments. Eshkol's speech was meant to inspire the public to patriotically tighten their belts, but instead it provoked anger and contempt, disappointment and anxiety. The "concession movement" turned out to be illusory; it disappeared as abruptly as it had emerged.[35]

The government's role in creating the recession remains controversial. The U.S. ambassador to Israel quoted a report stating that the government had indeed initiated an economic deceleration, but that the process had gone out of control and matters had never been intended to reach such a low point. "Having diagnosed the disease and prescribed the correct treatment, the doctor was still showing hesitation and some ineptitude in his handling of the patient," wrote the British ambassador in his assessment of the recession. A report presented to Walt Rostow, special assistant to President Lyndon Johnson, however, commended the Eshkol government's "courageous policy," and a *New York Times* editorial also praised Israel for its economic policy.

Another school of thought held that the government had initiated the recession, although not for the reasons it gave—rather, the downturn was politically motivated. "Mapai could not continue to maintain growth and full employment, although this was its purpose," wrote one historian, "because these phenomena only strengthened the workers and undermined the authority of the Histadrut"—the labor federation, which was controlled by Mapai. The recession, in this view, was meant to ensure that the Histadrut—meaning Mapai—would maintain control of the workers.[36]

IN THE SUMMER OF 1966, *HA'ARETZ* SENT REPORTERS OUT TO STORES TO ASSESS THE RECESSION's effect on consumers. Not surprisingly, they found that people were buying less and being more choosy. Significant losses were recorded in stores that sold home appliances, furniture, and rugs, as well as in art galleries and the like—places selling nonessential items. But people also bought less fresh meat and more frozen; there was no change in the consumption of poultry. In the groceries, there was a drop in sales of imported chocolate, butter, and liquor. At Herli, a well-known Tel Aviv café, fewer cakes were ordered. Restaurant owners in the city said reservations were no longer necessary. Clothing and shoe store owners complained of a 10 percent to 15 percent drop in revenues.[37]

"People are starting to think twice before spending money," wrote one Israeli to a friend in the United States. Many were taking their cars out of commission temporarily, he said—turning their licenses in to the Licensing Bureau to save on taxes and insurance premiums. People who had previously taken the bus for two stops now chose to walk. On Saturday nights, when the Sabbath ended, you could get tickets for the cinema in Tel Aviv because they weren't selling out. Several months later, *Ha'aretz* found that the effects of the recession were becoming more noticeable. Thousands of apartments stood empty throughout the country. In March 1967, an American who had come to settle in Israel wrote to friends in Boston, "The situation in Israel is very difficult. . . . If you're interested in buying an apartment here, now is the time." And he quoted a price: a three-bedroom apartment in northern Tel Aviv, which would have cost 90,000 to 100,000 liras a year ago, could now be bought for 75,000 liras.

The recession also affected institutions that primarily served the elite: the Hebrew University's finances had never been worse, according to its president. Similar news came from the Haifa Theater and the Israel Museum in Jerusalem. Among the headlines: "Villas Await Buyers"; "Growth in Vehicle Fleet Halts"; "Crisis at the Hilton Hotel." In the fall of 1966, one newspaper wrote, although with some degree of astonishment, of a "Certified—and unemployed—engineer." Everyone was talking about the general state of dejection. A "psychology of decline" was evident, wrote one observer of the recession. "There is no denying it," admitted Yehuda Gothelf, the editor of *Davar*, "an ill wind is blowing in the country these days." Quoting the minister of finance, Pinhas Sapir, he added, "More prevalent than the effects of economic factors at the moment are the symptoms of psychological factors. . . ." The mood slowed economic activity even more.[38]

The recession hit Rishon Lezion, too: almost a dozen factories closed down, leaving hundreds of workers unemployed. "Things are very difficult. They've known for years that the 'economic miracle' was no miracle at all, and still the government made no preparations, unemployment is growing . . . the human suffering is vast," wrote the father from Sokolov Street to his daughter Edna in New York. Her boyfriend wrote of a series of economic scandals that seemed typical of the government's failure and haplessness. One involved Meir Halevi, who obtained a government guarantee for a loan of millions of liras to establish a shipping company called Somerfin.[39] "It turns out he's a cheat and a thief, and now the government has to pay off his debts," wrote the economics student to Edna. He also diligently reported the events at Feuchtwanger, a small bank that got into trouble and almost collapsed. He had good reason to follow the affair, as Edna was one of its customers. He told her about the four hours he had spent at the local branch. "What a mess. You go in and stand in line, you take a number, there are policemen standing in the door to maintain order. And the yelling and the bitter, heartfelt crying. Just imagine all sorts of elderly men and women who can't read or write, being told their money, which they have saved over years of hard work, has gone down the drain. What do people like that know of currency trading? All they know is they gave the branch manager money and that's who they want it back from." He estimated that the Bank of Israel would compensate Feuchtwanger's customers, otherwise "there will be a small uprising in this country." He was ultimately able to salvage about 80 percent of Edna's money.[40]

There is nothing like a bank collapse to undermine confidence. And then the government decided to sell the *Shalom,* the luxury passenger ship belonging to the state-owned shipping company, Zim, which was millions of liras in the red. The buyers were German investors, which added a dimension of national humiliation to the failure. The day on which the ship's flags were changed was a day of "grief and insult" not only for the State of Israel, but for "the Jews of the Diaspora," said one member of the Knesset. Another described how the ship's German owners would take over its synagogue and set up a bar or a dance hall "or something else" in its place. The minister of transportation gave the Knesset an extremely detailed review of the history of this venture, but all his efforts to explain the *Shalom*'s economic failure were seemingly shattered by one heckler whose question spoke for the general "psychology of decline": "What else are you planning to sell?"

The prime minister received countless letters, from both Israeli citizens and Jews abroad, with emotional pleas not to sell the ship, especially not to Germans. A seven-year-old girl from Haifa received a reply from the prime minister's special assistant: "Only if we all work hard and with devotion will we create the opportunity to own such ships." He suggested that the girl study diligently, "so that our country will grow strong." The artist Danny Karavan demanded that a shipboard mural he had painted be restored to him before the *Shalom* was delivered to the Germans.[41]

Along with the scandals, a rumor mill spread news of government waste and corruption. A *Ha'aretz* journalist covering the effects of the recession on restaurants observed a certain deputy minister, some members of the Knesset, and a few senior officials dining at Yarden, an upscale restaurant. A report on the two thousand guests at the wedding of the daughter of Minister of Finance Sapir was published next to the headline "Minister of Finance Won't Give Up His American Car." The paper determined: "It's time ministers served as role models for the ordinary taxpaying citizens from whom the treasury constantly wrings taxes, especially from owners of small and mid-sized vehicles." In a similar tone, the paper reported on the remodeling of the plane that took the prime minister on his tour of Africa. The new accoutrements included "luxury chairs," a refrigerator, and a love seat, at a cost of 50,000 liras. In January 1967, word came of plans for a new building for the Israeli embassy in Paris, second in size only to the U.S. and Soviet embassies.[42]

THE CRACKS IN ISRAELI OPTIMISM CREATED BY THE RECESSION RAPIDLY DEEPENED. LETters from Israel became more and more pessimistic and increasingly cynical: "Nothing much is new here, everything bad is only getting worse." Internalizing the depression around him, Uri from Rishon Lezion began describing mainly bad news: fifty people had been killed in motor accidents; an Israeli ship, the *Hashlosha*, sunk off the coast of France, killing eighteen crew members and a woman who had gone on a honeymoon with her sailor husband; the former minister of police, Behor-Shalom Sheetrit, had passed away. There was no reason for the death of an elderly politician to concern the boy or his sister in New York, but it fit in with the overall mood his letters now conveyed. "The situation is not good," he wrote in one. He also told his sister about the recession, but claimed it was mainly something that "you heard a lot about." They weren't aware of it at home, he assured her.

"The truth is that here in Jerusalem we don't even feel the recession," wrote a resident of the city to his friend in America. He belonged to an entire class of Israelis that were immune to the distress, but nonetheless saw the recession as something inflicted on "us"—meaning the state— against all expectations, and that mainly harmed immigrants from Arab countries, the Mizrahim, or Orientals. "The most suffering is in the development towns, and that is of course what's worrisome."[43] Similar sentiments were expressed by Israelis whose lives were still relatively comfortable. The damage to "others" truly troubled them, and they found the enforced awareness of other parts of the population unpleasant. Most had tended to ignore the other—non-European, or Ashkenazi—sectors of society up until then: it was convenient for them to assume that "the state" was handling the population as necessary. The recession brought home the extent of their self-delusion, forcing them to recognize that Israeli reality was different from the pictures projected in Ascot cigarette ads, and less homogenously Ashkenazi than was perceived by the swimmers at the Weizmann Institute pool. And there were Israeli "others" who were Arab, or who lived on kibbutzim. These people led different lives.

CHAPTER 2

OTHER PEOPLE

1. MIZRAHIM I: "IT'S BETTER TO BE ASHKENAZI"

The houses in Jerusalem's Musrara neighborhood faced the walls of the Old City, right along the Jordanian border. The first Israelis to inhabit them moved in as soon as the houses were emptied of their Arab residents during the 1948 War of Independence. The neighborhood was given an official Hebrew name, Morasha, but as with most of the formerly Arab areas, everyone kept calling it by its original name, and when they said "Musrara" they meant poverty and distress. In the 1960s, close to 4,000 people lived there. They were construction workers, sanitation workers, maids, carpenters, locksmiths, painters, and owners of small shops. Some 60 percent of them came from Morocco, and like most Mizrahim in Israel, they had to make do with a lower quality of life than that of the average Ashkenazi.[1]

DURING THE SECOND HALF OF THE 1960S, ISRAEL WITNESSED ITS MOST DRAMATIC REVO-lution since the state's inception: the Ashkenazis stopped being the majority. When the state was established, eight out of every ten Israelis were Ashkenazi; only two out of every ten babies were born to Mizrahi mothers. Over the years, more Mizrahim than Ashkenazis settled in Israel, and they produced twice as many children. In 1967, six out of ten children in the first grade were Mizrahim. That same year, the Mizrahi population matched the Ashkenazi, and soon overtook it. In 1968, only three of every ten babies in Israel were born to Ashkenazi mothers.[2]

"It is never a good thing to be Mizrahi, not under any circumstances," *Yediot Aharonot* concluded on the basis of an official survey. "It's better to be Ashkenazi, a veteran of the country, with a small family, living in Haifa or Tel Aviv and earning a living in one of the liberal professions. In any profession in which one might engage, Ashkenazis will earn more." That was true for people at every level of employment, from the agricultural laborer to the physician, and it was independent of how long a person had been living in Israel: new immigrants from Europe made more money than new immigrants from Arab countries working in the same field. In many cases, Ashkenazi immigrants made even more than veteran Mizrahim.[3] An average Ashkenazi family had a household income of 825 liras a month, a Mizrahi family 536 liras. Many more Ashkenazis than Mizrahim lived in spacious apartments, with a bedroom for each family member. Over the years, most Mizrahim managed to get hold of gas heaters and electric refrigerators, but telephones and car ownership were still clear identifiers of Ashkenazis.[4]

There were various reasons for these discrepancies, including deliberate discrimination. Most longtime Israelis were Ashkenazis, and most of the Mizrahim had arrived after the establishment of the state—the majority destitute. Many came with neither the education nor the professional skills required to succeed in the Western society that Israel emulated. More than 250,000 Israelis, survivors of the Holocaust, were receiving reparations payments from Germany, and that money was often spent on better apartments. The average income of those who received German reparations was some 30 percent higher than those who did not. This was another factor in the deepening ethnic gap between Ashkenazis and Israelis from Arab countries.[5] In Musrara, less than 15 percent of the residents were Ashkenazi.

Houses in Musrara were, for the most part, outwardly attractive. Built of Jerusalem stone, they were a remnant of an old architecture of prosperity, with lemon trees growing in beautiful courtyards, where staircases and balconies and other ornamentation reflected the taste of the Arabs who had lived there previously. Inside, however, everything was rotting and musty, wrote Shoshanna Yovel, a community worker who visited the neighborhood on behalf of the municipality. The houses had once been home to one or two families; the entrance led onto an expansive foyer that opened up to the other rooms. Now there was one family crowded into each room. Many of the new residents set up kitchenettes in the entrances to their rooms, so they cooked in their bedrooms. The community worker described elderly women sitting on the floors, cooking on portable Primus stoves. They used a variety of spices bought at the market and ground at home, and cooking oil splattered in every direction. Yovel noted that the pots, coffee finjans, and copper trays were always polished to a shine. Cooking stations equipped with gas rings were available, but the women preferred the Primus stoves on the floor, because they found it strange to cook while standing up and did not know how to operate the gas rings. Even many young women also cooked this way. Cooking was a daily ritual that went on for a long time, and the people of the neighborhood made fresh dishes every day, rather than cooking for several days ahead, probably because the families were large. According to Yovel, nutrition was markedly deficient: the food was filling but not nourishing. They ate lots of bread. Apart from the cooking area, bedroom furnishings consisted of beds and a cupboard. Showers and toilets shared by the families were at the end of the hallway, or sometimes outside the house. "They miss having their own apartments, they see that as a real luxury," Yovel noted. Many wanted to leave the area and the neighbors, but were afraid to set off on their own into new environments. Most residents did not imagine they could afford better apartments. They thought of the housing projects built by the government as too small. The women had many children, which made it difficult to keep things clean. Yovel recounted the story of one neighborhood woman.

She had gone to elementary school. At fourteen or fifteen she had started work as a maid, and at sixteen or seventeen she started going to parties with boys, and to the movies. She had spent most of the money she made on clothes and shoes. She did her hair at home. "A common sight in the neighborhood: young women peeking out of the window or from the balcony with rollers in their hair." At some point she had found a boyfriend and started going out with him. After obtaining parental approval, the couple decided to marry. Many weddings in Musrara were held under pressure from the young women, Yovel noted. As was customary, the wedding was as lavish as possible. "In contrast to the difficult financial situation, the inadequate nutrition, and the insufficient education, we find some conspicuous consumption in the neighborhood," wrote Yovel disapprovingly. "Almost every family holds celebrations: brisses, bar mitzvahs and weddings. These celebrations entail huge expenses. Custom outfits are tailored even for the children. The young women borrow wedding gowns from friends, but a restaurant is rented, dinner is served, and sometimes a band is hired. Where do they get all this money? They go into debt for many years." A prominent Israeli sociologist attributed the showy celebrations to the loss of original cultural identity and the search for a new one. In summer, some weddings were held in the courtyards, which pleased Yovel. "Everything is wonderfully decorated, all the relatives are recruited to help cook, bake, and organize, and everything is done with a great deal of love and devotion."

Somehow the young couple found a room to live in and began raising their own children—again, in difficult and crowded conditions. Two years went by. "The well-groomed seventeen-year-old, who was so attractive when she used to go to the movies with her boyfriend, has become an irritable, nervous woman, neglected, depressed and apathetic, busy with housework all day long," wrote Yovel. The young mother complained that her husband did not help; he was short-tempered and hit the children. They had an infant and an eighteen-month-old girl. The husband was apologetic: he worked all day, and when he came home and the children cried, he lost his temper. The children looked pale and spotty—like, Yovel noted, many of the neighborhood children. They cried at night and woke people up, said the parents.

Sometimes a grandmother might help and even enable a young wife to hold a job. But the children kept coming. Family planning was practically unheard of in Musrara; around half the residents were under the age of eighteen. Yovel worried about the damage children might suffer from sleeping in the same room as their parents. One woman told her, "My husband and I behave like two strangers in the house, we show each other no affection, so the children won't see." But the couple's bed would be in the center of the room, surrounded by the children's beds in the corners.

A boy coming home from school in Musrara would grab a hunk of bread and hurry back to the streets, returning whenever he pleased. In the evenings, if it wasn't too cold, one could still find children running through the streets. The mothers complained, but as the community worker wrote, "What is there at home that would make the children want to stay inside? The home is messy, the mother is always busy, there are no toys, no corner where a child can sit quietly with a friend." Most mothers spoke Moroccan Arabic to their children.

Parents usually bought their children the cheapest clothes they could find, which quickly wore thin. Many children walked around with torn clothes that were not warm enough. Yovel found that the children were physically underdeveloped, short and thin for their age. Their hands and faces were always dirty. She often heard of children with rickets, made worse by the damp and mold. The residents' grasp of medical terms and institutions was "slightly confused." Those who belonged to the Histadrut's health fund used its services, but others neglected illnesses and only went to Hadassah Hospital when their health deteriorated badly. Still others preferred to take counsel of an elderly woman who had been known as a healer back in Morocco.

The municipality of Jerusalem tried to set up a sewing club in Musrara, but the women did not come. A parents' meeting organized by the municipality was also poorly attended.[6] The residents had little cause to trust the city. Their letters to the municipality expressed a sense that they had been abandoned, and the replies they received, if any, were disrespectful. "I have not yet received a response to my letter," wrote Sa'adia Marciano from block 13/35, two and a half months after complaining about sewage running past his front door. Government ministries also failed to provide the neighborhood with services. In January 1967, Victor Suissa, of block 15, sent a second copy of a letter he had sent two years previously to the district engineer of a state housing company, in which he complained of the damp in his building. The company had sent someone over, but the damp persisted. "All the furniture and the walls are ruined because of leaks," wrote Suissa.

Residents complained of having no street lights at night, despite the neighborhood's proximity to the border. The Ministry of Defense built a public bomb shelter, but neglected to remove the construction debris. Zvi Sela, of Hahoma Hashelishit Street, notified the Ministry of Health that after two years of complaints, the sewer was now overflowing into the middle of the road. Children were playing in the filthy mud and catching diseases. "The children can't stay at home all day, but we also can't send them out to the yard where there's filth flowing. We can't open the windows because of the stench and the mosquitoes, and inside it's stifling and hot," wrote Sela. Later the sewage flowed into the kindergarten, too.

THERE WERE TWO SCHOOLS IN MUSRARA. IN APRIL 1967, FOR THE FIRST TIME IN THE neighborhood's history, ten graduates of the elementary school got into the high school affiliated with the Hebrew University, one of the most prestigious in Israel. It was an impressive feat, but it did not alter the national statistics. The older the class, the lower the percentage of Mizrahi pupils: from 63 percent in the first grade to 15 percent in the twelfth grade. Only in vocational and agricultural programs were Mizrahi pupils a majority. They were less successful academically, too: only 31 percent of Mizrahi pupils achieved a grade of 70 or higher on the Survey Exam conducted in the eighth grade, compared to 70 percent among Ashkenazis. "The Survey [results] are a real blow to us," said the minister of education,

Zalman Aran. In 1966, Mizrahi children constituted 46 percent of Israelis of graduating age, but only 13 percent of them were eligible for matriculation. Ashkenazi pupils did far better on the graduation exams. Only 13 percent of university students were Mizrahim, and only 8 percent of doctoral candidates. The proportion of Mizrahi students studying medicine was even lower.

Prime Minister Eshkol asked Aran what could be done to reduce the disparities between Mizrahim and Ashkenazis, and was given a sobering response: "The past casts a long shadow," wrote Aran. There were plans to provide extra attention to Mizrahi kindergarteners, and Mizrahi students went to high school practically for free. One aim of instituting a junior high school system as part of the education reforms was to narrow the gap between Ashkenazis and Mizrahim, wrote Aran. But to remove the shadow of the past, the income of the Mizrahim had to increase and their living conditions improve.[7]

At some point the name "Musrara" came to signify not only distress, but also violence. An IDF unit decided to "adopt" the neighborhood, but just before the Central Command entertainment troupe was scheduled to perform there, an argument arose between the IDF and the municipality over who would pay for the chairs and benches that would be broken during the performance; the assumption was that there would be vandalism.

Poverty and distress also touched other neighborhoods, among them Katamonim, Kiryat Yovel, and Bak'a. The condition of these areas stood out in contrast to the prosperity of other Jerusalem neighborhoods, such as Rehavia, most of whose residents were Ashkenazi. In some of the "distressed neighborhoods," as they came to be known, street gangs sprang up, comprising youngsters who did not work or go to school. Full of anger over their situation, they spoke of rebellion. At their mildest, they would sneak into the movies downtown or the swimming pool in the German Colony neighborhood; not infrequently, they broke into cars, shops, and apartments, drank alcohol, used hashish as well as harder drugs, and committed assaults. One of the spots in the Bukharim neighborhood was tellingly given the nickname Hopeless Square.[8]

In Tel Aviv, some twenty thousand families lived in low-income housing. The deputy mayor, Avraham Ofer, promised that the problem of poverty would be solved within ten or twelve years, but later said he might have been overly optimistic. Previously Arab, Wadi Salib Street in Haifa's lower city symbolized not only poverty but also a national trauma: in the summer of 1959 it had been the site of Mizrahi riots that spread to other parts of the country. Seven years later, the Wadi was still an area of extreme distress. The poverty-stricken city suburbs were the worst. Living conditions in the development towns established by the state for new immigrants were more spacious, but there too the hardships took their toll. In almost all of these towns, most residents were Mizrahim. During the recession, many of them became unemployed.[9]

Economists, statisticians, and politicians argued among themselves over how many Israelis were left jobless during the recession. The figures hovered between 11.6 and 12.4 percent of the workforce—in either case, more than 100,000 people. Unemployment spread "like wildfire," as Eshkol said, and there was no argument over the very real damage it inflicted, both psychological and political. The papers dealt with it extensively.[10]

After the initial shock over losing one's job, after the sense of failure and frustration, came the shame. One newspaper report about the unemployment office described the people who had been sitting there every day for weeks. When a new person came in, his facial expression and all his body language said, I don't really belong here, I just came to get something sorted out and I'll be gone soon. The veterans would sit and snigger: they'd seen it before. An unemployed house painter who wished to remain anonymous told a reporter that he left home every morning, walked around town, and before returning dirtied his fingers with paint so his children wouldn't know he had no job. "I'm afraid of the moment when my kids ask for bread and I won't have any to give them," another man said. Most of the jobless people quoted in the papers were construction workers born in Morocco, Iraq, and other Arab countries.*

Unemployment hit young people especially hard and the Mizrahim among them even harder. Eight out of every ten applicants seeking job counseling for discharged soldiers were Mizrahim. Many shunned the counseling and avoided registering at the unemployment office out of shame. Various parts of the country reported an increase in crime due to the recession.[11]

ESHKOL'S HEART WAS HEAVY. HE HAD NO IDEA HOW TO CURB UNEMPLOYMENT. THE governor of the Bank of Israel and the finance minister were losing no sleep over it, he grumbled, and he did not know what to tell people: "First I said this and then I said that. What are we doing about it?" One evening

---

*One reporter, for *Maariv*, also quoted job seekers who spoke Yiddish.

he telephoned Yosef Weitz at home and asked if the JNF could provide forestry jobs to the unemployed. It was eight o'clock, the holiday of Shavuot had just ended, but Weitz sat down at once to work on a plan. By ten that night, it was ready. He recommended entrusting its implementation to Pinhas Sapir, the minister of finance. Sapir was unenthusiastic; he believed that unemployment would restore the economy. "The Jewish heart is unable to tolerate people without jobs," Sapir complained to members of Mapai; but "we must accept the pain and the anguish." He insisted that the recession had to continue. When he heard the arguments in his party, "the self-flagellation," particularly when there were journalists around, he became angry and bitter, he said. He also complained of "demagoguery and wickedness"—these, he claimed, aided the party's opponents, who were overestimating the number of unemployed. To him, this was the real scandal. Sapir objected to the worrisome, almost magical number of 100,000, and even when speaking at government meetings he went out of his way to refute it.[12]

Sapir, born Pinhas Koslowski, was sixty at the time. Originally from Poland, he settled in Kfar Saba in 1930 and became a Mapai activist almost on the day the party was established, in his first year in Israel. He began his political career as an assistant to Levi Eshkol, was involved in several development projects, and excelled at raising foreign investment. As Eshkol's heir in the Ministry of Finance, he looked to many, with his bald head and thundering voice, like an omnipotent economic tyrant. Sapir was no great believer in systematic decision making, preferring to manage the state's economy from a little notebook he carried everywhere. Like many of the country's leaders, he tended to think in Yiddish.[13] In his party speeches, he flitted from topic to topic without exhausting any of them, often digressing from the main argument to recount an anecdote from the past that had just entered his mind. He often got into personal arguments with his colleagues. The economy and politics were, for him, one entity, and entirely personal.

In light of the unemployment, he could not rest for even one moment, said Sapir. And no, he did not want to see the country living with many thousands of unemployed, since he, too, feared an outbreak of violence. "It will end with the destruction of government buildings," he cautioned. But he claimed the recession was already yielding initial results: the discrepancy between imports and exports had shrunk, interest rates were down, workers had stopped demanding cost-of-living increases. Another year or two, or five, and the economy would recover. Sapir swore that he was constantly at work, and that he had his finger on the pulse. "I meet with the public too, not only with my driver," he told his friends, and to reassure them, he said that close to 20,000 unemployed people were taking public works jobs, many of them in JNF forests. "Yosef Weitz thinks this work contributes something to the country," he said.*

YOSEF WEITZ WAS ABOUT TO RETIRE FROM THE JNF, SOMETHING HE WAS HAVING TROUBLE accepting. Like many of his colleagues, he needed to be active, and was miserable without something to do. He found old age loathsome. "I am not afraid of death," he wrote in his diary; "what I fear is life without interest." His Zionist faith was unblemished by question marks—it was adorned entirely by exclamation points. But rather than ideas and words, the tools of his trade were clods of earth and saplings. He knew the country's every field and tree, every path and water hose, and believed that these were the foundations of the Jewish state. The state was the objective and he identified with it wholly: "I yearned for it, I dreamed of it, and I have lived my private and public life for its sake." His personal diary was to a great extent the diary of the Zionist dream: the country would be as large as possible, with as many agricultural settlements as possible, its lands farmed and covered with woods. The more Jews and the fewer Arabs in it, the better.

After forty-seven years of activity, the doors of government offices were still open to Weitz. He spoke with ministers and with the chief of staff, trying to advance settlement plans that included a moshav to be named Hazon, "Vision." In early January 1967, Weitz wrote to Eshkol to caution him against granting unemployment benefits, an idea in which he detected "severe corruption." Educated people, people with dignity, would refuse the aid, while "the masses" would prefer to take the money instead of public works jobs, such as forestry and path maintenance, in service of the JNF. "The masses will defect," asserted Weitz, as if public works were a national duty like military service. He recounted a long list of settlement plans that the government, he said, had delayed for three years: only one moshav, Netua, had been set up. He argued that the widespread unemployment was an opportunity to renew the settlement drive, including in those areas with an Arab majority. Weitz gave details and urged the prime minister to "turn your attention to your first love, the earthly one—agricultural settlement!" After this appeal to sentiment, Weitz

---

*One of the newspapers published an article about 400 residents of Kiryat Gat who took forestry jobs, and hated every minute of the work.[14]

noted that a ministerial committee headed by Eshkol had invited him to join a discussion about settlement in the Galilee. He had refused the invitation, of course: why was he merely asked to "join" a discussion instead of being a full member of the committee?

The prime minister invited Weitz to his office. When Weitz arrived, he found Eshkol busy with other people. He waited for twenty-five minutes and then a delegation from a minor political party arrived; their appointment was after his, but they were allowed to go in first. "There was no secretary in sight," Weitz recounted in his diary. Eventually, he was called in. Eshkol was only four years younger than Weitz and also believed that the Zionist future depended on agricultural settlement. "He sits in his chair wearing a cardigan fastened up to his neck, with a white shirt collar and no tie," noted Weitz, who had come armed with maps and plans. But Eshkol began the meeting with a complaint: "Where is Raanan?" Weitz's son Raanan was the head of the Jewish Agency's settlement department, a position Eshkol himself had occupied in the early fifties. Eshkol thought the younger Weitz was taking too many trips overseas and this was why "nothing was moving ahead." Weitz senior tried to interest Eshkol in a series of projects, but the prime minister said there was no money. Perhaps Weitz would come to visit him at home one of these days, on Shabbat, Eshkol said, and then they would talk about everything.

"I saw him bogged down by internal politics," wrote Weitz. Several ministers were demanding cost-of-living increases for workers and threatening to resign if their demands were not met. Others were threatening to step down if the demands *were* met. "And he sits on the fence," wrote Weitz. He was disappointed, not necessarily by Eshkol himself but by his office, which was drowning in problems and had no time to analyze them properly. Eshkol needed advisers, Weitz wrote. In a letter sent to Weitz after their meeting, Eshkol wrote that there was no getting around unemployment benefits. "We must remember that times have changed and we must consider the education of the unemployed and their professions. We cannot offer road-paving jobs to academics, although in our day we were not above that—quite the contrary." It was not the government, he said, but rather the Zionist organization that was not doing enough to encourage agricultural settlement. Raanan was going abroad too often and perhaps that was why he was not paying enough attention to the needs of the country, Eshkol reiterated. But he did not neglect to appease the elderly Weitz and make up for past disrespect: of course Weitz was invited to be a full member of the Galilee settlement committee; he apologized for the misunderstanding.[15]

. . .

IN NOVEMBER 1966, THE GOVERNMENT HAD DECIDED TO EXTEND THE LENGTH OF men's IDF service to two and a half years, which had been the term in the past. The length of women's service remained unchanged, at twenty months. The extension of service postponed a deterioration in unemployment for a few months. The following February the government decided to provide a job for anyone who sought one, although no one knew exactly how this would be accomplished. A few weeks later, the public witnessed a riot in Tel Aviv by unemployed people. Most of them were Mizrahi, which was particularly alarming. Those in government were not surprised. "Today, this Mizrahi population is our proletariat," said one participant in a discussion held by the prime minister sometime earlier, adding, "It is a completely different world from the one we know."[16]

Beginning in 1966, newspapers had begun to write about the plight of the Mizrahim, especially in the development towns. "It seems that of the ten measures of filth that have descended on Israel, the development towns have taken nine. . . . Most of them are dirty and many of them look like garbage dumps," wrote *Ha'aretz*. The pressures of poverty were reported all over the country. "Whenever someone gets sick, we have to walk more than a mile to Bet Shemesh to call a doctor," said a resident of Mahseya, a moshav in the Jerusalem corridor. Not far from there, in an all but abandoned moshav, lived Eliyahu Amsalem, father of twelve, unemployed. His daughter Sarah wrote a letter to the prime minister on his behalf: "Mr. Prime Minister, if you do not help me, I will kill myself."

Irene Arbiv, a widow, lived near the airport at Lod, in a township named after President Truman. Her husband had died in an electrocution accident, leaving her to raise eleven children on her own in a two-bedroom house. Snakes crawled into the house through cracks in the walls. In Lod and Ramle, unemployment was on the rise, although the local labor unions reported that there was no starvation in their towns—not yet. Similar reports came from Or Akiva and Carmiel, from Yokneam and Upper Nazareth, and from Ma'alot. Kiryat Shmoneh, where roughly 70 percent of the population was originally from North Africa, was described as a dying town. Some eighty thousand people had lived in the town since its establishment in 1949, but by the beginning of 1967 only fifteen thousand remained. Between forty and fifty thousand people had settled in Beit She'an after the establishment of the state, but by 1967 only twelve thousand were left.[17]

On a December day in 1966, four reporters from Kol Israel radio went to Beit She'an. New archeological findings had revealed that this immigrant town was built on a site that had been inhabited almost continuously for four thousand years. A Talmudic scholar determined that it lay at the gates of Eden. The reporters met a thirteen-year-old girl named Yaffa Cohen. Asked if she was hungry, she replied, "Yes." Yaffa Cohen was not the only poverty-stricken child in Beit She'an, and she later revealed that she hadn't been hungry at all but had simply said what she had been told to say. The daily *Maariv* had already reported on hungry people in Beit She'an, but the power of radio was greater and Yaffa Cohen became a symbol. The broadcast shocked the entire country. "The State of Israel has the power to face any enemy," said one Knesset member after the broadcast, "but it cannot face a boy or a girl who says, 'I am hungry.'" Hunger was relative, wrote *Ha'aretz*, and Israel was no India. But the paper offered a definition: severe hunger in Israel was a condition whereby a family of nine subsists on bread, potatoes, or a little rice, and tea. Such hunger existed, the paper determined, and added that the recession was hurting Mizrahim more than Ashkenazis. Statistics confirmed this assertion. "The situation is explosive," *Ha'aretz* cautioned.[18]

Former prime minister David Ben-Gurion sensed desperation in the southern town of Dimona. There was no confidence in the future, "as if the situation is hopeless," he wrote in his diary. One of the city's residents, twenty-eight-year-old Prosper Lazimi, said, "Blood will be spilled here." Blood had already been spilled in the port town Ashdod on the first of May, international workers' day. A few hundred unemployed people took part in a demonstration that turned into a confrontation with the police. Two dozen people were injured, including eight policemen. The unrest in Ashdod had taken on the characteristics of a civil uprising, wrote one of the papers. Violent demonstrations occurred elsewhere, too.

A reporter for *Ha'aretz* described the atmosphere in Yeruham, a development town. He observed two girls playing hopscotch on the sidewalk outside the local council building. One was in the advanced stages of pregnancy. There were a few other unmarried pregnant girls with them. In the unemployment office, one sixteen-year-old girl threatened the staff that if she couldn't find work, she would become a prostitute "like those other girls." At Makhluf's café, more unemployed people sat around. One discharged soldier said that as far as he was concerned, "the whole country can go down the drain." The reporter warned: "The soldiers and the prostitutes are dangerously flammable material. One spark could result in an explosion that would shock the whole country."

A reporter for *Yediot Aharonot* described life in Kiryat Shmoneh as a disgrace to the memory of the heroes for whom the town had been named, among them the pioneer Yosef Trumpeldor, who, before being killed in an attack, had uttered the memorable words, "It is good to die for our country." If Trumpeldor knew of the conditions in town, he would have kept his famous words to himself, the reporter wrote. Another newspaper wondered: "Ashdod, Dimona, Beit She'an, Kiryat Shmoneh: of these we knew. But who imagined unemployment would reach Tel Aviv?" There were people on the verge of starvation in the center of the city, another paper reported. The media reports and the message of helplessness emanating from Eshkol's office quickly gnawed at Israel's self-image, frightening even those people who had at first described the recession as merely something one heard about. More and more Israelis began to fear that the recession was not simply a discrete economic crisis, but something that was undermining the country's very foundations. Obviously, the crisis was deepening.

The U.S. ambassador, Walworth Barbour, informed Washington of a profound disparity between "Occidentals and Orientals" in education, housing, and employment. Alongside the disparity, he said, was deliberate discrimination against the Orientals. They lived in a sort of ghetto, effectively isolated from true contact with the Occidentals. It could therefore be said that, to a great extent, a person's ethnic origin determined his future. This was the greatest danger facing Israel, the ambassador concluded.[19]

2. MIZRAHIM II: "IN EUROPE, PEOPLE DO NOT EAT ON THE STREETS"

One evening in October 1966, Yosef and Ruhama Weitz went to the Haifa Theater to see Moshe Shamir's *He Walked in the Fields*. In the play, a young man named Uri, born and bred on a kibbutz, falls in love with Mika, a Holocaust survivor. He enlists in the fight against British rule and, like Yehiam Weitz, is killed, apparently on the Night of the Bridges. The widowed Mika bears his son and names him after his father, Uri. "A pleasant, enjoyable play, its subject and the acting leave a great impression and will surely be a good influence on the youth," wrote Weitz in his diary, observing that most of the audience was young.

The play may have been appreciated in Haifa, but residents of Ofakim, originating predominantly in North Africa, said they did not want Shamir's heroic Ashkenazi play in their town. Their chosen heroine was the star of a lighter play in which Aliza Mizrahi, a cleaning woman, becomes a detective and solves a murder mystery.[20] This was not the world envisioned by the first Zionists.

The Zionist movement had been born in Europe, the cradle of the ideas it went on to cultivate: national identity—as well as nationalism—liberalism, socialism, and Marxism; all were anchored in European thought. Having determined that the solution to the Jewish question required relocating the Jews to the land of Israel, the Zionist leaders were thinking of the Jews in Europe. The state they envisioned was to be culturally a part of Europe, and when they traveled to European capitals asking for support, they promised a bastion of European culture in the Middle East. This was the image in which the Jewish state was built, under the auspices of the British empire. But the murder of Jews in the Second World War depleted the state's potential population, and the Zionist movement began to look elsewhere for possible immigrants, to the Jews of Arab countries. Prior to the Second World War, they had aroused, at most, anthropological curiosity within the Zionist movement; they were not considered partners in the dream.[21]

Tensions between Ashkenazis and Mizrahim (or Sephardim, or, as they were also then called, "members of eastern communities") had plagued the Jewish settlement in Palestine since its inception and worsened upon the establishment of the state, as the balance of numbers changed. Israel's basic goal was to achieve a "merging of diasporas," in the spirit of the American attempt to create a "melting pot" society. The state had at its disposal two primary means to reach this end: schools and the military.[22] But when Zionist leaders spoke of a "merging of diasporas," they meant that the Mizrahim would assimilate into European society—which they hoped would be strong enough to absorb them—without requiring it to give up Western values and culture. This attitude still prevailed in 1966. "We must try and bring European culture to the Mizrahi communities," said the writer Haim Hazaz.

The story of this attempt is one of accomplishments and errors, illusion and sobriety, goodwill and arrogance to the point of racism, deliberate and nondeliberate discrimination, and affirmative action both useful and harmful. Above all, it is a story of alienation: the Ashkenazis found it difficult to live with the Mizrahim, who in turn found the Ashkenazis trying. The intermarriage rate in 1967 was approximately 15 percent. A study conducted among young people revealed that Ashkenazi youth felt alienation, and even hostility, toward Mizrahim.

One teacher, Bilha Noy, documented accounts of growing up in Israel and heard many references to this hostility. Some of her interview subjects told her that in the fifth or sixth grade, Ashkenazi and Mizrahi students were separated and streamed, ostensibly according to scholastic ability. "We weren't told this openly," one person recalled, "it was the kind of thing you didn't talk about, but everyone knew. Then at some point the school decided that it didn't seem nice to have 'our' class and 'their' class. They didn't actually change anything, they just announced that there was no difference between us. The classes were renamed with the names of flowers, but the cosmetics didn't deceive us—or them. The fact is, in the afternoons we had no contact whatsoever."

Sociological studies confirmed the existence of a great deal of ethnic tension and even mutual hostility. "The hearts of the Mizrahi ethnicities bear envy and hatred of their Western brethren," determined a writer for *Ha'aretz*, who also noted that among "Westerners," only the educated were free of contempt toward the Mizrahim. Studies also exposed "internal" hostility among Ashkenazis and Mizrahim originating from different countries.[23]

Citizens from Arab countries sent furious letters to Prime Minister Eshkol. One of them accused the government of being comprised of "an unadulterated representation of the European race."[24] Indeed, Israel had not yet had a Mizrahi president, chief justice, or Knesset chairman, or a Mizrahi prime minister or chief of staff. Only one Supreme Court judge, Eliyahu Mani, was of Mizrahi descent. Only twenty-five of the 120 members of the Sixth Knesset were Mizrahim, only two government ministers, not a single IDF general, and none of the mayors of large cities. Mizrahi representation in other centers of political power—the Histadrut and the senior civil service—was also disproportionate to their share in the population.[25]*

The postal minister, Eliyahu Sasson, himself Mizrahi, said that many people turned to him to protest the meager representation of Mizrahim in politics, and he cautioned that Mapai was losing its influence among Mizrahim. Sasson was one of the two non-Ashkenazi ministers in Eshkol's government, but like the minister of police, Behor-Shalom Sheetrit, also Mizrahi, he was an old-timer in the country and did not represent the newer immigrants. In early 1966, Eshkol met with the Mizrahi Knesset members to discuss the advancement of their constituents and proposed that they establish a team to report on the needs in the development

---

*The deputy director general of the Ministry of Foreign Affairs once drew up a list of those among the hundreds of senior officials in his ministry who "belonged to the Mizrahi ethnicities." It was a short list. Among the forty-nine Mizrahi officials were six ambassadors. A similar list was prepared in the prime minister's office. Yaacov Herzog, the director general of that office, tried to reassure the head of the Sephardic Committee, Eliyahu Elyashar: "In my opinion there is no objective foundation to the claim that Sephardic children are inherently retarded."[26]

towns. When Minister Sheetrit resigned, shortly before his death, Sasson was given the Ministry of Police, and the Postal Ministry went to Israel Yeshayahu, the first cabinet minister of Yemenite origin. *Ha'aretz* declared that this appointment refuted the repeated claims that Mizrahim suffered discrimination. "One may with satisfaction note that a person who came here as a young man thirty-seven years ago has managed to climb up the party rungs until reaching the post of minister," wrote the paper, as proof that the door was open to any diligent, talented activist.* Most government members came to Israel as young men and had not had to wait nineteen years before becoming ministers—but they had come from Europe.

University students of North African origin tried to establish a movement named Oded in Jerusalem, aimed at improving the image of Mizrahim and neutralizing the Ashkenazi sense of them as foreigners. They received assistance from the government, and the press supported them, but the U.S. embassy was pessimistic about what they could accomplish. As long as the disparities between them and "the Ashkenazi minority" were not eradicated, the embassy charged, Jews from North Africa, and Mizrahim in general, would continue to exist as passive observers on the margins of society. The embassy attributed their condition to the "superiority complex" of the Ashkenazi establishment.[28]

Many Israelis acknowledged the discrimination. A reporter for *Maariv* wrote, "One day they will share the seats at the government table. So it would be a good idea for those who are sitting in those seats today to consider the issue, to make sure that when that day comes their children are not appointed to the Postal and Police Ministries." Even Ben-Gurion, no longer prime minister but now speaking as an ordinary Knesset member, admitted, though cautiously, that he was not certain that all Mizrahim enjoyed the same treatment afforded to Ashkenazis.[29]

In early 1967, two women were making headlines in the papers, one from Yemen and the other from Morocco. The Yemenite woman implied that she blamed herself for her predicament, while the Moroccan woman projected gratification and a certain self-righteousness. The mother from Yemen was Hamama Tan'ami, a resident of Gedera. Some seventeen years earlier, shortly after her family arrived in Israel, her four-month-old son, Yehuda, had disappeared. Infant mortality rates in Yemen were high and were predictably elevated among the Yemenite Jews who had recently im-

---

*The headline was "Ethnic Ministers," meaning Mizrahi ministers: Ashkenazi Israelis were never described as "ethnic." In another piece, the paper noted that Yeshayahu was a fine choice for postal minister, because he was a frequent letter writer.[27]

migrated. They were housed at first in transit camps where conditions were extremely harsh: there was insufficient nutrition, poor health care and sanitation, and inadequate shelter from the cold. Hundreds of children fell ill and died. But at the beginning of 1967, Moshe and Hamama Tan'ami received two notices from the government, one informing Yehuda Tan'ami that he was now eligible to vote, the other summoning him for IDF service. Similar notices were received by dozens of Israeli families who had lost their babies, virtually all of them from Yemen. The notices reopened the wounds and restarted the wave of rumors that had circulated over the years: the children had not died but been stolen and possibly even sold for adoption.

Hamama Tan'ami's account was echoed by hundreds of others. She was at the transit camp in Rosh Ha'ayin; her baby was in the special infant housing. "Every day I went to nurse him," she told a *Maariv* reporter. "One day I came early. A man cleaning the ward told me to wait outside. I stood by the window. Two ladies were standing near my Yehuda's bed. They were arguing. Each one said, 'He's mine.' Then they spoke in a foreign language. I walked around and heard two nurses talking. One said, 'So what? She has lots of children!' The other said, 'Yes, but this is wrong.' My heart was burning. I asked to go inside immediately. I went in and one of the nurses told me Yehuda had died. The nurse said, 'Go to the office, he's there.' I went. He wasn't there. I went to the tent to tell my husband. On the way, I heard them calling over the loudspeaker for me to come straight away. I ran to the office. There was a man called Ozeri there and he said, 'You should know that your boy did not die. I'm in charge of burials here. Go and look for him.' I searched and searched and searched and I couldn't find him. We were like blind people in a new land. There was no one to talk to. No one listened to us. We yelled, we cried. We begged—nothing."

In 1967, the government set up an investigative committee to look into the issue of the missing children. The committee located the graves of most, but not all. They found no evidence of children having been kidnapped or given up for adoption illegally. The induction order and voting notices sent to the deceased children seemed to reflect the general disorder that characterized the handling of immigrants. The committee found that Yehuda Tan'ami had died of malnutrition, malaria, and pneumonia, and that he had been buried in a plot that the committee had located.[30] But the rumors were extremely persistent and haunted Israel for years to come. Some of the infants' bodies were subjected to autopsies without their parents' knowledge. Most of the parents were devout; they may have found it easier to blame the disappearance of their children on the government than on God. Either way, it is doubtful that any incident could better have illustrated the great sense of injustice felt by Mizrahim, and the chasm between them and the Ashkenazi establishment.[31]

The woman from Morocco was Amalia Ben-Harush, of Kiryat Ata. In the middle of May 1967, she gave birth to a son, whom she named Israel. He was a chubby, healthy baby. The nurses in the maternity ward tied a red ribbon around his neck in celebration of his birth. A few days later his mother received an enthusiastic letter from David Ben-Gurion, expressing his admiration of her heroism as a mother in Israel, "unique in her generation and perhaps in all generations." As a gift, he sent her a check for one thousand liras. Little Israel was the twentieth child of Amalia and Meir Ben-Harush, and Ben-Gurion wished to laud her as a heroine to boost the Jewish birthrate.*

The press took part in this familial celebration. Journalists made a valiant effort to commend all twenty children, and to record their names, their birthdates, and their occupations. Various papers produced different lists, but they created a single myth: Meir and Amalia Ben-Harush emerged as ideal Moroccans. They were happy. So happy and so thankful. And so quiet. They taught their children to speak quietly, too. They were not bitter about their deprivation; they did not set fire to cars or make demands, but only asked politely for what they lacked. The Ben-Harushes did not yet have a refrigerator, a fact the newspapers observed as if to demonstrate the family's modesty and commendable willingness to make do, for the sake of the country. The family was so exalted that *Maariv* assigned it a biblical romanticism by describing it as "a tribe." Meir Ben-Harush was a religious man, but the secular *Maariv* assured its readers that he wore only "a small yarmulke," thus posing no real threat to secular Ashkenazi culture. Going out of its way to sanctify the family, the press positioned it at the heart of Israeli iconography and compared it to a kibbutz.[32]

Denial of discrimination was evident in other spheres, too. The stage hit of the season was *Kazablan,* starring Yehoram Gaon and written by Yigal Mosenzon. *Maariv* praised it as a fascinating musical "about the Moroccan man Kazablan, who is unable to find a place for himself after his discharge from the army." Much like *West Side Story,* which producer Giora Godik had imported a few years previously, *Kazablan* obliquely

---

*The check was transferred via the Haifa branch of Ben-Gurion's party, Rafi. Up until 1960, the government gave grants of 100 liras to every mother giving birth to her tenth baby. Nearly 5,000 women received these grants. After 1960, child allowances of 100 liras were distributed through the National Insurance Institute. In the second half of 1966, the birthrate decreased, apparently as a result of the recession.

hinted at true social distress and, as on Broadway, turned it into an entertaining spectacle that angered no one and, consequently, worried no one. Minister Haim Gvati was impressed. "A dynamic play, very impressive," he wrote in his diary. "It's no wonder it has been running for several months."[33]

Yet Mizrahim were asserting themselves against such complacency. The day after Passover ended, a few thousand Moroccan Israelis had held their Mimouna celebration, an annual festivity that had been customary in Morocco and renewed in Israel only in 1965, in a forest near Lod named after Theodor Herzl. More than reinvigorating a popular folkloristic ritual, the resurrected Mimouna sent a message: we too, the natives of Morocco, have something to contribute to Israeli society. Some viewed this as a threat. A senior editorialist at Ha'aretz, Shabtai Teveth, warned that "Israel is taking on an Oriental tone." This anxiety surpassed even economic and political concerns. More profound than the worries regarding poverty and unemployment, even violence, it touched on the foundations of the Israeli dream and Israeli identity.

UNEASE OVER THE DESTRUCTION OF ISRAELI CULTURE HAD BEEN WITH THE ASHKENAZI establishment since the first days of the state. "Indeed, there is cause for anxiety," wrote Yosef Weitz as early as 1950. Over the years, more and more Israelis registered the fact that the country was losing its Ashkenazi character and looked on with distaste as Mizrahi culture made inroads. "We cannot turn into a Mizrahi people," said the author Haim Hazaz; what he meant was we *must* not become such a people. "I have a great objection," he explained. "We have traveled for two thousand years to become a Jewish European cultural entity. We cannot now turn back the wheel and accept the culture of Yemen, Morocco, and Iraq." Hazaz further cautioned, "We are nearing the precipice with regards to Levantinism."[34]* Shabtai Teveth feared a generation in which three out of four Israelis would lack any affinity with Western culture. Such a generation might be closer to "the culture of our surroundings," he wrote, implying a proximity between Mizrahim and Arabs. His concern, Teveth explained, stemmed from the fact that the government was not doing enough to

---

*The term "Levantine" connoted something culturally inferior, but not necessarily Mizrahi. When Ben-Gurion protested "Levantinization," he meant that in Tel Aviv there were too many commercial signs in English. "Levantinism is wrapping itself in a cloak of Americanization," a kibbutz movement publication once cautioned.[35]

eradicate the gaps between Mizrahim and Ashkenazis—that is, to bring Mizrahim closer to European culture. "The greater the proportion of descendents of Africa and Asia in the population, the lower the education level might drop and the greater the breach with European culture." Teveth drew encouragement from the fact that most teachers tended to be women, which he believed delayed the entrance of Mizrahim into the profession, but it would not always be so. "Given the relative increase of natives of Asia and Africa, surely they too will join the population of teachers. . . . Can we assume that a teacher born in Asia or Africa, or born in Israel to parents from there, will be able to maintain the level of instruction of teachers from Europe?" The question was rhetorical. Teveth determined that to prevent a deterioration in the level of education, and even to improve it, the country should avoid "too great a drop in the proportion of teachers of European origin." One reason for Teveth's view of the country's European character as essential was the importance of the relationship between Israel and the rest of the Jewish world. "Most Jews in the world lean on the culture of Europe, not on 'the Levant culture,' " he wrote. Only in Israel was there a growing Jewish community that was not European. If the government failed to instill European culture in Israeli children, Israel would be "a mirror image" of the Jewish people, which would deter Jews from prosperous countries from settling there.[36]

Ha'aretz monitored the daily manifestations of Levantinism. "People eat while walking along Dizengoff Street," the paper reported in early 1966, and described with distaste a new "steak house," the brainchild of three cab drivers, that sold grilled meats in pita. Abie Nathan's California also served steaks in pita. Like falafel and *shwarma*, this dish came "from the fringes," wrote *Ha'aretz*, noting that "in Europe, people do not eat on the streets."[37] *Ha'aretz* also campaigned to preserve the customary two-hour period of afternoon silence. This effort seemed to be intended to educate noisy Ashkenazis, too, including music teachers, who had been tainted by the manners of the Levant. The paper devoted an editorial to the topic: "The boy whose music practice wafts from the neighbor's window, complete with grating, screeching, and off-key notes, might or might not be a future Paganini. But will the child's genius be thwarted if he does his homework until four and only then picks up the violin?"[38]*

---

*S. Y. Agnon wrote to the paper that he spent most hours of the day in stern contemplation of the evil of man, thanks to the racket caused by people near his home in Jerusalem. In response, Mayor Teddy Kollek ordered that a sign be posted next to Agnon's house, asking people to be quiet.[39]

In the opinion of Avraham Harman, Israel's ambassador to Washington, the battle over culture was virtually a lost cause. "A Jew like myself does not in fact represent the current Israeli reality," he proposed. As ambassador, he of course gave voice to the concerns of Mizrahi Jews and presented their claims, but in his manner of speaking and his outward appearance he did not truly represent them, he said. This notion troubled him not only as an Israeli but as a professional diplomat. There he was, on a television show, debating the representative of an Arab state. "He speaks English with an Arab accent," said Harman, "I speak British English. And he may well ask me—indeed, throw it in my face—'What are you even doing in Israel?' You were born in London, your parents came to London from Russia, what are you doing there?'" This would not happen, for example, to an Israeli born in Iraq, Harman explained as if with professional envy, because he could say, "I, too, am from the Middle East, I am in Israel because it is my homeland. It is the land of my forefathers. I have a historic right to it, although of course I could have remained in your country and waited for you to hang me in the town square." And then the Arab ambassador in the television studio would have to shut his mouth, Harman concluded.[40]*

Clearly, the Israeli unity that Harman ostensibly represented in Washington was far more fragile than many Israelis had perceived. The recession opened their eyes.

ONLY FOUR OUT OF EVERY TEN JEWS LIVING IN ISRAEL IN 1967 HAD BEEN BORN THERE. The other six-tenths, amounting to more than a million people, came from practically every other place on earth. Most were from Eastern Europe; many of these were Holocaust survivors. About half came from Islamic countries. More than half the Jews had settled in Israel after the establishment of the state. Nearly half a million, one out of every five, had lived in Israel for less than a decade.[42] Many Israelis had not settled there of their own free will, but as refugees, and many of those would have preferred to stay in their own countries. Neither Zionist ideology, the emerging Hebrew identity, patriotism and a willingness to sacrifice, nor anti-Semitic persecution, nor even the memory of the Holocaust sufficed to erase from many hearts the vague sense that they had left behind

---

*Another Israeli diplomat in the United States, Yisashar Ben-Yakov, estimated that Jewish Americans were finding it more and more difficult to understand the changing face of Israel. He therefore proposed appointing a Mizrahi publicity official.[41]

a better life, or at least the chance for a better future than what they found in Israel.

In "The Spotted Tiger," writer Yaakov Shabtai gave his character, Shoshana, a Vilna-born owner of a small restaurant in Tel Aviv, the following line: "If I had stayed there, and I had gone to the academy, I would have been in the opera by now." Her chances of ending up in Auschwitz would have been greater, but Shabtai was expressing, through Shoshana, a common perception. Like many European Jews, a large number of Jews from Arab countries would have also preferred to stay in their countries. They came because the War of Independence and the establishment of the state had made their lives among the Arabs impossible. The loss of home was the price they paid to realize the Zionist dream. Like many newcomers, both Ashkenazis and Mizrahim, they were a lost generation, doomed to lives spent in the misery of immigration. In a conversation with a reporter from *Yediot Aharonot*, one immigrant sounded as if he had stepped straight out of Shabtai's story: "If I had stayed overseas, I would have owned a shop by now, maybe even two." André Chouraqui, an Algerian-born lawyer who became a deputy mayor of Jerusalem, wrote: "Algerian Jews in France enjoy the wide variety of social services offered to families, including free education from kindergarten to university."*

On almost every continent conditions harsher than in Israel could be found, but when Israelis talked about "abroad" they were referring not only to a higher standard of living, but often to a better quality of life and even better human relations. "If, for example, you purchase an inferior product," wrote Shmuel Schnitzer in *Maariv*, "and it breaks before you have the chance to enjoy it, can you expect to get your money back from an Israeli store (even a reputable one)? Can you be sure that when you go and complain they will even listen to you and believe you? In civilized countries they believe you and they apologize and give your money back. Here . . . in no case and nowhere will they do that." Amos Oz found it hard, when young, to see Israel as "a real place," about which there was something to write. "A real place," he wrote, was Paris, Madrid, New York.[44]

As long as the country seemed to be forging a stable society that was integrating within the Western world and offered its population both shared and personal growth, people could believe in the Israeli dream, as

---

*Representatives of the Ministry of Foreign Affairs in Europe reported that many North African Jews were hesitant to immigrate to Israel because of the economic situation, preferring the "fleshpots" of Brussels and Paris.[43]

many did until early 1966. People like Yosef Weitz, Yehoshua Bar-Dayan, and even Uri, the young boy from Rishon Lezion, knew it was their task to lead those who came later, including the weak among them, to a safer and better future. They were the elite and they knew it. The recession, Mizrahi poverty, and mounting anxiety about the loss of Western identity abruptly showed them how distant that dream really was.

3. ISRAELI ARABS: "MY NAME IS AHMED"

Yossi Mizrahi spent almost a year on a kibbutz in the north before the time came to decide whether he would be accepted as a full member. In the meantime, he had fallen in love with a kibbutznik, Rivka. The first time they were together she had asked him, "You're Yemenite, aren't you?" Yossi was startled. "Good God, what is she thinking to herself right now?" he wondered. But he found an acceptable answer: No, he told her, he wasn't Yemenite. He was Israeli-born. There was nothing he found more troublesome than the kibbutz members' probing questions—who was he, where was he from, who were his parents, why didn't they come to visit? The kibbutz secretary, Selig, told him that before they could accept him as a member, they had to know everything about him. Yossi Mizrahi told Selig he had grown up on another kibbutz. This opened the path to an investigation, which exposed the true facts. "You're not Jewish!" said Selig, which was true. Yossi Mizrahi was an Arab posing as a Jew. Would the kibbutz still accept him?

Yossi Mizrahi and Rivka and Selig were characters in a novel, *In a New Light,* published by Atallah Mansour in 1966. Mansour, a journalist for *Ha'aretz,* was thirty-two years old at the time, one of the few Arab journalists employed by the Hebrew press. He had been born in the Christian village of Jeish, in the biblical Gush Halav region. In 1946, he was sent to high school in Lebanon, where he was still living when the War of Independence broke out and cut him off from his village. In 1950 he crossed the border back into Israel illegally and studied Hebrew on Kibbutz Sha'ar Haamakim. He lived as an illegal alien in Israel until 1960 and then, already writing for *Ha'aretz,* obtained Israeli citizenship. *In a New Light* was written in the first person.

The kibbutz members are conflicted. "Look, Yossi," says Selig, "we returned after two thousand years of exile from countries all over the world to be with our people." Yossi asks whether Selig is certain that his ancestors were really Jews who had lived in this land, and Selig replies, "The personal dimension does not matter!" Well, then, asks Yossi, why does his own personal dimension matter? "I thought it did to you!" replies Selig. But he agrees to raise the issue at the kibbutz assembly. "We face a historical decision this evening," he begins at the meeting. "We have no choice. This evening we must decide on our continued path. We are at a crossroads." Yossi tells them that when he was five, during British rule, his father was murdered; he does not know by whom. Perhaps the murderer was an Englishman, perhaps a Jew, perhaps an Arab. A man named Mizrahi took him in, and later he moved to a kibbutz and grew up there as a Jew, but the kibbutz was too homogeneous for him and so he left. He could have stayed, but the kibbutz members' views differed from his, perhaps because of his past. He could move to a city, of course, but he loves kibbutz life and he also loves Rivka. He wants to stay, he tells the members. He believes he can live with them and that they can live with him.

One member asks whether he is a Jew or an Arab. His papers, he replies, say he is Jewish. The members demand to know how he feels. "Like everyone," he says. One person comments, "The truth is, my friends, that we are faced with a fundamental problem of the utmost importance. True, we were brought up on ideals of full equality among men! But I believe our first duty is to be the pioneering force for our people in its struggle to implement socialism. Yosef's place is not among us. He must live among his people and wage his battle there." Someone else says that Yosef is not an Arab in much the same way that they are, in fact, not Jews: who among them is aware, for example, that the discussion is taking place on the eve of *Tisha B'av*, the holy fast day? But one member raises the question of future children. She wonders whether they should not be considered and their tragedy prevented. Yossi responds, "I will strive for my children to be human beings. Not Jews or Arabs." But the member stands her ground. "He is planning certain disaster for his children!" she maintains, and proposes that they reject his request. One member says that they should decide whether their kibbutz, of all places, should be a center of racial mixing, and the debate briefly becomes an argument over discrimination against blacks in America. Then Selig stands up and proposes a compromise. Yosef will be accepted for full kibbutz membership, but no protocol will be recorded. The kibbutz will simply be accepting another member. Not an Arab, not a Jew. "Furthermore," he adds, "I move that this debate be kept secret by every member. That's that. Are there any other proposals?" Everyone breathes a sigh of relief. Even the members who had initially objected now agree. "Selig has found the golden mean. We are not a forum authorized to decide on such a sensitive matter, but we cannot ignore our education as socialists and as Jews." And so Yossi is allowed to stay.[45]

The Zionist movement had adopted liberal democratic ideals from the first. Jewish leaders in Palestine were committed to socialism and social-democratic principles. But during the thirty years prior to independence they were often forced to choose between humanistic socialist principles and the national interest, and they usually chose the latter. Zionism rejected the idea that the Jews of Europe could ever attain equal rights in their countries, and so it called for them to move to their own state. Many of the founders believed that the Arabs in Palestine should also move to other countries, as if it were a historical rule that minorities could not achieve equal rights. "These Arabs should not be living here, just as American Jews should not be living in America," said David Ben-Gurion in 1950.[46]

The first Israelis were aware of their past as a persecuted minority and as Holocaust survivors, and they spoke often of the moral humanistic obligation that history had placed upon them. The newly founded state's Proclamation of Independence promised equality for all, regardless of religion, race, or sex. By 1967, Israeli Arabs represented what Atallah Mansour's Yossi Mizrahi was on his kibbutz: a litmus test for Israel's basic principles.

EIGHT OUT OF EVERY TEN ARABS LIVING IN PALESTINE PRIOR TO THE ESTABLISHMENT of Israel became refugees; some 20 percent of Palestinian Arabs—approximately 160,000 people—remained within the borders of the new country. Shocked and defeated, they became citizens of a state at war with their own people. The language, religion, and culture of the new nation were foreign to them. By 1967, their numbers had almost doubled, to 312,000, making them roughly 12 percent of Israel's population. In the Galilee and the so-called Triangle area in the north, they were the majority. Most were Muslims, with a minority of Christians, Druze, and others. They lived predominantly in villages. The population was relatively young; there were six people in an average Arab family, as opposed to four in a Jewish family. By 1967, six out of ten Israeli Arabs had been born after the establishment of the state.[47] As Israeli citizens, they were entitled to vote and run for the Knesset, but they were not Israelis with equal rights, or equal duties. Very few served in the IDF. The state viewed them as a security risk, and since Israel's establishment they had been subject to martial law.

Martial law was the product of emergency laws imposed by the British in Palestine, laws that had been designed to, among other things, subjugate the Jewish population. Jewish lawyers who had tried to fight these regulations at the time had compared them to Nazi policy. In daily life, martial law was manifested mainly in restrictions imposed on residents' mobility. Whenever they wished to leave their area of residence they had to appear at the military governor's offices and obtain a permit, which stated not only the destination and the date, but also the time of departure and return. The permit was required for every purpose, whether for travel for work, business, medical treatment, or to visit relatives. Weddings, funerals, surgery, going to the movies in the next town—all required a permit. Obtaining permits meant standing in lines. There were different types of permits, issued on forms that periodically changed. Permits often entailed extensive interrogation and petitions. Granting and withholding permits were done at the discretion of the governor, and often depended on his mood or other arbitrary factors. Not all of the governor's representatives were immune to accepting favors of various kinds. Naturally, the travel permits served as a means of oppression and control: people were asked to spy on their neighbors, to denounce them, all in order to obtain travel permits. Thousands of people were punished by means of orders forbidding them from leaving their places of residence, or even by deportation orders that forced them to live away from their homes.

Martial law was imposed not only because of security considerations but also to facilitate the state's confiscation of land from Arabs and to control their political activities. Over the years, the state confiscated roughly half of all Arab-owned land and transferred it to the Jewish National Fund's authority. As a director of the JNF, Yosef Weitz had significant influence over the allocation of appropriated lands to Jewish communities. The JNF was also involved in a national campaign to destroy the remnants of Arab villages that had been emptied of their inhabitants during the War of Independence.

Mapai, which did not accept Arab citizens as members, set up Arab satellite parties. By the end of the sixties, most Arabs were voting for Mapai and its satellites. Some gave their votes to other Zionist parties, as well as to the Communist parties. Out of 120 members, the Sixth Knesset included seven non-Jews. The parties bought Arab votes with money and various methods of threats and intimidation, some coordinated with the military martial-law administration, the security service, and the police. Their common goal was to prevent Israeli Arabs from starting their own political organizations. To this end they also used the educational system: to be hired as a teacher, one needed authorization from the security service. Teachers, as well as students, were forced to serve as collaborators. Teachers were questioned about what went on in students' homes, students about what teachers said in class.* Politics among Israeli Arabs was still based, to a great extent, on family affiliation. Government offices and parties dispensed favors based on political considerations, not only to different sectors but also to individuals.

The treatment of Israeli Arabs was always extremely contradictory. Martial law was supposed to ensure isolation in their villages, but the confiscation of land meant that one out of every two Arab breadwinners had to work for a Jewish employer. Many worked in agriculture or construction, receiving authorization from the military administration to go to work.[48]

By 1967, most Israeli Arabs were living in poverty and under precarious conditions. Although their circumstances had improved over the years, they suffered discrimination in practically every aspect of life. Their average income was less than half of the general average in Israel. Seventy-four percent of Arab villages were not hooked up to the electricity grid, 75 percent were not connected to the national water system, and 20 percent had no access roads. Not a single Arab village had paved streets, nor had sewage infrastructure been laid. Public housing was seldom built for Arabs. Only three out of ten Arabs were insured by the national health fund, whereas eight of every ten Jews were. In six out of ten Arab villages there was no clinic operated by the health fund. Fifteen percent of students in elementary schools were Arab, but the state allocated only 3 percent of its education budget to Arab education. An Arab farmer made between 30 and 50 percent less than a Jewish farmer. A Jewish construction worker made up to twice as much as an Arab. In the spring of 1966, during the economic recession, the unemployment rate among Arabs was twice as high as among Jews.[49] Until then most Israelis had tended to ignore the Arabs' plight, but it too became unavoidable, reinforcing the sudden and painful recognition that the Israeli success story was, to a great extent, only a myth.

Ha'aretz reported Arab laborers' destitution and exploitation in a series of articles published in early 1966, which included a detailed description of their appalling living conditions in abandoned barns and packing houses and in leaking tin shacks. Some even lived out in the open, in

---

*In February 1963, Ben-Gurion, speaking in the Knesset, used quotations from the notebooks of students in Arab schools as evidence of growing admiration of the Egyptian president, Nasser. He did not say how he had obtained the children's notebooks.

junkyards or garbage dumps. Not confined to distant villages, enclosed and cut off from the Israeli community, these conditions existed right in the heart of the country, between Tel Aviv and Rishon Lezion. Most Arab laborers were afraid to give the newspaper their names. Their spokesman was Ahmed Masrawa, from the village of Ar'ara.[50] He worked in a diamond-cutting business owned by David Ehrenfeld, who gave money to reconciliation efforts between Jews and Arabs. Ehrenfeld financed a seventeen-minute film that documented the plight of Arab laborers and caused a scandal.

My Name Is Ahmed was a powerful film. It did not deal with the Israeli-Arab conflict, did not even mention martial law, and did not expose the deprivation in Arab villages. Its producers—Avshalom Katz and Ram Levi, both employed by Kol Israel radio—accompanied one young man, a high school graduate, as he set off for work in Tel Aviv. His name was Ahmed Masrawa. With him on the bus were other young Arabs, including children who had not finished elementary school. They worked hard. Contractors preferred to hire Arab laborers because no one tried to enforce their rights. Masrawa described their attitude toward the laborers. To goad them, the boss would say, "Don't work like an Arab," because "Arab work" was considered substandard. Some Arab workers disguised themselves as Jews. One, Jamal, wore a Star of David and went by the name of Yitzhak. Before that, said Ahmed, he had been called a "dirty Arab." The young men tried to rent rooms. The camera followed them to six addresses, where, as soon as it became clear that they were Arabs, the landlords would say they were sorry, the room was taken. At the seventh address they were explicitly told: We don't rent to Arabs. Ahmed's friend suggested they introduce themselves using Jewish names. Ahmed refused. "My name is Ahmed," he said, and went to sleep on a mattress in a shantytown.

He understands the Israelis, Ahmed tells the camera. This is a land under siege. Almost every day there's a terrorist attack. But the terror comes from outside, it's not the workers' fault. He walks around Tel Aviv, alone among the twinkling lights, watching couples out having fun. He wants to live with Jews in friendship and reconciliation, but they treat him as if he were invisible. "They're afraid of me, they hate me," he says. They do not want him here, with them, with their women; they would like him to go to America or Canada. But he still has hope, he says. He still has dreams. The last scene shows the Capitol building in Washington, D.C.

The film hit a nerve. "A harsh film," wrote Minister Haim Gvati in his diary. "It tells the truth, but not the whole truth." The prime minister's adviser for Arab affairs, who had at first agreed to help fund the film, changed his mind in a panic as soon as he saw it, so the producers agreed to modify a few lines. Instead of having Ahmed say, "Once we had a lot of land, now the kibbutzim have it," they agreed to have him say, "Before the war we had lots of land." Instead of saying that Arabs were employed because few Jews were willing to take on hard, dirty work, they said, "Contractors hire Arabs who are willing to do hard, dirty work." But the self-censorship did not help. Mapai officials asked why the film didn't show Israeli Arabs being treated by the health fund, or the Arab villages that were connected to power and water grids. Where was the Histadrut club? they asked in the Knesset. Some claimed the film might incite Arabs against the state, and there were those who argued that it could damage Israel's reputation in the world. *Ha'aretz* concluded from these responses that most Israelis were unwilling to look at the true nature of their society.[51] Since the day Israel was established, the Arabs had indeed posed a challenge to its identity as a Jewish and democratic state.

On occasion, Arab members of the Knesset accused the state of trying to force Arabs to leave the country; some did leave. The prime minister's office found it difficult to monitor the phenomenon because many of those who left did not declare that they were doing so permanently. But according to one estimate, the percentage of Arabs leaving the country for good was twice as high as their proportion in the population. The prime minister's adviser on Arab affairs noted, however, that this amounted to only a few hundred people. Prime Minister Eshkol said he regretted the emigration of Arabs and called on them to stay. He added this expression of sorrow by hand to a draft of a speech prepared by his office. Someone put a large question mark next to his note.

Ha'aretz called for the integration of Arabs into civic life and gave fairly broad publicity to private initiatives meant to reconcile Jews and Arabs, such as those organized by the Tel Aviv socialite Nina De-Nur. When a few Arabs founded a public committee to enhance their status as Israelis with equal rights, they gained support from *Ha'aretz*.[52] But alongside the ideological, moral, and political difficulties involved in living with the Arabs, there was a genuine fear of them as spies and terrorists. The press attributed to them extreme nationalism and anti-Israeli sentiments, and portrayed them as agents of the enemy: "15 spy networks in 7 years," announced *Maariv*, apparently on the basis of information obtained from the security forces.[53] In August 1963, the mayor of Netanya, Oved Ben-Ami, said, "Netanya is the only urban center that stands as a force against Arabs in the Triangle area, who are increasing and flourishing. I'm not even talking about the temporary border between us and the other Arabs, the cease-fire line. As the years pass, we'll also see a problem at Tul Karem and Nablus [in the West Bank] as well. We must have a large Jewish center to stand against the Arab sector. We cannot allow the country's central area to become too weak."[54]

A debate arose over whether to include Arab students in the weapons training administered to Jewish students as part of the Gadna youth battalions program. In mixed cities, such as Haifa, there were close to a thousand Arab students involved. Everyone agreed they could not be allowed to participate in weapons training. So as not to discriminate against them, the Ministry of Education ruled that in mixed schools the Jewish students would not have weapons training either. The army objected, and Chief of Staff Yitzhak Rabin demanded that Eshkol step in. It was proposed that those exempt from military service would also be exempt from pre-military service. This meant that Arab students would not take any part at all in the Gadna training. The Ministry of Education charged teachers with explaining this new policy to students "in an inoffensive way."[55]

The Hebrew papers wrote about Arabs as they wrote about the Mizrahim, with a sort of anthropological fascination. "Even Dowry Prices Are Up . . ." announced *Maariv*, the ellipsis signaling that this was something ridiculous. *Ha'aretz* reported enthusiastically on the first Bedouin to study medicine in Israel. But its liberalism did not prevent it from running headlines such as "Eight Arabs Arrested for Assaulting a 15-Year-Old Girl" and "Foreigners Farming the Land at Megadim," the foreigners being Arabs. In the second half of 1966, *Ha'aretz* ran two short stories in which Arabs were featured as murderers.[56] But above all they were feared as the mothers and fathers of future children.

IN A SHORT STORY PUBLISHED BY *HA'ARETZ* IN THE SUMMER OF 1966, A JEWISH MAN meets an Arab man. "Does your father have one wife or two?" asks the Jew. The Arab responds, "That's what you always want to know. . . . He has two." The Jew then asks, "What's it like to live with two wives?" and the Arab replies that they are all one family.[57] Herein lay the real danger. "In the year 2000 there will be a million and a half Arabs here," warned one member of the Knesset in a debate devoted to encouraging the Jewish birthrate. The average Jewish woman had 3.1 children, while an average Muslim woman had 8.2. "This is a horrifying phenomenon," said Knesset member Yitzhak Rafael of Mafdal (the National Religious Party). "Arabs who adhere to their healthy national inclinations will continue to grow among us: Shall we not learn from them?" asked Rafael. "Should we not also adhere to our own national inclinations?" Another member of the Knesset, Mordechai Haim Stern, appealed to Jewish mothers' patriotism: "Every newborn child increases the security of the child already living and serving in the Israel Defense Forces." Stern said he often envied the good fortune of his wife, who was at home raising their children. But some women preferred to hold jobs and even employed maids, and some feared that having more children would restrict their freedom. They were to be reminded, Stern said, that they too, as women, bore a national, religious, and familial responsibility.

Opposition Knesset member Uri Avneri protested the state's attempt to enter citizens' bedrooms and to introduce biology into politics. Human beings are human beings, said Avneri, adding, "I do not want to mention regimes that we all abhor, which at their base had this dangerous mixture of biology and politics." In a similar discussion held in the Knesset, Meir Vilner, of the Communist party, said, "My entire family was destroyed because they were Jewish. As a Jew, I object to nationalistic anti-Arab tones. It offends my dignity as a Jew when racist questions such as these are raised in the Knesset."[58]

The government appointed a committee of experts to find ways to raise the Jewish birthrate without increasing that of the Arabs. The assumption was that the state could encourage people to enlarge their families through economic incentives, such as child support grants; but how to ensure that only Jews would receive these incentives? Ben-Gurion had an idea: the whole subject should be taken out of the government's hands and given to the Jewish Agency, which by definition served only the Jewish population—if the government began to pay out birth incentives, "it would spend all its money on families with many children, and they are of course almost all Arabs."* A government statistician, Roberto Bachi, wrote to Eshkol that the national peril posed by family planning must be explained to Jewish parents. This kind of campaign would best be left to some kind of nongovernment association. At the same time, information on family planning methods should be disseminated among the Arabs, and this, too, of course, would require "the utmost discretion." Earlier, the government had decided on an effort to curb abortions.[59]

---

*Several years prior to this, Ben-Gurion had asked to look into the possibility of converting Israeli Arabs to Judaism.

In August 1966, Yosef Weitz wrote to Ezra Danin, an adviser on Arab affairs in the Foreign Ministry, "I do not see a remedy or solution to this problem, which poses a danger to our state, other than by way of 'transfer.' There is no place for this minority among us. We dreamed of transfer and we addressed it before the establishment of the state. But its realization at that time was not possible. This is not the case now: transfer to countries near and far." Weitz seems to have been referring to a population transfer that would be arranged between Israel and its neighbors, in the framework of a peace agreement. That December, a senior IDF officer, Shlomo Gazit, explored an old fantasy of attaching some of the Arab villages in the Triangle region to an independent Arab state in the West Bank.[60] However, from elsewhere on the political spectrum, increasingly loud voices were calling for the lifting of martial law.

Opposition to martial law came at first from the left and was expressed by the Communists and the Ahdut Ha'avoda party together with Mapam, both socialist parties with many constituents among kibbutzim. They gained reinforcement from the right: Menachem Begin, the leader of the Herut party, demanded repeal of the emergency laws, which were left over from the British Mandate and had been designed to repress him and his movement. He called to replace them with Israeli statutes. The Knesset repeatedly debated lifting martial law. While prime minister, Ben-Gurion had insisted that the relevant laws not be repealed, but to appease his opposition he agreed to periodic improvements in the Arabs' living conditions and introduced various measures relaxing the severity of their governance.[61] Ben-Gurion's resignation in 1963 gave momentum to the fight against martial law. It was now the main cause of the liberal left and the war was waged in the spirit of the civil rights movement in the United States, with rallies, strikes, and even civil disobedience: activists entered closed areas in order to provoke arrest. The hero of this fight was a philosophy student named Uri Davis, a pacifist and a conscientious objector from the small town of Kfar Shmariyahu. His campaign against land confiscation in the Galilee to found the city of Carmiel had landed him in prison. Intellectuals and professors, including Martin Buber, lent their names to the cause of lifting martial law. Uri Avneri and his weekly magazine, *Ha'olam Hazeh,* gave voice to the Tel Aviv leftists, among them well-known artists and media figures.[62]

At the beginning of 1966, Isser Harel, a former head of the Security Service and the prime minister's adviser on security affairs, voiced support for revoking martial law, thus opening the door to dismantling the legal apparatus.* On November 8, 1966, Eshkol announced in the Knesset that martial law had "come to an end." It was a dramatic announcement, but not accurate: control had simply been transferred from the army to the police. The prime minister's office judged that the change would have a positive effect, "especially psychologically." Eshkol's biographer, Yossi Goldstein, wrote that lifting martial law did not reflect Eshkol's humanism: he continued to view the Arabs with suspicion and believed that Jews were entitled to settle the entire country. However, he believed that transferring supervision over the Arabs from the military to the police would reduce their hostility toward the state, and that this clearing of the air would make it easier for the state to set up a few dozen Jewish villages in the Galilee. Judaization of the Galilee had always been one of Eshkol's primary interests. He was also at the head of a parliamentary alignment between Mapai, his party, and Ahdut Ha'avoda, which had long been demanding the revocation of martial law, so his decision on the matter was also a function of coalition politics.

However, the police enforced the law more rigidly than the military had, and over the next few months conditions for Arabs worsened. Arab laborers who had worked illegally for years in closed areas now lost their jobs. "There was great anticipation of the revocation of martial law, but since in practice there has been hardly any easing of the restrictions, the result has been no small disappointment and much criticism, among both Jews and Arabs," wrote Eshkol's adviser on Arab affairs, Shmuel Toledano. "All our propaganda efforts . . . have yielded no results: the general opinion, unjustly, is that the government has fulfilled very few of its promises." Toledano therefore recommended further relaxing the restrictions.[64]

Similar pressure continued to come from the kibbutzim, as well. Many had been founded on the ruins of Arab villages whose inhabitants had fled or been deported, and whose land the kibbutzim were now farming. But the kibbutzim also frequently declared their commitment to the principle of equality for all Israelis, including Arabs. Kibbutz Yehiam's newsletter published a lovely poem for the Jewish new year, hoping for "Peace for both peoples, under the shade of one fig tree . . . For red wine sparkling with grapes / For a thousand flowers, with no hatred or grief / For the sword to return to its sheath forever / For a child to free a white

*In a discussion between Eshkol and Harel on martial law, the closed military areas were described as "cages."[63]

dove."[65] Perhaps the incongruity here between loftily declared ideals and sober reality reflected a real moral and ideological dilemma, or perhaps it was a means of exploitation and hypocrisy. In this regard, the poets of Kibbutz Yehiam were no different from most other Israelis.

4. KIBBUTZIM: "IT'S ALL A CARDBOARD SET"

Whenever Yosef Weitz visited Kibbutz Yehiam, he came away impressed. "From year to year, the place grows more magnificent," he wrote in his diary. He was enchanted by the trees, the flowers, and the lawns.[66] There was a lemon grove and a chicken coop and a herd of cattle. The members grew cotton and bananas.

Kibbutz Yehiam's founders had come to Palestine as children, from Czechoslovakia and Hungary. Their parents, who had remained behind, were murdered by the Nazis. The newcomers set up the kibbutz, at the foot of the isolated Crusader fortress in the Galilee, within six or seven years of their arrival. Less than two years later, in 1948, they had to fight for their lives. After the Israeli victory, Yehiam was allotted more territory, land that had belonged to Arabs. On its twentieth anniversary the kibbutz had roughly 450 full members, four times as many as in its first year. There were plans for expansion, as well as many apprehensions. "We go back and forth between hope and fear," kibbutz members wrote in their newsletter.[67]

By 1967, Yehiam was one of 232 kibbutzim, whose total population was approximately 81,000, about 3.5 percent of the Jewish population of Israel.[68] There were large kibbutzim and small ones; some were more leftist than others, and a few were religious. They were organized within a number of political movements. Yehiam was part of Hashomer Hatzair, the youth movement to which Yehiam Weitz had belonged.

THE FIRST KIBBUTZNIKS ARRIVED FROM EUROPE IN THE 1920S. DREAMERS AND PIONEERS, naïve revolutionaries, they believed in the power of choice—the choice to settle in Palestine, to stay there, to join a kibbutz, and to remain in it. They wanted to live together without private property, each person working to his or her utmost ability, mainly in agriculture, and each person receiving according to his or her needs. Everyone was supposed to make decisions together at the kibbutz assembly. Early kibbutzniks even showered together, shared clothes, cooked together, and ate in communal dining rooms. When children were born, they were housed together in "children's houses."[69] These children were commonly called Sabras, for a local cactus; they grew up, like Yehiam Weitz, into the fight against the British and the War of Independence. Many of them fought, again like Weitz, in the exclusive ideological framework of the Palmah.

The Sabra, the "new man," born in Israel, is a person whose existence is as part of a group that preserves its uniformity and tends to stifle independent thought and personal initiative: the *I* retreats in the face of the *we*. He suppresses emotion, reveres stringency, scorns politics, and, frequently, disdains education and words in general. The Sabra is supposed to be direct, a blunt talker: he speaks *dugri* (an Arabic word adopted by Hebrew slang, meaning "coarsely," "straight from the shoulder"). He was supposed to be a revival of the biblical hero: upright, proud, brave, masculine, defending his honor and that of his people. This was the origin of the Hebrew expression "From the Tanach—the Bible—to the Palmah." As the first generation of Israelis, these young men and women nurtured their love of the homeland through hiking and a near cultish devotion to archaeology. "The Land of Israel club on our kibbutz is the oldest and most stable of all the other clubs," asserted a member of Yehiam.[70]

In the thirties and forties the kibbutzim were considered the jewel in the Zionist crown. During the first years of the state, nothing epitomized Israel more than the kibbutz, and the country was often depicted precisely as some of the kibbutz movement's founders had dreamed: as one big kibbutz. Their foundation throughout Palestine played a large part in determining the borders of the state, and no one did more than they to celebrate it. But as the years wore on, the kibbutzniks began to lose their elite status, and by 1967 they found themselves engaged in the somewhat pathetic struggle of a dying aristocracy. New elites had sprung up in their place: politicians, administrators, scientists, industrialists, academics. These groups had gained in strength partly at the expense of the kibbutzniks' political and moral status; the primary remaining stronghold of the kibbutzniks was the army. "Since the establishment of the state, kibbutz members have felt despondent," said a leader of the kibbutz movement, Yitzhak Ben-Aharon, adding: "The kibbutz has seemingly been pushed aside."[71]

The ideological standpoint of the kibbutz movement was reflected during the sixties in its attitude toward three countries: the United States, the Soviet Union, and Germany. The United States was perceived as corrupting its youth with a deluge of commodities. Elvis Presley symbolized the decadent bourgeois culture. As the influence of American culture grew, the kibbutzim sensed that the threat from the outside world was growing.[72] The USSR, by contrast, represented the sought-after "world of tomorrow." The songs of the Red Army were considered Israeli folk songs. One kibbutz movement leader, Yaakov Hazan, described the USSR as "our second homeland."[73] As more and more news came of the Soviet regime's crimes and corruption, the kibbutzim became engaged in debates over the essence of true socialism. Later, Moscow's increased hostility toward Israel and the persistent news of anti-Jewish repression in the Soviet Union plunged the kibbutzim into much soul-searching. With regard to West Germany, kibbutz representatives were members of Eshkol's government, which had diplomatic relations with that nation, although the kibbutz movement had rejected any such contact for many years. After reparations for Holocaust crimes began, however, the kibbutzim started exporting to West Germany. The kibbutzniks debated, as only kibbutzniks could, if it would be fitting to sing Schubert in German.

To the outside world, according to historian Alon Gan, the kibbutz movement continued to voice familiar slogans against American capitalism and ties with Germany, against consumerism and slavishness to fashion, against private property and salaried work. But in practice, Western consumerist culture attracted every kibbutz household, as did salaried work outside the kibbutz.[74]

IN SEPTEMBER 1966, A REPORTER FOR *YEDIOT AHARONOT* WENT TO VISIT FRIENDS ON A kibbutz. When he wrote about his visit he deployed a plethora of foreign terms, as if to indicate that the world at large had finally reached the kibbutz. "With milk or without?" asked his hostess as she pulled the lever on an espresso machine. Some of the guests sat on bar stools at a marble-like Formica counter. Coffee was served in decorative ceramic mugs. The young woman operating the espresso maker leafed through a glossy magazine. Soft lighting from an unseen source gave the low-ceilinged room a relaxed atmosphere, as background music drifted through. One young couple engaged in a slow dance. This was the members' club on a young kibbutz.[75]

The writer's anthropological tone was not unusual: papers reported on kibbutz life as if visiting an exotic tribe. Kibbutzniks were pondering the observance of mourning customs, wrote *Maariv*, which also reported in amazement on kibbutz members finding success as factory managers in the cities. The status of kibbutz women supplied material for many articles, and *Yediot Aharonot* reported for the thousandth time that in the early days of the kibbutz, children "went through hell" because they were "prey" for all sorts of educational ideals and "guinea pigs for things like common showers for boys and girls under the age of eighteen."[76]

Meir'ke, the friend of the *Yediot Aharonot* reporter who wrote that story, took him to his apartment, which had one bedroom, a living room, a kitchen, and a bathroom. Out of habit, Meir'ke still referred to it as his "room." He had a bar across one entire wall, and they both sipped 777, a well-known Israeli brand of cognac. This is the life, thought the reporter; things have changed. And at this point, in the second of the article's nine columns, he mentioned the swimming pool, a symbol of the good life on the kibbutz.* The reporter and his friend reminisced: Where had they met last? Was it in Paris, London, or Stockholm? Meir'ke said that everyone on Kibbutz Nahal Oz had been overseas and they were starting a second round of travel. "Why not? If they can, why shouldn't they go? Everyone travels. Why does a guy from northern Tel Aviv deserve it more than a kibbutznik?" Meir'ke said the kibbutzim were still an equal society, with ideals and a value system that had not changed for the last fifty years.[78] This was not true: by 1967, life on the kibbutzim had certainly changed, leaving many of the old-timers with a bad taste in their mouths.

Kibbutz members had discovered the electric kettle and the record player, the refrigerator and the television, all of which made it more enjoyable for members to spend time in their rooms, thus threatening kibbutz togetherness. The new way of life necessitated new regulations. Typically, kibbutzniks argued these matters heatedly. The television was considered a true enemy, a monster, and then there were the transistor radios, the cameras people received as gifts from their relatives in the cities—all detrimental to the principle of equality. These changes were discussed in Yehiam, too.[79]

Kibbutzniks began reading the general national newspapers *Maariv*, *Yediot Aharonot*, and *Ha'olam Hazeh* in addition to the daily papers published by the kibbutz movements, and often instead of them.[80] The Yehiam newsletter attributed this phenomenon to the fact that the ideological newspapers, Mapam's *Al Hamishmar* most prominently, no longer met kibbutz members' needs. The newsletter was mainly troubled by the members' inclination to read *Ha'olam Hazeh*, which was so much a product of Tel Aviv. "This is unfortunate and sad, because this

---

*Many kibbutzim built swimming pools with the reparations their members received from Germany. They also used the money for sports fields, dining rooms, and clubhouses.[77]

weekly in all respects belongs at the bottom of the barrel," observed the newsletter.

One member of Kibbutz Ruhama who went to town was asked to bring back the weekly journals *La'isha* ("For Women") and *Kolnoa* ("Cinema"). What a peculiar request, thought the man, and promptly reported it to his kibbutz newsletter. He couldn't even find the time to read everything in *Al Hamishmar*, he wrote. He asked around the kibbutz and discovered that there were girls there who took an interest in Elizabeth Taylor's future marriage and Sophia Loren's wedding gown and the extramarital affairs of a third actress whose name he could not recall. He viewed this phenomenon "with concern and pain." More and more kibbutzim were restoring to families the roles they had taken from them when the movement began. In the twenties, the family unit was considered a threat to the community. In 1967, the children of Yehiam were still sleeping in communal children's houses, but parents were playing a larger role in their upbringing.

KIBBUTZ YEHIAM CELEBRATED ITS TWENTIETH ANNIVERSARY IN DECEMBER 1966. THE newsletter tried to project satisfaction, pride, and optimism, but between the lines one could read disappointment and muted sorrow, an echo of the bleak mood in the country as a whole. Less romantic and more sober than at the beginning, Yehiam members opened up their newsletter to the question of their happiness together and whether they would choose the same path they had taken in their youth if they could do it over again. "The number of members and membership candidates who have failed and left and are not living with us is almost equal to the number of members with us today," the article noted. One member, Avri, concluded that "there have been painful failures that the kibbutz could have prevented."

The contradictions between ideology and the daily routine became increasingly troubling as the years went on. "Salaried work has become a regular feature in recent years," wrote a Yehiam member, referring to people from outside employed by the kibbutz. There were repeated reminders that individual wedding gifts, inheritances, insurance payouts, and German reparations belonged communally to the kibbutz, as if this were no longer obvious. Despite the stated equality between men and women, there were nonetheless separate educational programs for boys and girls. The boys learned draftsmanship and how to dismantle and assemble agricultural machinery; the girls took sewing, cooking, psychology, and education. Women began getting their hair styled; some wore jewelry and even demanded cosmetic products. In the spirit of the kibbutz movement's values, the newsletter published a lively article describing the dangers of smoking—but one source of kibbutz income was tobacco.

The members of Yehiam deliberated at length over the internal contradictions. Relations among the members were not ideal. "Despite the accomplishments, we should not delude ourselves," wrote Esther G.; "deep in our hearts there is a sense of social unease and coolness in our human relations." Hanoh complained about the "members' lack of identification with the kibbutz," and Rina claimed that people shut themselves up in their rooms. The clubhouse was a disappointment. More and more members, particularly women, felt lonely. They did not all speak Hebrew fluently. Throughout the kibbutz movement, the second generation of members no longer formed a close-knit, committed group as their parents had done, but rather simply a community that viewed the kibbutz as, above all, a home, not necessarily a mission. Only 18 percent of members in the sixties said that they lived on kibbutzim for ideological reasons; others reported reasons such as ties with family and friends, work, or the landscape. Forty-four percent said they lived on a kibbutz out of habit. Most no longer placed society and the state at the center of their being, but rather just their own interests.[81] In this context, a bitter conflict began to rise to the surface between kibbutz members and the new Israelis— the Mizrahim.

The more the kibbutzim flourished, the deeper the rift grew between them and their neighbors in the development towns. One kibbutz member recalled, "I remember they would come on Saturdays to look at the swimming pool, and the same scene would occur every week: they would come and watch us from behind the fence, staring longingly at the pool— I don't think they ever swam in it—and we would chase them away, yelling, and sometimes someone would throw a stone. I can see in my parents, who lived on a kind of island of European Ashkenazis, that to this day they do not know that other world."

The Ashkenazi character of the kibbutz was an assumed fact, often mentioned in the press. An article about the town of Kiryat Shmoneh published in *Yediot Aharonot* at the height of the recession noted, "In the surrounding area are Kfar Giladi, Kfar Szold, Hagoshrim, and Lehavot Habashan—fattened kibbutzim with a plumply sated population. And in the middle, a large town silently wasting away."[82] In September 1966, *Maariv* published a prominent full-page feature reporting that the government planned to grant the northern kibbutzim land that would further increase their quality of life, and that this would entail leaving 250 families from Kiryat Shmoneh "without any employment or bread." According to the paper, "this cruel plan" could only be implemented because the kibbutzim had strong support in the government and the residents of Kiryat Shmoneh had none. The plan was for a few of the kibbutzim in the north to receive sizable parts of the drained Hula Lake region. *Maariv* wrote that the kibbutzim were planning to grow cotton and alfalfa on the new land, which would allow them to replace their crops of peanuts and vegetables; these crops, less labor intensive, would reduce the need for hired workers—work the residents of Kiryat Shmoneh had done. "Time is running out" for the kibbutz ethos, reported *Maariv* with open hostility. Members of Kfar Giladi were already walking around the area talking like landowners.*

The kibbutz already had a fair number of hired workers, according to one member. "There is no doubt that they were looked down upon—how else would they have been treated? It was an unpleasant time. How can you educate people to be socialists if a hired worker is cleaning their kitchen?" The hired workers did the "dirty work," which was the source of a "long conflict" in the kibbutz, said another member. On International Workers' Day, May 1, 1967, the Yehiam newsletter published worrying details of the gaps between Ashkenazis and Mizrahim. "What will we tell our children?" the writers wondered.[84]

Many kibbutz members found it difficult to adapt to living with "the other Israel," as the Mizrahim were described. Alon Gan writes, "Most of the new immigrants were utterly alien to the values of the labor movement in general and, more important, the kibbutz lifestyle in particular. Thus the dream of creating a new Jewish culture in Palestine collapsed and shattered in the face of a flow of immigrants who were distant strangers to this dream world." The Yehiam newsletter stated, "Our people do not like Mizrahi music. . . ." Thirty-two immigrants from France and South America were set to join Kibbutz Yehiam in 1967, and only one from Morocco.†

Israelis who attacked the kibbutzim for not doing enough to absorb new immigrants often did so to blur the responsibility of society as a

---

*The topic also preoccupied Yosef Weitz, who in addition to his many other positions was also a member of the Hula council. In the context of the growing unemployment in Kiryat Shmoneh, he positioned himself at the head of those who objected to the project, opposing Minister of Agriculture Gvati, who supported it. Weitz managed to obtain a two-year postponement.[83]

†Until the mid-sixties, about 4 percent of all immigrants were sent to kibbutzim, but few stayed. Nor did the absorption of newcomers reflect the ethnic makeup of immigrants overall: most who went to kibbutzim were Ashkenazi.[85]

whole for having neglected the Mizrahim. The kibbutzim aspired to be leading society down the right path, and so it was pertinent to criticize them for this failure. But the recognition that kibbutzim were not meeting expectations deepened the cracks in the foundations of Israeli unity. In addition, the kibbutzim soon found themselves having to defend what had been virtually the last remaining justification for their unique image: their caliber as fighters and their contribution to the IDF.

IN THE WINTER OF 1966 YEHUDA AMIR, A PSYCHOLOGIST AT BAR-ILAN UNIVERSITY AND in the IDF's psychological research unit, published an article in a professional journal, *Megamot*, in which he concluded that kibbutz members were superior soldiers. According to his findings, kibbutz members were more intelligent and better educated, with a better command of Hebrew; they were notable for having the range of personal qualities that the army sought in its officer material. According to Amir, these qualities explained the fact that kibbutz members frequently volunteered for command positions: they represented 22 percent of officers in compulsory service, more than five times their proportion in the population. Most of them had been born in Israel, and most were Ashkenazi, Amir noted.[86]

It was one of those sociopsychological studies that provide scientific confirmation of something everyone already knows, but the Yehiam newsletter gave it prominent publication, with unconcealed pride. The study's findings were also published in the daily press, where they aroused hostile responses, mainly on a topic Amir had not examined: motivation. "Volunteering in and of itself does not attest to the personality level of a soldier, because the motives for volunteering could be negative," wrote Benjamin Amidror in *Ha'aretz*, adding, "SS officers were volunteers." Until then it would have been difficult to imagine an Israeli newspaper publishing such a remark. "Those who see in volunteering for the army definitive proof of the moral, social, or military nature of a person do not know what they are talking about," wrote Amidror. Volunteers, he explained, always operate out of personal motives. There are kibbutz members who volunteer for the army because kibbutz life does not challenge them; some wish to leave the kibbutz, and the army offers them a transitional stage; some join to make money or out of adventurousness or an urge to prove a personal capability or because they are attracted to uniforms and medals. The exaltation of volunteerism as a value, Amirdor went on, may also result in a concentration of superior soldiers in the volunteer units, such as the paratroops, at the expense of other units, like the infantry. Young men from the cities fill the ranks of officers in armies all over the world and there is no reason to assume that their quality in Israel is any worse, he added, warning that kibbutz members were an endangered minority and that the army would do well not to build its future on them.[87]

The kibbutzim had never suffered such a brutal assault, reflecting profound disappointment in the kibbutz as the standard-bearer of Israel's fundamental values. Boaz Evron, a senior writer for *Yediot Aharonot*, attacked not only the kibbutz members' pretensions as fighters, but the very essence of their way of life. The pioneering days of most kibbutzim had ended even before the state was established, he said, and ever since, the kibbutzim had enjoyed an average bourgeois lifestyle. They had contributed in the past to the accomplishments of the Zionist struggle, but the state couldn't go on repaying that old debt forever, particularly when it had compensated the kibbutzim for their past sacrifices with extremely generous loans and support. Second, Evron asserted, the kibbutzim did not have a monopoly on the pioneering spirit. The residents of Jerusalem were also pioneers, as were others, yet only the kibbutzim had turned pioneerism into a source of profit. Yes, admitted Evron acidly, perhaps kibbutz society was more just, more kind, and happier, as it claimed—although the country was full of kibbutz refugees and the kibbutzim were having trouble finding people to join them. And so the question remained, if kibbutz life was so good, why was it so bad? Amir's study, wrote Evron, proved at most that kibbutz members were better soldiers, but it did not prove that they were better people. "We do not find that kibbutz members are better scientists, artists, or managers." They were probably better soldiers because that was how they were brought up, Evron suggested, and this was a question of taste, to his mind. "Some view Napoleon as the supreme human ideal, while others prefer Newton or Bach."

Evron had something to say about how kibbutzim were managed, too. "Is their equipment exploited to the fullest? Are their per capita expenses not in excess of their production? Is the kibbutzim's agricultural product capable of competing in foreign markets without subsidies?" The kibbutzim, he wrote, represented a burden on the state no less than car manufacturers and other industrialists. He asked, therefore, "Why must the workers of Ashdod and other development towns pay the price for industrialists' villas and the kibbutz swimming pools?" The answer was that the state was based on false pretenses, as were the pioneer values ascribed to the kibbutzim. "It's all a cardboard set," wrote Evron—meaning the manicured lawns, the spacious dining rooms, the gospel of Zionism and socialism.[88] This was another pronouncement that would never have found its way into the newspapers in the past. The assault on the kibbutzim thus joined the general gloom and made it all the more profound.

5. POLITICS: "THE BIGGEST LIAR IN OUR COUNTRY"

At the beginning of March 1966, Levi Eshkol came to the Wise Auditorium at the Hebrew University in Jerusalem for a question-and-answer session with students. An uncharismatic seventy-two-year-old, Eshkol was a life-sized politician who had replaced a giant, David Ben-Gurion, and he was haunted by his shadow. "I walk with slight trepidation and seek cover," he wrote several days after becoming prime minister. Eighteen months later he was all but pleading with Ben-Gurion: "Give me credit! . . . Please do not let me believe that my fear of becoming prime minister for all these years was justified."[89]

The evening at the Hebrew University was difficult. More than a thousand unruly students crowded into the auditorium. They stood up, shouted, stamped their feet, and heckled the prime minister continuously. Only a few supported him. A few days earlier, the student newspaper, *Nitzotz*, had appeared with an all-black cover bearing a single Hebrew word: *Hamatzav* ("the Situation"). The confrontation with Eshkol was, therefore, not merely a show of rudeness and chutzpah, nor a simple youthful rebellion against a representative of the old guard. The students were expressing a sense that something fundamental was going wrong in Israel.

One student asked Eshkol why he didn't resign, or at least call for new elections. Eshkol replied that the question was childish. He tried to explain that elections for the Knesset had been held less than six months prior, and that his government was built on a coalition comprising 75 of the 120 Knesset members. He was drowned out by the students' shouts. Someone asked why Eshkol had come to the university at the invitation of his own party's student division, but had refused to come when he had been invited by the student union. Did he only dare appear before his supporters? Was he afraid to hear the entire student body? The prime minister seemed to be uninformed of the details behind his appearance. An adviser handed him a note and Eshkol tried to explain, but the head of the student union shouted at him, "Mr. Prime Minister, you are knowingly lying!" Then the power in the auditorium suddenly failed and the lights went out, not an uncommon occurrence. The students started singing a lullaby, then moved on to a folk song: "We will build our country, our homeland, because this land belongs to us!" A few minutes later the emergency generator kicked in and three dim rays of light came on. They revealed the prime minister still standing on the stage, and although his two bodyguards were now at his side, he looked lonely and bedraggled. Someone brought a kerosene lamp and Eshkol tried to salvage the evening, but without a microphone he had no chance. According to *Yediot Aharonot*, he and his handlers left the place "in great darkness."

This would not have happened to Ben-Gurion. A few days earlier, people had crowded around his car when he passed through Beersheba. One woman pointed to him and told her child, "That's the king of Israel."[90]

Ben-Gurion had stepped down from his position as prime minister in 1963, and shortly thereafter he had a falling out with Mapai, his party. He left it and started the Israel Workers' List, known as Rafi. This schism had come in the aftermath of the "Lavon affair," a political earthquake that had begun with a botched act of terrorism carried out by Israeli intelligence agents in Egypt in the early fifties. The revelation of the failed operation embroiled Israel in a complex network of intrigues and quarrels, threats and blackmail, lies and fabrication of evidence, and brought on a tormented and reproachful self-examination regarding Israeli democracy and the basic values of society in general.[91] When he left Mapai, Ben-Gurion took with him a few major players, including Moshe Dayan, the former IDF chief of staff. But most Mapai supporters remained loyal to their party and to its new leader, Levi Eshkol. The latter formed an alignment (in Hebrew, Ma'arah) with the smaller Ahdut Ha'avoda party. In the elections held in November 1965, the Ma'arah list won forty-five seats of the Knesset's 120.

Ben-Gurion's Rafi party won only ten seats in the Knesset. The leader of the right-wing opposition, Menachem Begin, ran with Gahal, a partnership between his Herut party and the Liberal party. They won twenty-six seats. Most members of this Knesset, the sixth elected since the founding of the state, were men in their fifties and sixties, predominantly from overseas: more than half from Eastern Europe, mostly Poland and the Ukraine. Only ten members were women, twenty-two Mizrahim, twenty-two Jews born in the country. Three out of every ten had sat in the Knesset since the day it was established.[92] One of these was the prime minister.

Levi Eshkol had spent most of his life developing the country and its economy and was described as "one of the greatest go-getters of Jewish settlement in the land of Israel."[93] He had come from the Ukraine as a Zionist in 1914, when he was nineteen years old. His father had stayed abroad and was later murdered in a pogrom. Most of Eshkol's days in Palestine were spent under foreign rule—first Turkish, then British. The Zionist enterprise often called for devious and evasive methods, and Eshkol knew each and every trick to get around prohibitions, restrictions, and obstacles; this deviousness was a skill learned in the Jewish Diaspora. Shkolnik—his surname then—began life in Israel as an agricultural laborer and was among the founders of Kibbutz Degania Bet. He entered public life almost immediately after his arrival and was a founder of Mapai. The party was destined to control events in Palestine for many years; before the establishment of the state, it based its power on the labor union federation, the Histadrut, and on a number of economic centers of power. During the first decades of independence, the party won every election in which it stood.

In 1933, on the basis of an agreement between the Zionist movement and the Nazis, Eshkol facilitated the transfer to Palestine of property belonging to German Jews. He founded Mekorot, which assured the supply of water to Jewish settlements, and oversaw the settlement department of the Jewish Agency. Among its other responsibilities, after 1948 the department prepared housing for hundreds of thousands of new immigrants, at first in villages abandoned by the Arabs, then in transit camps, as well as in permanent housing in hundreds of new towns and villages. He believed the best way to take control of the country was by developing and populating it, step by step, "acre after acre and goat after goat."

In 1952, Eshkol became the minister of finance in Ben-Gurion's government, a position he occupied until he was himself appointed prime minister and minister of defense when Ben-Gurion stepped down. In the fifties he was associated with the difficulties and failures that accompanied the absorption of immigrants, including the discrimination against Mizrahim. Like others, Eshkol felt that the Mizrahim were a burden on the state, and he often spoke of Israel's need for immigrants from Western countries. In the early sixties, he was identified with the country's rapid economic growth. His practical involvement in security affairs was minimal, restricted primarily to his support of Ben-Gurion. Like Ben-Gurion, he accepted the need to partition the country between Jews and Arabs; but, like others, he also wanted it to be as large as possible. "The eastern bank of the Jordan has been the constant dream of every young man and woman in Eretz Israel since time immemorial," he wrote in 1927. Thirty years later, he proposed annexing the Gaza Strip after it had been conquered in the Sinai Campaign.

His status in the party was strengthened as a result of his handling of the Lavon affair: more than anything, he wanted it to disappear. Ben-Gurion, in contrast, wished to dig further and further into the matter until his own conduct could be vindicated. Their differences in this led Ben-Gurion to develop a profound hatred of Eshkol, who he felt had betrayed him. Ben-Gurion's personal prestige and influence were far greater than Rafi's strength in the 1965 elections, while Eshkol's were less significant than Ma'arah's strength as a party; to the public he represented party hackery and political pettiness, rather than statesmanship or leadership. In the twenties he had once interfered in a quarrel between two of the first settlements, Kinneret and Degania, which were fighting over trash removal. Eshkol wrote to them that life was based on mutual agreement and a willingness to compromise. This was his basic outlook as a politician. Not necessarily indecision, not compromise at any cost, but a combination of caution and an intuitive assessment of what could be achieved.[94]

A man of the people, lacking in pretense, Eshkol did not instill much respect. He thought and often joked in Yiddish, and was proclaimed by *Time* magazine to be "simply *haimish*," homey, familiar. Reviewing IDF troops while wearing a black beret, he appeared "an almost grotesque figure," the magazine continued.* Eshkol's military secretary, Israel Lior, wrote that Eshkol sometimes reminded him of his late father: he had a lifetime of wisdom, experience, and a keen instinct for people. Lior praised Eshkol's ability to listen to others. He knew how to make a direct connection to people and he liked them. But, in an echo of Yosef Weitz's impressions after his visit to Eshkol's office, Lior also criticized Eshkol's tendency to talk with too many people: everybody came through his office, and they all had something to say about everything. The office operated in constant chaos, wrote Lior. At least one of Eshkol's ministers also felt that too much time in government meetings was wasted on trivial matters.[96]

Eshkol was indeed a long-winded speaker. Like his minister of finance, Sapir, and many members of his generation, he spoke in a disorderly, unfocused, and purposeless fashion. He repeated himself, and his audience often lost patience before he had finished. Known as a ladies' man, he was married twice (once divorced, once widowed) before becoming prime minister, and in 1964 he married the Knesset librarian, Miriam Zelikowitz.

---

*For some reason, Eshkol insisted on wearing a beret. His military secretary kept a supply of them in his car. Before Independence Day in 1967, the IDF published a glossy book of photographs. According to one source, at the last moment someone instructed that the picture of Minister of Defense Eshkol be pulled from the book and replaced with a more flattering photograph, minus the beret.[95]

• • •

AS THE ECONOMIC RECESSION DEEPENED, EVERYONE BEGAN TO SPEAK OF THE NEED FOR stronger leadership. The U.S. ambassador hurried to update Washington on the commonly held opinion that the next prime minister would be either Yigal Allon, the leader of Ahdut Ha'avoda, or Moshe Dayan of Rafi. In March 1966, Ma'arah sent out questionnaires to ten thousand citizens asking what they thought were the burning problems of the day. The responses were not encouraging. Not even half the respondents (48 percent) praised the government for its handling of foreign and security affairs. Daily life was even more troubling. Approximately 51 percent cited unemployment and inflation as the most pressing issues. "Why has the price of eggs gone up?" asked one respondent. Forty-three percent complained about bureaucracy and the arrogance of government officials, demanding a higher quality of life. "Why aren't there afternoon office hours?" "Why can't we take care of things over the phone?" "Why do letters go unanswered?" Many demanded an "improvement in the terrible state of the postal service." People wanted better and more effective treatment at the Histadrut's health fund, of which some two million Israelis were members. "It is doubtful whether there is a single other institution so bitterly criticized by so many people, in such a focused and frequent way," wrote *Maariv*. "The Histadrut health fund provides clear—and very strange—evidence that such a huge institution can continue to exist despite the massive scale of discontent, disappointment, and harsh criticism."

Forty-one percent of respondents to the Ma'arah questionnaire complained about the high cost of high school education. "How can anyone manage with 900 liras and two school-aged children?" Some demanded more male teachers instead of female ones. Thirty-nine percent protested ethnic discrimination; 19 percent demanded legislation to prevent strikes. The remaining issues troubling respondents included governmental compliance with the demands of the Orthodox (18 percent); the sorry state of public transportation (12 percent); the difficulties of getting a phone line (10 percent); and neglect in the cities (10 percent).[97] There was also a particularly irritating branch of Amisragas, the national gas supplier: "Every time you order a container of gas, they promise to deliver it on a certain date and you know in advance that they won't keep their promise," wrote a columnist for *Maariv*. "After a few days you contact them again, and you know their second promise will be worth no more than the first. The third will be no better than the second. And no one will ever apologize for the lies of the day before, and when you complain, the manager will tell you that you can write to the newspapers about it—he isn't afraid of the press."

Disgruntlement over the poor quality of life was relatively new and was gaining attention. "Despite all the criticism, they persist in building a singularly ugly place," wrote *Maariv* of the new town of Carmiel, "a soulless town built from a random mixture of concrete 'boxes,' those same ugly 'boxes' that mar most of the country's landscape." Others denounced the "jungle atmosphere" prevailing on Israeli roads. This array of factors sustained a dissatisfaction that deepened the general gloom spreading over Israel in 1966. The feeling was also reflected in Israelis' letters to friends abroad. As the months went by, more and more of them began to express distrust of the political system itself, with a fair degree of cynicism. "Our system and our government are rotting," wrote *Ha'aretz*, quoting Haim Gadol, a tailor from Haifa: "I feel that the country has no father and there's no one who can lead, who can give inspiration, encourage, energize, and serve as an example to citizens."

Eshkol blamed the press and launched a personal attack on the editor of *Ha'aretz*, Gershom Schocken. He has "a strange tendency" to denigrate Jewish reality in Israel, said Eshkol in the Knesset. Schocken "systematically poisons the souls of his readers." The editor of *Davar* used a similar metaphor: "well-poisoners." But he was referring to *Maariv*.

Six months later, in September 1966, *Ha'aretz* conducted its own survey of the big cities. Forty-two percent of respondents wanted Eshkol replaced. Ben-Gurion received the results of a poll his party had conducted, which indicated that Eshkol's popularity had dropped by 50 percent over the past three months, while his own had doubled.[98] It was a birthday gift: on October 16, 1966, Ben-Gurion turned eighty.

Just before his birthday, Ben-Gurion said that he was not turning eighty but rather sixty plus six days, since he counted the years of his life from the day he came to Palestine and saw himself as having been born there. Only in the land of Israel had he discovered the true meaning of Zionism and socialism, he said. Only in the land of Israel had he begun to truly comprehend the Bible, and through it the people of Israel, their history and destiny. The Bible, he said, united the people of Israel in their moral superiority, which had enabled them to face all enemies and to survive as a people of eternity.[99]

No one else possessed Ben-Gurion's ability to internalize the history of the Jewish people, identify with it, and present his politics as a reflection of history's course. He often appeared to himself and to others as the personification of this history. When he resigned, he devoted himself to writing his own version of the history of Zionist settlement. Day by day, hour by hour, Ben-Gurion also wrote in his diary. He summarized meetings and events and copied down statistical charts, only occasionally adding a personal impression. He seldom wrote of what he felt. Although he was now only a member of the Knesset, at the head of a small splinter party, he remained one of the strongest figures in the state. As such, he was careful to maintain his relationship with the military forces. When Ariel Sharon was promoted to the rank of general, Ben-Gurion wrote to him with the salutation "Dear, great Arik" and promised him, "You are destined for great things!" He praised Sharon for having overcome "some faults" that he had identified in him previously.*

He wrote thousands of letters, usually in answer to correspondents he did not know personally. As the gloom in Israel increased, he received and archived letters from citizens pleading for him to return to a leadership post; without him, they said, they were like orphans. People did not hold his role in creating the current failings against him. They missed the days of national glory he symbolized. As a great man, he also seemed to be someone to whom they might address great questions, as if to a biblical prophet. No, wrote Ben-Gurion to Amos Frisch of Tel Aviv, who asked him about Israel's status as a chosen nation: It was not God who chose Israel, but Israel that chose God. Many wrote from abroad. Ruth Todd of Denton, Maryland, received the following reply: "According to my belief there is no question: Jesus was born in Nazareth and not in Beth Lechem." To Stanley Blumberg of Baltimore, Maryland, Ben-Gurion wrote: "*Uncle Tom's Cabin* . . . is one of the first books which I have read in my youth, when I was 9 or ten. I read it then in a Hebrew translation and it made on me a very deep impression." Once in a while he read the writings of Plato.[100]

Israel observed Ben-Gurion's eightieth birthday with dozens of ceremonies and other events, as if it were a national holiday. Ten thousand people came to Sde Boker, his kibbutz in the Negev, for a grand celebration in the local amphitheater. The IDF loaned the kibbutz two floodlights whose beams formed an arch in the sky. The Habima company actor, Aharon Meskin, spoke two lines: "The nation loves you, Ben-Gurion. Thank you for what you have done and good luck in the future." The president, Zalman Shazar, was there, as was S. Y. Agnon. Eshkol stayed in Jerusalem.

---

*Ben-Gurion admired the young Sharon, but as prime minister had caught him in a lie more than once. He said that Sharon admitted as much.

The next day, on October 17, Ben-Gurion wrote an entry in his diary that those in charge of his archives have seen fit to conceal from researchers for these past four decades. Perhaps he had repeated nuclear secrets he had been told, or perhaps the archive is simply trying to protect his image: in his old age, Ben-Gurion grew bitter and often embarrassed himself. As time went on, he burrowed deeper and deeper into the Lavon affair, with a grumbling obstinacy and compulsive vindictiveness. He wrote more and more letters on the matter, filled with minute details, dates, names, and quotes. He became increasingly derogatory toward Eshkol, describing him as a swindler who ruled the country with distorted justice, fear, and deceit. Eshkol, he said, was "the biggest liar in our country." Only toward Menachem Begin did he display comparable virulence. Nor did he confine his opinions to his diary. "The upper echelon is covering up the embarrassing and shameful behavior of a man serving as prime minister, and accepting moral deterioration within the party, which could undermine and destroy the state of Israel," he wrote to a Mapai leader. The state's well-being depended on security assistance from the outside, and therefore it could not exist if the nations of the world did not trust and respect Israel's leaders, he warned. And with a leader like Eshkol, Israel would not last long. Starting in 1966, Ben-Gurion also began blaming Eshkol for a mysterious "security breach." He took this accusation all over the country, but revealed no details. He may have been referring to Eshkol's handling of Israel's attempts to obtain missiles.*

Ben-Gurion repeated his claims over and over, both in public appearances and in press interviews; no other topic so preoccupied him. He claimed to be able to see what was going on "with complete objectivity," and nothing could budge him from his stance, even if he were the last of Israel's defenders. "I am willing to be lonely and isolated and even ostracized and vilified," he wrote. "I choose to be ostracized—but I will not lend a hand to those who distort truth and justice and undermine the existence of the state of Israel." He also excoriated the leaders of Mapai, friends and partners for decades, accusing them of viewing political power as a supreme goal that sanctified all means. He wondered where the Ma'arah had found the hundred million liras he claimed it had spent on the most recent election campaign: "Where will we get with such corruption?" In one letter he compared himself to the prophet Isaiah.

---

*Eshkol instructed his military secretary to look into Ben-Gurion's accusations, but Lior said he was unsuccessful. Eshkol was troubled. "What does he want from me?" he would ask in Yiddish; according to Lior, "His heart was wrenched."[101]

His pathetic behavior made him seem like a child deprived of his toy—or, in this case, of his state. But no other person in Israel was capable of provoking such a strong public response, and when "the father of the nation" voiced such harsh accusations against the prime minister, using such sharp words, he deepened the sense that something terrible was happening. Ben-Gurion even toyed with the idea of having Eshkol forcibly removed from office. He discovered that four "prominent, dedicated, and important members" of Mapai had come to the party leadership demanding to get rid of him. Two were Knesset members, and Ben-Gurion was quick to spread the news.[102] This happened in the aftermath of the murder of Ben Barka.

MEHDI BEN BARKA WAS THE EXILED OPPOSITION LEADER OF MOROCCO. WHILE THERE were no official ties, Israel had covert links to the king and his head of security and former interior minister, Mohammed Oufkir, which enabled Moroccan Jews to leave the country for Israel. Reportedly, Oufkir had asked the head of the Mossad, Meir Amit, to help him do away with Ben Barka, who disappeared in October 1965 and was never seen again. According to Amit, the operation itself was ultimately carried out by French mercenaries. "We came out completely clean," he later wrote.[103]

In December 1966, the pornographic tabloid *Bul* was about to go to press with a story implying that Eshkol was to be replaced by Yigal Allon because of the involvement of Mossad agents in the murder of Ben Barka. The Security Service and the police confiscated the issue before copies could be distributed. The editors, Shmuel Mor and Maxim Gilan, were tried behind closed doors and each sentenced to a year in prison. The trial was kept secret, the tabloid went on being published, and Mor and Gilan remained on the masthead as editors to prevent the exposure of the episode. But in February 1967 the entire story appeared in the *New York Times* and a firestorm erupted. The details of the Ben Barka operation were not published, but the *Bul* affair provided a temporary focal point for a continuing struggle over freedom of the press in Israel.[104]*

The excitement surrounding Ben-Gurion's birthday bolstered his public support and popularity, despite his ongoing obsession with the Lavon affair. "The future will tell what consequences this development will have

---

*There is no reason to assume that Ben-Gurion himself would not have authorized such an operation, but he found it difficult to pass up a chance to attack Eshkol. President Shazar sent him an emotional, handwritten letter, urging him to abandon the matter. At least some of the details of the affair remain classified, stored in a file kept in the state archives and in sealed portions of Ben-Gurion's diary.[105]

within the internal political landscape," wrote Yaacov Herzog, the director general of the prime minister's office, in his diary. Herzog, who was born in Ireland to a chief rabbi, had been ambassador to Canada and was a private adviser to both Ben-Gurion and Eshkol. The diplomatic skills of this brilliant man were tested by his dual loyalties. Shazar had been planning to hold a national celebration for Ben-Gurion in the presidential residence, but Herzog explained to him that Eshkol would not be able to participate and therefore the government ministers would not come. To prevent a scandal, the president should go to Sde Boker instead. Herzog then had to find the words with which Eshkol's government could congratulate Ben-Gurion. Eshkol refused to laud him for "developing the country," because he held his contributions to be greater than Ben-Gurion's. The minister of education came to Herzog with his own troubles: should the government's message praising Ben-Gurion for his contribution to state security be translated into Arabic? Herzog suggested that in Arabic they mention only the establishment of the state and Ben-Gurion's contribution to the advancement of all its citizens.[106]*

IN FEBRUARY 1967, *MAARIV* PUBLISHED A DEBATE OVER THE QUESTION OF THE IDEAL type of leader. The debate appeared in "Square Table," a personal column written by the well-known journalist Geula Cohen. One of the participants, the poet Haim Gouri, said, "I believe this era requires a strong person with clear and unflinching vision, who takes something of a philosophical view of the Israeli revolution."[109] He was probably referring to Yigal Allon, an admired commander in the 1948 war. In all the parties there were young members who were trying to reach prominence, but the great original leaders survived: Menachem Begin in Herut, Meir Ya'ari in Mapam, Haim Moshe Shapira in Mafdal. Only Mapai was left without its leader, Ben-Gurion.

Born in Poland in 1911, Menachem Begin was a follower of Ze'ev Jabotinsky, the father of Revisionist Zionism, who had challenged the

---

*At the beginning of 1967 there was an uproar over the "Ben-Gurion" entry in the *Hebrew Encyclopedia*. The author was the encyclopedia's senior editor, Yeshayahu Leibowitz, a professor at the Hebrew University and a long-standing ideological opponent of Ben-Gurion. "I think Ben-Gurion is the greatest disaster to befall the people of Israel and the state of Israel since its establishment," the professor told *Maariv*, and this view was reflected in the encyclopedia.[107] Ben-Gurion was hurt. "I don't care what Professor Leibowitz writes. I care what I do, if it's good or not," he responded to an admirer; to the encyclopedia's publisher he wrote, "Leibowitz is consumed with hatred."[108]

leadership of the Zionist movement with his demand for a faster, more energetic realization of Zionist objectives, throughout the whole of Eretz Israel, through resistance to compromise and territorial concessions. Begin came to Palestine only in 1942, where he became the head of Etzel, a terrorist organization that fought against British rule. Upon the establishment of the state, he took the helm of the Herut party. In contrast to Ben-Gurion's willingness to accept the 1949 borders, Begin aspired to "the whole country," extending to both sides of the Jordan River; against the centralized economic policy rooted in Mapai's social-democratic ideals, Begin demanded a free market in the spirit of classical liberalism. In his party, which he always made a point of describing as a "movement," he was virtually a unilateral leader, as was Ben-Gurion in his. And like Ben-Gurion, Begin was surrounded by worshipers. Always a smart dresser, polite and well-spoken, he was blessed with a sense of drama, history, and symbolism, complete with uniforms, torches, songs, flags, and slogans. A town square demagogue, he knew how to inspire his audience with rousing nationalistic speeches. "Sometimes his entire body was shaken by pathos and he rocked from side to side; his musical voice rose to a crescendo and fell to a whisper," wrote one journalist. *Ha'aretz* compared him to Mussolini; Ben-Gurion used to compare him to Hitler. While still prime minister, Ben-Gurion concluded that Begin and his movement were unacceptable partners in any coalition, as was the Communist party, and he was always careful not to mention Begin by name. Begin was a brave man. It was not easy to stand up to Ben-Gurion, and no other politician made a greater contribution to Israel's democratic parliamentarianism.

Eshkol, on the other hand, introduced a conciliatory style in Israeli politics, as when he instructed that Jabotinsky's remains be brought to Israel for burial. The leader of the Revisionist movement, who had died in America, had desired to be buried in Israel in a state funeral; Ben-Gurion had refused. The role of the State of Israel was to bring living Jews to the country, not bones, lest it become "a land of graves," he argued callously. Eshkol, on the other hand, agreed, and Jabotinsky's remains were buried on Mount Herzl. Later, a plaque was hung on his house in Jerusalem.[110] It was a peace-making gesture to the right wing, a display of Eshkol's willingness to do things that Ben-Gurion had blocked. But the transfer of Jabotinsky's remains to Mount Herzl was more than a political gesture: it brought Herut into Zionist history. Until then, the Labor movement had monopolized that history, an important asset in a society still molding its national identity. Eshkol may not have been aware of the magnitude of his concession to Begin, but Begin certainly was.

In the summer of 1966, Herut held its national congress, where something occurred that no one could have predicted: a twenty-one-year-old named Ehud Olmert demanded that Begin resign because the party had lost repeatedly in elections and was unable to attain government power. Olmert was the son of a Knesset member whom Begin had ousted, yet the assault was not interpreted as settling personal accounts but rather as an effort to undermine yet another cornerstone of Israeli life. Begin immediately acknowledged his failure and announced that he would step down as head of the party. The response was predictably hysterical. The delegates roared, "Begin to power! Begin to power!" and some burst into tears. "Don't leave us, you're like our father!" a delegate shouted out. One woman said, "He's like God. If he goes—everything's lost." He stayed.[111]

A few restless people, young and less young, attempted similar maneuvers against the legendary leaders of Mapam, Meir Ya'ari and Yaakov Hazan, although the two old men succeeded in quashing them.[112] A new generation also sprung up in Mafdal. One young member of the party, Yoel Yinon, wrote to a friend in America about an article written by Rabbi Haim Pardes, a Mafdal leader: "I read it with disbelief because this is the same Haim Pardes we knew ten years ago. [He] writes as if he's at least seventy years old. The conservatism and narrow-mindedness are truly amazing. In the article he laments the fact that nowadays people don't come to ask for the rabbi's advice like they used to. I thought to myself that if his thinking is as old-fashioned and frozen as his article indicates, it's no wonder people don't come to him. I only hope there are young rabbis with a different attitude. If not—woe to us." But the leader of the party, Haim Moshe Shapira, sixty-five years old, also held on.[113]

In the shadow of these giants, Eshkol found himself in a nearly untenable situation. People began mocking him with cruelty and bitterness. Uri in Rishon Lezion wrote to his sister in New York about a little book called *Complete Eshkol Jokes* that was being passed around at his high school. "In my opinion it's gone beyond the limits of good taste," he admitted, but he told her a joke anyway, one that wasn't in the book but was still probably doing the rounds of his fellow students: Eshkol almost drowns at sea. Someone saves him and Eshkol asks how he can show his thanks. His savior replies, "Just don't tell anyone about what I've done." *Ha'aretz* wrote, "There have never been so many jokes about a prime minister as there are now," and quoted one of the more painful examples: "A waiter asks Eshkol if he'd like tea or coffee. 'You know what?' replies Eshkol. 'Give me half and half.' "* His wife, Miriam, later recalled that she and the prime minister had each gotten hold of the joke book and hid it from the other. When they discovered they had both read it, she asked him what he thought. "I could have come up with better jokes," he said. But the gibes upset him. "I cannot recall another government that faced such destructive, bitter and arrogant opposition," he once said in a cabinet meeting.[114]

6. JEWS I: "LET US DIE IN PEACE"

On the evening of Saturday, August 13, 1966, just after the Sabbath ended, the sculptor David Palombo left his home on Mount Zion in Jerusalem and headed downtown on his moped. A few minutes later, he hit an iron chain stretched across the road. Palombo died shortly afterward of the injuries he sustained.

At the top of Mount Zion stood a German church that marked the place where, according to Christian tradition, the mother of Jesus had fallen asleep for the last time. At the foot of the hill was a darkened cluster of domed, charred, and semi-ruined buildings; before the hill was conquered in the War of Independence, they had belonged to Arabs. In one of them lay a large stone legendarily identified as the tombstone of King David. Thousands of people used to visit the tomb. Its folklore attracted predominantly Mizrahi Israelis, who saw it as a substitute for the Western Wall, which was in the Jordanian part of Jerusalem. From the tomb, one could see the Temple Mount, and some even believed they could see a corner of the wall. With its many legends and sacred vantage point, Mount Zion formed the focus of a passionate power struggle over the character of Israeli identity. Various factions also viewed the mount as a locus of political power. The dispute centered around the shaping of national memory. The director general of the Ministry of Religious Affairs, S. Z. Kahana, established the Holocaust Basement on Mount Zion, which consisted of a gloomy display of charred Torah parchment and ancient lamps made of such parchments or even of human skin, as well as bars of soap allegedly made from the bodies of Jews murdered by the Nazis. There the chief rabbinate buried remnants of Torahs salvaged from European

---

*According to his daughter, this was the only one of all the jokes' punch lines that Eshkol actually said. Although it came back to haunt him, he had intended it as a joke. He usually preferred tea.

synagogues, and even urns supposedly containing the ashes of Holocaust victims. There was an incinerator that could be lit. "When I go up to Mount Zion, I am outraged at the way things have been done, which, in my opinion, is not in keeping with the spirit of Judaism and verges on idolatry," complained Moshe Kol, a director of Yad Vashem, the national Holocaust memorial, with which the Mount Zion site was meant to compete.[115]

The road on which Palombo was killed had been paved in 1963 in preparation for the visit of Pope Paul VI. The chain stretched across the road was intended to prevent motor traffic on the Sabbath, but Palombo had not seen it in the dark. He and his wife, also an artist, were among the few people who lived on the mount. He had designed the entrance gates to the new Knesset building. Many secular Israelis came to see him as a victim of "religious oppression." The Sabbath was defined as the Jewish weekly rest day but while the use of transportation was forbidden in Jewish law, only a few roads were actually closed to traffic; in Haifa and the surrounding area there was even public transportation on Saturdays.

The struggle over the role of religion in public life in Israel had been a part of Zionist politics from the outset. David Ben-Gurion had instituted a series of basic accommodations—referred to as the status quo—that allowed coexistence between secular and religious Jews and included exemption from military service for religious women, separate religious educational systems, and kosher food in the army. In 1967 he was still defending the status quo. "This is not the time to ignite a dispute among the people over absolute separation of religion and state," he wrote.[116] Most Israelis were similarly unwilling to fight for such a complete separation: the majority were not entirely secular and almost everyone observed Jewish law to some extent. For the most part, they were willing to live with the status quo's concessions to Orthodoxy, albeit often grudgingly. The partnership between secular and religious necessitated a constant, almost daily reaffirmation.

As of early 1967, Israelis were still unable to agree among themselves on the crucial question of who was and was not a Jew. A naval officer named Benjamin Shalit wished to register his children as Jewish or of the Hebrew nationality, despite the fact that their mother was not Jewish. The issue soon reached the Supreme Court, which deliberated over the case for years. The Orthodox monopoly on conducting Jewish weddings was another divisive issue. In one case, a man who wanted to marry a divorcée had to do so in New York because as a "Kohen," or descendant of the priestly caste, he was forbidden to marry a divorced woman, according to Jewish law. The man argued that his intended wife was a widow, since her ex-husband had since died. The legal aspects of the case prompted a public dispute and the story caused a scandal, because the applicant was Supreme Court Justice Haim Cohen, and his fiancée, Mihal, was the daughter of the first president of the Israeli Supreme Court.[117]

Another story that made headlines was that of Benjamin Getieh, born in Ethiopia, whom the rabbinate refused to marry because it did not recognize Ethiopian immigrants as Jews. Getieh presented the rabbinate with the testimony of a woman who had taken part, with her husband, in one of the great adventures in the history of the Jewish people. Miriam Faitlovitch had been with her husband, Jacques, when he "discovered" the Jews of Ethiopia in the early twentieth century, on a mission funded by Baron de Rothschild. He had brought a few young Ethiopians to Palestine, where they were trained as teachers, and then returned them to their country. One of these young Ethiopians was Yirmiyahu Getieh, Benjamin's father. "Benjamin Getieh was born a Jew, and not only his father Yirmiyahu but also his mother was Jewish," Miriam Faitlovitch testified. But the rabbis repeatedly refused to marry him, at which point Getieh went to the press: "Am I a dog who does not need to be answered? What must I do to be allowed to marry—convert to Christianity?" Eventually, he was married in a private ceremony.[118] Kibbutz Yehiam's newsletter reported on no fewer than fifty couples from the kibbutz who had been married "in civil or semi-civil ways," and whose marriages were not recognized by Israeli law. "The conscientious decision over the form of marriage is a private matter," argued the kibbutz movement, demanding "equal legal opportunity for all"—that is, the establishment of secular marriage.[119]

There were those who felt that Jewish law—halakha—comprised racist elements, and some compared the rulings of the chief rabbinate to Nazi law.[120] Dr. Israel Shahak, a chemistry professor at the Hebrew University and a Holocaust survivor, once found a visiting student from Africa unconscious on a Jerusalem street. It was on the Sabbath and a nearby resident refused to allow Dr. Shahak to use his telephone to call an ambulance, claiming that the sanctity of the Sabbath could not be violated to save the life of a non-Jew. Shahak went to the chief rabbinate, which confirmed this interpretation of the Sabbath laws. He sent letters to the newspapers about the incident, and one respondent was Israel's ambassador to Austria, Michael Simon. "This is the most horrific and shocking thing I have ever read," he wrote to Prime Minister Eshkol. He wondered how the story would affect the country's standing in Africa or how Israel could continue to denounce discrimination against Jews in the Soviet Union. *Maariv* asked for the opinion of the minister of religious affairs, Dr. Zerah Warhaftig. The minister did not refute the rabbinical ruling, but quoted from traditional Jewish sources according to which Jewish doctors had saved the lives of non-Jews on the Sabbath, although they were not required to do so. *Maariv* was not satisfied. "The argument over this serious matter is only just beginning," read its editorial, asserting that in the battle he had started, Shahak "would not remain alone."[121] People like Shahak and Ambassador Simon represented Israel as it was: a largely free country, built on the foundations of secular democracy, despite its limitations.

From time to time Israelis examined and expanded the boundaries of their tolerance, similar to the process in other countries during the sixties. When the Jewish Reform movement held its first public prayer service in Israel, a heated debate broke out.[122] The minister of justice, Yaakov-Shimshon Shapira, was asked whether the time had not come to revoke the law prohibiting homosexual relations. "The truth is that although I have read a fair amount of material on the topic, it has not really preoccupied me," responded the minister uncomfortably. "Perhaps I am not progressive enough," he added; "there are things that I don't take much of an interest in." He made a point of observing that there were no homosexuals among his acquaintances, nor had he known any as a youth. But with respect to the matter at hand the minister set forth a liberal position: "I myself do not understand why these kinds of things should be a matter for the authorities—something a person does privately and which harms no one. . . . If two adults wish to stand on their heads and it does not disturb anyone—I think criminal law should not interfere." He also pointed out that there was no law actually forbidding Israeli citizens to transgress Jewish law.[123]

A Jerusalem writer, Dan Omer, was tried and convicted because the state found that his novel, *On the Road*, was pornographic; a debate ensued. One program director on Kol Israel radio prohibited the broadcast of a popular song with lyrics by the poet Haim Hefer. The song, "El El Yehezkel," was a humorous take on the story of the Prophet Ezekiel, but the director claimed it ridiculed the prophet. Another argument ensued. The street in Jerusalem named after Rabbi Kook was frequented by prostitutes, sparking a debate over whether to remove them or change the street's name.[124]

The dispute over the status of religion reflected dilemmas of identity—Jewishness versus Israeliness—and also touched on the relationship with

Diaspora Jews. Should the state president go to see the Lubavitcher rebbe in New York, or should he expect the rabbi to honor him as the head of state and come to his hotel? (Shazar went to the rebbe.) "For years I had an aversion to the Diaspora, to the Jew-boy syndrome," recalled Tikva Sarig of Kibbutz Beit Hashita. Her husband was a founder of the Palmah and had been an esteemed officer in the War of Independence. "Nahum and I were the first generation in Israel, the first generation to be free of Diaspora customs and mentality. And the teachers did everything they could to make us forget the Diaspora. We simply hated it." This disdain for Diaspora Jews strengthened Israelis' self-image as proud Hebrews. Their new life in Israel was supposed to embody not only the revolt of Jews against enslavement and persecution, but also the "rebellion against the Jews," as it was described by Berl Katznelson, a labor leader and ideologue, the founder of the newspaper *Davar*. He saw life in Israel as "a declaration of war against the Jews' aptitude to suffer and be subordinate."[125]

This rejection troubled religious people, however. In April 1967, *Ha'aretz* published a letter from a reader named Haim Schechter from Givatayim, in which he told of his disappointment as an immigrant. "Your expressions are full of contempt for this simple Jew who so misses simple Jews like himself," he wrote. "You took our children from us and injected their hearts with poison and scorn against their parents, Diaspora Jews. You turned them from Jews into Israelis, and now this youth is like the young generation of goyim from whom I fled."[126]

Most Israelis were searching for the best way to be "secular Jews." The minister of education, Zalman Aran, gathered a select group of scholars to advise him on how to deepen the Jewish awareness of Israeli schoolchildren. Young Israelis should not grow up feeling cut off from the Jews of the Diaspora, said the minister. The experts thought that a more profound identification with the Holocaust and with Soviet Jews might characterize a "secular Judaism." Aran proposed requiring every student to pass an exam on "Jewish and Israeli history," similar to the national history exams required in the Soviet Union. But the participants feared that this would nurture Israeli chauvinism. They were at a loss for what to do.[127]*

The question of the appropriate attitude toward Jews overseas was also full of contradictions. The press often reported on the persecution of

---

*The complexity of the issue was also apparent in the controversy over government ministers' vehicles. The ministers' cars bore blue license plates, while other vehicles had orange ones. On the Sabbath, ministers used to switch to orange plates, because it was deemed less than respectable for an Israeli minister to publicly violate the prohibition against driving.[128]

Jews, in headlines that left no room for doubt that life in the Diaspora was more dangerous than in Israel: "Jewish Woman Murdered in Harlem," "Two Blacks Beat and Rob Rabbi in New York." But the papers also boasted of Jewish successes abroad, as if Israelis had some part in these accomplishments: "38 Jews in British Parliament," "Four Jewish Members in Multi-National Council on Cancer Research." The editor of *Yediot Aharonot* protested the staging of the musical *Oliver!* in Tel Aviv because of the character of Fagin. Protective of the Jewish image, he viewed the play as "a horror," and its production in Tel Aviv as a form of masochism.[129]

THE PREVAILING THESIS WAS THAT THE JEWS OF THE WORLD LIVED IN SAFETY DUE TO the existence of the State of Israel. "Thanks to the might of Israel, even Diaspora Jews can hold their heads up high," asserts one protagonist in Amos Oz's novel *Elsewhere, Perhaps*.[130] Meanwhile, the prime minister's office had created a secret unit named Nativ to oversee the international campaign for Jews in the Soviet Union, who were not allowed to leave the USSR and many of whom were persecuted on the pretext that they were involved in Zionist activity. The head of Nativ was Shaul Avigur, who had been a prominent figure in the security establishment in Palestine, a labor movement leader, and secret adviser to Ben-Gurion and Eshkol. A 1966 report on Nativ activities enumerated roughly seventy supposedly spontaneous public protests all over the world, including a demonstration outside the Soviet consulate in Canberra, a resolution proposed at a Guatemalan authors' congress, and an agenda item offered at the British Communist party's conference. Like Mossad agents, and in coordination with them, Nativ agents acted under the guise of being Israeli diplomats. The poet Emanuel Litvinoff acted in support of Soviet Jewry on behalf of the philosopher Bertrand Russell; Litvinoff was in fact an agent for both Nativ and the Mossad. Russell probably knew nothing of his connections.*

The government often had to choose between the state's security, political, and economic interests, on the one hand, and its responsibility to protect persecuted Jews—primarily in the USSR—on the other. Some

---

*One Nativ operation involved a literary initiative: Leon Uris, the author of *Exodus*, looked favorably on an Israeli suggestion to write a novel about the plight of Soviet Jews, according to a Nativ agent's report to one of Prime Minister Eshkol's assistants. The request was made under a heavy cloak of secrecy. "Uris is interested in a cover for the operation, so that it cannot later be claimed that his inspiration for the book was the Israeli government," reported the go-between, Dr. Yoram Dinstein.

claimed that Israel was not doing enough for the Jews. The context of this argument was the lingering debate over the failure to rescue Jews during the Second World War. Ambassador Harman strongly denied the existence of a conflict, although he claimed that Israel was trying to institute a "division of labor" between itself and Diaspora Jews, so that "Jewish issues" would not get in the way of its diplomatic ties. "The problem that frequently troubled me was a different one," said Harman. "The problem was whether we were not harming" Soviet Jews by intervening in their situation. "I had never experienced such a regime. What was I, who was I, to do something that might put them in harm's way?"[131] This argument had also been voiced during the Holocaust. Most of the Nativ files are classified, so there is no way of knowing how exactly this covert organization operated and whether it restricted its activities to advancing the humanitarian, religious, and Zionist interests of Soviet Jews, or whether it also engaged in anti-Soviet activities such as espionage, subversion, and anti-Communist propaganda.*

Nahum Goldman, the president of the World Jewish Congress, attacked Israelis for their patronizing attitude toward the Diaspora and reminded them of the unpleasant truth: without the Diaspora, the State of Israel would not exist. Goldman, who also served as president of the World Zionist Organization, frequently angered the Israeli press. "Why doesn't Goldman keep quiet?" fumed *Maariv* after he said he supported a revival of Jewish life in Germany.[133] Goldman was highly voluble on the "moral and emotional crisis" in Israel, but Eshkol dismissed his comments: since the World Zionist Organization was unable to bring Jews to Israel, the views of its president were of no interest.[134]

MANY RELIGIOUS ISRAELIS, PARTICULARLY THE BRAND OF ULTRA-ORTHODOXY THAT OPposed the modern Jewish state as sacrilegious, found it difficult to quell the fear of a secular country they had felt since the declaration of independence and Israel's early years. They were afraid that the state would

---

*Jewish fate brought to Israel a diplomat whose life story was fairly dramatic and who did everything to keep it secret. Dr. Ricardo Subirana y Lobo was born in Hanover, in northern Germany, to a Jewish family named Wolf. An engineer and an inventor, he immigrated to Cuba before World War I; there he made a fortune. In the late fifties he supported Fidel Castro and helped finance the revolution that brought him to power. Castro accepted Subirana y Lobo's request to serve as Cuba's ambassador to Israel. He came with his non-Jewish wife, Francesca, set up one of the most lavish estates in Israel, and did volunteer work; Abba Eban wrote that he was a "loyal son to an ancient people."[132]

harm their way of life. Rather than attempting to impose Jewish law upon the rest of Israeli society, they were primarily focused on defending their community's interests. The battle waged by the ultra-Orthodox against autopsies was one example of their concern. "Let us live our lives our own way. We believe that our bodies must not be tampered with after death," wrote Rabbi Kalman Kahana. Autopsies were not a new battlefield; they had been a part of the conflict between religious and secular Israelis for years. Prior to 1967, the Knesset had begun debating a proposal for a legislative amendment that would reduce the number of autopsies done. As in other conflicts, non-Zionist ultra-Orthodox were not only fighting the secular establishment but were also demonstrating their higher loyalty to the commands of Jewish law compared to their competitors, the Zionist Orthodox camp.

The struggle was passionate. While thousands of people rallied under the slogan "Let us die in peace," the ultra-Orthodox disseminated gruesome posters and horror stories about "abuse of corpses" that went against the law, overrode the desires of the deceased and their families, and even ignored the explicit assurances of physicians. They also claimed that Israel was selling soldiers' body parts to Syria.[135] A woman from Bat Yam wrote about the body of her mother, the ninety-two-year-old widow of a rabbi: "After the women bathing the body went in and cleansed her, they came out sobbing. They had found the deceased with her eyes removed and her head smashed and her entire stomach empty and full of cotton wool and even her thigh was open." Ultra-Orthodox Knesset member Shlomo-Jacob Gross announced in the Knesset that he was in possession of a photograph of a crate containing the brains of deceased people. The minister of health confirmed that close to three out of every ten bodies underwent autopsy; the ultra-Orthodox claimed the number was much higher.

In March 1967, a related and rather macabre argument took place in the Knesset. Shlomo Lorincz, an ultra-Orthodox member, protested the fact that some two-thousand-year-old human skeletons uncovered in excavations at Masada had been removed for scientific study in Israel and abroad, instead of being buried according to Jewish law. The rock of Masada towers majestically over the Dead Sea, an emblem of the heritage of Jewish heroism in Palestine. Masada marked the last stand Jewish rebels had made against Roman rule; almost a thousand men, women, and children had held out in the fortress, besieged, for three years. When defeat became inevitable, they proudly committed suicide instead of shamefully surrendering. During a dig at Masada, Yigal Yadin, Israel's most senior archeologist and a former chief of staff, discovered twenty-five skeletons, which he surmised were the remains of some of the defenders. Three years after the discovery, research on the skeletons was still ongoing. Knesset member Lorincz thought this was shameful: "Thousands of young people and IDF soldiers climb to the peaks of Masada and swear to follow in the path of those heroes. They repeat the vow 'Masada shall not fall again.' I am sorry to announce today that Masada has fallen again. Not to an enemy or an outside conqueror, but to the cynicism of our times, to the spirit of wheeling and dealing that has taken over and knows no shame." His speech was highly emotional. "This is secularism and these are its fruits," he shouted. Eshkol tried to halt the political uproar over the skeletons and the treatment of corpses, as some doctors published opinions stating the value of autopsies.[136] But the death of one rabbi's wife had caused the debate to spread beyond the state and now threatened to upset Israel's status in the United States.

Rabbi Hersch Kohn had lived in New York for thirty years before moving to Jerusalem, where his wife died. Since she had died on a Saturday, Hadassah Hospital performed an autopsy without being able to obtain her husband's consent. The hospital director later claimed that this was the result of a misunderstanding: when the woman's death was pronounced, the hospital had sent an ambulance driver with a note informing her family. For some reason, the driver did not hand deliver the note, but rather left it in the mailbox where the family found it only after the Sabbath had ended. "The doctors believed in good faith that you had received the notice in the morning, and since they heard no objection on your part and the wife's death was sudden and unexplained, they performed the autopsy in the early evening after obtaining the necessary signatures." He apologized and promised to prevent similar cases in the future. The fact that the director even wrote the letter reflected increasing religious pressure on the Hadassah organization in the United States, which sponsored the hospital. Rabbi Kohn was also the father of a senior writer for the English-language daily, the *Jerusalem Post*. When Kohn phoned the Israeli consulate in New York after his wife's death, he was treated with hostility at first. "I was rude to him," acknowledged a consulate staffer, in a report that did not conceal his hostility to ultra-Orthodox Jews. He assumed that the rabbi had returned to America to "bad-mouth Israel"—and maybe to make some money by giving out a few *kashrut* certificates. Kohn had assured the diplomat he was not an Israel-hater.[137]

Israeli diplomats in the United States and Britain, meanwhile, reported on embarrassing articles about the affair that appeared in Jewish papers and in the *New York Times*. Ultra-Orthodox Jews held protest rallies outside the Israeli consulate in New York and planned similar ones outside the White House. There was even a fear that one of the leading American rabbis, Moshe Feinstein, would publish a religious ruling forbidding Jews to settle in Israel. In Washington, Ambassador Harman tried to moderate the ultra-Orthodox opposition to autopsies, but felt it was a lost cause: American Jews would not support Israel on this matter, particularly since in America the wishes of the deceased and the family were respected. The ambassador suggested to the government that it amend the relevant legislation on its own initiative; otherwise, it would have to do so under pressure from the ultra-Orthodox in America.[138]

THE RELATIONSHIP BETWEEN ISRAELIS AND AMERICAN JEWS WAS COMPLICATED AND OFten tormented, reflecting mutual dependency, exaggerated expectations, stereotypical perceptions, hypocrisy, and a fair amount of guilt. As Zionists, Israelis believed that Jews should leave the United States and settle in Israel. Apart from the ideological reasons, Israel also needed immigrants from "prosperous countries," meaning Ashkenazis from the United States, to balance out the waves of immigration from displaced persons camps in Europe and Arab states, as well as the high Arab birthrate.[139] Israeli Jews constituted only about 17 percent of the world's Jewish population.

Fewer than twenty thousand immigrants came from the United States during the first two decades after independence. Most U.S. Jews did not even come to visit. Many Israelis derided them for preferring "the humiliations of life in the Diaspora" and anti-Semitic persecutions to national sovereignty in their own land. Presuming that Jews in the United States felt some guilt about not living in Israel, many Israelis expected their American brethren to shower them with hero-worship: whenever the admiration from America seemed to be waning, Israelis felt reason for concern. But these heroes also expected American Jews to help them, and often they saw this assistance as an obligation, practically a tax. They assumed that most Jews agreed with this view, and that when American Jews helped Israel, they were in essence also ensuring their own existence.[140] But a special envoy for the prime minister, Eliezer Livneh, who was sent to the United States in 1967 to learn about the attitudes of Jews there, reported upon his return that many of them looked down on Israel for not being able to survive without their money. The need for assistance "greatly decreases the country's moral standing," wrote Livneh to Eshkol, and asked that Israel demand that American Jews help increase immigration. There was a certain degree of self-contempt among Israelis because of the willingness—and the need—to accept donations from America. "No one knows exactly how many Israelis have their hands held out to the Jewish benefactor in America," wrote one paper with disgust. People who had been willing to sacrifice their lives for the independence of the state were living on "foreign charity," wrote Benjamin Tammuz.* "Your money prevents us from working hard," said Livneh in one forum promoting dialogue between Jewish scholars from America and their Israeli counterparts. "The only thing we need from you is immigration."[141]

Livneh's report to Eshkol was pessimistic. He was extremely concerned that American Jews were neither sufficiently aware of their identity as Jews nor sufficiently Zionist. The relationship between Israel and American Jews was approaching an impasse, he said, partly because American Jews were undergoing a process of Americanization and losing their Jewish uniqueness. Tensions between them and the American blacks were leading them to be more concerned about their own standing than about Israel. Livneh reported to the prime minister about a new book, *Herzog*, by Saul Bellow. "Israel is not mentioned in the novel at all . . . even though its Jewish protagonist spends three hundred pages prattling on about an array of spiritual, social and political problems from all corners of the world," he wrote. Meir Rosen, at the Israeli consulate in New York, complained of an American Jewish diplomat who hesitated to promote the inclusion of anti-Semitism in any charter against racism: he was afraid to define Jews as a nation, lest it damage their image as Americans.† Jewish intellectuals from the United States who participated in the annual dialogue with their Israeli colleagues claimed they were more interested in the life of the mind. One of them said, "Jewish intellectual life in the United States is developing faster than Jewish intellectual life in Israel." Many of them demanded that Reform Judaism be recognized in Israel.[142]

As for Jewish students in the United States, *Ha'aretz* reported that Israel had ceased to interest them. A group of American students visiting Israel expressed disappointment and bitterness to a *Maariv* reporter. They complained of a depressing grayness, a lack of respect for the individual, ethnic discrimination, chauvinism and hypocrisy, narrow-mindedness,

---

*This was also Ben-Gurion's basic stance, but he too sometimes turned to American Jews, as he did in mid-1966, partly to raise funds for Sde Boker College.
†Similar reports came from London regarding the "poor state of British Jewry."

and intellectual boredom: one could find twenty sets of the complete works of Pushkin in the library, but not a single book by Hannah Arendt, they claimed. *Ha'aretz* quoted the writer Elie Wiesel: "The Jewishness of Jewish youth can still be reached, but not through Israel. Perhaps through the problems of the Jews in Russia. Perhaps through questions about the Holocaust. Not through Israel." Ambassador Harman argued that the public campaign for the rights of Soviet Jews was contributing to a Zionist awakening among American Jews, thereby helping Israel.[143]

Influential Jews in the United States often helped promote Israel's interests in other countries, and were sent on missions intended to make life easier for persecuted Jews in Arab states and in the Communist bloc. Harman described this diplomatic effort as "lobbying," an insulting term in Hebrew, reminiscent of the helplessness of Jews before the establishment of the state, but his embassy also emerges from his descriptions as a hugely influential Jewish agency active in precisely the same sort of interventions.[144] At the same time, the question often arose as to what extent the Jews of the United States were obliged to abide by policies of the Israeli government and act in its best interests.* This was not a new dilemma. Many years before, Jacob Blaustein, the oil tycoon and president of the American Jewish Committee, had managed to get a written undertaking from then prime minister Ben-Gurion that Israel would not interfere in the affairs of Jewish Americans and would not demand dual loyalties from them. Ben-Gurion thereby relinquished, in effect, Israel's Zionist monopoly on Jewish identity, and acknowledged the legitimacy of Jewish life outside Israel, in contradiction to the principles of Zionism.[146]† This pragmatic approach made it easier for American Jews to stand by Israel.

7. JEWS II: "IT'S GOOD TO HAVE THIS SORT OF FAUCET"

Ambassador Harman spent much of his time fostering the relationship with the nearly six million Jews in the United States, whom he viewed as an integral component of his political contacts. Jews who were close to President Lyndon Johnson helped the ambassador plead Israel's case directly, and the president also relied on their help for talks with Israel.

---

*The question also came up regarding ties with Jews in other countries. Jon Kimche, the editor of the *Jewish Observer*, a British weekly, was removed from his post because Eshkol believed he favored the Rafi political line.[145]

†Blaustein suggested at one point that he meet with Egypt's Nasser. The fact that he was not a Zionist might be of help, he claimed. It is unclear whether he was joking, but he did help Israel on other diplomatic matters.

These contacts were often maintained on a daily basis, sometimes even hourly, and they included frequent phone calls with the president's assistants as well as meetings at social events in Washington and on the president's ranch in Texas.[147] Israel enjoyed an extremely close relationship with the Johnson administration. Israel's special envoy to Washington, Ephraim Evron, once reported a conversation with the U.S. ambassador to the United Nations, Arthur Goldberg. Goldberg confided in the Israeli diplomat about the personal tension between himself and his superiors at the State Department, in part concerning ties with Israel. "His comments on the matter were a mixture of anger and pain," reported Evron, and noted that Goldberg was a personal friend. Evron also developed a friendly relationship with President Johnson himself: they played golf together twice.[148]

The position of Jewish Americans in relation to Washington was a complex one. Jews did not control the world or America, but the anti-Semitic myth of their power was helpful to the Zionist movement and to the State of Israel, and so it was in the Zionists' best interest to nurture it. Theodor Herzl had deployed the myth of Jewish power to enlist support for the Zionist idea; Chaim Weizmann had done the same to obtain the Balfour Declaration from the British; Nahum Goldman knew how to create the impression that his influence was boundless during negotiations with the German government on reparations for victims of the Nazi persecution. Goldman, a diplomat without a homeland and with half a dozen passports, frequently irritated Harman, but according to the ambassador he had learned from Goldman about the secret of the "Jewish myth" and how to employ its influence. "It's good to have this kind of faucet," he said of the Jews of America; "we have certainly gained all sorts of things thanks to this faucet, and it is doubtful we would have gotten them purely on the basis of merit. But with this kind of faucet you always have to consider when to turn it on: it's easier to turn on than off."[149] The battle of American Jews against Coca-Cola was, he felt, one example of the troublesome faucet.

Moshe Bornstein, a Holocaust survivor, was the owner of the Israeli beverage company Tempo, and had been trying for years to win the Israeli franchise to make Coca-Cola. The company had repeatedly turned him down, apparently fearing that manufacturing the beverage in Israel would lead to its boycott in Arab countries.* Israel and Jewish organiza-

---

*Coca-Cola even sued Bornstein, claiming that with one beverage he was imitating their bottles and the name "Cola." The case was settled: the Israeli bottle remained unchanged, but the name was now to be spelled "Kola."

tions in America consistently fought against the Arab commercial boycott, and Israel even kept a special consul in New York specifically for that purpose. In 1966 the consul was the journalist Yuval Elitzur, a writer for *Maariv*. Elitzur frequently worked with Arnold Forster, an official of the Anti-Defamation League of B'nai B'rith, who, as Elitzur described, launched an initiative called "Operation Coca-Cola." When the company repeated its refusal to grant Bornstein the franchise, Forster went to the U.S. press; before long, a "counter boycott" was under way among American Jews; they probably switched to Pepsi. Even the well-known hot dog chain Nathan's announced it would no longer serve Coca-Cola. The Israeli press attributed near existential importance to the issue. "Our country, in its political security condition, is unusual," said *Maariv* in an editorial. "While in any normal country, Coca-Cola is a drink and, at most, a symbol of American civilization, we see Coca-Cola not only as a drink but also as a political factor." The papers depicted an arduous battle against a far-reaching evil empire. When the soda company finally capitulated, it was as if the Jewish people had gained a glorious victory worthy of comparison to David's over Goliath.[150]

Behind the scenes, there had indeed been great drama. Moshe Bornstein had come to New York in April 1966 to join the struggle, and one Friday, at the height of negotiations, he left to spend the Sabbath out of town. He had given a contact number to Consul Elitzur, but apparently it was not the correct number. Just before the Sabbath began, an American Jewish Committee board member, an intermediary, phoned Elitzur with Coca-Cola's proposed settlement and asked for the Israeli government's approval: the company would authorize production of Coke in Israel, but it would award the franchise not to Bornstein but to an American Jewish businessman, Abe Feinberg, who had also been pursuing it for years. Elitzur could not get hold of Bornstein, but he phoned Ambassador Harman, who responded that the State of Israel was hardly in a position to dictate terms to Coca-Cola. Forster, who was also contacted, decreed that Feinberg would take the franchise and then transfer it to Bornstein, and the settlement was approved. When Bornstein came back to town, he discovered that Feinberg intended to keep the franchise for himself, and, feeling cheated, he threatened to create a scandal.

Ambassador Harman thought the entire matter was needlessly damaging to Israel. He said, "Israel needs Coca-Cola like a hole in the head"; the country had plenty of orange juice. Elitzur saw the whole thing differently. "Since the Allies' victory in WWII, this international beverage, for better or for worse, has become a symbol of American culture," he wrote, and warned that foreign investors might be put off if they concluded that big companies did not do business with Israel. Nor would tourists come if they couldn't find the drinks they were used to in Israeli hotels.[151]

Most Israelis would have agreed with Elitzur: they needed Coca-Cola for the same reason they took so many trips abroad and bought television sets long before there was anything to watch: they felt the claustrophobia of the borders and longed to be part of the great wide world, with America at its helm. Most of them had no way of knowing that the man behind the bottle, Abe Feinberg, was a key figure in the relationship between Israel and the United States.

FEINBERG HAD STUDIED LAW IN NEW YORK, BUT RATHER THAN GO INTO PRACTICE HE entered into a partnership with his father, a hosiery manufacturer. He was successful in business and a few years later became a banker. The persecution of Jews in Europe motivated him to become active raising money through the United Palestine Appeal. He organized activities among his partners and other hosiery manufacturers, and distinguished himself with his generous donations. While still in his twenties, he had become interested in politics. Now, impatient, he decided to skip the standard stages of activism and go straight to the president himself. He knew someone who knew someone who knew someone who had gone to school with one of President Franklin Delano Roosevelt's aides. Feinberg met with the aide to talk of the needs of the Jews, presenting himself as more of a moderate than the leader of the Zionist movement in America, Abba Hillel Silver, a Republican. Feinberg promised he had no interest in putting pressure on the president or extorting him or making threats. He was not looking for publicity. He wanted simply to pass on information regarding the needs of the Jewish people and to consider informally what the president could do for the Jews and what they could do for him and the Democratic Party. Roosevelt's aide suggested he first meet the vice president. Feinberg was none too impressed: people barely knew who Harry Truman was at the time. But Roosevelt's man arranged for Feinberg to be invited to a small party with Truman, and the two struck up an acquaintance. A few months after this meeting, Roosevelt died and was replaced by Truman. Feinberg had the beginnings of a friendship with the man in the White House.

Feinberg now became involved in the efforts to bring Holocaust survivors to Palestine, which was still under British rule. He financed and even personally accompanied ships full of illegal immigrants. He helped purchase arms for protection and once got mixed up in an espionage episode that led to his arrest. In Palestine, Feinberg was asked by the Hagana to deliver a report to Ben-Gurion, who was at the time in Paris. The report had come from Damascus from the journalist-spy Eliyahu Sasson, later the Israeli minister of police. The British, suspicious of the Hagana, arrested Feinberg but released him thanks to his ties with the White House, and he was able to carry out the mission. He claimed to have had a part in defining President Truman's position that 100,000 Holocaust survivors be allowed to enter Palestine. He was a guest of Chaim Weizmann in his hotel in New York when the UN decided to partition Palestine in 1947, and said he was among those who influenced Truman to recognize the State of Israel.

Before the presidential election of 1948, Truman gathered a few of his acquaintances, including Feinberg, and told them that his chances of winning depended upon his ability to reach out to the voters. He wanted to travel by train from coast to coast, and to do that he needed money. Feinberg promised to raise $100,000, and he succeeded. Most of the donors were Jewish: Feinberg told them they had to help Truman because he supported the State of Israel. Although Feinberg was exaggerating when he took credit for Truman's election, the president's gratitude did enable him to cement his status as a liaison not only between the administration and prominent Jewish Democrats, but also between the White House and the Israeli government. Once, he later recalled, Truman sent him to Israel to mediate between President Weizmann and Prime Minister Ben-Gurion. The United States wanted Israel to allow a few thousand Arab refugees to return to their homes as part of a family reunification program. Weizmann supported the proposal; Ben-Gurion objected. Feinberg talked to both men and was able to bring about the return of some of the refugees.

Feinberg recounted all this in a long interview he granted the Truman Library, years after the events.[152] Not everything he said is verifiable, but White House and State Department documents, as well as Israeli government materials, confirm that he was Israel's man in the White House for many years.* He also had ties with President John F. Kennedy, but his key personal connection was with Lyndon Johnson. Their acquaintance began during Truman's presidency and continued throughout Johnson's terms in the House and the Senate when Johnson was already a supporter of Israel.[153] Over time, the former hosiery manufacturer became more so-

---

*Although he was not Israeli, Feinberg's personal archives are housed in the State Archives in Jerusalem.

phisticated, overcoming his awe of the presidency. Though always respectful to the president, he talked with him as an equal. In April 1966, he sent Johnson a note thanking him for an invitation to Texas: "I cannot tell you how much I appreciate the fact that you invited me on the trip to Houston. The speech was great, the plane was magnificent, the White House bed was long enough, and your pajamas fit perfectly." He wrote on his bank's official letterhead and added a handwritten note in which he commented on how well the president, his wife, and his daughters looked. A White House assistant wrote to him that he was among the president's closest friends.

Johnson and the White House used Feinberg as a link to Prime Minister Eshkol and to Jewish public opinion. They expected him to attract political and financial support, and they were not disappointed. Feinberg did not represent official Jewish organizations, but Johnson saw him as an ambassador of the Jews, or, as they were careful to say in the White House, Feinberg's "friends" or "the friends of Israel." Johnson repeatedly sent him to deliver messages to Eshkol and to handle business he preferred not to put through official administration pipelines. Once, meeting Ambassador Harman at a reception, Johnson told him, "Tell Abe Feinberg I would like to see him and talk to him." The two men sometimes spoke on the phone.[154]

At the beginning of 1967, when Johnson wanted to communicate that the United States would find it hard to respond to all of Israel's requests for assistance, Feinberg was the man who received the news. This was shortly before one of his trips to Jerusalem. When he returned to America, Feinberg brought the White House Israel's response. In preparation for another meeting with Feinberg, Johnson was given memos detailing Israel's requests for financial and military aid, including information on the relevant credit ratings and interest rates. Feinberg was proficient in all the details. The particulars were accompanied by a memo analyzing the foundations of the relationship between the United States and Israel, which stated that "the existence of a large, well-organized group of Israel sympathizers within the U.S. body politic obviously puts a limit on the degree to which the USG [U.S. government] might contemplate a different policy" toward Israel. This relationship was Feinberg's domain. The White House opened a file named "Feinberg Good Works," which contained an article in support of the president that had appeared in a Jewish paper.[155] Johnson once called Feinberg to convince him that Israel should back the supply of American arms to Jordan, since it, too, had an interest in "the little king" maintaining power. But Johnson said he was willing to accept Eshkol's position on the matter, so that he, Johnson, should not be perceived as imposing anything on Israel. If that impression were created, Johnson said, he'd have Jim Novy on the line in five minutes protesting—something he'd like to avoid. Novy was a wealthy Jewish scrap-iron dealer, born in Poland, who had been helpful to Johnson at the beginning of his career. Johnson assured Feinberg that he wanted to please the Jews, not irritate them.[156]*

WHEN IN 1966 THE WHITE HOUSE WANTED TO FIND OUT HOW THE JEWISH COMMUNITY would react to a proposed arms deal with Jordan, a conversation with Feinberg did not suffice; two other Jewish men, David Ginsburg and Arthur Krim, were also brought in. The three conveyed that both Israel and the Jews could live with the deal.[158] Ginsburg, an attorney, had been a longtime friend of Johnson's. "It was fun being with him," Ginsburg later recalled. A Harvard graduate, he had law offices near the White House and served on various public boards from time to time. Although he held no government position, he spent a lot of time at the White House "as a friend of the President."[159] Johnson told Feinberg that Ginsburg was one of the most talented people he knew and that he would like to bring him into the government. That was in March 1967, during a discussion of a series of requests Israel had presented to the administration. In the same conversation, the president told Feinberg that he had given Ginsburg a mission. This was an unusual episode, even for the Johnson-Jews-Israel triangle, and an apparently astonished Ginsburg had been quick to report the matter to Israeli representative Evron: he had met with Johnson on a different matter entirely—to present the findings of an arbitration committee convened to address railroad workers' demands. When Ginsburg had finished, the president pulled him aside and asked him to prepare a memo specifying what he, Johnson, could do for Israel over the next few months. Administration officials wouldn't like it, Johnson said, but he was certain he could arrange passage of whatever plan Ginsburg came up with. He knew that most Jews had voted for him and he did not forget his friends, the president explained. There was no doubt that he was thinking ahead to the 1968 elections. He urged Ginsburg to hurry; indeed, two

---

*Novy was the man who, in the 1950s, first introduced the Israeli ambassador, Abba Eban, to the Democratic Senate majority leader, Lyndon Johnson. Israeli diplomats in the United States cultivated ties with Novy, and one of his acquaintances asked Eshkol to help promote his business in Israel.[157]

days later he ran into him and asked if he'd started working on the plan.

The Israelis treated the president's request as a windfall. As a first response, Ambassador Harman fantasized about a U.S.-Israeli defense pact and an official visit to Washington by the prime minister. He quickly sent Jerusalem a memo draft enumerating a long list of proposed requests: plane engines, tank engines, armored personnel carriers, economic aid, and political support. Figures, credit terms, supply and payment dates were all written down in great detail. The memo Ginsburg ultimately gave Johnson was very similar to this hasty draft, and Ginsburg reported that Johnson received it favorably. They sat together for two and a half hours, and then, in Ginsburg's presence, the president phoned Secretary of State Dean Rusk and Secretary of Defense Robert McNamara and invited them to discuss the matter. A few days later, Ginsburg, accompanied by Feinberg, went to Jerusalem to meet with Prime Minister Eshkol. The whole matter was top secret: embassy telegrams referred to Feinberg as "Andre," while Ginsburg was "Harari."* Ginsburg told the prime minister that President Johnson was willing to do more than any other president, including Truman, for Israel's sake. However, the relationship between Israel and the United States, he claimed, depended on one thing: Johnson wanted evidence that Israel was not building a nuclear bomb. There was no matter of greater importance, Ginsberg reiterated: Feinberg backed him up. The two seemed to have known more about Israel's nuclear program than most Israelis, and this intimate knowledge presented them with a serious dilemma.† Ginsburg's memo to Johnson reflects a fairly acrobatic attempt to represent Israel's position on the matter, but he suggested that Johnson go over the details with Eshkol himself.[162]

The whole episode was so extraordinary, and Ginsburg and Feinberg were so deeply involved in such profound, confidential matters, that the Israelis felt it necessary to be prudent. "The president personally needs us very much and his personal status may weaken even more in the coming period," wrote Harman to Eshkol, referring to the war in Vietnam and his bid for reelection, but "we cannot give him the impression that we are extorting a pound of flesh in light of his serious personal situation."[163] Moshe Bitan, an official at the Ministry of Foreign Affairs, sent Ambassador Harman his theory regarding what he called the "magic circle": the more

---

*President Johnson was "Issahar" in Ministry of Foreign Affairs telegrams; Eshkol was "Yehuda."[160]

†Feinberg was a central figure in raising the funds Israel invested in its Dimona nuclear plant.[161]

Johnson was inclined to do for Israel, the more his people rejected Israel's requests. Johnson, Bitan explained, acted personally on Israeli matters, even trivial ones. This angered both the State Department and the Pentagon, and so when they leaned on Israel, they were not acting out of practical considerations but responding, first and foremost, to the fact that Israel was going directly to the president and that he was talking to the country through its friends. Since the officials could not blame the boss himself, they took their anger out on Israel, wrote Bitan. He suggested doing everything possible to mend relations with the administration branches. These were the limits of the "Jewish myth" of power.

Many years later, Ginsburg believed it had been wrong to pigeonhole American Jews as Democrats: the wealthiest among them supported Republican candidates, he said. But in his memo to Johnson he emphasized that the Jews had supported Democrats for years. However, one could not rule out the possibility that a Republican candidate might make a special effort to gain their support, Ginsburg cautioned, and that obliged Johnson himself to make a special effort.[164] In his striving to comply, Johnson sought the assistance of a couple who added a certain glamour and romance to the story: Arthur and Mathilde Krim. He was a Jewish movie producer, she a former Israeli.

WHILE STILL A YOUNG ATTORNEY, KRIM HAD HANDLED THE AFFAIRS OF THE ZIONIST ACtivist Meyer Weisgal, Chaim Weizmann's representative in America. Weisgal was a journalist and theatrical producer who had a knack for befriending the rich and famous. In 1937 he produced *The Eternal Road* in New York, a play commissioned from Franz Werfel about the history of the Jewish people, with music by Kurt Weill; the director was Max Reinhart. The critics praised the play, but Weisgal went into debt and sought Krim's help. Weisgal was later a founder of the Weizmann Institute of Science, in Rehovot; to support it, he recruited many of his American acquaintances, including Abe Feinberg and David Ginsburg. One day he invited Arthur Krim, who had just purchased United Artists from Charlie Chaplin, to visit the institute. When Krim came to Rehovot, Weisgal introduced him to the biologist Dr. Mathilde Danon, who was, as Weisgal put it, "the most beautiful woman scientist" at the institute. In her twenties, she was indeed a beautiful blonde.

Mathilde Galland had been born in Italy to a Swiss Calvinist father and a Catholic mother. While she was still in high school, the news emerged of the extermination of Jews in the war, and she responded with profound shock. During her studies at the University of Geneva, she met a few concentration camp survivors. Her knowledge of the Holocaust drew her to Jewish circles and she soon fell in love with a Bulgarian-born student from Palestine, David Danon, who was also active in Etzel, the Jewish underground organization fighting the British Mandate. Mathilde Galland saw in him not a terrorist but a freedom fighter, a Jewish hero. She herself began to participate in Etzel activities in Europe, crossing borders on a bicycle to smuggle information and explosives. Together with Danon, she took part in purchasing arms to be shipped by Etzel on board the *Altalena*.* They drove from village to village in a jeep, buying rifles from farmers who had kept them since their anti-Nazi underground days. She married David Danon in 1948 and their daughter, Dafna, was born in 1951. When their studies were over they settled in Israel and both got jobs at the Weizmann Institute in Rehovot. Mathilde Danon, who had converted to Judaism, worked on chromosome research. She remained at the institute even after separating from her husband.

Meyer Weisgal, she later recalled, asked her to give Arthur Krim a tour of the institute, and he asked where he could get a good steak. The best steaks in Rehovot were hers, she said, and she invited him to her home. Krim visited her often over the next few months, and she eventually agreed to marry him.† When she came to the United States, Krim continued her scientific work and emerged as a glamorous hostess, too: their guests were a who's who of entertainment and politics. She was also involved in her husband's political activism. Arthur Krim supported Kennedy and helped raise funds for his presidential campaign. He was good at matching wealthy people with movie stars and politicians, and was a frequent namedropper; Harry Belafonte, Rudolf Nureyev, Woody Allen. When Kennedy became president, Krim started an exclusive "club" of donors who were privy to occasional political briefings, sometimes from the president himself. No one received tangible benefits in return for their

---

*The *Altalena* reached the shores of Israel in June 1948, carrying some 850 immigrants as well as the arms. Prime Minister Ben-Gurion demanded that Etzel hand over the arms to the newly formed IDF. Negotiations were conducted by Menachem Begin and Levi Eshkol, among others. When talks failed, Ben-Gurion saw the affair as a test of the state's sovereignty and ordered that the ship be bombarded.

†Weisgal also benefited from the matchmaking: a few years later he helped Otto Preminger film the story of the *Exodus*, the ship of illegal immigrants. The movie starred Paul Newman, with Weisgal himself in the role of Ben-Gurion. It was perhaps the greatest achievement of the Zionist movement's propaganda efforts, greater even than the actual sailing of the *Exodus*. United Artists, owned by Krim, distributed the movie and promised the Weizmann Institute a share in the profits of approximately $1 million.[165]

money, Krim later insisted, but they all enjoyed the proximity to power and charisma.

In May 1962, the Krims threw a party in their New York home. President Kennedy was among the guests, as were Marilyn Monroe and Maria Callas. Vice President Lyndon Johnson was "somewhat ignored," Arthur Krim recollected, although Mathilde Krim tried to entertain him. Johnson ended up staying till one or two in the morning, and it was the beginning of a wonderful friendship.

After the Kennedy assassination, Krim was reluctant to continue his fund-raising activities. Like many of Kennedy's supporters, he was planning to abandon politics but Johnson urged him to continue. As the widowed Dr. Krim later recounted, Johnson told him: "You have no other president." Krim had to stay the course "for America." Krim stayed. In a series of interviews he did for the Johnson Library, Krim recounted in great detail how Johnson had befriended him and his wife with a series of surprising gestures. Once the president suddenly called them at home and asked Dr. Krim to leave for Paris that night, to escort a delegation of U.S. astronauts. He explained that her command of French and her European manners would prevent the astronauts' wives from embarrassing the delegation. Dr. Krim stayed over at the White House prior to the trip—the Krims were to do so often, in a regular room on the third floor, number 303. She also visited several times on her own. Johnson occasionally invited the Krims to accompany him on his helicopter and even on Air Force One, when he flew to his ranch in Texas. His displays of friendship were lavish and at some point he even tried to convince the Krims to buy a ranch neighboring his. Dafna, Mathilde Krim's daughter, received a letter from him while she was serving in the IDF. He once told Golda Meir on the phone, much to her astonishment, that he was coming to Israel to visit Dafna.

The friendship between Johnson and the Krims was no secret, and yet the three preferred that the press not write about them or photograph them together. A photographer once shot Mathilde Krim sunning on board the president's yacht. The picture was published the next day with the caption "Who Is the Blonde on President Johnson's Boat?" Johnson was furious. White House logs show that the two spoke on the phone frequently, sometimes when she was staying on the third floor of the White House and he was in the Oval Office. Many years later, Dr. Krim was asked whether it would be true to say she was "Israel's woman in the White House." She responded that she had never been asked to deliver an official request from the Israeli government to the president. Yes, she said, she might have given him messages from David Ginsburg or others. She described her relationship with the president as "a very, very close friendship." Asked whether it was a romantic relationship, she replied in the negative. But, she added, it was not the first time she had been asked.

Arthur Krim said that Johnson communicated through him with the Israeli government when he wanted to circumvent the State Department and the Pentagon.* Johnson once asked him what he thought of Eshkol, but Krim knew the prime minister only in passing. Mathilde Krim, on the other hand, told the president that he would like Eshkol because they were alike: "Both came from the soil, and [were] very blunt, strong, pragmatic men." She might have added that they had both been required to step out from behind the shadows of great men, Ben-Gurion and Kennedy.

The Krims assumed that Johnson was grateful for their ongoing assistance. According to them he was hurt by the attitude of Kennedy's people, many of them New Englanders and Harvard graduates who looked down on the Texas rancher. Johnson felt compassion toward people who had suffered discrimination and could identify with them, the Krims said. He appreciated people who had made it the hard way, because he felt that he, too, had faced discrimination and had worked hard to get where he was. They thought he identified with Jews and with Israel much as he did with the plight of the blacks and the poor, and at times they said they would have expected to find such warmth only in someone who had Jewish roots himself.[166]

BEYOND GINSBERG, FEINBURG, AND THE KRIMS, THE MOST SENIOR FIGURE TO INFLUENCE President Johnson's policy on Israel was Associate Justice of the Supreme Court Abe Fortas. In early 1967, Fortas gave a speech in Chicago to delegates at a regional convention of the United Jewish Appeal. He reminisced about his childhood as a Jewish boy in Memphis during the days when there was some doubt as to whether Jews could survive in America as Jews. They did so, he argued, partly thanks to their pride in Israel's success. It was a warm Jewish speech, and Fortas charmed his au-

---

*He once asked Krim to tell Abe Feinberg that he had decided to support the candidacy of Feinberg's brother for a judgeship, not neglecting to mention that he was thereby angering other influential Jews in New York.

dience. He told a joke: Two American Jews visit Israel. They go to a night-club and see a comedy act. One of the two rolls around laughing. "Since when do you understand Hebrew?" his friend asks. "I don't," the first says, "but I trust the Israelis." In the same speech, Fortas also recounted how he had once invited David Ben-Gurion to breakfast at his home. They had talked about the similarities and the differences between discrimination against Mizrahim in Israel and blacks in America. According to Fortas, Israel had overcome discrimination and America would follow suit.*

Ambassador Harman would often meet with Fortas, and later said that Fortas could see Johnson whenever he wanted, "even ten times a day." But Fortas was more than a conduit: he also gave the president advice and played an extremely important role in talks that preceded the Six-Day War. Like Israel's other liaisons to the White House, Fortas was careful to keep these talks strictly confidential. In Israel's diplomatic telegrams he was identified as "Ilan." Many years later, the former envoy Ephraim Evron still denied that Fortas had served as a liaison to the White House.[168] Fortas's situation was particularly delicate because of his position on the Supreme Court. Although he was not the first Jewish judge to serve as a political adviser to a U.S. president, his status in the White House and his involvement in many key issues generated criticism. Arthur Krim later commented that he had been surprised at the president, and mainly at Fortas himself, for not being sufficiently sensitive about this. Johnson knew that his relationship with Fortas was problematic, and once instructed that a White House brochure be shelved because it featured a photograph of him with his advisers, including Fortas. Johnson's close adviser Walt Rostow was also Jewish. His brother Eugene was a senior official in the State Department. Ambassador Harman reported to Jerusalem that "unlike his brother," Eugene was positive about his Jewish identity and saw himself as part of the Jewish people.[169]

Johnson's special feeling for the Jews prompted a legend that found its way into the press and into research on the president. The story's origins go back to December 1963, when the president attended the opening ceremony of the Conservative Agudas Achim community's new synagogue in Austin, Texas. The event seemed to be of no particular importance, warranting twenty-one lines at the bottom of page 16 of the *New York*

---

*Prime Minister Ben-Gurion came to Fortas's house to meet Johnson when the latter was still the Senate majority leader in 1960. But Johnson had to attend a senator's funeral that day and it is unclear whether he had time to meet Ben-Gurion. Either way, in his car on the way to the airport, he spoke with Ben-Gurion on the phone and showered him with questions about the situation in Israel.[167]

Times, alongside an even shorter story covering the appointment of Sheldon S. Cohen, a partner in the law firm of Abe Fortas, as the new commissioner of the Internal Revenue Service.[170] Johnson's host at the synagogue was his old friend Jim Novy. In his welcoming speech, Novy said that early in World War II, Congressman Johnson had helped forty-two Jews leave Poland and Germany via the U.S. embassy in Warsaw. In 1940, he continued, Johnson had arranged for another group of persecuted Jews to be housed in Texas. Johnson did not deny the details, and his wife, Lady Bird, even reinforced it. At the end of the ceremony, she wrote, "person after person" came up to her and told her that they would not have been there that day if not for her husband. "He helped me get out," she said they told her, adding that this was one of the most memorable events of the day.[171] In its next incarnation, the story told of "hundreds of Jews" persecuted by the Nazis whom Johnson had helped smuggle into the United States and housed in Texas, illegally. The University of Texas awarded a doctorate to a student who made the rescue the subject of his thesis, even giving it a name: Operation Texas. Others copied the story from him.[172] Had the episode been true, Johnson would have been entitled to plant a tree on the Avenue of the Righteous Among the Nations at Yad Vashem, in Jerusalem, an opportunity Israel would not have been likely to pass up. But the story was completely unfounded.

In the Johnson Library in Austin there is a thick file documenting the efforts of a senior archivist named Claudia Anderson to track down the evidence, partly at the request of Johnson's daughter. Anderson discovered that Johnson, or someone in his office acting on his behalf, had helped the renowned Jewish conductor Erich Leinsdorf remain in the United States after the Anschluss; other members of Congress had assisted Jews in similar ways. Johnson probably also helped the relatives of a Texas Jewish businessman reach the United States. Anderson made extensive efforts to locate Jews supposedly rescued in "Operation Texas," and she publicized her search widely, hoping some of the survivors would come forward. She found no one. The Novys were also unable to help. Anderson searched various archives but could find no confirming documentation. She did, however, expose a little lie in which Johnson had indulged. He had spoken of visiting Nazi concentration camps after the war; indeed, he did go to Europe with a congressional delegation, Anderson concluded, and the delegates did visit Dachau; but he himself was in Paris that day.[173] And so the mystery behind Johnson's special treatment of the Jews remained mysterious.

"I think he is part Jewish, seriously," said Johnson's special counsel,

Harry McPherson, who oversaw ties with the Jewish community. "He really reminds me of a . . . slightly corny version of a rabbi or a diamond-merchant on 44th Street. . . . He has the kind of hot nature that one associates with Jews." McPherson remembered a Jewish writer who had once entertained other White House guests by comparing the "non-Jewish Jew" and the "Jewish non-Jew." He described the "Jewish non-Jew" as a Texan: frank, amusing, always complaining, always exaggerating. That was Johnson, said McPherson: "He was outrageous and he talked too much and demanded too much and was never satisfied and was a lot of fun." Speaking more soberly, McPherson explained that Johnson spoke of Jews with the somewhat amused tone often heard among Texans, which mainly expressed a sense of otherness: "I wouldn't call it anti-Semitism; it was a little of the southern country attitude toward urban, very different Jews." When Johnson praised Arthur Goldberg before appointing him U.S. ambassador to the UN, he said that Goldberg "understands our country well" and that "he understands us better than other Jews." As a Jew, Goldberg was apparently not part of the American "us" to Johnson. Mathilde Krim felt that Johnson identified in U.S. Jews a powerful political factor, one with which there could and should be collaboration.[174] He seems to have seen the different aspects as one: the Jews of the United States, including their financial support of his party, their public support of his policy, and their votes; the Middle East; and the United States' support of Israel, including economic, military, and political aid. All these elements were pieces in one puzzle to Johnson. Another piece was Vietnam.

THE ESHKOL GOVERNMENT WAS CAREFUL NOT TO IDENTIFY PUBLICLY WITH THE U.S. INvolvement in Southeast Asia, a focal point of the conflict between the Communist bloc and the West. The obligation to protect Soviet Jews was among the factors that shaped Israel's policy on the Vietnam War, as well as relations with France, which denounced America's involvement. Israel valued the support of several prominent intellectuals in Europe who also objected to U.S. involvement in Vietnam. Mapam ministers were among the war's detractors, and they rejected any hint of identification with the war.

By 1967, two out of every three Israelis said they were following the war closely. A little over half said it was an attempt by the Communists in the North to take over the South, while just under half said the war was being waged over the United States' attempt to take over the North. "A crazy war," proclaimed Ze'ev Schiff, the military commentator for

Ha'aretz, after returning from Vietnam. Schiff accepted the premise that if the United States were to lose, the security guarantees it extended to its friends would be worthless. In December 1966, and again in March 1967, a prominent ad denouncing the war ran in *Ha'aretz*, signed by some three hundred academics, writers, and artists, most of them well-known. Many had previously signed petitions condemning the imposition of martial law on the Arabs in Israel. Most Israelis, however, did not join the protest. On Kibbutz Yehiam there was an attempt to raise money to aid the Vietnamese, but the majority of members remained indifferent: the money they were being asked to send to North Vietnam would come back to them via Syria, they said. The fund-raisers admonished them: What would they tell their children, who had been raised on principles of absolute justice? On a wall opposite the American embassy in Tel Aviv someone spray-painted the slogan, "Yankees Quit Vietnam," and a couple of dozen people held a protest vigil. The U.S. consul in Jerusalem reported that only about forty-five people took part in a demonstration there, and that at one point there were more police than demonstrators.

Cautiously refraining from supporting the war, Israel was also careful not to join the countries denouncing it, instead doing its best to avoid taking a clear position. There were occasional signals of goodwill toward Washington: perhaps Israel could host students from South Vietnam? Humanitarian aid to South Vietnam was worth discussing, but not diplomatic relations. Walt Rostow believed that humanitarian aid to South Vietnam would give American Jews the impression that Israel supported the war.*

In June 1966, President Johnson called a meeting with the editors of Jewish newspapers to talk about his administration's aid to Israel. The meeting was part of a campaign to elicit support from American Jews for the Vietnam War, to which many of them objected. Israel's consul in New York sent Jerusalem a telegram with the results of a survey that showed 44 percent of U.S. Jews supported Johnson's policy in Vietnam, while 41 percent objected to it. Johnson's response to the survey was fury that so many Jews opposed his policy: Jews should support the war, he said, because he supported Israel. He repeated this contention often, as when he met with the national commander of the Jewish War Veterans Association. Israeli diplomats, as well as Foreign Minister Abba Eban himself,

---

Ha'aretz supported the establishment of diplomatic relations between Israel and South Vietnam.[175]

tried to help Johnson by attempting to convince Jewish community leaders to tone down their opposition to the war.[176] This was a difficult point
in the history of American Jews. Johnson treated them as if they were
agents of Israel, questioning their right as citizens to shape their own position on the war—for or against—on the basis of their own reasoning
and conscience. One Jewish community leader later accused Johnson of
trying to blackmail American Jews. Israel was troubled by this, too. David
Ariel, from the Israeli consulate in New York, sent Jerusalem a detailed report on a confidential meeting of the Conference of Presidents, the um-
brella organization of the leaders of large Jewish organizations in
America. The question was whether to declare a united "Jewish position"
on Vietnam. It was a tense and emotional debate, wrote the Israeli diplomat, with a mixture of personal bitterness, competition between organizations, and opposing ideological standpoints. According to the consul,
the debate exposed an insecurity—whose existence had been denied
until then—regarding the participants' very status as Jews in America.[177]
Consul Michael Arnon sent a similar report: President Johnson's demand
for support "uncovered the fear hidden in the hearts of many Jews—
although they of course like to deny it outright—that there is in America
a serious danger of anti-Semitism." Arnon believed, however, that Israel
could benefit from this fear. Recently, he complained, Jewish activists had
been neglecting "the purely Jewish domain" and focusing their activities
on general issues, such as U.S. policy in Vietnam, human rights, and so
forth. The consul pointed out that many were even ignoring Jewish issues
in their blessings for the Jewish New Year, Rosh Hashanah, "and preach-
ing general moral sermons" instead. But President Johnson's insistence
on support had shaken them out of their complacency, and the imposed
Jewish awakening might help "restore the correct balance," wrote the
consul.[178]

   In both Jerusalem and Washington, the state of affairs was causing significant alarm, partly because of a letter from the president of the American Jewish Congress, Joachim Prinz, to Foreign Minister Eban, in which
Prinz made clear that American Jews' commitment to Israel was not so
profound as to influence their position on Vietnam.* Israeli envoy Ephraim
Evron hurried to the White House and urged Johnson's special counsel,
McPherson, to "lay off" on this issue, assuring him that he was speaking

---

*Israeli diplomats soon became actively involved in the question of Prinz's replacement; Is-
rael's choice was the president of Hadassah, Charlotte Jacobson.[179]

as a personal friend and that he only wanted to ensure that the president's political interests were not harmed. Two Jewish leaders went to see the president to discuss the matter and Evron, who briefed them before the meeting, urged them to try to bring the conflict to an end. Johnson denied having demanded a unified position from the Jews and sent Arthur Goldberg to appease the community. The newspapers gave prominent coverage to the whole affair, and the Israeli consul in New York also reported on his efforts to rein in the press.[180] For a while it seemed the matter was fading from the headlines, but then the most famous and admired of all Israelis, after David Ben-Gurion, announced that he was going to tour Vietnam. This was Moshe Dayan.

Ten years after his last war, two years after resigning as minister of agriculture, Knesset member Dayan was finding life as the manager of a small fishing company boring. He was fascinated by Vietnam. "There is a war being fought in Vietnam with conventional weapons and on a limited scale," he explained, "and in which the guerrilla element plays a significant part. I think we have a lot to learn from this war and the way it's being conducted." He traveled as a reporter for *Maariv* and the *Washington Post*, but wherever he went the general was welcomed as an esteemed military leader. His trip was covered extensively in the United States and people awaited his pronouncements—not because they were hoping to learn something from his perspective, but because everything Dayan said and wrote made headlines that fit into the greater debate over the war itself. Rejuvenated by this new wave of fame, Dayan enjoyed every minute. The Israeli government, on the other hand, was unenthusiastic and anxious about his travels: Dayan was a Rafi man and Eshkol had no interest in any revival of his glory as a military leader. The Ministry of Foreign Affairs feared that any statement from Dayan would be identified with the State of Israel and might implicate it. Dayan had not asked for authorization for the trip, and Foreign Minister Eban rebuked him on the Knesset floor. Within the ministry, opinions were divided. Israel's ambassador to Paris demanded that the state explicitly disavow the visit, while Harman in Washington warned that such a declaration would be interpreted as a denunciation of the war itself. The government declared that Dayan was entirely responsible for the trip, and the Ministry of Foreign Affairs sent instructions to the Israeli embassies involved on how Dayan should be treated when he arrived at the various stops on his tour. Official contact with him would only exacerbate the "awkward situation," they were told, and they should therefore not initiate contact, lest he later claim that Israel had tried to oversee or censor him. If he got in touch with the embassies himself, he should be offered assistance "as is customary for a man of his stature." Under no circumstances should he be accompanied to meetings.*

En route to Vietnam, Dayan stopped off in Paris and Washington, where he met with the U.S. defense secretary, Robert McNamara, among others. A message was waiting for Dayan when he visited Ambassador Harman at home: Abe Feinberg had called. When Dayan returned the call, Feinberg explained that the Jews were among the sharpest of Johnson's critics and so it was important that whenever Dayan spoke publicly, he should emphasize the similarity between South Vietnam and Israel: the United States was defending Vietnam just as it might one day be required to defend Israel. Feinberg of course was concerned about a new spotlight focused on the Jewish position on Vietnam, so he had arranged for Dayan to meet Walt Rostow; at the end of the meeting Dayan could make this point, as an expression of Jewish support. Feinberg had previously written to Rostow that he would "arrange" for Dayan to "make the necessary remarks." But Dayan declined.[181]

Most Israelis knew of the influence wielded by American Jews. Only a few, however, knew just how indebted they were, and many did not wish to know. A report presented to Prime Minister Eshkol went so far as to claim that the good standing of U.S. Jews should be troubling to Israel, for "the existence of an affluent and well-organized Jewish community in North America encourages emigration from Israel and helps the emigrants become settled there."[182] Only Arab plans to destroy the country worried Israelis more than what seemed, by 1967, to be a mass escape from a sinking ship.

8. EMIGRANTS: "A DISGRACE TO THE COUNTRY"

In early 1966, a reporter for *Ha'aretz* spent an evening in a small strip club in Hollywood. He sat at the bar watching a brightly lit stage where one woman after another took her clothes off. He was bored. A young woman who might have been a waitress or a stripper served "decidedly mediocre" whiskey, he recounted. He was with an Israeli friend, who told him in Hebrew that he should take his time over the drink, because as soon as his

---

*Not long afterward, Dayan said that had Eshkol asked him not to go, he would have canceled the trip. But Eshkol did not. *Ha'aretz* supported the visit, contending that the government should not be allowed to monopolize the debate on foreign relations.

glass was empty the semi-naked young woman would pounce on him with the bottle and refill it. The waitress overheard him. "Almost naked, yes—that's true," she said in perfect Hebrew, but added that she wouldn't pounce on him with the bottle because in this bar they didn't force the customers to drink. The reporter was stunned: Hebrew in this remote spot? The woman replied "with forlorn laughter" that central Hollywood was hardly "remote."

When the two spoke later, she told him she was originally from Tel Aviv. She had been beautiful as a young girl and was always hearing that she had talent, so she had come to seek her fortune in the movie capital. She arrived to find Hollywood full of young women like herself, from every country in the world, all dreaming of becoming movie stars. The strip club paid pretty well, she said: "You have to make a living, don't you?" She had been there for five years, and her dreams had faded. The reporter asked why she didn't go home. In Hollywood, she explained, she was not embarrassed, but to go back to Israel and tell people she'd failed—she was ashamed. *Ha'aretz* published her story as part of a series about the lives of Israeli emigrants in the United States. The headline was "Hollywood: Grave of Illusions."[183]

The reporter also went to visit a childhood friend who had been living in Washington, D.C., for several years. He lived in a five-bedroom apartment, ran a successful business, and owned a year-old Buick. His wife told the reporter about the weekend they had spent in New York and praised the quality of their television sets. When the children came home, they said, "Hi, Mom," and sprawled on the rug to watch a western. After the noise had died down and the wife went to make dinner, the reporter's friend gave him a truer picture. "When we opened our first store, nine years ago, this was a quiet, calm neighborhood. Over time it became rowdy and dangerous. Not long ago there were race riots in a few places in the country and we were afraid. We still don't know what each day will bring. We feel foreign, and sometimes afraid, and there's the lack of connection you feel here every day. That doesn't go away when you drive a new car or buy two color TVs." The headline of this story was "Apartment, TV, Buick, and Homesickness." Another piece in the series depicted the reporter's encounter with a family that was simply ashamed of having left Israel, and that headline was "A Family Lowers Its Eyes."[184]

This was a prevalent trend in the Israeli press—emphasizing that emigrants were unhappy in their new homes and that they had not been wise to leave. All the newspapers saw emigration as a major story, devoting special investigative series to the subject and covering it extensively in both the news and editorial pages.[185] "They're fleeing like rats from a sinking ship," reported *Yediot Aharonot* on emigrants from Ashkelon, and *Maariv* informed its readers that central Ashdod had become "a bargain market" of emigrants' possessions. "Just like the stock market, the price of televisions goes up and down, the value of Persian rugs fluctuates, and silver and crystal sell high today, low tomorrow." One paper even reported on a new profession: "emigration pimps" specialized in finding employment in other countries for people before they had left Israel.[186]

The consul in New York reported worriedly that many U.S. Jews were starting to wonder what was causing so many Israelis to flee. In Queens and Brooklyn there were entire streets of Hebrew speakers, he noted. Most Israelis knew that emigration was widespread, and they were concerned, angered, and saddened by it. Nothing undermined faith in the future of the state so much as emigration. For along with the rise in emigration there was also, for the fourth year running, a steep decline in the number of immigrants—just over eighteen thousand in 1967. Only twice in the country's history, in the early fifties, had the number been lower.[187]

No one knows for certain how many Israelis left permanently in the eighteen months preceding the Six-Day War, but their number may have exceeded the number of immigrants. U.S. embassy figures indicate that approximately half of the emigrants settled in America. It issued only roughly 1,500 immigration visas a year, but the figure is misleading since most Israelis entered the country on tourist visas: only a few declared their intent to leave Israel permanently. Many went abroad to study, or took a job for only a few years and then came back, and many did not know when they left that they would not return. Either way, writer Haim Gouri was right when he said that the number of Jews from Israel who became Americans was greater than the number of Jewish Americans who became Israelis. It was not the statistic that bothered him, but the underlying issue: "I heard a man say that the number of people who would die in a war against the Syrians is smaller than the number of people leaving us."[188] Much like the recession and even unemployment, the "emigration plague," as it was called, was to a great extent a moral and psychological problem. It forced Israel to come to terms with the fact that people had, of their own free will, chosen the Diaspora over the Homeland. There could be no greater blow to the Zionist ego.

Israel's consul in Sydney reported that emigrants from Israel were receiving assistance from Catholic charities and were spoken of as "asylum seekers"—a term tremendously wounding to Zionist ears. *Yediot Aharonot* printed a similarly insulting piece of news on its first page: Jewish charities in France were having trouble meeting the needs of Israeli emigrants seeking assistance. Other Israeli diplomats reported the appearance of emigrants in many countries, from Canada to South Africa, Sweden to Nigeria. "It is the tragedy of our people," wrote Yosef Weitz.[189]

Israeli emigrants were referred to by the Hebrew word *yordim*, which literally means "those who descend." Immigrants coming to settle in Israel, on the other hand, were called *olim*, "those who ascend." Both words have biblical origins, but their modern usage is charged with heavy ideological significance: a person coming to live in Israel was "ascending" in a moral sense, whereas someone who "descended" had failed and was to be shamed.* The press often treated *yordim* rather as the kibbutzim did those who left for the cities. "It is not the good people who emigrate, but the bad ones, the ones whose Zionist and Israeli consciousness is lacking, out of an unwillingness to put down roots—the ones who give in to trivial difficulties and go off to roam the world," wrote one newspaper.[190]

The government weathered the occasional outcry over the emigration figures and tried to comprehend why people were leaving the country and what could be done to staunch the flow. It commissioned a detailed study meant to locate the factors that might be swaying Israeli students to stay in the United States. The minister of health told the Knesset that the number of young doctors, graduates of Hadassah's medical school, who were leaving for the United States had increased "tremendously," from 9 percent to 40 percent. He proposed conditioning the acceptance of new students on their commitment not to leave Israel during the first few years after graduation. In February 1967, the government censored a news item reporting that immigrants from the Soviet Union wanted to return home because of difficulties integrating into daily life.[191]

The widespread emigration necessitated a series of decisions, such as whether *yordim* should be allowed to give up their Israeli citizenship, whether their passports should be extended despite their residence abroad, and whether they should be given various benefits upon returning to Israel, of the kind new immigrants received. These questions provoked arguments within the various government ministries, arguments that often became debates over principle. Israel's ambassador to Sweden believed that *yordim* should not be made to encounter difficulty when they wished to extend their passports, but he was reprimanded by the Ministry of the In-

---

*Both terms are still in common usage today. Over the years, however, they have taken on a more neutral tenor, referring simply to the entry and exit of Jewish migrants to and from Israel.

terior, which found it odd that an ambassador would defend these people. The ambassador, Yaakov Shimoni, retorted, "I am acting in defense of my country, which I wish to prevent from looking like an arbitrary state that sets cruel or unreasonable regulations. Even *yordim* are human beings and are entitled to reasonable and humane rules by which to regulate their status."* The parliamentary opposition argued that "the high tide of emigration and the ebb of immigration" justified replacing the government. "You are dismantling the state," accused Knesset member Shmuel Tamir, and compared the decline in immigration during Eshkol's tenure to the prohibition on Jewish immigration to Palestine during the British Mandate. Since the establishment of the state there had not been such a predicament, said Knesset member Arieh Ben-Eliezer. Emigration was widely denounced and could never be justified, Ben-Eliezer claimed, but it was undeniable that people's decisions to leave resulted primarily from the government's policies.

Eshkol responded that this was not the first time there had been more *yordim* than *olim*. But, of course, there was a difference between the people who left the state during its early years, most of whom had been new immigrants, and those who left as Israel approached its twentieth anniversary. Eshkol was aware of this, and so he attacked the *yordim* themselves: "Many of the *yordim* are defectors, because they are leaving and defecting even though their economic situation does not require it and even though there is no explanation and no excuse—apart from the Gypsy inclination still deep within us, the urge to wander from one country to another."[193]

Eshkol's statement is worth another reading. In his clumsy, disorganized way, Eshkol had defined the credo of Israeli Zionism. Although he recognized that certain economic difficulties might justify emigration, he considered life in Israel to be an obligation, like military service, and emigration was defection. The term was used routinely by other politicians, too, including Minister of Education Aran and Minister of Finance Sapir, as well as by the newspapers. Some described *yordim* as "fallout," and Haim Gouri said, "Every emigration is a betrayal."[194] This was more than just invective. One reader wrote to *Davar*, "They leave their parents here—the pioneers who founded the state and who have grown old— and their little brothers and sisters, and the Holocaust survivors among

---

*As the Vietnam War intensified, there were reports from various places in the United States that Israelis residing there were asking to restore their Israeli citizenship, fearing they might be drafted.[192]

us. What will happen if, God forbid, a war breaks out?" *Davar* printed a letter from an eighteen-year-old boy who denounced a friend of his brother's for wanting to immigrate to America. A soldier at war does not abandon the battle, wrote the young man. "There is no forgiveness for emigration," wrote *Davar*, and demanded that Israelis make do with what their country could offer, maintaining that it did not owe them everything. "If Edmund Hillary was Jewish and immigrated to Israel, would we be required to give him a Mount Everest? . . . This is our country and these are its possibilities," wrote the author Haim Ya'ari, "Today no one is asking an engineer to be a dairy farmer, but he should at least be an engineer in Israel and not in America. . . . And if indeed opportunities for professional advancement here are slighter or slower than in America— well, that is the fate of people born in Israel and not in America, and that is the price one pays for fate." The affinity for one's homeland is what sets man apart from beast, wrote one reader.[195]

The writer Hanoch Bartov attributed emigration to "some unnatural attraction to self-destruction." Commentator Shmuel Schnitzer wrote in a similar vein that he viewed the *yordim* as someone for whom Israel was a hotel, not a home, someone who had exile in his heart and whose decision to move to another country was the symptom of a disease. Schnitzer claimed it was "the Jewish genetic disease of parasitism and an inability to connect with the homeland." Another commentator, Eliezer Livneh, wrote: "Emigration is an expression of the nature of many Jews after emancipation, who are rootless, agile, and shrewd, and whose primary (and sometimes only) motive is the increase of profit and material income. Their 'homeland' is wherever the profit is greater." No anti-Semite could have said it better. *Yediot Aharonot* particularly denounced *yordim* who settled in Germany, where they would "live in proximity to Fritz and Adolf, who a mere two decades ago were sending them to the crematoria." In short, they were "a disgrace to the country."[196]

Careful not to justify leaving Israel, the papers still allowed a self-critical tone to creep into their articles, and once in a while even a sharp sense of failure. When the minister of finance described *yordim* as defectors, *Ha'aretz* responded by declaring that "faced with such a leader, they have no choice but to desert the war." The paper wrote that travel overseas was arousing jealousy, making "overseas" seem a better place in public perception. "Israel Pushes, America Pulls" was the headline of another article.[197] As part of this trend, the papers gave voice to people threatening to emigrate due to the recession. "I ask myself what to do," one unemployed man told *Ha'aretz*, adding, "I am now at the point of taking an interest in foreign countries to see if there's work there." Young people who had finished their military service told *Maariv* they had registered at the consulates of Canada and Denmark, and others said they were considering doing the same. "We'll have no choice," they said. A graduate of the Israel Institute of Technology, whom a *Maariv* reporter met at the Australian embassy, asked, "Who has the right to stop me from going?"[198]

The case of two immigrants from Argentina who fled Israel as stowaways on a German ship led to a series of articles expressing understanding of the difficulties immigrants from South America faced in becoming part of Israeli life, and indirectly of their decision to leave. "One of the important factors leading to desperation among these immigrants is an almost daily trampling of the dignity and pride they felt in their countries of origin," wrote *Ha'aretz*. Other papers began to take on a similarly self-accusatory tone. "We do not accept the immigrants living among us," concluded *Maariv*, and *Yediot Aharonot* attributed the emigration to the contrast between the ideal world the immigrants had hoped to find in Israel and the reality they discovered. In a somewhat philosophical tone, the paper wondered if this were not a problem faced by all Israelis.[199]

LETTERS SENT BY ISRAELIS TO THEIR RELATIVES IN THE UNITED STATES DID NOT REFLECT the disapproval expressed in the papers. These people shared the family's daily events with their relatives as if they had never left. An accordionist played at the children's birthday party; a mother had surgery to remove a suspicious lump; there was trouble at work; the daughter started her army service, her mother was worried, but then the daughter was assigned to office work in a nearby base and came home every day. And there was the gossip: this young woman went out with that young man and her parents thought, "Any minute now," but then he left her, so she married a Hungarian doctor fourteen years her senior. Israelis often asked relatives to send things they could not get at home, such as medication, but also clothes, which could be bought in America "on sale." This was not the way loyalists addressed defectors and traitors. But emigration was undoubtedly a central topic.

"I don't know exactly what Hana told you," wrote a man named Israel, from Ramat Aviv, to his relatives in Boston, "but . . . leaving was never a real thought for us and I hope it never is. It would come up only in case of a serious emergency." He gave two hypothetical reasons for leaving: if he could not make a living or if a security situation developed that endangered the children's lives. Then he changed his mind and crossed out the words with thick lines and an apparently determined hand. He left only one word: "lives." As long as their lives were in no danger, there was no thought of emigrating, he wrote. But he left himself an opening for further consideration: "If the situation gets really bad, I may ask for your help." Hana, his wife, added a few lines. "We're not coming yet," she wrote, but she liked to take all possibilities into account, even the worst. Emigration was not at all attractive to her, "especially if it involves changes for the children." Meanwhile, the little girl's bronchitis was better and she was back at kindergarten, and Hana and her husband had seen a nice movie, *The Russians Are Coming, the Russians Are Coming*. A few months later, Israel wrote again. "I'm planning to get passports for the kids after all, just in case, and if it is possible to arrange for an affidavit valid for, let's say, three to five months, I would like to do that. It's best to have papers ready for them, it can't hurt."

Many letters mentioned acquaintances who had left. So-and-So's daughter and her husband, So-and-So's brother. This one already had a visa and the others were going to live with the wife's brother in Detroit, where they would get along pretty well, but they weren't taking the aunt and she was in tears—to be left alone at her age! The idea of leaving Israel emerges from these letters first and foremost as a relocation from one place to another; the considerations were personal and familial, not national or ideological.[200]

The papers looked for deeper meaning. Shmuel Schnitzer of *Maariv* attributed emigration to the compromise between the State of Israel and the Jews of the world, a compromise over the reason for Zionism itself. "Because if living in the Diaspora is positive as long as one donates to the Jewish Appeal and learns Hebrew and avoids intermarriage, why should an Israeli Jew not also live in this way? If living in Israel and living in the Diaspora are the same, why shouldn't all the Jews live in a place where life is easier?" He argued that in all the 120 nations in the world there was no other state where children were allowed to grow up with so little awareness of a homeland, as in Israel. States without heroes invented them, he said, while Israel, which had so many heroes, neglected them. *Yediot Aharonot* also complained that "we don't provide heroes for our youth," and determined that "militarism is the only state value that arouses any enthusiasm." *Ha'aretz* found that education in Israel was failing in many ways, and described emigration as a result of a crisis

among the younger generation.[201] It was only a small step from here to the
question raised by Geula Cohen's "Square Table" column in *Maariv*: Does
emigration begin in the schools? The answer was unequivocal: schoolchildren did not know enough about the history of Zionist heroism—or,
as Cohen put it, "They might get a bullet before finding out how the state
they live for was established." Many Israelis felt they were losing the
young generation.

9. YOUTH: "THERE IS BITTER DESPERATION EVERYWHERE"

In January 1966, journalist Shabtai Teveth caused an uproar when he
quoted in *Ha'aretz* three high school seniors who said they didn't really
know why they should stay in Israel. They had nothing against the country, they said, they even loved it, but they did not feel like Jews, and if
there was a better place to study and live, why shouldn't they go there?
The three were not identified by name, and even if they were figments of
the writer's imagination, the paper presented them as the spokespeople of
a generation, children of affluent parents in north Tel Aviv.

Horrified readers sent in letters that appeared under the headline,
"Who Is to Blame for the Attitudes of the Youth?" Geula Cohen went to
speak with high school students. "I know more about Napoleon than
about Herzl," said one, and another found it difficult to recall the words of
"Hatikva," the national anthem.* One pupil said he was willing to tell Jewish Americans that they should immigrate to Israel, but that in his heart
he knew that some of them should stay there to influence U.S. policy
toward Israel. Many of the students argued that emigration was justified.
Cohen also went to talk with several educators. One told her that some
students were not convinced that the Jewish people had a right to the
land, and another said, "The way literature and history are taught in
schools must be drastically revised." One teacher admitted that the school
was doing "very little" in the area of teaching national awareness, and another accused the Ministry of Education of not encouraging teachers in
that area. Geula Cohen was not alone in her criticisms. The editor of
Davar, Yehuda Gotthelf, first made a jokey attempt to defend Eshkol's
government—"As far as I am concerned, the crisis began with the expulsion of Adam and Eve from the Garden of Eden"—but then admitted, "We

---

*The director general of the Ministry of Education promised the reporter that the instruction
of the "Hatikva" was mandatory in four out of the eight years of elementary school, but was
later embarrassed when it turned out that this was in music, rather than in civics.

have not sunk our youth's roots deeply enough in the homeland, history, and destiny of the chosen people." *Davar* had previously published an article stating that Zionist education was needed "to save the country."

The state of Israeli youth was at the center of public discourse, addressed by the Knesset in a debate that lasted for months.[202] Besides security tensions, the repercussions of the economic recession, and emigration, no issue was of more concern. Compulsive and emotionally charged, the debate over the future generation reflected the distress of the present, and involved tormented and anguished soul-searching by a doubt-ridden society.

The Zionist revolution identified itself from the first as an expression of youthful rebellion. "Do not heed, son, the morals of the father, and to the mother's teachings do not lend your ear," wrote the poet David Shimoni (Shimonovitz). The second generation of Zionists in Palestine tended to adopt their parents' ideological foundations, resulting in fairly common conservatism. "Our world was created for us by our father. In that respect, Father was God," wrote the son of a labor movement leader. But those fathers now found it difficult to live with their children, who had been born in Israel and grown up into the sixties. They had stopped treating the state as if it were a historical miracle. "How have we reached such a steep decline in all areas of life, and in such prominent contrast to our aspirations and ideals?" lamented an editorialist in *Davar*.[203]

The deputy minster of education, Aharon Yadlin, confirmed: "This generation has no sense of being borne on the wings of history." He described Israeli youth as practical, unsentimental, purposeful, and career-driven. They were cynical and distant from abstract ideas, as well as politically indifferent and reluctant to identify with Zionist ideology. "It is as hard as the parting of the Red Sea to 'cloak' them with 'our world,'" wrote Haim Gouri.[204]

Ha'aretz reported that Israeli children in the fifth and sixth grades were already forming so-called ballroom societies. As early as the ninth grade, girls were going to ladies' hair salons. More and more young girls were using makeup and following the latest fashion trends. Young boys wore dress pants to parties, and by the twelfth grade they were used to wearing suits and ties. Ballroom societies, *Ha'aretz* explained, involved Western-style ballroom dancing. The hosts served refreshments, often at a cost of twenty or thirty liras, including cold cuts (or lox, in wealthier homes), pickles, pistachios, cakes, and coffee. Girls in the twelfth grade who were expecting soldiers to attend also served beer. The parties were held in the parents' homes, but most apartments were too small, which led to the invention of the rooftop dance party. "A friend with a good roof is not to be taken lightly," said the paper. Many neighbors complained about the noise, so the municipalities set up dance clubs. The ballroom societies competed with the youth movements that operated under the auspices of political parties, and with the Scouts.[205]

The first Zionist pioneers brought local folk dances with them from Eastern Europe, such as the hora, and cultivated them as part of the Israeli identity they were hoping to create. Folk dancing was the norm on kibbutzim, in urban youth movements, and at national ceremonies. To many in the older generation, ballroom dancing represented a daring, almost reckless deviation from prevailing values. "Indeed, vanity has affected all layers and levels of our youth," wrote *Davar*, and complained about the devaluation of ideological youth movements, which it attributed to the influence of movies, "a pipeline to vulgarization, exploiting the masses to admire violence and material success." The paper printed more and more articles raging against the destructive influence of cinema, a wellspring of adultery, prostitution, trickery, violence, and murder, "a terrible poison" and a "primary breeding ground" for crime.[206]

Shabtai Teveth, writing for *Ha'aretz*, recounted a visit to a student discotheque in Tel Aviv named Bar-Barim (a name that both employs the English word "bar" and plays on the Hebrew word for barbarians, *barbarim*). His report conveyed an astonished anthropological tone, as if he had returned from visiting some remote tribe. "The young are taller, thinner, better groomed, and more supple than we generally think of the children of Israel," he wrote. "Nowadays, girls mature biologically a whole year earlier than in their mothers' generation, and two years sooner than in their grandmothers'," reported the deputy minister of education in the Knesset. One writer for *Ha'aretz*, Amnon Rubinstein, maintained, "Israeli young girls are more shapely, womanly and pleasant" than the previous generations.[207]

The Bar-Barim disco held about three hundred people, and the main activity was on Friday night, the Sabbath eve. For three liras, guests received a half-hour entertainment program, dancing, and a choice of ice cream, sodas, or cake. Additional refreshments cost 35 aguras for soda water and 75 aguras for a bottle of beer. Teveth told his readers that the Gashash Hahiver comedy troupe was the most popular among the young generation. The singer Arik Einstein comes in a close second, he added. Both were among the architects of Israeli culture. The wordplay of the name "Bar-Barim" reflected a self-directed irony and a good command of the Hebrew language, enabling a playful adaptation to Western culture.

Once a week there was an open mike jazz evening at Bar-Barim, when whiskey was also served. On other days the disco did not serve hard liquor, which meant that there was no great reason for alarm, but Teveth nevertheless felt as if he had found himself in another world. "Visiting this place, one scarcely recognizes one's own people. To see the young men wearing trousers that look like hosepipes and the young women in half-skirts and big hairdos, one would think one had landed in Stockholm, Paris, or Greenwich Village." The editor of *Davar* scolded the students for their inferior "degree of spiritual-moral awareness."[208]

Many young people went to London, to soak up what *Yediot Aharonot* described as "a revolution of spiritual being and new moral standards." The editors of *Davar* perceived dangerous competition here. "We do not yet have a large movement of beatniks, but many of our finest youths are attracted to the circle of influence projected by the culture of the absurd," they cautioned. The paper explained why Israelis should be more cautious than others: "The phenomenon of beatniks and so forth exists in all the nations of the world, but there, this youthful insolence is nothing more than foam on a great ocean. Here in Israel, such a phenomenon could undermine our foundations, leading to deterioration and complete destruction."[209]

Dissenting voices were occasionally heard. "I don't see myself rearing my children as criminals by allowing them to wear jeans," said Knesset member Shulamit Aloni.[210] In January 1966, Amnon Rubinstein published an article called "Shake," in which he argued that ballroom dancing might "shake off the dust that has gathered for generations." This was a social and political statement: he was referring to the fossilized mentality of the founders of the state, many of whom were still its leaders. For all his abhorrence, Shabtai Teveth also felt that Israel failed to encourage its youth. "There is no competition in Israel over young people, not in the economy, not in higher education, not in research institutes." The only organization eager to take in educated young people was the army, he wrote, and this was partly because the state was still clinging to a moribund ideology that favored collective responsibility over individual initiative. Rubinstein further defended the young by claiming that the outcry over its loss of values was unfounded. He saw young people in concert halls, at plays, and in art galleries. The veteran educator Baruch Ben-Yehuda also felt that the youth of the sixties was not inferior to that of previous generations, and David Ben-Gurion agreed.[211] A few young people on Kibbutz Yehiam demanded the right to listen to "a certain type" of music, late into the night, and went to see movies in the nearby town of

Nahariya. The religious youth movement, Bnei Akiva, conducted a survey among its members after two twelfth-grade students, Yaakov and Hana, were seen kissing. Thirty-eight percent said the kiss should be permitted.

For most young Israelis, things did not go much further than that. Sixties culture largely reached Israel in the form of music and fashion. It changed relationships between young men and women, and some of the men grew their hair long. But it did not threaten the founding principles of the state. A few sociologists later explained that a real upheaval could never have occurred in Israel as long as the Zionist revolution was ongoing, manifested partly in the war between Israel and the Arabs. But public discourse during the eighteen months prior to the Six-Day War reflected an extremely solemn mood, almost one of bereavement, as if the younger generation were lost and the parents were somehow bereft. "Zionism, as an idea and as a dead movement, is no longer relevant to the Jewish question today," wrote Haim Gouri in response to a radio interview with a student named Eilon Kolberg, who wondered why he should even stay in Israel. Gouri was expressing a common sentiment. Against this background, an editorial in *Ha'aretz* wondered, "When all hope is lost, what else can one hope for if not a miracle?" A few days later the same paper stated, "There is bitter desperation everywhere."[212]

During the year and a half leading up to the Six-Day War, the following headlines appeared in the papers: "How Did They Manage to Destroy This Country?"; "The Seed of Destruction"; "The Crisis"; "The Shattering of a Dream"; "Death of a Vision"; "Vision and Failure"; "Israel Is Not a Challenge."[213] The papers described "demoralization," "bitterness," "distress," "indifference and desperation," "ill wind and suffocation."[214]*

Teveth believed that Israel was simply boring its youth, and Amos Oz also described "the burden of boredom," which he saw as "utter weariness that seeks not rest, but rather its opposite." Oz expressed the sentiment in a short story named "Tired Man." The protagonist lives in Jerusalem for fourteen years and then returns to Tel Aviv, where he finds neglect and wretchedness, and the apartment building he used to live in crumbling

---

*During that time, a woman with a reputation came to live in Israel, having married an Israeli businessman. Mandy Rice-Davies had been involved in the sex-and-espionage scandal that eventually resulted in the resignation of the British secretary of state for war, John Profumo. The *Ha'aretz* reporter Silvie Keshet wrote a fictional dialogue between two Israelis in honor of the guest. "She's all we need here," says the first man, while his friend responds, "Why not? She fits right in, the whole country is one big—" The missing word was probably the Russian *bardak*, which had been adopted into Hebrew slang to mean "total chaos" (literally, "whorehouse").

from dampness due to its proximity to the sea. The story projects an aura of death: an empty lot with the chassis of a dead truck, a bus's final stop, and, worst of all, the tedium that the city casts upon the man. His father, who seems to have been a member of Mapai, was injured in a terrorist attack on a bus after the UN decision to partition Palestine. Before dying, he told his children: I believe we will have a state. The mother, who suffers from bouts of insanity, has married another man and moved to the United States. A novel published by Pinchas Sadeh in 1967 is similarly pervaded by the grayness of daily tedium and the routine of Israeli despondency. "The situation," mumbles the protagonist in the book's final lines, "the situation is therefore worse than I thought."*

Yaakov Talmon, the dean of Israeli historians, asserted that Israel had entered the "postrationalist" era, by which he seemed to be saying that the dream was over. Another scholar, Yosef Salmon, wrote, "Israeli society has lost its national social vision and is thereby entering a new, post-Zionist crisis in the history of the Jewish people." Shmuel Schnitzer of *Maariv* feared that Israel was losing its historical uniqueness, becoming just another Hong Kong.[215]

In their state of grieving, the papers often dwelled on anniversaries: seventy years since the publication of Herzl's *The Jewish State;* fifty years since the Balfour Declaration; thirty years since the Arab Revolt; twenty years since the UN partition resolution; ten years since the Sinai Campaign. This near-compulsive preoccupation with history reflected what Haim Gouri described as the second-day crisis of the revolution. The time of dull routine seemed to have come too soon.[216] Some of the papers began to wax nostalgic over the figure of Avshalom Feinberg, "the wondrous hero of Eretz Israel," as *Yediot Aharonot* wrote, on the occasion of the fiftieth anniversary of his disappearance in the desert.

Fearless, tough, and brave, the paper recounted, Feinberg was also delicate and sentimental. A horseman, fencer, marksman, and boxer who struck fear into the heart of the entire country, he was also an intellectual, a philosopher, a writer, and a poet. An intrepid and flawless knight, as one of his acquaintances said, he was handsome and refined, his eyes as fiery as fireflies in an autumn night. He was considered the first Sabra, and was indeed one of the first children born among the Zionist settlers in Palestine. In 1917, Feinberg joined the underground resistance movement

---

*The well-known literary critic Baruch Kurzweil denounced both authors for turning their backs on Zionist ideals and lamented literature's "bankruptcy." If Satan had any talent, he wrote, he would write like Amos Oz.

Nili, whose purpose was to help the British wrest Palestine from the Ottoman Empire. When his group was discovered by the Turks, he fled to Egypt but never made it, presumably dying in the desert. According to Bedouin legend, he was carrying a few dates in his pocket to eat on the road, and after his death one of them sprouted and grew into a palm tree.

The nostalgia for Avshalom was nostalgia for the once-great revival of the Jewish people in their land, and for the glorious early days—days of challenge, vision, and inspiration, valor and excitement. Historian Alon Gan identified a similar feeling among kibbutz members: "The first generation lived the transition from dream to reality, while the second generation is searching for a path from reality to dream."[217]

The country had known difficult periods before; but never had so many Israelis felt that the situation was so bad for so many reasons as during Eshkol's time. The level of distress even reached those who knew practically everything that was going on in the country. Yaacov Herzog, director general of the prime minister's office, and his wife, Pnina, invited Ella and Shimon Agranat over for tea one day; Agranat was president of the Supreme Court. "The conversation, like most conversations these days, revolved around the country's socioeconomic crisis, the confusion of the younger generation, the dangers of emigration, the sense of helplessness," wrote Herzog.[218]

PART II

BETWEEN ISRAEL AND PALESTINE

Gabriel Stern eventually became a journalist, writing for *Al Hamishmar*. He got his biggest international scoop during a Saturday walk along Jerusalem's partition line. Looking out toward the Mount of Olives, he noticed the Jordanians were building a large hotel on the grounds of the Jewish cemetery. An uproar followed, leading to a debate in the United Nations Security Council. Any number of Jerusalem journalists could have landed the story, had they only known to observe their surroundings as Gabriel Stern did. During the two decades between the War of Independence and the Six-Day War, Stern seemed unwilling to acknowledge the partition of Jerusalem. Every few years, when snow fell in the city, *Al Hamishmar* would report: "Our diplomatic correspondent has learned from sources close to UN observers that it is snowing in the Jordanian part of Jerusalem and in the Old City too."

CHAPTER 3

MAPS AND DREAMS

1. FATAH: "THERE IS ALSO PALESTINIAN ZIONISM"

In early January 1966, a dot on the northern border that most Israelis had never heard of made headlines. "Fatah terrorists have done them a favor," said *Maariv*. "The assault on the Kfar Yuval swimming pool has put the forgotten moshav back on the map." The few hundred poultry farmers who lived in Kfar Yuval had never been in the limelight before. Originally from Cochin, in southern India, they were the fourth or fifth cycle of residents to live in the place. The first residents had been Arabs; the village was called al-Zuk al-Fawqani. The Arabs had been driven out during the War of Independence. They had been replaced by Jews who had been driven out from the Old City of Jerusalem in 1948. New immigrants from Iraq also came, but they fought among themselves and eventually left. They were replaced by new immigrants from North Africa, who, according to *Maariv*, "took one despondent look around and scattered." The Cochin Jews who came next stuck with the place, but they felt that the government had abandoned them. "We are closer to Beirut and Damascus than to Jerusalem," they said, and *Maariv* added, predictably, "To this day they are looked down upon by the established kibbutzniks in the Upper Galilee." It would only take a basketball court and a kind word for the residents of Kfar Yuval to feel less anonymous and remote, the paper said.[1] Other distant communities were occasionally covered in the press when their existence was recalled as a result of terrorism, and they too were quickly forgotten.

During the eighteen months before the Six-Day War, almost 120 acts or attempted acts of sabotage were carried out in Israel—an average of almost one every five days. Most of the Fatah saboteurs came from Syria and operated in small towns and villages close to the border. Other terrorists came from Jordan. They bombed pipelines, water pumps, warehouses, and power plants, and laid land mines on roads, highways, and railroad tracks. They usually managed to get back to their point of departure in one piece. Eleven Israelis were killed in these operations, including three civilians, four Border Guard policemen, and four soldiers. More than sixty Israelis were injured, approximately half of them civilians; in other words, a rough average of one casualty per week. The number of incidents rose steadily, doubling between 1966 and 1967.[2] As a permanent phenomenon in Israel's daily routine, terrorism exacerbated the overall depression. Its psychological effect, like that of the recession, was far more profound than the tangible damage it did; and, much as Israelis found it difficult to live with the recession, they also felt that they should not have to live with terrorism.

Fatah first became known in January 1965, when its operatives attempted to sabotage the national water supply system. In an effort to fill in the background of this debut, *Maariv* quoted official IDF sources who pointed to ties between Fatah and Syria, but the precise nature of the affiliation remained unspecified. The headline said the organization "draws inspiration from Damascus"; the story went on to assert that "the authorities in Damascus are behind" Fatah and that the organization "is probably operated by Syrian authorities." *Yediot Aharonot* ran a more decisive headline: "Syrian Sabotage Attempt Thwarted."[3] The papers did not know much about the Fatah organization. Even the name was somewhat mysterious: spelled backward, it was the acronym, in Arabic, of the "Palestinian National Liberation Movement." The press was at first derisive of this Palestinian force, as if they were unworthy of being considered a true enemy. They had not demonstrated much operational ability thus far, and so they needed the sponsorship of the Syrian intelligence service, one paper explained. Moshe Dayan dismissed them as "a few bandits."[4]

Yediot Aharonot quoted Israeli commandos who had infiltrated the Jordanian village of Kala'at in May 1966 to blow up the houses of residents who were suspected of collaborating with Fatah. They found them in wretched conditions. One soldier told of how his unit burst into the home of a village elder and found him standing in a room, surrounded by four children. "He was a huge man, maybe six five," the soldier recounted. The children were crying; their mother was beside herself. The man begged, "What have I done to you? Don't kill me." He protected the children with his body. The commander replied that no one was going to hurt him or his family, but their house would be destroyed as punishment for his support of Fatah. The man responded, "I curse Fatah! Long live the Jews!" The visit to the house of the village *mukhtar* was "far more amusing," according to the correspondent. The unit commander described a huge house with beautiful furniture. The *mukhtar*, a middle-aged man, welcomed the soldiers "by bowing and pleading for his life." His wife was in the next room with an elderly woman, probably her mother. At first the *mukhtar* tried to conceal his true identity. "We explained to him the purpose of our visit," the commander told the reporter. "When he picked up the word 'Fatah,' he started showering juicy curses on the heads of the organization and its members. 'There's no Fatah in our village,' he said." The commander said the *mukhtar* advised him to attack another village, where he said there was Fatah. He was not the only one to disavow the organization. "They disassociated themselves from Fatah activities so excessively that it disgusted the IDF soldiers," the reporter wrote.[5]

Several intelligence organizations around the world tried to piece together a picture of Fatah. Although it was a new organization, everyone believed it was directly continuing the war over Palestine that had begun at the turn of the century. Jews and Arabs had used terrorism as early as the 1920s, both against each other and to get rid of the British, observed intelligence reports written in Britain and the United States.[6] The saboteurs who had infiltrated Israel left notes at the sites where they struck, giving their names and units. One unit was named after the Palestinian fighter Abdel Khader Husseini, who was killed in 1948 in the battle for the Kastel, near Jerusalem. One newspaper explained this historical context to its readers, noting that Husseini was a relative of the Grand Mufti Haj Amin, the leader of the Arabs in Palestine during the British Mandate. The former mufti was still alive, and his travels and speeches were reported in the papers from time to time.*

The press soon turned its attention from the image of the mufti to Ahmad Shukeiri, the first chairman of the Palestine Liberation Organization—the PLO—which had been established earlier in 1964. Shukeiri, an attorney and a refugee from Acre who had become a diplomat, was portrayed in Israel as a corrupt and laughable crook. Fatah and several other

---

*In the early sixties, Mufti Haj Amin's name came up during the Adolf Eichmann trial, when the prosecution recounted a meeting between the mufti and Hitler in great detail. In March 1967, the episode was reported again, as if newly revealed.[7]

Palestinian organizations arose as competitors to the PLO. It was some time before Israelis heard a new name they could associate with terrorism instead of Shukeiri's, but at the end of September 1967, *Ha'aretz* reported a revelation that came directly from a captured Fatah operative taken hostage: "The chief of operations in the Fatah gangs is a Syrian Palestinian by the name of Yasser Arafat, known as Abu Amar."[8]

The renewed clashes reminded everyone of the fundamental causes of the conflict in Palestine. Fatah, explained one newspaper, wanted to revive the Palestinian question and convince the world that it was not an issue of refugees wishing to return to their homes, but rather a struggle for national liberation. As one Israeli commentator asserted, "There is also Palestinian Zionism."[9]

Eshkol thought it necessary to reassert the tenets of the Zionist faith: "We are not a foreign entity that just happened to fancy this country to live in. The Land of Israel and the People of Israel have been intertwined and bound together since the dawn of history. Israel has returned to its land and its home, and there is no power that can sever the eternal bond between our nation and its land." One Knesset member said, "Our national revival began almost at the same time as the Arab liberation movement rose against Ottoman rule, a few decades ago. Only bitter fate determined that these two movements, which should have been complementary, are not, and we find ourselves in a position where the other movement is hostile toward us."[10]

Yehoshafat Harkabi, an army general and Middle East scholar, who was the IDF chief of intelligence and oversaw strategic research during the fifties, observed the rise of a new generation. The young Palestinians who were children when their parents fled or were expelled from their homes in 1948 and who had grown up in refugee camps were now ready for the second round. A security study archived in the prime minister's office concluded that as long as there were refugees, there would be terror.[11] Foreign Minister Eban also studied the topic, viewing guerrilla warfare as the classic weapon of the weak against the powerful. In his view, since World War II guerrilla groups had been given cause for hope: hand grenades, land mines, and small arms had proved effective in various corners of the world, even more than nuclear weapons. One paper noted that the "guerrilla mystique" flourished everywhere, from Fidel Castro's Cuba to Ho Chi Minh's Vietnam.

Respect for Fatah's military capabilities was on the rise. *Ha'aretz* described the organization's members as "excellent soldiers in the field who know the area they operate in well." One Knesset member suggested to his colleagues that they reread a poem written by Yaakov Cohen after the violent conflicts in Palestine in the twenties: "In the place where one falls, ten shall rise; in the place where ten fall, glorious thousands. Every stone in the ravine shall testify, every knoll shall be a sign, for this land is ours since the dawn of time."[12]

ON FRIDAY NIGHT, OCTOBER 7, 1966, JUST BEFORE MIDNIGHT, THREE EXPLOSIVE DEVICES blew up beneath the supporting pillars of two apartment buildings in Romema, a neighborhood in the western outskirts of Jerusalem, a few hundred yards from the border with Jordan. A fourth device failed to detonate. One woman sustained eye injuries and was hospitalized. Two other women, a young girl, and a boy had minor injuries. The explosions were audible all over town. This was the first terrorist incident in Jerusalem since the War of Independence.

Most of the buildings' residents were in bed at the time the attack occurred. Margalit Shafir in Apartment 7 on the second floor heard the explosion and felt a strong shock wave. She thought it was an earthquake. But her husband, Eliyahu, a worker at the Friedman stove factory, smelled gunpowder and realized immediately that it was an explosion. Before he could even get to the light switch, the second explosion rocked the building. The apartment was showered with broken glass, and cracks appeared in the walls and ceiling. In the apartment next door, the geologist Ze'ev Benyamin Begin lived with his family. They were not hurt. His father, Knesset member Menachem Begin, arrived later that night. The next afternoon, on the Sabbath, the prime minister and the IDF chief of staff also came. Eshkol's military secretary said the prime minister chose his words carefully in advance. "The ledger is open and the hand is recording" was his way of saying that Israel would not respond immediately but reserved the right to do so later.[13]*

General opinion held that the operation, carried out by Palestinians from Fatah, was intended to entangle Israel in a conflict with Jordan. Yaacov Herzog, who oversaw relations with Jordan, wrote in his diary that he hoped Israel would not respond with force. Most newspapers also urged restraint. "It is true that the attack occurred in Israel's capital," wrote

---

*While Eshkol's statement might have sounded like corner-store accounting, in keeping with his image, it also reflected his Jewish learning. The line, which was to become one of the most famous in the Arab-Israeli conflict, was borrowed from the Book of Ethics, the "Pirkei Avot," where it is attributed to Rabbi Akiba (Masehet Avot, 3:16, "The hand is writing").

Ha'aretz, "and the explosives could have killed and injured dozens of people. But Jerusalem is a border town that is not difficult to penetrate, and the actual damage was minor. Let us be thankful for that and remain levelheaded." The paper praised Eshkol's response: "We should record, but we should not strike, at least not now and not in Jordan." But the Herut movement's publication, *Hayom*, demanded action, as did *Yediot Aharonot*. The army began plans for a security fence meant to prevent further infiltrations.[14]

Forty-eight hours after the attack, on the day the papers published Eshkol's "open ledger" statement, four Border Guard policemen were killed when their vehicle drove over a land mine not far from the Syrian border. Two had been born in Morocco, one in Yemen, one in Bulgaria. *Maariv* described their families' hardships and prominently quoted Meir Gigi, the brother of one of the men killed: "Tell Eshkol not to be so quiet; he should avenge my brother's blood!"

Ha'aretz called for restraint again. "The rules of blood vengeance cannot serve as a basis for Israeli policy. . . . It is not grief and anger that should dictate the steps to be taken by the government toward Syria; the account must be settled logically and cold-bloodedly, not on the basis of an eye for an eye."[15] But amid the general gloom, doubts now arose as to whether Israel was capable of protecting the lives of its citizens. The question was presented to Eshkol, as it had been in the fifties to David Ben-Gurion in light of attacks by Palestinian terrorists, most of whom had come from the Gaza Strip. Ben-Gurion had ordered a series of cross-border retaliations, culminating in the Sinai Campaign. The tenth anniversary of that campaign was around the corner. Alongside the news of the four policemen's deaths, *Maariv* ran a large headline quoting the British *Sunday Times* of London: "Syria Fears a Suez-Style Israeli Invasion." The Suez anniversary prompted the press to reveal details of a trilateral pact made in 1956 between Israel, France, and Britain, with the aim of removing Nasser from the Egyptian presidency and ensuring Western control of the Suez Canal. Most of the details had previously been classified, or had been published only abroad.

A short while earlier, Moshe Dayan had published his war diary. The prevailing view at the time was that the Sinai Campaign had strengthened Israel's security, led to an almost complete cessation of terrorist acts, opened the Red Sea to Israeli shipping, and had brought UN forces to Sinai and Gaza. *Maariv* stressed that the campaign had been "an existential necessity," partly for psychological reasons with which most readers were personally familiar: the terrorist attacks that had preceded the campaign had sunk Israel into deep despair, and the atmosphere had become intolerable. *Maariv* depicted the Sinai Campaign as a personal victory for Ariel Sharon. "Arik and his young commanders gave the chief of staff considerable confidence," the paper determined, as if Dayan had been short on confidence in the first place. It quoted praise for an armored corps commander that made reference to one of Hitler's military leaders: "He fought like a tiger. A real Rommel!" But the press also projected disappointment with the campaign's outcome, because Israel had been forced to withdraw from Sinai and the Gaza Strip. The sense was that the UN and world powers had robbed the country of a justly acquired piece of land. During the months around the anniversary, *Maariv* also published chapters from a book by Ben-Gurion, in which he revealed details of conversations held in the thirties with leaders of the Arab population in Palestine. The preoccupation with this chapter of Israeli history was part of some national soul-searching; the conclusion was that not much had changed, and that all attempts to talk with the Arabs met with refusal.[16]

2. SAMUA VILLAGE: "MADNESS"

On the evening of October 25, 1966, a cargo train traveling from Jerusalem to Tel Aviv struck a land mine that derailed two engines and two cars. A passenger train had traversed the same tracks about two hours earlier. The papers quoted a statement issued by a commando unit named after Abdel Khader Husseini: "Get out! Get out of our lands, you Zionists!" The next day, *Yediot Aharonot's* front page cited a broadcast heard over Radio Palestine, the PLO station, from Gaza: "Tomorrow we will reach Netanya and Eshkol's office." Headlines have the power to create reality, and Eshkol was finding it more and more difficult to ignore the question of what should be done. Terrorism took center stage at almost every government meeting, and public pressure to act was steadily increasing. "Restrain Fatah Immediately!" demanded *Yediot Aharonot*. A few days later the paper cautioned, "The success of the Fatah terrorists and their Syrian backers in evading punishment seems to have encouraged others. . . . If the impression is created that Israel does not respond—and the mistaken conclusion that Israel has been weakened is not far behind—Nasser may also support 'activist' enemies as the leaders of Syria have done."[17]

On Friday night, November 11, three paratroopers doing their compulsory military service were killed when their command car drove over a land mine not far from Arad, in the south. They were on their way back from Mount Hebron, where they had collected some soldiers after setting an ambush for terrorists. Tracks leading to the border with Jordan were identified at the site. The next day, the Sabbath, Israel had to decide how to respond. The General Staff met in the morning, and the generals agreed that there was no way to prove Syria responsible and that action could only therefore be taken against Jordan. The military had been demanding permission from the government to act against a Jordanian village for months. They wanted to operate in daylight and with a large force, to compel the civilian population to drive out the terrorists and prevent them from infiltrating Israel. The government had refused, authorizing only limited action that the military commanders deemed useless. Now the army proposed entering the village of Samua, less than fifteen miles south of Hebron, and bombing a few dozen houses there. Chief of Staff Rabin went to see Eshkol at his home in Jerusalem. Eshkol would have preferred to take steps against Syria, but he agreed that the circumstances demanded action in Jordan, despite the risk of unwanted conflict with the Jordanian army.

Foreign Minister Abba Eban later wrote that the deaths of the three soldiers had constituted an escalation: "There is an increasing impression in the country of 'open season' for murders and attacks, as our neighbors sit by securely." Eban felt that a government incapable of ensuring regular train service and the existence of normal life in the national capital "is in grave condition by any standard." Eban was referring to Israel's ability to deter attack, but he might have added that a prime minister who was mocked for his indecisiveness even by his own supporters had also found himself "in grave condition."

Eshkol could not ignore the military's demand to avenge the three paratroopers' deaths; "Israel's patience is not unlimited," he told the security cabinet. Military secretary Israel Lior documented an argument among the ministers. Three of them, Minister of Health Israel Barzilai (Mapam), Minister of the Interior Haim Moshe Shapira (Mafdal), and Minister of Tourism Moshe Kol (Independent Liberals) wanted assurances that the operation would have a more limited scope than what Rabin was proposing. Others, mainly Yigal Allon (Ma'arah), supported Rabin. The newspaper editorials on Sunday mirrored this disagreement. "We may have to get used to the thought that the penetration of these infiltrators, well trained in field operations and sabotage techniques, will continue," wrote Ha'aretz, calling for defensive and preventative steps. Maariv, conversely, quoted the relatives of one of the soldiers, who demanded that the government "avenge his death."[18]

King Hussein of Jordan, apparently assuming Israel would not let the three paratroopers' deaths go without a response, quickly expressed his regret in a message to the United States government. Records kept by the director of the prime minister's office show that the content of the king's message was relayed to the Israeli embassy in Washington on Saturday evening and sent to Jerusalem that night in encoded form. Eshkol was informed of the message on Sunday, November 13, at nine A.M., by which time the Samua operation was already drawing to an end.[19]

Selma Nasser Salameen, an eighty-five-year-old woman, told UN investigators about the bombing of her house in Samua. "Yesterday morning at nearly 0700 hours LT, I was in my house at a-Samua. I heard shooting all over the village and I heard aircraft roaring in the sky in the a-Samua area. I took shelter in my house; then Israeli soldiers came to my house. They ordered me in Arabic to leave my house, because they wanted to blow up the house. After I left the house for a few meters, the house was blown up and I was hit by fragments from the explosion." The soldiers destroyed dozens of homes in this way, without allowing the residents time to bring out their belongings. Furniture, rugs, stored food, kitchen equipment, personal documents, family photo albums—everything was buried under the rubble. Jordan later claimed that more than a hundred homes were blown up; Israel admitted to destroying forty, although an internal report gave the number as sixty. The military attaché at the U.S. embassy in Amman, who visited Samua, estimated that the number of houses destroyed was much higher than Israel's figure. Israel's envoy to Washington, Ephraim Evron, reported that the attaché had seen "many civilians' bodies," which suggested that not all the houses were evacuated before being blown up. Some of the bodies were those of elderly women who had not been able to escape in time, Evron reported.

Operation Shredder, as it was called, grew far beyond the cabinet's expectations, culminating in an air battle with Jordanian forces. A regiment commander in the paratroopers was killed and ten IDF soldiers were wounded. On the Jordanian side, fourteen officers and soldiers were killed and thirty-seven injured; the casualties included a pilot. Upon returning from Samua, the participants in the operation took part in a victory parade of sorts through the streets of Beersheba.[20]

On the day after the operation, three out of four citizens surveyed in a quick poll conducted by *Ha'aretz* said that they supported it. *Yediot Aharonot* wrote, "We knew we were dealing with an irrational and hopeless factor, with saboteurs and murderers who have no self-restraint. . . . They cannot stop, because when an animal, driven only by its urges, tastes blood, it is not sated, but rather grows thirstier." According to *Maariv*, "It was not with joy that the IDF crossed the border, but rather because there was no choice." The paper was reminded of the circumstances during the War of Independence, when Israelis were similarly faced with a powerful enemy, knowing full well that they had no option but to win.[21] Israel had no interest in entering a conflict with Jordan, and the Samua incident was a severe departure from its operational intentions. But even the critics shied away from condemning the army. "As successful as this raid was militarily, doubts remain as to whether it was as successful politically," wrote *Ha'aretz*, and maintained that the operation had exposed Israel's weakness. "It is difficult to avoid the impression that Jordan was chosen as the target because the defense of Syria by the USSR prevented an attack on the right target."[22]

Behind closed doors, more critical voices were heard. Six cabinet members, including the two ministers for religious parties, expressed anger over the extent and results of the operation. Eshkol tried to mollify them by pointing out that Israel spent 1.5 billion liras every year to build up its deterrent forces—should it, at the moment of truth, make do with a simple mezuzah on the door? "And even with a mezuzah there, is there any guarantee that devils will stay outside the house? Here is Israel telling the whole world that it has deterrent forces, but when our blood is spilled should we just utter the Shema?" Yes, Eshkol added, he too had said the Shema once, twice, even three times, but eventually something had to actually be done. Although he also believed that the IDF had gone too far, he nonetheless defended the army, telling the cabinet that it was not true that the operation had gone wrong. He expressed his full support of the chief of staff, and talked of how touched he had been, while visiting soldiers wounded in the operation, to see their steadfast spirits. Rabin himself, and Aharon Yariv, head of the intelligence branch, admitted they had been wrong to estimate that the Jordanian army would not react. Rabin now feared the Jordanians might try to hold up trains to Jerusalem and slaughter passengers. But he did not agree that recommending action against Jordan had been wrong.[23]

Foreign Minister Eban requested and received permission from the government to explain "candidly" that the operation's scope had been unexpectedly expanded, and that intentions did not always determine results—in other words, that they had failed. In a conversation with UN secretary-general U Thant, Eban said that the operation "got out of hand." The need for "candor" had arisen owing to the United States' blistering response. When President Johnson heard what had happened he was "deeply distressed" according to one report, "extremely upset" and even "furious" according to another.[24] The Americans opposed retaliation by Israel in Jordan, reasoning that the Jordanian army would not be able to adequately defend the country and the king would be humiliated. An American intelligence report from May, analyzing the factors that could ignite war between Israel and its neighbors, put border incidents and terrorist attacks at the top of the list. The Americans passed messages between Jerusalem and Amman in an effort to bring about the dismantling of Fatah. One of the president's assistants, Robert Komer, was sent to tell Ambassador Harman that if Israel continued to strike in Jordan, the United States would be forced to "reexamine" its supply of arms to Israel.

It was not every day that Israel was threatened in this way. Harman tried to explain that Eshkol had acted "under heavy pressure from his own conscience," but this did not satisfy President Johnson, who sent Komer to see Abe Feinberg. Komer heard that Feinberg had just spoken with the director general of the prime minister's office, Herzog, who told him they had intended to blow up only four houses in the village. Komer replied that they should have thought about the possibility of escalation before they acted, not after. Feinberg asked whether he should convey Komer's message to Ambassador Harman, but Komer said he would manage Harman himself, and asked Feinberg to give Eshkol the message. As usual, Feinberg accepted the assignment. On behalf of his president, he explained to Eshkol that Johnson was afraid that there were officers in the Jordanian army who might take action against Israel, in opposition to King Hussein's wishes, and that Israel's response could result in an uprising against the king.[25]

A senior official in the State Department, Nicholas Katzenbach, explained to Foreign Minister Eban the absurdity of the situation: it was as if he, Katzenbach, had wanted to slap the Israeli ambassador in the face, but because he could not do so, he slapped the ambassador's secretary.* Ambassador Harman viewed the Samua operation as "madness," and claimed that not a single Israeli diplomat in the United States thought otherwise. He regretted, however, that Israel had not taken action against Syria after the deaths of the four Border Guard policemen a month earlier. The IDF had sought to act against the Syrians at the time, but was stymied by the government, partly because of American pressure. Instead of attacking, Israel went to the UN Security Council, but the Soviet Union

---

*Levi Eshkol's daughter later attributed the following quote to her father: "We meant to give the mother-in-law a pinch, but instead we beat up the bride."[26]

blocked the council from even censuring Syria. "That was the original sin," Harman later said. If the government had agreed to act against Syria in October, perhaps it would not have had to succumb to the military's demand to act against Jordan in November.

Following the Samua operation, demonstrations were held against Hussein in Jordan. The Israeli press voiced concern, and *Ha'aretz* reported that 17 percent of Israelis now disapproved of the operation, three times as many as on the day after it took place. Herzog, also worried, made sure that Hussein was sent an expression of regret through a London physician who functioned as a covert liaison between the two men. Herzog hoped the king would view the letter as an Israeli apology of sorts.[27]

THE UNITED STATES OFFERED ISRAEL AN ARRAY OF ELECTRONIC BORDER SURVEILLANCE devices meant to impede Fatah operatives; the hope was that such defenses would not only halt terror but also restrain Israel. The offer was widely publicized, but Israel examined the technology and responded that it was inadequate.[28] Eshkol, meanwhile, was flooded with letters from concerned citizens suggesting ways to fight terror. One demanded the death penalty for Fatah members; another suggested erecting an electrified fence along the border. Ehud Buch, a student from Jerusalem, sent Eshkol detailed diagrams of security system improvements. Some civilians warned against explosive devices that could be placed in public places like sports stadiums and cinemas. One suggested checking the bags of every person entering a theater, with particular attention paid to anyone who left the auditorium before the program ended. Another citizen was especially concerned about Israeli Arabs, who could easily place bombs anywhere. Some suggested retaliatory terrorism. "Why not organize saboteur units like Fatah's and make their lives hell?" asked Rahaman Mizrahi. He received a brief but courteous response: the letter would be brought to the prime minister's attention.[29]

During one of the closed meetings Eshkol held periodically with editors of the daily newspapers, Herzl Rosenblum of *Yediot Aharonot* asked whether Israel might employ retaliatory terrorism. "There is a demand to that effect in security circles, for us to have our own commandos," said Rosenblum. He was well informed. The possibility that Israel might employ its own guerrilla forces to carry out terror attacks had in fact been discussed by the General Staff. The proposal was made by Israel Tal, commander of the armored corps, and he was supported by the director general of the Ministry of Defense and the inspector general of the police. "We will use the same weapon, but with greater power and a wider effect," said Tal. Ambassador Harman also spoke of this option. Eshkol did not rule out an "eye for an eye" policy in principle, and even insinuated that "certain things" (but "not many") were being done in this respect. He described the operational difficulties for the editors: "It's not that simple. They're sitting on the mountain, and so we have to send two or three men up the mountain, into houses, to remove women and children. And then the men have to get back—it's not simple. But it is possible, if the situation deteriorates, that we will have to take that route."*

When they had to act against terrorism, IDF generals raised various ideas but always reverted to the same proposal: large-scale operations against Syria and Jordan. A dispute soon arose between Eshkol and Rabin. The prime minister and many of his ministers believed in defensive mechanisms, such as fences, ambushes, and various electronic devices. The chief of staff and the generals demanded an offensive policy. More than a simple tactical and political argument, this was also a generational conflict—and an ideological and psychological one. Eshkol and the cabinet feared the political repercussions of large-scale offensives. The IDF, however, was designed not for response and defense, but for initiative and offense. The state's borders were not fortified or fenced, and this was not by chance, as Moshe Dayan explained in April 1967: "The Israel Defense Force is a decidedly aggressive assault army in the way it thinks, the way it plans, the way it implements. Aggression is in its bones and its spirit."

For Rabin and the generals, most of whom were Israeli born, this was not merely a professional military issue, but a question of their prestige, their dignity, and their image as Sabra warriors facing weak-spirited politicians. They viewed these Eastern Europeans, some of whom were three decades older than they, as clinging to "Diaspora psychology." The belief that terrorism could be overcome by defensive means might bring about the construction of electric fences along the borders, said Rabin, and "they'll turn Israel into another ghetto." When speaking at General Staff meetings, Rabin used to refer to Eshkol and his ministers as "the Jews."†

---

*He told them about a young man who had infiltrated Israel from Syria, crossing the Jordan River by boat. The man was caught and was found to have a good command of Hebrew. He was carrying over twenty-five pounds of explosives, as well as threatening letters addressed to a few statesmen and newspapers. His mission was to carry out an assault in a populated area.
†Eshkol liked to call the generals "Preissn"—Prussians, in Yiddish.[30]

3. CONTRASTS: "TWO PEOPLES OF ISRAEL"

About ten days after the Samua operation, Eshkol received a letter from
an elderly historian named Yitzhak Baer, one of the first professors at the
Hebrew University, urging him to remember that "the government's decisions must correlate with the historical character and the religious and social ideals of our nation, and any action must be inherently persuasive of
its justice and have educational force." Baer was from Germany, a founder of the "Jerusalem school," which provided academic support for the
Zionist idea. In 1966 he was seventy-eight years old. He said he was writing "on behalf of a few friends," and added an apologetic note: "These
words stem from a sense of responsibility for the image and fate of our
state and our people."

One could still find in Jerusalem a few of the founding members of the
Hebrew University who had proposed a binational alternative to the
Zionist program: instead of a Jewish state on part of the land, there would
be a binational Jewish-Arab state on all the land. Within the colorful Israeli mosaic of ideas there was room for this position, expounded by the
philosopher Schmuel Hugo Bergman, the Kabbalah scholar Gershom
Scholem, the educator Akiba Ernst Simon, and others, but it had next to
no influence. These scholars came from Central Europe and lived within
walking distance of one another in the Jerusalem neighborhood of Rehavia and nearby. Although they were fluent in Hebrew, they felt more
comfortable in German, and as they grew old they distanced themselves
from the Israeli experience. Bergman recorded in his diary a conversation
among guests at a reception held by President Shazar, where Simon's new
book was being discussed. It had been published, of course, in German,
and everyone agreed that it simply could not be translated into Hebrew.

A few professors were vocal in demanding military restraint and efforts
to talk with the Arabs. One of them, the philosopher Yehoshua Bar-Hillel,
said as early as April 1967 that the Arab refugees' right to return to their
homes was no less valid than the right of Soviet Jews to settle in Israel,
and that the Israelis' moral duty to accept them was as great as their obligation to take in the Jews of Russia. A physician named Shimon Shera-
shevski also suggested restoring the refugees to the villages they had
abandoned. Although these and similar opinions had no real impact,
they were notable as part of the constant clash of fundamental values
that was occurring in Israel, and that occasionally escalated into a culture war. It was a conflict between Athens and Sparta; between optimists
and pessimists; between those who championed humanistic values and

believed in the possibility of peace with the Arabs and those who saw war as predestined and held that the Arabs would never accept the existence of Israel. Both sides spoke in the name of the "People of Israel," but it often seemed they were talking about two different nations.

"There are two Peoples of Israel," wrote Bergman. "There have always been two dueling currents in Judaism. The first is isolationist; it hates the goy, emphasizes at every opportunity the imperative to 'Remember what the Amalekite did unto thee'"—Bergman was referring to a biblical massacre—"and cultivates this Amalekite-syndrome. And there is the other Judaism, which I would perhaps characterize with the verse 'Thou shalt love thy neighbor as thyself.' This is a Judaism that prays, 'Let me forget the Amalekite,' a Judaism of love and compassion." Herein lay the deeper layer of the political disagreement between "left" and "right," between "doves" and "hawks." The dilemma was how to determine whether the state was in actual danger; at what point and to what extent was it essential or desirable for the IDF to act; and whether restraint would result in moderation across the border or simply be interpreted as weakness and so encourage aggression.[31]

The Communist party spoke of Israel's need for accepted permanent borders and for recognition of the Palestinian refugees' right to choose between returning to their homes or receiving compensation. Mapam raised the possibility of Israel taking in "an agreed-upon number" of refugees. Uri Avneri, of *Ha'olam Hazeh*, did not rule out the return of refugees, either. Mapam proposed a confederation between Israel and Jordan, while Avneri suggested a federation between Israel and a "Republic of Palestine." Israel Baer, a well-known military commentator who was also a senior officer with close ties to David Ben-Gurion, proposed a federation between Israel and a Palestinian state that would rise in place of the Kingdom of Jordan.

But the Israeli peace movement had trouble offering immediate solutions and was perceptible only on the margins of public discourse. The Communists spoke with the voice of the USSR, and Mapam represented kibbutzim built on Arab lands. Avneri published his positions alongside pictures of scantily clad women in *Ha'olam Hazeh*, and Israel Baer was a traitor: he had been arrested in 1961 and sentenced to fifteen years for spying for the Soviet Union. Although his story aroused a great deal of attention when it was made public, he remained uninfluential and ultimately died in prison.[32]

The elderly Professor Baer did not mention what had prompted him to write his letter to the prime minister, apart from a vague reference to "recent events," by which he meant the Samua operation. The weak tenor of his protest reflected not only his personal aversion to political involvement, but also the decline of the alternative position. As the years wore on and the universities' dependence on the state increased, the professors from Rehavia sounded more and more like an echo of the past. Eshkol had good reason to view the academics as his allies, for they had extended moral support in his great struggle with Ben-Gurion over the Lavon affair; many had opposed Ben-Gurion even before Eshkol did. From time to time he sought their advice on how to improve the gloomy national mood, although they were as helpless as he.[33] Eshkol was also receptive to their demand to revoke martial law.

Baer received a long reply from Eshkol that was probably meant for posterity, as is often the case with such correspondence. Eshkol detailed at length the peaceful intentions he had expressed in the past, and described the acts of terrorism. "I do not know whether you met with the residents of Romema after the explosions in that neighborhood's homes, whether you saw the demolished train on the way to Jerusalem, or whether you visited the families of soldiers killed in the recent attacks along our borders. You can surely imagine that one who does come in contact with all these, one who bears the responsibility of securing the country's borders and ensuring the safety of its citizens, must act as best he can to ensure peace and fortify the borders." Eshkol mentioned that the UN Security Council had not sided with Israel. He went on to ask, "What further justification and inherent persuasion did we need so that we could exercise our right to protect ourselves? After all, we have practiced restraint more than once, more than twice, more than seven times. Must we allow ourselves to be worn down and killed bit by bit, if not destroyed in a future all-out war, as promised by Nasser? Must we wait for Hannah Arendt to write articles about our failure to resist?"*

A seventh-grade schoolboy from Rehovot, Eitan Galon, asked Eshkol why the IDF had set out to kill innocent civilians in Jordan instead of striking against Syria. An assistant replied that Jordan was responsible for the infiltration of terrorists over its borders, and promised that "decisions about military actions are made in the government following serious debate and extensive consideration."[35]

---

*Eshkol was referring to an extremely painful argument that had surfaced in public life in Israel after the Holocaust, reawakened following a series of articles written by the Jewish American philosopher Hannah Arendt after the Eichmann trial. Arendt condemned the "Jewish councils" that had collaborated with the Nazis, and was severely critical of Israel. Contrary to Eshkol's insinuation, however, she did not admonish the Jews for having failed to defend themselves.[34]

• • •

IN 1966, THE IDF ENLISTED THE FIRST GENERATION OF ISRAELI-BORN SOLDIERS, A JUNC-
ture Yitzhak Rabin saw as symbolic of the state's independence. Most Israelis identified the establishment of the state with its victory over Arab
armies in the War of Independence and trusted the IDF to ensure its continued existence in the face of Arab intent to destroy it. Almost every
young man and woman knew they would serve a few years in the army
and be called up for annual reserve duty well into mid-life. They also accepted the possibility of losing their lives in the course of military service.
Yitzhak (Iki) Kotler of Kibbutz Givat Brenner wrote to his girlfriend about
a friend who had been killed in a training accident, and shared with her
his response: "To simply . . . continue being ourselves and go back to routine, because such is life and sometimes it demands victims of us and
there is nothing to be done against this."*

Most Israelis tended to assume that the army's operations were usually
necessary and appropriate. People knew the units and the commanders,
and many carried into their civilian lives ties forged during military service. They talked knowledgeably about IDF equipment, analyzed operations, strategies, and tactics, and whispered military secrets to one
another. The IDF was part of routine life, a component of Israeli identity.
At least once a year, on Independence Day, the power of the IDF took center stage as military parades and displays drew thousands of spectators.[37]
According to *Maariv*, they came to "visually caress the metal and the muscle of their army." In July 1966, an air show was held in the center of Israel to celebrate Air Force Day. *Ha'aretz* reported that the demonstration
included the use of napalm bombs.[38]

The Israeli ethos ruled out "militarism," a term reminiscent of malignant regimes in Europe. Israelis liked to brag about their peaceful aspirations, and the army was deployed in a series of civilian missions,
including agricultural settlement, the absorption of immigrants, and education. It was supposed to fight only to protect the state's existence. The
day after the Syrians shelled a kibbutz in the north, Tel Katzir, a *Yediot
Aharonot* reporter met with children on the kibbutz. Six-year-old Zehava
said that the Arabs in Israel should be deported, and a boy named Nir
asserted that "anyone who speaks Arabic is a bad man." The reporter
explained that "a foreigner hearing such words from these children may
mistakenly conclude that the militaristic viewpoint is imbibed here along

---

*Iki Kotler was killed in action a few years later.[36]

with mother's milk. However, any experienced kindergarten teacher will tell you that this is a child's emotional response to the experience of fighting for one's rights." The kindergarten teachers told the reporter that they tried to prevent the children from developing hostile feelings. They told the children about the Arabs who lived in Israel and emphasized that there were good Arabs in Syria, too. Only the bad Arabs wanted war. The reporter was impressed by the children's toys. "In vain I searched for model tanks, cannons, or rifles, like the ones children play with all over the world. But the children of Tel Katzir apparently do not need them. They have plenty in real life."

There were those who were proud that the victory in the War of Independence had not produced great myths of heroism or songs of glory. One literary critic praised the children's writer Israel Menahem Weisler, who wrote under the pseudonym Poochoo, for his antiwar book. The book did not justify the war; rather, the hero, Yoram, and his friends were born into a situation where the war was "imposed on them by reality," said the critic. He added, "War is like an upper class in high school, which you reach naturally and without too much thought. Whoever does not go on to the next class is the odd one out and is to be shamed."

At the beginning of 1967, enrollment in the Gadna youth battalions was approximately seventy thousand. This training program under the IDF's auspices instilled the basic precepts of military service in high school boys and girls. Khaki uniforms were mandatory at the weekly meetings. The training included camping, topography, sports, first aid, self-defense, and marksmanship. Older students went on excursions across Israel and took part in National Service army camps, where they had target practice. The children's weekly *Davar Leyeladim* pointed out that many Gadna trainees were engaged in nonmilitary activities, such as volunteering at hospitals, restoring antiquities at Masada, and planting trees. But the magazine also linked academic achievement with the possibility of becoming an IDF officer. "Talented students" with suitable qualities took part in squad commander training during their Gadna sessions, and most of them were admitted to officer training programs when they joined the army. *Davar Leyeladim* also ran an editorial entitled "Good Guys Go to Military Boarding School." These were institutions that accepted elementary school graduates and combined high school studies with preparation for military service, encouraging camaraderie and a sense of shared destiny—values highly praised in the article. Before Independence Day in 1967, a particularly patriotic issue of the magazine was published, featuring a story about children who had saved a soldier's life and who distinguished themselves by other heroic acts, as well as an article about the IDF's British-made Centurion tanks. That same issue carried the first installment of a comic strip about the War of Independence.

A similar spirit was projected by other papers. The Independence Day edition of *Maariv Lanoar*, the daily paper's magazine for young people, looked like something published in the Soviet Union. The cover, featuring the black silhouette of a soldier against a red background, bore the caption "Israeli Youths Send Blessings to the IDF on the Nation's Nineteenth Independence Day." First-graders in Beit Lehem Haglilit sent a poem to David Ben-Gurion in praise of Tzahal, the Hebrew acronym by which the IDF is widely known: "Tzahal / Our Tzahal / So strong / Protects us / From all trouble / You are our bravest army / You we salute / For you we cheer / And you we love more than anything." Ben-Gurion kept the poem in his personal papers.[39]

"Ben-Gurion and his associates conferred an almost sacred aura on the IDF, and the public accepted that image," wrote Yosef Lapid in a *Maariv* article whose headline ran the whole width of the page: "Is There a Danger of the IDF Taking Over the Government?" Military coups were a daily occurrence around the world, Lapid argued, not just in Indonesia, Ghana, and other Third World countries, but also in Greece, for example, the country that gave the world the term "democracy." "With the exception of Britain and the Scandinavian countries, not one country seems to be immune to the possibility of a putsch," he explained. That term, of course, evoked the events preceding the rise of the Nazis. "Why, then, does no one entertain the thought that the IDF may decide one day that it has had enough of chaos, moderation, and chitchat—it's time to put things in order?" But Lapid did not believe that the IDF was considering this idea. The Jewish mentality would not accept any form of dictatorship, and historical experience had made the prospect unthinkable. The IDF's senior command had been educated in the bosom of democracy, and although the top brass had all come from a similar ideological background, they held a range of political views. The frequent turnover of officers prevented the formation of a military cult, and the people would not accept a coup: the Histadrut would paralyze the economy, the kibbutzim would protest.*

Having said this, Lapid went on to describe the IDF as extremely influential, partly because many officers became directors of financial organi-

---

*The question also preoccupied the British military attaché. He did not rule out the possibility of an IDF coup, but thought the chances were slim. He did assume, however, that there was a reasonable chance that army officers would influence government policy by legitimate means—for example, through public opinion.[40]

zations after their discharge. Although the IDF was often called "the people's army," Lapid saw a proclivity to social isolation, exemplified by special housing for members of the standing army. "Friday-night dinner conversation focuses on military topics, while the wives discuss products sold at the army canteen," Lapid explained. "The dominant topics are not those that preoccupy other Israeli neighborhoods. For example, the recession is a purely theoretical issue, because it does not affect army people." IDF members had their own language and their own class consciousness: the distinctions included "a senior officer with a car and driver, an officer with a car, an officer without a car. An army boy might tell his friend, 'My dad is a lieutenant colonel; yours is only a captain.'" When a residential neighborhood was built in Nazareth for members of the standing army, the senior officers' wives did not want to live next door to the families of noncoms. A colonel would not fool around with the wife of a lieutenant colonel, said Lapid, quoting a senior officer.*

Israelis worshiped the IDF, wrote Lapid, and that was as it should be. But the danger of projecting such a perfect image was that the army itself might start to believe in it. "An officer who reads in the papers every day that the government appears powerless and the Knesset is helpless, and at the same time reads only praise for the IDF, will sooner or later start to believe that he is made of better stuff," Lapid concluded, and observed how rarely the press criticized the army.[42]

The papers did cultivate admiration of the army and often sang the praises of its commanders. Speaking to *Yediot Aharonot*, Avraham Vered, a photographer for the IDF weekly, *Bamahane*, described the paratroopers whom he often accompanied on missions: "From the moment they crossed the border, our boys showed a kind of masculinity and dedication. They suddenly matured and became as one muscle, taut and invincible." Until that experience, he had viewed the soldiers as innocent curly-haired boys, kibbutzniks who liked folk dancing and dabbled in ideological arguments. "I could see them working quietly on the kibbutz, herding sheep or driving tractors, taking pity on a poor kitten suddenly caught in their path." But en route to their mission, they changed. "When

---

*The army's elitist sense of itself was illustrated in typical fashion during a General Staff discussion about supplying soldiers with windbreakers. One of the generals, Uzi Narkis, complained about teenagers who adopted military fatigues as a fashion statement, something he saw as insulting to the army: "All sorts of teenagers, construction workers who may or may not have jobs, are walking around in camouflage clothes. It is unbelievable chutzpah." Another general, David Elazar, commented that in Nazareth even the Arabs wore fatigues.[41]

given an order to carry out a mission, one that will clearly involve killing—with the cruelty inevitable in any war—they will do it perfectly, without hesitation, without philosophizing. That's the way they are!" Vered was impressed that the paratroopers did not "play hero." Their attitude was businesslike, practical, straightforward.

Such was "the double identity of the paratroopers," noted Ilan Kfir, the author of the article that quoted Vered. They included not only kibbutzniks but city men, among them "the lions from Hatikva," a poor neighborhood in southern Tel Aviv; but the entire corps (here Kfir quoted Vered again), "these wide-eyed, golden-haired boys, was touched by an earthy spirit." It was a spirit of mischief, he continued, which at the right moment turned into a mood of vengeance, a crushing fist. Vered described a target being stormed: "Never in my life have I seen a more shocking and magnificent sight." Above all, the soldiers dreaded failure, and this left no room for the fear of dying. "If a paratrooper knows he is alive because he fled or backed down, he will despise himself, and will no longer see his life as having any value," said Vered. In a historical vein, he added that they reminded him of Ezekiel's prophecy of the dry bones coming back to life: "This is the resurrection. This feeling did not exist among Diaspora Jews. They were content to preserve their lives. Here we have something entirely different."

When Colonel Ariel Sharon was appointed head of the army's training department, *Maariv* raved, "The much-praised commander of the paratroopers will now pass his courageous doctrine on to the entire army."[43] Similar articles appeared about another commander, Ezer Weizman, nephew of Chaim Weizmann. The two generals were referred to by their nicknames, Arik and Eyzer.[44] Sharon spoke of his attitude toward the Arabs: "I do not hate Arabs, but I certainly feel strongly about our historic right to Palestine, and this of course intensifies my attitude to the Arabs. But that attitude is not, under any circumstances, hatred. I fully believe that our existence depends upon a resolute insistence on our rights and that we must retaliate relentlessly when there is a need." He talked of his feelings during one operation: "The moon was shining and I looked back and saw the mighty line of men following me. It gives a great sense of strength, of power."[45]

Uri Avneri's *Ha'olam Hazeh* also cultivated admiration of the IDF as one of the components of the Israeli ethos Avneri was trying to create through his magazine. Other figures identified with dovish positions also venerated the army: "We are proud of our army and we love it," wrote

Nathan Rotenstreich, a well-known professor of philosophy.[46] In the gloomy, doubt-ridden atmosphere that pervaded Israel, the IDF was practically the only institution still enjoying public confidence.

IN JULY 1966, A LARGE ADVERTISEMENT APPEARED IN *HA'ARETZ* PROTESTING THE INTRO-duction of nuclear weapons into the Middle East. Many of the dozens of signatories were the same professors who had opposed other aspects of Ben-Gurion's Israel, including martial law.[47] Israel claimed it had no nuclear weapons and that it would not be the first to "introduce" them into the region.* Nuclear development in Dimona, begun in the early 1950s, remained shrouded in secrecy. Israel took various steps to conceal it, but the circle of those in the know seems to have been larger than was thought at the time. In early 1966, Eshkol gave details of the project to the Knesset Foreign Affairs and Defense Committee. Besides sixteen Knesset members, a few senior IDF commanders were also present. Statements made by Moshe Dayan about Dimona at that meeting left little room for doubt as to what was involved in the project.[49]

A few journalists knew about Dimona, but were forbidden to publish their information; they made do by quoting the foreign press, often in headlines.[50] It became increasingly clear that Israel was arming itself with nuclear weapons. Professor Ernst David Bergman, head of the Israeli Atomic Energy Commission, an official organization, stopped just short of saying so outright: in developing atomic energy for peaceful purposes, one attains nuclear capability anyway, he told *Maariv* in an interview. The paper called him Mr. Atom. Yuval Ne'eman, a scientist involved in the nuclear project, wrote, "On the eve of the Six-Day War, Israel had a broad nuclear infrastructure, with the security potential inherent therein." Washington's assessment was that Israel had two bombs.[51]

Israel's nuclear project had been begun partly in response to the Holocaust. The mass murder of European Jews gave rise to the view that the State of Israel needed an atomic bomb to prevent a second Auschwitz. The strategic supposition was that only a powerful Israel could deter the Arab states from attempting to destroy it, and that if Israel had nuclear arms, its enemies might even be persuaded to recognize it and make peace.

---

*Eshkol once asked Abba Eban what, in fact, was meant when English-speakers used the verb "introduce" in the context of nuclear arms—was it that Israel should not be the first country to use the bomb, or that it not be the first to manufacture one? Eban replied, "It means that something that didn't exist suddenly does exist."[48]

"The fear of nuclear retaliation prevents an Arab attack against Israel": thus *Yediot Aharonot* quoted a report produced by a British research institute.[52] But opinion in Israel on the subject was divided.

Among military men and politicians, the Dimona project aroused strategic, economic, and political controversy; naturally, power struggles, prestige, and ego were involved as well. Some information was made public. The military commentator Israel Baer, who wrote a book on the topic, rejected the inclination to base the state's security on deterrent abilities: "In the final analysis, Israel's security problem has no military solution, only a political one." It would be better to attain nuclear disarmament of the Middle East, wrote analyst Eliezer Livneh.[53] Yigal Allon feared that nuclear weapons development would take money out of IDF budgets and thus limit the army's ability to build up its conventional forces. It might also spur the Arab states to attack, as they had threatened more than once. A member of the Knesset's Foreign Affairs and Defense Committee pointed out that since the first atomic bomb was dropped on Hiroshima there had been countless conventional wars, in particular guerrilla wars. This was the main danger, and nuclear arms would be useless against it.[54] Because they believed almost exclusively in preemptive attacks, IDF leaders worried that a nuclear capability would restrict the military's operational abilities to the point of near paralysis.[55] If the General Staff had read Israel Baer's book on Israel's security, they knew that nuclear arms would come at the expense of conventional equipment, and if they were persuaded by the argument that nuclear weapons would prevent war, they might have concluded that their time was up. The officers may have feared that the possession of nuclear arms would constrain them and even make them redundant. Perhaps it was this anxiety that made them so pugnacious. [56]

Herzog's diary, as well as American records and the few documents made available by Israel's state archives, all indicate the centrality of the topic to the relationship between Israel and the United States. "We have no evidence that Israel is actually making a bomb," wrote the American undersecretary of state to President Johnson in May 1967, but the assumption was that it could do so "at reasonably short notice should the need arise." It was highly probable that Israel was hiding the truth from the United States, the undersecretary added. American suspicions were based on, among other things, Israel's refusal to tell them what it had done with between eighty and one hundred tons of uranium concentrate it had purchased from Argentina four years earlier, and its evasions of the U.S. demand to conduct a regulatory visit to Dimona. Time after time, the Israelis deliberated over how to respond when the United States demanded details of the Dimona project. Ambassador Harman suggested that Eban not go to the UN General Assembly, so as to avoid meeting U.S. Secretary of State Dean Rusk. In preparation for the possibility that U.S. ambassador Barbour would ask Eshkol about the Argentinian uranium, it was decided in the prime minister's office that he would try to laugh off the matter.[57]

The Israeli public was never asked to choose between those who supported having the bomb and those who opposed it, but as long as most Israelis felt that the state's existence was threatened, there was probably no chance that the majority would object.

Living without final or internationally recognized peaceful borders, Israeli citizens were not only in a state of constant anxiety, but also subject to the unease of temporariness, which hampered their efforts to define their identity. More and more people began to speak of the need for the state to restore the country's biblical borders, including East Jerusalem. In September 1966, *Yediot Aharonot* hosted a discussion with Jewish Agency officials about the state of the Zionist movement. One reporter, Eliyahu Amikam, asked how many Jews the agency thought could be settled in Israel "within its current borders." *Yediot Aharonot's* editor, Herzl Rosenblum, clarified the question: "Is it possible to bring millions of Jews to Israel given its current borders?" They could not have presented the Zionist movement's spokespeople with a more fundamental question, and the agency leaders evaded it.

A few weeks later, *Maariv* published a letter to the editor from a reader grappling with the foundations of secular Israeli Zionism. "Instead of Judaizing Hebron, the site of the Tomb of the Patriarchs, we built Ramat Gan; instead of protecting the Tomb of Rachel, we protect Kibbutz Hanita in the Galilee; and above all, instead of ascending Jerusalem's Mount Moriah, we built Tel Aviv." Divided Jerusalem was indeed an open wound, still painful to many. "The true Jerusalem is the one within the walls," the poet Uri Zvi Greenberg had declared in 1949, referring to the Old City. As a member of the First Knesset, he had asked, "Why would we want a state without Jerusalem?"[58]

4. JERUSALEM: "GOING DOWNTOWN"

The Green Line, which partitioned Palestine, left Israeli Jerusalem at the edge of a narrow corridor, virtually isolated from the rest of the country, and divided the city with a belt of ruined houses, barbed-wire fences, cement walls, and mine fields. This was a no-man's-land. On the other side

were the ancient Old City walls. The Israeli part of town projected a
dreary gravity and weariness: in 1967, nineteen years after being cut off
from most of the sites that comprised its religious and historical uniqueness, including the Western Wall, Jerusalem was also lagging behind the
new secular Israeliness that flourished in Tel Aviv. There, the bright American future set the city's tone; in central Jerusalem, the atmosphere was
shaped by a past left over from the British Mandate. The city was veiled in
a dust of misery.

In the second half of the nineteenth century, most of Jerusalem's residents had been Jewish, but Zionist leaders, primarily Theodor Herzl himself, nonetheless approached Jerusalem with hesitation, sometimes with
hostility: the city was too religious for them and, unlike Tel Aviv, the capital of the Zionist enterprise, it was considered a bastion of Orthodox opposition to Zionism. The British saw it as the country's capital, but Jewish
leaders neglected it. By accepting the UN partition plan in 1947, the Zionist movement gave up on Jerusalem, accepting that the undivided city
would become a *corpus separatum*, a separate entity. Jerusalem was declared the capital of Israel only some eighteen months after the establishment of the state.

Residents of the city were zealous about their identity as Jerusalemites,
and that was practically all they had in common. Most were Jewish, but
the ultra-Orthodox who grew up in Mea Shearim rarely found themselves
in the secular neighborhood of Beit Hakerem, or vice versa. Residents of
affluent Rehavia did not usually go to distressed neighborhoods such as
Musrara, nor the other way around. Only a few Jerusalemites ever reached
Beit Tsafafa, an Arab village in the south that was split down the middle
by the Green Line. The city was a colorful mosaic of isolated neighborhoods and communities, each with its own borders and distinct personality, some projecting a captivating air of stone and faith. To an extent
unique among all the cities of the world, Jerusalem inspired writers and
poets. It had no single story: almost every cliché and generalization about
it had a grain of truth.[59]

During the nineteen years of Jerusalem's partitioned existence, the
population of its Israeli side doubled; with close to 200,000 residents at
the beginning of 1967, it was the country's third largest city, after Tel Aviv
and Haifa. The population had grown mainly thanks to the new immigrants sent there to strengthen the city, although in reality they weakened it both economically and socially. They settled at first in rented
rooms or in houses abandoned by Arabs in the War of Independence.
When the immigrants kept coming, the state housed them in *ma'abarot*,

neighborhoods of tents and tin shacks. Later the state began building big, ugly apartment houses. These complexes almost immediately became poverty-stricken zones, most of whose inhabitants were immigrants from Arab states.[60] Most of the city's residents either worked for public institutions or received public assistance, including the poor, who survived on various stipends; the ultra-Orthodox, who lived on community charity; and teachers and clerks working for the government, the Jewish Agency, the municipality, and the university. Jerusalem had few industrial factories, because it was more cost-effective to open them almost anywhere else in the country.

Many spoke highly of the Jerusalem air, but one resident, Eliezer Livneh, complained about a persistent foul smell that welcomed visitors. One acquaintance, Livneh recounted, had come to town on a rickety old train; it had seemed so romantic as it passed through the wonderful mountain landscape. The man was admiring a charming creek that wound among the rocks alongside the train tracks, spraying a lovely foam. How nice it was to see a mountain creek on a hot summer day, he thought, opening a window—only to discover that what he was admiring was Jerusalem's sewage. Piles of garbage covered the streets, and the trash cans were overflowing, where there were any. Beggars sat at every corner, a city-wide plague. The buses were cumbersome and noisy, giving off noxious fumes, and were neither heated in winter nor air-conditioned in summer. Their windows, floors, and seats were filthy. Even when the ancient local bus company, Hamekasher, merged with the nationwide Egged concern in 1967, there was no immediate improvement. Residents complained about the infrequency of buses and the lack of schedules. Every few years, when it snowed in the city, Jerusalem was completely cut off from the rest of the country.

When Jerusalemites said they were "going downtown," they were referring to the triangle formed by Jaffa, King George, and Ben-Yehuda Streets, with the central post office and the Frumin building, home of the Knesset until 1966, at one point of the triangle; Café Ta'amon, Steimatsky (the bookstore in Zion Square), the Schwartz Department Store, Café Atara, Friedman (the bookstore for those with refined taste), and Rosenblum Women's Fashions were nearby. Another side of the triangle led from Zion Square through Rosenfeld (toys) and Freimann & Bein (shoes) to Tarablus (a restaurant). The triangle's third side stretched from King George Street past the Café Allenby and Hakol Lanoar (notebooks and textbooks) to Heihal Shlomo, seat of the chief rabbinate. A little beyond the triangle was the Mahane Yehuda outdoor market, a particularly filthy area.

Many Jerusalemites preferred to shop in Tel Aviv. According to Uri

Scharf, a reporter for *Ha'aretz*, the buying power of most residents was fairly negligible and, unlike Tel Aviv and Haifa, Jerusalem was not surrounded by smaller towns with additional consumers, which meant that it had fewer stores and a smaller selection. The variety of clothing and shoes, especially for women, was extremely poor, Scharf reported. "A style will be seen around Tel Aviv and Haifa for months before it makes its pilgrimage to the holy city. And if a store does offer an original style at a moderate price, one immediately fears that buying it will be a mistake, because in a matter of days there will be countless women on the streets of Jerusalem wearing the same item." Scharf listed only six reasonable clothing stores. Shoes were cheaper in Tel Aviv, as were furniture and electrical appliances. There was one store that would darn nylon stockings, two businesses that fixed electric shavers. The usual refrain was "We'll have to send it to Tel Aviv." Shops closed at lunchtime.

There were a few cinemas in the center of town where one could see fairly new movies after they had already been screened in Tel Aviv. The Zion, Orion, Orgil, and Tel Or cinemas had no air-conditioning or heat, and their creaky wooden seats were often broken. Tickets were not sold in advance. The screens were cracked and torn around the edges; the sound systems were grating. Before the movie the projectionist showed slides advertising local businesses; after the Moch launderette slide, the movie would begin. The projectors often broke down in the middle of a movie. Empty bottles rolled around noisily between the seats, and cars could often be heard honking through the thin walls. Smoking was prohibited, but only rarely did anyone enforce the ban. Only the Hen cinema offered a slightly higher level of comfort. There was no theater in Jerusalem, and one *Maariv* reporter compared the city to Ofakim, an immigrant town in the desert.[61] The Knesset and the Supreme Court lent a conservative gravity; this city of scholars and scientists, words and ideas, was also the home of the university, with its National Library and student life.

DIVIDED, JERUSALEM LIVED WITH THE TENSIONS INHERENT TO BORDER TOWNS. DEFENsive walls built outside houses during the War of Independence were still standing, and a wall full of bullet holes stood on King George Street, above the park looking out on the Old City. The borderline attracted those visitors who liked to take potentially dangerous tours. Eccentrics from all over the world, as well as children, often crossed the border by mistake or intentionally entered the no-man's-land to collect scrap iron for sale. Occasionally they stepped on land mines. Jordanian soldiers could be seen in some places, and anyone trying to take pictures of them was liable to be fired on. Jordanian snipers opened fire frequently, and there were some incidents involving casualties. Severe incidents were dealt with by the UN Security Council, while those of only local import were settled by the Mixed Armistice Commission. The Jordanians claimed that Israel was violating the cease-fire agreement by preventing access to the Jordanian side along Bethlehem Road. Israeli renovations of abandoned houses along the border, such as Tanus House, often caused tensions. Israel, for its part, claimed that Jordan was required to allow Israelis to pray at the Western Wall.

"Our demand for access to the Western Wall is eternal," declared Prime Minster Eshkol in the spring of 1966. That summer, on the holy fast day of Tisha B'av, an article about the wall in *Maariv* ended with the words "The Wailing Wall weeps today for the children of Israel who are not at its side." The Jewish holy places in the Old City had been "pilfered," wrote the paper in January 1967: "Your soul cries out to them but your feet may not tread there." *Yediot Aharonot* reported that the Jordanians had named the street leading to the Western Wall after the Prophet Mohammed's horse, Alborak. Jordan allowed Jewish tourists to approach the wall, but not Israelis.*

Many people pined for homes in the Jewish Quarter that they had been forced to leave during the War of Independence. "I had a huge longing to go back to the Old City, to wander among the Jerusalem alleys, to see the walls," said Hana Rivlin. Nostalgia for the Old City was nurtured among schoolchildren. "Oh, how I longed to see the Old City!" wrote a girl at Arlozorov Elementary School in the fifties. "I told my mother—Oh! If only I could go there! My mother told me what the Old City looked like. . . . While I saw the Old City in my imagination, my mother showed me pictures of it. They made me very happy and I said to her, 'May it happen that I shall see the yearned-for city not only in pictures but in reality.' "

Not far from Mount Zion, which looked onto the Temple Mount, stood the YMCA bell tower, from whose heights one could see the edge of a street in the Arab part of the city and sometimes even cars driving by. The roof of the Notre Dame monastery also offered a romantic glimpse of a foreign and forbidden land, at once threatening and fascinating. One could even make out people. The partly destroyed French monastery was

---

*An Israeli-Jordanian committee was supposed to regulate a series of unsettled issues, including access to the Western Wall, but after a few years it ceased operating, "fell into a deep sleep," and finally "died."[62]

even closer to the Old City walls than the YMCA tower; its garden was in the no-man's-land.[63]

Apart from the railroad and the Tel Aviv highway, the only legal departure points from the Israeli part of Jerusalem were the Mandelbaum Gate and Armon Hanatziv, the former British headquarters. Both had an air of international intrigue. The Mandelbaum Gate was an Israeli roadblock painted in black-and-white that opened onto a small square, on the other side of which was a red-and-white Jordanian roadblock.* Tourists were permitted to enter Israel from the Jordanian side of town, while Christian clergy, UN officials, and diplomats were allowed to cross in both directions. Israeli Arabs were sometimes allowed to meet relatives living in Jordan at the square between the two roadblocks. They referred to the site as the Gate of Tears. Once a year, on Christmas, Christian Israeli citizens could cross over to pray in the holy places. Israeli and Jordanian officials would exchange newspapers and there were friendly relations between the two sets of policemen, which lent the gate an almost surreal detachment from reality. It was once described as "a porthole in the wall of hostility."†

In the southern part of the city one could get as far as the iron barrier blocking access to Armon Hanatziv, the building that had once served the British high commissioner and was now the headquarters of UN observers. The building itself could be seen only from a distance, rising above a hill identified as the biblical "hill of evil counsel." Hidden from view in the distant valley was "the Line"—the border, manned by Israeli soldiers— a secret passed among children in whispered awe. The various prohibitions in the Armon Hanatziv area were much disputed among Israel, Jordan, and the UN. Secrecy also hovered over the abandoned buildings of the Hebrew University and Hadassah Hospital on Mount Scopus. The mountain was surrounded on all sides by Jordanian territory, but according to the cease-fire agreement it remained an enclave under Israeli control. Once every two weeks, an Israeli police motorcade would drive up to Mount Scopus, as permitted by the agreement. The motorcade would

---

*The gate owed its name to Yakov Mandelbaum, who had built his home there many years earlier. The Jordanians wanted to change the name, and debated whether to name it after Salah a'Din, who had retaken Palestine from the Crusaders, or simply to call it the Gate of Return— meaning the return of the 1948 refugees.

†An Israeli citizen named Nahum Takson once asked the UN secretary general for permission to enter the Old City so that he could visit the grave of his brother, who had been killed in 1948. Another citizen, Avraham Stavsky, demanded that the UN undersecretary general allow Israelis free access to the Western Wall. The undersecretary, Ralph Bunche, politely replied to both men that he could be of no help.

leave through the Mandelbaum Gate and cross Jordanian territory, protected by UN forces. In fact, Israel was transporting troops—soldiers and
officers disguised as policemen or even as scientists—to scope out the area.
It was a game of cat and mouse, another of the secrets whispered by so
many Israelis. The head of the UN observer team complained that the Israelis were also smuggling weapons and even disassembled military vehicles up the mountain, which was true. Over the years, too, the university
staff managed to remove most of the books that had remained on the
campus after the War of Independence. The Mount Scopus situation led to
frequent disagreements between Israel and Jordan, stemming from the
claim that Israel was trying to take over territories that did not belong to it,
and from the demand of villagers in nearby Isawiya that they be allowed
to farm lands that were off-limits, according to the cease-fire agreement.[64]

Most countries, including the United States, honored—at least
officially—the UN partition resolution and refused to recognize Jerusalem
as Israel's capital. Nor did they recognize the annexation of the city's eastern part by Jordan, but Jordan, unlike Israel, did not declare the city its
capital. Most foreign embassies were in Tel Aviv, while the consulates in
Jerusalem retained the special inviolate status they had enjoyed since the
nineteenth century. The effort to gain de facto recognition of Jerusalem's
status as the capital of Israel was a focus of the Foreign Ministry. Israeli
ambassadors urged heads of state, including President Charles de Gaulle
of France, not to address letters to "President of Israel, Tel Aviv." Foreign
Ministry officials tried to convince foreign reporters to use Jerusalem as
the dateline of stories filed from Israel. There were attempts to organize
international conferences in Jerusalem, and one success in this area was
an international book fair. But efforts to "strengthen Jerusalem" in more
practical ways, for example with investment in development, generally
amounted to a rather pathetic series of letters written by the city's mayors
to the successive Israeli prime ministers and grandiose announcements
in the Knesset. In June 1966, the Knesset discussed the problems of
Jerusalem and heard Minister of Finance Sapir make several promises to
improve the city's economic state. Among his plans was the opening of a
Hilton hotel.

Until the occupation of East Jerusalem in the Six-Day War, the government tended to view demands for the development of Jerusalem as a nuisance, particularly when they entailed spending money. In early 1967,
the mayor of Jerusalem, Teddy Kollek, asked Foreign Minister Abba Eban
to give the city one million liras to benefit a Jerusalem Day that would

reinforce its status as the capital. The events were to include an "international prayer for peace." Eban offered 100,000 liras. Kollek wanted a special law to require the government to invest in development of the capital, but Sapir and Eshkol were opposed. The prime minister suggested postponing legislation "until there is an improvement in the economy." The minister of justice also objected. But Kollek was relentless, and the government made several secret decisions that would incur no monetary costs: meetings with ambassadors and foreign reporters were to be henceforth held in Jerusalem, and the Foreign Ministry would look into enticing foreign diplomats to come to the city by inviting them to concerts at the city auditorium, Binyanei Hauma, and similar events. One government minister took it upon himself to talk to the IDF chief of staff about holding ceremonies and military displays in Jerusalem. In reality, Jerusalem was the capital for only three or four days a week, since every Wednesday (or, at the latest, Thursday) it was abandoned by most Knesset members, ministers, and other senior officials. Those who remained in town were said to hide from public view, in case word got around that since they weren't required elsewhere in the country, they must be superfluous. Kollek wrote to Eshkol that he felt as if he were battling the wind.[65]

Teddy Kollek was a rising star in Israeli politics. He had previously held various national positions, including that of director general of the prime minister's office. The mayoral elections in Jerusalem were his first experience as a political candidate, at the age of fifty-four. He took office at the end of 1965, promising to bring Jerusalem into the twentieth century. He used to get up early and walk through the town making notes on what needed to be done: an unemptied trash can in one neighborhood; a rose bush that needed watering in another. Here he found a site that could become the public park that the millionaire from Chicago wanted to fund; there they could put the statue that the movie producer from Los Angeles wanted to buy for the city.* When he arrived at the office, usually before other municipal employees, he was liable to call department managers who had displeased him, waking them up and roaring at them over the phone, but he often sent warm notes of appreciation to those whose work he liked. He was bored by the routines of management, preferring

---

*Early on in his first term, Kollek hosted Marlene Dietrich in his home. *Ha'aretz* printed a large picture showing him sitting on a rug at her feet. The religious party representatives in Jerusalem protested, and Kollek explained that although he had been sitting at the most beautiful feet in the world, he had been thinking only of the city's monetary problems, as evidenced by the sorrowful expression on his face.

to delegate authority. But on the first anniversary of his taking office, *Ha'aretz*'s municipal affairs reporter wrote that Kollek had not made good on his promises and services had not improved. The opinion was echoed in other news outlets. "Teddy Kollek's smiles have not improved the cleanliness of Jerusalem," wrote one. Kollek also found it difficult to take an interest in social distress. He wanted momentum; he wanted international prestige. A conversation with an important American journalist would do more for the city than a meeting with the manager of the welfare department, he believed.*

Shortly after his election, Kollek canceled a plan to move the municipal offices out of their building near the border; he reasoned that there would come a day when the city was reunited, and then the existing building would be in its center. Speaking to delegates at the annual Herut political conference, Kollek publicly promised that Jerusalem would one day be united. In December 1966, Kollek told the Bar-Ilan University student newspaper, *Bat-Kol*, about other steps the municipal government had taken to further the city's reunification. Jerusalem's master plan ensured that when the border was opened there would be a smooth connection with the Old City. Newly built roads, such as the Hebron Road, were being constructed in such a way that they could easily connect to the Old City's access roads when the time came. "I hope peace will bring about an open border between the two parts of the city. Certainly I do not wish this to occur in a nonpeaceful way," said Kollek.

In April 1967, Kollek dedicated a monument to a convoy that had tried to reach Hadassah Hospital on Mount Scopus two decades earlier. Several dozen people in the convoy, doctors and nurses among them, had been killed when Arabs attacked it. The memorial was built on Hanevi'im Street, not far from the border. At the ceremony, Kollek said he prayed for the divided city to be unified so that the memorial could be erected at the site of the attack, next to Sheikh Jarrah on the Jordanian side.[66]†

Many of the soldiers who had fought in the War of Independence felt

---

*Talking with a *New York Times* reporter, Kollek once compared Jerusalem with a Jewish village in Eastern Europe. The shtetls, he pointed out, had not been beautiful. An Israeli diplomat in the United States hurriedly responded that the shtetl had spiritual resonance, and the mayor's derision was to be condemned. He asked Kollek, "Incidentally, what would your friend Marc Chagall say if he were to read your comment?" Kollek promised to choose his words more carefully in the future.

†His predecessors had made similar statements. One of them, Gershon Agron, described the partition of the city as a disgrace. His words were published in a glossy book of photographs of Jerusalem. Of the eighty photos, almost a dozen showed sites in the Jordanian part of the city.

that David Ben-Gurion had blocked them from conquering territories they could have taken, including the Old City and the West Bank. "I never forgave the Israeli government under Ben-Gurion for not letting us finish the job in '48–'49, both militarily and politically," said former general Yigal Allon. A few weeks before the signing of the agreement that demarcated the Green Line between Israel and Jordan, Allon demanded that Ben-Gurion give Israel "strategic depth" by setting its borders along the Jordan River. He felt similarly about the Gaza Strip: if only he and his men had been given a few more days, they would have occupied it. But the government had succumbed to American pressure and ordered a withdrawal. Many of Allon's comrades in arms shared his frustration, and some of them went on to become senior officers, including a few generals. General Ezer Weizman used to say that a Jewish state without all of Jerusalem, without the Western Wall, without Shiloh and Anatot (on the West Bank), was "a fragmented, defective state that would have trouble staying alive."[67] In Israeli history, this failure came to be viewed as the cause of "weeping for generations," and its mark was the Green Line.

5. NOSTALGIA: "THE AXIS AND BOND"

The border demarcated by the Green Line far from coincided with the map of the Zionist dream. Under British rule, the Zionist movement had been forced to exclude fairly extensive territories from its ambitions. The War of Independence gave Israel larger territory than that allocated to the Jewish state by the UN, but did not remove the sense among Israelis that they had compromised on the original dream, waiving their historical right to the entire land. Although Israel did not demand territories that remained outside the Green Line, there was a consensus that the borders agreed to under the cease-fire made it difficult for the country to defend itself.[68]

Shortly after taking office as prime minister and minister of defense, Levi Eshkol discussed a possible expansion of Israel's borders. In June 1963, the IDF chief of staff was Zvi Zur; Yitzhak Rabin was his deputy. Rabin described to Eshkol the ideal boundaries of Israel: they would follow the Jordan River, the Suez Canal, and the Litani River in the north. Although he did not propose military action to alter the existing borders, Rabin believed such alteration would be desirable—not essential, but worthwhile if the opportunity arose. A few months later, the IDF had a plan, code-named Whip, to occupy the West Bank, including East Jerusalem.

A more limited proposal, code-named Mozart, involved "grabs"—takeovers of various spots that were not controlled by Israel at the time, such as Armon Hanatziv, Latrun, on the road to Jerusalem, and other areas.* According to a plan named Bnei Or ("Sons of Light"), in the event that the Arab states attacked Israel, the IDF would attempt to relocate the battlefields in their territories. Israel would be slow to vacate territories it was able to occupy, unless such withdrawals took place in the context of peace agreements that assured safer borders between Israel and its neighbors Jordan and Syria.[69] For years, Israel tried unsuccessfully to reach an agreement with Jordan to improve the border in the Latrun area. Israel's representative on the Mixed Armistice Commission felt that the state could achieve its objectives piecemeal, by simply farming the lands. "But we must make sure these steps do not make headlines." Rather, things should be done quietly, "by the JNF method, acre by acre." To the representative, access to Mount Scopus and the holy places was "a vision for the future." Eshkol devoted a great deal of thought to the situation on Mount Scopus. He asked the army for a plan to take East Jerusalem and join up with Israeli forces on the mount, in the event that the Jordanians tried to conquer it. This was considered a strategic objective not only for the sake of national dignity, but also because it was generally held that anyone controlling Mount Scopus was easily in a position to take over the entire West Bank.

A few of the generals who believed that Israel should expand its borders discussed taking over the West Bank and even debated what to do with it once it was conquered. The options were either to annex it to Jerusalem, or to set up a Palestinian buffer state. Shimon Peres, then the deputy minister of defense, said that the day of geography had passed and had given way to the day of technology: nuclear deterrence could make border expansion irrelevant. However, even if Israel's nuclear capabilities ultimately led to peace, as hoped, it might still be advisable to take preemptive steps to ensure more comfortable borders. The idea that the IDF might actively seek to expand Israel's borders came up repeatedly during the mid-1960s. The discussion was always confidential and the generals' positions did not figure much in public discourse. Eshkol told the General Staff that he ruled out any takeover of territories beyond the Green Line and cautioned against thinking of preemptive war and border

---

*One IDF general explained that Armon Hanatziv was worthy of occupation partly because of its "sentimental value."

alterations. But he, too, was unable to resist: for years, he had dreamed of the waters of the Litani River in Syria.*

Many Israelis, old enough to remember the days before the Green Line, were loath to internalize it as a permanent settlement. Some nurtured the memory in the context of an ideology that rejected partition of the land. "The West Bank was a part of my childhood landscape," wrote the historian Meron Benvenisti. Born in Jerusalem, he often went hiking with his father in Bethlehem, in Hebron, and at the Dead Sea. Benvenisti's father was a geographer who used to tell his son stories of treks through the Judean Desert. Benvenisti was a young boy during the War of Independence. On a January evening in 1948, he was playing basketball with a group of Hagana members in the Beit Hakerem school gym. Two days later they were all dead: they were part of the famous "Thirty-five," a group that had tried to reach the Gush Etzion region of Jewish settlements, which had been cut off from Jewish Palestine. The Gush settlements were conquered by Jordan. "We may not have felt, as others did, that the story began thirty-seven hundred years ago, when Abraham purchased the Tomb of the Patriarchs [in Hebron] from Ephron the Hittite. But for my generation and for my older friends, the West Bank was not a foreign land," Benvenisti wrote.

"I never lost Eretz Israel," Azariah Alon reflected. A member of the Mahanot Olim youth movement, Alon was known for his weekly radio broadcast on Saturday mornings, in which he directed his listeners on hikes around the country. Each Independence Day, he devoted his program to a site beyond the Green Line. In 1967, two weeks before the war, he spoke of Wadi Kelt, in the West Bank.

Mahanot Olim was part of the labor movement. It went through many incarnations, and its members founded several kibbutzim. The party to which it was affiliated, starting in the fifties, Ahdut Ha'avoda, was led by a much admired white-bearded old man named Yitzhak Tabenkin. Two of its primary figures were influential ministers, Israel Galili and Yigal Allon. Since the 1920s, Tabenkin had opposed all plans to partition the country; and he had agreed only reluctantly to the 1947 partition plan. His party objected to Israel's withdrawal from the territories occupied in October

---

*Early on in his term, Eshkol had raised the possibility that the Ba'ath party in Syria would agree to closer relations with Israel on an ideological basis, seeing that it shared Mapai's socialist principles. He hoped this would also bring about a thaw in relations with the Soviet Union. He understood that the idea was naïve, he said, but still he promoted it: Israel would be neutral, like Switzerland, and would withdraw from the UN.[70]

1956. The right to control the Gaza Strip and the Sinai Peninsula stemmed, Tabenkin claimed, from the Ten Commandments and from the blood of the soldiers killed during the campaign. He compared Nasser to Hitler, and the withdrawal to the Munich agreement.

Mahanot Olim members took excursions all over the country as part of their efforts to implement their right to the land. "I learned my love of the land through my feet," recalled Rina Klinow. "Every beautiful spot we hiked to, every lovely corner of landscape outside the communities where we camped—we would decide to go back when the time came and build a settlement." The poet Haim Gouri also participated in these trips; he said they added "a valuable component to the secret of the ancient connection between the People of Israel and the Land of Israel." The excursions were part of the collective biography of the founding generation, an ongoing initiation ceremony of sorts, in which the hiker seemed to be "entering a covenant with the land and discovering its expanses and its times." This was both an emotional phenomenon and an aspect of the Zionist ethos. "We turned our affair with the landscape into the primary force in our emotional world," wrote Benvenisti. "But we were not allowed to love the land with a quiet love, because our familiarity with it was an act of occupation: we were taught that by hiking in the desert, we were conquering—with our feet—its mountains and valleys. The roads and mountain paths would become Jewish when an Israeli vehicle drove across them. Archaeology, bird-watching, or plant identification was not simply a hobby or a profession but a means of taking title. Knowledge of the homeland and cultivation of the wilderness were firmer evidence of ownership than a property deed. After all, who makes an effort to cultivate something that is not his property?" In schools, geography was called homeland class.[71]

The establishment of the state within the Green Line did not alter the tendency thus expressed. A few hundred members of the Scouts set off to reenact the 1948 battles on the hills of Jerusalem, defending their camp against an attack by a gang of "Arabs." The students then reenacted the failed attempt of the "Thirty-five" to reach the Gush Etzion settlements. Since the area was now in Jordan, the Scouts' goal was an abandoned Arab village not far from their camp. On their way, they met "an elderly Arab" (one of the counselors) who misdirected them, in accordance with the story the students knew. In 1967, on the eve of Independence Day, prior to the war, a hundred students from the Or Etzion yeshiva held a race in memory of the Gush Etzion fighters. The race began at a point where the Gush was visible and ended at two settlements, Ein Zurim and

Masuot Yitzhak, which had been part of the original Gush bloc but had been "resettled" in the south of the country.

In 1966, Nathan Shaham and Shmuel Katz published a coffee-table book entitled *A Journey Through Eretz Yisrael*. Although Shaham, the author, and Katz, the illustrator, limited themselves to territory within the state's borders, they waxed nostalgic for the days when the land was wide open and expansive. The Yehiam newsletter reported that the book was extremely sought-after among kibbutz members. Amos Oz described kibbutzniks hiking among the ruins of an Arab village, searching for ancient shards and other "junk," as if only such a site, from before 1948, could represent the true Palestine. "The border itself is invisible, and there is no knowing precisely where the State of Israel ends and the Kingdom of Jordan begins," wrote a *Yediot Aharonot* reporter who visited the border village of Mei Ami. "The same hills, the same landscape, the same wonderful mountain air—one perfect continuum of a beautiful picture." This attitude had led a few adventurers to trespass into Jordan, attempting to reach Petra. The longing for the "Red Rock" of that city fostered a romantic legend of illegal border crossing, which fired the imaginations of many young people.[72]

Israeli students were not, on the whole, explicitly taught to long for territories beyond the Green Line. But some textbooks sent a double message, and there were frequent discussions of how schools should present the issue. In an interview with *Maariv* in 1963, the archaeologist Yigal Yadin said, "Our educators, as they stand before the children, and our authors, as they write their books, will have to decide: Shehem [Nablus]—is it ours or not? The Old City—is it the past or the future? In my opinion, the foundation of all education is truth. We must tell our children the truth: Hebron is not ours today, but it was in the past, when King David ruled. The fact that we have had to give it up today does not mean we should erase it from our people's history."[73]

Students could internalize the concept of "Greater Israel" just by glancing at the series of blue plastic binders published by the IDF's education corps in May 1959, under the rubric, "Israel from Dan to Eilat." Two of the booklets included the Gaza Strip and the Sinai Peninsula, and three the regions of Judea and Samaria. There were dozens of pictures of Jerusalem, but only two showed simply its Israeli part. Children who referred to the *Speaking Maps* atlas illustrated by Friedl Stern would have needed to be particularly attentive to notice that Judea, Samaria, and Gaza did not belong to the State of Israel, because Stern's illustrations gave the maps an attractively colorful uniformity. Some of the Arab towns and villages beyond the border were labeled with their Hebrew names from biblical times, including Eshtamoa, for Samua village. The Gaza Strip was included in the map of the Ashkelon region, with a note reading, "The city of Samson is surrounded by hostile refugees." The editors of the atlas, published jointly with the Ministry of Labor, reminded young readers that, as a result of the Sinai Campaign, Israel had controlled the Gaza Strip for four months. "We had to withdraw from it, but there is still great confidence and faith in a better future. . . ." Of Jerusalem, they said one could look out from a tall building to the Judean Desert, Bethlehem, and Anatot—all of which were in Jordan: "Expansive areas, rich in memories, that are under enemy control and toward which our eyes gaze longingly."

Many children during those years played Concentration, a real estate board game that was a precursor in Israel to Monopoly. Concentration included transactions involving a house in Hebron and a hotel in Jenin, or a house in Nablus and a hotel in Gaza, all outside Israeli territory. Palestine was depicted as one undivided entity, as it had been when the game was invented during the British Mandate.*

During the sixties, Yitzhak Tabenkin repeatedly maintained that the partition of the country would one day be revoked, either peacefully or by war. He did not back down from this position, although he did soften it for political advantage: while negotiating an alignment with Mapai before the 1965 elections for the Sixth Knesset, his party did not bring up the issue. But in June 1966, he said, "Anywhere war will allow, we shall go to restore the country's integrity." This was also the approximate position of Menachem Begin, the leader of Herut.

Begin's party was committed to Ze'ev Jabotinsky's views, also rooted in the twenties, thirties, and forties. Herut members sang an anthem with lyrics by Jabotinsky: "Like the pillar supporting a bridge / Like the backbone of man / The axis and bond of my country / Is the Jordan, the holy Jordan." This verse was followed by the refrain, "Two banks has the River Jordan. One is ours, the other one too."[†] In the fifties, Herut's logo was a map of Israel with a hand grasping a bayoneted rifle and it bore the slogan "Only Thus." The day after the declaration of independence, Begin

---

*The most popular radio station among Israeli youth was broadcast from Ramallah. A female DJ whose velvety voice gained her some notoriety played more current British and American music than did Kol Israel or the IDF station.[74]

†Other important poets, including Shaul Tchernichovsky and Uri Zvi Greenberg, expressed yearning in their poetry for a region that extended all the way to the Euphrates in Iraq.[75]

said, "The State of Israel has been founded, but let us remember that the homeland has not yet been liberated. . . . The soldiers of Israel will yet raise our flag above the Tower of David; our plow will yet till the fields of the Gilead." Begin often demanded that territories beyond the Green Line be "liberated," and he maintained that Hebron and Bethlehem, Shechem and even Amman were all an integral part of the Jewish homeland. His party's daily newspaper made a point of referring to the Kingdom of Jordan in quotation marks, and gave the same typographic treatment to the title of "King" when it preceded the names of the rulers of Jordan, Abdullah, Talal, and Hussein.

Upon the IDF's withdrawal from territories occupied in the Sinai Campaign, Begin chastised Ben-Gurion's government: "You have abandoned a liberated part of the homeland and delivered it knowingly to the enemy." Like Ahdut Ha'avoda, which underplayed its views on Greater Israel when it entered an alignment with Mapai, Begin was astute enough to establish Gahal, a parliamentary bloc with the Liberal party, without compelling his partners to accept his position. The demand for Greater Israel obligated only Herut, not the Gahal bloc.* "The integrity of the homeland is an irrelevant slogan, and in fact is no political slogan at all," concluded *Ha'aretz*. But in March 1966, Begin was still speaking in the Knesset of Israel's right to the homeland, "the land of our forefathers, which is one," and the members of his party's youth movement, Betar, were brought up in this spirit. Conquering Palestine was at the center of the discussion that year at the annual conference for biblical research; among the lecturers was a Jerusalem scholar named Israel Eldad, who presented a paper entitled "Conquering the Land as a Moral Act." Similar views were expounded by a few of the religious Zionist leaders. In a sermon on Independence Day in 1967, Rabbi Zvi Yehuda Kook told students at the Mercaz Harav Yeshiva in Jerusalem how he had grieved upon learning of the UN partition resolution two decades earlier. "Where is our Hebron—are we forgetting it?" he asked. "Where is our Shechem? Are we forgetting it? And where is our Jericho—are we forgetting it? And where is the eastern bank of the Jordan?"[77]

---

*The pragmatic establishment of Gahal enabled Ben-Gurion to offer Begin an absolution of sorts. "If Herut would be willing to join a government that strives for peace based on the status quo, it should not be rejected because it believes in 'Greater Israel,' which shall come when the Messiah comes," said Ben-Gurion, who by 1965 hated Eshkol even more than he hated Begin.[76]

• • •

THE DAY BEFORE THE INCIDENT THAT LED TO THE SAMUA OPERATION, *YEDIOT Aharonot* prominently featured a story related to the "weeping for generations"—a phrase that referred to grieving for the loss of territory left outside the 1949 cease-fire borders. The background was a chapter in a biography of Ben-Gurion, by Michael Bar-Zohar. According to Bar-Zohar, Ben-Gurion claimed that he had proposed conquering the West Bank during the War of Independence, but that the proposal was rejected by the government. The article sent a clear message: a weak and hesitant government had curbed a strong, battle-ready army. On the eve of Independence Day in 1967 *Maariv* published an interview with Yigal Yadin. The former IDF chief of staff did not often speak publicly about the War of Independence, so the interview was widely read and prompted heated responses. Yadin projected sorrow, regret, disappointment, and even pain over the fact that the Old City and other areas had not been conquered. His statements were interpreted as a personal attack on David Ben-Gurion. Yitzhak Rabin also assumed that Ben-Gurion had not wanted to conquer the West Bank. "Whatever Ben-Gurion truly desired, he could have made happen," he said.

That same week, *Ha'aretz* also recalled the omissions of 1948. Ze'ev Schiff, the military correspondent, published a piece about the failure of the battle for Jenin, the essence of which was regret that the city had not been taken and the IDF had withdrawn. One reader reinforced this thesis: had the IDF been victorious and taken the city, the Arab front on the Jordanian border would most likely have collapsed, the Iraqi army would have retreated, East Jerusalem would have been liberated, and the Jordan River would have become Israel's border. This scenario was assumed to be preferable to the existence of the Green Line.[78]

6. REFLECTIONS: "WE HAVE NOTHING TO OFFER"

As riots in Jordan intensified in the wake of the Samua operation, Israeli opinion makers and officials were thinking about how to divvy up the spoils. Herzl Rosenblum of *Yediot Aharonot* wrote of the possibility that Egyptian and Syrian forces would enter Jordan and carve it up between the two of them: "We should also have a share in the booty. Because before Jordan was 'Egyptian' or 'Syrian,' it was part of our own country and of the mandate we were given. Let the 'looters' beware."

Israel would not accept a foreign military presence in Jordan, declared

Minister of Labor Yigal Allon, and Moshe Dayan spoke of forming a confederation comprising Israel, the West Bank, and Jordan. Prime Minister Eshkol proclaimed that Israel reserved the right to act if the situation in Jordan deteriorated.[79] However, King Hussein managed to quell the protests, and a report authored by the Israeli Ministry of Foreign Affairs stated that his power had been underestimated. The king had in fact increased his prestige by mobilizing the army to challenge the Israeli forces attacking Samua. Egypt's failure to come to his aid constituted a warning to Syria, said the report; if terrorists operated from within Syrian borders and Israel attacked, Egypt would not help. The Syrians should be made unequivocally aware of this through appropriate leaks to the press, proposed the memorandum's author, Moshe Sasson, but the headlines appeared even before he had finished writing. "Egypt did not interfere in Samua out of fear of a surprise Israeli response," announced *Yediot Aharonot*. As *Maariv* put it, "The cannons roared but the Egypt-Syria defense pact was not implemented."[80]

The immediate question had been what Israel would do if the demonstrations had toppled Hussein's regime and brought down the monarchy. This was not the first time the question had concerned Israel. Shimon Peres had once suggested that if Hussein's rule collapsed, Israel should "appoint" an Israeli Arab in his place.[81] The discussion continued even after Hussein succeeded in quelling the riots. The prime minister's office accumulated information about Hassan, Hussein's brother and potential heir. Foreign Minister Eban thought that the West Bank could not exist as an independent state and it was therefore unlikely that Jordan would be dismantled, although it might become a republic. "How big is the West Bank?" Eshkol enquired. If Jordan were to become a republic, Eban continued, it might ask Syria and Egypt to post forces within its territory. Israel should be prepared for any eventuality. In response to a request by the director general of the Foreign Ministry that there be some "planning," Eban replied, "We could meet to analyze a few paradigms." But Rabin responded impatiently, "We can come up with 200 speculations," but there was no way to know exactly what would happen in Jordan. Rabin did not think an Iraqi battalion entering Jordan with tanks would compel Israel to "descend" on the country, and he also expressed confidence that the USSR would not interfere if Israel attacked Syria, even if it reached Damascus. "They may threaten us at worst," he believed. He seemed to be satisfied with the existing contingency plans. But Aharon Yariv, head of the IDF intelligence branch, was in favor of "sitting down together" to outline a plan of action.[82] In fact, Yariv was proposing deliberations that were already going on.

The most comprehensive political and strategic discussions preceding the Six-Day War began in November 1966 and concluded in January 1967. There were two working groups. The first examined relations with Jordan, the second those with Egypt. The participants, representatives of the Mossad, the IDF's intelligence branch, and the Foreign Ministry, labored to formulate joint answers to a series of questions posed by Abba Eban. The documents they prepared were approved by Rabin and Eshkol, and therefore reflect Israel's thinking six months before the war. The National Defense College also held extensive debates on the future of relations with Jordan, the conclusions of which were presented to the chief of staff.

The surviving protocols and position papers reflect certain disagreements, but on the whole the discussions were virtually devoid of emotionally or politically charged arguments. They were conducted in secret, although a few Knesset members, journalists, and professors were ultimately included.

The Mossad representative, Yitzhak Oron, asked whether Israel should "clean up" the West Bank, meaning to put an end to Palestinian centers of hostility. Shlomo Gazit, from army intelligence, said opinions on this in the IDF were divided. Some thought Hussein's regime was harmful to Israel because as long as he ruled, Israel could not invade the West Bank, which, in its current state of unrest, constituted "a catastrophe for Israel." Others believed that Hussein was "good for Israel." Gazit presented the compromise position: "The IDF accepts the current situation, but would welcome an opportunity to change the status quo to create a new and more comfortable one." Under the present conditions of hostile coexistence, he added, the Green Line represented a threat to the center of the country. But were the IDF to occupy the West Bank, Israel would have to consider what to do with it and, more specifically, whether it could annex it "without the annexed territory becoming a cancer that would gnaw away at Israel from the inside." In any event, Israel would not be annexing empty territory. To neutralize the dangers of the West Bank, continued Gazit, Israel should found an independent Palestinian state that would be completely dependent on the IDF for defense and internal order; in addition, Israel would oversee its foreign policy. Mordehai Gazit of the Foreign Ministry, the brother of Shlomo Gazit from military intelligence, responded unenthusiastically that this would be "a puppet regime."

The document Shlomo Gazit offered on behalf of the IDF gave a Palestinian protectorate only a slim chance. He presented another option, which he considered less advantageous to Israel: to post emergency forces on the border, whether as part of an international administration that would govern the area or as a buffer between Israel and Jordan. No such arrangement was likely to ensure a long-term solution, he said, and its purpose would be to afford a transition period "until the introduction of unconventional weapons into our region."[83] The Gazit brothers argued over this question. Shlomo Gazit said that the IDF's responses were appropriate "at least as long as the region does not enter the nuclear age," and added, "There are those who believe that the moment we enter the nuclear age there will no longer be any thought of destroying Israel." Mordehai Gazit responded, "As for the matter of nuclear weapons raised repeatedly in the document, I do not believe it holds the answer to terrorism."[84]

In a lecture at the National Defense College, Mordehai Gazit spoke of the possibility that Israel would occupy the West Bank. The countries of the world would not allow annexation, he said, and added the following consideration: "We had better be honest with ourselves. We are not interested today in annexing the West Bank, because our small state would immediately face an extremely dangerous situation. What would we do if the population in the West Bank, our sworn enemy, did not flee across the border?"[85]

In December 1966, General Elad Peled, the commander of the National Defense College, sent a highly confidential memo to the chief of staff, entitled "Jordan as a Military and Political Problem for Israel." Peled felt that the best situation for Israel was Jordan's continued existence as an independent and relatively weak state. He did not rule out having to attack Jordan—if the king were to be toppled, if he sent tanks into the West Bank, or if Jordan entered an active anti-Israel coalition and foreign Arab forces were placed in the West Bank. In any of these eventualities, Israel would not confine itself to a defensive posture, but would initiate preemptive attacks. The assumption was that this meant occupying the West Bank, and Peled reviewed at length the question of what to do with it. The document was a decisively secular and democratic one, with no mention of Jerusalem. Peled opposed any occupation, reasoning that the world would neither recognize the West Bank's annexation by Israel nor accept a puppet regime there. The UN could not govern the West Bank, so Israel would have to do so by itself. Any occupation of the West Bank would ultimately lead to a binational state in all of the country.

The college had commissioned a study of the West Bank's economic viability and the effects of occupation on Israel's economy. Zvi Zussman, who authored the study, concluded that Israel could afford to occupy and annex the West Bank, economically speaking. However, employing an old Zionist term that had fallen out of use, Peled argued that "the Yishuv"—the Jewish community in prestate Palestine—would move into white-collar professions, while Arab laborers would focus on "manual work," with the economic and social implications of such a division. Peled also analyzed at length the demographic significance of the West Bank. At the latest, he found, the Arab population would catch up with the Jewish population in 2050, but this was more likely to occur as early as 2035, perhaps sooner in certain areas of the country. He assumed that Israel would not deport the Arab population of the West Bank and that it could not deprive them of civil rights. A bloc of thirty to forty Arab seats would emerge in the Knesset. Arabs would become the second largest or even the largest party in the Knesset, Peled wrote. Israel would have to accept a large number of Arab ministers, and at least one of them would have to receive an "important" ministry overseeing large budgets. Some ambassadorships would have to go to West Bank residents, as "these positions cannot be given only to our own people for long." Some Jewish groups might try to withhold these rights from the Arabs, who would in turn revolt, forcing the Jewish majority to enact an iron-fisted policy that would include imposing harsh regulations and creating restricted areas of residence. This process could deteriorate into racism and oppression, which "we, as a people and as Jews, abhor, and which may cast the state in a dubious light and make its international position difficult." The concept of "restricted areas of residence" evoked the limitations on domicile and movement imposed on Russian Jews under the czars.

The Arabs, Peled continued, might form opposition movements, and Israel would then have to take steps characteristic of "a police state." If the Arabs were not enlisted in the IDF, their young people might come to constitute a hard core of national liberation fighters. The concentrated areas of Arab populations might serve as shelters for terrorist bases. It would also be necessary to provide the Arabs with education. Within a short while, there would emerge an educated Arab class demanding white-collar jobs. The separation between Jews and Arabs could not be preserved for long. Arabs would begin living in the big cities along the coast, and poverty-stricken Arab suburbs would develop. This would give rise to social problems necessitating large expenditures. The Arabs would influence the culture of those Israelis with similar cultural origins, namely the Mizrahim. There would be intermarriage, Peled further cautioned.[86]

The deliberations over a possible occupation of the West Bank and Jordan were thorough and profound, taking into consideration both advantages and, more often, disadvantages. In the end, everyone agreed that it would be to Israel's advantage for King Hussein to remain in power: he had, in effect, accepted Israel's existence, so Israel naturally had an interest in strengthening his regime. Hussein was also endeavoring to unify the West Bank with the East Bank and was encouraging West Bank Palestinians to migrate to the east. Over the preceding fifteen years, their numbers had reached 200,000. Moreover, Hussein allowed Palestinians to emigrate from Jordan, and approximately 100,000 of them had done so. "This is a positive phenomenon from Israel's point of view," concluded the final position paper that emerged from that winter's debates. In fact, Hussein was acting to eradicate the Palestinian question, and this was an excellent reason— indeed, an existential one—not to take the West Bank away from him.[87]

THE WORKING GROUP DISCUSSING THE CONFLICT WITH EGYPT ALSO INCLUDED PEOPLE from the Foreign Ministry, army intelligence, and the Mossad. The debate over Egypt was initiated by Eban, following a meeting in New York with an American businessman named Robert Anderson. A friend of Nasser's, Anderson had made unsuccessful attempts to mediate between him and David Ben-Gurion in the past. In August 1966, Anderson told Eban that Nasser's approach "had not changed for the worse," and Eban heard from others that Nasser's position was considered "moderate." In light of this, and of Nasser's proclamation that "the time is not right" for war with Israel, Eban asked for an analysis of whether there was a chance of negotiation.

At the end of November 1966, roughly two weeks after the Samua operation, there was a sudden flare-up along the normally quiet Egyptian border, and the Israeli air force shot down two Egyptian MiGs. In another development, Israeli intelligence learned that Egypt was reinforcing its troops in the northern Sinai. The IDF called up some two thousand reserve soldiers, but released them after a few days.[88]

The participants in the Egypt consultation were given two working papers, one prepared by IDF intelligence and classified as "confidential," the other written by the Mossad and classified as "highly confidential." Army intelligence asserted that Egypt aspired to destroy Israel and that there was no chance that Nasser would revise his position. Only deterrence would convince him that Israel could not be destroyed, and that recognition might one day lead him to a willingness to accept its existence. Israel could achieve this objective solely through military strength. The Mossad agreed that Egypt still aspired to eradicate Israel, but also examined the prospects for talks. If Israel could provide hundreds of millions of dollars in economic aid, Egypt might be interested in relations. But in aiding Egypt, Israel would be strengthening it, against Israel's own interests. The Mossad suggested that Israel could encourage Egypt to tone down its propaganda, and perhaps offer to establish a Palestinian state "in place of Jordan or as a result of Jordan's dismantling."

There was one more option: Israel could offer to halt its nuclear program, in return for Egypt's ending the arms race and leaving in place the current balance of power. Egypt, the Mossad argued, lagged behind Israel by five to ten years in this area, and the attempt to catch up was a heavy burden on its economy. The Mossad's conclusion was that "at the present time, the only significant interest shared by the two sides is to be found in this issue." But the Mossad estimated that Egypt would not wish to limit its military power with respect to other states in the region. "The question that comes up repeatedly is whether Israel is capable of exploiting its advantage over the next few years in the nuclear area, putting pressure on Egypt. This question is today perhaps the most important one in the overall relationship between Israel and Egypt." Both parties had an interest in preventing accidental war, but even in this regard it was doubtful that Egypt would agree to a fail-safe arrangement, the Mossad believed, and so it concluded that the chance of talks occurring was slim. The agency did not rule out, however, the possibility of an "open channel," a pipeline that could be activated from time to time.

Another argument arose between the two Gazit brothers on this issue. Shlomo, from army intelligence, held that there was no chance that Egypt would revise its position on Israel. He posited two theses that, within a few months, turned out to be mistaken. First, he said, "it is clear to us that the Egyptians cannot risk war against Israel for the next five years." Second, "while in the past it was clear that Israel could occupy the Sinai, it is now apparent that if the Egyptian army were to concentrate its forces there, Israel could not conquer it." He therefore emphasized the need for "qualitative superiority" of an unspecified nature, and said that in the meantime Israel must maintain peace along the borders. However, Mordehai Gazit, the diplomat, searched for ways to open talks with Nasser. "At some point we will even be able to influence the U.S. president to supply food aid to Nasser, reasoning that in return we could strengthen our relationship with him." His brother objected. Such an initiative could cause more harm than good, he said. But, like the Mossad, he did not rule out an attempt at secret talks with the Egyptians.*

---

*In early 1966, Meir Amit, head of the Mossad, who had ties with a senior figure in the Egyptian regime, proposed that Eshkol allow him to travel to Cairo to pursue negotiations. Eshkol thought such a step would be too dangerous. Amit believed that Israel thereby missed a historic opportunity.[89]

One Foreign Ministry official asserted, "If Israel obtains atomic weapons it will be safe from destruction. If it does not obtain such weapons, it must not be satisfied with the current situation and must act to thwart Nasser." The ministry officials were slightly more optimistic than the military and Mossad people, but they were basically in agreement: Nasser had not abandoned his dream of destroying Israel, and the safest way of stopping him was to preserve Israel's deterrent forces. This was also the view of the National Defense College, after months of studying the topic. "The current regime in Egypt sees the obliteration of Israel as one of its fundamental policy objectives."[90]

This, in effect, concluded the debate on Egypt. But the head of the Mossad, Meir Amit, believed that the pessimism projected by the team's final document necessitated further examination: "The truth is that it is so pessimistic that we ourselves were alarmed after reading it." And so one evening he invited a few Knesset members to his home, as well as two distinguished professors from the Hebrew University and three commentators from the daily press. They were met there by officials from the Foreign Ministry, the army intelligence, and the Mossad.

The identity of the head of the Mossad was one of Israel's top secrets. Knesset members and senior media figures probably knew who he was, but Amit's opening of his home for such a consultation was an extraordinary event. His intellectual open-mindedness reflected a fundamental characteristic of Israeli society: the senior elite was composed of people who were privy to state secrets, and they all knew one another, trusted one another, and commonly boasted not only of knowing secrets but also of keeping them. There were senior journalists who belonged to the Israeli aristocracy of secrets, and they did not usually feel that this status conflicted with the fundamental requirements of their profession. In this respect, Amit was not taking a real risk by inviting them. The three journalists were Dr. Shlomo ("Poles") Gross from *Ha'aretz*, Shmuel Schnitzer from *Maariv*, and Arel Ginai from *Yediot Aharonot*. Amit told the group that their goal was self-examination, and asked Knesset member Yaakov Riftin, from Mapam, to begin.

Mapam was in the coalition government, but Riftin was known for his dovish positions. He suggested that Israel support the return of Palestinian refugees, "under specified conditions," and proposed "saying something about a federation with Jordan." He believed that contact with Egypt could be made through neutral countries, and he offered a few other suggestions. But he did not delude himself: he did not expect peace to prevail, and would be content with the avoidance of war. Dr. Gross raised the idea that Israel might allow Egypt to take control of the entire Middle East; in return, Egypt would "stop this nonsense about the refugees" and recognize the State of Israel "as it is." But he did not truly believe this could happen: "We have nothing to offer." Knesset member Yizhar Harari, from the Independent Liberals, had an original proposition: "It is worthwhile developing nuclear weapons, so that we will one day be able to give them up." But like Gross, he had little faith in his own proposal: "I do not think that we can compromise [with Nasser] on much of anything." Schnitzer brought up the territorial claims. While Israel could perhaps renounce some parts of Palestine in return for peace, he did not believe that doing so was practical. "We cannot buy anything from Nasser," he said, because the Egyptian president's position was a matter of patriotism, and patriotism was not for sale, not even with Nasser. The sociologist S. N. Eisenstadt said there was no chance of a broad agreement, but only of "small deals" over "insubstantial things" that would bring about the creation of trust: one could unload as much baggage as possible, thaw things out, and try to maneuver in a limited way, "very slowly." In the meantime, there was nothing to be gained by the media's hysterical propaganda against Nasser. The rest of the participants, including a prominent Middle Eastern scholar, and another Knesset member from Mapam, agreed there was no chance of talks with Nasser.

And so the guests of the Mossad chief parted. Most Israelis would agree with their basic conclusion, which was partly based on a statement attributed to Nasser himself, in an interview with *Life* magazine that was published in full in Hebrew. The only way to solve the conflict with Israel, said Nasser, was to return all the refugees to their homes. The Israelis, after all, wanted immigrants from other countries, such as Russia, so why should they not take in the Palestinians? Nasser asserted that all the refugees wished to return, in case there was any doubt. He understood, of course, that this was not feasible, but he claimed that financial compensation could not be considered a substitute for the right of return. If this was the case, the American interviewer suggested, then war was inevitable. True, Nasser confirmed, but he added that there was no rush: the Egyptians had inhabited the Nile Valley for thousands of years, and had always been victorious. Time was on their side. He repeated this thesis over the next months.[91] The Israeli army, meanwhile, was conducting extensive discussions on the future of relations with Syria.

CHAPTER 4

THE SYRIAN SYNDROME

1. CONFRONTATIONS I: "IS DISHON WORTH DYING FOR?"

At the beginning of 1966, Syrian artillery shelled the northern kibbutzim of Tel Katzir, Gadot, Ein Gev, and others. "We weren't afraid," a child from Kibbutz Ha'on was quoted as saying in *Maariv*, "but we wanted to go outside and pick flowers." The children did not understand why plowing their fields was leading to bloodshed. "Why do they want our fields?" a child from Tel Katzir asked in *Yediot Aharonot*. According to *Maariv*, farming lands along the border was the most courageous job of the day. "These strong, young tractor drivers, operating armored tractors, and these kibbutz members going about their daily business, are the heroes who protect the sovereignty of vulnerable sites along the border." The paper offered a historical perspective: "World War II first saw the Japanese kamikaze pilots. These suicidal pilots crashed into Allied ships as if to declare, 'Let us die [like Samson] with the Philistines!'" Unlike them, said the paper, the tractor drivers were not suicidal: they were young men with a thirst for life. But they knew full well that the job must be done and that it demanded great courage, "no less than the kamikaze fliers demonstrated in their time."

Over the next few months, tensions between Israel and Syria increased and the air force was eventually deployed, shooting down a Syrian MiG in July. Ze'ev Schiff of *Ha'aretz* determined, "There is no chance of reaching any settlement with the Syrians, even one from which the Syrians would derive the most benefit." He explained that, unlike other states, Syria was ruled by "unregulated Arab gangs. Even when there is a chance of reaching an arrangement along the border, we do not know if the person talking with us today will be there tomorrow to fulfill his promises." A few months later, Schiff wrote, "Syria is dragging Israel into war."[1] The military held the same view.

The conflict with Syria developed on three tracks: the struggle over water and the Syrians' attempts to divert the Jordan River, quarrels over agricultural lands in the demilitarized zones along the border, and the Fatah operations. The water issue was especially dear to Eshkol's heart, according to the prime minister's military secretary, Israel Lior, since he had once been involved in the development of the water system. According to Lior, Eshkol used to surprise his staff by spontaneously recalling facts and figures about the water supply. He understood that without control over water Israel could not realize the Zionist dream. Eshkol later attributed to himself the phrase, "Water is blood." Historian Ami Gluska, who focused on the question of Israel's struggle with Syria over control of the water supply, wrote, "In the battle over water, the IDF gained an easy and cost-free victory, managing to disrupt the Arab diversion plan by simple, cheap, and effective means, striking locally without risking full-scale military conflict." But Syrian attempts to divert the Jordan's waters did not stop completely, and the IDF occasionally intervened. Yitzhak Rabin later confirmed that Israel had "staged" at least one incident that enabled it to bomb Syrian tractors working on water diversion.*

The 1949 cease-fire line between Israel and Syria did not correspond to the international border between the two countries, and there were demilitarized zones to which neither side was permitted entry. The question was whether Syrian or Israeli farmers were allowed to work these lands. The dispute sometimes seemed to be a conflict between farmers and shepherds, while at other times an argument among experts in international law. Some of the landowners were Syrian, some Israeli, some were neither. Some of the lands belonged to Baha'i citizens of Iran. One plot was a square within a square: the owners of the outer square were Israelis, while the owners of the inner square were Syrians who could not farm their land without crossing the Israeli perimeter. Some farmers, both Syrian and Israeli, claimed that over the years they had purchased "right of possession" to certain lands. There were also areas to which Israel and Syria attributed strategic value. Some bore names like "Horseshoe," "Little Table," and "Legume Plot."[2]

---

*Rabin revealed how he had forced residents out of two villages in the demilitarized zone and into Syria. "How did we do it? There were threats, of course, and then they signed documents stating that they were moving of their own free will."

Not all the incidents in the demilitarized zones were instigated by the Syrians. Moshe Dayan later claimed that 80 percent erupted as a result of Israeli attempts to farm there, and that they were unnecessary. "It would go like this. We would send a tractor to plow the earth in some plot you couldn't do anything with, in a demilitarized zone, knowing in advance that the Syrians would start shooting. If they didn't shoot, we would tell the tractor to go farther, until finally the Syrians would lose their temper and shoot. And then we'd fire back, and later send in the Air Force." Dayan explained that the tension caused by Israel on the Syrian border did not reflect a strategic approach, but rather the fact that Israel did not take the cease-fire seriously. "We thought at the time, and this went on for quite a while, that we could move the cease-fire lines by using military action that was less extreme than war. Meaning, taking over some land and holding on to it until the enemy gave up and let us keep it." One could say this represented "a certain naïveté on our part," Dayan conceded, but one also had to remember that the state had not existed for very long. Either way, he said, "we thought of the cease-fire lines as a temporary arrangement." He claimed that the Syrians did not treat the agreement seriously, either.

The head of the UN observer team, General Odd Bull, proposed various agreements to enable agricultural work to proceed along the border. Rabin invited him to lunch and told him it was difficult to reconcile the Syrians' interest in an agreement with their terrorist activities. After lunch, Rabin went to the IDF's Command and Staff School, where he gave a speech that made headlines the next day: "Syria Operating 'Popular War' and Sabotage Units in Israel." Bull wrote to Ralph Bunche that Rabin's declaration would not make his efforts any easier.[3]

Relations between Syria and Fatah were ambiguous. In August 1966, Yaacov Herzog, director general of the prime minister's office, wrote in his diary that the Syrians were trying to take over Fatah, restrict its independence, and integrate it into the army as one of its commando units. "It is clear to us that the recent operations are the acts of the [Syrian] units and not Fatah," wrote Herzog, but he also thought it possible that the commando units were operating without the knowledge of the Syrian authorities. Information was scant, Herzog wrote, but he maintained that Syria was training Fatah, and that as far as Israel was concerned, it was therefore responsible for the organization's activities. He assumed that had the Syrian army wanted to rein them in, it would have done so. Roughly three months later, a Foreign Ministry official reported to the Israeli embassies that Syria was demanding that Fatah exercise restraint. It was acting out of fear of Israeli retaliation, as well as in response to pressure from the Soviet Union, which had an interest in preventing escalation. Fatah, wrote the official, still maintained a degree of independence, and it was unclear to what extent the Syrians could exert control.[4]

The newspapers, the primary source of information for most Israelis, favored the opinion that Syria was to blame, just as they had believed in the fifties that Egypt was responsible for commando activities carried out by Palestinian guerrillas. A state with a capital and a government and an army could be related to. The still nascent Palestinian organizations were more elusive. They had no clear address and were difficult to explain to readers. The papers usually painted a straightforward picture: the Syrians were harassing Israel because they hated it. When S. Y. Agnon received the Nobel Prize in Literature, *Maariv* wrote, "There is no doubt that bestowing the literary award on a Hebrew author who resides in Israel will arouse much anger in Damascus, as well as in Cairo and the other centers of hatred and incitement."[5]

ONE DAY IN THE SUMMER OF 1966, AN ISRAELI NAVY PATROL BOAT RAN AGROUND ON A sandbank not far from the eastern shore of Lake Kinneret, in the Galilee. It was a sensitive area, as the Syrians were only a few yards away. The patrol had needed authorization from the prime minister, and according to Israel Lior, Eshkol had given permission because it was fishing season, he had a sentimental fondness for the fishing business, and the patrol would provide protection for the fishing boats. But when he heard that the patrol boat had gone almost as far as the Syrian shore, he "grew very angry." The night before, he had gone to bed late and so his staff chose not to wake him to report the incident. When Eshkol's military secretary phoned, he was not available to take the call. But he did later take part in the technical discussions of how to free the ship. When he was told that the IDF did not have the right kind of cable, he fumed, "I will personally get hold of the cable!" He asked for Moshe Yulish, the director of the Koor building concern, recalling having once seen the proper cable in his yards. The story illuminates much about Eshkol's intimate relationship with the army, and about the dynamics of the entire Arab-Israeli conflict. Eshkol spent the whole day overseeing the efforts, demanding to know where Yulish was and what was going on with the cable. He also wanted to know exactly how the cable would be attached. Rabin himself, in civvies, boarded the boat.

According to Lior, Rabin requested and received permission from Eshkol to send out patrol flights over Syrian military posts while the rescue attempt was under way. In a report by Odd Bull, it is unclear which country deployed its aircraft first. Either way, both Lior and Bull agreed that the situation brought the two countries to the brink of war, because at some point an air battle ensued during which the Israeli air forced down two Syrian planes. The military correspondent for *Maariv*, Yaakov Erez, observed the fight: "They descended upon us like birds of prey. Birds of prey after our lives . . . all they wanted was blood." When the Israeli planes arrived, "I tasted for the first time the flavor of sweet revenge."

A downed Syrian plane and its pilot plunged into the Kinneret, which complicated the situation to no end. In the background was a struggle among the army, the Foreign Ministry, and the UN: Bull wanted to delay any further military activity, and Eban, who was inclined to agree, bought time by suspending contact with the prime minister's office so they could not find him. The IDF was pressing for more action, without the involvement of the UN. "My impression was that the IDF and the Ministry of Defense did not want UN assistance, if only for reasons of prestige," wrote Lior. In the end the correct cable was found. Efforts to free the boat went on all night, and Eshkol did not rest, but in the morning he was told the attempt had failed. The boat was only extricated a few days later. According to Bull, Syrian frogmen had managed in the meantime to secretly retrieve their pilot's body. The IDF was startled by what it saw as the Syrians' willingness to attack the boat, and their boldness was interpreted as a new stage in the conflict.[6]

"I had a bad feeling," Lior wrote, reviewing the whole incident. "I kept thinking Yitzhak Rabin was suffering from what's called Syrian syndrome." As he explained, the syndrome affects almost anyone who does military duty on the northern border, himself included. "Serving on that border, opposite the Syrian enemy, inflames extraordinary hatred toward the Syrian army and people." He maintained that there was no resemblance between Israeli attitudes toward the Syrians and the attitude toward the Jordanian or even the Egyptian army. He did not explain the roots of the "Syrian syndrome," but noted, "We loved to hate them."*

Eshkol was aware of the phenomenon. When Rabin once suggested that Israel begin to farm a piece of land nicknamed the Yellow Plot, Eshkol feared an incident. Rabin tried to reassure him: "We're not sending tanks or anything. If there is an incident, we'll get out." Lior was

---

*When the Syrians refused to give back a soldier who had crossed the border, apparently by mistake, Lior wrote, "This added a little to the heavy sense of bitterness [in Eshkol] and the desire to hurt the Syrians, even to take revenge."

afraid of a trap: if an exchange of gunfire took place, there would be no choice but to bring tanks into the area, and this would send the whole region up in flames. Eshkol asked, "What will we do if they don't let us farm it?" and Rabin promised, "We'll bring you a proposal." Eshkol feared for the safety of the tractor drivers: "Maybe we should put four thick steel plates around the driver's compartment?" Rabin replied that a driver in a steel box without a roof could be hit from above. "Then make a roof," Eshkol replied; "we're not going to just send people out there." Rabin said if that was the case, it was better to send in armored tractors. He confirmed that their use could be interpreted as a provocation, but Eshkol opted for the drivers' safety.[7]

Discussions among the General Staff and statements made in other IDF forums confirm Lior's opinion that the generals viewed Syria as Israel's foremost enemy and thought it should be attacked forcefully in a large-scale military operation.[8] The press was also recruited to give voice to this view. During the eighteen months leading up to the Six-Day War, the papers often printed threats against the Syrians. It is difficult to say when the reporters and analysts were speaking for themselves and when they were expressing the opinions of the political or military figures who briefed them. "We are determined to protect the country from any incursion, and anyone who infiltrates our territory must take into account that Israeli security forces will pursue them, even beyond the border," wrote *Ha'aretz* in August. That same day, *Maariv* wrote, "The border will no longer protect the Syrians."

Against this background, a dispute arose between Rabin and Eshkol. Rabin was popular with the media and impressed readers with his analytical skills; he often voiced political opinions. Eshkol generally trusted Rabin—to a great extent, the IDF chief of staff served as the true minister of defense—but he felt that Rabin was stealing the spotlight. Lior thought Eshkol was jealous, observing graciously, "Even the prime minister is only human."[9]

The IDF weekly, *Bamahane*, published the traditional holiday interview with the chief of staff on Rosh Hashana. Eshkol authorized the interview on condition that Rabin restrict himself to technical military matters and avoid political pronouncements. The interview included the following remark: "The response to Syrian acts, be they terrorism, water diversion, or border hostilities, should be aimed at those who carry out the attacks and at the regime that supports them. . . . The problem with Syria, then, is essentially a clash with the regime." The choice of words was unfortunate. Amplified by subsequent inaccurate quotes in the daily press, they were interpreted as a plot to bring down the Syrian government, whose leaders had seized control in a military coup only six months earlier.

Eshkol lost his temper in response to the interview and decided to reprimand Rabin. He summoned him and, in his presence, asked Yaacov Herzog what he thought of the comments. Herzog was in an awkward position: "I wondered why the prime minister could not speak with the chief of staff on his own and why he was setting me up against him." The scene reflected the essence of Eshkol's relationship with Rabin. The prime minister did not want a confrontation with the popular chief of staff; he probably feared he would lose. Rabin claimed that *Maariv* had twisted the things he had said to *Bamahane*. He asked to compare the two versions. Herzog said that even the *Bamahane* interview gave the impression that Israel was planning to attack Syria. Rabin said that this was not so, but that he did not mind if the prime minister publicly disagreed. Eshkol told Herzog to draft a government statement for the press. Herzog realized that Eshkol had found an opportunity to put a stop to Rabin's political statements. "Maybe he'll get the hint and tone down the self-promotion," Herzog wrote, echoing Eshkol's own thoughts.

The difficulties of phrasing the statement reflect the extent to which ego and politics were involved in formulating Israel's security policy. The problem was that three things had to be achieved simultaneously, wrote Herzog: the statement must "imply" a reprimand of the chief of staff, but "not go too far"; outline a policy toward Syria that would clarify that the chief of staff's view did not reflect the government's position; and yet still contain a warning to the Syrians. It was a task well suited to Herzog's diplomatic skills.

The government made only "slight revisions" to Herzog's proposed wording: Israel did not interfere with the internal affairs of other countries, and it wanted peace. The statement thereby seemed to diverge from Rabin's. The greatest difficulty was what to say about Rabin himself. Herzog suggested that Eshkol declare, "I have spoken with the chief of staff regarding a certain section of the interview," and add that the chief of staff had "explained that in certain newspapers his words were misinterpreted. Security and political announcements are made solely by the prime minister and the minister of defense." Rabin, arguing that the newspapers should not be accused of distortion so casually, refused to accept this language. That part of the statement was struck. Rabin also demanded that the paragraph discussing him come at the end of the statement rather than the beginning. And he objected to Eshkol saying that Israel did not interfere with other states' affairs: would it not interfere in Jordan if King Hussein were to lose power? Herzog thought this was a "baseless" objection and sought advice from Minister Israel Galili, himself a master of rhetoric. They went to see Eshkol, with three of his senior assistants, and found him with Foreign Minister Eban. Eshkol was asking Eban for a response to an interpretation of Rabin's interview given on Radio Moscow. Then they all discussed whether the reprimand Herzog proposed was severe enough. Rabin might resign, Eban cautioned. "The prime minister sighed and crossed out the harshest words."

Furious, Rabin enforced military censorship, to which all the media were subject, to limit discussion of the affair. "It is interesting to see how extremely sensitive people seem to be insensitive when it comes to hurting others," Herzog observed. "Rabin finds no fault in his own infringement of the prime minister's authority day and night with political statements, but when someone else calls his behavior into question, the world turns upside down." Eshkol said he had handled Rabin with kid gloves and wanted to know why he was kicking up such a fuss.[10]

Eshkol himself began issuing frequent warnings to Syria, probably in part so as not to be outdone by Rabin. In October he said in the Knesset, "If the acts of sabotage and murder continue, we will take steps to stop them." The possibility of Israel acting against Syria had of course been in the air for months. "The Syrians seem to be doing everything they can to leave Israel with no choice but to halt their acts of terrorism and sabotage through unequivocal and conspicuous retaliation," asserted *Maariv*.[11]

ON THE SABBATH OF JANUARY 14, 1967, FATAH MEN STRUCK AT A REMOTE MOSHAV NOT far from the Lebanese border. Most Israelis had probably never heard of Dishon, inhabited primarily by immigrants from North Africa. This time the Palestinians attacked with a force that prompted even the normally restrained *Ha'aretz* to declare, "We cannot ignore the psychological implications of what happened in Dishon." One resident, Yosef Cohen, was killed when he stepped on a mine hidden in a wooden box. Cohen was an eighteen-year-old soldier home for the weekend. The mine had been laid in the local soccer field and exploded during a league match. Another undetonated mine was found on the field. A few hours earlier, an explosive device had blown up near the moshav's pumping facility, and subsequent searches revealed additional devices.[12]

The attack affected the residents' morale. *Yediot Aharonot* wondered on their behalf, "Is Dishon worth dying for?" There was a danger that they would leave the moshav. "It's time to take control," the paper continued, and then tried to divine what UN observers might be thinking: Dishon, they feared, might become a small-scale Sarajevo, a dot on the map that started an all-out war. The military commentator for *Ha'aretz* reported, "Israel is considering its response." According to Israeli intelligence, the Syrians feared that an attack might occur "within minutes."[13]

Roughly two weeks earlier, the IDF had renewed a practice of firing at Syrian farmers and shepherds who crossed into the demilitarized zones. This usually involved small arms and was meant to force the Syrians back, a tactic referred to in military parlance as buffer fire.[14] Over the previous six months there had been a cease-fire in the area, mediated by the UN, but Rabin managed to convince Eshkol that the agreement served Syrian interests: the farmers and shepherds were expanding their land, while Fatah continued to receive support. The Syrians responded immediately to the Israeli fire, deploying tanks and heavy artillery against tractors in fields belonging to Kibbutz Ha'on and Kibbutz Tel Katzir. The government restrained the army at first, forbidding it from returning tank fire. The policy of restraint was championed by the minister of the interior, Haim Moshe Shapira. There was a distinct confrontation between doves and hawks, and the military eventually won out. Over Shapira's protests, the army was allowed to respond with tank fire and Eshkol was authorized to deploy the air force.

Then, within days, the Syrians opened tank fire on an abandoned spot called Nutra. Eshkol refused to allow a response—thus, Rabin claimed, diminishing the IDF's status as a deterrent. Rabin had a strong case, as the IDF's deterrence capabilities were considered even by doves to be the best way to protect security without resorting to war. Because the government could not accurately assess the degree to which deterrence had been weakened, it was difficult to argue with Rabin. The government required a significant amount of fortitude to hold back the army. Demanding a "restoration of deterrence," Rabin proposed provoking the Syrians. If they opened tank fire again, the IDF would respond with tank fire; if they fired artillery, the air force would be activated. Shapira faced off with Yigal Allon, the minister of labor, who supported Rabin and objected to ministerial interference in military actions "on issues that are not matters of principle." However, the question of principle was, of course, whether these remote fields were worthy of a military conflict whose outcome was unpredictable. "We know that using airplanes will open the door to more serious clashes and this may bring about war," said Shapira. Allon responded, "If we exercise more restraint, the provocations will intensify."

Eshkol told the cabinet about his visit to the northern kibbutzim. "The members are on pins and needles and say they cannot continue this way." He noted that incursions by Syrian farmers and shepherds in the demilitarized zones had cost Israel about two hundred acres of land. He did not rule out activating the air force. But Shapira threatened to resign if he did so, and the minister of religious affairs, Zerah Warhaftig, joined him, as did the Mapam ministers. Their threats led the government to decide against calling in the air force. Israeli farmers were restricted to working in undisputed areas, but the IDF was permitted to open tank fire if Syrian tanks appeared.

According to a book published years later by the Ministry of Defense, Rabin himself determined that had Israel allowed the Syrian farmers and shepherds to work in the demilitarized zones, tensions would not have escalated. The intensification along the border was a result of Israel's decision to resume buffer fire, following six months of quiet.[15] And then Yosef Cohen was killed on the soccer field in Dishon.

Two days after Cohen's death, various assessments were presented at the General Staff meeting. Rabin said the device had been a mine with shrapnel, obviously homemade. "Fairly similar to our own mines," added Ezer Weizman, and Israel Tal commented that in World War II the Germans used to lay similar mines in wooden boxes, so that the victim would not be killed but only have his leg blown off. "All in all, it was a well-executed operation," Rabin continued, "outperforming [Israel's] operations up to this point." A search of the site revealed food scraps left by the assailants, which led investigators to believe that they had returned to Syria, although they were unsure whether that was where they had set out from. Tal wondered why the terrorists had chosen such a remote target, and Rabin explained, "There are Dishon people among the Palestinian commandos."[16] Dishon had been built on the ruins of the Arab village of Dayshum, whose inhabitants fled in 1948.*

On the same day as the General Staff meeting, a special session of the Mixed Armistice Commission was convened. "In view of the meeting, the possibility of response to Dishon was immediately dropped," said Rabin.[18] Eshkol took advantage of this restraint to win points in Washington. "Today I made the most difficult decision not to authorize a military reaction to the brutal Syrian provocation that took place yesterday morning," he wrote to President Johnson, and described the attack in Dishon

---

*A few of Dayshum's inhabitants had arrived in the mid-nineteenth century from Algeria, as had some of the Jews who settled in Dishon in the early 1950s.[17]

as the apex of Syrian aggression, following ten days of shelling Israeli populated areas and shooting at Israeli fishermen on Lake Kinneret. "The country is seething with indignation," wrote Eshkol. Johnson quickly expressed his regret for the tragedy in Dishon, admitted that no government could remain indifferent to such events, and mentioned the technology the United States had offered Israel to help stop border infiltrations, technology he said was better than retaliation. He promised that the U.S. ambassador to Damascus would clarify the gravity of the situation to the Syrians.[19]

THE RELATIONSHIP BETWEEN JERUSALEM AND WASHINGTON AT THE TIME WAS CLOSE TO ideal. In October 1966, Abba Eban had conferred with his American counterpart, Dean Rusk, on various issues. Ambassador Harman summed up the significant points of the conversation, which, he wrote, was conducted in a "decidedly intimate" atmosphere. "When the problem of Syria was mentioned, Rusk gave us to understand that he knew this was a special problem for us and he had not a single word of criticism over our policy toward Syria."

The USSR, on the other hand, supported Syria's military rulers, though it also denounced the Fatah operations. The Soviets declared that Israel had aligned itself with the imperialist camp and was planning to attack Syria. They also vetoed proposed UN Security Council resolutions denouncing Syria. The Russians had previously cautioned Israel against attacking Syria, and Ambassador Dimitri Chuvakhin even claimed that Israel was deploying forces along the border. Eban suggested he visit the north to see with his own eyes that there was no military deployment, but the ambassador turned down the offer. A few weeks later, the Soviets tried to clarify the issue of troops deployment with the heads of the Israeli Communist party. Toward the end of 1966, Eshkol had again invited Chuvakhin to tour the north, and the ambassador once again refused.[20] Israel denied the Soviet claims. "Instead of warning the aggressor, they warn the victim," Eshkol complained. To the assertion that Israel was aligned with "the imperialists" he responded almost with insult: "Israel the liberator, which freed its people from the generations-long bonds of exile and ghettoization; Israel, a victim of pogroms all over the world, that now returns to its homeland after thousands of years; Israel, the first to rid itself of a foreign power when it realized that this power could not fulfill its hopes—*we* are being driven by imperialism?"

But at the end of December 1966, Shlomo Argov at the Israeli embassy in London raised a question that had troubled him for some time: was it possible that Israel was unwittingly becoming a pawn of foreign oil companies? The Soviets believed this was the case, and Argov wondered whether it might not hold "a grain of truth." Argov was an independent thinker as a diplomat. "I was struck by the way the British ambassador to Israel [Michael Hadow] practically encouraged us openly to strike against the Syrians," Argov wrote. "To my knowledge, Hadow moved among various circles in Israel offering encouragement in this direction. Today we are witnessing a confrontation between IPC [the Iraq Petroleum Company] and Syria. Is it conceivable, then, that Hadow's campaign was connected with British oil interests, whereby a destructive Israeli blow against Syria would have brought down the radical regime and prevented the current crisis? It may sound absurd, but is it, perhaps, not that absurd?"

Meanwhile, Israel continued to warn the Syrians and eventually turned to the Security Council. "One can restrain oneself until it is simply intolerable," said Eshkol at Tel Katzir; he made similar comments to the cabinet. "Israel will not accept this," "an intolerable situation," "the end of patience is nearing," and other such statements were intended, it seems, to appease the cabinet. Eban, too, said, "We will not accept this."

The Syrians and the Russians had no reason to take these remarks lightly. The U.S. ambassador in Damascus was instructed to convey a harsh warning, almost a threat: "We believe Israel is on the brink of an attack and [the Syrians] cannot count on us to hold Israel back." According to "credible information" obtained by Israeli intelligence, the Russians were also pressuring the Syrians not to tangle with Israel.[21] This prompted a debate in the General Staff at the end of January 1967 on the future of relations with Syria; Eshkol was among the participants. The discussion was, at times, rather embarrassing.

2. CONFRONTATIONS II: "WE'RE NOT GOING TO KILL SEVEN MILLION SYRIANS!"

Much like the analysis of Israel's relations with Jordan and Egypt, the Syria discussion touched on fundamental questions. The minutes reflect the General Staff's opinion that Israel had been rendered virtually helpless in the face of Fatah infiltrations, and therefore must conduct a large-scale operation against Syria. Eshkol tried to rein in the army.[22] Colonel David Carmon, the deputy head of army intelligence, named the various Palestinian organizations and proceeded to describe the leaders of the

Syrian regime. They were intelligent and flexible; they took the initiative, and they knew when to take chances and when not to. They acted despite their very strong sense of threat and were prepared to take risks, even if doing so elicited retaliation, which they estimated would not be too severe. Eshkol wanted to understand the Syrian interest in the demilitarized zones. Carmon said the Syrians wanted to farm that land. He began analyzing the situation in the demilitarized zones region by region: here, the Syrians were on a sounder legal footing than Israel; there, Israel was better off. But Rabin interrupted him, claiming the legal and agricultural issues were secondary. The central problem was that Syria wanted to be the spearhead in an Arab war against Israel. The diversion of the Jordan River was another essential problem, as was the "popular war"—the Palestinian infiltrations. These problems demanded immediate solutions, but there were no clear answers.

Rabin proposed a number of options. First, Israel could increase its intelligence effort using secret agents born in the countries in which they would operate. Another option was the "Star of David line," which involved sealing all Israeli borders with fences and land mines. There was a third option. "Gentlemen, the Syrian operations against us are harassment. We can lay seventy mines for every one of theirs, and we can lay them deeper. We will begin a war of harassment against their war of harassment at a ten-to-one ratio." This option must be made clear to the Syrians, Rabin said, at which point he began speaking in the second-person plural, as if the Syrians themselves were sitting in the meeting. "You want a small war—we will respond with a greater blow." He suggested inflaming tensions along the border and exploiting them as an excuse to act, and described the increased number of border incidents as a "gold mine."

Eshkol asked what could be done in the meantime, including defensive steps. "Is what we are doing worth anything? When there are borders and there is an army, the army protects the borders. But faced with these acts of harassment, is what we are doing of any value? If it is not, what should we do that would be valuable, especially in a war? Will we occupy Syria? And what do we do afterward?" He suggested offering a reward to terrorists who turned themselves or others in. But it occurred to him that perhaps these people were acting in a spirit of self-sacrifice and true dedication, and he asked again what should be done. The prime minister could not have made it any clearer: the army had no answers.

General David Elazar, head of the Northern Command, wanted to go beyond Eshkol's practical questions. Syria, he argued, was the ideological force driving the "popular war." It saw itself as a pioneer in the struggle, and its support of Fatah compelled other countries and organizations to become involved as well. And so Elazar maintained that the original sin lay with Syria. Fatah's success could not be ignored, he cautioned. In the two years since its formation, it had conducted approximately seventy operations. Elazar was inclined to ignore the plight and aspirations of the Palestinians themselves; he viewed them as fighters in the service of Syrian ideology, which opposed what it saw as Israel's complicity in imperialism and reactionism. This was why a partial, military, defensive solution was not enough: there needed to be "a total, military, political" solution. Elazar was not talking about war, but he opposed petty harassment, since the Syrians were better at it and there was no point competing with them. He supported the idea of dealing significant blows to the Syrians. "The time has come," he said.

In response to a question from Eshkol, Elazar said he did not completely rule out defensive steps. A lot was being done, he said, and mentioned the nocturnal ambushes: every night three or four companies lay in ambush in the freezing cold, and sometimes they got frostbite and had to be evacuated to hospitals. But this had limited value, Elazar believed, since the enemy was three hundred yards away and could often see the ambush party. It was enough for a soldier to drop his Uzi, and the ambush was exposed.* Eshkol had some knowledge of techniques and costs. He asked about paths and roads, and which was better—dirt roads on which tracks could be detected, or asphalt roads with fencing and lighting. At times he sounded like a landowner conversing with his guards, not a minister of defense at a General Staff meeting. Elazar believed it was best to invest in sophisticated electronic devices. It was true that no device was infallible, he said—in Algeria, people had discovered that radar could be detected with transistor radios—but he believed it would take time for the Palestinians to develop such skills, and so he rejected defenses that the "primitive" enemy could overcome, such as a fence along the border. Even Fatah would find ways to cut through a fence and slip past IDF patrols, he said. He did support building fences around populated areas, however, with good lighting, and proposed allocating more manpower to accomplish this. Dishon was fenced, but the soccer field and

---

*Some two months after this discussion, Ze'ev Schiff from *Ha'aretz* accompanied a nighttime ambush party against Fatah, and although he tried to praise the soldiers and supported the increase of passive defenses against terrorist infiltration, he left no room for doubt: the ambushes served no real purpose.[23]

water facility were outside the fence, he reported. And not all settlements were fenced, because no money was budgeted for doing so. Eshkol was astonished: "We're talking about pennies. Why wasn't this done? Two hundred and twenty thousand liras?"

General Uzi Narkis, head of the Central Command, offered the assumption that terrorism would not stop. "One of the great things the Chinese said is to have patience," he explained. "They usually have patience. They have ten thousand years, until Vietnam and all the rest is over. The Arabs have time, and I think we do, too. So I say—there's time. We shouldn't decide that we'll do something tomorrow and it will be over. It won't be over." Narkis believed, however, that the Arabs should be hit repeatedly. "We are dealing with the Arabs, and the Arabs, mentally, for the most part, what characterizes them is that when they get hit, they retreat." He gave a biblical example. "Let's say, during the Prophets, that the People of Israel had trouble. They struck a blow against their enemy, and everything was quiet for forty years. In modern terms, two weeks is like forty years. . . . It says, anyway, that the Arabs, when they get hit— they calm down for a while." Eshkol was dubious. "We're getting into psychology. Is that really just the Arabs?" he asked. "It's pretty Arab," Narkis replied, "it says about the Jews in the Haggadah that the more they were afflicted, the more they multiplied and grew." Eshkol was still unconvinced. "At the moment they're the ones who are multiplying," he grumbled, but Narkis held his ground, offering recollections from the British Mandate: "When the Arabs take a hit—I remember this from before there was a state—they quiet down. It's all relative."

Narkis spoke positively of the Samua operation. "I think that today everyone has come to see the justice of that operation." But the prime minister corrected him once again: "One could replace the word 'justice' with the word 'effectiveness.'" Narkis responded, "I'll tell you why I say it was just: there were considerations and a decision was made, and in my opinion it was not only effective, but also just." He meant that Hussein, as a result of the operation, had increased his efforts to prevent Fatah activities.* Narkis was concerned about Central Command's limited role in the war effort; despite the fact that Syria, "the father of all sin," was pulling the strings in the north, his sector was also important, he stressed, and he

---

*A few days after this meeting, Rabin commented in a General Staff discussion that the Samua operation had in fact strengthened Hussein's position. This was not to say that the king's enemies would not try to kill him: "A bullet can always find him." But he added that the Samua operation should not be viewed as having been intended from the beginning to strengthen the king. "I wouldn't say we were that smart."[24]

suggested harassment of the Palestinians beyond the border. "We are far more vulnerable than they are, but it wouldn't be so pleasant for them, either, if twenty groups went into twenty villages and stopped them from sleeping, there'd be explosions, shootings, a couple of guys killed every night. Then they'd run to the authorities crying, 'Save us!'" The more the debate went on, the more political and even fantastical it became.

General Rehavam Ze'evi, from the operations branch, known to all as Gandhi, proposed all-out war on Syria. Eshkol attempted to steer the discussion back to defensive measures. Rabin tried to prevent an argument between the two, but his own position was clear: "I completely agree with Gandhi." Ze'evi thought in terms of overall national security. Everything that could be done against the terrorists' incursions had already been done. There wasn't a country in the world whose military was capable of doing things the IDF could not, with the possible exception of the USSR. But even then, some people managed to breach the Berlin Wall. And so the solution was not defensive—that approach had never succeeded anywhere in the world. Any analysis would show, Ze'evi said, that the only way to finish off a war was to address its cause—in this case, Syria.

Ze'evi gave three reasons that had led him to this conclusion. First, the IDF was not designed for small wars. Second, the civilian communities could endure only so much. He gave Kfar Yuval as an example. "A moshavnik living in Kfar Yuval, he hears his tenant farmer digging outside at night and thinks it's someone come to kill his children—he can take it for a week, a month, a year. But one day he'll have to vote with his feet." The third factor that led Ze'evi to believe that radical steps against Syria were essential was the economic damage wreaked by terror, primarily on tourism. He recalled the Sinai Campaign, which had demonstrated to the Egyptians that there was no such thing as a half war. "We can try treating the wound with defensive medicine or limited operations, but it needs to be cured by surgery, and that means explaining to the Syrians what needs to be explained unequivocally." War with Syria, according to Ze'evi, would also solve the dispute over water and the demilitarized zones, and would prevent the spread of terror by deterring other countries.

The IDF had three plans for initiating an attack against Syria, including Operation Ax, which involved occupying Damascus; Tongs, an intermediate plan to occupy the Golan Heights all the way to east of Kunetra; and Concoction, a plan to take over just the Banias area.[25] Eshkol tried to bring the debate back to the idea of halting terrorist infiltrations by means of a fence. Ze'evi said erecting a fence would set down political facts in places where the border was unclear, and Israel might lose certain territories. Besides, both Arabs and Jews might simply sneak through. Fences had sometimes failed in Algeria, Morocco, and Berlin, he said. "I did not suggest surrounding all of Israel with a fence," Eshkol replied, but he thought that where there were fences, there would be less of a need for manpower. Rabin came to his aid on this point: there was no doubt that defensive means had prevented terrorist infiltrations, although there was no way to tell how many because only successful infiltrations were recorded. Eshkol liked the argument. "It's almost tricky, it's a good explanation," he said happily: "You never know what might have happened without the fence."

Somewhat encouraged, the prime minister proposed another idea. "This fear that they can see [our men], because we go out at sundown, that they're under a rock watching us. Wouldn't it be possible to switch [the men's] positions as soon as it got dark?" He admitted, however, that he was not telling his colleagues anything new, and compared himself to the Jew who came to Moscow with a new invention: a bicycle. Rabin explained dryly that if they began shifting people around after dark, as Eshkol suggested, the IDF would have more casualties than the terrorists. And so Eshkol wondered about night vision binoculars. How many did the military have? How much did they cost? How many did the IDF need? He was excited. "It's clearly a worthwhile idea." He criticized Ze'evi's comparison with the Sinai Campaign. "First of all, I know a little about geography. We do not have the same type of situation with Syria as we had in the Sinai Desert, or that we have with Jordan, where you go in and that's that. But you can't do that every month, the world would be outraged."

Eshkol did have some good news for the General Staff. At a reception in Paris for the "non-Jewish New Year," as he called it, President de Gaulle had approached the Israeli ambassador, Walter Eitan, and wished him peace, quiet, and calm. "Since you are strong, you should also be peaceful," de Gaulle had advised, "and in any case don't attack Jordan." The statement surprised Eshkol, who would have expected the French president to be concerned for Syria, considering the two countries' historic ties, but this was not the case. "They're not the worst," Eshkol commented, regarding the French, and asked about the binoculars again. Rabin cut him off: binoculars could improve the situation, but would not put an end to the infiltrations. Eshkol clung to what little he could, saying an improvement was better than nothing. "Am I asking for a one-hundred-percent solution?" But Rabin said that even 500 pairs of binoculars, 220 infrared sensors, and 60 miles of fence, would do no more than help strengthen local residents' feeling that the IDF was standing by them. "To my mind that is worth more than any strike against the infiltrators," Rabin said, but to solve the problem they essentially had to hit within Syria, "at least in a Samua formula." Eshkol said Samua had not provided "a permanent solution" in Jordan, and Rabin responded that they had not struck at the right address. Eshkol said out loud, "Syria? What a thing! We're not going to kill seven million Syrians!"

Rabin observed, "But after Sinai we had ten years of quiet on the Egyptian border." Eshkol responded, "I'm not sure if that's the way to look at it. Other thoughts have come to Nasser. I'm not sure. It's impossible to prove. Same as you can't prove that without [defensive measures against terrorism] things would have been worse. It's hard to prove that Syria wants to be a spearhead so much as Nasser wants to avoid" being in that position. "I'm not saying this so as not to do it," Eshkol went on. "I'm saying that anyone who thinks a few strikes will finish it off—I don't know. We'll have to learn as we go." He added that in case of an attack against Syria, "all the Arabs together with Jordan" might unite against Israel. But Rabin reminded him that "Samua divided them." Egypt and Syria had not come to Jordan's defense.

Three other generals then spoke—Elad Peled, Israel Tal, and Amos Horev—as well as the director of weapons systems development, Meir (Munya) Mardor. Only Horev, the deputy chief scientist in the Ministry of Defense, did not propose major steps against Syria, but instead a significant effort to prevent terrorist infiltrations. Terrorists could place a bomb in a movie theater, he said, in which case not even a conversation between de Gaulle and Ambassador Eitan would do any good. Eshkol ignored the jab and Horev went on to quote proposals for retaliatory terrorism, such as "laying mines using planes. Let them get their legs blown off." He felt that these ideas expressed the mood of the General Staff, and suggested another solution: dig a canal along the Syrian border.

And that was how the meeting ended. The General Staff felt they had been talking with an elderly man who had little faith in the power of the IDF. But Eshkol might well have noted with real anxiety that he had been talking to men who were narrowminded—and, worse, helpless. When the generals guaranteed, in their authoritative and opinionated way, that war with Egypt was improbable before 1970, and that it was unlikely Egypt would interfere if Israel hit Syria, Eshkol looked at them with his wise eyes and said, in Yiddish, *"Tomer efsher"*—Maybe so, maybe not, maybe you are wrong.[26]

• • •

FOR THREE AND A HALF MONTHS, UNTIL THE MIDDLE OF MAY 1967, THE TERROR CON-
tinued. Israel dealt punishing blows to the Syrian army, and Eshkol and
Rabin made a series of combative declarations before Independence Day.
During those fifteen weeks, Israel suffered thirty-one attacks and attempted attacks—two per week. Half the terrorists crossed into Israel
from Jordan, but some of those may have entered Jordan from starting
points in Syria. The Palestinians laid mines along roads (and one bridge);
they set explosive devices on the railroad to Beersheba and damaged the
water tower in Arad as well as pumps and pipelines in other places. Four
Israelis were injured, one seriously. When Eshkol visited the northern kibbutzim, members of Ha'on and Tel Katzir demanded IDF operations to
enable them to work "on all their lands" and to prevent the Syrians from
bringing flocks and shepherds onto fields the kibbutzim wanted to farm.

At the end of March, Eshkol and Rabin had made a decision. "We will
ask General Bull to explain to the Syrians that we do not intend to take
control of all the demilitarized zones, but that we will protect the areas
farmed by our people. We will hint to General Bull that he should find a
way to make the Egyptians aware of these facts as well." This was a formula
both Eshkol and Rabin could live with. Lior wrote: "Finally Eshkol understands that there is no turning back, and that if farming for political reasons is authorized, it is essential to follow through all the way, even if we
have to use heavier weapons (tanks and planes)." That same day in March,
Rabin requested and received permission to bring in armored tractors near
the Syrian border, not far from Kibbutz Tel Katzir. The prime minister
should know, he said, that it might be necessary to deploy the air force.

Foreign Minister Eban became suspicious. On April 4, 1967, he wrote
to Eshkol that he was surprised to see almost identical articles about Kibbutz Ha'on in *Ha'aretz* and *Yediot Aharonot*. *Ha'aretz* had also run an editorial arguing that "we are obliged to repel any attempt to prevent Jewish
farmers from working land in Israeli territory, including in the demilitarized zones." Attempts to stop land within Israel from being farmed could
not go unchallenged, said the paper. The press reported prominently on
the incidents within the demilitarized zones and took a belligerent tone.
Eban wrote to Eshkol, "The fact that these articles were written primarily
by the military correspondents, and are almost identical in content, indicates the possibility of guidance." It was no wonder, he wrote, that even
the opposition parties had picked up the impression that tensions were increasing and had submitted an item for the Knesset agenda. Knesset

member Yosef Shofman, of Gahal, spoke sharply. The Syrians had infiltrated Israel's sovereign territory 770 times in the last few months, he
claimed, while Israel sat idly by and watched. He complained about Israel's "miserable role" and asked, "Will Israel consider the question of the
significance of our sovereignty—the sovereignty of the State of Israel—
over our national territory?"

On Friday, April 7, 1967, two tractors entered a fifteen-acre lot, Number 52, according to plan. The Syrians opened fire. The IDF returned fire.
"Their tanks, our tanks," wrote Lior. By afternoon, Eshkol had to decide
whether to stop the work or call in the air force. Lior, from his Tel Aviv
office, listened in on the phone conversation between Rabin in the north
and Eshkol in Jerusalem. Rabin broke off every few moments to report
excitedly, "Now I see shells falling near the tractors!" Eshkol said the
work should go on, and if there was no choice, the air force should be
sent in. Then he added an instruction that no civilians be harmed. Lior
suggested sending a helicopter to bring Eshkol to Defense Ministry headquarters in Tel Aviv, which made him "very happy." By the time he arrived, the air force had shot down two Syrian MiGs. Rabin proposed
halting the work, but Eshkol demanded that it continue until dark. By
the end of the day, Israel had shot down six MiGs, including one near
Damascus.*

The press was elated. This was the greatest achievement in the history
of the air force, said *Yediot Aharonot,* and reported how the kibbutzniks
had left their bomb shelters and run out to watch the incredible scene of
"avenging airplanes." *Maariv* wrote, "This was not an 'incident,' but a real
war," noting that it was the largest battle in the north since the War of Independence. "Six in One Blow!" shouted *Yediot Aharonot.* At first there
had been an air of utter disbelief, the paper reported, and people had hurried to their telephones to call one another and find out if the newscaster
on Kol Israel radio had not made a mistake when she announced that six
planes had been downed. Ze'ev Schiff declared in *Ha'aretz,* "The Syrian pilots proved that they are little more than airplane drivers. Not one of
them even tried to offer any resistance to the Israeli planes." The editorial
described the incident as "a glorious accomplishment." For many months,
Israel had not had such cause for rejoicing. Silvie Keshet, who wrote

---

*One of the Israeli pilots, Yiftah Spector, who reached the outskirts of Damascus, was later
asked what the city looked like. His response became a staple of Israeli political folklore: "Like
an Arab village that grew up."

imaginary dialogues for *Ha'aretz*, gave one of her characters the line: "Even in Vietnam, I don't think they take down six in one day." A French general telephoned the IDF attaché in Paris to congratulate him, said *Maariv*, because the Israeli air force had used French Mirage fighters. The assessment in Paris was that the defection of the Iraqi pilot who had brought the MiG to Israel many months earlier had helped in the battle. "There is no doubt that Israel's prestige has skyrocketed," said *Maariv*. "The Syrians have been stripped of their illusions." The paper devoted five pages to coverage of the operation.

One Israeli officer from Haifa was killed in the confrontation. A few of the kibbutzim in the area were hit hard by Syrian bombardment, including Gadot, which had been founded by Holocaust survivors in 1949. There were gaping pits in the kibbutz, and punched-through walls; bombs had destroyed the roof of the children's house, ripped up the playground slides, and left a bed covered with shattered glass. A second earlier there had been a room there, *Maariv* recounted, with a vase of sweet peas, an African statuette, an embroidered tablecloth, and a bookshelf—a warm oasis, a lovingly tended nest. Now the kibbutz members rummaged through the ruins, retrieving an old photograph and a child's toy. The children of Gadot had a beloved, loyal dog named Tzah. When the bombing began and everyone ran to the shelters, there was no time to find Tzah, and he ran around through the explosions, finally taking shelter in a warehouse. As he cowered in a corner, a shell hit the warehouse, shattering a bottle of acid. It spilled over the dog and after the bombing they found him writhing, covered with burns. They poured water on him, but to no avail. The children dug a grave.

"The Syrian ledger is filling up," *Yediot Aharonot* declared. Eshkol, however, received only a fraction of the glory: one or two paragraphs, with no headline. He had been "somewhere out there" during the action, it was said, and had received updates. The reports said he had shared in the passion of the battle, but rather than showing excitement, had "quietly considered the situation and made decisions." *Maariv* politely noted that in the past Eshkol had allowed the air force to take steps against Syria a number of times. The paper tried to say a few kind words about the prime minister, but it is doubtful that these compliments warmed his heart: "Although D. Ben-Gurion exceeds Eshkol when it comes to decisiveness, the operations carried out during L. Eshkol's term of office, and the achievements of the day before yesterday, have proved that the prime minister's personality is not the only factor that determines events, but rather the situation, the conditions, and the circumstances."

Rabin, on the other hand, was predictably hailed as a personal victor. "I am not certain whether the Syrians are good students, and I am not convinced they will be capable of learning their lesson in one go," he said.* A military commentator added, "Damascus and its surroundings will no longer be immune in the event of a serious clash." He called once again for Israel to farm the lands it had ignored. "It is important to insist absolutely on this territory we have neglected for years." Eshkol tried to wrest at least some of the glory from Rabin, and three weeks later *Maariv* rewarded him with the headline "I Gave the Order." It was true: he, not Rabin, had been at the center of command, and Mordechai Hod, the commander of the air force, had received the necessary operational approvals directly from him. In fact, Eshkol seemed to have been swept up in the combative excitement, allowing Hod to act to a great extent on his own initiative, according to Ami Gluska.

This was not the large-scale operation against Syria that the IDF had demanded, but it did provoke a dramatic escalation of tensions. Eshkol knew that that was what the army was after, and he could reasonably have been expected to know that it would be the result of deploying the air force. He could have avoided involving the air force; its deployment would not prevent a single Fatah operation. Eshkol was instinctively skeptical of the intelligence assurances that Egypt would not interfere on Syria's behalf. The excesses of the Samua operation were still fresh in his memory. But he was neither strong enough nor bold enough to curb the army, and was probably not utterly convinced it was the right thing to do. In the background there was always the need to prove that he was not the weak man depicted by his adversaries. And so Eshkol allowed the army to accelerate a dynamic that was at odds with Israel's basic national interest: the prevention of war. Ezer Weizman later recalled Moshe Dayan's response when the Syrian planes were shot down: "Have you lost your minds? You are leading the country into war!" Israel Lior agreed: "From my point of view, the Six-Day War had begun," he wrote.[27]

---

*This was a common cliché. Israel had always wanted to "teach" its enemies "a lesson." *Maariv* wrote of "an exemplary, crushing lesson," and its editorial was entitled "Crime and Punishment and Lessons."

3. CELEBRATIONS: "WHO KNOWS HOW MANY?"

About ten days before the Syrian MiGs were shot down, a guest at the Tchernichovsky Writers' House in Tel Aviv generated great excitement. The invitations were printed on glossy paper, as the poet Dalia Ravikovitch later wrote, and it was no wonder that by eight-thirty the main auditorium was filled with dozens of members of the Writers' Association, along with their spouses and sons, daughters-in-law and grandchildren, interpreters and neighbors. People in the third row worried that they wouldn't be able to see the guest, who was a short man.

Jean-Paul Sartre was ushered into the auditorium and sat behind a table laid out with glasses of juice and stale egg-and-tomato sandwiches. "Almost immediately one could see nothing but a dense cluster of dignitaries and their families, each one tugging at the hem of the diminutive guest's overcoat, trying to obtain at least one thread of the lining as a timeless souvenir," Ravikovitch wrote in *Ha'aretz*. The writer Azriel Uhmani opened the event. He told Sartre that he was in Eretz Israel, the cradle of the Jewish people, whose dialogue with God had been conducted in its ancient language, a language that now mediated between the Jews and modern times. Uhmani invited Sartre to lend a hand to the peace efforts of this persecuted, pacific nation. Then he spoke about the great poet Shaul Tchernichovsky, his writing and his translations. This long speech, wrote Ravikovitch, "swept away any ignorance Sartre might have had of the renewal of the Hebrew language and the literary endeavors of Tchernichovsky."

Sartre, responding in French, thanked the many writers for their warm welcome and said he would like the opportunity to study the country's problems. He spoke briefly, wrote Ravikovitch. "His words contained no flattery, but they were courteous. . . . If he chose to describe the jabbing in his ribs as warm—he no doubt believed it was the local custom: in Israel one jabs, much as in Russia one hugs and in France one kisses." The audience shouted out, "Translate, Uhmani, translate!" Uhmani tried to relay a message to Simone de Beauvoir, but instead of wishing her a speedy recovery from her troublesome cold, he mistakenly congratulated her on having caught the cold. Yigal Mosenzon, assisted by his own personal interpreter, told Sartre about his play *Kazablan*. Then the masses crowded around the guest for autographs. The singer Braha Tzfira tried in vain to get Sartre's attention, and when she was unsuccessful she sang out in her huge soprano, *"Vive la France!"* Sartre turned pale, wrote Ravikovitch. The writer Ehud Ben-Ezer later tried to excuse Tel Aviv's provincialism by criticizing Sartre himself: he had nothing to say, except for five or six trivial lines of niceties. "Something like a speech by a minister forced to give a toast at his driver's son's bar mitzvah."[28*]

In his meeting with Eshkol, Sartre mentioned how impressed he was that since his previous visit, in the early fifties, immigrant camps had vanished from the landscape. He expressed strong support for Israel, but said he felt that the key to solving the Israeli-Arab conflict was the return of the Palestinian refugees. Eshkol replied that the demand to allow refugees to return was no more than an indirect way of destroying Israel. In fact, he explained to Sartre, the number of Jews who had left the Arab states and settled in Israel was almost identical to the number of Arabs who had left Israel, and so one could say that there had been an exchange of populations. The most just solution of the problem was to settle the refugees in their countries of residence. Sartre should know, said Eshkol, that the State of Israel included no more than 20 percent of the territory within the original boundaries of Palestine.[30†]

MEANWHILE, ESHKOL DEDICATED A MEMORIAL TO A KEY BATTLE OF THE WAR OF Independence—the battle that had allowed the IDF to lift the siege of Jerusalem. The memorial was erected along the road to the capital and suggested nothing so much as a launching device for huge, rocketlike arrows. The sculptor, Noemi Hanreck, wanted to create the sense that the monument was "built into the living rock of the hillside," according to the announcement published by the Postal Ministry's Philatelic Services, which produced an image of the sculpture on the annual Memorial Day stamp. "And indeed," the explanation continued, describing the monu-

---

*Prior to Sartre's visit, the Israeli prisoner Maxim Gilan wrote him a letter, introducing himself as the translator of Jean Genet and asking Sartre to visit him in prison. Gilan was still serving time for his attempt to publish information about Israel's part in the Ben Barka kidnapping in the weekly *Bul*. The letter seems to have gotten only as far as the prime minister's office, where it was placed in a file. Eshkol told the cabinet that various foreign entities were pressuring Israel to release Gilan and his colleague, Shmuel Mor. The two were abruptly pardoned and released just before Sartre's visit.[29]

†A few weeks later, Israel was told by another visiting celebrity that it must allow the refugees to return: Pete Seeger announced in Tel Aviv that proceeds from his concert in Israel would fund the education of a Palestinian boy who was living in a refugee camp near Beirut and who dreamed of becoming an engineer. *Maariv* responded, "Obviously, the good Pete . . . has not heard about the refugee problem in India and Pakistan, in Poland, and elsewhere."[31]

ment, "the wall shall be broken by these arms, which seem as if they are cleaving and rupturing it."* Three other Independence Day stamps depicted planes representing different periods in the history of the air force: a British Auster, a French Mystère, and a French Mirage. The picture of the Mirage showed it flying over the cliff at Masada.†

In the weeks following the downing of the six MiGs, the Syrians continued shelling the northern kibbutzim and there were further acts of sabotage. By mid-May, there was a growing sense that the IDF would soon take broader action against Syria. On its front page *Yediot Aharonot* reported that "Syria is establishing a new terrorist organization." On May 4, the security cabinet met to discuss the situation on the northern border. Chief of Staff Rabin and a few senior officers also took part. They decided to issue a warning to the Syrians, using the United States as an intermediary, stating that if they dared to continue the provocations, Israel would respond with military action.[33]

The country's nineteenth Independence Day was approaching. For the first time since the establishment of the state, the Jewish date and the Gregorian date, May 15, were to coincide. Traditionally, it was the season for the prime minister and the IDF chief of staff to offer declarations, and this year Eshkol and Rabin sounded particularly aggressive. Eshkol told his party that it might become necessary to take more steps as harsh as shooting down the six planes, and his statement was widely publicized. In an interview with *Bamahane* and on Kol Israel radio, he delivered a warning to the Syrians: "There will not be calm only on one side of the border." He described Syria as the spearhead of hostility against the country, and promised that "Israel will continue to respond."[34] Rabin also addressed the Syrians, as did the head of the IDF intelligence branch, Aharon Yariv, in a briefing for the foreign press. Rabin enumerated Israel's options, including the occupation of Damascus. The papers, too, employed emotional language that stemmed directly from the victory celebrations after the shooting down of the planes. "It seems there will be no escaping a head-on clash with Syria in the future," said *Ha'aretz*.[35] *Yediot Aharonot*'s military commentator, Arel Ginai, who was known for having reliable sources and who often expressed government, Mossad, and military positions, learned from Rabin and Eshkol's declarations that Israel was laying the groundwork for a large-scale operation. "After the clear

---

*These words were omitted from the English-language version of the announcement.
†The decision to issue these stamps was made by the government on January 23, 1967, as tensions raged.[32]

warnings voiced in recent days by Israeli leaders, first among them Mr. Eshkol, there is no longer any doubt that Israel will respond to the recent Syrian actions against its territory." Ginai wrote that the Israeli strike would be "powerful and impressive," but would not involve seizing territories "that are far beyond the Syrian border," meaning, apparently, that conquering Damascus was not an option. In his view, Russia and Egypt would respond only if Israeli forces occupied Damascus. *Maariv* concluded that same day, May 12, that a letter sent by Israel to the UN was "a final warning."[36]*

Eshkol attributed great importance to the U.S. position, but the Johnson administration had no objection to Israel striking against Syria and therefore did not demand that he temper his public utterances. In preparation for a meeting with Abe Feinberg and David Ginsburg, President Johnson was given briefing papers by Walt Rostow, which included the statement, "We sympathize with Eshkol's need to stop these raids and reluctantly admit that a limited attack may be his only answer." According to Rostow, the administration wanted Eshkol to "think twice" before commiting the IDF to such an attack, but the United States also did not want to give him reason to blame Washington for having held Israel back, particularly if it transpired that a small-scale attack was the best course of action. Hal Saunders of the National Security Council reported to Rostow that during his visit to Damascus he had been told explicitly by Syrian officials that they intended to disrupt life in Israel to such an extent that Jews would stop settling there and Israelis might leave. Saunders's impression in Jerusalem was that the Israeli government, in particular Levi Eshkol, saw Palestinian terror as the main threat to Israel's security.[38]

On the eve of Independence Day, *Yediot Aharonot* asserted on its front page that there was "Fear in Syria in Light of Israel's Warning." On the second page appeared the headline "Damascus Reassures Itself That Egypt Will Come to Its Aid." On the third page, the paper settled scores with Nasser, calling him "a thug." Eshkol himself had words of warning for Egypt: "We shall thwart any attempt to hinder free passage to and from Israel through the Red Sea, whoever the assailants may be." Earlier, Eshkol had mocked the dream of Arab unity that Nasser was attempting to realize and had taken a swipe at him over Egypt's failure to protect Syria from Israel.[39]

A close reading of the Independence Day statements indicates some

---

*The next day, the Soviet ambassador complained to the director general of the Ministry of Foreign Affairs that "military circles" were creating provocations along the Syrian border in an attempt to topple the Syrian regime.[37]

divergences. Eshkol spoke of the need for preventative action—in other words, defense—while Rabin argued that the terrorists' activities could not be stopped by defensive means. Eshkol spoke in the semiofficial Mapai newspaper, *Davar*, while Rabin made his declarations in *Lamerhav*, the organ of the hawkish Ahdut Ha'avoda. But the general impression was clear: Israel was planning to act against Syria, and these belligerent statements were intended to create the appropriate atmosphere. Abba Eban wrote drily, as only he could: "Had there been a slightly greater measure of silence, it transpires that nothing would have been lost to the treasury of human wisdom."[40]

Eshkol was under particular pressure to prove his mettle as Independence Day approached. The Syrian question was not the only challenge to his fitness as Israel's leader. In the previous few months he had been charged with an awful accusation: that he was incapable of defending the special status of Jerusalem and the dignity of the army, and that this failure was the reason why the IDF could not hold its traditional annual military parade in the streets of Jerusalem.

THE PARADE IN JERUSALEM WAS AN ANNUAL ISSUE, OR, AS ONE OF THE U.S. PRESIDENT'S assistants wrote, an "annual hassle." The cease-fire with Jordan allowed only a small number of troops to enter the city and prohibited heavy equipment, including tanks.* A parade held in Jerusalem in 1961 led to a reprimand of Israel in the Security Council, and since then the parades had taken place in other cities.

Jerusalem was the last refuge of the Israeli patriot. "Accuse your enemies of betraying Jerusalem, and you are exempt from any further argument with them," wrote Uri Avneri; "prove that you are the only person who truly cares about Jerusalem, and you no longer need to bother trying to find real answers to real problems." In this spirit, Knesset opposition members and a few editorialists annually demanded that the parade should take place in Jerusalem, and Eshkol was required to explain why this was not possible. The opposition thereby emerged as the champion of national dignity, while the government was depicted as a group of weaklings, meekly succumbing to American pressure. In 1966, the opposition on this issue had been strengthened by the additional support of David

---

*The agreement also prohibited planes from entering Jerusalem's airspace, except by special authorization. This gave rise to one of the many characteristics attributed to Jerusalemites: when they hear a plane, they always look up.

Ben-Gurion, a powerful orator. That year, the parade was held in Haifa, and Ben-Gurion announced vociferously that he would boycott it.[41]

Ha'aretz had come to the government's defense and, in a rare moment, even criticized Ben-Gurion, reminding readers that during his final years in office the parades had not been held in Jerusalem either. The director general of the Foreign Ministry cautioned that a military parade in Jerusalem would damage Israel's standing as a country that kept its word, would strengthen the Palestinians vis-à-vis Jordan's Hussein, and would push the king to take extreme steps.* The mere holding of the parade did not reinforce Jerusalem's status as the capital, any more than conducting it in Haifa gave that city special status, asserted the director general; but he added that on the following anniversary, the state's twentieth, the IDF would have to demonstrate its full power.

Eshkol's military secretary, Lior, seems to have keenly understood the domestic dynamic behind Israel's foreign policy: the claim that Eshkol was not courageous enough to hold a military parade in Jerusalem was damaging to him, in light both of Rabin's popularity and that of the entire military, and because he was also the subject of ridicule to so many Israelis. To prove his adherence to Jerusalem's status as the capital of Israel without provoking international anger, Eshkol decided to hold a limited military parade in the capital, one that would not overstep the rules of the cease-fire with Jordan. There would be no tanks, no aerial demonstrations. "A mini-parade," mocked Uri Avneri. This decision created an all-encompassing array of pressure: the Arab states pressured Jordan, Jordan pressured the United States, and Herzl Rosenblum, the editor of *Yediot Aharonot,* and David Ben-Gurion both pressured Eshkol. Rosenblum wrote an editorial entitled "Scoundrels," in which he claimed it was the prime minister's weakness that was causing the world powers to pressure Israel. Ben-Gurion protested against the "phony parade" planned by the government, and announced that he would not attend it either.[43] Eshkol responded heatedly: Had he not sent the IDF to Samua? Had he not sent the air force to shoot down Syrian MiGs? Three times he had unleashed the air force, and Israel had shot down no fewer than eleven Arab aircraft that year.

The United States, Britain, and France could not ignore the parade, for the simple reason that they had to decide whether their ambassadors

---

*A popular march to Jerusalem was also held every year, shortly before Independence Day. In the 1967 march, some citizens carried signs reading, "Next Year in Old Jerusalem." The march was held under the army's auspices, and *Ha'aretz* asked Chief of Staff Rabin what he thought of the slogan. "Let the young people celebrate," he responded. He conceded that some of the sloganeering was unnecessary, but said there was no point in censoring it.[42]

would accept the invitation to sit on the dignitaries' stage. The question became the topic of a voluminous correspondence, as a State Department official put it. Everyone treated the subject with the utmost gravity, as world powers had always done whenever Jerusalem was concerned. Ambassador Walworth Barbour had attended the dedication of the new Knesset building, and Secretary of State Dean Rusk accompanied this gesture with an internal memo in which he maintained that the dedication of the Knesset should be seen as a onetime affair and that the ambassador's presence did not change the U.S. position that in principle Jerusalem was not a part of the State of Israel. The American ambassador's presence at the parade could be handled in a similar way, and this was the Americans' intention, but when Britain and France announced that their ambassadors would not attend, the Americans also balked. A few administration officials took the opportunity to voice fairly hostile positions toward Israel. The U.S. ambassador in Damascus wrote to Washington that the time had come for Israel to stop leading the United States around by the nose, as this was not an election year. One White House official saw the affair as an example of the general problem that characterized relations with Israel: the Israelis were not entirely honest. Yes, he wrote, the American ambassador could simply attend the parade to be nice to the Israelis on their day of celebration, but the problem was that the Israelis tried to turn everything to political advantage, and they had lost all sense of proportion with regard to the parade.[44]

The Israeli press followed the affair closely. The military correspondent for *Ha'aretz* quoted "security sources" who suggested that if the U.S. ambassador did not attend, Israel should respond with a full military parade without observing the cease-fire limitations. The paper, however, took a moderate position, arguing that the presence of the ambassadors at the parade was of no great significance, and it repeated its rebuke of Ben-Gurion.[45] At some point the matter landed on President Johnson's desk.

Walt Rostow all but apologized for the nuisance: in his view, the question was trivial, but the president should know that the ambassador's absence from the parade might cause "trouble," and he felt obliged to warn him. The issue at hand, he continued, was Jerusalem's status. The British had raised an important point: there was no doubt that the Israelis were using "salami tactics"—trying to take the whole salami slice by slice—and much as Rostow liked them, they were unfortunately not people to content themselves with a friendly gesture. They were always determined to get something, always negotiating. The Israelis were threatening that the ambassador's absence from the parade would bring about a crisis in the relationship between the two countries, but this was "nonsense" and they could probably be talked out of taking that line, Rostow believed. However, they might interpret the ambassador's absence as "the kind of aloofness that doesn't help you here at home." He, Rostow, would hate to see the president get into hot water over this. But the question was not easy: was the United States prepared to give in to all the Israelis' demands, or was it still interested in maintaining a degree of balance between them and the Arabs? The Israelis felt they had achieved a breakthrough with the president on the issue of tanks and planes they wished to purchase, and they were trying to "exploit it to the hilt." The State Department recommended siding with the British and the French, which necessitated choosing between two options: boycotting the parade or attending. Johnson ultimately decided that the ambassador would not sit on the dignitaries' stage on Independence Day itself but would take part in a sound and light show to be held in the Hebrew University stadium the evening before. He instructed his assistants to minimize damage to relations with the Israelis and to inform David Ginsburg of his decision.[46]

Independence Day celebrations began in the traditional way, on the evening of May 14, with a sharp transition from Memorial Day, with its ceremonies in memory of Israel's war dead. As mourning gave way to joy, ten men and two women were chosen to light torches by the grave of Theodor Herzl, representing eleven settlements founded in the Negev at the end of Yom Kippur in 1946, "a settlement operation," as *Maariv* characterized it, intended to protest against British rule. At the Hebrew University stadium, President Shazar entered accompanied by mounted troops, and then there was a show of torches and lights, standard-bearers and groups of soldiers in formation. The press coverage expressed the pride of a small state struggling against isolation. Among the guests, noted *Yediot Aharonot*, were not only foreign ambassadors, but also the vice president of the African Malagasy Republic, who had come to Israel for the occasion. Throngs of Israelis went out that night to dance in the streets and crowd around outdoor performances. There were also fireworks.*

The military parade was held the following day. UN observers monitored the event as if it had the power to determine the future of world peace. Some of them ascended David's Tower, within the walls of the Old

---

*Careful to avoid provocation, the prime minister's staff instructed that a few lines be omitted from a poem by Nathan Alterman that was to be recited at the display. The lines in question included the words "Arabia, consider your ways before it's too late! . . . This may be the final hour." Predictably, the instruction was leaked and Eshkol was once again portrayed as a coward.

City, to count precisely how many vehicles, how many soldiers—both male and female—and how many flags appeared in the parade. The UN secretary general, U Thant, later opined that the parade had triggered the dynamic that ultimately led to the Six-Day War. Some 200,000 people crowded the streets of Jerusalem that morning. "It was not a particularly impressive event," wrote *Yediot Aharonot*, characterizing it as more of a march than a military parade. Many spectators were disappointed and left with a bitter taste in their mouths. "A lot of people were depressed by it," wrote David Ben-Gurion.[47]

Independence Day was the only secular holiday in Israel, except for election days. Israelis went hiking and picnicking. Students reenacted the battles of 1948. The extreme ultra-Orthodox in Jerusalem, who did not recognize the state, boycotted Independence Day. Spotting an Israeli flag waving from a parked car that belonged to people who had come to Jerusalem to watch the parade, some of them tore it and drew a swastika on it. The car owner's wife, reported *Maariv*, was a Holocaust survivor. One can imagine how shocked she was at this barbaric act, wrote the paper; the desecrated flag had been handed over to the police. The winner of the International Young People's Bible Quiz, Yitzhak Hagiz, won first prize thanks to his knowledge of seven verses that included the phrase "from Dan to Beersheba." Eshkol was present at the event, as was Ben-Gurion, who was extremely impressed by the winner's proficiency. Many Israelis listened to the annual quiz on the radio "with the sort of tension reserved in most countries for big sporting events," as Abba Eban wrote.[48]

On the occasion of the holiday, *Maariv* published a sort of report on the state of the argument between "the two peoples of Israel"—the practical and the messianic, historically represented by Mapai and Herut. Geula Cohen, the high priestess of the Greater Israel proponents, conducted a dialogue with David Ben-Gurion. "The old man," who demonstrated such fierce patriotism when compared to Eshkol, appeared, in the face of Cohen's impassioned vision, as pragmatic and even lacking in faith.

"Grandpa," Cohen asked him, speaking in the persona of his grandson, "what are the borders of my homeland?"

Ben-Gurion replied, "The borders of your homeland, my grandson, are the borders of the State of Israel, as they are today."

Cohen would not back down. "Grandpa, when did Sinai stop being mine? They told me that you were there in 1956 and you declared to the whole world that all of it was mine."

Ben-Gurion replied that the Sinai Peninsula had stopped being his at the moment Israel was forced to leave it in 1957.

In that case, Cohen asked, do borders shift with power?

Ben-Gurion confirmed that: "There are no absolute borders. If the Arabs had accepted the 1947 UN partition plan, our borders would have been even narrower. Borders are not an abstract principle. Historical borders are a concept for the days of the Messiah." His practical conclusion was this: "We are interested in peace based on the status quo, but if the Arabs desire war rather than peace, then we will fight and perhaps the status quo will change."

Geula Cohen wanted to talk about the Messiah. His arrival depended on faith, longing, and education, she said. "Would you encourage a child living in Israel today to write a song of longing for all of Jerusalem, including the Old City?" she asked.

"If a child wants to write such a song, he may write one," Ben-Gurion responded; "I would not."[49]

At the end of that Independence Day, Israelis got just such a song. "Jerusalem of Gold" united its audience with the emotional power of a national anthem. It originated as one of the gimmicks Teddy Kollek excelled at. For Kol Israel radio's annual Independence Day song contest, known as the Song Festival, Mayor Kollek suggested that the selection include a few songs about Jerusalem. The festival's producer, Gil Aldema, commissioned the songwriter Naomi Shemer to write the lyrics and music.* It was a very beautiful song, performed by Shuli Natan, a young woman with a crisp voice. And it was a very political song, in which Shemer lamented the partition of the city. She described its Arab half as a deserted wilderness, apparently unpopulated: "Where the water wells have gone dry / The market square is empty / And no one visits the Temple Mount / In the Old City."

Shemer, a native of Kibbutz Kinneret, always denied the political intentions attributed to her songs. Before the festival she played the song for Rivka Mihaeli, a popular radio host, who asked why it was so short. "Before you have time to cry, it's already over," she complained. In response, Shemer said, she added another verse, expressing longing for the Temple Mount. *Ha'aretz* printed the lyrics in its news section, and many Israelis quoted the song in letters to friends and relatives abroad. "Jerusalem of Gold" cast a mysterious spell. Shuli Natan was said to have appeared on stage like a priestess in a holy ceremony, and her song was the prayer of a nation.[50]

---

*The song that actually won the contest was "Who Knows How Many?," performed by an American-born actor-singer, Mike Burstein.

PART III

THE FORTY DAYS OF PRIVATE YEHOSHUA BAR-DAYAN

Once, a young boy asked Gabriel Stern to explain what a border was. A border, Stern said, is not a line that separates good people from bad. There are good people on the other side of the border, too. But they do not know that there are good people on our side—and that is why we have war.

CHAPTER 5

THREE WEEKS TO WAR:
WHAT DOES NASSER WANT?

1. SURPRISE: "IF YOU BLOW SMOKE"

Private 216777, Bar-Dayan, Yehoshua, served as a driver during his yearly stints of reserve duty. A few hours after saying good-bye to his wife, Gila, and their son, Yariv, at their home in Rishon Lezion, he arrived at the Requisitioned Vehicle Base in the south of the country, somewhere between Nitzanim and Julis. He drove there with his friend Uzi Avrahami. They picked up the newspapers on the way. It was May 19, 1967, a Friday. At the base, he was told to pick a requisitioned vehicle. He considered a Studebaker, but then settled on a familiar Willys truck in good working order. In the glove compartment, Bar-Dayan found a year-old pocket calendar with a green plastic binding. The diary belonged to the truck's owner, who lived on a moshav named Netaim. On one of the first pages he had written, "Aliza, birthday." There was a passport photo of a young woman tucked under the plastic sleeve on the inside of the cover. Most of the pages were empty, and Bar-Dayan began to use them to record his impressions, beginning with the events of the previous day, when he had taken his Sussita for an oil change with his son, Yariv. Over the next few weeks, he wrote daily, often hourly, filling every available space with tiny, barely legible handwriting. He wrote a total of three hundred pages. One of his first entries was the question preoccupying every reservist: "What does Nasser want?"[1]

A FEW DAYS EARLIER, PRIME MINISTER ESHKOL HAD STOOD ON HIS OFFICE BALCONY with a glass of orange juice and looked out toward the Hebrew University stadium, which was filled to capacity for the events of Independence Day eve. The stadium was lit up with huge floodlights, and Eshkol could hear the crowds roaring even from his balcony. His wife, Miriam, was also there with some guests. Before leaving for the stadium, Rabin had come by to tell the prime minister that information from Cairo indicated the Egyptians were moving forces into the Sinai Desert. News agencies reported seeing troops on their way, marching through the streets of Cairo. Eshkol was surprised, Israel Lior later wrote, but did not seem worried: despite lingering doubts, he agreed with the army's assessment that Egypt would not initiate war before 1970. And so there was reason to believe, on the eve of the controversial military parade in Jerusalem, that Nasser was just flexing his muscles. That Egyptian military forces were making their way to Sinai so openly seemed only to reinforce this view.

On the day of the parade itself, as the procession was under way, the telephone rang under the seat of General Yeshayahu Gavish, head of the Southern Command. The caller was Rabin, who was sitting a few rows ahead with other dignitaries. He updated Gavish about the Egyptian troop movements and instructed him to return to his command.[2] But the chief of staff was not worried yet, and neither was Ezer Weizman, the chief of operations. This was not the first time Egypt had expanded its forces in Sinai; the last occasion had been only two months earlier. While the move necessitated some readiness on Israel's part, even a limited call-up of reservists, it did not necessarily imply an intention to declare war. This was the assessment that was now given to the government.

The Egyptians' intent, Eshkol told his ministers in a cabinet meeting, was to deter Israel from carrying out its threats against Syria. Adding that recent Israeli warnings seemed to have alarmed the Syrians, he noted that it was quite an achievement for Syria to have drawn Egypt into supporting its extreme position. But at this point, Eshkol did not seem to believe that his and Rabin's Independence Day declarations had instigated a process that would lead to war. He felt the situation did not call for a revision of the view that Egypt would act only if Israel began a far-reaching attack against Syria that included seizing and holding territory. Foreign Minister Eban told the government that the United States was demanding that Israel not act against Jordan or Lebanon, but with regard to Syria they "did not speak." Minister of Education Aran asked whether preparations had been made for a possible emergency, and Eshkol replied, simply, "Yes." There was no sense of anxiety at the meeting. Afterward, one cabinet minister wrote that the Egyptian military movements might be a bluff, and the press agreed. *Maariv* called the maneuver "a showcase response" and *Yediot*

Aharonot termed it "a war of nerves." *Ha'aretz* also viewed the Egyptian move as "a show of strength."[3]

Just a day later, however, Egypt asked the UN to remove its peacekeeping force from the Sinai border; the UN Emergency Force, known as the Blue Helmets, had been posted between Israel and Egypt roughly a decade earlier, as part of the IDF's withdrawal from territories occupied during the 1956 Sinai Campaign. Surprise over the Egyptian redeployment turned to shock when Secretary General U Thant agreed almost immediately to Nasser's demand. This development produced piles of paper documenting numerous diplomatic, historical, and legal debates. U Thant spared no effort in attempting to convince the world—and history—that he had acted as he should have, both legally and politically, as he had an obligation to protect his men's lives and remove them upon the Egyptians' demand.[4] U Thant, a former teacher from Burma, was thus revealed as a man lacking in initiative, concerned only with international law and not with the real world, as rigid as the UN building in New York. Ambassador Harman later observed, "I am convinced that Hammarskjöld [U Thant's predecessor] would have responded to the Egyptian demand by saying, 'Slowly, slowly, *shwaye, shwaye*—I'm getting on a plane and going to Cairo, first of all, to at least try to buy some time, try to calm things down.'" Had U Thant been more creative, more shrewd, more open to criticism, more daring, he might have been able to prevent the war. As Eban told the government, Nasser had not in fact demanded a fundamental realignment of UN forces, only that they vacate the Sinai and concentrate in Gaza. In response, however, U Thant demanded an all-or-nothing clarification from Nasser—that the peacekeepers either stay or go—which left the Egyptians little choice but to ask for their total withdrawal. Eban observed that the secretary general, "a stubborn man," was leading the crisis from one mistake to the next, and called his justifications "a bunch of insulting nonsense." At this point, Eban suggested making it clear to Nasser that hindering Israel's freedom of navigation meant war.[5]

There was, of course, another way to respond to the problem, which was to move the UN emergency forces to the Israeli side of the border. Israel's ambassador to the UN, Gideon Rafael, was asked about this option when he met with U Thant. The ambassador exclaimed: "Ridiculous. Israel is not the Salvation Army and would not be willing to accept UN discards from Egypt." The United States tried, albeit rather limply, to convince Israel to accept the idea. The presence of UN forces would have limited Israel's ability to act against Egypt. But this, like so many other issues, was seen more as a question of national dignity: posting the UN force on the Israeli side of the border would have been interpreted by the Arabs as a humiliating defeat for Israel, and Eshkol's adversaries would have exploited it. The question was raised in a government meeting. "What will the UN forces do here," asked the minister of justice, "recite the book of Psalms?" Eban replied, "They can play cards for all I care."[6]*

EGYPT'S DEMAND THAT THE UN FORCES BE REMOVED DID NOT HELP PRIVATE Yehoshua Bar-Dayan and his friends comprehend Nasser. Yitzhak Rabin, addressing the Knesset Foreign Affairs and Defense Committee, seemed equally uncertain. He did not really know what Nasser wanted, but he assumed the Egyptian president had decided to heat up the southern border so that Israel would not attack Syria, in the north. General Aharon Yariv, head of the IDF intelligence branch, offered the General Staff a fairly lucid explanation: "Nasser's move is a result of Syrian pressure, and the last straw was the Israeli declaration regarding possible action against Syria if the acts of sabotage continue."

Israel Lior surmised that Nasser's move was primarily part of a psychological face-off, and believed the process had started with the air battle near Damascus on April 7. That flight had constituted a provocation and, above all, a humiliating insult to Syrian Arab dignity, he wrote in his diary.[8] A few members of the Knesset Foreign Affairs and Defense Committee also felt that the April 7 incident had caused the crisis, and the most outspoken of these was Moshe Dayan. Egypt was responding to a series of Israeli actions, Dayan maintained, which included the extension of military service, the April 7 incident including the flight near Damascus, and the Israeli propaganda line, which blamed Syria exclusively for the terrorist attacks. He also mentioned the Samua operation. Nasser could not remain indifferent to all these, Dayan said, and added that he was not surprised by the Egyptian demand to remove the UN force: if that step was not taken, Nasser's promise to protect Syria was worthless. Nasser was not planning to invade Israel, but the steps he had taken up to this point would no longer suffice. To preserve his prestige and secure his status, he

---

*A few Israelis agreed that the UN force should be moved to the Israeli side of the border. One of them wrote a letter to *Ha'aretz* in support of the idea; another suggested it in a letter to David Ben-Gurion. Uri Avnery proposed posting UN forces on both sides of the border. In an announcement on behalf of his Knesset party, Avnery demanded that every effort be made to prevent war: "The one-hit-and-we're-done system has failed for nineteen years; let us not continue with it now."[7] Had the idea been implemented, the 1967 war might have been avoided. These isolated voices, however, remained uninfluential.

had to take more provocative steps, which would inevitably elicit an Israeli attack. Dayan mentioned two possibilities: bombing the nuclear reactor at Dimona, or closing the Straits of Tiran. Nasser probably estimated that the Egyptian army could withstand an IDF attack, which explained the defensive alignment of his forces.

At this point, two days after Egypt's demand regarding the UN forces had escalated tensions, there was already a feeling that Israel was on the verge of conflict with Egypt, and that this was against the national interest. "I would like to maintain the status quo for fifty years," said Eshkol. Dayan gave the impression that he himself would never have gotten into this mess: "If you blow smoke, you have to understand that the other side will think a fire has been lit."

Rabin and Eshkol were furious at Dayan. "What are you complaining about?" Eshkol asked. "It was you who demanded ages ago that we do something to get rid of the UN force!" Dayan had taken jabs at Nasser in the past—writing, "It is doubtful that any of the other Arab leaders fail to understand that the UN soldiers are on Egyptian soil not to prevent Nasser from harming Israel, but to serve as a fig leaf over his naked weakness and his inability to do so." Dayan had believed it was best to remove the UN force. Rabin later recalled "an atmosphere of hostility against the government and the IDF brass" at the meeting. These were the first signs of the political and personal rivalry that was to play such an important role in this drama. During the meeting, it was reported that two Egyptian MiGs had invaded Israeli airspace; they had circled over Dimona, among other places.[9]

The fear that the Egyptians would bomb the Dimona reactor or even try to attack it with paratroops became a central concern in the debate over the next few days. Although he still believed the Egyptians would not attack, Eshkol said on May 17, "You never can know what might happen." A few days later he conceded, "One can assume they will have an interest in bombing Dimona." Not all the government ministers believed that a strike on the Dimona reactor would justify all-out war, partly because they felt the world would support Egypt if it destroyed the reactor. The United States did not discount the bombing of the reactor as a possibility.

By May 21 there was talk of outright war. According to one minister, Israel Galili, any infringement on the free movement of shipping would mean war, as would an attempt to bomb Dimona. Rabin sounded confident. If Egypt attacked, he said, Israel would deliver "a very severe blow," although that same day he noted that the results of an air war between the two states would depend on who attacked first.[10] The assumption was that whoever struck first and destroyed the enemy's air force on the ground would win.

There were those who surmised that Nasser was acting partly in response to insults directed at him by the Jordanians, who mocked him for not coming to Syria's aid. Eshkol urged King Hussein not to provoke Nasser, as did the Americans. There was also a theory that the Soviets were to blame. Yaacov Herzog assumed from the outset that Nasser would not risk conflict with Israel without Russian support, and he told Eshkol so.[11]

Foreign Minister Eban had informed the cabinet that information on the Israeli alignment in the north had reached the Egyptians through the USSR, and he blamed the Soviet ambassador, Dimitri Chuvakhin. Eban did not explain the basis for his view, but said he had no doubt of it, and rejected the contention that Israel's threats against Syria had caused panic in Damascus and Cairo. He also expressed his suspicion of the USSR in a conversation with the U.S. ambassador, Walworth Barbour; the accusation was reiterated by an Israeli embassy staffer in Washington, Nehemiah Levanon, who was in charge of the struggle against oppression of Jews in the Soviet Union.[12]

The Israeli press adopted Eban's version of events almost immediately. "Perhaps this is not merely a theatrical demonstration, but a Russian-inspired operation," conjectured *Yediot Aharonot* on May 17. *Maariv* concurred: "If Moscow has been and still is pushing the Arabs to the brink of war and even beyond, it is because it hopes, among other things, that it will succeed in turning the Middle East into a second front with the United States." *Ha'aretz* published the thesis as a front-page scoop: "Nasser's moves fit into a political conspiracy behind which stands the Soviet Union." The Soviet connection theory was attributed to "political observers in Jerusalem."

This view was ultimately adopted by many historians. The Mossad's Meir Amit never ceased believing it. After communism collapsed in Eastern Europe, a secret speech given by Leonid Brezhnev, who had been general secretary of the Communist Party of the Soviet Union since 1964, was revealed, in which he said that the USSR had told Egypt that Israel was about to attack Syria. Other sources confirm this, but do not remove the question marks surrounding the matter: What was the exact nature of the information and what was its source? Did the Russians give Egypt intelligence obtained in Israel, or did they pass on what they had heard in Damascus? Did the Russians believe the information was true? Why did they give it to Egypt? In one Israeli government meeting, the view was expressed that the Russians wanted to open a second front in order to weaken the United States in Vietnam. But this thesis originated with the minister of religious affairs, Zerah Warhaftig, and had no verifiable basis.[13]

The USSR hardly needed an Israeli mole, and Arabs had no need of Soviet intelligence to calculate that Israel might attack Syria. What one government minister called the "abundance of remarks" by Eshkol, Rabin, and other Israeli spokespersons before Independence Day left little room for doubt. Eshkol had been explicit: the main problems in relations with Syria were the water dispute, the demilitarized zone, and the acts of sabotage, for which there was no proven remedy. Syria, therefore, needed "to be dealt a serious blow." A few days later Abba Eban determined that the "first link" in the chain of events that had brought Egypt and Israel to the brink of war was Fatah.[14]

MEANWHILE, LIFE PROCEEDED AS USUAL. PEOPLE WERE PREOCCUPIED BY JUICY REPORTS from the trial of a district court judge, Eliezer Malhi, accused of taking bribes, as well as by the ongoing campaign against autopsies. Erich Leinsdorf came to conduct the Philharmonic in Brahms's Third Symphony. *Yediot Aharonot* devoted a few columns to the Gashash Hahiver's new show. *Ha'aretz* was still busy with an interview Yigal Yadin had given to *Maariv*, in which he criticized the IDF's failure to occupy Bethlehem in the War of Independence, a failure he attributed to Moshe Dayan.[15] Yadin had good reason to make his claims in public: he was vying with Dayan for the leadership of a "nonpartisan" movement that would act to change the electoral system. *Yediot Aharonot* reported that David Ben-Gurion's maneuvering to set up a new government led by Dayan had failed. This news was important, for it suggested the possibility that Ben-Gurion himself, or Dayan, would soon replace Eshkol.

But then the shock Israelis had felt when they learned Nasser was kicking out the UN forces gave way to fear. Nasser might well get involved in a war, maintained *Ha'aretz*. Nasser's move might bring about an explosion even against his own will, *Maariv* added. The military commentator for *Yediot Aharonot* wrote that the war of nerves begun by Egypt could deteriorate into real war, and, as if to remind readers what real war might mean, the paper published excerpts from a new book about the Sinai Campaign.[16]*

---

*Ben-Gurion spent the weekend reading books about the talks that had preceded the campaign, including one by Mordechai Bar-On, the former head of Chief of Staff Dayan's office, and another by the British writer Anthony Nutting.[17]

The day Yehoshua Bar-Dayan was called up for reserve duty, Eshkol told his party's political committee that the situation was far worse than it seemed at first sight. Earlier, at a reception for the president of the Malagasy Republic, Eshkol gave Rabin permission to call up between fifteen thousand and eighteen thousand reservists. By Friday, May 19, more than forty thousand had been called up.[18] Yehoshua Bar-Dayan was no longer merely anxious. For the first time in many years, he wrote in his diary, he was afraid.

On Friday evening, the day after his call-up, Bar-Dayan was moved farther south, toward Kibbutz Revivim. He did not know exactly where he was headed. He wrote two names in his diary: Gili and Yariv. Near Beersheba, he saw long convoys of military vehicles. He ran into an acquaintance and sent regards to his family. At first he camped in a eucalyptus grove, then at a repair facility used by an armored corps unit for its tanks, half-tracks, trucks, pickups, "everything." Bar-Dayan was troubled by the oppressive heat. At the field showers, he met soldiers on their regular army service. "Kids," he wrote. Someone was giving a running commentary on the situation, predicting that Nasser would close off the Straits of Tiran and the IDF would set out to reopen them by force, with American support. One officer let slip that they were in for "a little excursion to the Sinai." Rafi Zur, who worked for the Veterinary Institute, tried to comfort himself and his friend Bar-Dayan: there would not be a war. "Who wants war?" wrote Bar-Dayan. "We just want to live quietly at home. Just live. Gili, Yariv, what will happen?"

Like most Israelis, Bar-Dayan had in fact lived from one war to the next. The figures populating his childhood memories included Eliyahu Golomb and Shaul Avigur, founding fathers of Israel's security apparatus. His parents had hosted Levi Eshkol and Eshkol's second wife, Elisheva, in their home. On November 30, 1947, Shuka Bar-Dayan was supposed to have taken a math exam, but his mother woke him during the night and said, "We have a state." She had just heard on the radio that the UN General Assembly had voted to partition Palestine. The family went out into the street to dance with the crowds, and the next day, of course, there was no school. Outside the local police station, Shuka saw a bus stained with blood after it had been attacked on its way from Netanya to Jerusalem. His mother said the war had begun; it would be long and hard. The day independence was declared, the Bar-Dayans went to see the Golombs; Moshe Sharett talked about the struggle ahead. The next day, Tel Aviv was bombed. Three members of Kibbutz Degania went to Tel Aviv to beg David Ben-Gurion to send in larger forces to defend the

Jezreel Valley. On their way, they stopped off to visit their former physician. Bar-Dayan remembered them sitting with his father, looking worried and tearful.

Shuka went on to study at Mikveh Yisrael, an agricultural school. One of his classmates, Roi Rotenberg, later joined Kibbutz Nahal Oz, in southern Israel, and was shot in April 1956 by Arabs from the Gaza Strip. Moshe Dayan gave a memorable eulogy at his funeral: "Today, let us not hurl accusations at the murderers. How can we argue with their hatred of us? For eight years they have been living in the refugee camps of Gaza, while in front of their very eyes we make our homes on the lands and villages where they and their forefathers lived." During the Sinai Campaign, Bar-Dayan had been among the troops who occupied Gaza City.[19]

2. TENSION: "YITZHAK WAS DEPRESSED"

On Saturday, May 20, Eshkol and Rabin visited the Southern Command of the IDF. Aharon Yariv, head of the army intelligence, had reassessed the situation, and now believed the Egyptians were deployed for offense, rather than just defense. This was a dramatic change, because Yariv had frequently repeated his view that the Egyptians were not preparing for war. "As head of the Intelligence Branch, I failed," he later admitted to colleagues on the General Staff. "I did not anticipate the eventuality that befell us." His revised position was based not only on the tensions created by the IDF along the Syrian border, but also on a perception that the Egyptians wanted to destroy the reactor in Dimona before Israel acquired a nuclear bomb. It is unclear why Yariv needed the concentration of Egyptian forces in Sinai to reach this conclusion. In any event, Eshkol could not ignore it, but the sudden transformation of the fundamental assumption that had guided Israel for years gave him good cause to doubt the information he was now receiving from the military. The IDF also suffered a loss of confidence: events in the Sinai not only disproved the intelligence sector's ability to predict the enemy's intent, but also exposed the weakness of Israeli deterrence.

The power of deterrence was supposed to prevent an Arab attack on the reactor, on military airfields, and on Israeli cities. Virtually the entire strategy was based on the assessment that the Arabs would be afraid to strike. Psychology played an important role. The army had asked repeatedly for permission to carry out operations meant to ensure that the IDF would not be "humiliated" before the Arabs, lest they perceive weakness. This strategy was now collapsing, and panic was not far behind. The country was vulnerable, and the best way to protect it was to attack the Egyptians first.

At the end of his tour in the south, Rabin took Eshkol home and told him about the IDF's various plans. The air force would destroy first the Egyptian air force, next the Egyptian armored corps, and only then would the IDF take over Sharm el-Sheikh, the southernmost point of the Sinai Peninsula. In one variation of this plan, code-named Atzmon, the IDF might occupy Gaza "for negotiation purposes." The two agreed that it was not yet time to act, because political means of reducing tensions had not yet been exhausted. Eshkol asked Rabin to consider the economic burden of a general mobilization.[20]

YEHOSHUA BAR-DAYAN HAD BEEN ISSUED A UNIFORM, A HAT, AND A MESS TIN, AND HIS diary entries began to adopt military slang for the tanks, trucks, and jeeps that surrounded him. One of his friends was given leave to go home and see his newborn son, but was told to return immediately without waiting for the bris. Bar-Dayan missed Gili and Yariv; he wrote Gili letters in which he did not say exactly where he was. "Only here do you realize what home is, and a beloved wife and a precious son," he wrote. He had a lot of time to think, and what he thought about was home. "The balcony doors should be kept closed and the screws on the bottom of Yarivi's crib need tightening. Check them every two days." If Gili needed oranges, he could arrange for a friend from work to bring her a crate of Valencias, and if she needed money, his father would give her a loan. He had forgotten to pay the municipal tax; the bill was in one of the drawers in the bureau. He read a lot. Some people had brought English paperbacks to read. The Nahal entertainment troupe had put on a show.[21]

AT THE BEGINNING OF THE SECOND WEEK OF THE CRISIS, A NEW TONE APPEARED IN THE media, probably because of the new intelligence assessment. Ze'ev Schiff wrote that, contrary to what he had reported three days earlier, Israel was now under threat. The ball was in Egypt's court, the UN force was no longer there to prevent direct conflict between the two countries, and incidents might blow up because not only were there Egyptian soldiers posted in Gaza, but also Palestinians. The conflict had turned into a struggle over prestige, and this phase was primarily psychological. For Nasser, the matter of prestige was extremely important, Schiff judged, and he quoted Dayan's words before the Foreign Affairs and Defense Committee, to the effect that the humiliation of Nasser had only stoked the fire. Israeli leaders had talked too much; their style was too boastful. If they kept it up, Israel would find itself faced with a blockade of the Straits of Tiran and a fight to reopen them. Israel should explain that hindering the free passage of shipping was a cause for war, but in doing so it must avoid provocations and insults. Each of the two countries would have to respond if the other took a "provocative step."

Concern was growing in the security cabinet and the government as a whole. Besides the danger that the Egyptians would try to hit the nuclear reactor and block access to the Straits, there was also talk of the possibility that they would initiate a general attack. One minister, Haim Gvati, considered the situation "fairly serious," but no one seemed to know for sure what Nasser wanted and how far the Russians would go along with him. Criticism of the military was increasing among some of the ministers. Haim Moshe Shapira, the minister of the interior, sounded disgruntled: until two weeks ago, the government had been assured that Syria stood alone and it was therefore time "to teach it some manners." Now all of a sudden there was a danger of war. The inadequately protected borders needed "fifty thousand guards," meaning reservists. Shapira said it would have been advisable to invest more in protective means long ago. He was concerned about terrorists, not the Egyptian army's presence in the Sinai. Minister of Education Aran added, "I will not agree to a war over acts of sabotage. I am not ready for this, either intellectually or spiritually." Mordehai Bentov, the minister of housing, disputed the basic assumption guiding IDF strategy: "The time has passed for the idea that if there is a danger it is better to strike first." Most of the ministers saw no need to reach an operational decision. Only the minister of transport, Moshe Carmel, believed that Israel should be preparing for war. His party colleague, Yigal Allon, was not present at the meeting because he was visiting the USSR at the time.

The ministers tried to set a positive tone. The minister of commerce and industry, Zeev Sherf, said that the state's food supplies would last for several months. Deputy Minister of Defense Zvi Dinstein said there was enough fuel for limited consumption for 120 days, but he promised that fuel from Iran could reach the port of Ashdod by sailing around Africa; fuel could be purchased from other countries, as well. Israel was well prepared for a state of emergency. The minister of education therefore proposed that the public be informed there was no reason for alarm, but Eshkol objected: any such announcement would have the opposite effect. Minister of Finance Sapir commented, "The Israelis are capable of shifting within a few days from the rooftops to the pits and back again."

Eshkol was already hinting at the prime consideration that was to motivate him later on: no action should be taken without prior permission from the United States. Eshkol and Eban reported that Ambassador Harman had been told at the State Department that nothing should be done against the Egyptians as long as the straits were not closed. The Americans said that in any case Israel should not act without "prior consultation," but Eshkol and Eban understood that in the event that Egypt closed the straits, the United States might allow Israel to act, just as it had not opposed action against Syria. This was a good reason to wait and see how things developed.

Eshkol summed up: Israel did not want war, and the call-up was intended to prevent it. If Egyptian aircraft entered Israeli airspace and bombed any target whatsoever, there would be an immediate and forceful response by the air force. The initial five minutes of all-out war would be critical: whoever hit the enemy's airfields first would win. Meanwhile, the situation at Sharm el-Sheikh should be played down. "Let's not give the Arabs cause to celebrate while the Jews stand by and whine," he said. The minutes of the meeting include the words "apprehension" and "fear." Eshkol said he was "praying" that the Egyptians did not initiate a full-scale attack. Shapira sighed, saying, "Who knows where this will end."[22]

IN THE EVENING OF MAY 21, ESHKOL TRAVELED TO AVIHAIL, NORTH OF NETANYA. THE founders of the moshav had served in one of the Jewish brigades set up by the United States and Britain in the First World War, and that evening the community was commemorating the brigade's fiftieth anniversary. The event was intended as a reminder of an old Zionist truism: only Israel's strength could deter the Arab desire to destroy it. In 1918, Eshkol had enlisted in one of the Jewish brigades. He considered canceling his appearance at the event, but the cabinet wanted to project "business as usual."

Some three thousand people filled the local amphitheater, including many veterans of the brigades. "Decorated with medals and standing tall," wrote *Maariv* the next day, "they nostalgically recalled the great era of comradeship in arms and the national pursuit of independence." David Ben-Gurion, also a brigade veteran, had spoken to the crowds earlier in the day. He gave his speech in Yiddish.[23] He did not attend the assembly with Eshkol; instead, he met with Yitzhak Rabin, at the latter's request. Ben-Gurion said he was surprised that the IDF chief of staff wanted to see him, and found Rabin in need of encouragement and emotional support.

"I felt lonely," Rabin later wrote. He felt Eshkol was "exhausted" and that "his wings were clipped," partly because of the erosion of his standing. Although Rabin said Eshkol knew there was no avoiding war, "he did not have the strength to impose his authority on the government." Rabin claimed that he "pitied" Eshkol and felt the army was not getting clear instructions from the government. Existing documentation does not corroborate this. Eshkol was not yet certain that war was inevitable, and at this stage he had no difficulty uniting his ministers around him. The army was given perfectly clear instructions: be prepared and wait. The one who was "exhausted" was not the prime minister but rather Rabin himself. According to Moshe Dayan, "Yitzhak not only looked tired—which was natural—but also confused, less than confident, irritable (he chain-smoked), and extremely unenthusiastic about the battle ahead." Abba Eban wrote that Rabin was "feverishly irritable." Israel Lior reported to Eshkol that something was happening to the chief of staff: "He's not the same Yitzhak."

Rabin shared the opinion that the IDF's job was to deter the Arabs so that there would not be a war. He knew that he bore a significant part of the responsibility for the deterrence failures that, in his view, necessitated immediate war. As chief of staff, he was accountable for the intelligence assessment that had dismissed any chance of war with Egypt in the next few years and had therefore seen no reason for restraint on the northern border. Over and over he had lobbied Eshkol to allow an attack against Syria; he had led the campaign of threats against the Syrians, pulling Eshkol along with him. Now he hoped Ben-Gurion would strengthen his resolve. Like most Israelis, he admired Ben-Gurion. But their meeting was miserable, because instead of encouraging Rabin, the old man showered him with accusations not unlike those Rabin had already heard from Dayan in the Foreign Affairs and Defense Committee. Like Dayan, Ben-Gurion believed that neither Egypt nor Syria, but Israel itself, was responsible for this crisis. It is unclear to what extent Ben-Gurion blamed Rabin and how much of the situation he attributed to Eshkol.

Ben-Gurion explained that the national call-up, which had already involved seventy thousand reservists, was "a political and social error." He also spoke of "other mistakes." He denounced the operation in Samua, "a civilian village in nonhostile Jordan," and criticized the April 7 air battle with Syria. He also accused Rabin of the worst: loyalty to Eshkol. "I told [Rabin] he was not telling me everything that was in his heart, because he had to follow orders from the minister of defense and was not permitted to criticize him," wrote Ben-Gurion. "Yitzhak was depressed," he added.

According to Ben-Gurion's biographer Michael Bar-Zohar, he also told Rabin that Eshkol was "a liar and a coward." Rabin was stunned: "I had never felt such a deep sense of disappointment and distress."

The next day, May 22, Rabin went to seek Moshe Dayan's counsel. According to Dayan, he told Rabin that Nasser would close off the Straits and Israel would have to take military action. They spoke about various strategic options. Rabin suggested occupying the Gaza Strip, but Dayan was opposed to Israel taking control because of the refugee camps. Rabin said the success of the air force depended on delivering the first blow; Dayan said the government as currently constituted would not authorize this. They discussed the causes of the crisis. Rabin seemed to blame himself, not only for having brought about an escalation of tensions, but also for not being able to convince Eshkol to attack Syria more forcefully. Dayan disagreed: a stronger blow would have accelerated Egyptian intervention, and a blow strong enough to deter Nasser from intervening could not be delivered except in war. "Yitzhak was unable to say what would have constituted a stronger blow, either," Dayan noted. "My main impression from the evening was Yitzhak's low spirits. If this is apparent when he is with his subordinates, too, that is not good."[24]

AT MIDDAY, YEHOSHUA BAR-DAYAN WAS ORDERED TO DRIVE CAREFULLY, AS THE BRIGADE commander, Colonel Shmuel Gorodish, was coming that evening. "Chilling words; the situation is deteriorating. We will go out to strike and destroy the Egyptians." Bar-Dayan documented his response: "My heart beats powerfully—I may not return from this. What does this have to do with me?" He had trouble sleeping. He kissed the photo of his wife and son. "Little *mamaleh*," he wrote.[25] He slept in the requisitioned pickup truck, which had a transistor radio.

3. NERVES: "HOW DARE YOU!"

On the morning of Tuesday, May 23, Israelis learned from the six o'clock news that Nasser had blockaded the Straits of Tiran. "That's it," Bar-Dayan wrote in his diary. "War. Almost certainly." The mail would be picked up soon, so he quickly wrote another letter to his wife and son: "I miss you very much and that is the most difficult thing. I feel love and endless longing for you and I pray that the tension will be diffused and we will come home quickly." He reminded Gila to drain the water out of the washing machine—one of the neighbors could help. If there was a problem, the Amcor appliance insurance was in Yariv's room, in the closet on the left, on the bottom shelf. "Blessings to you, my love, and to you my little boy."[26]

Once Israeli shipping was barred access to the Straits of Tiran, Israel would lose the most important advantage it had acquired in the Sinai Campaign. Eshkol heard about the blockade from Israel Lior and immediately departed for the IDF command post in Tel Aviv. Rabin, Weizman, Yariv, and Mordechai Hod, the commander of the air force, demanded action without delay. For the first time, it seems, they were explicit and insistent. There had to be "a serious blow," they stressed. Yariv said that if they did not take action, "Nasser will keep up his obstreperousness and tomorrow there will be sabotage." Rabin said the dilemma was simply "to be or not to be." The war would not end in a day or two, and one had to take into account that there would be "massive destruction" in populated areas. Hod promised he could handle the Syrian air force. They did not discuss a limited action to open the Straits, but only an all-out war. "Let's be honest with ourselves," said Rabin: "first we will attack Egypt; then we will also attack Syria and Jordan." From this point on, Eshkol had to repeatedly push back against Rabin and his cohort. Throughout the day, Rabin over and over demanded a preemptive attack, claiming that the Straits would remain closed otherwise. Ezer Weizman tried to scare Eshkol by saying he "hoped" Israel would be able to destroy the Egyptian air force, "assuming they do not use gas."*

Eshkol said a week would pass before the first tanker would reach the area, and that time should be utilized for diplomacy. In any case, at the Foreign Affairs and Defense Committee, which had convened the previous day, he had said the situation in the north was far more dangerous than in the south because the Syrians could destroy all the Israeli settlements.[27] The United States asked for a forty-eight-hour moratorium on any response, and the security cabinet met on the morning of May 23 to discuss the request. Eshkol was in favor, arguing that the Americans must not be allowed to claim that Israel had "ruined things" by hindering an attempt to resolve the crisis without war. But he cautioned that a waiting period might last longer than forty-eight hours. "From two days it becomes two weeks, and two weeks could become two years," which would be a victory for Nasser. Minister of the Interior Shapira disagreed: "If it takes two years, that's not a bad thing." Eshkol was surprised: "Closing the shipping at

---

*Rabin later wrote, "We were not prepared for chemical warfare at that time; we grew more worried."

Sharm el-Sheikh for two years?" But Shapira proposed that Israeli ships could proceed to Eilat with foreign warships escorting them. At this point Rabin revealed a fact that was top secret: the Egyptians had already decided that ships under American escort would not be stopped.

Minister of Transport Carmel asserted that closing the Straits was an act of aggression that necessitated a response. Minister Israel Galili proposed a resolution that the closure of the Straits amounted to a declaration of war. Rabin repeated that if Israel did not respond, it would lose its deterrence capability. Some of the ministers asked if postponing the action for forty-eight or even sixty hours would lessen the element of surprise. "A difficult question," Rabin responded, and refused to say that such a delay would be critical: "I don't think I can say to you in all honesty that forty-eight hours would make a difference here." But he added, "As difficult as the situation is, and knowing that this is no picnic, it seems to me that we are dealing here with an extremely serious matter for the security of Israel." When questioned, he said that in a battle with the Egyptian air force, Israel would lose fifteen to twenty planes. Sapir said, apparently for the first time since the crisis began, "We are talking about our very existence here."

Tempers flared at times. Galili shouted that he could not be held responsible for failing to respond to the closing of the Straits; he then apologized for raising his voice. But most of the ministers were loath to take action. Minister of Health Israel Barzilai suggested waiting two or three weeks. Shapira maintained that Egypt did not want war. They all agreed that closing the Straits was "an act of aggression" and decided to send Foreign Minister Eban to the United States. Eshkol raised the idea of bringing in opposition members to join the cabinet.[28]

AFTER THE MEETING, RABIN TESTED HIS FRAZZLED NERVES YET AGAIN AND SAT DOWN TO talk with Haim Moshe Shapira. "I brought the distress upon myself," he later wrote. The leader of the Mafdal party objected to unleashing the IDF in response to the closure of the Straits; Rabin tried to soften his opposition, unsuccessfully. "How dare you!" Shapira exclaimed. "How dare you? Ben-Gurion did not dare—how dare you!" According to Rabin, Shapira suggested "hunkering down" instead of fighting. "War will risk Israel's existence."

Like many Israelis, Shapira was thinking of Ben-Gurion's management of the Sinai Campaign. "Explain to me, just explain to me," he said to Rabin, "do you really think the Eshkol-Rabin team should be bolder, more courageous, than the Ben-Gurion–Dayan team was? Why? The Straits were closed until 1956—did it threaten Israel's security? It did not!" Shapira, who was in the government at the time, reminded Rabin that Ben-Gurion had not gone to war before securing the support of Britain and France; he had known that Syria and Jordan would not intervene. The current situation was different. No one was standing by Israel; the United States was demanding that it wait at least forty-eight hours. "I understand—they attack us," said Shapira, "we will go out and defend our lives. But to start a war? To bring this curse upon ourselves with our own hands? Do you want to be responsible for putting the existence of Israel at risk?" The more he spoke, wrote Rabin, the more agitated he grew.[29]

IN THE KNESSET CAFETERIA, THERE WAS TALK OF A NATIONAL EMERGENCY GOVERN-ment. To forestall any attempt to exploit the crisis and topple his government, Eshkol made a dramatic gesture: he invited opposition delegates—Knesset member Menachem Begin and two of his people, and Moshe Dayan—to a briefing, where they learned, among other things, of the disagreement between Eshkol and Rabin. Eshkol explained that he supported the U.S. request to wait forty-eight hours, so as not to give America an excuse to renege on its commitment to Israel. Were the United States not mired in Vietnam, everything would be much easier, Eshkol observed. Rabin repeated once again that if Israel did not respond, it would lose its deterrent capability, which would lead to war under more difficult conditions. The war he was proposing now would not be easy, either: what began as a conflict with Egypt might snowball into war with Syria, and perhaps Jordan. But, as he saw things, there was really no choice. The Egyptians had to be hit.

He shared the war plans with the participants. First, there would be a surprise strike on the Egyptian air force; the aerial advantage gained would then be exploited in a land war. Begin asked Rabin to clarify whether he was saying that the air force would strike the Egyptian air force while it was still on the ground. Rabin confirmed that it would. He was convinced they could deliver a devastating blow against the Egyptians. There would be losses, he said, that much was clear; in the north, too. The Syrians might bomb Israeli settlements and it would take some time before the air force completed its mission in Egypt and could turn its attention to suppressing Syrian fire. Some of those present responded with discomfort, wanting to know how much time might pass until the Syrians were quelled. Rabin was evasive. Perhaps several hours, he said. Knesset member

Yosef Serlin, who had accompanied Begin, demanded a more specific answer. Rabin said that the stronger the strike against Egypt was, the freer the air force would be to handle the Syrians. "How long is several hours?" Serlin persisted. Rabin said, "Eight to ten. That's the picture."

David Hacohen, the chairman of the Knesset Foreign Affairs and Defense Committee, and Knesset member Arieh Ben-Eliezer, another of Begin's allies, were stunned. Until that moment, they had believed the IDF could fight on all fronts simultaneously. No, said Ezer Weizman, that claim had never been made. But the two Knesset members persevered: they had always been given the impression that the IDF could repel a multifront attack. This was another basic assumption, like the intelligence assessment of no war with Egypt before 1970, and it, too, was crumbling. The discovery bolstered their opinion that it was best to wait, as the United States had asked.

Foreign Minister Eban raised a proposal that had come up earlier that day in the security cabinet, whereby U.S. warships would escort Israeli ships to Eilat. Begin asked for clarification: Was the foreign minister recommending that? Eban replied that it would be an act of protest—someone had to show that Nasser could be overruled. Golda Meir, the secretary of Mapai, objected. Either there was freedom of navigation or there wasn't, she argued. Dayan said that if the Americans committed to deploying the Sixth Fleet to the area to assure freedom of passage in the area, he would not object: "I will swallow my Israeli pride." But he ruled out the idea of escorting each ship individually. He pointed out that Nasser had in fact ordered his forces not to fire on ships entering the Gulf of Aqaba with American warships. Rabin interrupted: "I alert you to the fact that this is extremely confidential material," he said, but he agreed that escorts might provide an avenue to resolving the crisis.

Eshkol tried to build on the idea, grasping at Dayan's willingness to put aside pride. The United States was not suggesting that it would go into Egypt and slaughter twenty million Egyptians, he said, but it might agree to send destroyers to the Red Sea to escort Israeli ships. It could be a temporary arrangement—a year and a half, two years. Meanwhile, Israel would build its own large naval force and would no longer need American escorts. Dayan responded coolly: "I'm not a partner to this." One participant reminded Eshkol that the United States had not offered such an arrangement, and that in the meantime they were playing chess with themselves. "True," said Eshkol, "but don't put the king in your pocket." He was encouraged by the fact that those present did not view the idea as a nonstarter and did not reject it outright.

But Dayan led the meeting in another direction. Nothing would change during the next forty-eight hours, he said; the Americans would not secure Sharm al-Sheikh. Israel would go to war with the Arab states. Jordan might be first. The situation at the outset was graver than in 1956, and far more so than in 1948. As an aside, Dayan said, "We should also take the Israeli Arabs into account." Over the next few weeks there were persistent fears that they would aid the Arab armies.

Then those present spoke of the need to obtain gas masks and reviewed the state of the bomb shelters. War seemed inevitable. Eban amended his proposal: instead of asking for escorts for its ships, Israel should demand that the United States "fulfill its promises." The next suggestion was equally legalistic: Israel should send a vessel of some kind into the Gulf of Aqaba, but do nothing until Egypt attacked it, in case it later had trouble convincing the world that it was acting to assure freedom of the seas.

Before the meeting was adjourned, Rabin again cautioned the participants not to reveal under any circumstances the information about Egypt's order not to shoot at ships accompanied by U.S. vessels. Hours later, he had a nervous breakdown.

"DURING THOSE FINAL DAYS, WHICH WENT ON WITH NO END IN SIGHT, WITHOUT regular meals, with little rest, I was smoking like a chimney," Rabin later wrote, "but it was not only the excessive smoking. A strong sense of guilt, which had troubled me recently, surged that day, May 23. I can't forget Minister Shapira's punishing words. I had dragged Israel into this crisis. I was not able, as chief of staff, to prevent the development of the great danger the country now faced." He noted that he had prepared the army adequately for war, but wondered, "Perhaps I had failed as the main military adviser to the Prime Minister and Minister of Defense. Perhaps that is the reason Israel is now in such a difficult situation. Maybe Ben-Gurion was right to say that there should not have been such a large call-up of reservists and that this had caused an escalation that led Israel to war."

Rabin summoned Ezer Weizman, his deputy, and proposed that he step in as chief of staff. Weizman later claimed he had noticed days earlier that Rabin was growing unsteady: "Rabin was spreading a lack of confidence." At Rabin's home, Weizman found the chief of staff sitting alone in the living room, "depressed and broken." Leah Rabin, his wife, called a doctor, who gave him a shot that left him incapacitated for the next twenty-four hours.[31]

• • •

MEANWHILE, WEIZMAN ATTEMPTED TO HASTEN THE BEGINNING OF THE WAR. IN THE
morning hours of May 24, war seemed "very close," an IDF report noted.
"Preparations for starting war on the twenty-fifth of the month are being
made final." At midday on May 24, with Rabin still at home in a stupor,
Weizman presented Eshkol with a plan code-named Expanded Atzmon,
whose essence was destruction of the Egyptian air force and occupation
of the Gaza Strip. Contrary to what he had claimed the day before, he
now promised that the military could operate against Egypt and Syria at
the same time. When he met with his people before seeing Eshkol, there
was talk of the operation commencing the next day, May 25. With
Eshkol, he spoke of "operational readiness" on May 26. According to another summary, he said action could be taken "immediately."

Weizman asked Eshkol to come to the war room to meet the IDF generals, who also did their best to convince the prime minister to strike.
They were told that Rabin was at home, feeling unwell. Mordechai Hod of
the air force and the head of the Southern Command, General Yeshayahu
Gavish, promised the plan would succeed. General David Elazar of the
Northern Command guaranteed that even without the assistance of the
air force he could put a dent in the Syrian artillery, although there was
no doubt that Israeli settlements would be hit. General Uzi Narkis of the
Central Command, still a minor voice in the discussion, promised that
his forces could also carry out "limited aggressive operations." The plans
were ready, he declared. All the generals emphasized that the operation's success depended on Eshkol allowing them to act as soon as possible; otherwise they would lose the element of surprise and flexibility.
They also pointed out that it was difficult to maintain the requisite level
of alertness among the reservists. Weizman said he would prefer a political solution, but according to Lior, "the atmosphere at the General Staff
headquarters was as if war was about to begin at any moment."[32]

In fact Weizman began winding up the war machine that very night.
"We're on the move," Yehoshua Bar-Dayan wrote in his diary; "a good
feeling, realistic, confident." They joined a convoy of tanks belonging to
the 79th Regiment and traveled south with dimmed lights toward Kibbutz Gvulot. There were Shermans, Pattons, Centurions—"a force of steel
and humans and dust," wrote Bar-Dayan.

"I issued orders to the Southern Command to move units and divi-
sions," Weizman later wrote, and claimed that none of the officers asked
where the chief of staff was or questioned Weizman's orders. But some of

them thought Weizman had lost his mind, because there seemed to be no reason for his order to move units from one point to another. It was "a mad race of uncoordinated forces," Ariel Sharon later recounted; "I had no idea whether the General Staff knew what was going on, and we had no idea what was going on at the top." Sharon tried to get hold of Rabin but was told he could not speak with him. "I think the army is really sick," he wrote to a colleague, Avraham Yaffe, who replied, "Yesterday the war was directed by our mutual friend, and it showed."

According to General Gavish, "It was no easy task to move all the troops in one night just because of one man's craziness." He demanded that Haim Bar-Lev replace Weizman as deputy chief of staff. Herein, apparently, lay the primary motive behind Weizman's entire futile exercise: Bar-Lev was threatening his dream of becoming the next chief of staff and he wanted to take advantage of Rabin's absence to demonstrate leadership.[33]

PRIVATE YEHOSHUA BAR-DAYAN WROTE A LETTER TO HIS WIFE, AS WAS HIS CUSTOM every morning. When he wrote to Gili, it was like being with her, which gave him some comfort. The conditions were fine, he assured her. He continued to sleep in the pickup truck's cabin, curled up in a blanket and a sweater. There was no danger where he was, he promised. Only he missed her so much, which was not something you got used to. The blinds had to be fixed. "There are so many things I didn't take care of when I was home, and here it really annoys me." He met with Uzi Avrahami and Rafi from the institute. They'd already had three entertainment troupes, and a movie. There were books and newspapers. The papers were unequivocal. "Nasser wants war," asserted *Maariv*. *Ha'aretz* went a step further: "Nasser Declares War on Israel." Everyone was talking about revisiting 1956.[34]

Only an extremely experienced man, determined not to lose control of events, could have withstood such pressure as the country stood on the brink of war, with a chief of staff recovering from emotional collapse and an out-of-control acting chief effectively forcing him into war despite the government decision that had just sent Abba Eban to Washington. Eshkol bore some responsibility for the situation, since he had allowed the military to drag him toward an attack on Syria. He had not offered any principled objection to the military's demand to respond with force to the closing of the Straits, but he still hoped to resolve the crisis without war. Above all, he believed Israel should not act against U.S. opinion. For the moment, he was unbroken. A report compiled by the General Staff summed up the drama in a few words: "It is reported that there is no chance of a decision before Saturday, May 27, 1967."[35]

THE HEAT WAVE SUBSIDED A LITTLE. YEHOSHUA BAR-DAYAN DID NOT DO MUCH. HE read and now felt afraid. "We lack confidence, hope, and initiative," he wrote in his diary. Rafi from the Veterinary Institute had a stroke of luck: the vehicle he had chosen had no front-wheel drive, so it seemed he would not go out with the rest of the force. "Strange," Bar-Dayan pondered, "only a few days ago, I was busy packing oranges." He spoke with Gila on the phone. "My heart is lighter," he wrote. And he started getting used to the idea of war: "Increasingly, I realize that we can't escape fighting. It is our destiny, which has brought us to this place."[36]

CHAPTER 6

ELEVEN DAYS TO WAR: NOA'S FATHER IS WAITING

1. EXPLORATORY MOVES: "YOU'RE THE ONLY ONE"

On the morning of May 25, Private Yehoshua Bar-Dayan woke up in his truck cabin in the Julis camp, in southern Israel, and quickly wrote a letter to Gili and Yariv. He asked his wife to buy him a new pair of sandals, so he could step right into them as soon as he got home. There were some great guys with him, he wrote; they helped one another ease the loneliness and cope with the homesickness. He would have given anything to be able to hug and kiss his wife and son, but he was where he was so that he could do so in the future, and there were thousands upon thousands of others along with him. A few hours later he was able to talk with Gili on the phone, and he detected extreme anxiety in her voice.[1]

The mass call-up disrupted life in almost every household. Buses ran on reduced schedules; the school day was shortened. It was suddenly easy to find parking in front of the California restaurant at lunchtime. The few cars on the road had their headlights painted blue, so they could drive during blackouts. Men of eligible age who had not been called up were ashamed to be seen on the streets. Masses of Israelis, including schoolchildren, volunteered to dig trenches, fill sandbags, sort mail, distribute milk, drive ambulances, work in hospitals, and do guard duty on kibbutzim. "Eve-of-war tension," wrote Yosef Weitz in his diary.[2] Most Israelis assumed that war was inevitable, and a growing number concluded that Levi Eshkol was incapable of leading the country at such a time. They demanded a national unity government under David Ben-Gurion. The demand was spontaneous, an authentic expression of the sense that the country was teetering on the brink of the abyss.

Rafael Halevi, a ninth-grader from Ramat Hasharon, wrote to Ben-Gurion two days after Nasser's demand to remove the UN forces. "The enemy is ready for battle," Rafael wrote, and begged Ben-Gurion to return to lead the country. Over the next few days, Ben-Gurion was inundated with similar letters. "You're the only one who could, today, with a lightning attack, turn this miserable moment into a historic crossroads and create a unique chance for normal life," wrote a citizen named Yaakov Bermes. He suggested seizing the Old City and expelling the country's Arabs, who would receive financial compensation. A group of anonymous soldiers from the southern front sent a letter signed only with their initials, emphasizing that they were voicing the anguish of hundreds of their comrades: "We are asking you, great captain, to liberate the ship of the People of Israel, which has run aground, and lead it to safe shores." Letters to the president, the prime minister, and Moshe Dayan also demanded Ben-Gurion's return. Some wrote out of great distress. "My husband goes from one hospital to the next, I've three sons in the army, I'm alone and living in terrible fear," wrote Batya Gotlieb from Tel Aviv; she begged Ben-Gurion to join the government immediately. "A depressed and fearful man is writing to you," wrote Haim Elimeleh Ohon. Many others expressed such feelings as well, and similar letters flooded the office of the chairman of the Knesset. "Say yes to the old man," wrote one citizen.[3] Almost all the writers asked Ben-Gurion to take charge as the head of state and lead Israel to victory. They did not know that he was opposed to the war.

According to Rabin, Ben-Gurion did not believe that the IDF could win. Rabin attributed this view to the fact that Ben-Gurion was behind the times and his ideas were old-fashioned. Ben-Gurion thought that getting rid of the UN forces and closing the Straits would be enough for Nasser, and that he would not allow Palestinians in Gaza to carry out terrorist attacks in Israel. Yet he viewed the situation as "an unprecedented and difficult test." He supported limited action to open the Straits, but thought that any steps should be taken only after support was assured from the United States, Britain, and France, or at least from one of them, as in the Sinai Campaign. He was concerned primarily by weapons supplies, and believed that without support from the great powers, the IDF would fail. "It will be the end. Our army is wonderful, but these days one cannot fight the way David fought Goliath."[4]

Ben-Gurion was not alone in his skepticism. General Yehoshafat Harkabi, a Ministry of Defense staffer at the time, believed the war should somehow be delayed. Harkabi feared the death toll even in an Israeli victory might be as high as 10,000, while a defeat would bring about the "decisive and final" destruction of two million Israeli citizens. He suggested waiting six months. "What will be different in six months?" Ben-Gurion asked, and Harkabi replied, "They will attack and then we will defend ourselves." He was probably surmising—or perhaps he knew—that Israel was close to a dramatic improvement in its warfare capabilities. Parts of Ben-Gurion's account of this conversation are classified, and many of the classified sections in his diary concern the development of nuclear weapons.[5]

Over the next few days, the political system seemed stricken by frenzy. Everyone ran around frenetically, swept up in a storm of initiatives and proposals, plots and conspiracies, trickery and political maneuvers, a whirlwind of contradictory interests and massive egos; Israel had never known such feverish activity. The question of whether the war could be prevented was pushed aside, the focus having shifted to how to get rid of Eshkol and who would replace him. The two central figures in this drama were Shimon Peres and Menachem Begin. As opposition members, they both wanted Eshkol gone. Peres, a member of Rafi who shared Ben-Gurion's assessment, was also hoping to prevent war. He agreed that they should try to delay the war for at least six months and spend the interval in preparation. He knew, however, that a delay might be even more shocking to Israelis and undermine their confidence, and he believed that the only person who could manage the situation successfully was Ben-Gurion. He should therefore return to the prime minister's office and Eshkol moved to a different position. "In our opinion the country is in the worst situation since its establishment," Peres told members of his party. "There is no clear-cut solution. The central thing required is leadership that can handle the situation."

Begin also demonstrated responsible statesmanship at that time, despite his image as a town-square demagogue. "If this government were to resign tonight, I would recommend to the president that he appoint Ben-Gurion to form a new government" and lead the country as it prepared for war or, as Begin put it, "bloodshed the likes of which we have never seen." He too was apparently unaware of Ben-Gurion's opposition to war.

Together, Peres and Begin took upon themselves an extremely difficult task: Peres agreed to ask Ben-Gurion whether he would serve in a government led by Eshkol, and Begin agreed to ask Eshkol whether he would step down as prime minister, or at least as minister of defense, in favor of Ben-Gurion. But Ben-Gurion refused either to join Eshkol's government or to accept Eshkol in a new government of his own. He would, however, support Eshkol remaining in a government led by Dayan, but he himself would remain outside, he wrote in his diary. Nonetheless, Begin went to Eshkol to persuade him to act as Ben-Gurion's deputy, claiming Ben-Gurion had sanctioned the idea. "Who told you that?" Eshkol asked. He suspected Peres was behind it, and so was skeptical. If the idea had been Dayan's, he might have put some stock in it, he said.

It is unclear what led Begin to claim that Ben-Gurion was willing to accept Eshkol as his deputy. Perhaps he was trying to mislead Eshkol; perhaps he himself had been misled by Peres. Rafi members also heard from Peres that Ben-Gurion had agreed to take on Eshkol as his deputy. Either way, the conversation was friendly. Begin and Eshkol were old acquaintances. Begin thanked him once again for allowing Jabotinsky's remains to be brought to Israel, and said he knew the rift with Ben-Gurion was more painful to Eshkol than it was to Ben-Gurion. Eshkol said, "I've already got it out of my system," but added bitterly, "Over the last decades I have perhaps educated a few young boys and girls to admire Ben-Gurion." Which was why he now bit his tongue, he said; once in a while something negative slipped out, and he regretted it, but generally he tried not to get dragged into responding to Ben-Gurion's slanderous remarks. As to the matter at hand, he said there was no one who could succeed as Ben-Gurion's deputy. He was not willing to be a second Moshe Sharett—referring to the foreign minister and prime minister whom Ben-Gurion had pushed around. But Begin would not let it go: "After all, it's me that Ben-Gurion makes out to be a Hitler, not you," he said. "He spoke very nicely, in a Polish, gentlemanly way," Eshkol later told the cabinet. But his response to the proposal was unequivocal: "Out of the question. These two horses will never again pull the same cart." He assured Begin that "the fool sitting before him" was capable of leading the country even without Ben-Gurion, and told him about the steps he had taken to strengthen the IDF. "We will be able to sustain the campaign," he promised.[6]

One day later, Shimon Peres spoke with Meir Yaari, the head of Mapam. As Yaari's associate Yaakov Hazan recalled it, Peres said that Israel was not ready for war and that the country was under the threat of a "true holocaust." Yaari quickly called Hazan, and Hazan called Peres to hear from him first-hand. According to Hazan, Peres added further details that made the situation sound utterly dire. Hazan asked to speak with Golda Meir, the secretary of Mapai, and within fifteen minutes he was in her office. There he found Shaul Avigur, who was widely trusted in matters of politics, security, and covert operations. Avigur said he had been with

Ben-Gurion that day, and he wanted to talk with the military leaders before deciding whether to return to the government; but one thing Ben-Gurion knew: if he came back into the government, Eshkol would have to leave. Avigur had reportedly told Ben-Gurion to forget about his contempt for Eshkol, but Ben-Gurion was insulted: he didn't need to be told what to remember and what to forget.

Golda Meir told her colleagues that Paula Ben-Gurion had phoned her and said, in English, "Come to Ben-Gurion, he loves you." But Meir's colleagues agreed with her that Eshkol should not be replaced and the government should not be expanded to include Ben-Gurion's party. The matter was closed, Meir therefore decreed. The important decisions should be left to the IDF chief of staff and the government, led by Eshkol. Ben-Gurion himself did not have much faith in the proposal to bring him in, for he had predicted that Golda Meir would oppose it.[7]

An intriguing question remains unanswered: had Ben-Gurion returned to the government, would he have been able to prevent the war, or at least restrict Israel's goal to reopening the Straits? Another question left unanswered is which of these two horses, Eshkol or Ben-Gurion, should have placed the prevention of war ahead of his own ego.

SHUKA BAR-DAYAN COULD SCARCELY BELIEVE HIS EARS. "WE'RE GOING TO TEL AVIV," announced a young officer named Yoram. Shuka was sure Yoram was pulling his leg, but it turned out they were going to the Tel Hashomer army base to bring back spare parts, which meant he would be able to go home. Bar-Dayan was thrilled. When they stopped for lunch in Ashkelon, he was so excited he couldn't swallow his food. In Rehovot he dropped in to give his father a quick kiss, and then went to his apartment. Gila was wearing pink. They exchanged kisses and hurried to Yariv's kindergarten. It was the first time Bar-Dayan had visited his son there, and he was choked up. The boy came to him hesitantly. "Dad, are you home from the army?" "No, son, not yet—look at my boots, my little son whom I love so much." He didn't have much time. He kissed Gila and was gone. "The visit home was a dream," he wrote later, "I'll never forget it."[8]

He brought some newspapers back with him to Julis, and sat around analyzing the situation with his friends. They all agreed that war was inevitable, and that it was all because of the Russians. Preparations in the camp had intensified to a buzzing swarm of tanks and cannons. Bar-Dayan met a young man, Captain Yohanan, who had also been born in Afula. He was cheerful but taciturn, confident and energetic. Bar-Dayan felt he could be trusted. Yohanan said there would be casualties. "Good God," wrote Bar-Dayan, "I could die. And never again see Gila and Yariv. Each man to his own fate and luck. God—to live! To live!" He was no longer afraid, he wrote, because he had become realistic. But he kissed the pictures of his loved ones again and again. "It's not superstition, but I hope they bring me luck." He consoled himself with the thought that he was not on the front line: he would be driving behind the forward tanks.

THE PAPERS WERE CALLING FOR THE GOVERNMENT TO EXPAND. SOME SAID THERE should be a broad national-unity government, others an emergency government, and *Maariv* simply called for "a war cabinet." The press was impatient and bluntly intolerant of the negotiations that were supposed to lead to an expanded government. Instead of "petty accounts and partisan calculations," *Maariv* demanded that a "war leadership" be set up, composed of figures representing "experience and strong leadership, personal prestige and public backing." Not Levi Eshkol, in other words—or, at least not him at the helm.* Other papers made similar demands. "There is no need to say very much about the necessity to lift the nation's spirits at this moment," explained *Ha'aretz*.[9]

2. DIPLOMACY: "ALL TO CREATE AN ALIBI"

Spirits were indeed at a low point. Even those who had access to accurate information, including the former head of the Security Service, Amos Manor, began digging trenches around their homes. General Uzi Narkis told Colonel Mordechai Gur that in Tzahala, the residential neighborhood for the senior military ranks, they were digging trenches. Gur himself, a regimental commander in the paratroopers, dug a trench to protect his wife and children.[10] But Manor apparently did not know how to prepare a trench, so one of his neighbors, an American, helped him out. The American, however, noted that the whole effort was superfluous: if there was a war, Israel would win, perhaps within six or ten days. He claimed to know this for sure, and indeed he did.

---

*The editor of *Maariv*, Arieh Dissentchik, committed his paper to the campaign to appoint Moshe Dayan minister of defense. He did so in coordination with Dayan, but did not confine himself to his role as journalist: in keeping with the excessively close relationship between newspaper editors and politicians, he went to Eshkol and tried to persuade him to give up the defense portfolio.

His name was John Hadden, and he was the CIA station chief in Israel. His main job seemed to be spying on the progress of Israel's nuclear project. He was once observed wandering around the Dimona reactor's employee housing, copying down residents' names from mailboxes. When asked what he was doing, he claimed he was looking for a Mr. Tzafriri. An experienced spy with a sense of humor, he began each day with an attempt to learn what was going on in Israel by studying the well-known caricaturist Ze'ev's daily cartoon in *Ha'aretz*. He knew a little Hebrew; at the Mossad he was referred to as "the bastard."[11]

When he told his neighbors there was no need for trenches, Hadden was reflecting an assessment prevalent in Washington and accepted by the administration. U.S. analysts gave Israel complete military superiority over every combination of Arab forces, and they assumed this imbalance would hold for at least another five years. At the same time, the view in Washington was that Israel expected to need an atomic bomb within a fairly short time, and was planning for this eventuality.[12] A year earlier, the Americans had predicted that Palestinian terror attacks might lead to war. In that event, they believed, Israel would destroy the Egyptian air force and "within days or weeks" would occupy areas of the Sinai, the West Bank including East Jerusalem, and the Golan Heights—all, evidently, taken as bargaining chips. There would be heavy casualties, but Israel would win.[13]

THE DAY AFTER INDEPENDENCE DAY, PRESIDENT JOHNSON HAD MET WITH DAVID GINSburg and Abe Feinberg, who had just returned from Israel, to discuss the aid package Israel was requesting. Ginsburg and Feinberg mentioned specific numbers and costs; the Israeli ambassador had simply been told that the package would substantially match Israel's requests. Walt Rostow had advised Johnson to tell his guests that a "miscalculation causing a Mid-East blowup" at this critical time "would make life awfully hard" for him.[14] A week later, Johnson decided to sell Israel a hundred APCs, spare tank parts, expertise for repairing HAWK missiles, surplus food, and more, for a total of over $72 million.[15]

Meanwhile, the crisis was developing on the Egyptian border. As it unfolded, the most important contacts between Israel and the United States were made through Jewish and intelligence (meaning Mossad and CIA) channels. Through a phone call from Rostow to Feinberg, Johnson conveyed his request that Israel delay for forty-eight hours any action in response to the closing of the Straits.[16] Rostow also called Ginsburg and asked, on behalf of the president, that he do what he can to cool down U.S. public opinion "for a short while." The Israeli envoy told Ginsburg to reply that this request was "unrealistic."[17] In fact, the Israeli embassy in Washington had already begun to implement instructions from Jerusalem: "Create a public atmosphere that will constitute pressure on the administration in the direction of obtaining our desired goals, without it being explicitly clear that we are behind this public campaign." Moshe Bitan, director of the North America department in the Foreign Ministry, suggested "organizing" letters, telegrams, editorials, and public statements aimed at different parts of the administration, "in a variety of styles"; they should also criticize U Thant and depict the dangers involved in a surge of Nasser's prestige. "Our purpose is to create a public atmosphere (Jews and non-Jews) that will strengthen our friends within the administration and lessen the influence of those who treat us with distance and disdain (for instance, Zevulun)." Zevulun was Secretary of State Dean Rusk's code-name. "The main thing is that Issahar [Johnson] himself is influenced by the many communications sent to him, so that he feels that despite his troubles in Vietnam he must pay attention to the dangerous situation developing in the region," wrote Bitan, and he explained that the danger would affect not only Israel but also American interests.[18] Israel demanded that the United States act to reopen the Straits, and threatened that otherwise it would take action itself.[19] Some Israeli emissaries spoke in extremely emotional terms, emphasizing the fear in Israel. Eban called the atmosphere "apocalyptic," while Evron declared, "For us it is not a matter of prestige, but of life and death."[20]

"Yesterday we gave instructions to Harari [Ginsburg]," one telegram reported. "He happened to have been hosting Haim last night. . . . Harari feels that the problem is Zevulun, whose attitude to us is more than averse. . . . Haim said he would recommend to Issahar that he—Haim— go immediately to meet with Yehuda and with the Kitchen Ruler." "Haim" was Vice President Hubert Humphrey; "Yehuda" was Eshkol; the "Kitchen Ruler" was Nasser.[21] Foreign Minister Eban instructed Evron to invite "Andre"—Feinberg—to Washington and show him a letter from Eshkol to Johnson, so that he could explain to Johnson that his reply was critical.[22]

At this point in the crisis the Americans were still trying to prevent the war. They said the Gulf of Aqaba was an international shipping channel, which Egypt had no right to close. But they did not want war to break out over the matter and hoped that instead the UN would be able to broker a settlement. They also spoke of establishing an "armada," an international fleet that would pass through the gulf to demonstrate support of freedom of the seas.[23]* But that would not be enough. Before his crucial meeting with President Johnson, Eban explained to administration officials that to be able to hold off the hawks in Israel, he had to go home with a real promise of American steps to reopen the Straits.[25] As he was preparing for his meeting with the president, the Israeli government was already discussing bringing him home.

Aharon Yariv maintained it had been a mistake to send Eban to Washington in the first place. Israel should start the war immediately rather than waste more precious time. A similar attitude prevailed in the Ma'arah's political committee and in the Foreign Ministry. Adi Yaffe, Eshkol's assistant, told the director general of his office, Herzog, that the prime minister himself would be glad if Eban's meeting with Johnson could be canceled. "The temperature in Tel Aviv has risen," said Yaffe, referring to the military's increasing pressure on Eshkol. Rabin had recovered from his breakdown and was back at work; Eshkol, in his wisdom and humanity, had rejected his offer to resign.[26]

On the morning of May 25, two days after the closing of the Straits, Eshkol took another tour of the south that included a visit to Ariel Sharon's command. Sharon assured him that the crisis would enable the IDF to destroy the Egyptian army: "This is a historical opportunity." Labor Minister Allon, who was back from the USSR and traveling with Eshkol, proposed "inventing a pretext" to allow Israel to claim that the Egyptians had started the war. A long argument ensued over the best way to do this. Amit of the Mossad suggested sending a ship through the Straits so that the Egyptians would attach it. Yariv cautioned that the Egyptians might respond, conversely, by bombing the Dimona reactor. The more they talked, the more the men worked themselves up and generated a climate of war, as if it were inescapable.[27] In that climate, Eshkol sent Eban a telegram, in which he claimed that "there has been a far-reaching change" in the situation: the Egyptians were reinforcing their troops in the Sinai; the Syrians were concentrating most of their army along the Israeli border; Iraq, Kuwait, and Jordan were also redeploying, and the Egyptian minister of war was in Moscow. It was therefore possible that the Arabs were about to initiate a comprehensive attack. Every passing hour strengthened their forces and increased their appetite, audacity, and boldness. In light of all

---

*At some point, both White House and Israeli embassy staff contacted former president Dwight Eisenhower to inquire what exactly the United States had committed itself to do, a decade earlier, in order to preserve freedom of movement through the Straits.[24]

this, it must be made clear to Johnson that the issue was no longer merely the reopening of the Straits, but first and foremost a threat to Israel's very existence. He must be asked what practical steps he was prepared to take "at the eleventh hour" to prevent an imminent explosion.

In the evening of May 25, Eshkol became part of a move that, according to Foreign Minister Eban, reflected "momentous irresponsibility."[28] It began in a discussion in the Tel Aviv office of the minister of defense. Yariv said "all signs indicated" that there was a chance that the Arabs would offer a provocation, and this eventuality was "becoming increasingly likely." Rabin said, "We're approaching the moment of explosion." He suggested demanding a clear and public commitment from the United States that any attack against Israel was tantamount to an attack on the United States itself. If Johnson agreed to make such a statement, Rabin explained, "We've lost out on having the war"; if he did not, there would be no choice but to act. Rabin preferred war over a statement: "It's obvious that the IDF will take care of it best."

The director general of the Foreign Ministry, Arye Levavi, offered to wire Ambassador Harman that Israel was about to initiate an all-out assault. Eshkol responded with his own proposal: "Better say there is danger of an attack on Israel." Rabin developed the idea: "We'll say there is danger of a comprehensive Egyptian-Syrian attack on Israel. I want the record to show that, before we acted, we did everything we could to exhaust diplomacy." Herzog explained that Johnson would not be able to deliver the statement Rabin was asking for even if he wanted to, as the U.S. Constitution prevented him from doing so without authorization from Congress. But Eshkol responded, "That's all right. If the president cannot [offer the commitment], then we'll have to explain to him that he must understand we have no choice but to act." The discussion resulted in a second telegram to Washington.[29]

Addressed to Ambassador Harman, this telegram took an even more alarming tone than the one Eshkol had sent to Eban a few hours earlier: "Immediate implementation of the American commitment is essential with a declaration and immediate—repeat, immediate—action, namely, an announcement by the U.S. government that any attack on Israel is tantamount to an attack on the U.S. This announcement should be accompanied by instructions to U.S. forces in the region to coordinate action with the IDF against any possible attack." The telegram reiterated the assertion that there was a danger of an all-out Egyptian-Syrian attack on Israel. This development, Eshkol said, had arisen in the last twenty-four hours, since Eban's departure. If Eban had arrived in Washington, Harman should coordinate with him, but if he was still en route, the ambassador must act alone, "because of the urgency of the situation," and relay the message to the president himself or, in his absence, to Secretary of State Rusk.[30]

Eban conveyed the content of the telegram to Rusk, who hurried to the White House, which ordered an intelligence reassessment. Eban "strongly recommended" revealing to the Americans the source of the information on which the telegrams were based, but the Americans, relying on their own sources, determined that the Israelis' claims were unfounded, and that Egypt was not about to attack. They did, however, agree to caution the Egyptian ambassador.[31] Walt Rostow told Johnson that the Israeli intelligence assessment, which had also been sent to CIA director Richard Helms, reflected the explosive growth of Israeli anxieties.[32]

Eban was stunned when he received the messages from home. "I found it difficult to comprehend how such a radical change could have occurred in our military situation since I heard the reports from our generals in Tel Aviv," he wrote in the Hebrew edition of his memoirs, adding diplomatically that it might be worth examining the meaning of the sudden nervousness reflected in the telegrams. In the English edition, he attributed the telegram to Rabin's nervous breakdown and its influence on the decision makers.[33] "I cannot overemphasize the impression this affair made," Ambassador Harman later recalled. It was as if " 'everything is lost, we're like lambs to the slaughter.' . . . Terrible panic, truly terrible panic. Because what it really meant was that only the Americans could save us."[34] The telegrams disrupted the plans for the Johnson-Eban meeting. Instead of asking for a few vessels, the Israelis were now speaking as representatives of a nation facing a holocaust, said Harman. Looking back, he thought that Eshkol's telegrams reflected the hysteria in Israel, but that in order to ascertain who really "cooked up the affair," it would have been best to set up a commission of inquiry.[35]

The Israeli intelligence assessment of the same evening was fairly different from what had been wired to Washington: "There are initial signs that the Egyptians may be preparing not only a holding action but also an assault." Nothing was said about a dramatic change in the deployment of Syrian and Jordanian forces. Nor did the possibility that Israel's existence was threatened occur to the intelligence agents.[36] Eshkol knew that no such danger had suddenly emerged over the past two days. He was obviously trying to mislead Eban, and through him President Johnson, in order to ensure U.S. support.[37] On a copy of the telegram to Harman, Eshkol added in his own handwriting: "All to create an alibi."

At the next government meeting, Arye Levavi explained that the telegrams' purpose was to put pressure on the Americans: "The demands to the United States were intentionally phrased in an extreme way." The intent was partly to enable Israel to take independent action, without President Johnson being able to protest. Some of the ministers demanded to know how truthful the telegrams were. Aharon Yariv and Rabin were forced to admit that they did not know exactly what the Egyptians were planning. Coordination between Egypt and Syria had increased since the shooting down of the MiGs on April 7, said Yariv—meaning, not necessarily in the past forty-eight hours. The ministers noticed that he made frequent use of the word "perhaps." His central statement was a far cry from the panicked certainty of the telegrams to Eban and Harman: "Before this whole affair began, Nasser was unwilling to go to war with Israel and unready for such a war; in the last few days, he has moved from that to a state of unwillingness to initiate war, but a readiness to accept it . . . a state of readiness to enter into all-out war with Israel, and perhaps even—perhaps; I'm not saying certainly—perhaps even to initiate it by means of a provocation at a time of his choosing."

Rabin said that at the moment there were only "signs" indicating "the possibility" of an attack. "I'm not willing to say with certainty that there is an intent to launch an overall attack on Israel." Shapira would not let him off the hook: "Is there information that they are about to attack us at any moment?" Rabin was evasive: "I wouldn't suggest addressing that." Eshkol came to his rescue: "We sent the telegram . . . on the basis of an intelligence assessment. Obviously, Nasser is not going to tell us about it himself."[38]

In a conversation with the editors of the various dailies when he returned from Washington a few days before the war erupted, Eban hinted that he did not trust the intelligence. Aharon Yariv sent him a note of apology, claiming that he and Rabin had not seen the telegrams before they were sent. Yaacov Herzog quickly disputed this: not only had Yariv known about the telegram to Eban, but he had taken part in phrasing it, as had the chief of staff. Yariv and Rabin denied this, but Herzog repeated his version in some detail. Rabin looked dazed, Herzog wrote in his diary, and said he might have forgotten. Eshkol listened to the argument and observed that perhaps, under different circumstances, this too should be investigated.[39]

The most current Israeli research, based partly on Egyptian material seized by Israeli intelligence, asserts that on the evening of May 25, the

Egyptian military did authorize a plan for an air attack on the southern Negev starting on May 27. That Yariv could have known about this "is extremely questionable," concluded a book published by the Ministry of Defense.[40]

"I'M IN THE BESOR AREA OF THE NEGEV," WROTE YEHOSHUA BAR-DAYAN. "NIR Yitzhak, Tze'elim. Fields of ripe grain, bowing down in hope for the harvest, flourishing. What I would not give to take a pair of shears and go out to the orchard, prune and gather it up, as in the past, instead of being in this war." He could not fall asleep in his truck. "Thinking about home, hearing the rhythmic pumping of the sprinklers quenching the thirst of a Negev orchard. So near and yet so far, beat after beat. Thoughts swirl around me, and hopes, to go home alive to Gili and Yariv."[41]

A FEW HOURS BEFORE EBAN HAD BEEN DUE TO MEET WITH JOHNSON, JOHN HADDEN OF the CIA came to see Meir Amit of the Mossad at home; there were raised voices, Amit recalled. He and David Carmon, the deputy head of military intelligence, tried to convince the CIA representative that the situation had changed dramatically. The Egyptians had reinforced their troops in the Sinai; the entire Arab world was offering to help. Twenty-four hours earlier, Amit had still believed that the Egyptians did not want war; he now thought they did. The change had occurred because Israel had not acted as soon as the crisis began. He further revealed to Hadden that the Mossad supported immediate action and he tried to convince the American that the Russians were behind the crisis. The fires had spread and needed to be put out right away; otherwise Israel would lose its deterrent capability. Furthermore, the reserve call-up could not be drawn out indefinitely.

The Arabs and Nasser also believed war was inevitable. "We have it from confidential sources and it has been published in *Al-Ahram*," Carmon said. He said he was basing his information on wiretaps of telephone calls made by an Iraqi diplomat in Cairo. This was not enough for Hadden. He knew that the Israelis had grown up with the grand legacy of Masada. At this point they were no longer just thinking about the Egyptians, but about a full-scale conflict. Hadden said Israel should help the United States help it by sending a ship to Eliat, for example. If the Egyptians shot at it, Israel would have cause to attack. "Give us a good reason to take action on your side," he repeated, and added a threat: "If you attack, the United States will land forces in Egypt to protect it." Amit did not believe the threat, but Hadden stood his ground: a good cause for attack "is what will determine whether the United States stands by you or against you."

Hadden demanded that Israel not act before the end of the waiting period it had agreed to. "It's better to be slightly in the wrong but alive than dead and innocent," said Amit, but Hadden was familiar with this rhetorical style and repeated his threat: "It's important for you to ensure that the United States is on your side, not on the other side." Amit wanted to know what was going on in Washington. Hadden said he was up-to-date: if Israel acted without cause, Johnson and the United States would support Egypt "all the way." He cautioned Amit against surprising the United States. Amit said surprise was one of the secrets of victory.

Hadden kept threatening: "I don't know how important American aid is to you." He then added, "Do not create a situation where we'll have to act against you." Amit and Carmon said that action against Israel would damage U.S. interests in the Middle East, and so the United States would not take that route. But Hadden responded, "We will act." Amit asked whether they were prepared for such action; Hadden replied, "I assume we are."[42]

This was an explicit threat, mere days after Johnson had authorized a generous aid package to Israel. Eban, already in Washington, had traveled via Paris and London, where President Charles de Gaulle and Prime Minister Harold Wilson had given him no reason to hope they would act to reopen the Straits. Everything depended on Johnson.

The army was expecting the war to begin at any time. Yehoshua Bar-Dayan wrote, "The engines are roaring, we must be going soon. A huge noise of steel engines and human hearts."[43] But the war didn't start this time either. At about nine in the evening of May 25, according to a military report, it transpired that an attack had been postponed. A senior officer on the General Staff telephoned the Southern Command and reported, "Noa's father is gathering his friends for a meeting, tomorrow at nine." The reference was to the government meeting; Noa was Eshkol's eldest daughter.[44] The next day, Moshe Dayan revealed an important secret to Ben-Gurion: there had been orders to storm the Gaza Strip—but they had now been changed.[45]

SHUKA BAR-DAYAN AND HIS FRIENDS PREPARED FOR THEIR SECOND SHABBAT ON RESERVE duty. He was the oldest in the group and had become a father figure. This was not only a question of age, he thought, but also of personality: "I get my own spirits up, and then theirs go up, too." He made sure the men had newspapers and cigarettes. People came to tell him their troubles. One of them was Benjamin, whose son had been born a week earlier. "He's going through the whole process like I did, becoming a realist—whatever happens, happens," Bar-Dayan wrote. Shuka consumed the weekend papers. "My conclusion is simple—realistic. We will definitely go to war. Today? Tomorrow at daybreak?"[46]

CHAPTER 7

TEN DAYS TO WAR:
WHAT DOES AMERICA WANT?

1. PRESSURES: "NO ONE CAN ASK ME TO BECOME A DOORMAT"

On Friday, May 26, at the government meeting, Rabin asked a clear-cut question: Are we launching an attack on the Egyptian army, and if so, when? Minister Israel Galili proposed authorizing Eshkol and Rabin to initiate action when they saw fit. The Mafdal ministers, Moshe Haim Shapira and Zerah Warhaftig, were strongly opposed. "We must not attack first," Warhaftig cautioned. Rabin responded, "The first one to attack creates an aerial advantage."

This was a conflict between the military and the political ranks—soldier against civilian. Previously, the military's demand to attack Syria in response to terrorist infiltrations had been at odds with the ministers' insistence on defensive means. Now, too, the debate over the crisis with Egypt emerged as a clash between the perfect, upright "new Hebrew" of Palestine and the "old Jew," whom many Israelis of Rabin's generation derided. Rabin was a strong, handsome forty-five-year-old, secular, red-headed, in charge of the army. He incarnated the narrative of Israel's courageous fight for independence. Zerah Warhaftig, a Holocaust survivor from Poland who spoke with a heavy Yiddish accent, was a short sixty-one-year-old, a politician wearing a black yarmulke, the minister of religious affairs. To the army generals, he symbolized Diaspora meekness, cowardice, hesitation, and the annoyance of Israeli politics. Even his name prompted scorn: "All sorts of Warhaftigs," said Rehavam Ze'evi, an officer of Rabin's generation, when he wished to express the sense of repugnance he felt toward the ministers in Eshkol's government.[1]

Dr. Warhaftig, a jurist, had been involved in wartime efforts to save Jews from the Nazis, and was among the signatories to the Declaration of Independence. He was a wise man, whose life experience had left him with a tendency to be cautious in his deliberations. "I am a father of four children," he said at the meeting. "Two of them are on the front lines, paratroopers. I do not know what we are heading into." The minister of health, Israel Barzilai of Mapam, suggested not bringing personal considerations into the debate: "We all have sons in the army." Warhaftig, however, was speaking not only of himself, but of "the nation's future." He felt the situation demanded more responsible leadership, and he heatedly demanded the appointment of David Ben-Gurion as minister of defense. If this was not feasible, the job should go to Dayan.

The first man to speak with Eshkol about the need to expand the coalition "in light of the grave situation" seems to have been Haim Moshe Shapira. The ministers from the religious parties wanted to prevent the war and assumed that Ben-Gurion could stand up to the military. If there was no avoiding war, it would be better to have him leading the country, instead of Eshkol. The other ministers objected; most of them were still not convinced that a preemptive attack on Egypt was required. One minister, Mordehai Bentov of Mapam, said that expanding the government would indicate that it had lost its mind; even Ben-Gurion "is no longer the same Ben-Gurion," he asserted, and suggested setting up a forum of former chiefs of staff (Dayan, Yigal Yadin, Haim Laskov), together with Yigal Allon, to act as consultants. But calm should be maintained: "To immediately panic and expand the government—this is uncalled for." Shapira interrupted him: "How many people have to die?" Pinhas Sapir said he would also oppose handing over decision-making authority to an eighty-one-year-old man, and he proclaimed that those who talked of expanding the government were in fact plotting to replace it. Minister of Police Sasson said a new minister of defense would not save the day. Minister of Agriculture Gvati was also opposed, although he accepted the military's estimate that the situation necessitated an attack on Egypt.

The minister of education, Zalman Aran, who was at the forefront of those objecting to war, said there was no reason to enlarge the government: the whole idea was nothing but a ruse to restore Ben-Gurion, which would be tantamount to establishing a dictatorship. "What has the government done wrong that it should be replaced?" he asked. While the meeting was in session, two Egyptian MiGs infringed Israeli airspace again. Eshkol grumbled, "Egyptian planes are photographing Dimona and we're sitting here talking about Ben-Gurion." The proposal to bring Ben-Gurion into the government offended him. "I will not coexist in a government with him," he declared. Ben-Gurion had called him a cheat and a liar—how could they manage a war together? "No one can ask me to become a door-mat," Eshkol said. The meeting went on for five hours, and according to Minister Gvati, it was "very harsh."

That morning, Eshkol still had a reasonable degree of faith that his colleagues' support would assure his continuance in office as both prime minister and minister of defense. Soon, however, he had to contend with another attempt to impose immediate war upon him.

Rabin, who left the government meeting to look into the reports about the Egyptian planes, returned and asked Eshkol to step out for an urgent consultation. "We've picked up a worrying and strange transmis-sion," he told Eshkol. It seemed to indicate "some sort of deployment" of the Egyptian air force. "It's still unclear what it is," Rabin said, but he did not rule out an attack on Dimona. He had brought Ezer Weizman with him. The chief of operations knew no more than Rabin about the inci-dent, but asserted unequivocally: "All signs indicate that the Egyptians are planning to attack Dimona today. Therefore, there is no choice but to attack the Egyptians today." The demand could hardly have been stated more urgently: Weizman wanted the prime minister to agree that they would go to war immediately.

Eshkol, as he often did at that point, preferred to rely on his intuition, which advised him not to lose sight of the main issue, the meeting be-tween Eban and Johnson. Rabin agreed, and although Weizman was forced to concur, he said, "I suggest the latest time for action be set for to-morrow morning." Upon returning to the meeting, Eshkol observed that Rabin was usually more "*gellasen*" ("calm," in Yiddish), while Weizman was "temperamental." He told the ministers that the two had made it clear that the air force could not protect the reactor continuously around the clock, because that would wear out the planes. He quoted them as saying, "There is a limit to our erosion capacity," but did not add that Weizman had demanded that Israel act that same day. The Egyptians did not attack Dimona, and Eshkol could add this episode to the list of mat-ters demanding "investigation."[2]

JOHNSON TRIED TO AVOID EBAN, POSTPONING THE MEETING SEVERAL TIMES, UNTIL Eban announced he would have to return to Israel for the government meeting scheduled for Saturday night. Walt Rostow telephoned the Israeli envoy Ephraim Evron and told him the president was angry: he resented being pushed around.* Johnson, meanwhile, was consulting his people. Abe Fortas suggested that the president guarantee the passage of an Israeli ship, but Johnson refused.[4] Later that day, he received a written proposal from David Ginsburg: to open the Straits, two American merchant ships or tankers would enter the Gulf of Aqaba, one heading toward Eilat, the other to Aqaba. The ship to Eilat would be carrying oil, the one to Aqaba food. They would not be armed. According to Ginsburg, he had not cleared the plan with Eban or with anyone at the Israeli embassy, and so did not know what their response would be. It was far from what Eban was hoping to take home, but it was a possible solution. Ginsburg's letter was shelved.[5]

While still waiting for the meeting, Eban heard from top officials in the administration that the United States would act to reopen the Straits of Tiran, but not right away, not alone, and not at any cost. The secretary general of the UN was on his way to Cairo and everyone should wait for the results of his trip. There must be international action. Under no circumstances would the Americans give Israel the commitment Eshkol had demanded in his telegrams, but the Israelis had no reason for concern—they would win anyway. "You'll whip the hell out of them," Johnson himself said.[6]

The military attaché in Washington telegrammed the IDF chief of staff to inform him of assessments he had heard: there was almost no chance of independent American action to open the Straits, and the military people weren't even sure they would help if Israel came under Egyptian attack. General Earle G. Wheeler, the chairman of the Joint Chiefs of Staff, felt that Israel was capable of beating the Egyptians even if it suffered the first airstrike. The attaché reported a vote of confidence in the power of the IDF. The only thing worrying the Pentagon was the need for Israel to back up its actions with arguments the world would find convincing.[7] But, as Johnson himself repeatedly stressed, Washington was not speaking with one voice. There were doves and hawks, the former nearly bullying Israel in their attempts to keep it from attacking Egypt, the latter all but encouraging it to do so. Arthur Goldberg, the U.S. ambassador to the UN, urged Eban to keep in mind that only one man really called the shots in the United States, and that was the president.[8]

Johnson let Eban speak first when their meeting finally materialized.

---

*The White House also reiterated its request that Israel stop applying pressure through its domestic letter-writing campaign. "Of course we are continuing it," Ambassador Harman reported to Jerusalem.[3]

The discrepancy between the two men's styles was no less profound than the chasm between Rabin and Warhaftig. The Israeli foreign minister, a Cambridge graduate, viewed diplomacy as a vocation and an art, and was known for his polished language and elitist pomposity. Addicted to the pleasure of words, he detailed the chain of events at length, asserting that the United States had at one time committed itself to ensuring the free passage of ships in the gulf, and emphasized that the situation was no longer a question of Israel's welfare but of its very existence as a country. Johnson, who reiterated the American commitment to unobstructed passage through the gulf and promised to work to restore it, barely deviated from what Eban had already heard from his staff; only his choice of words was more colorful. "We should not jump," he said, and that was the essence of his message. He said he was not a king in his country, and that commitments the United States had made in the past were not worth five cents without reauthorization from Congress. Nor was he a feeble mouse or a coward, he said, but there was no point jumping the gun, in case doing so only increased Nasser's standing; he did not want "to call Nasser and raise his hand." He also told Eban that according to his intelligence there was no chance that Egypt would attack Israel in the immediate future, contrary to the telegrams Eban had brought to his attention. Johnson was essentially saying that he did not believe Israel. Eban asked him to at least clarify whether the United States would intervene if Israel was attacked. Johnson nodded, although he seemed to be saying, "That won't happen, anyway." At times he read from prepared notes. He cautioned Israel against initiating an attack on Egypt. His key statement, formulated by Dean Rusk, comprised both a threat and a promise: "Israel will not be alone unless it decides to do it alone."[9]

The Israeli account of the meeting differs from the American minutes, partly with respect to the last portion of the conversation, when Johnson and Eban spoke of the need to establish an apparatus for military coordination, including joint intelligence assessments. According to the Israeli version, Johnson said that Ambassador Goldberg had expressed doubts about the reliability of American intelligence. The president did not discount the possibility that the United States might be wrong—after all, General Douglas MacArthur had been misled into thinking the Chinese would not invade Korea. And so he had instructed that all Israeli intelligence claims be examined on the assumption that they were correct. It turned out they were not. Egypt was not about to attack.

The president walked Eban to the elevator and asked how he thought the Israeli government would respond to their conversation. Eban said it all depended on what he could tell the government about the president's position, and asked again whether he could report that the president would do everything possible to assure freedom of passage in the gulf. Johnson said yes, and shook Eban's hand so vigorously that Eban thought he might lose the use of it. "It was undoubtedly a disappointing conversation," said Ambassador Harman. "The Israelis were hoping for more."[10]

Johnson was satisfied. "They came loaded for bear," he said immediately after the meeting, "but so was I. I let them talk for the first hour and I just listened and then I finished it up the last fifteen minutes." His assistants were also extremely impressed, the president boasted: one of them said it was the best meeting of its kind he had ever attended. Secretary of Defense McNamara was so enthusiastic according to Johnson, "he just wanted to throw his cap up in the air."[11] Johnson seems to have felt that he had got out of a trap the Israelis had set for him. He later mimicked Eban's stuffy style of speech, saying he acted like "a mini–Winston Churchill." But essentially, Johnson assumed he had not been successful at preventing the war: the Israelis were going to attack, he figured, and there was nothing he could do about it.[12]

2. MISGIVINGS: "MOSHE DAYAN, MOSHE DAYAN"

While Eban and Ambassador Harman were meeting with Johnson on Friday evening, it was already two A.M. in Israel, on the Sabbath morning. Because of the tensions, the prime minister and his wife were staying at the Dan Hotel in Tel Aviv. Just before three, Eshkol was awoken and informed that Dimitri Chuvakhin, the Soviet ambassador, was waiting in the lobby and insisting that he see Eshkol immediately. Eshkol asked his wife what to do; she said, If the ambassador wants to see you in your pajamas, let him come up. The ambassador delivered a fairly restrained letter from Premier Alexey Kosygin. The USSR declared once again that it was interested in peace, and called on Israel to resolve the crisis without war. Eshkol promised there were no concentrations of military forces in the north, and offered again to take the ambassador to the field to see for himself. He also suggested a meeting with Kosygin.[13]*

---

*Many years later, Chuvakhin said somewhat critically that he had supported a meeting between Eshkol and Kosygin, and that had it been held, the Six-Day War might have been averted. But his recommendation was overruled by Moscow. Eban described Chuvakhin as a "sadist"; he told the ministers that once, when he had spoken with Chuvakhin about the terrorist attacks, the ambassador had denied that the Syrians were behind them and insinuated that the CIA might be carrying them out.[14]

· · ·

IT WAS ALMOST DAWN. ABBA EBAN WAS ON A PLANE ON HIS WAY HOME. SHUKA BAR-
Dayan traveled again to a nearby workshop for spare parts. He showered
and shaved in the Kibbutz Tze'elim cowshed. Soldiers crowded around
the kibbutz pay phone. Bar-Dayan tried to call home, but there was something wrong with the phone. A few good bangs and it started working.
Gili wasn't home, but her mother was there. At least he'd been able to get
in touch. Suddenly he spotted a civilian car: it belonged to Levi Yitzhaki,
a greengrocer from Rishon Lezion, who was visiting his son. Bar-Dayan
sent a note home to Gila with him. Back to the tanks. Lots of rumors flying around. There was a target for their operation: the village of Khan
Younis in the Gaza Strip. The air force would strike first, to weaken resistance. Shuka would not be in the first line of assault, but what if the air
strike led to them being cut off? "Troubling thoughts. We will hope and
pray that everything goes well."

ESHKOL CONVENED HIS PEOPLE AND TOLD THEM ABOUT HIS NIGHTTIME MEETING WITH
Chuvakhin. Rabin, Yariv, and Weizman were present. Eshkol repelled another attempt to take a step toward war: Minister of Labor Allon restated
a proposal to authorize Eshkol and Rabin to go to war. Rabin supported it:
"There is no escaping action." He had received new reports saying that
the Egyptian army had been deployed so as to besiege Eilat and the southern Negev. He believed the war would start that same day, and proposed a
feint: announce that the government would wait until the next day at
noon to hear Eban's report. This would give the impression that they
were still temporizing. Minister Sapir objected: First let's hear Eban, he
said; and that was what they did. They also debated what to do with
Moshe Dayan, who wanted to return to the army. Eshkol offered him
membership in a special ministerial committee, but Dayan refused.

A few days earlier, Eshkol had agreed to let Knesset member Dayan
take a tour of the IDF, in uniform, and meet with commanders, which he
now felt was a mistake. As the days of waiting for war passed, Dayan had
gained the aura of a savior and a hero: the military leader of the Sinai
Campaign had held himself above politics. Chasing power, women, and
money, infinitely egocentric, cynical, and unstable, Dayan was loyal only
to himself. His tour created a dynamic that could hardly be forestalled
any longer: he was making a comeback.

· · ·

WHILE MEETING WITH SENIOR OFFICERS, POLITICIANS, JOURNALISTS, AND OTHER PUBLIC figures, Dayan ran into the man he called "his Arab," Amos Yarkoni. The meeting occured in Beersheba, in the evening hours. Dayan had gone out alone for a breath of fresh air, when suddenly a car stopped and flashed its lights to signal him to approach. "I was very surprised," he wrote later; "how could anyone recognize me in the dark, while driving at high speed?" But the driver who had stopped for him could have spotted almost anything: he was the best scout Dayan had ever known, a Bedouin whose birth name had been Abdel Majid Khader al-Mazarib.

Dayan had known Abdel Majid since childhood, when his tribe had settled near Dayan's moshav, Nahalal. He was a smart boy, a shepherd, a few years younger than Dayan, and they became friends. During the Arab riots against the British and the Zionists that raged during the second half of the 1930s, Abdel Majid was an expert at blowing up oil pipelines, but he was suspected of betraying his fellows and was thrown into a deep pit. He managed to escape to nearby Nahalal, where he sought refuge with his childhood friend, who had meanwhile become a commander in the Hagana. When the IDF was founded during the War of Independence, Abdel Majid enlisted in its minority unit and was given a cover name: Amos Yarkoni. During seventeen years of IDF service, he rose to the rank of lieutenant colonel.

That night in 1967, Dayan went with Yarkoni to his home, where he met his four children and his wife, who had converted to Islam from Christianity. They talked about the adventures of the daring religious leader and Arab guerrilla fighter Izz al-Din al-Qassam, in whom Dayan was interested. He had been killed by the British and became a Palestinian national symbol. Abdel Majid promised to arrange for Dayan to meet a veteran who had fought alongside al-Qassam.

Dayan's diary projects a romantic, paternalistic, almost colonialist approach to Abdel Majid, who had earned his admiration by betraying his own people and linking his fate to that of the Jews. "He was a sweet boy, short for his age, who played the recorder and eagerly awaited the bread and jam we would give him from our meals." In the 1930s, he and Abdel Majid had both been imprisoned in Acre, where they were held by the British, one for operations against the Jews, the other for targeting Arabs. According to Dayan, he bore no grudge against Abdel Majid then, and even gave him some money for cigarettes.

As chief of staff, Dayan had pinned the officer's stripes on the shoulder of his distinguished protégé. He could not hide his excitement: here was a boy who had never been to school, but thanks to his natural intelligence had learned to read and write Hebrew. Dayan doubted Amos Yarkoni had also in the meantime learned to read and write Arabic. "I hoped—and indeed I was not disappointed—that Western education had not caused him to forget his natural tracking skills, and that he could still follow the traces of stolen cattle even on rocks," wrote Dayan, and added: "I saw it with my own eyes."

After the visit to his home, Abdel Majid took Dayan back to town, where he wandered through the streets. Young men and women standing outside cafés recognized him and called out, "Moshe Dayan, Moshe Dayan!" and a trail of people followed him. An old drunk came up to him and asked, with tears in his eyes, if he could kiss him. A policeman helped Dayan escape the man's grasp. His driver brought the car and took him back to his hotel.[15]

ON FRIDAY, MAY 26, DAYAN HAD MET WITH BEN-GURION AND TOLD HIM ABOUT HIS DE-sire to return to the army. Ben-Gurion said he understood, and that if he were younger he would also volunteer. He also tried, unsuccessfully, to persuade Dayan that war right now would be a disaster. Although Dayan agreed that Israel was responsible for the crisis, he thought there was no longer any way to avoid going to war, and he was already thinking ahead. To make the war look like an effort to reopen the Straits of Tiran, Israel must stage an attack on Sharm el-Sheikh, but the main goal would be to destroy the Egyptian military. Having accomplished that, the IDF would take over the Straits. Dayan remarked that no attempt should be made to occupy the Gaza Strip, which was populated with refugees; he described it as "a swarm of bees." He also thought Israel should not seize the Suez Canal, for if it did so it would anger the countries that relied on the canal, which he described as "a wasps' nest."[16]

Eshkol and his colleagues found it difficult to decide, on Saturday morning, whether to enlist Dayan in the army or invite him to join the government. In either case, they were not sure whether they would be calling on him personally or as a member of Rafi. Some were afraid of him. "Before you put him in uniform, ask him here for a meeting," Golda Meir suggested.[17]

That same afternoon Dayan returned to Ben-Gurion's home to meet party members. The question was whether to join the government. Dayan was opposed: the goal should be to replace the government, not reinforce it. Ben-Gurion also objected, suggesting that Dayan become the prime minister and minister of defense, while he himself could act as adviser, if Dayan wished. Shimon Peres brought information that the war would begin the next day. He took Ben-Gurion into another room and suggested appointing Moshe Dayan as chief of staff, not minister of defense, so that he could postpone the war for a few days. "I would not agree to this," Ben-Gurion wrote.[18] If Ben-Gurion's account was accurate and he was not confused, as he sometimes was at that time, then Peres's proposal was yet another indication of the general befuddlement that had taken over everyone, because Dayan was in favor of the war.

In the course of the discussion, Ben-Gurion told those present what Dayan had revealed to him the day before—that there had been an order to occupy Gaza, but that it had been revoked. At this point, Dayan grew furious and left the room. He had passed on the information in confidence, and Ben-Gurion had promised not to repeat it. "I suppose that is true," Ben-Gurion conceded, "but I didn't remember." The first IDF chief of staff, Yaakov Dori, followed Dayan and tried to convince him to come back, but Dayan refused. He went to meet with the editor of *Maariv* and that night he drove south, to visit the 7th Brigade, under the command of Shmuel Gorodish.[19] He found Gorodish addressing his soldiers, one of whom was Private Yehoshua Bar-Dayan.

"SOME TREMBLING," WROTE BAR-DAYAN BEFORE GORODISH'S SECOND VISIT. "I'M NOT sure why, but he is the man who controls our fate and the fate of victory. May God—if he is here—lead him to success." Jeep headlights illuminated Gorodish as he addressed his soldiers. "Short, stocky, sunglasses, firm as a rock, confident talk, a certain crudeness," Bar-Dayan noted. He recorded his commander's words: "This evening is the eve of battle. Tomorrow, the battle. Its importance is even greater than the War of Independence. If we don't win, we have nowhere to come back to. Nasser wants to destroy us. We'll destroy him. You are the fastest brigade in the IDF and I'm counting on you. Your mission is extremely difficult. We storm the Rafiah posts at dawn. The battle must be decided within twenty minutes. I want to see their tanks [become] flaming torches. Don't waste munitions on infantry. They should be run over right where they are. Kill the enemy. Kill them. We won't repeat the mistakes of Sinai, when we didn't run them over. The brigade will be helped by gunners and we'll proceed to victory, hoping there won't be a delay. We'll meet at the radios."

He left the troops in silence. Bar-Dayan looked around at the chemist from the Weizmann Institute, at the high school literature teacher. Parents of children, like himself. "What the hell am I doing here?" he wrote.[20]

BEN-GURION RECEIVED A SECOND VISIT THAT SATURDAY, FROM MENACHEM BEGIN AND a few of his people. Only the sense that Israel was facing calamity, coupled with a searing hatred of Eshkol, could have prompted such a visit. Paula Ben-Gurion was very moved. Ben-Gurion told Begin that Israel should wait until it could coordinate with the United States, and only then carry out a restricted operation to reopen the Straits. This seems to have been Begin's first inkling that Ben-Gurion did not support an immediate war and was opposed to a full-scale attack on Egypt. He and his men decided they would not support Ben-Gurion's return to leadership; instead, they would push for Moshe Dayan, as Haim Moshe Shapira was doing as well.[21]

These conversations reflected panic and confusion. People bandied about Ben-Gurion's and Dayan's names without knowing exactly what the two men thought. Yigal Allon was also mentioned as a candidate to replace Eshkol. Shapira was wary of Allon because he supported the war, and yet his demand to appoint Dayan helped to hasten the beginning of war. "You want Dayan but you don't want war?" Eshkol asked him, and told his friends that Shapira was "torturing him."[22] Shapira apparently assumed Dayan would follow Ben-Gurion. Like others, he acted "according to my heart," as he told Eshkol.* Pinhas Sapir later judged that some ministers feared Dayan because of Eshkol's weakness; they were also wary because of Rabin's breakdown. According to Sapir, he had heard from Rabin's physician long ago that Rabin could not be in charge if a crisis developed; this was not a well-kept secret. "This crisis seems to be too much even for the chief of staff," Zalman Aran told friends. "The situation is that the chief of staff, who is supposed to be made of steel, is not made of steel."[24] Shapira felt the need for "national unity." This was partly an emotional position, rooted in his religious conviction, and not the result of a rational examination of the best way to prevent war. This was also why he wanted Begin included in the government. Most Israelis at the time also wanted "national unity," but unlike Shapira, most Israelis thought the country should go to war.[25]

---

*If the Mafdal ministers believed that Dayan could stop the escalation toward war, they were not alone. The U.S. and British ambassadors made a similar assumption.[23]

• • •

ABBA EBAN LANDED AT LOD AIRPORT AFTER TEN ON SATURDAY NIGHT AND WAS TAKEN directly to meet with the cabinet. On the way he heard about Rabin's breakdown for the first time. His impression was that the atmosphere was "approaching panic." Before his arrival, Rabin had told the ministers that "the noose is tightening." Eban gave a detailed report on his meetings with President de Gaulle and Prime Minister Wilson, and read long excerpts from the transcript of his conversation with President Johnson. He emphasized Johnson's promise to act to reopen the Straits. In Washington, he said, there was an air of suspicion toward Israel, as if it were intending to entangle the United States in a war. Eshkol said he had no faith in Johnson's promises, because what the United States actually did was up to the State Department. Rabin supported the idea of exhausting the diplomatic avenues, but repeated over and over that this should be done as quickly as possible. Nine of the ministers supported his position. At times, the discussion slipped into self-examination of an almost existential-historical tenor.

Yigal Allon feared a comprehensive attack by the Arab states, perhaps coordinated with the USSR. He rejected the view that no action should be taken without support from the great powers. Had we gone it alone in 1956, he said, we would have accomplished more. The IDF could act on its own. He suggested taking action the next day. Israel Galili felt that years of accomplishment were being undermined; he was concerned about the IDF's deterrent capabilities. Minister of Transport Carmel said any future war would be waged under far more difficult circumstances. He also warned that Israel's deterrent ability might collapse, and pointed to the danger that the Egyptians would bomb Dimona. "Whoever claims we will not be able to withstand the battle might as well claim we have no right to be here."

The question of the Straits was secondary, said Minister Gvati, seeing it an opportunity. He assured his colleagues that war would not lead to a loss of Western support, but rather the contrary: the West did not want Nasser victorious. Israel Yeshayahu, the postal minister, observed that the public now had the impression that the government could not make up its mind. Shapira said the government should not act on the basis of public opinion. Israel had never initiated an attack alone. He believed the Americans' assurances more than he believed in the IDF's power. He did not think Nasser would attack, and in his view a reopening of the Straits by the United States would hurt him more than a defeat at the hands of

Israel. The United States should be trusted to restore freedom of navigation. "It's never too late to fight," said Shapira, and meanwhile Israel could grow stronger. Warhaftig also said he believed the Americans would help. He called the notion of acting against U.S. opinion "adventurism, real adventurism." Aran spoke mainly of the losses Israel would suffer. The minister of tourism, Moshe Kol, said that without friends Israel could not last long. Ministers Mordehai Bentov and Israel Barzilai maintained that it was sufficient for Israel to break the blockade. There was no need for all-out war.

Eshkol said they had to decide in whose hands to place the fate of that generation: America or Chuvakhin. If Israel avoided taking action against Egypt, it might also be asked to exercise restraint with Syria and the terrorists: "And from now on we will sit as quiet as water and low as the grass." Sapir remarked that "to get a country was very difficult. To lose it may be very easy."

Aran exclaimed that they were in a no-win situation, and Haim Moshe Shapira sighed. "How will we hold out against all the Arab states?" he asked. Israel Yeshayahu, who supported the war, raised a new argument: "What will we tell the army? 'Go back home. It was all for show'?"[26]

At eleven o'clock that night, while the argument was still going on, the phone rang at David Ben-Gurion's house. It was the editor in chief of *Ha'aretz*, Gershom Schocken. He asked to see Ben-Gurion. "Why so late?" Paula protested, but Schocken said it was important and Ben-Gurion agreed to see him. A native of Germany, the owner and editor of the newspaper for almost thirty years, Schocken showed Ben-Gurion an editorial he was planning to run the next day.

Dr. Shlomo Gross, a senior commentator at *Ha'aretz*, had written that evening that there was no longer any point in waiting: Israel must act immediately. "On the one hand I, too, was of this opinion," Schocken later recounted. "On the other hand, I thought back to the group we used to belong to, in Weimar Germany. We were members of a set that was antiwar, pacifistic, and the most unacceptable thing, the worst thing, was incitement to war. And here I was, calling for war. It was dispiriting." Ben-Gurion was, as Schocken saw it, "the greatest military leader of the people of Israel," and so, although the two had not always had a good relationship, he decided to show him the draft.*

---

*"What is a newspaper, anyway?" Ben-Gurion once said, according to Schocken. "A landlord hires some workers and tells them what to write. The fact that Schocken told his people to write this and write that—this means it has some importance?" Usually, Schocken said, he found Ben-Gurion too nationalistic, like Begin, "determined to stand against the world, with a back that was too straight and a chest that was a little too puffed out."

"Ben-Gurion was lying in bed in a very dreary room, reading a book in English about Greek philosophy," Schocken recalled. He quickly read through the editorial and handed it back without a word. "What do you say?" asked Schocken. Ben-Gurion replied that he had only one request: take out the demand that he return to the government. Schocken asked what he thought about the war. Ben-Gurion said, "I think it's a disaster, but that's your business." Schocken had no idea before then that Ben-Gurion opposed the war. He hurried back to the paper, where, he said, he "weakened" the editorial.[27]

THE SOLDIERS SERVING WITH SHUKA BAR-DAYAN HAD TAKEN TO CALLING ONE ANOTHER "sweetie." Strange, wrote Bar-Dayan. He drew encouragement from two soldiers in their twenties, "the tank kids," as he dubbed them: Arieh and Leon. "Bold men, cool-tempered, fearful but confident, proud, and realistic," the tank kids lifted his spirits. He hugged them and gave them some cigarettes he had been keeping in case someone needed them. Then he kissed the photos of Gili and Yariv and fell asleep.[28]

THE CABINET MEETING WENT ON INTO THE SMALL HOURS. EBAN SUGGESTED ADJOURNing the discussion for forty-eight hours, and left to brief members of the Knesset Foreign Affairs and Defense Committee, who were convened on the floor below. When he returned he found that the cabinet had decided to put off the decision only until noon the next day. Nine ministers said they supported immediate action, including Eshkol, his party colleagues Yaakov Shimshon Shapira, Israel Yeshayahu, Eliyahu Sasson, Haim Gvati, and Zeev Sherf, and three other ministers from Ahdut Ha'avoda: Israel Galili, Yigal Allon, and Moshe Carmel. Nine wanted to wait, including Eban, Zalman Aran, and Pinhas Sapir (Mapai); Haim Moshe Shapira, Yosef Burg, and Zerah Warhaftig (Mafdal); Israel Barzilai and Mordehai Bentov (Mapam); and Moshe Kol (Independent Liberals). No vote was taken.

If Eshkol had wanted to lead Israel to war, he would probably not have had much trouble convincing one of the ministers opposed to change his position that night, or at least to remain silent, just as, in 1948, Ben-Gurion could probably have rallied the support had he truly believed that the West Bank should be occupied. Eshkol did not yet support immediate war, but in a stalemate between the supporters and the objectors, he risked nothing by aligning with the former. Perhaps he was considering his historical image as a patriot. More likely, he was thinking of a possible leak to the press. Ironically, he opposed the war for the very same reason as Ben-Gurion: he believed that Israel should not go to war as long as the United States was opposed.

Aharon Yariv formulated the following assessment: "The Americans view a preemptive strike on our part as reasonable, as long as they themselves are not required to take action. They will act only in the case of a defeat of our side." But at this point Eshkol no longer had reason to believe the IDF intelligence branch's political judgments, once again preferring his gut feeling and Eban's report: the United States had not yet authorized Israel to go to war.[29]

The presses at *Ha'aretz* had started spitting out the early editions of the paper. "The editorial was printed as proposed," wrote Ben-Gurion in his diary, disregarding Schocken's last-minute changes. The editorial asserted that steps should be taken to reopen the Straits, but did not call for "immediate action." It argued that the schedule must not be dictated by "Israeli impatience" but by the country's military and political leadership. The paragraph pertaining to Ben-Gurion was worded vaguely: Schocken did not tell his readers that Ben-Gurion opposed the war. "In large parts of the nation there is a sense of mistrust toward the government as currently constituted. . . . To the people and to the world, Ben-Gurion embodies Israel's determination to face the most difficult trials. He has proved more than once that he is cautious when the occasion demands caution."

It was four in the morning. The cabinet was about to disperse. Ezer Weizman was claiming that army morale was deteriorating. He viewed any postponement as a lack of confidence in the air force and a personal failure, he said, but the ministers were too tired for this sort of argument. "When I got home, daylight was breaking," wrote Haim Gvati in his diary. "Despite my weariness, I could not fall asleep and had to take a pill."[30]

Yosef and Ruhama Weitz with the Yehiams, 1951: "The children of the dream"
(Central Zionist Archives)

Dizengoff,
more than a street
(Israel State Archive)

The Sussita. The models below are the
Sabra sports car, the Carmel sedan,
the Sussita commercial, and the Sussita
station wagon. *(Government Press Bureau)*

Abie Nathan,
pilot for peace, 1966

A tale of two cities: a Tel Aviv country club; Jerusalem in winter *(Moshe Freidan; Moshe Milner)*

Musrara: life on the line in Jerusalem (*Moshe Freidan*)

The Mandelbaum Gate (*Fritz Cohen*)

"The parade was pathetic": the Hebrew University Stadium, Independence Day, 1967 *(Ilan Bruner)*

The 13th Government, January 1966. Standing *(from left)*: Moshe Kol, Zerah Warhaftig, Moshe Carmel, Eliyahu Sasson, Yigal Allon, Yosef Burg, Israel Barzilai, Haim Gvati, Yaakov-Shimshon Shapira, Mordehai Bentov, Israel Galili, Haim Tzadok. Sitting *(from left)*: Pinhas Sapir, Behor Shalom Sheetrit, Levi Eshkol, President Zalman Shazar, Haim Moshe Shapira, Zalman Aran, Abba Eban

The unemployed protesting in Tel Aviv, March 1967: "I'm afraid of the moment when my children ask for bread and I won't have any to give them" *(Israel State Archive)*

The Complete Book of Eshkol Jokes

Teddy Kollek with Marlene Dietrich: "Sitting at the most beautiful feet in the world, but thinking only of the city's monetary problems"

Fatah terrorist attack, October 1966: a train derailed on the way from Jerusalem to Tel Aviv (*Moshe Milner*)

Syrian bombardment, June 1967: a children's house on Kibbutz Tel Katzir (*Asaf Kotin*)

Samua, November 1966 *(Moshe Milner)*

"Through This Wall": the commemorative letter sent to bereaved families for Memorial Day, May 1967

"If Nasser wins, we were born in vain": Tel Aviv high school students dig trenches. *(Ilan Bruner)*

CHAPTER 8

NINE DAYS TO WAR: A TERRIBLE SITUATION

1. ANXIETY: "KEEP UP YOUR APPEARANCE"

The fear triggered by Nasser's acts, beginning on Independence Day, rapidly escalated into panic. "We are in a cold war, with the hot war close on the horizon, ready to erupt at any time," wrote Yosef Weitz in his diary. "The people of Israel are in a state of anxiety." The public was demanding the immediate appointment of a war cabinet, he noted, but the ministers were negotiating as usual to expand the coalition. He thought this was madness. It was hard for Weitz to work in his garden, hard not to be involved. He felt as if he were outside of things. But his grandson Nir was called up and Nir's wife, Mira, was going to visit him in the Negev with fresh socks and underwear. She left their two-year-old son, Amir, with Weitz, who went with his great-grandson to the park, played ball with him, and took him to the supermarket. "A nice boy, intelligent, perceptive and talkative," he noted, trying to console himself.[1]

"The children know every detail and at school they have prepared them for a state of emergency," wrote Riki Ben-Ari from Tel Aviv to her relatives in Los Angeles. Many Israelis were going overseas. "Every day people call me and say So-and-So has left the country," Ben-Ari wrote; those leaving included women and children.[2] "Planes arrive empty and take off full," reported *Ha'aretz*. The conductor Erich Leinsdorf canceled his concert and fled, like most tourists. According to a report given to the chief of staff, the southernmost city of Eilat was emptying out; thousands had already left. The IDF feared that the Egyptians or the Jordanians might attack the city and cut it off from the rest of the country.[3]

People hoarded food; there were buying panics almost everywhere. "Mothers and wives who are ordinarily wise, moderate, and capable women are rushing to the grocery stores in loud confusion, buying up in virtual hysteria whatever is needed and whatever is not," wrote the Jerusalem author Yeshurun Keshet in his diary. Grocery stores stopped extending credit. "What will happen if, God forbid, there isn't any bread or water or dairy when the war really does break out?" wrote Keshet; he had no doubt that it would. "They are not to be blamed, I guess," wrote Edith Ezrachi of Jerusalem to her relatives in Nashville, North Carolina; she assumed they were "remembering their suffering and near starvation in 1948." She also went out and bought rice, noodles, and sugar, and she filled a spare bucket with water.* Anxiety took over the kibbutzim, too. On Yehiam they prepared for the worst, partly under the sway of recollections from the War of Independence. They dug defensive trenches between the houses, as if expecting the enemy to invade kibbutz territory. "If you take shelter in a house or a hut, seek cover beneath a bed, table, etc.," members were instructed. The shelters were for the kibbutz children.[5]

Yehoshua Bar-Dayan's impression was that the situation on the home front was worse than where he was, and many soldiers shared this sense. "The calm and confidence in the military are completely different to the sense of panic felt by the little man," wrote one soldier in a letter home. Another wrote, "I never imagined the situation was as terrible as what you described to me in your last letter. . . . If what you wrote is true, about women crying all day and running to get in line early at the grocery store in case, God forbid, there is no food left, then all the nice stories in the papers and on the radio about people volunteering are just that—nice stories."[6]

The newspapers tried to lift public spirits with reports of unity between the people and its army, with accounts of steadfastness and willingness to sacrifice. This was Israel's "secret weapon," *Maariv* believed: the Israeli. Such was the story of a kindergarten teacher from the south who took her class of thirty on a day trip. They happened on an encampment of reservists. The five-year-olds started clambering happily on the military vehicles. Some of the soldiers hoisted them onto their shoulders. One soldier was equipped with a recorder and a harmonica, and he gathered the children in the shade of a tent to play some tunes while they sang along. Other soldiers gave the children cookies and candy from their battle ra-

---

*The onslaught on grocery stores stopped a few days later. The minister of agriculture wrote in his diary that the buying panic had reflected temporary supply problems, caused by the call-up of so many drivers.[4]

tions, and let them drink out of their canteens. Finally they all sang songs together. One of the boys recited: "Soldiers, take care of us and of the country and of our flag." He was showered with kisses. "The soldiers, most of them fathers, seemed to enjoy the visit even more than the children," *Maariv* concluded.

The paper told of a shoemaker from Ness Ziona who wanted to give all of his savings to the IDF; the army refused his donation. An elderly couple donated their pensions to the IDF. The Helena Rubinstein cosmetics company promised its Israeli customers it was doing everything possible to keep production going. "Our duty and yours in these days of emergency is to stay level-headed and continue our daily activities, even step them up, and not to get into a bad mood or fall into panic," declared the company. Its advice to the women of Israel: "Keep up your appearance, put on makeup, look beautiful, and smile, even if it takes an effort."[7]

Letters sent overseas also reflect an attempt to repress anxiety, but it nonetheless was often visible between the lines. There's nothing to worry about, everyone is healthy, we feel fine, spirits are up, it all looks worse from the outside, wrote one woman from Tel Aviv to relatives in Boston, probably trying to reassure herself first and foremost, but the opening words of her letter were "Taking advantage of the Friedmans' leaving Israel, I'm writing you this letter," as if she feared it might be her last opportunity to make contact. Some letters were warm and calm, the writers seeming to have internalized the official spirit of resolve; others were official and cheery. "The main thing is the greatness of the people at this hour, which proves over and over again that the spark exists in each and every person from Israel and becomes a great flame of dedication and a love of Israel," wrote Yoskeh Shapira to overseas delegates of the Bnei Akiva movement. "We are keeping calm and trusting Him who dwells in the heavens," wrote parents from Kibbutz Ein Hanatziv to their daughter in Los Angeles. The kibbutz members were collecting underwear and towels so the soldiers camped nearby could shower and change, wrote the mother: "A spirit of volunteerism and generosity prevails in the country; everyone looks out for everyone." On the balcony at Café Roval in Tel Aviv they set up a blood donation station. The owners offered donors complimentary coffee and drinks.[8] Penina Axelrod, in Boston, received letters from her family assuring her that the mood was cheerful, but she also got a request from her sister to send their father's medication quickly: "I don't want Dad left without a supply."[9]

But the letters from Weizmann Street in Rishon Lezion showed how hard it was to stick to a routine. Rina and her baby moved in with her parents when her husband, David, was called up for reserve duty. The toddler made everyone happy. A real little boy, as his grandmother wrote, he was starting to walk and chatter, saying every word twice. He could recognize his grandfather and say "Saba," the mischievous little devil. But he also called out for his father all the time, saying, "Come, come." His grandmother wrote, "It breaks your heart." Uri, the young brother, now in high school, kept up his good grades and did his homework "tip-top, as if nothing is going on." But his father, who remained unwell, "felt the situation keenly," wrote his wife. "I never imagined I would go through this horror again in my lifetime," he wrote to his daughter, who was still in Manhattan but was now thinking of coming back. "Everyone has betrayed us." The parents refused to advise their daughter to come home. They knew no more than she did from the papers in New York, they wrote. But on May 28 the mother said, "Father's opinion is that you shouldn't send your things over yet. If you haven't sent them, wait until the situation becomes clearer."[10]

Riki Ben-Ari, a fashion commentator whose drawings appeared in *Maariv*, found it difficult to concentrate and was doing almost no work, but she wrote to family that she was more optimistic than many because she believed in fate: "You could die by accident, too." While weeding his garden, Yosef Weitz noticed an unusual silence that had settled on Hahalutz Street. Almost no vehicles were going by, he wrote in his diary. "Everyone looks up at the sky as if planes will appear at any moment."[11] Civil defense representatives went through houses in Rehavia to check on the basements (which served as bomb shelters), Edith Ezrachi told her relatives in Nashville. "It's hard to say there's a good mood." The civil defense authorities instructed residents to buy black paper and tape to darken their windows. Across the street, Ezrachi noted in another letter, was the Gymnasia Rehavia high school, its windows piled high with sandbags. "It's a very sad sight."

The first volunteers soon began to arrive from overseas. "It's wonderful to see them," *Yediot Aharonot* wrote cheerfully. Some celebrities came, too, to show solidarity with the embattled country, including the pianist Daniel Barenboim. Foreign reporters also started arriving, among them the grandson of Winston Churchill, who went to see Ben-Gurion almost as soon as he landed.[12]

As tensions mounted, so did the fear of Israeli Arabs. The crisis sharpened suspicions that always hovered over Arab laborers, and the number of Jews traveling to predominantly Arab Nazareth dropped. The police denied, however, that Arabs were distributing anti-Jewish leaflets. The author

Yeshurun Keshet thought about Israeli Arabs that week. There were no assurances of their loyalty to the state, he wrote in his diary: "The soul of the eastern man is a dark abyss and his thoughts are a mystery." Naturally, "the voice of blood and racial belonging" drew Israeli Arabs to the Arab world, and were stronger than the material advantages Israel offered them. It followed that no arrangement in the relations between Jews and Arabs in Israel could be natural or sustainable. "This is not a temporary problem, but a curse for generations." Keshet had no delusions: "No final solution is feasible."[13]

Eshkol's military secretary, Israel Lior, had met with the head of the Security Service, Yosef Harmelin, and suggested he heighten the state of alert. Harmelin proposed "preparing actions against the local population." It was decided that in the event of war, military supervision over Israeli Arabs would be renewed; among other things, overnight curfews would be imposed and Bedouin residents would be moved from the north of Israel to the south. A few dozen Arabs were arrested under military directives. The military advocate general, Meir Shamgar, however, cautioned against a second Kafr Kassem, an Arab village where, on the eve of the Sinai Campaign, several dozen residents had been shot dead after curfew hours by Israeli Border Guard police. "Curfew violation is not cause for opening fire. Use of firearms is permitted only when engaged in war. People who are late getting to their villages when a curfew is in force will be allowed to return home; if necessary they will be arrested. Under no circumstances should they be hurt."

Fausi Al-Asmar went to visit a friend on Kibbutz Galon, but no sooner had he reached her room than she was called to the kibbutz secretariat. When she returned, she told him the kibbutz had demanded that he leave immediately. He might be an enemy spy, the kibbutz secretary had explained. What could he be spying on in the kibbutz? she had asked. He could tell the enemy that all the young kibbutz members had been called up, and also that there were not enough bomb shelters. The army, which continued to monitor Arab activities, reported enthusiastic expressions of identification with Nasser and hopes that Israel would be destroyed, particularly among Muslims.[14] Kibbutz Lohamei Hagetaot, conversely, sent out a newsletter to its active-duty members reporting that Arabs from the surrounding villages had come to help the kibbutz with the farmwork. They came with their families, and looked sad and tense. "We set up lovely tables for them in the dining room," the newsletter continued. "We tried to honor and appreciate what they were doing, and they spoke of work and peace." *Ha'aretz* reported that the Galilee Arabs were afraid of the coming war and were depressed. There were also reports of Arabs offering to donate blood and money.[15]

Professor Akiba Ernst Simon, a longtime member of the movement in favor of a binational Arab-Jewish state, and Uri Davis, a leader of the struggle against martial law, were among the signatories to a petition published in *Ha'aretz* calling on Israel to wait before going to war: "He who gains time may also gain peace."[16]* But these voices were lost in the consensus of anxiety. Amnon Zihroni, an attorney, reexamined his worldview as a pacifist and draft resister; in 1954, he had held a prolonged hunger strike to force the government to recognize his right to conscientious objection. In May 1967, he still believed he did not have the right to kill a human being, in accordance with the principles of pacifism. While he blamed the government for the crisis, he nonetheless wrote to Eshkol asking to be enlisted "in some defensive capacity," such as a medic.[17]

Though always a positive thinker, even Edith Ezrachi was losing hope. "I must admit that up until about Friday . . . I was still fairly optimistic," she wrote to Norwalk, Connecticut. "I was still almost confident that some way would be found to avert a military confrontation. But by Saturday I was grasped by the nightmarish realization that there may be no way out." On Sunday, her husband, Eitan, was called up. She tried to amuse her relatives in America with descriptions of his efforts to fit into his old uniform. He looked as if he were back in the Boy Scouts. She laughed at his appearance, but really she wanted to cry. "Our anxiety is very great and very grave and our incomprehension is maddening."[18] This was a fear of destruction, and its source was rooted in the Holocaust.

2. HOLOCAUST: "NASSER IS HITLER"

During the first years of Israel's existence, the events of the Holocaust was shrouded in a great silence, making the topic virtually taboo. Parents would not tell their children what had happened to them, and children dared not ask. But after the April 1961 kidnapping of Adolf Eichmann and the trial that followed, Israelis became more open with respect to the Holocaust, ultimately making it a part of their identity.[19]

In the middle of 1966, some young Israelis went on a tour of the death camps. One of them, Mordehai Kremnitzer, wrote an article about

---

*Other signatories to the petition were familiar to *Ha'aretz* readers: Professors Yehoshua Bar-Hillel, Carl Frankenstein, and Nathan Yelin-Mor, a well-known intellectual, formerly a commander in the Lehi underground force and a member of the First Knesset.

the trip. "Israelis in Auschwitz. Tears in their eyes; gloomy, silent. Wanting vengeance. Promising to remember and not to forget—Israelis who feel they are the children of those who were murdered, who feel they are Jews, Jews at the graves of their fathers, the graves of their brothers. And there was also a sense of victory: we are the living." The three weeks spent in Czechoslovakia and Poland, wrote Kremnitzer, turned these young people into proud and sensitive Jews, but also into better Israelis: "Everywhere I went, the word 'homeland' called out to me."[20]

These were the first voices in a fairly slow learning process. Israelis began to internalize the foundations of their past, including their history in the Diaspora, and gradually stopped being ashamed of it, unlike the previous generation. At the culmination of the process it would be hard to find a young Israeli who would use the name Warhaftig as an insult. In January 1967, a few hundred students at the Lady Davis school in Petach Tikva gathered to hear impressions of the young Israelis who had been to Poland. Their elderly teacher told the children not to forget the Holocaust, and the next speaker explained why this was important: so that they would be strong.[21]

This was the emerging attitude, lucidly expressed in a 1963 letter written by a young man, Ofer Feniger, to his girlfriend following the Eichmann trial. "I feel that from all the horror and the helplessness, a hugely powerful strength is growing in me. Strong to the point of tears; sharp as a knife; quiet and terrible; that's how I want to be! I want to know that never again will hollow eyes look out from behind electric fences! . . . Not if I am strong! If we are all strong! Strong, proud Jews! Never again to be led to the slaughter."[22]*

Politicians, educators, and media figures repeated the lesson often. A small minority tended to emphasize the universal lessons of the Holocaust, such as the duty to protect democracy and human rights and the obligation to fight racism and refuse manifestly illegal orders. This was yet another arena of the conflict between "the two peoples of Israel."

THE STORY OF ISRAELIS AND THE HOLOCAUST ALTERNATES BETWEEN TRUE EMOTION and manipulative argument, which are not always easily distinguished. As soon as the crisis of war began, the press began comparing Nasser to

---

*In August 1966, Meir Amit reported to Eshkol about the attempts to track down two Nazi criminals: Martin Bormann, Hitler's private secretary and head of the party chancellery, and Heinrich Müller, the head of the Gestapo. He presented various possibilities of capture for Eshkol's consideration.[23]

Hitler. In the past, other Arab leaders had been compared to Hitler, but this had been done to insult them, not as part of the situational assessment and a reason to attack. "Nasser speaks clearly, as Hitler did on the eve of the Second World War," wrote Ze'ev Schiff. Nasser's speeches, Radio Cairo broadcasts, and the anti-Semitic cartoons in the Egyptian press prompted this assertion. *Ha'aretz* published an article by Eliezer Livneh called "The Danger of Hitler Is Returning." Livneh, a former Knesset member for Mapai, also sent a note to Eshkol: "Nasser is Hitler."[24]

Many compared Israel's situation to Czechoslovakia's prior to World War II, when it was abandoned to the Nazis. They recalled that the British prime minister, Neville Chamberlain, had forsaken the Czechs in the Munich accord, and they likened his appeasement policy to Eshkol's approach.[25] Letters and articles to this effect were published in *Yediot Aharonot* and *Maariv*. One editor, Shalom Rosenfeld, read a book about the dismantling of Czechoslovakia written by Israeli historian David Vital, and became so worried that he could not sleep all night.[26]

David Ben-Gurion said, "None of us can forget the Nazi Holocaust, and if some of the Arab leaders, with the leader of Egypt at their head, declare day and night that Israel must be destroyed . . . we should not take these declarations lightly."[27] This was also Israel's official propaganda line. The Foreign Ministry instructed the Israeli embassy in Washington to ask for an urgent meeting with James Reston, associate editor of the *New York Times*, to persuade him that the only difference between Nasser and Hitler was that Hitler had always claimed he wanted peace, while Nasser was explicit about his aim of destroying Israel. Minister Mordehai Bentov asked Eshkol to set up a "center for psychological warfare" that would focus on the comparison between Hitler and Nasser.[28]

Baruh Nadel, a prominent journalist at *Yediot Aharonot*, published impressions from a visit to reserve soldiers posted in the Negev. One soldier he met, apparently a Holocaust survivor, was sitting in the last row of trenches, "a little Pole, illuminated by red twilight, his black shadow cast far back to the hills, where the tanks, hidden under netting, point their threatening mouths of steel toward Gaza." Nadel returned home calm and reassured.[29] This was the Holocaust as propaganda.*

---

*In contrast, Boaz Evron of *Yediot Aharonot* warned against the inclination to compare Nasser with Hitler, suggesting instead that Israelis, unlike the Jews of Europe, "stand up like men."[30] In a cabinet meeting just before the war, Zalman Aran also maintained that "Nasser is not Hitler."[31]

. . .

BUT THE EXISTENTIAL ANXIETY THAT GRIPPED ISRAELIS WHEN THE CRISIS ERUPTED WAS real. Someone no doubt organized citizens to send care packages to soldiers, perhaps to unite the people around their army, but there is no reason to assume that anyone solicited the letter written by a woman who sent a package of goods to the soldier Arnon David Grabow. She told him she had been in Auschwitz, where her husband and four children were murdered. After many tribulations, she had reached Israel and managed to start a new family. She had small children, and she trusted the IDF and prayed for its welfare every night.[32] There is also no reason to doubt what members of Kibbutz Lohamei Hagetaot told their sons in a newsletter for enlisted soldiers. While digging defensive trenches on the kibbutz, the members recalled doing the same thing in 1939, in preparation for the Nazis' invasion of Poland. They believed there was no choice but to go to war with Egypt. When the situation was explained to young Amosi, one of the "second generation" kibbutz children, he responded, "This means that if Nasser wins, we were born in vain."[33]

"The situation is terrible," wrote Naomi Shukri from Ramatayim to a classmate living in Los Angeles. "You cannot imagine how lucky you are not to be in Israel right now." It wasn't the recession, she wrote, it wasn't money, it was life. People were walking around hunched over, the stress was exhausting. Who could think of work? The country was paralyzed. "No one knows what will happen tomorrow, in the next hour, the next minute. People keep asking each other: What will happen? What will happen? Only God knows." Sometimes she thought she was having a nightmare, that she would wake up and everything would be back to normal. But no, she wrote, this was cruel and terrible reality, and it had been going on for almost two weeks. "I suppose this is the fate of the Jews, even in our time, in our land. Will we also be a generation of war?" Her letter was not written to persuade James Reston. It was written from the heart and soul of Naomi Shukri, and she expressed the feelings of countless Israelis. "Who would have believed it?" she continued. "Who? Who could have imagined that all the stories about the fear before war would happen in our own lives?" Her husband had been called up for reserve duty. "Don't even ask how I stood there and packed his bag. May you never know such a thing your whole life. Your whole life." She wanted to believe that if, God forbid, "something happens," they could rely on the army; but, she enjoined her friend, "Don't dare regret not being in Israel."[34]

Rabin, who believed that Israel faced its most difficult trial since the War of Independence, instructed schools and other public buildings to be readied to serve as hospitals and casualty centers. Zerah Warhaftig later recalled asking the chief of staff how many deaths he thought the IDF might sustain, and Rabin estimated perhaps tens of thousands. Ten rabbis from the chief rabbinate and the Tel Aviv Hevre Kaddisha went through the public parks sanctifying them to serve as cemeteries. Only a society drenched in the memory of the Holocaust could have prepared so meticulously for the next one.[35]

ALL AT ONCE, IT HAD BECOME CLEAR HOW VULNERABLE AND DESPERATE ISRAELIS WERE. It was not Nasser's threats that had brought this about—or, at least, not only his threats—but the quicksand of depression that had pulled so many people down for so many months. It was the disappointment and the feeling that the Israeli dream had run its course. It was the loss of David Ben-Gurion's leadership, the father of the nation, coupled with the lack of faith in Eshkol and the general mistrust of politics. It was the recession and the unemployment; the decline in immigration and the mass emigration. It was the deprivation of the Mizrahim, as well as the fear of them—the fear that they would erode Israel's European society and culture, that they threatened the Ashkenazi elite. It was the difficulty communicating with the younger generation. It was the boredom. It was the terrorism; the sense that there could be no peace. All these feelings welled up in the week before the war, sweeping through the nation in a tide of insanity. The people had not felt this wretched and isolated since the Holocaust.

And so the ideas being put forth in the meantime by more stable minds in Israel, Washington, and New York never had much of a chance. There were a few proposals, all meant to provide a two- or three-week cooling-off period, during which it was suggested that Israel not try to move ships bearing its flag through the Gulf of Aqaba, and that Egypt not hinder the passage of other ships.[36] Arthur Goldberg, U.S. ambassador to the UN, suggested a settlement to Johnson that could both maintain Nasser's standing and assure the passage of ships to Israel: Israel would stop sailing under its flag, and Nasser would stop conducting searches of ships making their way to Eilat under foreign flags. Israel would have a difficult time accepting this, the ambassador wrote, but one must remember that in any case oil was shipped to Eilat in tankers that did not bear Israeli flags.[37] The State Department suggested a similar plan, pointing out that over the past two and a half years only one merchant ship flying the Israeli flag had gone through the Straits.[38]

The majority of Israelis knew nothing of the proposals to end the crisis without war. They listened to the Voice of Thunder from Cairo, an Egyptian radio station that broadcast propaganda in Hebrew.* "Your leaders will not help you—they will bring a Holocaust upon you!" roared the broadcaster. One Tel Aviv woman wrote to Boston that "anyone who can pick up Cairo television must have been wetting themselves with fear over the past few weeks." Many Israelis felt they should believe the broadcasts, just as people should have believed Hitler.† Countless letters from Israelis to friends overseas, as well as letters written by soldiers at the front, reflect a desire to avoid war. But the military leaders insisted there was no way out of it, and they were the only people most Israelis still trusted.

*The Hebrew word for thunder (ra'am), is also the acronym for the United Arab Republic, as Egypt was officially known during that period. (Translator's note.)
†The popular entertainer Uri Zohar responded with a morale-building song that he performed for soldiers: "Nasser is waiting for Rabin, ay-ay-ay / Let him wait and not budge / Because we'll be there for sure / He's waited twice before / And we gave it to him good / He'll be shouting, ay-ay-ay / Like in the Sinai Campaign / You'll see, the day will come / He'll beg for peace."[39]

CHAPTER 9

ONE WEEK TO WAR:
THE GENERALS' REVOLT

1. STAMMERING: "THE WAR'S NOT GOING ANYWHERE"

Sunday, May 28, began in a fever of anxiety for Shuka Bar-Dayan. Everything was so quiet. There was still no war. "I wish it would start already, so we can release the tension, and whatever happens will happen." He drank warm soda and gobbled crackers, and then someone came and handed him a gas mask. "Looks like they're going to gas us," he wrote hurriedly, his diary functioning as a barrier between himself and his fear.[1] A notice circulated among the reservists that week including the following guidelines: "An IDF soldier taken prisoner must act proudly. He must not try to ingratiate himself with his interrogators and must not be self-deprecating in front of his captors." The notice described a soldier named Jibli, who had been captured and managed to withstand torture "until his captors gave up trying to make him talk."[2] "Dear Gili," wrote Bar-Dayan to his wife, "I'm here simply because Nasser wants to destroy us and throw us into the sea with our children. And the world stands by silently. We will smash his plans with immense force. That's why you are going through this—and us, too." He could not help but feel homesick; he prayed for Gili and Yariv, hoped they were taking care of themselves and not panicking. "Endless love," he concluded, "Daddy Shuka."[3]

A few hours earlier, the Israeli envoy in Washington had contacted Walt Rostow to ask for permission to brief the Israeli press correspondents in town, a move initiated by Foreign Minister Eban. In advance of the day's cabinet meeting, Eban hoped the morning papers would project a degree of optimism about the chances that the United States would reopen the Straits of Tiran. Rostow conveyed the request to Johnson. The embassy would say only a few words to the reporters, he promised, and Johnson agreed. But Private Shuka Bar-Dayan was not impressed with what he read in the morning news: "Nasser is out of control and Johnson is not standing by us."[4]

AT FIVE-THIRTY THAT MORNING, AMBASSADOR BARBOUR HAD DELIVERED A LETTER from President Johnson to Eshkol in Tel Aviv. The Russians were claiming that Israel was about to attack its neighbors, Johnson wrote. As a friend, he was once again cautioning Israel that it "just must not take any preemptive military action." Barbour added a sharper message: any unilateral act by Israel would be irresponsible and even disastrous.[5]

The cabinet reconvened as scheduled at noon on Sunday, May 28, as had been arranged when the previous night's meeting had ended before dawn with a stalemate: nine ministers supported immediate war; nine wanted to wait. Eban assured the ministers that Johnson was trying to put together an international coalition to reopen the Straits, and that if he was unsuccessful, the United States would act alone. Johnson was "steady as a rock," Eban promised—he would bring in the Sixth Fleet if he had to. This had been conveyed on behalf of the president to Ambassador Harman, following Eban's meeting with Johnson, Eban claimed. He had reexamined the minutes from that meeting and repeatedly asserted that he had no doubt: the minutes contained an explicit commitment that if the United States was unable to coordinate international action, it would act alone. This was untrue, even according to the Israeli version of the minutes. While Johnson had firmly promised to make every possible effort to open the Straits, he had not expressly stated that the United States would act on its own to that end.

The cabinet discussion repeated positions already laid out: Eshkol understood that the Americans' communication must not be ignored; he proposed waiting for two or three weeks. Rabin said that postponing the attack would set Israel back to the situation it was in before 1956. He did not believe the world powers would reopen the Straits. In two or three weeks, Israel would be facing the same problem but under worse conditions. Meanwhile, the IDF's prestige was being damaged. He regretted having to say it, he added as if apologizing, but this was simply the way he saw things. This was his sense and his belief and he had to speak his mind. Eshkol insisted on rebuking Rabin—perhaps an expression of a new attitude toward the military's assessments—telling him, "I don't want to do what I've done with the others, back you into a corner and ask a simple yes or no question [on whether to defer to Johnson]. Even if you say yes, I'm not interested."

Similarly, Eban rejected the need to consider what Rabin described as "the army's prestige," maintaining, "There are no widows or orphans of prestige." The doves were setting the tone of the hour. Even Allon now supported a delay, albeit reluctantly, as he feared the Americans would demand international supervision over Dimona in return for their help. Minister Gvati said that compliance with Johnson's demands would mean delivering Israel's fate into American hands. "We'll just be patronage Jews," he said; but he, too, voted in favor of waiting. Only Carmel stood his ground: "The government is in a state of severe delusion." The cabinet decided to avoid military action, pending a new decision, to be made within three weeks. The ministers' willingness to comply with Johnson's request was based on the incorrect information Eban had given them. Eban had done to them precisely what Eshkol, Rabin, and Yariv had done to him and Ambassador Harman with their telegrammed reports of a worsening situation that threatened Israel's existence. Eban had not believed their telegrams; but the ministers, conversely, believed his report.

The decision draft made reference to President Johnson's "commitment" to ensure freedom of shipping in the Gulf of Aqaba, but a more guarded official deleted that word and replaced it with "promise." The stated reason for the government's decision was the "chance" that the United States would act to reopen the Straits "together with other governments or on its own."

"I do not know whether I was endowed with the personal courage to send our young men to war," Minister Aran said two days later, "but I had enough courage to not send them at that particular moment, given the overall assessment of the situation. It is very possible that we will be blessed for not having done so, and for having deflected the hell as much as we could." According to the minister, he had no illusions that the waiting period would prevent the war, but he thought they could not pass up the possibility: "The war isn't going anywhere," he said.[6]

"The General Staff took the decision very badly," wrote Gvati in his diary. He himself had "a heavy heart" and was not at peace with his choice. "I am afraid our decision was wrong and it may cost us dearly," he wrote.[7] Within a few hours, after hearing Prime Minister Eshkol's radio address, most of the country agreed with him.

EVERYONE WAS EXPECTING ESHKOL TO GIVE AN ADDRESS TO THE NATION, BUT INSTEAD he simply read the government's decision over the radio. It was phrased in clumsy, near-legalistic language, meant to be read, not spoken. At that point, life was more or less paralyzed. In almost every household, people were worried about their loved ones on reserve duty—fathers, husbands, sons. Eshkol's announcement offered neither reassurance nor warmth, not even a Churchillian blood, sweat, toil, and tears type of encouragement.

The first line of the resolution's second page included one handwritten change, made by one of Eshkol's assistants. Eshkol was not prepared for the change, which replaced "retreat of forces" with "shift of forces." Eshkol became confused as he read the paper. He stopped, whispered to his assistants, and mumbled something. On live radio. His horrified assistants desperately motioned for him to keep going. Reading the next line, Eshkol began to stammer.[8]

Miriam Eshkol was on her way from Jerusalem to Tel Aviv when she heard her husband on the radio. She was gripped with a sense of disaster. She did not know what exactly had happened, but realized immediately that the result was terrible. She hurried to the studio and found it filled with foreign reporters but almost none of the prime minister's assistants; they had fled like mice, she later said. Eshkol explained what had happened, rubbing his eyes; he had recently undergone cataract surgery. She was beside herself with fury. This could have been avoided if Eshkol had recorded his speech, or at least waited a few moments for a fresh typescript without handwritten corrections.[9]

Some of the cabinet ministers felt the radio broadcast was a central factor in the subsequent fervor. "Never was a country's political life changed so drastically because of a stammer," said Zalman Aran. "I realized immediately that Eshkol had made a mistake, possibly a fatal one," wrote Israel Lior, who had been with him in the studio. "For many days afterward, I kept hearing stories of soldiers and officers in the Negev bursting into tears when they heard Eshkol's stammering voice on their transistor radios. The low morale dropped even lower." General Yeshayahu Gavish of the Southern Command said the whole thing was frightening and extremely depressing. He had heard the speech on the way to a meeting with Eshkol and the General Staff. Ariel Sharon heard it on the way to the same meeting, and said it only heightened his sense of foreboding.[10]*

---

*Private Yehoshua Bar-Dayan did not hear the speech; he was on kitchen duty.[11]

2. THREATS: "YOUR HESITATION WILL COST US
THOUSANDS OF LIVES"

The meeting was tough; rage was in the air. Eshkol found himself facing a fierce, confrontational General Staff, worked up to the point of hysteria and particularly rude. Some of the officers were threatening, claiming that the state's existence was in danger. Eshkol put them in their place, but was evidently deeply shaken.

Aharon Yariv told those present about a few Egyptian officers who had defected to Israel, and said the information they supplied "basically confirmed our intelligence." He did not say whether, according to the soldiers, Egypt was about to attack. Next he reported that the "prevailing wind" in the Jordanian refugee camps was that "Palestine will soon be returned." Then Yariv summarized a statement Nasser had given to the press. At this point, General Gavish said, "Tomorrow is the last chance. The Egyptians are blocking every axis. Tomorrow we could swallow an Egyptian division." The minutes note that Gavish was speaking to Minister Allon, who had arrived at the meeting with Eshkol. No one seems to have asked Gavish why the next day was their last chance.

Eshkol told those of the generals who had not heard him on the radio about the government decision, adding that since he had been reading from a prepared document, he might not have managed to explain himself properly. The nature of the decision might make the generals "uncomfortable," he conceded, but they should remember that only a day earlier he had been one step away from deciding on war. Now there were "diplomatic problems" that necessitated a delay. "We're not alone in the world," he said. He spoke at length of his nighttime meeting with Chuvakhin, and reported confidentially on the message he had received from Johnson that morning. He said Johnson had warned that a preemptive strike by Israel would bring about "a holocaust." Eshkol was embellishing somewhat. Secretary of State Rusk had instructed Ambassador Barbour to caution Israel against bringing on a "catastrophe," but he had not used the word "holocaust," and the president himself had not warned of a "catastrophe." Following Eban's lead, Eshkol repeated the American commitment that if they failed to organize international action, they would go it alone.

The decision not to go to war had been preceded by lengthy deliberations, Eshkol said. At this point the minutes add a parenthetical question: "Moral ones, too?" It is unclear whether Eshkol spoke these words or whether they express the note taker's reservations. Either way, Eshkol described the decision as an expression of "political maturity."

Gavish said that in two weeks the Straits would still be blockaded and the situation would be worse. Rehavam Ze'evi said that the IDF's plan of action might have been leaked by then. Eshkol replied that if it transpired that Israel had been misled, it would act, but that on the basis of his personal acquaintance with Johnson he believed the president would keep his promise.

Ariel Sharon said: "Today we have ourselves chopped off the IDF's deterrence capability. We have chopped up our main weapon—the fear of us." He said Israel was capable of destroying the Egyptian army, but if they gave in on the question of free navigation, "we will open the door to Israel's total destruction." Like Yigal Allon, Sharon invoked the Sinai Campaign and claimed that cooperation with the British and French had been to Israel's detriment. Today Israel was capable of demolishing the Egyptian army on its own, he said, but it was clear that any delay would mean paying a higher price "for something we'll have to do anyway." Up to this point he had been speaking as Sharon the soldier; from here on, he became Sharon the politician: "We also have to keep in mind the domestic consideration of not undermining the people's morale by deciding to wait. The people are ready for a just war. All of our pleading makes us seem weak. The people understand this and feel that they're going to have to pay the price. We have to fight for what is essential."

Sharon's use of the word "pleading" reflected a Sabra's scorn for the old-fashioned Jewish way of conducting business in the Diaspora, and was probably intended to insult the prime minister. He cautioned that delay might reinvigorate terrorism and the "problem of the Arab minority." His conclusion was dramatic: "The problem is not the Straits—the problem is the People of Israel and their continued existence." Not just the State of Israel, but "the People of Israel," in its entirety. Eshkol tried to show that Sharon was being unreasonable, but Sharon interrupted him: "Inaction on our part shows powerlessness. We're making ourselves look like an empty vessel, a desperate state. We've never before been so humiliated." Then he went even further: "Your hesitation will cost us thousands of lives," he told the prime minister.

It would have been hard to put the case more hurtfully, but Eshkol showed restraint. He did not ask Sharon to leave, nor did he himself walk out or even demand an apology. "You are greatly exaggerating," he told the generals, and asked them to "take a deep breath." The cabinet had considered all the arguments. They believed the great powers were concerned for Israel's welfare. Destroying the Egyptian military would not be the end of the story; Egypt's army would be rebuilt. Israel, on the other hand, could not exist without outside help. If war could be averted, then everything must be done to avert it. There was hope that Britain and the United States would take action in Israel's stead, for the sake of their own interests. "IDF generals must understand the role of statesmanship and not allow their discontent to tip the scale. There is no room here for self-immolation," Eshkol rebuked the generals. The government, conversely, had to consider the whole picture—"the problem of blood, the problem of property, the damage to the military." Eshkol then lost the thread of his argument, as he often did. "Perhaps in fifteen years there will be a different Arab generation, one that will kiss us."

The generals kept up their onslaught. Avraham Yaffe said they were "disappointed" because the government had declared in the past that if freedom of the seas was hindered, it would bring in the army; he spoke as if the government had gone back on a commitment. The army that Egypt was building with the help of the USSR was intended for one purpose, Yaffe contended: to destroy Israel. And here was the IDF, ready and willing, but with its hands tied. "No one will help us if we don't help ourselves. If we're still pleading with France and the United States when the Egyptians attack, we're marching toward a holocaust." Yaffe went on to accuse the government of violating the people's right to employ their army. "As military men, we feel the army is not being allowed to fulfill the task it was established to do. But the army has a rear, which is the people. And the government's decision today will hurt it. People along the border, and not only there, want the IDF to defend the State of Israel and its dignity." He praised "the wonderful nation," argued that the people had not lost hope, but declared, "The wonderful spirit of the people is being destroyed." He warned that the people would be provoked to rebel. "It is inconceivable that our feelings will not spread. We won't leave this room with happy faces. If we pretend, they'll say we lied." Ezer Weizman declared, "Our leaders are incapable of forging national unity in the face of the Arab danger."

A whiff of mutiny, almost of a military coup, was in the air, and so when the next general spoke he felt it necessary to say, as if it were not obvious, "I do not dispute the government's right and obligation to make decisions." This was Israel Tal, commander of an armored division. But he also claimed they were contending with "the state's very existence." He tried to persuade Eshkol that there was no assurance that the United States would reopen the straits. Tal's forces could destroy a significant part of the Egyptian army, which would damage Nasser and might assure peace for the next fifteen years.

Quartermaster General Matityahu Peled also felt the need to stress that he was not questioning the government's decision. He hoped to convince Eshkol with economic arguments. There was no possibility of extending the reserve call-up much longer, which meant that Israel would soon face the Egyptians with a smaller army lacking response capabilities. "Every hour that goes by may hasten the destruction of the Third Temple," Peled said; was this the government's intent? He could not comprehend the decision, and asked for clear instructions.*

General David Elazar, of the Northern Command, also tried to soften the effect of Yaffe's outburst, saying his comments should be viewed as "information," not "criticism." He mentioned the need for a surprise attack on the Egyptian air force and concluded: "If the enemy achieves an aerial advantage, the IDF will not win—or, if it does win, the cost will be devastating." General Narkis of the Central Command harked back to the Second World War to prove that the Russians were deceitful. He then went on as if he were actually trying to help Eshkol: "Discontent in the IDF is a very serious matter"—but added a vague threat: "The army won't trust us if we say we're doing nothing." It's not the men in the room whom Eshkol should be worried about, he said: "We're not the problem. You can talk to us. The problem is the youngsters. Nothing we say here will leave this room, but everyone believes the war is starting tomorrow. It'll be hard to explain what happened." According to this argument, the country was supposed to go to war so as not to disappoint the "youngsters." "I don't know what you think of the military," Narkis said patronizingly to the prime minister. "All of us here have been in the army for twenty years or more, and I want to tell you—it is a fantastic army. There's nothing to worry about." Just to remove any doubt, Narkis added that the Arabs had not changed: "They're a bubble of soap, and with one pin-prick they'll burst," he bragged.

THE GENERALS WERE IN THEIR FORTIES, FAMILY MEN, BUT THEY CLUNG TO THE ISRAELI culture of youth; they were like adolescent boys or bulls in rut. They believed in force and they wanted war. War was their destiny. Almost twenty years had passed since the army had won glory in the War of Independence,

---

*Yigal Allon later cited the economic hardship caused by the call-up as a justification for the war: "A general mobilization in Israel means economic paralysis. They could drive us crazy every three or four months by redeploying and each time we would have to call men up and then let them go."[12]

and ten years since the victory in the Sinai. They had a limited range of vision and they believed that war was what Israel needed at that moment, not necessarily because they felt the country's existence was in danger, as they wailed in an almost "Diaspora" tone, but because they believed it was an opportunity to break the Egyptian army. And they thought that any delay would increase the number of casualties.

They knew no more than Eshkol did; and, unlike them, Eshkol was involved in the international repercussions of the situation. As Israel's leader, it was his responsibility to do everything in his power to prevent war. With a head of intelligence admitting that he had been wrong, a chief of staff recovering from a nervous breakdown, and the peculiar outbursts of Ezer Weizman, Eshkol had no reason to privilege the generals' statements over the other factors that had guided him, usually successfully, throughout his life: experience, wisdom, and intuition. Eshkol knew, of course, as everyone did, that Israel had "a fantastic army," and that very fact was a good reason to take a deep breath, as he had put it. He disputed the army's basic premise. Israel had managed for years without the Straits, he reminded the generals; and, he asked rhetorically, "What if we hadn't gotten the Straits in the Sinai Campaign?" He also rejected the thesis that the Egyptian army's presence in the Sinai necessarily called for war. Only two or three months earlier, the Egyptians had moved forces into the Sinai, and Israel had felt no need to start a war then. "It never occurred to me that large Egyptian forces near the border meant we should get up one night and destroy them," said Eshkol, and asked, "Must we live by the sword forever?"

Eshkol had given the generals everything they wanted, he said, sounding like a father speaking to his impetuous sons. "You wanted a hundred planes? You got them. And you got tanks. You got everything, so we can win if we have to. You didn't get all that matériel so that one day we would get up and say, Now we can destroy the Egyptian army—so let's do it. We were brought up not to wage preemptive war." Eshkol was extremely angry at this point. "There's nothing worse for me than to hear you all speaking this way and feeling as you say you do. What you're really telling me is, Give us a chance to blow up Egyptian aviation. Why didn't we attack them two months ago? Three? We can do it two months from now, too. Just like that. For no reason."

Israel Lior feared that the discussion was about to explode, a sense apparently shared by Minister Allon, who suggested suspending the conversation so that they could "come back and talk about the problem next week."[13] On his way out, Eshkol stopped to talk to Sharon, and told him he was under heavy pressure to appoint Moshe Dayan minister of defense. "For all I care, you can appoint Beba Idelson," Sharon replied, meaning that the appointment would not change the way he and his soldiers fought.[14] His answer was extremely insulting: the woman whose Diaspora name he had thrown out was a leader of the Mapai party; he might as well have said "Zerah Warhaftig." Eshkol was "torn and wounded," his military secretary wrote.[15]

AFTER ESHKOL LEFT THE MEETING, THE OFFICERS CONTINUED TO STOKE ONE ANOTHER up with speculations on the dangers Israel might face, including an attack on Dimona. As far as the minutes show, none of them referred again to the Holocaust or the destruction of the Third Temple. In fact, a sudden pronouncement by Uzi Narkis might have interested Eshkol: "I don't believe Nasser's about to strike." Rabin expressed his hope that Nasser, "out of drunkenness," might make a mistake that would let them go to war after all, before the two-week waiting period was up. But in the meantime they had to decide what to tell the soldiers and, perhaps, start discharging some of the reservists, who had heard Eshkol's speech and knew there was not going to be a war for now. General Tal suggested telling them exactly what the military believed: that the danger had not passed but that, for political reasons, the government was stopping the IDF from acting. That was how they should explain it, he said bitterly.[16] Meanwhile, Shuka Bar-Dayan was washing his socks.

3. NEW DEVELOPMENTS: "NOW HUSSEIN IS OUR ENEMY, TOO"

Bar-Dayan had trouble deciding which was worse: the tension or the boredom. "Another day has passed with no news either way—a real war of nerves," he wrote to Gili, and told her he needed his gas mask because his socks smelled so bad. This was his way of telling her that he and his friends had been trained to protect themselves in case of a gas attack. "What to do, my love? This is our fate in this country." He had joined his unit unwillingly, but he would do what he had to, all so "we will be free men and not slaves," and for Gili and Yariv. "They've simply imposed a war on us, and we have no choice but to win. It will be an even more important war than the War of Independence."

The papers reported on Begin's efforts to form a national unity government. "Well done, Begin, a true patriot," Bar-Dayan wrote. To pass the time, he gave his fellow soldiers a ten-minute lecture on one of his interests: the history of the Crusader Kingdom of Jerusalem. His conclusion was that Nasser was no Salah a-Din, the Muslim leader who had trounced the Crusaders, and he would not be able to destroy Israel. "My dear Yariv, I have not seen you for two weeks, except for one quick glimpse. The ink is wet with tears as I write these lines, I miss you my son, I love you so much, and I'm sure I will come home to you after the victory."[17]

At dawn on Wednesday, May 31, Bar-Dayan's brigade left the sands of Halutza and returned to the unit workshop. "It's like America," wrote Bar-Dayan, because he could finally take a shower. They camped near a grove of tamarisks that he knew well: as a student at the Mikveh Yisrael agricultural school he had helped to plant it. He started getting letters from home. His two brothers, Nissan and Ali, had also been called up. The first letter from his wife was heart-rending. He had always tried to nurture her patriotic loyalty, he wrote in his diary, and now, when crisis struck, it turned out she was feeling deep resentment. She wrote to him about men who had not been called up for active duty and did not have the guts to volunteer ("bastards"). She wrote about officers' wives ("hypocrites") whose only concern, even now, was that their husbands were coming home too late in the evening. "I was very, very depressed, without any ability to comfort, to support, to encourage," wrote Bar-Dayan. "There's no justice in the world: I'm on the front line, and they, my neighbors, are sitting in the sun on their balconies, complacent."[18]

Kol Israel began broadcasting a daily commentary by General Haim Herzog, the brother of the director general of the prime minister's office. Irish born, with his British accent, Herzog projected cool sobriety and familiarity with the situation. On June 1 he said something that later became an Israeli classic: "I must say in all sincerity that if I had to choose today between flying in an Egyptian bomber bound for Tel Aviv, or actually being in Tel Aviv, I would out of purely selfish desire for self-preservation opt to be in Tel Aviv."[19] Herzog favored the war—in this he was unlike Ben-Gurion, but they shared a similarity: Herzog, too, might have been able to convince Israelis that it would be best to turn aside from the war. People believed him. "With his level-headedness he really improves our mood," wrote Bar-Dayan. Glued to his transistor radio, "drawing strength" from Herzog's commentary, Bar-Dayan remembered that in his youth everybody in the moshav used to go out and greet Herzog's father, the chief rabbi, when he visited.[20]

Bar-Dayan asked his wife to send him two undershirts, two pairs of underwear, shaving cream, and a small bar of laundry soap. He assured her that there was money in the bank. "When I get home we won't spend even a minute apart," he wrote. He listened to the radio a lot. "The evening news is distressing. Hussein flew to see Nasser and signed a defense pact with him. Now even the reasonable Hussein is our enemy, too. It complicates things, but let's hope we can deal with the Jordanians too."[21]

Minister Gvati also found the news of the Egyptian-Jordanian defense pact "very depressing," viewing it as "another victory for Nasser." The "noose is tightening around our neck," he wrote. "What are we waiting for?" Gvati had just visited Kibbutz Lehavot Habashan. "I shudder to think that in a few days the kibbutz might be a pile of ruins," he wrote, but added, "There are a lot of troops in the area, and we have to hope that they'll repel all attacks and conquer the Golan Heights."[22]

IN HIS MEMOIRS, EZER WEIZMAN RECONSTRUCTED HIS MOOD IN THE DAYS BEFORE THE war. He visited army units in the south, where he found "tigers." The commanders he met with, including Ariel Sharon, were "burning" with one demand: "to do something, to act." Uzi Narkis "pumped him up" with the demand "to do something huge with the Jordanians."* Weizman also met with General Amos Horev, the deputy chief scientist of the IDF, and asked him what he thought was the best route into the Sinai. Horev replied that the ideal solution to the Straits predicament was to liberate the Old City of Jerusalem and the West Bank. In a discussion with the chief of staff, Horev repeated that the West Bank should be conquered. Weizman shared this view, grumbling that Rabin was the only one who thought differently. He felt that Rabin was always hesitating, tormenting himself with vacillation and doubt. He asked himself whether he should not have taken advantage of Rabin's nervous breakdown—"shown a more modest degree of friendship" and a greater degree of "responsibility toward the big issue"—and assumed the role of chief of staff, which he wanted so badly.[24]

The defense pact that Jordan signed with Egypt on May 30 motivated the IDF to prepare to attack and occupy the West Bank and to shift its priorities from Egypt, then Syria, then Jordan to Egypt, then Jordan, then Syria. Over several General Staff meetings, those officers thinking of conquering the West Bank considered, as they had in the past, the possibility that Hussein would either attack Israel, with or without assistance

---

*Moshe Dayan met with Narkis at Ariana, a Tel Aviv restaurant, and the two agreed that if the Jordanians attacked, Israel should seize Mount Scopus and the Latrun Road and not give them back.[23]

from Iraqi forces, or that he would be ousted. None of them assumed that the IDF would wait for a Jordanian attack, whatever the circumstances, and so planned for the eventuality of invading the West Bank to prevent Jordan from moving on Jerusalem. They assumed that the West Bank could be conquered within forty-eight hours, and they would then use it as a defensive zone. As one general put it, "Historically, we should take the West Bank, because it is more worrisome than the Sinai." Ezer Weizman said, "We are on the brink of a second War of Independence, with all its accomplishments." The last few words are underlined in the minutes of the General Staff meeting, apparently to stress that this war would be unlike the first, with all its flaws, including the failure to occupy the West Bank and the Old City. One way or another, the war was going to take place, said Weizman, "otherwise there is no State of Israel." He repeated his assertion that every passing day strengthened Egypt, but he also said something he had not voiced in front of the cabinet ministers: as a result of waiting, "the fruits of victory and the international support will be that much greater and more secure." Eshkol himself could not have put it better.

The discussions were practical, operational, virtually devoid of any patriotic or religious sentiment. The generals argued over whether to conquer Jerusalem or whether they should limit themselves to "grabbing" territory in the West Bank. They did not talk about the problems involved in conquering the Old City. One general mentioned that taking control of the West Bank would require a plan to establish a military government, but according to the minutes his point was drowned out with calls of "no need." Somewhere in some drawer there were plans for that eventuality, but at this point the IDF did not seem to expect to hold on to the West Bank for very long.

As was the practice, the debate went through various stages before finally reaching the chief of staff, at which point he shared his great dream with his colleagues. "Israel has not been forsaken," he said, quoting Jeremiah. Then he borrowed from the Passover Haggada: "If there were any assurance that we would come through a battle in possession of the West Bank and the Gaza Strip, and having defeated the Egyptian air force, *dayenu*"—that would be enough. He believed these goals were attainable, but the main task was to crush Nasser. "The plan for conquering the West Bank should not divert us from the main issue," he stated. The plan, code-named Whip and dated June 1, involved conquering the city of Jenin, but left open the question of what to do about the Jerusalem area.[25] One day earlier, Colonel Mordechai Gur had been on a tour of Jerusalem, where he had discussed with his colleagues how to break through to Mount Scopus. Gur, whose men were designated to parachute into Al Arish, in the Sinai Peninsula, raised the possibility of seizing the Old City. "Everyone was enthusiastic about the idea, but it is doubtful they put much faith in it," he wrote.[26]

The IDF intelligence branch had meanwhile prepared a paper on the implications of the decision to postpone the attack on Egypt by two to three weeks; it enumerated a long series of dangers, including the possibility that Egypt would use "primitive radioactive weapons, accompanied by advanced psychological warfare." The paper stated no basis for the sudden revelation that Egypt had "primitive radioactive weapons," nor did it explain what exactly these weapons were. The document was designed to serve the army's position, did not make the claim that Israel would be unable to defeat Egypt two weeks later, and it completely ignored the possibility that the risk of war might diminish as a result of a diplomatic settlement.[27]

4. SHARED DESTINY: "I AM JEWISH"

President Johnson spent Memorial Day weekend on his ranch in Texas with a few guests, including Arthur and Mathilde Krim. The week before, Dr. Krim had been a guest at the White House, spending the night, as usual, on the third floor.[28] On the way to Texas on Air Force One, Johnson told the Krims about his meeting with Eban, and again boasted of his listening skills: "Listening is the smartest thing one can do."[29]*

Arthur and Mathilde Krim were among the chosen few to fly in the private section of the plane, as well as in Johnson's helicopter. The president and his guests had a pleasant weekend. Johnson tended to his deer and discussed the electricity system, the plumbing, and fertilizers with his ranch staff. He dressed like a rancher and rode a bicycle. The Krims spent almost every waking hour with him and Lady Bird, and ate every meal with them. On Sunday, Johnson took another guest, the important Democratic donor Mary Lasker, up in his helicopter to show her the area. Johnson flew her to see the Krims' own nearby ranch, and showed her their house as if he owned it. The president made a few public appearances; local residents gathered to watch his helicopter take off and land. There were journalists, too. One news agency mentioned the presence of

---

*In the White House log, Eban is identified as the Israeli prime minister.

Arthur and Mathilde Krim, prompting Johnson angrily to instruct a staffer to find out how the information had leaked.

Arthur Krim and Johnson discussed a fund-raising dinner being held for the president the following Saturday in New York, which Krim was in charge of organizing. The White House log also notes that Johnson spoke with the Krims about the situation in the Middle East. Secretary of State Rusk called to update the president.[30]* He said Ambassador Arthur Goldberg had called to say that Israel might act alone, either "for psychological reasons" or if it concluded that time was pressing. Johnson said Israel had to make up its own mind what to do and whether it really could not wait any longer. "Menashe" (Ambassador Goldberg) reported this conversation to "Andre" (Feinberg), who passed it along to Israeli envoy Ephraim Evron.[32] This marked the first crack in the president's opposition to Israeli action.

On Sunday, May 28, Justice Fortas phoned the president's ranch. That same day, he also spoke with Ambassador Harman. There is no reason to doubt the sincerity of "Issahar," the judge told Harman. He was encouraged by news that the USSR was now willing to restrain Nasser, but added some friendly advice: under no circumstances should the matter be drawn out for too long, lest Israel "dallied," as the ambassador put it. Here was another hint that the United States would not oppose action if its own efforts to find a solution fell through. After mentioning to Ambassador Harman that their conversation must be kept completely secret, the United States Supreme Court justice agreed to hear the draft of a letter Eshkol proposed to send the president laying out Israel's position following the cabinet's decision that day. "Ilan" not only heard the message draft, but suggested revisions. He recommended that the letter emphasize the pressing time factor, as well as the fact that there was no knowing what Nasser might do. He proposed that Eshkol should say that he would consider what steps to take depending on developments. It should be especially stressed that the government's decision to postpone a strike was based on the absolute trust Eshkol placed in Johnson.[33]

More up-to-date than perhaps any other diplomat in Washington, Ephraim Evron was able to report on the news from the ranch to Jerusalem.

---

*The United States was holding direct talks with Nasser, and hoped to buy time by inviting his vice president, Zakaria Muhieddin, to Washington, and sending Vice President Humphrey to Cairo. Johnson received a conciliatory message from Nasser through an American attorney identified as a friend of Arthur Krim's.[31]

Abe Feinberg had heard from Krim that Johnson had looked and sounded very worried; he was making desperate efforts to organize an international action to reopen the Straits.[34]* More important, Walt Rostow had phoned to tell Evron that when the president received Eshkol's letter, he had been "troubled" by one particular paragraph, which implied that the United States would act on its own to reopen the Straits. The phrasing may have been an attempt to get more out of Johnson than he had given Eban. Or perhaps Eban was trying to create a commitment that did not exist but had already been reported to his government. Either way, the Americans might well have seen the letter as confirmation of a suspicion that Israel was trying to entangle them. Rostow reiterated that the president had not given Eban any such commitment, nor did he have the authority to do so, as Eban knew. Evron applied as much pressure as he could, saying that the Israel government could no longer withstand the public demand to act against the Egyptians. Rostow promised only to report their conversation to the president immediately.[36]

When he did so, Rostow took the opportunity to tell Johnson how Israel's decision to postpone a strike had come about. Harman and Evron had believed that the United States was determined to reopen the Straits, even if it ultimately had to do so on its own. According to Evron, Eshkol was not led to believe that Johnson had said this explicitly; rather, they only "shouldered the heavy burden of giving the government their assessment" of Johnson's intent. Evron added that he himself was considered a hawk in Israel, so that his judgment was therefore given special weight. Rostow then said that Evron had explained, with tears in his eyes, how important it was that Johnson not destroy Israeli ministers' faith in him. "So much hinges on this man," Evron had said of Johnson. Rostow had explained to Evron that the president wanted the Israeli government to fully understand the restrictions imposed upon him by the U.S. Constitution, and that Eshkol must be cautious in his pronouncements, including his planned speech in the Knesset the following day.[37] Israel sent Washington the text of the speech Eshkol was planning to give, and Secretary of State Rusk sent it back with revisions.[38]

---

*Evron also conveyed other impressions. The news columnist Joe Alsop was proposing that Israel take action—that it should not rely on the United States being able to enlist international support, and that the Russians would not intervene. This was also the opinion among "authoritative circles in Washington," Evron reported as per Alsop.[35]

· · ·

THE WHITE HOUSE, MEANWHILE, WAS INUNDATED WITH LETTERS FROM CITIZENS CALL-
ing on the president to stand by Israel. At least some of the letters probably resulted from the Israeli embassy's attempts to "organize" a writing
campaign. Many of the writers identified themselves as Jewish. A few tried
to convince the president that it was to his political advantage to support
Israel. One of them, Bill Moyers, the publisher of the Long Island newspaper *Newsday* and until recently the White House spokesman, wrote that
supporting Israel "provides a real opportunity to make some points on
Vietnam. . . . We have a chance to silence some of the carping criticism
from the Jewish press." The White House had also thought of this.[39]

Some of the letters came from a group of children in California. "Dear
President Johnson, Please help Israel if she has to fight a war. Egypt is going to fight a war with Israel. Don't let her," wrote Bonnie Weitzman, aged
seven, from Sherman Oaks. "I hope there is no more war in Israel or anywhere. I hope there is peace," wrote Steven Turner, aged seven and a half.
"I wish Israel wins the war, but I really wish that they don't have a war,"
said Howard Rothbloom, aged seven and a half, from North Hollywood.
Their classmate, six-and-a-half-year-old Stephen Bresnick, asked his president, "How can the United States help Israel not fight? I hope you know
how." Mrs. Maizlish, the children's Hebrew school teacher, sent a cover
note saying she had helped only with spelling, not with ideas. The White
House received many hundreds of similar, almost uniform, letters.[40]

The most dramatic letter President Johnson received came from Sheldon Cohen, the IRS commissioner, writing the day after Hussein and
Nasser signed their defense pact. Cohen had been born an American citizen
"by the grace of God," he wrote, "and the foresight of my grandfather,"
who had managed to immigrate to the United States sixty years earlier.
Those of his relatives who had remained in Europe were either murdered
and sent to the Nazi crematoria, or else had been miraculously spared and
found refuge in Israel. The ones who made it to Israel "now face a new
tyrant with a new crematorium." But this time they had nowhere to go.
When Cohen thought about Israelis, he saw himself among them, as did
his wife, Faye, and their children. As an American, he believed the United
States must stand by the only democratic state in the Middle East. "We
must find a way to help Israel defend itself—hopefully without bloodshed
or harm to any of its neighbors, but aggression must be stopped."[41]

This sense of solidarity was reflected elsewhere. Sue Sacks, a student at
UCLA, wrote from Jerusalem to her sister in California. She knew Mom

and Dad would be very angry, but she had decided to stay in Israel, even though she might be killed. She sent her sister a long explanation, whose essence was: I am Jewish.[42] The U.S. embassy in Israel was making preparations to evacuate such American citizens. The American consulate in Jerusalem sent an architectural consultant to the synagogue at Hadassah Medical Center to examine the feasibility of evacuating Marc Chagall's famous stained-glass windows called *The Twelve Tribes of Israel*.[43]

CHAPTER 10

FIVE DAYS TO WAR: THE OUSTER

1. INTRIGUES: "DROPS OF VENOM"

When Ephraim Evron told Walt Rostow that the Eshkol government was under heavy pressure from the Israeli public, he was not misleading him. But the people were not only demanding war: they wanted a new government. The campaign had begun even before Eshkol's stammered radio address. "Give Us an Emergency Government," demanded an unidentified "citizen" on the front page of *Ha'aretz*. A letter to the editor demanded that Ben-Gurion rejoin the government.[1] The poet Nathan Zach, the journalist Amos Kenan, and a group of professors from the Hebrew University's chemistry department, including the human rights activist Israel Shahak, also called for a national emergency government.[2] Expanding the government, wrote *Maariv*, should not be construed as a vote of no confidence in the current leadership, but as something similar to the call-up of reservists. "This may be your finest hour, leaders of the people," claimed *Maariv*, pointedly deploying Winston Churchill's wartime rhetoric.[3] The day after the stammered speech, *Ha'aretz* wrote of Eshkol: "He is not suited to be prime minister and minister of defense in the current situation; his many good qualities were not designed for this test."[4] The editors of *Maariv* proposed that in the future, the prime minister's statements should be read by an announcer.[5]

There was a putschlike atmosphere in the streets, Eshkol later commented.[6] The writer and translator Aharon Amir wrote to *Yediot Aharonot* suggesting the formation of a "military government" with Yitzhak Rabin at the helm, assisted by Moshe Dayan and Yigal Yadin, the former chief of staff.[7] Yadin had a visit from Professor Benjamin Akzin, a university colleague who taught law and political science, had been close to Ze'ev Jabotinsky, and was often mentioned as a possible candidate for president. Akzin came to "feel out" the possibility of a "military putsch." Yadin told him to forget it.[8] Yadin himself enjoyed tremendous prestige thanks to his history as a general untainted by politics, and as the archaeologist who revealed the glories of Masada.

Not for the first time, David Ben-Gurion feared that the IDF might seize control of the country, which led him to issue an extraordinary public statement. "The army in a democratic country does not act of its own volition or at the behest of its military commanders, but rather on the judgment and the orders of the civilian government," he said, as if this assertion could not be taken for granted. He emphasized that an army alone could not protect the state—diplomacy also played a necessary part. "We have many important friends, and wise and consistent work is required to maintain these friendships." In other words, Israel should not go to war without either the consent of the United States or at least one of the European powers.[9]

Although Eshkol was in complete agreement with Ben-Gurion, coming from him the statement would have been seen as evidence of fearful defeatism. A speech Eshkol gave in the Knesset on May 29 was firmer than his radio address, and it included repeated praise for the army.[10] Only those who knew of the ferment in the military could have appreciated the point; most Israelis did not.

But Ben-Gurion did not go so far as to express open support for Eshkol's government. "As long as Eshkol remains in power, we will tumble into the abyss," he wrote in his diary. He seems to have believed that Eshkol should be replaced in part to ward off the danger of a military coup. "The party wants me to replace Eshkol as prime minister and Moshe to be minister of defense," he wrote. "I support making Moshe both minister of defense and prime minister, or making someone else from Mapai prime minister."[11] Fear of a military coup might have also been the reason behind Mafdal's demand for changes in the government. "Shapira spoke about the military command with great concern," wrote Yaacov Herzog, as he praised Ben-Gurion's statement.[12] At times, the cabinet seemed to be as wary of the IDF as the Egyptian army was. "The army is rebelling," wrote Minister Gvati in his diary, while Minister Aran said the situation in the army had reached a boiling point.[13] Minister Galili described a meeting with seventy reserve officers as a visit "to the lions' den"; most of the officers demanded action. "They asked whether the government was a man or not," Galili recounted.[14]

The turmoil among the generals continued. "I left with a bad feeling yesterday," one of them said after their stormy meeting with Eshkol. Others felt that the ministers "don't understand" the situation, and started discussing how to make them change the decision to wait. "We have to find a way to bring about a decision," said Ezer Weizman. "There's no guarantee that in two weeks we'll be able to screw the Egyptians," said Rabin. "The Americans will place an embargo on us," he thought. Nonetheless, he promised to make another attempt to change the government's position.[15]

At least one general spoke openly of the possibility that the IDF would go to war without government authorization. This was Ariel Sharon, who recounted the story himself. He presented his plan of action to Rabin: "We get up and say: 'You listen now, your decisions are putting the state of Israel at risk, and since the situation is now critical, we're asking you to go into the next room and wait. And the chief of staff will go over to Kol Israel and make an announcement.'" Sharon did not remember Rabin's reaction, but he thought the ministers would have been "relieved."[16]

As members of the same establishment and sometimes even the same families, the generals were in close contact with the cabinet ministers and Knesset members. Uzi Narkis was married to the daughter of David Hacohen, the chairman of the Knesset Foreign Affairs and Defense Committee. "The government made no decisions without first listening to the generals, and I cannot remember a single case when we denied the General Staff permission to do whatever it wanted," Yigal Allon recalled. During the waiting period, he met with several officers, including the air force commander and General David Elazar. "You have to get us authorization to take the Golan Heights," Elazar told Allon. Sharon phoned Allon, urging him to get the government to hurry up and go to war. Allon himself asked Rabin to help convince the government that war was essential. But Rabin thought that the officers' impatience was a cause for concern. When Allon toured the front with Eshkol, he told the officers he met that another day here or there was not what would seal the country's fate. The officers trusted him as one of their own, Allon said.[17]

The unrest in the army was exacerbated by the sudden appointment of Haim Bar-Lev as deputy chief of staff. Bar-Lev had been called home from a leave of absence in Paris, in the wake of Rabin's collapse and Weizman's attempt to start the war. Weizman had considered resigning in response, but was persuaded by Menachem Begin to remain in the army. "I was walking around feeling like a beaten dog," he wrote.[18]

• • •

CITIZEN AND POLITICIAN MOSHE DAYAN, MEANWHILE, WAS ALLOWED TO CONTINUE his tours of the army and receive intelligence reports. One person he met with was Meir Amit, the head of the Mossad, who was about to go to the United States. The two often engaged in what Amit described as "heart to heart talks" lasting well into the night, in which they discussed "the world and everything in it." Dayan's outlook on the situation had evolved into a straightforward stance that Amit described as: Let's go to war! "As he often did, Dayan quickly lost his patience, and each night I saw his tolerance level drop," Amit wrote.[19] More and more people, including journalists, were subjected to Dayan's opinions on the best course of action. One night he invited the writer Ephraim Kishon to his home. Kishon wrote a political column in *Maariv* that was widely influential, mostly because of his wit. They sat talking until one A.M.; Shimon Peres was also there.

Peres, who was forty-four at the time, suffered from the vast gap between his accomplishments and his public image. Polish-born, he had come to Palestine at the age of eleven. He had endured a great deal as a result of his desire to be accepted among Israelis as an equal. His failure to do so stemmed partly from his accent, which always gave him away. He was addicted to politics from an early age, so much so that he gained a reputation as a sly fox always up to some intrigue. This tendency also distanced him from the New Hebrews of Rabin's generation, who loathed politics and words in general; Peres read books and wrote poetry. Many envied the trust Ben-Gurion placed in him. When Peres was twenty-nine, Ben-Gurion appointed him director general of the Ministry of Defense, despite—or perhaps because of—his lack of military experience. This lack earned him derision in many circles.

Peres turned out to be a brilliant man of action, cold and analytical, who took charge of setting up Israel's military industries and the nuclear reactor in Dimona. A tireless deal maker, never too lazy to visit the most remote branch of the party, he had a rich imagination, broad horizons, and an expansive appreciation of the larger world.[20] A member of Ben-Gurion's opposition party, he made every effort to bring about the ouster of Levi Eshkol. He spread rumors, forged alliances, weaved intrigues, lobbied journalists. This was Peres the politician. "Ministers and others told me that their positions had been influenced to various degrees by the smear and whisper campaign orchestrated by Shimon Peres," wrote Yitzhak Rabin. "Perceived by himself and others—thanks to his close ties with Ben-Gurion—as a security expert, he went around dripping venom in every available ear, saying, We must not fight, we must simply hunker down, the IDF is not ready for war, Israel cannot withstand this kind of war, and other such learned opinions." Eshkol despised Peres and made no effort to conceal his opinion from his friends in the government. He was not presenting an ultimatum, he said when discussion began about expanding the government, but he would find it very hard to work with Peres.[21]

But there was also Peres the statesman, and he did in fact believe that reopening the Straits called for thorough consideration; every decision had to involve long-term planning. "We can't go to war now," he told Ben-Gurion.[22] Peres agreed with Ben-Gurion and Eshkol that Israel should not go to war without prior coordination with the United States. But, not unlike Haim Moshe Shapira, his schemes to oust Eshkol and appoint Dayan in his stead effectively hastened the war. Perhaps, like Shapira, he was afraid that the army might revolt; unlike Shapira, however, he cannot have believed that Dayan would act to prevent war. His interest was to restore Rafi to power.

That night at Dayan's home with Ephraim Kishon, Peres asked the columnist to join the demand to appoint Dayan. Kishon, writing as he thought an objective observer from the moon might, saw the logic: "The people want the military leader of the Sinai Campaign to be the minister of defense."[23]

SOMEWHERE ALONG THE SINAI BORDER, PRIVATE YEHOSHUA BAR-DAYAN FOLLOWED THE news in *Ha'aretz* and felt "profound disappointment." He did not understand them, these politicians. "Is this the time for coalition calculations?" he wrote. "Why don't they just bring in Rafi, Begin's Gahal, and anyone who's reasonable, if that's what will save even one casualty? Is this the time for settling accounts? Is this the time to waste the talents of David Ben-Gurion, Dayan, and Peres?" He thought the failure to expand the government was "more than a crime." Above all he was angry with Golda Meir, who was opposing changes in the government. He was a die-hard Mapainik, but now he wrote: "Am I really finished with this party of old people that I've supported for years?"[24]

The day before, Golda Meir had told her colleagues, "This morning my driver got a call, then my son, and they were told that I shouldn't leave the house because the papers said that I was blocking the whole national solution to the composition of the government." Of the possibility that Dayan and Begin might join, she said, "We wouldn't be the first socialist party to hand over power to fascists without a struggle." She was referring to Germany.[25] About a hundred women gathered in front of the Mapai offices demanding that Meir "stop the hate." Eshkol later described them as "the Merry Wives of Windsor," prompting Dayan to observe dryly that they were anything but merry.[26]

2. TUMULT: "IT'LL BE HELL"

On Tuesday, May 30, a few hours after King Hussein made a surprise visit to Cairo to sign the Egyptian-Jordanian defense pact, Eshkol was warned that he faced a "blow-up," since almost all the Ma'arah Knesset members thought the Defense Ministry should be handed over to someone else. From a political point of view, the crisis was entirely personal and without reason. No one could explain why a new minister of defense was so essential. The assumption was that this was the price to be paid for the parties entering an "emergency government," but no one stopped to ask why Gahal and Rafi should be brought into the government at all. To go to war? To avert war? At this point, the question was hardly relevant. "There is a psychosis about a new government," one Knesset member said, adding, "The situation of the people is not good," although he was actually referring to the government and the party. The people simply did not want "fraternal conflict" and there was "intense demand for war." Only appointing Dayan would calm the public.

Some Ma'arah members tried to prevent Dayan's appointment by proposing Yigal Allon. The minister of labor was forty-nine at the time, with roughly two decades of political experience, but unlike other politicians he had managed to preserve his image as a military man. In 1945 he had been appointed commander of the Palmah, and during the War of Independence he was promoted to general. Twenty years later, he still had admirers. "Allon is a dream, he is a legend," said one Knesset member.[27] He viewed the Ministry of Defense as a stepping-stone to becoming prime minister. According to Allon, Rabin was also in favor of his appointment, and believed that they would "work together in harmony like a symphony orchestra."[28]

Some time before the crisis with Egypt, Allon had developed a theory that Israel's strategic circumstances necessitated a preemptive attack. In his 1959 book, *A Screen of Sand*, he described in great detail the danger that the Arabs might destroy Israel's air force on the ground. In an interview that was not supposed to be made public for many years, he claimed he had written this only to avoid complications with the Israeli censor: in fact, he had meant that Israel should destroy the Arab air forces. He called this "active defense," or "preemptive counterattack," and he maintained that "there is no substitute for aggression, in the positive sense of the word."[29]

Eshkol proposed an idea that had been raised in cabinet meetings: a national security council comprising the three former chiefs of staff, Yigal Yadin, Moshe Dayan, and Haim Laskov, plus a fourth member, Allon. One Ma'arah member said it was too little too late; only Dayan would do. "You, Eshkol, decide which minister he'll be, but he doesn't want the Ministry of Religious Affairs," said Deputy Minister Arie Lova Eliav. Postal Minister Israel Yeshayahu said, "I hope it's not the Postal Ministry." The argument escalated and Eshkol left the room. The meeting notes state that he "slammed the door."[30]* Before going home, Eshkol spoke with Haim Moshe Shapira, who repeated his firm demand for a national unity government. That night, a few ministers came to speak to Eshkol about agreeing to at least shift Allon from the Labor to the Defense Ministry. Deputy Minister Eliav, who was close to Eshkol, accompanied him to Tel Aviv the next day, May 31, and in the car tried to convince him to groom Dayan as his heir. Eshkol said there was no dynasty and he did not wish to appoint an heir. He had told the same thing to Allon, he said, who had found it insulting.

The Ma'arah ministers were waiting for Eshkol in the Ministry of Defense to pick up the conversation. They were united in their view that Allon should be made Minister of Defense. Eshkol asked bitterly, "And what's left for the prime minister?" But the real question was what post to give Dayan. "The people are very anxious, they see Moshe Dayan as their savior," wrote Gvati in his diary.[32]

Even at this point, still trying to prevent the war, Eshkol was concerned that Rafi might rob Ma'arah of the glory of victory. He warned his colleagues, "They'll say they saved the country, but it will be with our forces, that we set up." He tried to project a bellicose tone. The situation was serious now that Jordan was involved. "Maybe we should settle the score with Jordan once and for all." He restated Johnson's promise that

---

*At approximately the same time, Ben-Gurion heard on the radio that the parties of the Socialist International had expressed solidarity with Mapai. "They don't know that Mapai has no solidarity with the State of Israel," he wrote.[31]

the United States would reopen the Straits on its own, if need be, and he did not forget to mention Hitler. Just as people should have believed Hitler then, so Israel had to believe Nasser now, he said.* Eshkol said he was willing to continue in both capacities, as prime minister and defense minister, but that he would prefer Allon to Dayan. He was prepared to find a way to include Allon in security affairs even if he continued as minister of labor. But the party members rejected that idea. The inclination to replace the minister of defense was a healthy one, said Zalman Aran, although the notion that the new minister had to be Dayan, of all people, was mad. And so he too backed appointing Allon. Kadish Luz, the chairman of the Knesset, also supported Allon. "I'm a little afraid of Dayan," he admitted. He demanded censorship of the press to stop the campaign against Eshkol. "Yoel Markus wrote the most shameful things yesterday in *Ha'aretz*," said Abba Eban, quoting military circles in Paris to the effect that Nasser had moved because of Eshkol's weakness. Ezer Weizman was to repeat this argument at a later date.[33] Eshkol fumed. "The prime minister has to have a job, too," he said, and his friends discerned a threat to resign. If Eshkol resigned, Allon said, Nasser might attack the very next day.

And so the ministers flexed their political creativity, tossing out more and more ideas and suggestions and solutions to a problem that now seemed even more urgent than the war itself: what to do with Dayan. Eshkol suggested appointing him minister of the armies. "What is that?" asked Golda Meir, and Eshkol admitted, "I don't know." But he tried to improvise: "The minister of armies gives advice about the armies." Meir wouldn't give in: "What is he supposed to do?" Shaul Avigur, the party's trusted adviser, did not like this idea either. "Dayan is a very complex man and it'll be hell," he said—no one would know who the army was taking its orders from. Better that Dayan should be minister of defense than minister of the armies, he argued, but Eshkol did not want to hand over the defense portfolio.

The debate continued, back and forth. Eventually they decided to send Avigur to ask Dayan if he would agree to serve as deputy prime minister and military adviser to the prime minister. Allon would be the minister of defense. But Avigur did not want to speak with Dayan, and neither did Eshkol. They argued about who would ask him, and eventually agreed to do it together. Dayan refused to be deputy prime minister without an operational position. He asked to go back to the army to

---

*Eban, however, said in the same discussion that if the United States could not organize an international response, it would withdraw its objection to Israeli action.

command the southern front, above General Gavish. Typically, he saw no need to discuss this with Gavish.* Dayan said he was not a consultant but a "doer." When he heard that Allon would be minister of defense, he became "enraged," Eshkol recounted. "Moshe says the blood rushed to his head," Shimon Peres related the next day.[35]

Dayan argued that Yigal Allon was more of an adviser than he was. Eshkol persisted: "Let's say we meet every two days, me, Dayan, Allon, and Eban, for a consultation." Dayan said that after the consultation the others would each go back to their offices and he would have nothing to do. The problem, he said, was how to win the war with a minimum of casualties. The conflict would be quick, but even harder than the battle of El Alamein. He wanted the job and believed he could handle it. And he did not want to be foreign minister. If he was appointed minister of defense, he said, he would leave Tel Aviv and direct the war from the Negev.

The Ma'arah ministers then discussed among themselves Dayan's suggestion that were he appointed, his position be kept secret, so as not to provoke Nasser. The Ma'arah ministers were in pressing need of some good publicity, however, which led to a lengthy debate over how to formulate an announcement. Eshkol noted that if Dayan were appointed commander of the southern front, there would be no need to take the Defense Ministry away from his own control. That decision could at least be postponed. "But I can see that you're people who really love to make decisions," he said bitterly. Golda Meir wanted to keep talking about Dayan, apparently afraid that he would take over the army. "I caution you against bringing him in," she said. Allon, for his part, asked whether Dayan was supposed to replace Gavish. Avigur said the idea was for Gavish to report to Dayan. Then they realized that no one had spoken to Gavish, nor had they told Rabin. Naturally, Dayan had said nothing to Rabin either.

Rabin was horrified, but promised to consult the General Staff. Gavish threatened to resign and the other generals saw the proposal as an ouster. Rabin himself offered to resign so that Dayan could take over as chief of staff, but Dayan swore he had no interest in the post. Rebellious voices were now coming from members of the Mapai secretariat, more and more of whom wanted Dayan as defense minister.[36] "I am deeply upset," wrote Gvati; "instead of preparing for war we're busy with civil war."[37]

---

*According to Allon, Eshkol was willing to appoint him commander of the Southern Command, but unlike Dayan, Allon said, "I wouldn't do that to Shaike [Gavish]."[34]

A cabinet meeting followed, hurriedly convened at the request of Haim Moshe Shapira, who had heard that Eshkol was willing to give the defense portfolio to Allon. If Dayan were not given the Defense Ministry, he said, Mafdal would leave the government. A turbulent meeting ensued, full of emotion and mutual accusations. A harsh exchange of words led Shapira to say to Eshkol, "Nasser and Hussein can exchange kisses, but you and I cannot come together?" Shapira and Zerah Warhaftig were afraid of losing control of the army. "We are missing the boat," said Shapira. "The things the people are saying and the things the army is saying—I don't know how much longer we can last as a government." Warhaftig talked about his recent tour of the military. "The officers are saying, we're all fine, if only the government was doing as well." He believed that if Dayan did not join the government, "there'll be riots in the street, the sort of thing that borders on treason." Galili said people were worried about Nasser, but Shapira interrupted him: "It's this government they're worried about."

Voices were raised again. Eshkol told Shapira he could leave if he did not want to be in the government—if all he wanted was a *get*, a divorce, he could have just sent a letter. "I'll write a letter," said Shapira, and threatened, "We'll go to the Knesset and get it over with." Feelings ran high. People were furious that the war had been postponed, said Shapira. "We haven't seen the mothers whose sons are going to be killed," Eshkol struck back. It was all very personal, and often in Yiddish. "It breaks my heart that the defense portfolio is being taken from me," Eshkol said, but added that he did not want any more arguing. He wanted this to be over with. The meeting ended at one A.M.[38]

3. SURRENDER: "HISTORY, WHATEVER YOU'RE GOING TO DO—DO IT QUICKLY"

Eshkol gave up at around noon on Thursday, June 1. At the Mapai meeting that morning, Golda Meir presented the situation: Gahal would join the government if Rafi also joined. Rafi would join if Dayan became minister of defense. Mafdal was threatening to pull out of the coalition if that did not happen. Eshkol said Mafdal was fighting for Dayan as if in a holy war; he used the Arabic term jihad.

Eshkol almost certainly understood by then that he was being deposed. He told those present that he would speak as a historian, and much of his statement did sound like chapter headings for a future biography. When his intelligence people had said war would not be an issue before 1970, he said, he had not believed them. How could they be so confident, he had asked—what if war came a year sooner? Accordingly, he had prepared the army. He insinuated that Shimon Peres had limited Israel's arms purchases to France, while Eshkol himself had opened the path to deals with the United States. He then revealed confidential information: there was talk of Israel building planes and tanks. "I ask you, I implore you, if the future of the People of Israel is dear to you—if you feel it is worth a single penny—do not make this information public." He disclosed that Israel had asked the United States for engines to "revolutionize its tanks and build airplanes." One Knesset member protested: "Why are you telling us this? It will leak to the press." Golda Meir took advantage of the opportunity to scold those present because every word always showed up in *Yediot Aharonot* even before the meetings were over.

Eshkol went on to justify Eban's trip to the United States and the decision to postpone an attack on Egypt. He gave the impression that at least two weeks would go by before war broke out. He himself felt no great need to expand the government, he said. A broad government would basically be a second Knesset and everyone would want to have a say. If the party members were stronger, made of steel, iron, and stone, then perhaps there would be no need to enlarge the coalition. But sometimes he thought he could hear the opposition speaking through his own friends. He did not know how the idea of handing over the Ministry of Defense had come up. He was insulted, but was nonetheless willing to expand the government. Rafi's resentment was far greater than that of Gahal, but he was willing to try, he said, and left the meeting. He was going to meet Begin and other Gahal members.

Gahal was also pressing for Dayan's appointment to the Defense Ministry and demanded to know why Eshkol objected. In response, Eshkol told a joke about a Jew who wants a divorce. The rabbi asks him why he wants the divorce. The man says, "How can I speak ill of my wife?" After they get a divorce, the rabbi says, "Now can you tell me why you wanted this?" The man answers, "How can I speak ill of a stranger?" Similarly, Eshkol did not want to reveal the nature of his aversion to Dayan. "I am afraid to tell you," he said. "I may have to live with him. He may join the government. Why should I give you reasons? I have my reasons."

AT MAPAI, MEANWHILE, PARTY MEMBERS WERE THE VOICE OF THE PEOPLE: THEY wanted Dayan, not Allon. Rafi was plotting a coup, one member said, and only the appointment of Dayan could prevent it and save democracy.

Some suggested leaving the decision to Eshkol, but no one explicitly recommended that he continue as minister of defense.[39]

The decision was made at this stage, according to Eshkol's assistant Adi Yaffe. Yaffe himself went to have lunch with a reporter from *Time* magazine, Israel Shenker, who was writing a cover story on Eshkol. Yaffe was gone for about two and a half hours, and by the time he returned things had changed. In his absence Eshkol had been besieged by ministers, Knesset members, and others, all demanding that he appoint Dayan. Rabin had spoken with Eshkol too, and explained that the idea of giving Dayan the Southern Command was meeting with resistance in the army. He had been sent by some of the generals to pass on their "strong, intense, and angry objection" to giving Dayan the Southern Command. Yadin appealed to Haim Moshe Shapira to demand Dayan's appointment, and Shapira responded by asking Yadin whether he would take the position himself. Yadin did not rule out the possibility, but repeated his view that it would be better to appoint Dayan. Choosing Yadin would probably not have prevented the war, since he too believed Israel should attack immediately.[40]

After Yadin came Ezer Weizman. There are at least two versions of what happened next. According to Israel Lior, Weizman "burst into" the prime minister's office, where he found Eshkol having lunch with Minister of Justice Shapira. Weizman wept in front of the prime minister, according to Lior. "The country is being destroyed," he wailed, "everything is being destroyed." Eshkol and Shapira were stunned. "Eshkol—give the order and the IDF will go to war," Weizman yelled. "Why do you need Moshe Dayan? Who needs Yigal Allon? We have a strong army and all it's waiting for is your order. Give us an order to go to war and we will win. We will win and you'll be the leader of a victory." At that moment, wrote Lior, Shapira also burst into tears.

According to Weizman, he told Eshkol, "If you give the instruction, you'll go down in Jewish history as a great leader. If you don't, history will never forgive you." Yaacov Herzog wrote in his diary that the precise words were, "Commander—give the command and you will go down in Jewish history." Lior thought that as Weizman left the room he tried to tear his general's insignia off his shoulder, but he was not certain. "The truth is, I don't remember exactly what happened afterward," he wrote in his diary. "It was an event that is hard to describe in words." Weizman confirmed that something like this did happen: "I was fuming. With my right hand I removed the insignia from my left shoulder and threw them onto the table." But he claimed that this occurred on a different occasion, and emphasized that, contrary to other reports, he did not throw his insignia onto Levi Eshkol's desk.[41]

"THE CONSTANT TRICKLE," WROTE ADI YAFFE, "ONE PERSON COMING IN BEFORE THE last had even left," was what tipped the scales. He believed that had he been there, he might have at least provided some balance, although this is unlikely. Either way, at four-fifteen Eshkol offered Moshe Dayan the Ministry of Defense. He did so, said Yaffe, thinking, "I'm sick of this pressure. If there's no choice, let it be Dayan."[42] Dayan asked whether he was being invited alone or as a member of Rafi, although he was perfectly willing to accept even without his party's approval. "Better as the Rafi representative," Eshkol said, "so they won't send me Shimon, too."

Eshkol convened the Ma'arah ministers and announced his decision. Allon said he was withdrawing his candidacy. Eshkol thanked him, saying that he himself could hardly bear to part with the portfolio. "My only reward is that I am causing pain to someone else," he joked, meaning Allon. Then he reported Weizman's outburst.

Talking to his party, Eshkol said he had decided that it was best to put an end to the maneuverings. "I made a decision: History, whatever you're going to do—do it quickly." He later added that this was a saying of Leon Trotsky's. The whole thing had been "a thorn in his side," he said, and gave them some more news: Hussein was planning to close off the Mandelbaum Gate and thereby access to Mount Scopus in Jerusalem. The members of Mapai told him he had done a great thing and gave him a round of applause. They wanted to applaud Golda Meir too, but she cut them off: "I'm not dead yet."[43] Eshkol still had several phone calls to make; Ben-Gurion had not yet agreed.

Not all the Rafi members were in favor of joining the government. Knesset member Yosef Almogi suggested that without Ben-Gurion, the party should remain in the opposition. "What will the country gain from Dayan becoming minister of defense in a jungle with Eshkol in charge—a quick shot of morphine? So people will think this is a solution?" But Peres argued that they should first hear what Ben-Gurion had to say.[44] According to Peres, Ben-Gurion was furious, and he only came around for the sake of national security. But Ben-Gurion set one condition: Peres must tell Eshkol that although the party was joining his government, Rafi still believed he was not fit to serve as prime minister.

"I felt wretched the whole day," Peres later wrote, but he asked Eshkol for a private meeting. He said, "As you know, we have stated that you are unfit to be prime minister. Our opinion has not changed. Of course, after we join the government we will act with complete loyalty and all the old scores and personal differences will be put aside." Peres said he was flushed and perspiring when he said these things, but Eshkol responded generously, saying he knew of their opinion, but perhaps it would change in time.

Peres hurried to Ben-Gurion's house, but on the way he stopped at a café and phoned Eshkol. What now? asked the prime minister. Peres suggested that he go to see Ben-Gurion himself. It was time for a reconciliation, he said, and suggested sending Ben-Gurion to the United States to explain the new situation; this may have been Peres's attempt to postpone the beginning of the war. Eshkol was afraid that Ben-Gurion would refuse to see him and that he would be humiliated, but he asked for time to think it over. In the evening, he told Peres he had decided not to go. Maybe another time.[45]*

THE NEW GOVERNMENT WAS SCHEDULED TO MEET AT TEN THAT NIGHT. ESHKOL looked pale and tired; Yaacov Herzog noted in his diary that the prime minister appeared wrapped in a kind of "lassitude." Herzog formulated an announcement and scheduled a breakfast the next day with Yadin to discuss setting up a "committee" to facilitate relations between Eshkol and Dayan. "A great thing has occurred in Israel," Haim Moshe Shapira announced. "The prime minister has acted with restraint." The ministers praised Eshkol, who proclaimed a national unity government. Rabin and a few officers were waiting outside. "The chief of staff looks tired and stunned," wrote Herzog. Rabin said that had they acted at the beginning of the week, they might already have been at the Straits. Herzog recounted the chain of events that had led to a postponement, and then Begin arrived. He embraced Rabin, slapped his back, and declared, "We're proud of you!" He also embraced Herzog and reminded him of their first meeting, twenty years ago, when Herzog had accompanied his father on a visit to Begin when he was in the underground. Begin thanked him, saying he knew Herzog had helped to bring him into the government.

Dayan arrived late, walked in, and shook everyone's hand. Rabin asked

*Ben-Gurion's diary does not confirm Peres's account. On the contrary: according to Ben-Gurion, he sent Peres to Eshkol to tell him that Rafi would approve Dayan's appointment on condition that Eshkol step down as prime minister. Ben-Gurion claimed Peres told him he had relayed the message.[46]

to be excused from giving the customary update: it was late and he still had a lot of work that night. But the ministers wanted to hear from him. Dayan sat at the other end of the room, next to the military maps. "There is a marked change in the chief of staff," Herzog wrote. "For the past two weeks he had been speaking hesitantly and always looked as if he was buckling under the burden of his responsibilities. None of his recommendations were given firmly. His self-confidence seemed shattered, his eyes had lost their usual spark. His words and his orders seemed to come not from inside, but rather as a conditioned reflex." But now, wrote Herzog, for the first time, Rabin was standing upright and speaking clearly. Once in a while he looked at Dayan, and according to Herzog it was clear that the new minister's presence gave him confidence: "His face suddenly filled out." Rabin repeated that had Israel attacked five days earlier, it would now have a clear advantage.[47] Dayan demanded to know what the ministers wanted: if they wanted to attack, they had to do so immediately; if not, they had to prepare for defense. They decided to discuss it the next day.

ON JUNE 2, THE DAY AFTER ESHKOL WAS DEPOSED, *MAARIV* WROTE THAT THE PRIME minister was making frequent jokes in Yiddish, looking "as if he has been reborn." In fact, his authorized biography later stated, he felt injured and betrayed. His removal remained an open wound that, according to those close to him, never healed.[48] He approached Dayan with suspicion. "The 'Arab' has already started," he said to Yigal Yadin, meaning that Dayan was already putting his people in charge of the ministry. Yadin, meanwhile, was working on an agreement to demarcate the lines of authority between Dayan and Eshkol. Dayan could not declare war or expand the scope of a war, nor was he to bomb major Arab cities on his own initiative. "Eshkol is waiting for the moment when he can return to a government without Moshe," wrote Yadin.[49] The sole justification for Eshkol's removal was the public hysteria.

Dayan revealed himself to be precisely the way he was described by those who knew him: ruthless and hungry for power. His appointment dealt a blow to Golda Meir and an entire generation of veteran leaders. They had tried to preserve their standing by promoting their own militarist, Yigal Allon, but at the moment of truth it transpired that most Israelis did not share the admiration of Allon's friends. The chasm between his image as a fabled Hebrew warrior prince and the reality of his life as a mediocre politician made him seem quite pathetic.

Menachem Begin's entrance into the government broke a taboo. The man who until not long ago had been insulted as a Hitler had been legitimized, and Mapai lost its monopoly on power. Begin's legitimation was also a step on the way to a social and cultural revolution. Although part of the Ashkenazi establishment, Begin the opposition leader, long deprived of influence, had leaned on the support of many Mizrahim, cultivating a sort of alliance of the underprivileged. On the night he sat down at the government table, the road to power opened for the Mizrahim.

Few people took notice. The songwriter Haim Hefer, who responded to day-to-day events with verses published in *Yediot Aharonot*, saw the government's expansion as a late victory for the Palmah: warriors had triumphed over politicians. "Those who lived through the last week / And saw how Dayan and Allon stood tall / Those who saw the noise and the fury / The wheeling and dealing and the warmongering / Those who watched for a moment from the side / Knew that these two blossomed from a special, special root."[50]

Hefer was right, in that the Six-Day War supplied Israeli politics with a new reservoir of ministers and leaders. Of the eighteen generals serving on the General Staff at the time, eight went on to enter the Knesset, and some assumed government positions. Rabin became prime minister, as did two other officers who shone in the Six-Day War, Ehud Barak and Ariel Sharon. The frenetic whirlwind and the to-and-froing of the days preceding the war—the panic, the threats, the deals, and the spin—elicited the following comment from the editor of *Yediot Aharonot*, Herzl Rosenblum: "Long live the people's fighting government! Long live the IDF and its invincible commanders! Long live the free State of Israel! Long live justice, trampled by thugs and tyrants and the heirs of Hitlerist anti-Semitism! There will be no Treblinka here! This time its architects will be drowned at sea!"[51] Shuka Bar-Dayan was pleased with the turn of events. "Thank God," he wrote in his diary, "they're done fighting on the home front. . . . Security may be in better and more experienced hands."

BAR-DAYAN HAD NOW BEEN ON RESERVE DUTY FOR TWO WEEKS. YARIV MISSED HIM SO much, as did she, Gila said in a letter. He tried to console her with a joke: he knew it was hard for her, of course, but it was also hard for him to go without washing the car or doing the dishes. He told her how all the guys confided in him and called him Dad. One man, a thirty-one-year-old bus driver, showed him a picture of his son and started weeping. Bar-Dayan had trouble calming him down. It was the same with all the tough guys, he told Gila. Almost all the nonsmokers had started smoking, apart from him.

He hoped the slides he had taken on Independence Day had come back from overseas.[52] The heat wave was rough: he sweated a lot. People were starting to go on leave, but not him. Rumors circulated among the soldiers constantly, only to give way to new ones. Sometimes they had orders to start up the tanks, and they thought they were on the move. Then the order came to turn the tanks off. More waiting. The comedians Uri Zohar and Shaike Ofir had come to perform. "We laughed a little," wrote Bar-Dayan, but his homesickness for Gili and Yariv was overwhelming. "I pray that we return home healthy and in one piece after victory. Amen, may it be so." He suddenly thought of his mother. "Please return me to my son and wife," he wrote in his diary. His friend Uzi Avrahami gave him reason for great hope: maybe, just maybe, Gili would be able to visit.

CHAPTER 11

THREE DAYS TO WAR: THE DECISION

1. PROPOSAL: "TOP SECRET"

According to Israel Lior, the decision to go to war was made on Friday, June 2. Eshkol met with the General Staff again that morning, and this time he brought ten ministers with him, including the newly appointed Menachem Begin and Moshe Dayan. By Lior's account, the generals berated the ministers relentlessly: "I wondered at times if they meant to bring the ministers to their knees or reduce them to tears."[1] The minutes, however, do not confirm Lior's impression. The generals repeated their demand to go to war immediately and a few spoke disrespectfully to the prime minister, but Eshkol, though downcast and dejected, unflinchingly refused to promise war. He was waiting for the green light from the United States. Zalman Aran said afterward that the visit to "the pit," as the General Staff's command post was known, was convincing, but the ministers had nonetheless posed some tough questions.

Aharon Yariv spoke vaguely, as usual, repeating that every passing day "greatly diminished" Israel's chances of aerial supremacy and increased the risk of the Egyptians bombing the reactor at Dimona. He claimed that "many people in important places in the United States" would view an Israeli strike as a convenient way "out of this whole mess," because the Americans had no intention of breaking the blockade themselves. He provided no real information and there was no discussion of the possibility of getting "out of this whole mess" without resorting to war.

Rabin opened with a rather peculiar statement: the Egyptian army at this stage was "perhaps in a defensive orientation only," but he could not say that "this was where things would end." He went on just as vaguely: "I think we might find ourselves in a situation where we'll lose much of our advantage, and we might reach a situation that I don't want to describe too clearly, but it will pose a real threat to Israel's existence, and the war will be difficult and savage, with many casualties." He spoke as if he had no obligation to make the government aware of the danger he perceived. He then said: "Now that we've waited, and the Arabs have defined their political goal as a return to 1948, and this is clearly defined, we must not wait until there's a situation that makes things difficult, if not worse, and I don't want to say anything explicitly, in case we don't act immediately." Again, no one pressed Rabin to say what exactly he preferred not to "state explicitly," and the dim threat continued to hang over the room like a dark and terrifying cloud.

Rabin was essentially telling the cabinet that the ministers must not wait, which was the opinion of the sixteen generals at the meeting. Ariel Sharon was just as vocal as he had been in the past, stating that not since the War of Independence had Israel been in such a dangerous situation. He repeated his scornful dismissal of Israel's "scurrying" among the world powers for rescue. "I won't use the word 'pleading,'" he said, taking a jab at the prime minister. Sharon maintained that Israel's goal should be the total destruction of the Egyptian military, so that for the next ten or twenty years the Egyptians would not think of fighting Israel. He had been with the troops in the south for two weeks now, and he knew that the army was more ready than ever, with a first-rate fighting spirit. The people on the home front were also "wonderful," he said. He asked the ministers for respect: "Who, if not us, is authorized to tell you that the army is ready for war?" The government had to make a "quick and brave" decision. "You can leave the rest to us."

Matti Peled, the quartermaster general, also spoke boldly. He said he understood why Nasser had decided to act now, rather than in a year and a half as the intelligence had estimated originally: "In my opinion, he was relying on the government's hesitancy. He acted out of confidence that we would not dare to attack him." Nothing during that week irked Eshkol more than this claim. As Peled had said before, prolonging delay might destroy the economy. "The State of Israel does not have unlimited resources." There were now approximately 100,000 soldiers on reserve duty on any given day.[2] "We deserve to know why we are suffering this disgrace," Peled said. "Now might be the time to explain what we are waiting for." Mordechai Hod and Yeshayahu Gavish assured the ministers that the army was ready and strong, and that it would win.

The ministers were not so easily persuaded. "You said that a week, two, three, or four could be decisive," Eshkol confronted Yariv. "But there's a difference between one week and three or four." He was surprised that none of the ministers had raised this point. Rabin burst out, "I'm saying that every day is more of a burden, making operations more difficult and more costly." Shapira asked, "In your opinion, have they concentrated almost all their military forces in the Sinai? And if so, what's the difference between now and a week or ten days from now? Because they're already there, after all. We, on the other hand, may lose on the diplomatic front if we take action immediately. So what's the decisive factor here?"

General Peled responded: "Perhaps you can tell me what we're waiting for on this diplomatic front?" He was extremely annoyed, and a whiff of rebellion was again in the air. "What has the IDF done to deserve this skepticism? What does an army have to do, besides win every battle, to gain the government's trust? The questions we've been asked, now and before, indicate a lack of faith in our ability."

Minister Aran wanted to know how many airplanes Israel could expect to lose in an attack on Egypt. General Hod replied evasively: "In Vietnam, the rate of losses is now at four percent. I believe that the sooner we strike, the smaller the losses." He said it was impossible to defend the country against airstrikes; rather, the enemy's bombers would have to be hit on the ground. Then he added casually, "We can carry out our mission. And I believe we can do it even with a delay, but we'll have to invest more effort, more time, and absorb more casualties to reach the same goal we can reach today or tomorrow." Such statements could only make the ministers more skeptical of the military's urgency.

Moshe Dayan later wrote that the generals failed to communicate the problem well, that their approach was too political, so he—the politician—decided to talk tactics. But he too added no particularly convincing information. None of the ministers, including Begin, found the army's arguments persuasive. All of them relied on the same information. The ministers, with Eshkol as their head, were reckoning with broader considerations than the army was.

Eshkol responded as a statesman. He had wrinkled his nose when Sharon used the term "pleading," and also rejected Sharon's description of Israel as "scurrying." Everything "we have in terms of military strength comes from this scurrying. Let's not forget that. . . ." Eshkol assured the General Staff that hearing them "chastise the government" was always important. "But let's say that we broke the enemy today: tomorrow we'd have to start rebuilding our own strength, because we too will lose forces.

Even if we start building our own aircraft, we can't build engines that quickly. And if every ten years we have to fight, we can't just say that we don't give a damn about allies." This was why Israel should wait. The effort to convince the world that Nasser was acting like Hitler also took time, Eshkol said.

General Matti Peled erupted again: "We asked for an explanation! What are we waiting for?" Eshkol put him in his place: "If it's still not clear to you, I'm not going to explain any further." But he added, "I want to drill it into Johnson so he doesn't say we cheated him. We may still need him. I hope we don't need him in the middle of the war. . . . Military victory will end nothing. Because the Arabs are here to stay."[3]

Abba Eban was noticeably silent at the meeting. The evening before, after Dayan's appointment as minister of defense, Eban had changed his mind about going to war and told Rabin that diplomacy had run its course. In his memoirs, as well as in a letter to the American diplomat and historian William Quandt, Eban claimed that he revised his position after hearing a report on a conversation with a senior U.S. administration official. Sensitive to language, Eban noticed that the report discussed the waiting policy in the past tense, which led him to believe that the Americans now agreed that Israel should act to reopen the Straits. The report, by David Ginsburg, was quoting Clark Clifford, an associate of President Johnson's and a supporter of Israel.[4]

Eban was also aware of what Meir Amit had heard from some administration officials in the United States. "My conclusions at the end of the first round in Washington are that we should wait a short while longer for an international armada, and then find a way to strike. [U.S.] public opinion is in favor . . . I think that McNamara does not object, either. The only ones opposed at this point are the people in the State Department," Amit reported.[5] Eban might also have concluded that, with Dayan's appointment, war had become inevitable, and that his own opposition might harm him politically.

WHEN THE EXCHANGE CONCLUDED, ESHKOL CONVENED DAYAN, EBAN, AND ALLON and a few of their staffers. The next evening, they would hear from Amit, who was about to return from Washington. At that point, they would have their "final discussion," Eshkol said. He asked for the ministers' opinions. Dayan, predictably, said the war should start immediately. His plan was to destroy the Egyptian air force and occupy the Sinai, but not the Gaza Strip or the Suez Canal. Allon, who also considered himself a strategist, had his own plan. He suggested approaching the canal, threatening to close it, and taking advantage of the threat to transfer hundreds of thousands of Palestinian refugees from Gaza westward over the canal. Dayan said that deporting the refugees might turn into an "incomparably barbaric and inhumane" operation. Returning to his own vision, he proposed a timeline: a government decision on Sunday morning; war on Monday. Sensing that Eshkol now supported starting the war, Dayan left for lunch. Eshkol went home, but not before asserting, as recorded by Israel Lior, that "we have basically done all we can do politically. We can't wait any longer."[6]

But at least one man still believed, even that Friday, that Israel should avoid war. Shimon Peres had a proposal that, had it been accepted, might have set Middle Eastern history on a different course. He suggested conducting a nuclear test, a demonstration, that might have restored Israel's deterrence and prevented the war from breaking out. Peres's psychological reasoning was not unlike his proposal to restore Ben-Gurion to the prime minister's office: the move would alarm the Arabs, while soothing the fears of Israelis.[7]

THAT FRIDAY AFTERNOON, DAYAN GAVE AN INTERVIEW TO *TIME* MAGAZINE. THEN HE RECEIVED a visitor with a wonderful name, he wrote: Winston Churchill, the grandson. Churchill came on behalf of the British *News of the World*. He was a cute young man, Dayan said, so the minister of defense was surprised when Churchill asked him bluntly whether war would break out in the next day or two, or whether he might as well stop hanging around in his hotel and go home. Dayan told Churchill he could go home, he wouldn't miss a thing: it was either too late or too early to initiate an attack, and Israel still had to pursue diplomacy. "I was sorry to mislead him," he later wrote, "but in my heart I took comfort: if he was the loyal friend to Israel that he said, it was fitting for him to help mislead the enemy."[8]*

Later that Friday night, Dayan took part in a discussion with the chief of staff and a few generals. Gavish presented two plans of action, one that involved taking Gaza and one that did not. The generals argued the point. Rabin, who only a few days earlier had thought Gaza should be captured as a bargaining chip, had meanwhile shifted to Dayan's position,

---

*Earlier, Aharon Yariv had warned Rabin that the air force plans might be leaked, and mentioned that Churchill had telephoned overseas, saying that the air force would initiate an assault. The military attaché at the British embassy reported that Israeli intelligence people were beside themselves over how much Churchill knew.[9]

whereby Gaza was expendable. Others argued that conquering Gaza would protect Israeli settlements along the border. One general said simply, "It would be a pity to lose the headline 'Gaza Is in Our Hands.'" But Dayan explained that taking Gaza, at least in the first stage, would mean having to deal with the refugees. "We have to let someone else take care of them," he said, referring to the UN. He also said that occupying the Suez Canal could only cause harm.

The cabinet, having heard repeatedly that Israel's future depended on a first strike against the Egyptian air force, would have probably been amazed to hear Dayan's next statement: "We're working on the assumption of a surprise airstrike, but it's possible that things won't go exactly the way we expect, for example, if there's an aerial battle. In any case, Egypt will never have the aerial advantage, even if things don't start off with an Israeli surprise in the air."[10]

It was close to midnight when Dayan arrived at Shimon Peres's house to celebrate his new job with a few friends. Ben-Gurion was there. Teddy Kollek was also there, reporting that Dayan's appointment had led to the cancellation of a huge demonstration planned in the capital.[11]

2. GREEN LIGHT: "A WEIGHT IS LIFTED FROM MY HEART"

On Saturday, June 3, while the government was waiting for Amit to return from Washington, Yehoshua Bar-Dayan was waiting for his wife. It was his third Sabbath on reserve duty. Gili had promised to come even if she had to take a taxi the whole way, and he was as excited as he was on their first date. She and Uzi Avrahami's wife managed to get as far as Revivim. Bar-Dayan took a jeep and went to pick them up. She was wearing pink. They kissed and hugged excitedly. He told her his life was in no danger; in his diary he added in parentheses, "if only."

Gili told him someone had refused to give her a ride, saying that to do so would ruin his Sabbath. Bar-Dayan was furious: "Never in Israel have so few decent people taken risks and sacrificed so much, and their wives suffered so much, while others are mean and heartless. We'll settle the score one day." He felt his neighbors could at least have volunteered for something; "parasites," he called them. He and Gili drove to Beersheba to have lunch at Morris's restaurant. On the way, they saw a huge picnic going on among some trees next to a memorial for soldiers killed in the War of Independence. Throngs of citizens had come to visit their soldiers. Morris's was packed with soldiers and their wives and children. "I had a lump in my throat. Gili and I looked at each other sorrowfully, longingly, and lovingly, hoping everything would end peacefully and we could go back to our normal lives." Gili brought the slides Shuka had asked about. He looked at the pictures of Yarivi over and over, hardly able to stop, but he was worried that his brigade might move on that afternoon and leave him behind. They said good-bye.

The brigade had indeed started to move, and he only just caught up with it. The commander had noticed Bar-Dayan's absence and sent a jeep out to look for him. But even if he had gone AWOL for a few minutes, it was for Gili. That was understandable. They would move at night. Dark, dust, a black convoy. They drove for three or four hours. Bar-Dayan made a wrong turn and took a whole string of vehicles with him, but he was able to backtrack, and he felt great. He loved Gili so much.[12]

DURING THE SABBATH, ESHKOL TOLD ISRAEL LIOR: "THERE'S NO REASON TO WAIT. They can't help us," referring to the Americans. "We have to make the decision as early as tomorrow morning." Dayan called a press conference to mislead the Egyptians. He spoke of "a month, two months, six months." War was not imminent, he said.[13]

Amit arrived that night, bringing Ambassador Harman with him. They drove straight from the airport to Eshkol's house in Jerusalem, where they found the ministers showing signs of the recent stress. They were "bleary-eyed from lack of sleep, their movements irritable and impatient." Eban passed a note to Harman: "They think we've gained nothing by waiting."

Amit's trip to Washington had been instigated by Aharon Yariv, and its main purpose was to find out, through intelligence channels, what the Americans would really do if Israel attacked Egypt. Amit later wrote that he had never before left Israel feeling so distraught. "The helplessness and inaction at the top" angered him. The flight attendant had told him that planes over the last few days had been full of Israelis leaving the country; he said they made him sick. Amit replied, "It's all right—if people want to run away, let them." He considered the events as if he were the nation's teacher: he thought the terrible crisis would do the Israelis some good. Things had been too easy, and people had gotten spoiled. "Whatever we're left with will be healthier," he wrote. When this crisis was behind them, Israelis could begin a different era, a different reality, a new chapter in history. The CIA station chief in Israel, John Hadden, was also on his way to Washington, but not on the same flight.

The first person Amit met there was James Jesus Angleton, the head of counterespionage in the CIA. He was a controversial figure, obsessed by the belief that the USSR was the source of all evil in the world. "In his imagination, everything that happened, every event, every incident," wrote Amit, "was tinted by his suspicion and was somehow connected to his theory." CIA people mocked him, but Amit did not mind: "Angleton was an extraordinary asset for us. We could not have found ourselves a better advocate."* Angleton updated Amit on the goings-on in Washington and conveyed a few snippets of local gossip; then Amit went to meet with the head of the CIA, Richard Helms. The two were old friends: Helms and his family had visited Amit at his home in Ramat Gan, and Amit had visited Helms's home. Amit said that over the years they had developed a close and honest relationship, so he assumed that at this critical hour he would "reap the fruit of the seeds he had planted years ago" and hear reliable information from his colleague. He wanted to know the precise timeline for deployment of the multinational naval force that would break through the Straits, but to his surprise he learned there was none. According to his account, he was "stunned," as this revelation was "the polar opposite of all of Eban's reports." This was inaccurate. Eban had not claimed that such a force existed; he had reported that one was planned.

Helms arranged for Amit to meet with Secretary of Defense McNamara, and in the meantime introduced him to senior CIA staff. Amit reportedly explained to them that the more time went by, the greater the need for U.S. intervention. If the United States had allowed Israel to act ten days ago, there would be no need for their intervention now. He still spoke in terms of a multinational naval force, but in fact he was suggesting that Israel be allowed to act alone. Israel was asking the United States for nothing but arms and political support, which would include an effort to prevent interference by the USSR. The question of the Straits was secondary, Amit told his CIA counterparts: the main question was "What will the Middle East look like?" He warned against a domino effect, using the favored term deployed by the CIA in its justifications for the war in Vietnam. Pro-American countries, Amit said, were falling one after the other into Nasser's net. He appealed to the CIA staff's conscience, arguing that thanks to American pressure staying Israel's hand, the country must now prevail in a cruel and bloody clash. The casualties would be their responsibility and on their heads. "The entire staff sat hunched over and lowered their eyes," Amit reported when he returned.

---

*In a corner of a public park in Jerusalem, opposite the Old City walls and the Hill of Evil Counsel, lies a black stone cenotaph in honor of Angleton. It bears a slightly mysterious inscription in Hebrew, English, and, oddly, Arabic: "In memory of a dear friend."

In all his meetings, including the one with McNamara, Amit emphasized the economic burden of the general mobilization. He repeated that Israel was not asking the United States for anything but freedom of action. He heard no objections from McNamara, who asked how long the operation would take (Amit said one week) and how many casualties Israel would sustain (Amit said fewer than in the War of Independence— less than six thousand). When Amit mentioned the multinational fleet, McNamara responded skeptically. During their meeting, the secretary of defense was handed a note informing him of Moshe Dayan's appointment. Amit reported that "McNamara was very moved and almost kissed me," and that the secretary said of Dayan, "I admire this man." Amit reported back to Israel that his impression was that the Americans would give their blessing to an Israeli strike "crushing Nasser." In response to Eshkol's question, Amit said they might even assist Israel in such a strike. McNamara was called out of the meeting twice to talk with Johnson on the phone. He told Amit that the president knew he was there, and promised, "I read you loud and clear."[14]

McNamara found Amit's arguments persuasive, and he conveyed them to Johnson the same evening. The president understood that Israel was going to act; he set up a special task force to handle the situation, headed by McGeorge Bundy. Jim Angleton was enthusiastic: for the first time in the history of the Middle East, there was the possibility of solving the region's problems, making it less vulnerable to intrigue and extortion, safer for capital investment and development. The new situation must be quickly exploited. Helms had made sure Israel's positions were reflected in the CIA's recommendations to the president. Angleton stressed the issue's delicacy and asked to preserve complete secrecy.[15]

Ambassador Harman later commented, "I am certain that they told Johnson, 'The Israelis can do the job, you don't have to worry.' Clearly, the President would have asked, 'And what if the Egyptians attack them? Will they come to us to rescue them? I don't want to be involved.' And they would have said, 'You can rest easy. Amit says they can finish it off themselves and do it quickly. That's the truth. All you have to do is make sure the Russians don't interfere. You have nothing to worry about.' "[16]

Amit also posited that the Americans had given up on organizing a multinational fleet and they understood that unilateral action by Israel would not implicate them. Furthermore, it transpired that in 1957 the United States had assured Israel that the Straits of Tiran would remain open. "The Americans still seemed to attribute a certain value to moral considerations," wrote Amit. But he also identified more pragmatic reasons for U.S. support. Jim Angleton, whom Amit described as "the biggest Zionist of the lot," had intimated that the Americans "would undoubtedly look positively on a knockout," that is, an attack on Egypt. Amit reported that the other people he met with had "downplayed" this view, but they nonetheless shared it.[17] Johnson's weekend guests at his ranch might have helped to persuade him, and perhaps also Dayan's appointment. One State Department staffer maintained, contrary to the view put forward by Ambassador Barbour, that Dayan was a short-tempered militarist who did not understand political complexity and whose appointment increased the chances of war. Ambassador Harman felt that it was Amit himself who had effected the change in the U.S. position, an assessment confirmed by the Mossad representative in Washington.

Amit later wrote that his flight home was one of the strangest he had taken. He was on a huge jumbo jet full of military equipment, with only two passengers: himself and Ambassador Harman. They flew via London and Frankfurt, where they loaded up with gas masks.* People were waiting for them impatiently at Eshkol's house; Dayan was among them.[19]

"The United States won't go into mourning if Israel attacks Egypt," Amit said on his return. His official report states: "The Americans will hesitate to act against us and there is reason to hope that they will even support us." He repeatedly suggested giving them another week, and meanwhile sending a ship to the Gulf of Aqaba, expecting—or hoping—that the Egyptians would fire on it and Israel could then act without having taken the first shot. He pointed out that there was some dissent among the Americans. Ambassador Harman suggested considering the State Department's position, too. Before leaving for Israel, he had met with Secretary of State Rusk, and had allowed himself a fairly undiplomatic outburst. Those who bore the responsibility for Israel's fate would not accept another Munich, he had said; "Must Israel have to accept ten thousand casualties before the U.S. will agree that aggression has occurred?"[20] Back in Israel, Harman also thought that they should wait another few days, so as not to lose U.S. support. He urged Dayan to consider that the United States might force Israel to stop the war within 24 hours after it started, and then Israel's situation would be even worse. Unlike Amit, he still believed in the multinational fleet, and observed

---

*John Hadden recalled a similar experience. He returned to Israel via Rome, also on a plane loaded with gas masks. Both he and Amit, Hadden wrote, realized that the United States had given Israel the green light. Ambassador Harman remembered leaving Washington with a sense that the red light had changed, but not to green: "We've been given the amber light."[18]

that Johnson understood that he would lose the next election if he did not help Israel.[21]

Dayan responded furiously: "And after seven or nine days? We'll send a ship through the Straits of Tiran, and then what?" Yaacov Herzog recorded one more panic-stricken remark by Dayan, or perhaps it was meant to make everyone else panic: "Anyone waiting for the Americans to open the Straits has to know that this way we'd be losing the whole land of Israel." Yigal Allon said that sending a ship through the Straits as bait would alert the Egyptians that war was imminent and the army would lose the element of surprise. Dayan demanded to know what any of this would mean regarding the concentration of Egyptian forces in Sinai, and Harman replied honestly, "I have no answer." He told them what the State Department had asked his people: "Does the fact that Nasser has jumped off the cliff mean you have to follow suit?"

Eshkol tried to get through to Dayan: "We'll send a ship. They'll open fire. Then there'll be a cause for action." Rabin repeated that every passing day made it harder for the IDF to act. The Arab armies were getting stronger. Two battalions of Egyptian paratroopers had arrived in Jordan. Dayan said they could take Eilat. "We'll be busy with El Arish and they'll occupy Jerusalem," he continued. "If we wait for seven to nine days there will be thousands of casualties. It makes no sense to wait. I'd rather we start first. We'll strike and then we'll take care of the diplomatic aspect. We have to do it, despite the political disadvantages." He promised an easy war. "Within two or three hours we'll have a huge aerial achievement, and within the first day, by evening, other forces will also make significant headway. Within two days, we can reach the canal area."

Amit repeated his opinion that the Americans would be pleased: they wanted Israel to release them from the obligation to send a fleet. Yigal Yadin contributed his own reassuring thought: "No one will be able to prove that our planes went in first after we start spreading the word that we are besieged by enemies on all sides." Even Ambassador Harman now chimed in: his idea was to dispatch Abba Eban to New York as a diversion. Dayan made more promises: "After the air force strike, the Egyptians will be without an air force for at least six months." He quoted an assessment that it would take three days for the Egyptians to recover from an air attack and deploy their infantry.

Eshkol was now convinced. He wanted to know the soonest possible date for the operation. Dayan said he had given orders to prepare for Monday. "Can we do it this morning?" Eshkol asked, and Dayan said it would be difficult: there were some constraints.[22] Meir Amit's report from

Washington had relieved Eshkol of his lingering qualms; he felt that Israel had been given the go-ahead. No one had a better appreciation of Israel's connections in America. The importance Eshkol attributed to the United States was his contribution to the process of Americanization that had begun to change life in Israel. Weapons, money, Jews, political support—he rightly perceived all these as more important than the claims made by the army in recent weeks, often with much exaggeration, sometimes hysterically. Amit's report greatly diminished the gamble Eshkol now had to take, and he relied once again on his intuition: whatever the Americans would accept in a week, they would just as easily accept in two days. Even an urgent communiqué from President Johnson promising continued international efforts would no longer make much of an impression on him.

Eshkol emerges as a statesman with nerves of steel who withstood all pressure until he could achieve coordination with the United States. It is doubtful whether he believed Israel's existence was truly in danger, and equally doubtful that he was convinced Egypt would attack. He knew what the army knew: that even if Egypt had attacked, Israel would win. But unlike Ben-Gurion, or perhaps even Dayan, Eshkol was not the man who could lead the Israelis to decide against war. His weakness ate away at him, particularly after being forced out of the Ministry of Defense. He wanted to be remembered as a patriot, and at this point the public equated patriotism with war. He also agreed with Dayan and the military that a war might improve Israel's situation.[23]

AT SHUKA BAR-DAYAN'S CAMP, TWO TANKS FLIPPED OVER. HE MANAGED TO CALL GILA and she cried over the phone, wrenching his heart. He spoke to Yariv, who asked, "Shuka, where's your Uzi?" Yariv promised to be a good boy and Bar-Dayan wrote, "The worry and the homesickness are awful. One of the hardest days." He had a popular song stuck in his head: "Could it be / could it be / that it's already simply tomorrow?" But who knew what tomorrow would bring, he thought. "I hope there will be no war. That our statesmen, Moshe Dayan and Begin, will know to attack some other time." He suddenly thought back to a day when he was about eleven and his mother had refused to buy him an ice cream cone. It was a sad day, she said, because Devorah Dayan's son, Moshe, from Nahalal, had been injured and lost his eye. Bar-Dayan told himself he would be all right. Maybe he just needed a good night's sleep. He would write to Gili tomorrow.[24]

. . .

THE FORMAL DECISION WAS MADE THE NEXT DAY, SUNDAY, JUNE 4. EBAN GAVE HIS colleagues additional information that left no room for doubt: the United States had given its consent for Israel to go to war. He based his report on his contact with a man whose name he did not specify, although everyone knew it was Abe Fortas, whom Begin referred to as "the mystery man." The U.S. Supreme Court justice had asked Israel to wait just one more week, and three days had passed since then. Fortas had given only one injunction: "Do not fire the first shot." Ambassador Harman told the ministers this was a central issue, both diplomatically and emotionally. Israel had to appear to be defending itself. Eban asserted: "If the strike is defensive, then America is on our side." Another urgent message from Johnson had arrived, promising continued international efforts. Eshkol relied on his intuition, believing that "in his heart," Johnson's opinion differed from what the United States said officially. If Johnson really intended to reopen the straits and truly wanted to restrain Israel, he would have sent in the Sixth Fleet. Had he done so, Eshkol would have suggested waiting. But there was no sign of American vessels in the region.

In any case, Dayan was not impressed by the United States' military might: "Half a million marines in Vietnam, with the best tools they have, are unable to defeat 200,000 Vietcong fighters in three years." This was one of the main lessons Dayan had brought home from his trip to Vietnam. Earlier, Eban had reported that McNamara had told Ephraim Evron that Dayan's reports from Vietnam contained the most reasoned assessments he ever received.

Aharon Yariv told the ministers he was in possession of Egyptian orders that indicated a planned assault before June 5, meaning the next day. "I am not saying [an assault is] certain," he said, ever cautious, but Dayan was now pushing hard. If they did not act immediately, Israel might lose the war and there would be thousands of casualties. He insisted that Israel should no longer comply with Fortas's request, particularly as the week he had asked for was coming to an end. "The Americans aren't going shoot at us," Dayan promised, and described the demand to keep waiting as "stupidity." Begin suggested sending Johnson the speech given by President Kennedy during the Cuban missile crisis. Minister Yosef Burg brought up Chamberlain and Hitler, and Allon said, predictably, "Better they condemn us alive than eulogize us at our grave."

Dayan reported that the Egyptians were planning to seize Eilat:

"I find it very difficult to see how we will stand up to that." Nasser was now essentially a presence in Jordan, too. The Jordanians might invade Jerusalem. "What if they send a commando battalion to carry out carnage in the heart of Jerusalem?" As he delivered this dramatic scenario, shots were heard through the window. The Jordanians had opened fire on an Israeli plane that, according to Eshkol, was flying in Israeli airspace. Shortly thereafter, the Jordanians fired on the Musrara neighborhood; no one was hurt.

Eshkol now concurred that if Israel did not act, they could expect "slaughter." With a hint of remorse he even suggested that perhaps had Israel acted two or three days ago, everything would now be easier. Haim Moshe Shapira and Zerah Warhaftig still pushed for a postponement, as did Menachem Begin, surprisingly. Shapira said that even after all he had heard, he was not convinced the Egyptians could attack in the next few days. He believed they expected Israel to attack first. He said that two days earlier he had met with Ben-Gurion, who had insisted that Israel must not strike without the assistance of another power.

Dayan responded derisively: "If we take a hundred of their planes out of commission, that's worth more than any additional arms that the minister of the interior or Knesset member Ben-Gurion can get hold of in six months." He reminded them that over the last few weeks he had consistently been right: he had predicted that the Egyptians would kick out the UN forces, and he had known they would blockade the Straits.

Begin suggested sending Meir Amit on another mission, to Paris, London, and Washington, to explain Israel's predicament. Although he supported the war, he did not believe that a few days' delay would do any harm. But he did not insist on his position. Warhaftig asked Dayan how they could present an Israeli first strike as a response, and wondered whether they could stage something. "We need an alibi," said Minister Bentov. "I haven't got any tricks other than taking action. If someone has some other trick, I'll buy it," replied Dayan. Regarding the possibility of sending an Israeli ship to the Gulf of Aqaba as a provocation, Dayan said, "Absolute suicide." Allon thought the prime minister could announce to the world's heads of state that the Egyptians had attacked, and minutes later Israel would respond. The prime minister would risk a lie, but only historians would know the truth. "I don't think the Americans will dig around to check up on what exactly happened," Allon said.

Eshkol pointed out that their actions would be judged by history. The resolution that evolved asserted that Israel was acting against "the ring of aggression tightening around it." Eshkol and Dayan were authorized to decide on the time of action. "A weight is lifted from my heart," wrote Minister Gvati. Almost everyone was in favor. Only the Mapam ministers proposed waiting awhile longer, and said they could not vote in favor of war before receiving authorization from their party leaders, Meir Yaari and Yaakov Hazan. As camouflage for the meeting, the cabinet approved additional resolutions: participation in a diplomatic conference in Sweden, and approval of a cultural agreement between Israel and Belgium.[25]

Years later, Yigal Allon said that from a military perspective, a single week would not have sealed Israel's fate. The government and the military were afraid that postponing the war might increase the number of casualties, but there was no existential danger to the state. "The only crisis was psychological," Allon said. It was not the situation on the front that was the main cause of war, but the loss of faith in the government. "To this day I wonder whether, if not for that stammered speech on the radio, things might have developed differently."[26] Obviously, Israel was too weak to avoid war.

GILI BAR-DAYAN SAT AT HOME IN RISHON LEZION AND THOUGHT ABOUT HER HUSBAND. "You have no idea how terrible the worrying is," she wrote to him. "The news is so depressing and I don't know what will happen. Take care of yourself for us, because we love you so much and so want to see you back healthy and whole. . . . Your father called before and sent his regards. . . . Come home—I miss you so much and want you with me and with our sweet Yarivi. Who needs these wars . . . ?"[27] Her husband felt the same way, but by the time he got her letter he was already in Sinai.

CHAPTER 12

DAY ONE

1. THE FOG OF WAR: "BING BANG BOOM"

On Monday, June 5, at 7:45 A.M., Private Yehoshua Bar-Dayan wrote in his diary: "I believe the war has started. Two Mystère squadrons flew by low." By the time he made his next entry, forty-five minutes later, the war had been all but won: the planes flying overhead destroyed hundreds of Egyptian aircraft, most still grounded at their bases.

Bar-Dayan and his fellow soldiers in the 7th Brigade took the camouflage nettings off the tanks and prepared to move. Someone went around giving out syringes in case the soldiers were attacked with gas. The syringes might have been among the equipment delivered two days earlier on the plane Meir Amit and Ambassador Harman had flown back on, or perhaps they came in on the CIA agent's flight. Then everyone received a proclamation signed by General Israel Tal, commander of the armored division nicknamed the Steel Division.

"Today we shall go out to crush the hand that had reached out to strangle us," declared Tal, hurling accusations at the Egyptians. "This is a battle that the enemy wanted and the enemy began; we will strike the enemy twice as hard as he hit us." He stressed that they were facing a long war: "For the third time, the Egyptian dagger has been brandished at us. For the third time, the enemy has erred in its mad delusion of seeing Israel brought to its knees. With blood, fire, and iron, this time we shall purge this plot from their heart. . . ." Tal promised that Israel did not intend to make war on Egyptian civilians: "We do not covet their land or their property. We have not come to destroy their country nor to take possession of it." The Israelis had come "to defeat the plot of destruction," and they would win. "Today the Sinai desert shall know the force of the Steel Division. And the land will shudder at its coming." Tal was a man who appreciated quality work: the author of his proclamation was Amos Oz.[1]

Bar-Dayan wrote: "I hope we win, that it will be quick. My God, protect me and my family." He made sure he had a jack and a lug wrench for changing tires, and he kissed his wedding ring.

At David Ben-Gurion's house in Tel Aviv, a senior officer sent by Dayan came to inform him that the war had started. "There was no need for this," Ben-Gurion wrote in his diary. He remained steadfast in his view of the war: "I believe it is a grievous mistake." Dayan wanted Ben-Gurion to know that in the next few hours the IDF would storm the townships of Khan Younis and Rafiah, south of Gaza.[2]

For the Ezrachi family, in Jerusalem, the day began like any other. Father was on reserve duty, but the children went to school. Edith Ezrachi went out to the post office. Yosef Weitz, meanwhile, was looking forward to a productive day. He was writing a book on the history of forestation in Palestine, and had been agonizing for several days over the first paragraph in the chapter on the Carmel forests. That morning he found the right words and forged ahead.[3]

Bar-Dayan saw his brigade commander, Gorodish, driving by in a jeep. He waved to his friend Uzi. Dozens of tanks and half-tracks started moving in no apparent order. They were on their way to Khan Younis. He drove his pickup and wrote fragmentary diary entries during the frequent stops: "After the war we'll come here as tourists"; "They came to destroy us—and so we will destroy them." Then he thought about Yariv again. "There is great excitement. There is no fear. I am in the rear."

Sounds of explosions and gunfire thundered from every direction. The vehicles traveled through burning farmland. A shell landed twenty yards from Bar-Dayan's pickup, showering it with shrapnel. He was not hurt. "We're not going to die that quickly," he wrote. This was untrue: one man had already been killed, Yossi Algamis, twenty-three, of Jerusalem, an officer in the armored commando unit. His vehicle had been hit by a sniper serving in one of the Palestinian units in the Egyptian military.[4]

A Patton tank broke down and got stuck, and Bar-Dayan's team hurried to repair it. They drove through an orchard. "Young, beautiful, fresh graftings, second year, blooms and heartwarming growth," he noted with professional expertise, and added, "What a shame to lose it. The fault is not the farmer's, but Nasser's." They passed a village where Bar-Dayan saw laundry hanging on a line. The villagers had fled. "The poor people. Not their fault." The air force had meanwhile completed the destruction of most of the Egyptian air force. Only a few Israelis knew this; most were enduring hours of terror. Gila Bar-Dayan took Yariv and went to stay with her mother. She felt paralyzed with fear.

AT TEN PAST EIGHT, KOL ISRAEL RADIO ANNOUNCED THAT THE EGYPTIANS WERE AT-tacking Israel. Soldiers on leave were instructed to return to their units immediately. Edith Ezrachi heard an air-raid siren, but wasn't sure if it was a real warning or another test. She rushed home.

A Foreign Ministry official called the head of the UN observer team, Odd Bull, and asked him to hurry to the ministry. The general said he could come at ten-thirty but was told it was urgent, so he left immediately. The ministry informed him that at ten past eight that morning, Egyptian planes had invaded Israeli airspace. They asked him to give a message to King Hussein of Jordan: as long as Jordan did not attack Israel, it would not be attacked. If Jordan took action, Israel would respond with full force. The decision to warn Hussein had been made at the cabinet meeting a day earlier. General Bull perceived the warning as a threat, and he held that the UN's role was not to carry threats. He nevertheless conveyed the message to its intended recipient. A similar warning was delivered to Jordan via the U.S. embassy.[5]

At ten, Ruhama Weitz asked her husband to go to the supermarket with her. "As soon as we got there, we realized something was going on," Weitz wrote. "A long line of housewives and men outside the doorway, everyone trying to fill up their baskets." It was a "distressing" scene; many vehicles loaded with soldiers were driving through the streets. That was how Weitz found out the war had begun. They bought some food and went home. And then there was another siren.*

THE FOREIGN MINISTRY REPORTED TO THE EMBASSY IN WASHINGTON THAT AT AROUND ten-thirty that morning, gunfire was exchanged along the border in

---

*By this time, presumably, the British ambassador, Michael Hadow, was already feeling "some humility," as he later wrote; a mere twenty-four hours earlier, he had reported with confidence that there would not be a war. When he heard the air-raid sirens in Tel Aviv on Monday, he was certain they had gone off by mistake. The ambassador apologized to his superiors. Unfortunately, he wrote, foreign diplomats in Israel, including Her Majesty's ambassador, were not party to cabinet proceedings.[6]

Jerusalem, and at eleven—"Bing, Bang, Boom," as Edith Ezrachi later wrote—the Jordanians started shelling Jerusalem. Civil Defense people appeared on the streets and notified residents that it was time to protect their windshields with tape and shade their windows at home. Ezrachi quickly filled a few buckets with water. Her hands were shaking and her heart trembling, she wrote. The explosions were very loud; she felt as if they were coming from her backyard. It was harrowing.

About a dozen residents were killed, including two children, and a few hundred were injured, according to Mayor Kollek. Many buildings were damaged, including hospitals, schools, the Israel Museum, the president's home, the Knesset building, and the house next door to Eshkol's. A few stores burned down. In the Biblical Zoo some ninety animals died. There was heavy damage to streets, and trees were burned.[7]

YEHOSHUA BAR-DAYAN AND HIS FRIENDS SAW THEIR FIRST DEAD BODIES. THEY WERE IN an abandoned village. Only a few cackling chickens were left, and a blindfolded donkey dragging a thresher through a granary of barley as if nothing had happened. Khan Younis was also deserted when Bar-Dayan and his unit reached it. According to his diary, that was before noon.

JUST BEFORE NOON, RUHAMA AND YOSEF WEITZ LOCKED UP THEIR HOUSE AND WENT down to the public bomb shelter. It was under a new apartment building whose construction had necessitated uprooting a few of the trees Weitz loved so much. The shelter was a square room of raw concrete, just over fifty square feet. When they walked in, they found three women already there, one in an advanced stage of pregnancy, one with a two-year-old, and another with a seven-year-old. The women had a transistor radio. Weitz's son Ra'anan also came, and another two women and three children, who brought mattresses, food, and medicine. Water, electricity, and tools had been prepared a few days earlier. The mood was gloomy, wrote Weitz. No one knew what was happening.

Edith Ezrachi's sons had been moved into the school bomb shelter with all the other children. The older children, including Ilan Ezrachi, were allowed to run home. The little ones, including his brother Amiri, had to stay. His mother could not bear the thought of him sitting there in a dark airless shelter, hungry, so she went to fetch him home. The terrible noise of shells and gunfire went on and on. None of them could sleep, except for Amiri. He had nerves of steel, his mother wrote.[8]

Letters written from the bomb shelters depict a profoundly disturbing experience. "We were terribly afraid," wrote Dalia Herzog from Tel Aviv. "I cannot describe the worrying. It was intolerable. We were really losing our minds." The fear gave everyone stomach cramps and diarrhea. A little girl wrote from the bomb shelter at Kibbutz Ein Hanatziv, "The situation is horrible. Asi and Yair have been called up."[9]

The night before the attack on Egypt, Dayan had ordered the censor to maintain "a fog of war" until the evening. "For the first twenty-four hours we have to be the victims," he said. As long as the world thought Israel was defending itself and fighting for its life, there would be no pressure from the outside to stop the attack. The lack of information greatly increased the public's anxiety: as far as the people in the shelters knew, Arabs might burst in and slaughter them at any moment. The radio reported only enemy action. "The Voice of Thunder" from Cairo claimed, in Hebrew, that Tel Aviv was burning and Palestinian fighters were roaming the streets. "They are not afraid of death, they dispense death!" screamed the announcer. Most Israelis had no other source of information.

SOME DID, THOUGH. NEVER BEFORE HAD THOSE AMONG THE "ARISTOCRACY OF secrets" been more grateful for their status. At nine-thirty, two reporters for Kol Israel reported that the Egyptian air force "had suffered a devastating blow." Their report was not broadcast, but rumors began flying from ear to ear: switchboard operators, secretaries, producers, correspondents, editors, technicians, cafeteria workers, gatekeepers, drivers—they all had friends and relatives and neighbors who were consumed with worry and desperate to know what was happening.

Ezer Weizman telephoned his wife, Reuma, at ten and announced, "We've won the war." A few minutes later, the IDF spokesperson briefed military correspondents, who were not permitted to reveal the news. At ten-thirty, an assistant to the minister of defense, the former chief of staff Zvi Zur, called Ben-Gurion and informed him that 137 Egyptian planes had been destroyed, and only six or seven Israeli planes had been lost. Just before eleven, Dayan spoke on the radio. He did not report the destruction of the Egyptian air force, but at eleven, Kol Israel announced in Arabic that 120 Egyptian planes had been destroyed. The furious censor called, demanding to know how this revelation had happened. He was told that Arabic programming was a separate kingdom. Around the same time, someone called Minister Gvati and told him that 150 enemy aircraft had been destroyed. Meanwhile, *Maariv* issued its third edition of the day, with a headline based on Kol Israel's Arabic broadcast: "120 Egyptian Planes Destroyed." Someone from the Israeli embassy in Paris leaked to Reuters that the air force had destroyed 117 Egyptian planes on the ground.

A reporter for *Ha'aretz* in northern Israel heard the news from a police officer in Acre: 224 planes. The reporter, Yehuda Ariel, also worked for a German news agency. He hurried to the post office in Nahariya, many of whose residents were of German origin. Dr. Fritz Wolf was filling in for the postman, who had been called up. When he read Ariel's telegram, he initially refused to transmit it. "This is not possible," he said in German. "Who would even believe such a thing?" He thought Ariel had gone mad. Another clerk spread the news around town.

President Johnson's adviser Harry C. McPherson, Jr., came to see Eshkol at around noon. While he was waiting outside the prime minister's office, he later told Johnson, an air raid siren suddenly came on. McPherson asked worriedly whether they shouldn't all go down to the bomb shelter, but the intelligence officer accompanying him said, "It won't be necessary." McPherson understood from this that Israel had won.[10] Yehoshua Bar-Dayan wrote: "We're taking Rafiah."

BY THIS POINT, BAR-DAYAN HAD SEEN ISRAELIS INJURED AND KILLED. HIS FRIEND UZI WAS transporting a wounded soldier in his van. "He suffered serious head wounds," wrote Bar-Dayan, "the thunder of cannons, shells around us, I don't know if they're the enemy's or our own. Smoke is rising from the posts. The commander gave us ten minutes to finish with Rafiah. It seems to be a bit more difficult. Someone's been injured. I'm opposite the Rafiah train station. We're dying to find out where there's a medic or a doctor." Uzi's van came back with Uzi lying in the back, wounded. His head was bleeding. "The guys say it's nothing serious," wrote Bar-Dayan. "He gestured with his hand. I hope it's nothing. I think about Ora and the kids. Where's the doctor? I pray he gets out of it. At least he's done with the war. We've been fighting for Rafiah for an hour now."

Bar-Dayan's next diary entry came at twelve-forty. Scouts reported that the battle for Rafiah was over and the Egyptians were fleeing. "The posts of Rafiah are ablaze," he wrote. "They're bringing out casualties fast. Where the hell is the doctor? Another unit is passing by, the guys all giving the thumbs-up. Egyptian soldiers' corpses along the side of the road. To our left, cannons roaring. Is this a new battle?" Then he saw his brigade's tanks driving back out onto the road to keep fighting. "May the God of the armies of Israel be with them. Gili and Yariv, don't worry. The guys who came back from the front line said Uzi was only lightly injured. He'll probably be home in a few days." A vehicle was taking away wounded and dead soldiers. "The injured guys are naked, their faces burned and dusty. Gunfire has started up again in the field. Shells exploding and clouds of smoke. We heard Eshkol on the radio." The prime minister gave a radio address at noon. He did not reveal that the Egyptian air force had been destroyed.

2. VICTORY: "AMAZING AND WONDERFUL"

At twelve-thirty, Eshkol met with Dayan; Rabin, Allon, Yariv, and Yadin were also present. The situation report was that IDF armored and infantry forces were advancing into the Sinai. Dayan had changed his mind about the Gaza Strip and had allowed units to start occupying Gaza City. The air force was still striking Egyptian air bases. UN observers had tried, unsuccessfully, to broker a cease-fire in Jerusalem. The IDF was still returning fire. The Jordanians expanded their fire, threatening Ramat David, the main air force base in the north. Dayan suggested protecting the base by invading the area around the West Bank city of Jenin. "We won't take the city," he said. Eshkol agreed, but stressed: "If possible, leave the city." According to Dayan, he had already given orders to occupy Jenin before the meeting with Eshkol. He had also ordered the air force to strike at Jordan and Syria and for the IDF to start the operation to seize Mount Scopus. Eshkol authorized Dayan's orders.[11]

The meeting involved one of the most important discussions held during the war. On the surface, it was only a moment in the continuous management of the situation; in fact, it led to conquering the West Bank and Jerusalem. According to Israel Lior, Dayan said, "I suggest we avoid getting involved in two wars," as if cautioning against a war with Jordan. But Lior was aware that he was playing a double game. "Damn. What does Moshe Dayan want?" he wondered. Dayan also suggested seizing Latrun, a "grab" that had been planned long before. Yitzhak Rabin, who was reluctant to occupy the West Bank, said, "We're screwing their air force, why do we need to take land at this stage?" Earlier, Rabin had refused to authorize General Narkis's Central Command to strike at the Jordanians in response to their bombing of Jerusalem.[12]

KING HUSSEIN OF JORDAN WAS WELL-KNOWN IN ISRAEL. YAACOV HERZOG HAD SEcretly met with him for the first time some three and a half years earlier, and there had been a few more meetings since then. Roughly two years before the war, Hussein had also met with the then foreign minister, Golda Meir. Israel and Jordan maintained unbroken ties, both direct and indirect, partly via the United States.* The liaison with Hussein in London was through his Jewish physician, Dr. Emanuel Herbert.[13]

Some ten days before the war began, and again two days later, the IDF offered the assessment that the Jordanians would attack only if the situation on the southern front deteriorated and the Egyptians managed to "nail" Israel. Rabin estimated that the opposite was also true: "If [Hussein] sees that Nasser is taking a beating, he'll keep quiet." Yariv commented, however, that Hussein would have to "do something," or at least appear to. The assumption was that to hold on to power, Hussein would have to participate in the Arabs' war effort and perhaps even in their defeat. Yariv had restated this assessment in the discussion with Eshkol at midday on June 5.[14]

Hussein did in fact "do something": he began shelling Jerusalem and other places along the border. One shell landed in downtown Tel Aviv.[15] Israel could have responded by defeating the Jordanian army without taking the West Bank and Jerusalem. It would have been sufficient to destroy the Jordanian air force, and perhaps carry out the land "grabs" in Latrun, Mount Scopus, and the Armon Hanatziv area. But Rabin's reservations about the West Bank and Jerusalem were not shared by everyone on the General Staff. Ezer Weizman's memoirs reflect extreme hostility toward the "chirping" coming from "the little king," as he called Hussein. For some reason it was important to Weizman to humiliate Hussein. "At least Nasser was a real man," he wrote—he had attacked, while Hussein had waited until Nasser "filled his head with rubbish," claiming that Tel Aviv was on fire and that Israel was about to collapse and that it was time to divvy up the spoils. "He heard 'spoils'—and the blood rushed to his head," wrote Weizman. "He came to claim his share of the remains, to get his cut of the corpse's flesh." In retrospect, Weizman had no regrets. He said, in fact, that he had hoped Hussein would fight: "If we're destined to fight this war anyway, then I want to be able to slip a note into the cracks of the Western Wall." According to Weizman, it was Hussein who gave the war its historic-national dimension, the dream of returning to greater Jerusalem and the biblical areas.[16]

After the noon meeting with Eshkol, Rabin asked Dayan if the Jenin

---

*It seems, however, that the Americans were unaware of Hussein's direct contacts with Israeli leaders until the end of December 1966. They found out only when the king himself chose to inform them, and they reacted with amazement.

operation should include the village of Yabed in the Dotan Valley. It was a large village, and Rabin probably felt they should not seize it, just as they should not seize Jenin. But Dayan wanted Yabed. "It has a history," he wrote: it was the place where Jacob's sons had sold their brother, Joseph, and it was where an Arab woman gathering firewood had discovered the cave hideout of Izz al-Din al-Qassam, the Palestinian rebel who had fought against the British.

At three, Dayan convened the editors of the daily papers and told them—not yet for publication—that Israel had now destroyed four hundred Arab aircraft.[17]

AT AROUND THE SAME TIME, GENERAL ODD BULL GOT THE SURPRISE OF HIS LIFE: JOR-danian soldiers were coming in through the fence surrounding his headquarters at Armon Hanatziv. Bull hurried out, met the commander of the Jordanian force halfway between the entrance gate and the building, and asked what he thought he was doing there. The officer, a major named Daoud, told him he had orders to seize the site. Bull took him to the garage, where he telephoned his contacts in the Jordanian army to protest the invasion, but Major Daoud was receiving orders over his radio to enter the building itself. There were many people there, Bull recalled—UN workers, a few of them Jordanian, and some women and children. Daoud suggested evacuating them, but Bull refused. He took the major into his office and called the Jordanian army again. He had never been so angry, he later wrote. He threatened the soldiers that if they did not leave the building, he would telephone King Hussein himself. This made an impression on Daoud and he quit the building, but his soldiers remained on the grounds and started shooting toward Israeli Jerusalem. Bull called the Israeli Foreign Ministry, reported the situation, and insisted that IDF soldiers not approach the area. He tried to phone the Jordanians again, but the line had gone dead. He got into his car to try and reach someone on the Jordanian side, but at that moment the IDF started bombarding the site. Bull stayed where he was. The IDF entered the area a few minutes before four. The building and a few cars were damaged in the exchange of fire, and Bull's residential quarters burned down. The Israelis demanded that he and his people relocate. Having no choice, Bull obeyed. His officers were housed in a hotel.

Uzi Narkis later said that the Jordanian presence at the UN site had put the residential neighborhoods in southwestern Jerusalem at risk. "The enemy could easily have reached the Katemon area," he said. The U.S. consul quoted General Bull's expert opinion: "The Jordanians handled themselves very amateurishly and the Israelis very professionally." Bull hurried to the Israeli Foreign Ministry for the second time that day, to complain, among other things, that the IDF soldiers who had entered the building had cut off radio contact with UN headquarters in New York.[18]

DAYLIGHT WAS JUST BREAKING IN THE UNITED STATES. A FEW PEOPLE HAD ALREADY BEgun to grasp that the Middle East they thought they knew when they went to bed had changed. President Johnson's telephone had rung at four-thirty A.M. Walt Rostow was on the line, reporting the first details of the war. Johnson may not have found the news surprising: on Saturday night he had been at a fund-raising dinner, where he sat next to Mathilde Krim. At a certain point Abe Feinberg came over, leaned down, and whispered to the president that the Israelis had decided to go to war. Feinberg was in a position to know.[19]

The White House log carefully documents what the president did after getting up on the morning of June 5. He showered, shaved, and dressed, then left the bedroom and had chipped beef, a grapefruit, and a cup of tea for breakfast. Considering this meticulous account, the lack of detail about what the president did at around seven A.M. is rather striking. He went up to the third floor with two bodyguards and knocked on the door of room 303. Mathilde Krim opened the door in her nightgown. "We have a war," said Johnson, and turned and left without waiting for her response. Johnson was angry. To the end of his days, he never believed that the Israeli resort to war was anything other than a blunder.[20]

"What a crazy situation," Krim thought; when she recounted the episode later, she found it difficult to decide what was crazier: the war, or the fact that she had learned about it from the president of the United States as she stood before him in her nightgown. "The truth is, it was a little bizarre of him to come to me like that and tell me about the war. He probably felt he needed a little understanding, a little sympathy." The historian William Quandt suggested that at the time there were probably only three people who spoke with Johnson on the phone more often than Mathilde Krim: Walt Rostow, Dean Rusk, and Robert McNamara.

Typically for relations between Jerusalem and Washington, the Jewish channel rushed with activity. Israeli chief justice Shimon Agranat, a native of Louisville, Kentucky, phoned his childhood friend Arthur Goldberg in New York; the two had been active together in the Jewish student union. Agranat asked Goldberg to give Johnson a message from Eshkol:

the prime minister hoped the president understood Israel's motives, hoped the United States would not restrain Israel, and promised there would be no need for American intervention to open the Straits. Goldberg was alarmed: Agranat was speaking over an open telephone line. He asked that Eshkol not use this channel of communication again.[21]

YEHOSHUA BAR-DAYAN SUMMARIZED THE NEWS: "HUSSEIN AND THE SYRIANS ARE ON A rampage, attacking civilian targets. They didn't mention us at all." This annoyed him. "We're waiting anxiously for the rest of the battle in our area," he wrote, munching on an apple. They were still near Rafiah. A group of his men went off to repair a tank. The turret of one of the tanks that passed by was damaged, but when he pointed this out, his commander responded dismissively and said the Egyptians were fleeing. Zvika arrived in Uzi's van and said that Uzi had been injured because he wasn't wearing a flak helmet.

Bar-Dayan knew very little of the army's progress in the Sinai. Rumors had it that they were having trouble reaching El Arish. And so the men waited. Fifteen Egyptian prisoners were marched in with their hands up. "Will they kill them?" Bar-Dayan wrote. They walked between two tanks. "The heroes of the Egyptian army are coming toward us, the sons of bitches. Yes, I hate you," Bar-Dayan added. One prisoner, a large, clumsy man, drew up in a vehicle and stepped out. He had three stars on his shoulder: a colonel, the guys determined. He knelt down with the other prisoners, putting his face in the sand. A jeep came to take him away. "The guys are starting to walk around with Carl Gustaf submachine guns that belonged to the Egyptians," wrote Bar-Dayan. "One guy has an Egyptian radio. He says: Let's call Nasser! Smoking Egyptian Piccadilly cigarettes. The commander just went by. The guys' spirits are way up." Bar-Dayan felt strong and confident and prayed the Egyptian air force had been paralyzed.

They picked up the movement toward El Arish. "Two of our half-tracks on the way. Direct hits. Pieces of human flesh hang from them. God help us." A rumor came through that the air force had demolished 180 planes on the ground. "Good job. We're much safer." Black smoke was coming from the battlefields. Green, red, and yellow plumes of smoke rose up like signals for the helicopters. "On the way one of our half-tracks, burned with its men. They lie there burned, headless. We salute them. A depressing and horrifying sight. Gili and Yariv, I kiss you on my wedding ring, we will see each other again, I am sure that the fighting will be over in two days." At seven P.M. he wrote, "Twilight has fallen on the Sinai Desert."[22]

Around the same time, news reached the Jerusalem bomb shelter where the Weitz family had taken refuge: 157 enemy planes had been destroyed.[23] Most Israelis still had no idea what was happening and were as frightened as before, planning to spend the night in the shelters. Minister Haim Gvati spent several hours in the shelter with his neighbors, then left for the Knesset. By the time he arrived, the Jordanians had renewed their bombing. Everyone in the Knesset building crowded into the bomb shelter. It was an extraordinary scene, wrote Gvati. Eshkol was late. Allon and Begin also had trouble coming from Tel Aviv: they got stuck in a traffic jam of military convoys just outside Jerusalem.

The ministers crowded into a small room in the shelter and heard a report from Rehavam Ze'evi. El Arish had been conquered. The entire Gaza Strip, apart from Gaza City, was in Israeli hands. The armored corps was progressing as planned in three separate thrusts, commanded by Israel Tal (north), Ariel Sharon (central), and Avraham Yaffe (south). In Khan Younis, an entire Egyptian division had been crushed, its commander taken prisoner. The air force had demolished 362 planes, 300 of them Egyptian, the rest Syrian and Jordanian. Essentially, the air forces of all three countries had been taken out of commission. Military experts agreed that this was an unprecedented achievement. The Jordanians had bombed several towns, while the Syrians, oddly, were doing virtually nothing. Gvati could barely contain his excitement: who would have believed this?

When Eshkol finally arrived, he was welcomed with cheers and elation. The cabinet meeting was short, Gvati noted. "A proposal was made to take the Old City of Jerusalem. Since a force was on its way to secure the road to Mount Scopus anyway, the political implications were quickly analyzed and it was agreed that the General Staff should decide on the basis of the military circumstances." The idea of taking the Old City had been brought up by Yigal Allon and Menachem Begin. Their reasoning was primarily patriotic, not military; the Jordanian attack on the Israeli part of the city merely provided an excuse. Some participants suggested considering the legal and political complications of conquering the city, including the holy sites. Ministers Aran and Shapira suggested that the IDF seize the city and turn it over to international rule. Ministers Kol and Bentov suggested postponing the decision on Jerusalem, or alternatively, delegating authority to the prime minister and the minister of defense.

Eshkol wanted the Old City. He wanted the West Bank, too, but he believed the world would force Israel to withdraw from both. He suggested a peculiar resolution: "In light of the situation that has evolved in Jerusalem, because of the Jordanians' bombing and after the warnings that were sent, we may have an opportunity to enter the Old City." Allon added this gloss: "The government does not object to seizing the Old City if it becomes militarily necessary." David Ben-Gurion was also in the Knesset that evening. He supported taking the Old City.

After the cabinet meeting, the Knesset swore in two new ministers, Begin and Yosef Sapir. Dayan was there for the swearing-in, but the ceremony was delayed, and he lost his patience and went back to Tel Aviv. "The occasion was unforgettable," wrote Gvati. "It embodied the unity of the nation defending its existence at a time of unprecedented danger, and its pride in the IDF for demonstrating its immense talent and capability. The spontaneous singing of the national anthem that broke out at the end of the session expressed only a fraction of the feelings of those present at this great occasion."

Gvati went home through dark streets, to the sound of shells thundering. Back in the bomb shelter, he told his neighbors what Kol Israel had not yet reported. Then he went up to his apartment, but the walls shook and he returned to the shelter.[24]

YEHOSHUA BAR-DAYAN MANAGED TO GET TWO HOURS OF SLEEP, BUT AT TWO A.M. HE was awoken by a friend who told him Rabin and Hod had just been on the radio: four hundred planes had been destroyed. It was the broadcast the whole country had been waiting for. "Amazing and wonderful," wrote Bar-Dayan. "The news is spreading from one truck to the next and jolting the soldiers awake as they take in the enormity of the accomplishment—they can't contain their joy."

Hod also reported that the air force had lost nineteen pilots: eight killed, the rest missing, perhaps captured. David Ben-Gurion received a more extensive report on casualties—forty killed, four hundred injured. Bar-Dayan wrote, "Four of our fallen soldiers lie on the ground near the tank, as if they are asleep." He noticed that one of them was fair-haired and wore paratroopers' boots.[25]

CHAPTER 13

DAY TWO

1. ELATION: "MY GOD! THE COUNTRY IS SUDDENLY SO LARGE"

The 7th Brigade and General Tal's other armored units kept moving, as did all of Ariel Sharon's and Avraham Yaffe's forces. Fighting also continued in the Gaza Strip. Yehoshua Bar-Dayan and his friends moved down the desert along the coastal route. On the way they saw an armored commando jeep with three dead soldiers inside. The vehicle had been hit head-on. The dead men were still seated in their positions, one with his green eyes open. One of them had died clutching the wheel, his gaze fixed on the winding strip of asphalt ahead. Along the road Bar-Dayan also saw the bodies of Egyptian soldiers. Two Israeli Mirages flew overhead, apparently chasing down the last few surviving Egyptian aircraft.[1]

At around two A.M. on the morning of June 6, Eshkol had authorized Dayan's priorities for the rest of the war: destroy the Egyptian armored corps; seize Sharm el-Sheikh, the Latrun Road, the Old City, and the entire West Bank; seize the Banias in the Golan Heights, Tel Azaziat, and the demilitarized zones on the Syrian border. The battle for the road to Mount Scopus had already begun.[2]

General Odd Bull told his superiors in New York about an exchange of fire along the Israeli-Syrian border. He reported that the Syrians were shelling Israeli communities. Still exiled from his headquarters, Bull was using the American consulate in Jerusalem as a base of communications.[3] Aharon Yariv told the government that the Syrian attacks on a few townships in the north were less severe than expected.[4]

Just before daylight, Abba Eban left his house in central Jerusalem. He was on his way to the UN General Assembly in New York, with the aim of delaying a cease-fire resolution for as long as possible: the IDF needed more time.[5] His wife, Suzy, walked him to the car. They hugged, and when they pulled back they felt something like a gust of wind pass between them at face level. According to Eban, it was a bullet or a piece of shrapnel.[6]

At four in the morning, Yigal Allon heard on BBC Radio that the war would soon be over. He was afraid it would end without the conquest of the Old City. He telephoned Eshkol, who told him to come to his office. When Allon reached the building, he found Menachem Begin there, too. Begin had heard the same news on the BBC and, after speaking with Dayan, had called Eshkol with the same question: "What about Jerusalem?" Allon and Begin went in to see Eshkol together and declared ceremoniously: "It is time." Allon later recalled that Eshkol responded positively and told the two ministers the topic was to be discussed at the cabinet meeting later that day.[7]

YEHOSHUA BAR-DAYAN AND HIS COMRADES REACHED THE JIRADI THAT MORNING, A SEries of Egyptian strongholds on the way to El Arish. Fortunately, the area had been seized by advance forces after a tough fight. El Arish itself was already taken. There was a damaged tank whose commander had been killed. The turret was covered with blood and human flesh. Someone pulled out a blanket and went into the tank to bring out the body. Two female soldiers were there, too. "Golden-haired girls, not yet nineteen, walking among the tanks and the dead soldiers," Bar-Dayan wrote.[8]*

Bar-Dayan and his friends spread out and waited. Another pickup truck was parked next to his own. The driver, a young soldier, could not stop crying. "It really is very hard not to cry here. My God, let it be over," wrote Bar-Dayan. The sobbing driver started beating his fists against his head, his tears turning to wails. The two women soldiers near to him did not say a word. An officer asked Bar-Dayan to try and calm the young soldier because he was damaging the morale of the others. His name was Sander; he was a military driver, and his boss was the man whose body

---

*The president's adviser Harry McPherson told Johnson about two "good-looking girls in uniform" who rode in the back of a jeep one day when he was in southern Israel. One was wearing a spangled purple bathing cap, the other an orange turban. They were on their way to the front with two brawny young sergeants. "Incidentally," McPherson added, "Israel at war destroys the prototype of the pale, scrawny Jew; the soldiers I saw were tough, muscular, and sun-burned."[9]

had just been extricated from the tank. Bar-Dayan was shocked to discover that the dead man was a regimental commander, not a tank driver as he had previously thought. It was Ehud Elad: he and Shuka had just eaten lunch together at Morris's in Beersheba. They had gone to kindergarten together in Kfar Saba. He had been a patient of Shuka's father, the local physician.

Major Elad, originally Eidelman, a resident of Ashkelon, was thirty-one when he died, leaving behind his wife, Hava. He was the commander of a regiment of Patton tanks. "We were friends," Shmuel Gorodish later recalled, and said Elad had a powerful sense of patriotism and a warm heart; he was strong and knew exactly what he wanted from himself, his subordinates, and his commanders. Tall, bespectacled, "very imposing," he was a strapping man who looked tough on the outside, but one IDF publication said that he was not really that way inside. He liked taking photographs, he played tennis, he dreamed of traveling to Europe. According to Gorodish, he loved his Patton.* Elad's tank took a direct hit in the battle for Jiradi. He had been in his usual position, his head and torso protruding from the turret, and was killed instantly. At first, the commander tried to repress the news of Elad's death, fearing his soldiers' reaction. It was not easy to quiet Sander the driver. Bar-Dayan told him Ehud would want him to be a man, not to cry during battle. He slowly calmed down.

The convoy was still parked, waiting for orders. Big flies buzzed around. "The distinctive smell of burned cars and scorched bodies stays with us," wrote Bar-Dayan. He saw a few prisoners and picked up a rumor: the Mirages he had seen before had already shot down two MiGs. Two large transport planes flew low overhead and the guys in the planes waved. The sun beat down and the flies harassed them. Gili had left him some packaged moist napkins. Refreshing. Breakfast: canned corn, pea soup, peanuts, Valencia oranges. More burned half-tracks, both Egyptian and Israeli; more thundering explosions. At ten-thirty, Bar-Dayan heard on the transistor that Latrun and Jenin had been captured, and he wrote, "Hussein started it, the fool, and now the scoundrel has got what was coming to him."

The Latrun region overlooked the road from Tel Aviv to Jerusalem. The failed attempts to capture this area during the War of Independence were imprinted in Israeli memory as one of the more traumatic losses in IDF

---

*Major Ehud Elad was posthumously promoted to the rank of lieutenant colonel and given a commendation for his courage and tenacity in the mission.[10]

history. The mission remained to be accomplished, whether by means of a "grab" or otherwise.[11] The conquest of Latrun, therefore, had great secular symbolic significance—much like Armon Hanatziv and Mount Scopus.

"You stand in this historical silence and pinch yourself—is this not a dream?" wrote Menahem Talmi in *Maariv*. "Is my mind playing tricks on me?" He remembered the War of Independence: "You see the battlefields from '48 and they lie before you like a living monument. In the attempt to reach the place in which you stand today, many hundreds of Israeli fighters died; their bodies lay scattered over this westward-sprawling expanse and bloated in the terrible burning heat. . . . My God! The country is suddenly so large!"[12]

Fighting in Jerusalem continued; just before noon, Dayan reached Mount Scopus. "No conquest in Sinai would have made up for the loss in prestige had Israel failed to take Mount Scopus," Uzi Narkis said afterward. Dayan reached Mount Scopus via the Latrun Road. He took note of the date: June 6, D-Day.[13] Ezer Weizman traveled with him. On the way to Mount Scopus they stopped at a local hotel, the Ambassador. Weizman, somewhat childishly, took a few pieces of the hotel stationery "for history's sake." They toured the abandoned lecture halls and labs of the old Hebrew University campus. "Time seemed to have stood still: the clock had stopped," wrote Weizman. They went into the lab once used by his uncle, Moshe, a chemistry professor. On the desk he found notes in his uncle's handwriting, on the blackboard an announcement of his next lecture, in 1948. Weizman imagined he could detect a strong odor of chemicals. His sister, Yael, had studied here. Someone found one of her old notebooks. Weizman thought of her son, David, who was with Sharon's troops on the way to the Suez Canal. Looking out over the breathtaking view from Mount Scopus, Weizman contemplated his sister and the great family drama she had triggered.

Ezer and his sister were the niece and nephew of Chaim Weizmann, the leader of the Zionist movement and the first president of Israel. In her youth, Yael was in love with Haim Laskov, who had eventually replaced Moshe Dayan as chief of staff. The young Ezer, at thirteen, was also enamored of Laskov, who was seventeen at the time. He wrote that Laskov had stolen a place in his heart: "muscular, healthy, strong, the epitome of sports and youth in Palestine." Laskov was "a god" to him, and Ezer "was drawn to him with a bond of friendship." So he was sorry when his sister broke up with him. And then a tragedy occurred: Yael fell in love with a British officer. Weizman referred to him as a "gentile" and felt that Yael and fate had dealt the family a dreadful blow. "I was all fire and brimstone," he wrote. "Father—his world collapsed." His status as Chaim Weizmann's brother enabled the father to arrange the British officer's transfer out of Palestine, but Yael's love for her captain only deepened. Her father threatened: "If you marry that goy, it will be your bitter end and mean being totally cut off from this house and from this people, like a traitor." Ezer was also hurt: "I thought she had betrayed the Jewish people, Zionism, our parents, our home, Israel, and me." Yael and the British captain married anyway. Only one man in the family did not cut her off, and even helped the couple: Yael's uncle Chaim, president of the World Zionist Organization. Yael's son, David, was born in 1945. At fifteen he had come to visit his uncle Ezer, now a senior commander in the air force, and at seventeen he moved to Israel and enlisted in the armored corps. On May 15, 1967, he was finishing an officers' training course. Weizman asked Shmuel Gorodish to give David a pistol that his father had left him with the instruction to give it to the first grandson to become an Israeli officer. "What a crazy world," Weizman thought. "How history turns out! Where is it, that invisible computer, which computes these whims and oddities, sticks together the ends and joins the links, where is it?"

Weizman himself eventually married Moshe Dayan's wife's sister. Now he sat with his brother-in-law and Narkis on Mount Scopus, the Old City before them, his head in the clouds.[14]

BEFORE THE IDF'S ENTRY INTO THE OLD CITY, UZI NARKIS WAS A FRUSTRATED MAN, constantly fighting for status in the army and his share of glory. In his memoirs, he complained about the Central Command's low rank in Dayan's list of priorities; the forces at his disposal were minimal and insufficient. There had been no planning for the West Bank or East Jerusalem; it all just snowballed, he claimed, as if he were unaware that a plan had existed. A man with academic pretensions and, later, political aspirations, Narkis commanded the National Defense College before the war. He was among the Palmah alumni who found it extremely difficult to come to terms with the failures of the army in the War of Independence, including its unsuccessful attempt to occupy the Old City. In 1948, Narkis had led an effort to break through to the Old City's Jewish Quarter and rescue the residents, who were besieged by the Jordanians. Its failure haunted an entire generation of Israelis, and was greatly associated with Narkis. Now he felt he was getting another chance.

"We're hoping for action," he wrote to his soldiers, and told them the people of Jerusalem remembered the Old City and wanted to return to it.[15] According to his diary, Narkis told Teddy Kollek, "You may yet be the mayor of a unified Jerusalem." That was on the first day of the war, at ten minutes past nine. A few hours later, Narkis ordered Mordechai Gur to break through to the route to Mount Scopus, take over the Rockefeller Museum area in East Jerusalem, and prepare to take the Old City. "Today Jerusalem will be liberated," he announced to his troops. "Today the IDF will erase a stain left on the map of our country twenty years ago, when our holy and ancient capital was torn from the heart of the nation." He described his soldiers as the heirs of the zealous warriors from the time of the Second Temple. "The soldiers of the Central Command have the great fortune to be entrusted with the liberation of the city of eternity, the city of David, the city of the past and the future. Today they stand at the heart of the country, the heart of the nation, the heart of history." The conquest of the West Bank, Narkis said, would fulfill the command's "deep longings." But Dayan denied Narkis permission to take over the Old City— "that Vatican," he called it—and ordered that it be encircled instead.[16]

By June 6, the war in Jerusalem had claimed dozens of lives. In battles for the Jordanian officers' school and a fortified target known as Ammunition Hill, not far from the border, many soldiers had died. Some were killed by friendly fire: they were mistakenly targeted by the air force. Narkis wrote, "It is very easy to make such mistakes." He put more pressure on the General Staff, saying that Israel would have only itself to blame if the Wall remained in Jordanian hands.[17]

King Hussein requested a cease-fire, even begged for one. Ambassador Barbour sent the Foreign Ministry the four telegrams he had received from Amman, the first at 5:25 that morning. In it, Hussein had announced that without an immediate cessation of fire, his regime was finished. Half an hour later, a second message arrived, saying that the king was not requesting a formal cease-fire, but merely imploring Israel to stop what he described as its punitive action against the Jordanian military. Just before seven, he again cautioned that he might lose control of events. The king's messages reached Jerusalem at eight in the morning. They presented an opportunity to stop—before hundreds of thousands of Palestinians came under Israeli control. Dean Rusk instructed Ambassador Barbour to convince Israel to ease up militarily so as not to bring down the king, but he did not demand that Israel refrain from occupying the West Bank. Barbour conveyed the request to Eshkol, but his impression was that it was too late: Israel no longer had any interest in keeping the king on his throne, not after he had bombed Jerusalem, Kfar Saba, Netanya, and other towns well within Israel. Neither Eshkol nor Dayan wanted a cease-fire. Not yet.[18]

Hen Ronen, a medic from Kibbutz Yehiam, remembered an earlier time when he had been preparing to occupy the Old City with his unit. At the last minute, that operation had been canceled. He recalled himself and his fellow soldiers waiting near the Mandelbaum Gate. "I was just a kid then, without a wife and children. I was a fighter. But today? The Old City?" The idea that he would be one of the soldiers who conquered Jerusalem frightened him. The alleyways were so narrow: "Someone could pour boiling water on you from the window and get you that way." Still, he admitted, Jerusalem was a dream.[19]

YEHOSHUA BAR-DAYAN'S CONVOY WAS MOVING "METER BY METER," AS HE WROTE. They had reached El Arish and headed south, toward Bir Lahfan, a place Bar-Dayan remembered from the Sinai Campaign ten years earlier. He recognized the open-air cinema that had served as a canteen. Nearby were dozens of overturned railway cars. He was impressed with the area's development since his last visit; now there were fields of casuarinas, olive groves, and greenery. He saw two crashed planes.

They stopped often, meeting other soldiers everywhere they went. "Where's the fighting?" asked Bar-Dayan. He was afraid, kissing his wedding ring often. He saw more and more Egyptian prisoners, hundreds of them. Many had put on blue and green pajamas over their uniforms, in an attempt to disguise themselves as civilians; some wore only their underwear, and many were barefoot. They walked with their hands up in the air, frightened. Bar-Dayan said to them, in Arabic, *"Wein hua Jamal Abdel Nasser?"* (Where is Nasser?) Then he hurled some juicy Arabic curses their way. Some of the Israeli soldiers took the prisoners' watches off their wrists and started fighting over the loot, something Bar-Dayan also remembered from the Sinai Campaign. One soldier got hold of a Russian assault rifle and proceeded to bang it against a train car until it went off and he got a bullet in the face. An Egyptian tank that looked abandoned suddenly came to life and leaped toward an IDF vehicle in a sort of suicide mission, injuring several people. It was demolished at close range with machine-gun and bazooka fire. They repaired the tank of the dead regimental commander, Ehud. It was not battle-ready, but would keep going anyway—"a horse with no horseman," as Bar-Dayan wrote.[20]

. . .

MANY ISRAELIS WERE STILL SITTING IN BOMB SHELTERS, BUT NEWS OF THE ARMY'S progress had traveled quickly and fed the day's headlines. "Tuesday was a day of increasingly joyful news," wrote Yosef Weitz. "There is a noticeable inclination to conquer the West Bank." Life in the bomb shelter was settling down. The neighbors set up a "commune" and ate their meals together. "The children are amusing themselves. Two-year-old Danny keeps everyone busy, whether with his screaming or his dancing. The older boy, around ten, follows the IDF moves on a map he hung on the wall, marking each spot in the Sinai and Jordan as it falls." Weitz himself could scarcely tear his eyes off the map: "I see in my mind that western Eretz Israel is being unified and the longing we have had since 1948, to reach the Jordan River, is about to come true. A great happiness fills my heart and soul." He hoped the Arabs would flee this time too, but feared it would not happen, and wrote worriedly, "How will we take in this mass?"[21]

In the bomb shelter at Kibbutz Ayelet Hashahar, the children heard about the capture of Jenin and the Dotan Valley. They were very excited, even though the Syrians had bombed their kibbutz earlier that day. They had just learned in school about how Joseph's brothers sold him into slavery. "They want us to call the army and ask whether they've found the pit Joseph was thrown into," wrote kibbutz member Ruth Geffen Dotan.[22] A woman in the bomb shelter at Kibbutz Ein Hanatziv wrote to her children in Los Angeles that there was no longer any reason for anger at Eshkol. Everything was falling into place.[23]

2. A GAMBLE: "I ADMIT I WAS A COWARD"

The cabinet convened in the afternoon. First the ministers heard that the pope had asked for Jerusalem to become an open city, which constituted yet another opportunity to avoid the conquest. According to Israel Lior, however, it was too late: "That day, it was clear to all the ministers and every IDF general that the wheel of war could no longer be turned back." It seems that, unlike Narkis, Lior saw not "snowballing" but rather a reasoned and pragmatic response: "Hussein made a historic error, and we will exploit it fully."[24]

This discussion was very different from the one prior to the decision to attack Egypt; it proceeded without fear. There was no more talk of the threat to Israel's existence; on the contrary, the ministers heard encouraging reports from Yariv, who said the Egyptian army was in complete disarray.

The director general of the Foreign Ministry, Arieh Levavi, reported on Hussein's telegrams, the most recent of which had arrived half an hour earlier. Hussein was prepared for a cease-fire, preferably to be kept secret, but he would accept a public statement if necessary. His petition necessitated a decision over whether to seize the West Bank or not.

Having settled in Palestine more than fifty years earlier, Levi Eshkol found it easy to view the nineteen-year-old Green Line as a temporary, artificial arrangement, the result of military failure. His address to the cabinet that day was characteristically ineloquent: "Given the new situation that has emerged we must contemplate new definitions of our security and political goals, which in my opinion must be directed toward changing the nature of Israeli-Arab relations as they have existed since 1948, and in light of the defeat of the Arab armies we must form a plan that will assure Israel's proper standing in the Middle East, while achieving permanent peace and border security."

Eshkol was familiar with the discussions conducted by the Mossad, the IDF, and the Foreign Ministry following the Samua operation. They had concluded that Israel's national interest lay in allowing Hussein to continue the process he had begun—to destroy Palestinian identity by integrating Palestinians into Jordan and encouraging them to emigrate. Eshkol knew that taking control of the West Bank would place a million Palestinians under Israeli rule, inevitably deepening their national identity and posing a danger to Israel's Jewish character. But to guide his government to decide not to seize the West Bank, Eshkol would have had to know, or at least presume, that Israeli rule would remain for a long time. Did he have any way of knowing that? Perhaps not. Only the night before, he had expressed the view that Israel would have to give back the West Bank and Jerusalem. Perhaps he thought the West Bank would serve as a bargaining chip. He may have hoped the bargaining would lead to peace, with better borders and access to the Western Wall. In light of the past, he may have been anticipating a mass flight of Palestinians.

Meanwhile, the conquest was progressing rapidly and with relative ease, and there was ever greater temptation to take over the areas Ben-Gurion had failed to seize in the War of Independence. The destruction of the Egyptian air force and the initial successes in the West Bank had produced ecstatic headlines in the papers. "With All Forces of Body and Spirit—to Victory!" declared *Ha'aretz*. "Well Done! Well Done!" praised *Maariv*.[25]

At times Eshkol seemed like a gambler in a casino who tells himself, "I can stop any time I want"—and keeps on gambling. The party, the press, and the ranks of Holocaust-haunted Israelis who had taken the Defense

Ministry away from him because he had hesitated to send the IDF to war would not forgive him now if he denied them this great victory. From his vulnerable position, Eshkol was already thinking of the next round: the war over fame. Yaacov Herzog observed that he spoke slowly and indistinctly. He was faced with three ministers whose influence was greater than his own—Allon, Begin, and Dayan.

Allon offered the government an entire philosophy, evidently formulated before the war. They should strive to negotiate with Hussein. If that did not succeed, they should turn the West Bank into an autonomous region with economic ties to Israel. Meanwhile, the Old City should be conquered but not formally annexed. The Syrian border must be amended, which meant controlling the Banias. Israel should hold all the territories until a political settlement was reached, "even for months or years." They should not give up Gaza, but look for ways to get the refugees out of there.

Begin said that taking the West Bank meant "liberating the eastern part of western Eretz Israel," and demanded expanding the conquest to include the Jordan River, but not the land beyond it. He asserted that Israel should control the Old City, and was quick to suggest that the entire government, along with the two chief rabbis, should go to the Western Wall and recite a prayer. "The Christian world will understand that," he said. Begin also addressed the issue of the residents of the territories, whom he clearly wanted to leave. But he spoke cautiously, saying Israel must do everything possible so that "the Arabs are moved in a humane way."

Dayan suggested taking Sharm el-Sheikh, occupying the ranges of hills in the West Bank (but without descending to the Jordan), and encircling the Old City but not entering it immediately. In response to an objection from Begin, he added, however, that the IDF could enter the Old City at any time once the government gave the word. Dayan also hoped that fighting could be avoided. He believed that the people of the city would raise white flags and ask the army to enter. "Jerusalem has seen a lot of war and destruction in its day. We must try, as much as possible, to take the city peacefully," he wrote. According to Ben-Gurion, Dayan did not believe Israel would be allowed to keep the Old City. "Moshe does not want to take it because he doesn't want to have to give back the Western Wall," he wrote; he had heard this from one of Dayan's assistants.[26] In his own memoirs, Dayan claimed the question was not whether to conquer Jerusalem, but how and when.[27]

This was the decisive moment. If Eshkol truly believed that conquering the West Bank made sense so as to gain a bargaining chip, he should have in that case stopped short of taking the Old City. He should have known that no Israeli government, certainly not his own, would be able to give up the Old City, and that there was no chance that Hussein would give up his own claim, either. The seizure of Jerusalem threatened to return the situation to the stalemate that had preceded the war: once again, there would in fact be nothing to offer the Arabs. But Eshkol and the ministers did not ask themselves why, exactly, it was to Israel's benefit to control the Old City, as if that point were taken for granted. Haim Moshe Shapira and Zalman Aran feared that Israel would find itself in a difficult position, particularly in relation to the Christian world, but no one rejected the dream. At the center of the debate was not political logic, but an eruption of feelings, as if those present had suddenly found the light hidden within, had suddenly seen the truth and grasped what they had always known, whether secular or religious: that the Old City was the true Zion, the grail for which the nation had yearned for two thousand years, the rock of its foundation.

Israel Lior noted that the whole discussion proceeded in an improvised way, with no organized or systematic process, with no working papers. The ministers did not examine all the alternatives. They could, for example, have confined the IDF to opening the route to the Wall without seizing the entire city; this, they could have claimed, was in accordance with the 1949 truce agreement.

Mindful of their place in politics and history, some of the ministers who had supported waiting now tried to justify their hesitancy. "I admit I was a coward," said Shapira, but claimed that the delay had strengthened Israel's position with Johnson. Dayan admitted that the postponement was perhaps a blessing, but had the Egyptians begun the war and bombed Israel's air bases, seizing the Sinai would have cost "not thousands, but tens of thousands of lives."

Although he had joined the government, Dayan had not changed his view: he believed Eshkol should not be prime minister. Dayan had little faith in Eshkol's ability to run the country. "It was the first time I had to act without having an authority above me," he wrote. He was subject to the government and the prime minister, and, as he said, "security decisions depend on political decisions." But in reality, "and especially morally speaking," Dayan identified a profound difference between his role as chief of staff in the Sinai Campaign and his current status: then, he had answered to Ben-Gurion.[28] Now, Dayan did not first consult Eshkol about every move, and once or twice he sought government approval for actions that had already been taken; he simply kept Eshkol in the picture. Herzog noted that Dayan was irritable and rude during the cabinet meeting. He dozed some of the time, then gave vent to an angry outburst in which he told his colleagues that this was no time for a symposium. At other moments he seemed reasonable and considerate. Arieh Levavi passed Herzog a note saying that Dayan was like Dr. Jekyll and Mr. Hyde. Dayan sat at the end of the table, at a distance from the other ministers. Whether he intended it or not, he left the impression that he did not consider himself part of the group, according to Herzog. The meeting ended with no clear conclusion, but there was a sort of unspoken agreement with Dayan's position. No one had disputed his ideas.

Before leaving the meeting, Shapira asked to issue a special instruction to soldiers to exercise caution in dealing with Arab civilians and their property. He reminded the government of the Kafr Kassem incident during the Sinai Campaign. Dayan rejected the request: a special instruction would be interpreted as an admission that the soldiers were not acting properly, he said; then he left. Eshkol asked Dayan to come back and said he agreed with the request to be especially strict about appropriate behavior toward Arab civilians.

Hen Ronen from Kibbutz Yehiam was already in the center of Ramallah. "No one returned our fire," he later recounted. "They hid. White flags everywhere. A feeling of surrender. There would be nothing to tell. The radio station: now it was ours. And it was so easy. We didn't do any work!"[29] The takeover of Ramallah's popular radio station prompted particular excitement in many of the soldiers, symbolizing as it did a secular importance similar to Armon Hanatziv, Mount Scopus, and Latrun. One soldier recalled that while still preparing for the operation, they had been listening to a particularly captivating Jordanian DJ as she accompanied Adamo's "Tombe la Neige" with her silky whisper.[30] Meanwhile, fighting around the Old City walls was in full swing.

Haimito Mosowitz, also from Yehiam, was a paratrooper. He and his friends had been assigned to occupy El Arish, but instead were brought up from the south to Jerusalem. They penetrated the eastern part of the city, near the Mandelbaum Gate. "It was a little chaotic," Mosowitz recalled. He was cold. He asked the other men if they also felt the cold, but they did not. It must have been fear. Mosowitz was with the forces that broke through the Jordanian fortifications in the area of Ammunition Hill. He remembered one injured soldier almost entirely covered with blood. His face had been hit and his chin was coming off. "Our flak helmets had this kind of strap that protected your chin. So I put it on his chin. I held the flesh in place, put the strap on it and started crawling with him." They crawled along that way for fifty yards or so. "I told him, Don't be nervous, everything will be fine, calm down—he was pretty nervous, didn't know what to do. He thought he was going to die soon." Mosowitz started talking to him, and the soldier asked where he was from, having recognized Mosowitz's accent as South American; he himself was from Uruguay. "We were so happy," Mosowitz recounted. Bombs were falling all around. They crawled into a tunnel and found a medic with an eye injury. Mosowitz bandaged the medic, then went to get a stretcher. He laid his wounded soldier on the stretcher and, together with two other men, took him to a car that was evacuating casualties to Hadassah Hospital. The car was full and they barely found room.

Mosowitz kept on fighting. There were snipers everywhere. "I threw my bazooka away because I had no rounds left. I took an Uzi and some hand grenades. I took an ammunition clip from an injured soldier and went to clean out some houses." Mosowitz described how this was done: "First, when you go into the house, you open the door and throw in a grenade. I mean, not right away like that, because we had defense grenades, meaning four-and-a-half-second fuses. And it's pretty dangerous to throw them because if someone's inside, he can throw them back out and we could get killed." He went into one of the houses, waited a little, and threw the grenade. "I went in, of course I fired a round, and then I saw a pair of elderly Jordanians, dead. Well, of course it wasn't pleasant for me to see that and of course that wasn't my intention and . . . well."[31]

Besides seizing the hills in the West Bank, Bethlehem, and Ramallah, the government also decided on various "land grabs" in the demilitarized zones between Israel and Syria, without violating the international border.[32] Dayan ruled out occupation of the Golan Heights, including the Banias, for fear of a Soviet response. Political considerations also motivated him not to approach the Suez Canal. The ministers continued to monitor responses in Washington. Levavi concluded that the Americans would allow Israel to "finish the job."* Ben-Gurion was also receiving constant updates on the developments. "America wants us to finish off Nasser quickly," he wrote.[33]

BUT "AMERICA" WAS NOT SPEAKING WITH ONE VOICE. AT THE BEGINNING OF THE WAR, the United States had demanded to know who had fired the first shot.

---

*Levavi complained about Dayan's radio address the night before: his announcement that the Egyptian planes had been destroyed on the ground made it difficult for Israel to claim the Egyptians had attacked first and impeded the ongoing efforts to convince the world that Israel had not fired the first shot. Dayan admitted that his statement was "a blunder," and noted two more: the leak in France and the news of the air attack given on Kol Israel in Arabic.

Eban and Amit lied and claimed the Egyptians had started it; the lie may have been made with a nod and a wink.[34] Either way, "the great lie" that most troubled the Americans was not this, but rather the Arab claim that U.S. aircraft had taken part in the assault on Egypt. The telegrams exchanged on this issue reflect panic and a concerted effort to show the Arabs that the accusation was unfounded.[35] Israeli intelligence picked up, recorded, and published a telephone conversation between Nasser and Hussein, in which the two coordinated a story whereby the United States and Britain had participated in the attack. The conversation transcript was truncated and did not prove unequivocally that the statement was a lie: in any case, in light of the magnitude of their defeat Nasser and Hussein may well have truly believed that Israel had not acted alone, as even Dayan conceded.[36]

Dean Rusk tried to effect a cease-fire in the West Bank, if possible before Jerusalem was conquered, but even as the battles raged, he asked Ambassador Barbour what kind of settlement he thought Israel would agree to. Would it accept an agreement over traffic through the Straits of Tiran? What were its objectives in Gaza? And in the West Bank? At the State Department, proposals were already being drafted.[37]

Johnson himself was troubled by an announcement issued by the State Department on the first day of the war, saying that the United States was taking a neutral position "in thought, word, and deed." The announcement provoked a storm of protest because it read as if the United States had abandoned Israel to its fate, and Rusk was forced to "clarify" it. Johnson later saw fit to include this episode in his presidential memoirs. It marked the beginning of a wave of public pressure to stand by Israel. At no other time could Johnson have been more certain that when it came to Israel, there was no distinction between foreign policy and domestic policy.[38] For no sooner had the State Department spokesman finished his neutrality announcement than Johnson received a piece of legal advice from a friend: David Ginsburg called to direct his attention to the fact that invocation of the Neutrality Act would bar Israel from raising money for its war effort in the United States.[39] The president's advisers quickly contacted some of his Jewish supporters.[40]

John Roche, a Boston professor described as Johnson's intellectual in residence, sent him a firm letter that opened with a quote from the Book of Isaiah: "If favor is shown to the wicked, he does not learn righteousness; in the land of uprightness he deals perversely." The neutrality declaration had proven to Roche that State Department officials wanted to "kiss some Arab backsides." He found this to be "worse than unprincipled—it is stupid. The Arabs have to hate us—and the rougher the Israelis are on them, the more they will hate us NO MATTER WHAT WE DO. They must create the myth that the United States, not Israel single-handed, clobbered them." The Americans' "sweet-talking" of the Arabs would only make them view the United States with contempt and alienate American Jews.[41]

Johnson hated being pressured in this way, according to Roche.[42] The White House log documents the president's response to a commentary he overheard on a special CBS broadcast, in which the analyst took a pro-Israel position. "It's easy to tell that he has some sort of Jewish background," Johnson observed.[43] Levinson and Wattenberg, two Jewish assistants who advised the president to issue an announcement of support for Israel, got an earful from him in the hallway. "You Zionist dupes!" he yelled at them and raised his fist. "You're Zionist dupes in the White House."[44] By the evening of that day, he had received 17,445 letters and telegrams from citizens responding to the war. Ninety-eight percent of them supported Israel, approximately two percent warned him against intervening in the war, and only a handful expressed support of the Arabs.[45]

IN ISRAEL, NIGHT HAD FALLEN ON THE SECOND DAY OF THE WAR, AND DAYAN summed up the situation: Sharon and Yaffe's forces were progressing in Sinai. Along the El Arish–Bir Lahfan axis, on which Yehoshua Bar-Dayan was moving, there was heavy fighting. The Egyptians had lost about three hundred tanks. On the Jordanian front the war had essentially been won. Only three cities had not yet been captured—Nablus, Hebron, and Jericho—but they were encircled. The air force had shot down twenty-three more planes, about half Egyptian and half Iraqi, and had lost five of its own. The number of Israeli dead had reached 460: 225 in the south and 235 on the West Bank.[46]

The commander of Southern Command distributed General Order No. 2 among his troops: "Never before have so few pilots destroyed so many aircraft in such a short time." He urged them to keep up the good work: "Follow the enemy and strike him down, hit him again and again, until he is defeated by the sword of the fighters of the Southern Command," he wrote.[47]

CHAPTER 14

DAY THREE

1. TEARS: "I'M TOUCHING THE KOTEL!"

The sun rose large over the low hilltops in the east, wrote Yehoshua Bar-Dayan on the morning of his third day of war, Wednesday, June 7. He looked to the north—home. They had coffee and chocolate wafers for breakfast; he gobbled down about fifteen, calling them "the IDF's secret weapon." They had stopped across from Jebel Libni, just before Abu Agila. On the way there, he had witnessed a scene unlike anything he had ever seen before: dozens of Egyptian vehicles, tanks, APCs, and long-barreled cannons, exploding and burning. The roadside was littered with piles of discarded shoes. "These are Nasser's heroes who wanted to destroy us," he wrote. Since the Sinai Campaign, the abandoned shoes of Egyptian soldiers had come to stand as a symbol of their mediocrity.

Bar-Dayan moved in a small convoy of tank repairmen. A convoy coming toward them brought the news that the defeated Egyptians were still fighting, the bastards. Suddenly a rumor went around: someone swore he had seen paratroopers. The soldiers took up their positions and waited. Two planes flew over; Bar-Dayan was not sure whether they were Israel's or the enemy's. Nothing happened. He listened to the radio with a fellow soldier, Benjamin Cohen. The Security Council had proclaimed a cease-fire, which was welcomed by Abba Eban. There was no demand for a withdrawal. This made Bar-Dayan and his friend happy. "I hope it is over," he wrote.[1]

When Menachem Begin heard about the Security Council resolution he phoned Eshkol again to ask about the Old City. Eshkol called Dayan, and soon Begin did the same. Dayan replied impatiently that he did not need their advice; the IDF was doing all it could. That morning, he ordered that the Old City be taken as quickly as possible.[2]

Mordechai Gur's paratroopers had already reached the Mount of Olives, seized the stone tower of Augusta Victoria, built by the last German kaiser for his wife, and shelled the Muslim Quarter inside the Old City. The battle for Jerusalem involved many mishaps that led to IDF casualties. Gur wrote in his diary that he received orders to enter the Old City through the Lions' Gate at 8:04. At 10:00 he announced, "The Temple Mount is ours!" His radio code name was "Student."[3]

The first thing Gur saw at the Temple Mount plaza, to the right of the gold-domed building, was a motorcycle blocking the way. Behind it were the yellow tents of a Jordanian military camp. He did not know whether there were any soldiers in the camp nor what the motorcycle was doing there. "Will it blow us all up?" he wondered. The correct response would have been to stop the car and check out the situation, but what the conqueror of the Old City did was typical of the whole operation. "Ben-Zur, go!" he ordered his driver. They looked each other in the eye, Gur wrote later. "His eyes glittered with determination and excitement. We're on the motorbike. Our eyes are shut. An explosion? The half-track shudders—but only from the impact. We hear the motorbike dragging beneath the half-track's wheels."

The soldiers who followed Gur could not restrain their joy. "Hugging, yelling, overwhelmed, slapping each other on the back. Laughing, shouting, hugging again," wrote Gur. "I feel at home here. The object of our longing. The Temple Mount! Mount Moriah. Abraham and Isaac. The Temple. The Zealots, the Maccabees, Bar Kokhba, the Romans and the Greeks. They all tumbled together in my mind. But the feeling is steady and deeper than anything. We are on the Temple Mount! The Temple Mount is ours!"

Someone climbed to the top of the building and raised the Israeli flag. Others ran to find access to the Western Wall. They spied a spiral staircase and climbed down, and then the call rang out: "It's the Kotel! It's the Kotel!" They stopped: to their right rose up a massive wall. "Huge stones sprouting bushes," wrote Gur. "The wall of prayer, the wall of tears. We are dreaming. . . ." They looked for a way to reach the top so they could fly the flag there, too. They went back to the Temple Mount plaza and ran to the left, searching for the way. When they reached a gate, they broke through. A young man appeared with two women, one white and one black; the man was a Jew who had converted to Islam. He directed them to the top of the wall and they staked the flag. An officer pulled out a bottle of whiskey. "He'd thought about it ahead of time," wrote Gur. They opened the bottle and made a toast, passing the whiskey from hand to hand. "*L'haim!* To the state of Israel and the Western Wall!"[4]

AMONG THE SOLDIERS WHO ENTERED THE OLD CITY WITH GUR WAS HAIMITO Mosowitz from Yehiam. "We saw no enemy troops because they'd all run away. Only a few snipers were left, and a few who behaved like men and fought to the end. The others picked themselves up and fled. And the ones who couldn't get away dressed up as civilians. We saw their mortars with all their explosives ready for a fight, but no one was there. They'd left everything and ran. Almost at the last minute. Because we saw the explosives just thrown down next to the mortars. They didn't even load them."[5]

Uzi Narkis and Haim Bar-Lev hurried to the Old City in a jeep. On the way they saw General Shlomo Goren, the chief rabbi of the IDF, on foot with a few of his men, carrying a Torah scroll and a shofar. They all went in through the Lions' Gate. "I grabbed an Arab kid and asked him how to get to the Temple Mount," Narkis recounted. The motorcycle Gur had trampled was still there. They passed by a monument in memory of Abdel Khader Husseini, a Palestinian commander killed in 1948; Narkis had been the one who found his body. They reached the wall, where they drank whiskey and sang "Hatikva." Goren blew the shofar and kissed Bar-Lev. When Narkis asked how the kiss was, Bar-Lev replied, "I've had better." Many of the men were crying, including the Kol Israel broadcaster Rafi Amir. "I am not a religious man, and I am touching the Kotel," he sobbed into the microphone, "I'm touching the Kotel!"[6]

Haimito Mosowitz recounted: "Of course I went to the Western Wall to see it. And as soon as I go there—I see Rabbi Goren with a Torah scroll in one arm, a bottle of wine in the other, and he's drinking and toasting *l'haim*. So happy. I really wasn't pleased, I had no idea where he'd come from. We were the first forces there, of course, with the half-tracks, and then suddenly I see he's turned up at the Kotel, crying and drinking, really happy. I saw that there were some soldiers crying at the wall. Religious ones. They were praying. I was very angry. I felt nothing. I thought, Because of this so many people had to die? Then to hell with all the religious people. I wanted them all to die. Because I was very upset."

Then there was the "game," Mosowitz said: hunting for prisoners. He came across a man wearing civilian clothes with military boots. The man spoke a little Hebrew, and he said to Mosowitz, "Don't be scared, I won't do anything to you." Mosowitz thought he had misheard. "He—*he*—was telling me! I look at him, I don't know, what a character: he says that to me! And me with an Uzi and him with no weapon. I checked." Mosowitz ordered his prisoner to put his hands up, but the man kept telling him not to be afraid because he wouldn't hurt him. "Then I started losing my temper. I told him, Come on, put your hands up. And he was still laughing at me, doing like this—scratching his head. So I took my Uzi and with the butt I hit him on the head. He fell over. Of course I didn't mean to hit him that hard. He was injured. I bandaged him and took him away."[7]

DAYAN INFORMED ESHKOL ABOUT THE CAPTURE OF THE OLD CITY. ESHKOL WENT INTO consultation and said the military operation Israel had initiated had saved the country. In his memoirs, Dayan could not restrain himself: "When Eshkol said that, with pathos and pride, I wondered to myself whether he remembered that only three days before the military action, he had explained to the General Staff all the virtues of waiting."[8] The Knesset Foreign Affairs and Defense Committee heard similar statements from Eshkol, as well as his expression of hope that the conquered territories would open up "political horizons" that would improve Israel's position in the Middle East.

Eshkol gathered the members of his party's political committee. "We've been given a good dowry," he told them, referring to the territories, "but it comes with a bride we don't like"—the Palestinians. There was no choice but to give the Palestinians "special status." At that point he was ready to keep Gaza under Israeli control. "I have a great desire for Gaza," he had said while the war was still raging, "perhaps because of Samson and Delilah." But Gaza too, in his words, was "a rose with many thorns."[9] A committee of experts was already looking for areas where refugees could be settled. Of the West Bank, Eshkol said that the border would be at the Jordan River, and without peace Israel would not budge. The ministers reached two decisions: to seize all of the West Bank to the Jordan River, as Begin had demanded, and to take the demilitarized zones along the Syrian border. Eshkol said repeatedly that he also wanted the Banias. "There was a stormy argument," wrote Herzog.[10]

But before opening the third front in the north, Dayan was winning the war over history. Israel Lior, always loyal, wanted Eshkol to visit the

Western Wall right away, but was told by Dayan's office that it was too dangerous: there were snipers, it was impossible to get there. Meanwhile, Dayan rushed to Jerusalem in a helicopter and made sure the IDF photographer immortalized his entrance into the Old City with Rabin and Narkis. The photographer later recalled that Dayan had staged the picture carefully, attributing great importance to it—just like Allenby, the British general who had wrested Jerusalem from the Turks in 1917.

"We have returned to the most holy of our places," said Dayan at the wall. "We have returned, never to part from them again." The soldiers, and quite a few civilians who had managed to reach the site, welcomed his statement with roars of happiness, the photographer reported. He confirmed that there were still exchanges of gunfire in the area.[11] Meir Shamgar, the military advocate general, directed Dayan's attention to the flag flying over the Dome of the Rock, and Dayan ordered that it be removed.[12]

Lior, like Eshkol, was extremely angry: "Dayan stole the glory and it was impossible to erase that from the pages of history written in Jerusalem that day. There was nothing to do. Eshkol was left with a minor role." Lior was also angry at himself for his own naïveté in falling for Dayan's tricks. "He left not a smidgen of fame for anyone else—not even for Yitzhak Rabin, who was there in the photos and at the speeches like a back-seat driver in the chariot of history." Eshkol arrived later that evening. Thousands of citizens were already swarming the area. Eshkol said he saw himself as an emissary of the entire Jewish people. "The photographers took pictures," wrote Lior, "history recorded Eshkol's words—but they were merely a footnote. Dayan took us for a ride."* The rest of the cabinet was also furious.[14]

Ezer Weizman missed the historical photo op, too. That morning, he was hoping to reap the glory of capturing Sharm el-Sheikh, guarding the entrance to the Straits of Tiran and thus the reason for the war, so he joined up with the forces on the way there. When he arrived, he was "unbelievably surprised" to find that the navy had beaten everyone to it and the area was already empty of Egyptians, who had all fled. Weizman could scarcely conceal his disappointment, but he tried to contact Dayan to convey the news that the Straits were in Israel's hands, open to

---

*Lior was right: Dayan's speech at the Kotel was published the next day on the front page of *Ha'aretz* alongside his picture. Eshkol's statement ran with a small headline, beneath Dayan's piece and with no picture. *Maariv* published Eshkol's speech in a modest inset at the bottom of the third page.[13]

Israeli shipping. He was told that the message could not be relayed; Dayan was at the Western Wall.

"I crashed," Weizman later wrote. "This time I really crashed." He said to someone at his side, "My lousy luck! For years I've been going on about the Kotel. For years I've dreamed of it. And now, at this great historic moment, when everyone's at the Kotel, where am I? Stuck at the farthest outpost of the war. . . . I lost out on one of the greatest moments in Israeli history—a moment I dreamed of more than the others, who've all had their pictures taken by the Kotel."[15]

General Yeshayahu Gavish was also upset. When he heard on the radio about the conquest of Jerusalem, he was somewhere near remote Bir Gafgafa in the Sinai; he got out of his car, sat down on a rock, and shed a few tears. "They stole the show," he said. Then he spurred his soldiers on: "To the canal!"[16]

2. PRISONERS: "THEY LIE THERE, CUT DOWN"

While at Sharm el-Sheikh, Weizman saw many prisoners of war: "I see these Egyptians with their hands tied behind their backs, crouched on their knees on the ground. Pathetic enemy soldiers, beaten down, humiliated, lonely. It's a sad sight," he wrote. He ordered his men to give them food and water. One of the prisoners caught his eye and Weizman asked that his hands be untied. "A Sudanese, he was. Tall, strong, kind of solid. He had interesting features, all dark brown." He drank, ate, and looked at Weizman, who thought, "What business does he have with this war? Why is he here?" The prisoner was emotional as they spoke. He took out a photograph of his wife and daughter and, hesitantly, unsure of Weizman's reaction, held it out. Weizman looked at the picture. "A tranquil calm, beyond the war, the general of the victorious army stands in far-off Sharm and rests his eyes on a picture of the wife and daughter of a beaten, defeated Sudanese prisoner."

Some time later, Weizman visited a POW internment facility with Rabin and saw the man from Sharm. "I stop. I look again. It's him, dammit. Tall, handsome, dark." He asked for the man to be brought to him. "I have some sort of connection with him, beyond the fog of war, beyond all the wars, all the hatred, all the animosity between peoples. We almost embraced—almost, because thousands of eyes turned to us from every direction." Weizman was glad to find the man unhurt. He asked Weizman whether he could be assigned to a kitchen job. "I arranged it," Weizman wrote. The man thanked him. "The word of a defeated corporal," Weizman wrote.[17]*

Many Israeli soldiers and officers described personal encounters with enemy soldiers. The reports express a range of feelings from compassion to hostility, contempt, alienation, and, in particular, indifference. The Israelis were often able to view the men as not merely "the enemy," but also as human beings, reminding themselves that the defeated soldiers before them were not personally responsible for their leaders' initiation of the war. They often described the prisoners' wretchedness, not only as captives but also as fighters. Hen Ronen from Yehiam told of four prisoners he saw in the West Bank. "Hands tied at their backs, feet bound, led like dogs to interrogation. . . . They're terrible cowards. They're terrible sycophants. You meet this creature who is just like you, after all . . . and his hands are tied behind his back. . . ."[19] Uri Chizik, also from Yehiam, wrote, "Where I was, their treatment was certainly decent. They got water and cigarettes, a little food—whatever we could give them." Chizik saw them in the Sinai. "Thousands of soldiers wandered on foot in the direction of the canal, all at risk of death from dehydration. All the abandoned cars along the road had empty radiators. The Egyptians had taken the water to drink."[20]

The captives began to take up an increasingly central role in Yehoshua Bar-Dayan's war experience. "The Egyptian soldiers who hadn't been killed and hadn't abandoned their tanks took off their shoes and started running across the sand," he wrote to his wife. "If they had any sense, they turned themselves in immediately as POWs, and there are several thousand of them. But the ones who tried to escape on foot, or who weren't taken prisoner during the battle, kept moving barefoot toward the canal. The heat and the thirst finished them, and they started streaming toward our cars, our tanks, flocks upon flocks of people coming down from the sandy hills." In his diary, Bar-Dayan wrote, "Good Lord, what are we going to do with them?" They looked depressed, apathetic; some crawled on all fours; he saw them in the internment camps too, fainting from thirst, even dying.

The low point came on Friday. "After five days of hunger and thirst, the soldiers and officers were calling out from every hilltop, they had no

---

*Israel was holding roughly five thousand Egyptian POWs, including some 480 officers. Dayan met with them as well. Earlier, he had suggested to the government that they return most of the prisoners to Egypt and keep holding only the officers. The government rejected his proposal, fearing the POWs would go back to war.[18]

strength—water, water, water." According to Bar-Dayan, the soldiers gathered the prisoners, searched them, and took their papers. He heard some of them say, "Water—get it from Nasser, he'll give you some." He wrote, "They see our water canteens and lose their minds. It's a terrible thing to see."

Bar-Dayan and his friends did not have enough water themselves. There was a heat wave, and they were often thirsty. The Egyptians were close to death. "Dozens of young and not so young men yelling, 'Water!,' writhing in their holding pens—'please, captain, a little water.'" Soldiers gave out tin canisters of water. Some of the prisoners were first required to curse Nasser, and some cursed his mother too. Bar-Dayan noticed one prisoner who kept his wits about him and seemed to lose not a trace of dignity. He positioned himself as the leader, making requests on everyone's behalf, passing the water can to others before drinking himself.

Bar-Dayan saw a man who had been with him and Gila when they ate lunch in Beersheba— he was the one who ate rice because he had diarrhea, he reminded Gila in his letter. The man's truck was now being used to transport prisoners. Bar-Dayan went over to say hello. There was an Egyptian nearby, wearing brown civilian pants. "A sweet, handsome young man, writhing this way and that, he lifted his undershirt, wailed and shouted in every direction with what little strength he had left." The Egyptian addressed Bar-Dayan in English: "Captain, please, give me some water. I'm dying. I haven't had a drink for five days. I'm not a soldier, I'm an engineer. Two weeks ago I came home from England, please help me." He was twenty-four and studied mine engineering in Lancashire. Bar-Dayan pictured him taking part in the Arab students' union, slandering Israel, probably supporting resolutions calling for Israel's destruction. He knew them, the Arab students in England. But he told the prisoner that he had also been in Lancashire, and they swapped memories. Bar-Dayan found a can full of sand, cleaned it out, filled it with half the water from his own canteen, and gave it to the young man. When he turned to leave, the man cried out, "Captain, please give me some more if you can, just another bit." Bar-Dayan gave him another bit. "I saved his life," he wrote.

Bar-Dayan described a guard who "went nuts." First he bound the prisoners' wrists so tightly that their circulation was cut off. Then he picked up a bayonet, killed one man and injured two others. "Everyone was shocked," Bar-Dayan wrote. "He'll certainly be brought to trial, but when you see thousands of dead people—suddenly life becomes cheap, to the point where it's hard to describe how cheap it is."[21] In his diary, Bar-Dayan wrote about other soldiers who killed prisoners. He saw bodies.

"They lie there, cut down." Some of the soldiers told him, "Any prisoner who shows up—that's it, he's dead."[22]

"It was perhaps the cruelest possible war, from our point of view," Uri Chizik later said. "Our soldiers were sent to scout out groups of men fleeing and shoot them. That was the order, and it was done while they were really trying to escape. If they were armed, they got shot. There was no other option. You couldn't even really take prisoners. And sometimes you had to finish people off when they were lying on the ground with their heads on their hands. Simply shoot them." Chizik recalled that the men talked about this even as the war was still going on, trying to explain to themselves why they had to kill Egyptian soldiers who were trailing them just for water. "They may not have been dangerous militarily, but they were desperate and dying, and a dying man is capable of anything." They found it difficult to define for themselves the moment when a soldier became a prisoner, and they knew that sometimes Egyptian soldiers surrendered but then attacked their captors. "There was one prisoner who put up his hands and then threw two grenades and killed eight of our men," Chizik said.* He said that some of the Palestinians serving in the Egyptian army "were executed." These were men suspected of prior attacks on Israel.[24]

Gabi Brunn, a reporter for *Yediot Aharonot*, witnessed such an episode. It occurred at the El Arish airport, where Israel Tal's division—Yehoshua Bar-Dayan's unit—had set up its headquarters. Some 150 POWs were being held in an aircraft hanger surrounded with sandbags. They sat huddled on the ground with their hands at the backs of their necks. Not far away was a desk where two men in IDF uniform were sitting. They wore steel helmets and their faces were hidden by dust goggles and khaki bandannas. Every so often the military police would pick out a prisoner from the holding pen and lead him to the desk. Brunn could not hear the brief exchange, but he saw that when it was finished, the prisoner was led about a hundred yards behind the hanger and handed a shovel.

"I watched the man dig a large pit for about fifteen minutes," Brunn wrote. "Then the officers told him to throw away the shovel and one of them aimed an Uzi submachine gun and fired two short bursts at the man, three or four bullets each. The prisoner fell dead." Then more prisoners were brought out and shot. Brunn saw roughly ten such executions. An

---

*At the request of the Foreign Ministry, the IDF spokesman gathered information about a few similar cases from all fronts of the war.[23]

officer whose identity Brunn could not recall then explained to the horrified reservists that military intelligence had identified some Palestinian terrorists among the POWs in the holding pen, men who had killed Jews. They had disguised themselves as Egyptian soldiers and fled the Gaza Strip.*

Brunn only published this story many years later, when it accompanied an account of the same incident by the historian Arieh Yitzhaki.[26] But rumors of prisoner killings were circulating within days. "We've turned the Sinai Peninsula into a valley of death, into one big cemetery," wrote soldier Kobi Rabinowitz, from Kibbutz Na'an, to his girlfriend. "Unarmed men, prisoners with their hands above their heads, cut down against orders. . . . I've seen too many murders to shed any tears." Yet he was clearly shocked, writing: "Apparently it doesn't take years of Nazi education to turn people into animals."[27]

Ten members of Kibbutz Ga'aton, near Yehiam, turned to Meir Yaari, the leader of Mapam, whom they considered a moral authority. They wrote to him about soldiers home from the war who told stories of systematic killings of enemy prisoners, particularly in the Sinai Desert. The stories were precise and came from reliable kibbutz members. They also told of tens of thousands of people wandering through the desert without food or water, destined to die horrible deaths "that only Holocaust survivors can describe." Yaari advised them not to make too much of these tales. He himself was not indifferent to human rights, he promised—for example, he had interfered with a military governor who had expelled a group of people, leaving them without food, and thanks to his intervention the decree had been rescinded and the people had returned to their homes. "In every war there are aberrations," he concluded, explaining that at least some of these "aberrations" occurred in response to mine-laying and sniping from cover. "There are still Egyptian commandos around and there are cases when the local population gives them cover," he wrote. This kind of thing called for a drastic response. "One should assume that in Sinai, too, there were isolated cases of mistreated Egyptian soldiers," Yaari continued, "but government policy was to feed them and give them water and move them toward the canal. Even the Red Cross affirms this. On the contrary, it seems that Egypt is the one that refuses to let refugees cross the canal." Either

---

*The pursuit of soldiers from the Egyptian army's Palestinian units was delegated to the Shaked commando unit, whose commander was Amos Yarkoni—Abdel Majid—who had hosted Dayan in his home just before the war.[25]

way, "Things have worked out in the meantime, and the campaign to provide relief to the soldiers is coming to an end." He added a reprimand:
"The army should not be accused of massacres. We are very aware of the
aberrant behavior in the days after the war, but one must also be careful
not to blacken the image of Jewish soldiers."[28]

Accounts of Egyptian soldiers lost in the desert were brought up in the
Knesset, where Dayan denied that Israel had maliciously caused their
deaths, saying most had died because they tried to reach the canal on foot
instead of turning themselves in to the IDF. In his book about the war he
asserted that some sixteen thousand Egyptian soldiers were killed, "most of
them in retreat." Rabin noted in his memoirs that he gave orders that prisoners not be killed, and the operational orders do indeed state that prisoners were to be treated in accordance with the Geneva Conventions.[29]

PRIVATE YEHOSHUA BAR-DAYAN, MEANWHILE, HAD RUN INTO A PROBLEM OF HIS OWN,
for the first time since his call-up. His commander, First Lieutenant Nah-
man Wagner, was threatening to "screw him" after the war. For some reason he had suddenly remembered that Saturday when Bar-Dayan had
come back late from Beersheba. Wagner called him a deserter. "I hope he
doesn't give me trouble after the war, so I can go back to my family and
my job like everyone else," wrote Bar-Dayan. But he prepared his defense:
"Do I look like a deserter? I hope he only called me that as a joke. A man
like me, a soldier like me—I've never run and never would. But Gila was
sobbing that Saturday—how could I leave her in the lurch?"

The images of scorched IDF tanks and dead bodies would not leave him
in peace. "May Nasser burn," he wrote. They were still driving, always in
first gear, as one of his friends read from *Ha'aretz* and *Davar*. Bar-Dayan
was not pleased: "The descriptions of our fighting are incomplete and
bad." A helicopter landed to pick up their mail. "Dear Gili and Yariv," he
wrote. "We defeated the Egyptian army; their weapons of war, which they
wanted to destroy us with, are burning like torches. They've got thousands
of casualties. Now we're on the way to Ismailia. Pictures of Nasser, the dog,
decorate all our vehicles. There's a feeling that the whole thing's over,
praise and thanks to our pilots and men in the tanks who did the job—the
pilots covered us and saved us all." He told them how he had constantly
kissed their pictures and his wedding ring, and promised they had nothing to worry about: he was in a safe place. The war was almost over. He
wrote about Uzi Avrahami's wound, a small piece of shrapnel in the back

of his neck. He was keeping an eye on Uzi's vehicle for him. He listed the people he had met, sent regards to his father, and finished with a request: "Hold Yarivi up high and dance with him." He signed off, "Daddy Shuka."[30] Meanwhile, the helicopter waited and the pilot went around picking up letters. "In what army in the world does a pilot, a captain, stand in full battle gear and wait to pick up soldiers' letters?" Bar-Dayan wrote. The pilot was Mario Shaked, from Ramat Hasharon. He usually flew a Mystère, but his plane had been hit by the Egyptians near the canal and he had been forced to bail out. He had been rescued by helicopter.

Later, on the road, Bar-Dayan wrote in his diary, "There's no cause for worry. The skies are clear. The Egyptians are fleeing toward the canal. We're not letting them. We want to kill them. He who rises to kill you, rise and kill him first. Tomorrow or the day after, Gili will get the letter. We're getting desperately short of water. I hope they solve the problem." Suddenly he heard shouting from the vehicle behind him. The engines made it difficult to hear, and at first he could not believe it, but someone was screaming, "The Old City is ours!" "Sharm el-Sheikh is ours!" The transistor batteries were almost too weak for the soldiers to make anything out, but there was Rabbi Goren's voice, and Rafi Amir reporting from the wall. There was the singing of "Hatikva."

Yehoshua Bar-Dayan and his six fellow soldiers, without really knowing what they were doing, instinctively stood up and joined in with the national anthem coming over the radio. One of them, an electrician from Tel Aviv, sobbed with excitement. And so these seven men stood in the desert singing "Hatikva," as their voices echoed and passed from their truck to the one in front, where others joined in, and the singing went from one vehicle to the next, from trucks to tanks. Suddenly, four Egyptian soldiers appeared in the distance, wanting to surrender. One lay down and the men shot him. The others put up their hands and the men ran to them and grabbed them. Chaos took over the convoy and the route was blocked. Bar-Dayan volunteered to direct traffic.

The radio broadcast the chief of staff's statement to bereaved families. Bar-Dayan was moved and wrote in his diary, "A great man, Rabin." Later that evening he wrote, "Ancient Jerusalem is in our hands again. To have it and all the conquered Jordanian territory. We heard that Gush Etzion is ours again—our second Masada, it's come back to us. I hope we do not give back the Gush and the Kotel, but there are endless foreseeable political problems." As a history buff, Bar-Dayan decided that if he could, he would go to see Rockefeller Museum, where some of the Dead Sea Scrolls were on display.[31]*

Hen Ronen and his friends sang "Jerusalem of Gold." They were on their way to Ramallah. Ronen recounted: "We sang the song over and over again. Dozens of times. Everyone singing and singing. It sweeps you up. Hearing the shofar blown at the Western Wall. The paratroopers. We knew we had seven guys from Yehiam there. We were really worried. Had anything happened to them? Was anyone injured or killed? For some reason I was terribly provincial. I was concerned for those closest to me. An uncle, a brother-in-law, the kibbutz members. I couldn't see further than that. But that's the way it is. 'Jerusalem of Gold,' and again, 'Jerusalem of Gold.'"[33]

SOMEWHERE IN AN ARCHIVE, TWO TELEGRAMS FROM THE ISRAELI AMBASSADORS TO Britain and France are filed away. The British had offered to take advantage of Hussein's pleas for a cease-fire to make him sign a peace treaty. The ambassador in London, Aharon Remez, who had been the first commander of the Israeli air force, recommended giving this a try. Ambassador Walter Eitan, a senior Israeli diplomat, cabled from Paris: "I suggest immediately accepting Hussein's offer of a cease-fire and asking for a personal meeting with him to offer an Israel-Jordan peace treaty. Hussein fears for his regime anyway. We can give him full support, ask for the U.S. and Britain to get involved and put pressure on Hussein, to convince him of the logic of our offer." The ambassador assumed that the chances of a treaty were slim, but he believed they should still try. "We must act quickly, before we get into the thick of the political and diplomatic arguments." What he meant was that, if negotiations were held at all, they should take place before the conquest of Jerusalem.[34]

3. LEGENDS: "THE PEOPLE ARE DRUNK WITH JOY"

"The feeling was fantastic," Uzi Narkis said later. That Wednesday morning at the Temple Mount, he received the first of a series of preposterous suggestions that came up over the next few days and weeks, apparently

---

*Yigal Yadin, the archeologist and adviser to the prime minister, also spoke of the scrolls. Even before the war he had forged secret ties with a well-known Bethlehem antiquities dealer named Kando. When the IDF entered Bethlehem, Yadin ordered that they take one of Kando's scrolls, part of which he already owned, and then instructed that Kando himself be interrogated to find out if he had any more.[32]

under the influence of that same "fantastic feeling." General Goren, the chief rabbi of the IDF, told Narkis that this was the moment to blow up the Dome of the Rock. "Do this and you will go down in history," Goren said, and explained that such a thing could only be done under cover of war: "Tomorrow might be too late." Narkis threatened to throw the rabbi in jail if he did not drop the idea.[35]

At around the same time, David Ben-Gurion had a visit from Yosef Sapir, one of the new ministers in the unity government, who asked him, "What shall we do with the Old City and the west bank of the Jordan?" Ben-Gurion said they must first consolidate their victory. They still had to deliver a fatal blow to Syria. There were roughly a million Arabs living in the West Bank, Ben-Gurion said. "We don't need them on top of the Israeli Arabs." In Gaza there were some 200,000 refugees from 1948, he noted: "It won't be easy to get rid of them." That evening, Ben-Gurion went to Jerusalem and told Teddy Kollek they had to start settling the Old City's Jewish Quarter immediately. Kollek said he would talk to Eshkol, but Ben-Gurion asked him not to mention his name. He also wanted to discuss the matter with the minister of the interior, but Shapira was in Tel Aviv. When he came to Ben-Gurion's house there the next morning, the first thing he heard was, "We've already lost a day." Ben-Gurion wanted to talk to Moshe Dayan about settling the Jewish Quarter. When he was told the minister was in Jerusalem, he drove back there yet again.

Ben-Gurion was accompanied by his wife, Paula, Ezer Weizman, Mordechai Hod, and Shimon Peres. Weizman recalled that on the way, Ben-Gurion poked fun at Eshkol and Eban. They were cheered and applauded by soldiers en route. The scent of war was still in the air—a mixture of gunpowder, sweat, and dust, as Weizman wrote. "And that smell calls out, voicelessly, with the story of the battles and the heroism and the dedication, and pours a gravity into one's soul, even in moments of elation." At the Western Wall Ben-Gurion immediately noticed some structures the Jordanians had built. "I was astonished that no orders had been given to destroy these buildings," he wrote in his diary. He stormed ahead; his bodyguards had trouble keeping up with him.

Weizman recalled coming to the site as a young man, in a British military uniform. He used to go into the Dome of the Rock, always fearing he would be identified as Jewish. And now he was here, Jewish and victorious. "We approach the Kotel and I feel how my heart and my blood and my breath are pounding and coming faster and faster. I have no control. This is the history of my people, breathing here its breath of thousands of years." There were soldiers putting on tefillin, some praying with great intensity and extraordinary devotion, Weizman observed. "Each Jew bound to every other Jew. Whole groups. Swaying clusters of hands and feet and heads and bodies." And there were those who did not know what to do with themselves, he wrote: "nailed to the spot, perhaps not even feeling the tears rolling down their cheeks." Weizman wanted to rejoice with all the others, but his riotous joy was marred by a thought that he could well have addressed to Ben-Gurion, among others: "Where were you for nineteen years, when it was forbidden to say a word about the enormous importance of the emotional bond between an entire people and this holy wall?"

Ben-Gurion noticed a street sign in Arabic and English that read "Al-borak"—"Supposedly this was where Mohammed met the angel of God," he wrote in his diary. According to Muslims, Alborak (Lightning), Mohammed's horse, brought the Prophet in one quick leap from Mecca to Jerusalem, where Mohammed tied him to the wall. Like all street signs in East Jerusalem, this one was ceramic, painted blue and green, hand-crafted by Armenian artisans. According to Weizman, Ben-Gurion said, "Take it down," with the decisive diction that always made people obey him. A soldier by the name of David Kolitz jumped up to carry out the order. He climbed onto the shoulders of another soldier and tried to re-move the sign with a stick. That didn't work, so he smashed it with a small hammer. Ben-Gurion said nothing further, but Weizman had the feeling that the command to "take it down" expressed a need to wipe out nineteen years of all that Alborak represented—nineteen years of regret. For all that time, Ben-Gurion had borne the blame for failing to capture the Old City in 1948. It was a terrible indictment, rivaled in gravity only by the claim that he had neglected to rescue Jews during the Holocaust. It is doubtful whether anything upset Ben-Gurion more than the fact that the Old City was finally conquered during Levi Eshkol's premiership. He chose to focus all his fervor on the campaign to populate Jerusalem with Jews, and when he heard from Teddy Kollek that Arabs were currently liv-ing in the former Jewish Quarter, he responded, "They must be expelled. There's no need for any law. Occupation is the most effective law." The symbolism of shattering the street sign with its Muslim resonance touched Weizman, too. "In those few seconds I felt that we were standing at the gate of a new era, having our national reckoning."[36]

NOT SINCE THE STATE WAS FOUNDED HAD ISRAELIS BEEN SWEPT UP IN SUCH A WAVE OF excitement, wrote a veteran Jerusalemite in his diary. "The people are

drunk with joy," wrote the poet Natan Alterman.[37] Everyone went searching for the most elaborate superlatives; no flowery phrase or cliché was
left unused, including the repeated claim that words could not express
the feelings in one's heart. Exclamation points worked overtime. Even the
most prosaic writers turned to poetry, and die-hard secularists unearthed
Jewish sources. "The Messiah came to Jerusalem yesterday—he was tired
and gray, and he rode in on a tank," wrote Gabriel Tzifroni in *Maariv*.[38]

Yaffa Yarkoni, a singer who had been entertaining the troops since
1948, sang "Jerusalem of Gold" at the Western Wall. It was a decidedly secular gesture, but *Maariv* called it "pure prayer." The paper had printed the
song's lyrics in lieu of an editorial. Naomi Shemer hurriedly updated
the song with the following verse: "We have returned to the water wells,
the market, and the square / A shofar calls at the Temple Mount in the
Old City / In the caves of the rock, thousands of suns shine / Once again
we shall go down to the Dead Sea, by way of Jericho." Haimito Mosowitz
described a victory rally at the Mount Scopus amphitheater, where the
singer Nehama Handel tried to sing "Jerusalem of Gold" but burst into
tears, along with all the soldiers.[39]

The capture of the Old City was described as the correction of a historical error. The Central Command decreed that it had been "seized by the
enemy" and that "IDF soldiers restored the stolen holy site to the people."[40] "Ancient Jerusalem has been liberated," said *Davar*. The Bible was
also doing overtime. *Maariv* reported, in biblical terms, that the IDF was
at "the heights of Latrun."[41] Uzi Narkis's action report noted, "The gates
of Jericho have been surrounded, its walls have fallen." Of the conquest
of Hebron and Bethlehem, the general said, "The Tomb of the Patriarchs
and Rachel's Tomb are in the hands of the sons of Abraham, Isaac, and Jacob."[42] The editorial in *Ha'aretz* bore the headline, "Cry Aloud and Shout,
Thou Dweller of Zion!" and proclaimed, "The Western Wall shall never
again stand abandoned and silent; the glory of the past will no longer be
viewed from afar. Henceforth it will be part of the new Israel, and its
splendor shall disperse its rays over the building of a Jewish society that is
a link in the long chain of the nation's history in its land." The press described the previous few days as "days of miracles." "We were like them
that dream," they wrote again and again.[43]

Israelis writing to friends and relatives abroad responded spontaneously in the same spirit and with almost the same words. Just as the
anxiety they expressed before the war was sincere, as if they had always
feared that the Arabs would destroy Israel, they now wrote with the sudden realization that an eternal dream had come true. The conquest of the

Old City emerged as far more than an event in the news—more, even, than mere history: it was a profoundly personal experience.

"We are very confused. The radio is on twenty-four hours a day. Yesterday was Grandfather's memorial at Father's, and we were together when we heard the shofar being blown from the Kotel. We sang 'Hatikva' together and cried like little children when we heard kaddish recited there for the fallen soldiers," wrote a woman from Tel Aviv to her sister in Boston.[44] "It fills the heart, a real miracle," wrote Riki Ben-Ari from Tel Aviv to Los Angeles, minutes after hearing on the radio about the conquest of the Old City. "I am proud to have been born in this generation and to have lived to see the revival of Israel: such a fighting spirit, such heights of greatness—much will be told of this in the years to come."[45] Another woman wrote to relatives in the United States, "Praise God, praise God, a great miracle has befallen us and the entire people of Israel." A man from Tel Aviv wrote, "The great miracle that has happened surprises us all. We were so certain of destruction." The people who had watched the Arab television broadcasts had been most afraid: "The fear was awful," someone wrote, adding, "imagine now that Kol Israel is being broadcast from Ramallah."[46] Some wrote to their families that the war would now continue in America. They were referring to President Johnson's Middle East policy.[47]

ON THE THIRD DAY OF THE WAR, ALREADY SWEPT UP IN THE INTOXICATION OF VICtory, Levi Eshkol mocked Lyndon Johnson, "leader of the world, a man of no small accomplishments," who had made great promises of which nothing had come. Forty-five countries were said to be joining the international fleet that Johnson had promised to send to the Gulf of Aqaba, but when Israel looked at his promise closely, it turned out there were just two: the United States and Israel itself. "It's possible that, in the end, Johnson would have gotten out of the game too, because he has international interests," Eshkol told his party secretariat, and added that in general, they could not rely on the promises of the U.S. president. What would happen if they needed him urgently and he happened to be away for the weekend?

The White House was furious at this kind of talk. Ambassador Harman reported that Walt Rostow had phoned him, "extremely angry," to say that Eshkol's comments were "explosive." Abe Feinberg had also called, "in a real panic." Harman had another call from "Ilan," Abe Fortas, who reminded him of "the special sensitivity of Issahar" during this period, and asked that Israel be considerate. "Over the last few days, the president has showed particular sensitivity and is not pleased with the Jewish pressure on him," reported Ephraim Evron.[48]

At the moment of the conquest of the Old City, Mathilde Krim was still staying at the White House. She had seen the president in recent days, and had talked to him on the telephone from her room on the third floor; sometimes she called him, sometimes he called her. She lobbied him to stand by Israel; in this, she was apparently acting in coordination with the Israeli embassy. That morning, she was preparing to leave the White House. Johnson was still eating breakfast and she did not want to disturb him, so she left a message. She wrote that she thought the president was underestimating the lingering Israeli resentment of the U.S. neutrality statement. She had reports from Israel of severe anti-American feeling. The Israelis were saying that they had won the war not thanks to the United States, but rather despite it. The American Jewish community was finding it very hard to understand the administration's position. The president should know that the Jews had a deep persecution complex, and that before they knew they would win, it had seemed as if the United States was abandoning them to Nasser's aggressions—and they looked at Nasser like at a second Hitler. Many people, including her husband, had tried their best to explain the State Department's position, Krim wrote, but unsuccessfully: the man on the street still felt resentful.

A mass rally was being organized in Washington for the following day, and Krim felt that it might well become not a show of support for Israel but a protest against Johnson. Ephraim Evron was doing his best to prevent this, but even he feared that events were getting out of hand. Krim therefore urged the president to issue a pro-Israel statement that same day. She made it clear that she was speaking for her husband and for others. First, the president must declare that the United States would not maintain diplomatic relations with Egypt as long as Nasser was in power, because of "his attempts to provoke a major conflagration." Second, the president must say that this was the time to take action to allow Israel to live in peace with its neighbors. Krim suggested that Johnson announce a peace conference. Such a statement would help him "regain the sympathy he lost" from both Israelis and American Jews.*

David Ginsburg called to say that the keynote speaker at the next day's

---

*During a phone conversation with the secretary of state later that day, the president sent his secretary to look for Krim's memo, and when she brought it to him, he read parts of it to Rusk. Abe Feinberg asked to convey similar sentiments to the president.[49]

rally would be Morris Abram, the president of the American Jewish Committee. "It will be okay," Ginsburg said; he himself had reviewed the speech draft. Besides expressing solidarity with Israel, Abram would assert that the president was doing a magnificent job in the current crisis.[50] Levinson and Wattenberg, the two "Zionist dupes," reported to Johnson, on behalf of the Anti-Defamation League, that U.S. Jews were particularly afraid that Israel would be forced to withdraw from the areas it had seized without achieving a peace treaty first. The ADL asked the president to send a statement of some sort to be read at the rally.[51] Someone went to the trouble to carefully count and sort the letters coming into the White House. There were 5,241 that day: ninety-six percent supported Israel, 3 percent called on the United States not to intervene in the war, and 1 percent supported the Arabs.[52] Israel's representatives in the United States were satisfied. "Never before has American Jewry united around an issue as it has now around Israel," wrote one. He was concerned, however, that U.S. Jews might also unite yet again in opposition to the war in Vietnam.[53]

CHAPTER 15

THE FINAL DAYS

1. NIGHTMARES I: "MISSION: DAMASCUS!"

On Thursday, June 8, Shuka Bar-Dayan had been on reserve duty for three weeks. He thought back to the day when he had taken the car for an oil change with Yarivi. His letters home continued to express endless love and homesickness. He tried to sound optimistic. The fighting was over; driving around now was just like being on vacation, the desert was wonderful, the weather was pleasant, he felt great. Might it never be any worse. At night he looked for the north star: that was the direction where Gili and Yariv were.[1] But for the first time since leaving home, his letters and his diary began to diverge. The diary now described a chilling, blood-soaked, macabre routine. Bar-Dayan wrote to his wife that the convoys of burned-out vehicles looked like millions of sculptures by Yigal Tumarkin—the Israeli expressionist artist—but he censored the true horrors, voicing them only in his diary. Ambulances kept emerging from within the black smoke, carrying wounded men, dead men, including some of his friends. The roadsides were littered with hundreds of Egyptian corpses; the desert heat was making itself felt and the flies were swarming. That Thursday, at 5:15 P.M., he wrote, "Now we are driving—good lord—over human bodies, Egyptians, over limbs, another and another and another. God—we are driving over a human face; only his nose sticks up. His eyes are open. The guys in the truck bed are nauseated. Some of them are laughing hysterically."[2]

· · ·

AN AMERICAN SPY VESSEL, THE *LIBERTY*, WAS SAILING OFF SHORE NEAR EL ARISH THAT day. It was attacked by Israeli air force planes and navy torpedo boats. Thirty-four crew members were killed, 171 injured. Washington, initially believing the Russians had attacked the ship, sent in fighter planes, and the two countries came close to conflict. The incident threatened relations between Israel and the United States. Israel apologized immediately. Ambassador Barbour cabled Washington within minutes to say that "Israel is obviously shocked by the error and tenders sincere apologies." He recommended that publicity be avoided, lest the presence of the American ship near Gaza "feed Arab suspicions of U.S.-Israel collusion."[3] The ambassador's recommendation was followed by several instructions meant to prevent the story from becoming public.

Over the years, Israel and the United States have declassified many, but not all, of the documents related to the incident; some lingering question marks remain. The secrecy prompted countless conspiracy theories that have yet to dissipate even four decades later. Many have tried to prove that Israel bombed the *Liberty* intentionally to keep some secret from the Americans—perhaps something to do with Israel's nuclear capabilities, its intention to attack Syria, perhaps a massacre of Egyptian prisoners, or possibly something else.[4] President Johnson, CIA director Richard Helms, Secretary of State Rusk, and the heads of the Department of Defense disbelieved Israel's version too—or, at least, they never shook the suspicion that the *Liberty* was bombed intentionally.[5] But even they could not say what could have motivated Eshkol, Amit, Dayan, or Rabin to order such an act. When the security cabinet met that day, Eshkol reported that the *Liberty* had been struck by mistake. Begin commented that in Vietnam the Americans had mistakenly bombed their own ships a number of times.* The war abounded with operational errors, and so long as there is no clear evidence of motive, one can assume that the *Liberty* was bombed in error.

A FEW HOURS AFTER THE *LIBERTY* INCIDENT, THE SECURITY CABINET DISCUSSED A PROposal to seize the Golan Heights. That morning, *Ha'aretz* published an editorial entitled "Finish the Job," which discussed Syria. "It is time to settle accounts with that country," the piece said, and called for the defeat of

---

*Walt Rostow told President Johnson that when Yitzhak Rabin heard about the attack, he was with Golda Meir. Reportedly, he was so taken aback he almost fainted.[6]

the Syrian army in order to create "borders appropriate for our needs." The paper did not say exactly which territories should be conquered, but demanded "geographical and strategic realities that will afford long-term effective protection of the lives and property of the citizens of Israel." A short-lived daily newspaper started by Uri Avnery, *Daf*, published a huge headline on its front page: "Mission: Damascus!"[7]

"Finishing the job" was not the sole point of action against Syria. The conquest of the Sinai was the result of a surprise attack, and taking control of the West Bank could be seen as a large-scale land-grab operation; but Syria had been considered the primary source of trouble even before the war. Rabin and a few senior military figures were now demanding that they be allowed to seize the Golan, as they had wished to do as far back as early January. And Eshkol was still dreaming of controlling the sources of the Banias.*

The debate that preceded the operation on the Golan Heights resembled the one that led to the attack on Egypt. The principal argument against it was political, but this time it was not the United States that the objectors feared. On the contrary: as early as Wednesday, June 7, Meir Amit reported that the United States would accept an attack on the Golan. Eban later recounted that McGeorge Bundy had phoned him and "hinted" that it was time to act against Syria, though without going as far as Damascus. But a few of the ministers were apprehensive about the USSR. Some of them had also objected to the attack on Egypt, including the ministers from Mapam and Mafdal. Among the supporters, Yigal Allon was once again at the forefront. Dayan, in contrast, demanded restraint this time. He did not view Syria as a strategic threat. Before the war, he had believed that Israel was responsible for the escalation of tensions along the northern border. "I was afraid of the Soviets' response," he wrote. "Syria was under the USSR's protection, and they might have come to its aid." At first, he permitted the IDF only to take control of the demilitarized zones, without crossing the international border. As he had before and during the war, he was once again able to impose his position on Eshkol.

Rabin argued with Dayan: there was no point in stopping at a limited action in the demilitarized zones and the Banias area, he said, nor should they content themselves with Tel Azaziat, one of the Syrian strongholds discussed in recent days. One local community leader from the north later recalled hearing rumors that Dayan had claimed the operation on

*Miriam Eshkol asked General David Elazar, of the Northern Command, to take the Banias as a birthday gift for her.

the Golan Heights would take the lives of thousands of soldiers, but in the Northern Command there was talk of a mass resignation of officers in protest against the government's hesitation to take the Golan.

The main pressure to seize the Golan came from General David Elazar of the Northern Command, known to his friends as Dado. In the two years preceding the war he had broached the matter not only with his superiors in the military, but also with Eshkol and a few ministers, including Allon, with whom he even discussed the possibility of occupying Damascus. Allon objected. Elazar sent a friend, Uzi Feinerman, to lobby Dayan about the Golan. Feinerman deployed an emotionally and historically charged phrase: if Israel did not take advantage of the war to occupy the Golan, the result would be "weeping for generations."

On Thursday morning, the air force bombed the Golan Heights. Rabin claimed it was an "error." The Syrians bombed several Israeli communities in response, and Eshkol authorized the evacuation of children from the region. Elazar and his men pushed kibbutz members in the Galilee to exert pressure on the government to take the Golan, recruiting Allon to their efforts. Allon organized a kibbutz delegation to go to Tel Aviv and arranged a meeting for them with Eshkol, who, in an extremely rare gesture, agreed to let them speak at the cabinet meeting that day. Perhaps he was hoping their appearance would facilitate a decision to at least seize the Banias, despite Dayan's position, or perhaps he only invited them out of sympathy and identification with their plight: they were friends, agriculturalists, members of the labor movement. "I briefed them on what to say and how to say it," Allon recounted.

The kibbutz members described their lives as a nightmare. Kibbutz Gadot lay in ruins, they reported. One delegate, Shalom Hablin of Kibbutz Hagoshrim, had come straight from guard duty and apologized because he had not had time to change his clothes. He had been living in the Galilee for thirty-four years; his children and grandchildren had been born there. One of his sons was in the Sinai; a second had been injured by a shell. The grandchildren were in the bomb shelters, while he himself was on guard duty the whole time. They couldn't bear it any longer. Eshkol, himself a member of Kibbutz Degania, remembered that during the War of Independence a delegation from Degania had gone to talk to Ben-Gurion, to try and persuade him to assign more forces for their protection.*

---

*This was the same delegation that had stopped off in Petach Tikva, at the home of the local physician, Ben-Zion Borodianski. Their arrival was one of the childhood recollections of the doctor's son, Yehoshua Bar-Dayan.

The meeting's irregular and emotional beginning was effective. Nerves were on edge. Allon began by saying that as long as the Syrians controlled the Golan Heights, they would shell the communities to their south and terrorists would continue to slip across the border. Israel would have to respond, and doing so might complicate things with the Soviet Union. He did not believe that the USSR would break off relations with Israel, but even if it did, he preferred to have the Golan Heights without a Soviet embassy than a Soviet embassy without the Golan Heights. He could not see why the disputed border should be respected, nor did he understand why the Sinai and the West Bank could be seized but the Golan Heights could not.*

Zerah Warhaftig replied, "I think we must take care not to get caught up in the intoxication of victory." If the USSR cut ties with Israel, the ten other Eastern Bloc counties would do so too, additional countries might follow suit, and who knew—Israel might find itself outside the UN. The region was Syrian; it always had been. The Security Council had called for a cease-fire. If Syria violated it, there would be a war. But why initiate one?

Minister of Education Aran, who had objected to the attack on Egypt, sounded different now. "For four thousand years we have discussed the *akeida*—the sacrifice of Isaac—which did not ultimately take place. Here in these communities we have men, women and children threatened with sacrifice. It is an intolerable situation."

Dayan first refused to explain his position, and only following lengthy persuasion did he speak. The occupation of the Golan would complicate Israel's position not only with respect to the USSR but also vis-à-vis France, Israel's main provider of aircraft, and "the situation in the air force is not good." He also feared a combined attack by the air forces of Syria, Iraq, and others. The conquest of the Golan would require a complex operation, and it was of no benefit: the Syrians would never stop fighting.

Dayan spoke emotionally, sometimes angrily, as did others. Israel Lior wrote that Dayan once again sounded menacing. In general, Dayan said, he was not willing to have every military action come before the government for advance authorization. Although Zerah Warhaftig supported his position, Dayan chose the minister's name to express the depth of his scorn for his colleagues: "When my role and Warhaftig's decision carry the same weight, and a majority of two votes decides whether we go to

---

*There was another reason for Allon's desire to occupy the Golan that he did not mention at the meeting. He was toying with the idea of setting up a Druze state that would act as a buffer between Israel and Syria.

war over two more kilometers—I don't believe this is the way to manage a complicated war."

Dayan was like a god just then, and that was how everyone treated him, wrote Lior: "The proposal that military matters not be subject to the decisions of the majority was the demand of a tyrant, not of a minister in a democratic government."

Then Dayan said some of the harshest words ever spoken in a cabinet meeting. "This evening we've heard the kibbutz delegation give an emotional presentation. And I have to be the one to tell them, stay there and suffer. In my opinion, it's better to move ten kibbutzim fifteen kilometers out of the way and say that we're not dealing with [the Golan] now, if we're not able to."

It was as if the ministers had been struck by lightning, Lior wrote. Allon and Eshkol were quick to respond. "I cannot imagine evacuating kibbutzim," said Allon; "that would mean giving up part of the land of Israel." Eshkol was also shocked by the notion. "The Syrians would require no greater victory," he said, and added, "Could such a thing be done after consultation with only two or three people?"

Eshkol was alluding to Dayan's demand that the conduct of the war be removed from the government's purview. Typically, however, Eshkol found the words that allowed him to accept Dayan's position: "Just as wars aren't fought simply because the commanders want to, one can also say that wars aren't fought to make life easier for ten kibbutzim."

Dayan won: the cabinet decided to postpone the decision for a day or two. The chief of staff would bring them a proposal, and in the meanwhile he "would make an effort not to provoke the Syrians." The next morning, Dayan phoned General Elazar and on his own initiative ordered him to commence an incursion into the Golan. Elazar, wrote Yitzhak Rabin, "almost fell off his chair." He was not the only one.[8]

2. NIGHTMARES II: "THE HANDS ON MY WATCH STOPPED MOVING"

According to Dayan, he had found out early on Friday morning that the Syrian forces were crumbling and would be easy to defeat, although Syria was about to stop fighting, as Egypt had already done. His information came from a telegram sent by Nasser to the Syrian president, Nur Al-Din Al-Atassi, which had been intercepted by Israeli intelligence. "Last night I did not think Egypt and Syria (the political leadership) would collapse like this and abandon the rest of the battle," wrote Dayan to Eshkol, "but if this is the situation, it should be fully exploited. A great day."

"What a despicable man," was Eshkol's reaction. Intuitive as he was and always the politician, he naturally felt that Dayan was stealing his thunder on this front, too, which had great political value because of the kibbutzim. After all, Eshkol had been in favor of the operation, and only under Dayan's influence had he convinced the ministers to wait. Now it would look as if Eshkol's government had once again tried to curb the army and that Dayan, the Israeli hero, had once again taken it upon himself to do the patriotic thing. Eshkol fumed. But there was no point in revoking Dayan's order, particularly since he supported it.[9]

It is possible that Dayan was telling the truth and that he had changed his mind in light of new information. Perhaps he got caught up in the uncontrollable feeling that it was now or never, which to a great extent had prompted the conquest of Gaza, the West Bank, and the Old City— the urge that impelled Israel to act quickly, before the rest of the world could stop it. "Has Israel received official notice of Syria's decision to cease fire?" Dayan asked of Yaacov Herzog. At such moments Dayan tended to forget that not every territory that could be conquered should be conquered. He often reversed his positions, capriciously and at times spitefully.

"I came to understand that whatever I proposed, Dayan would propose the opposite," Yigal Allon later said. On Thursday, Yigal Yadin had observed to Haim Bar-Lev that Dayan's stance came from a desire to prove who was boss. Allon claimed that the government was in any case about to decide to seize the Golan; this, according to Allon, was reason enough for Dayan to beat the ministers to it.*

Yitzhak Rabin wrote that he did not understand Dayan's behavior during these events. In a conversation with Yaacov Herzog, he described Dayan as "a peculiar man." A book about the history of the war, published by the IDF in conjunction with the Ministry of Defense, left the question of Dayan's motives open, commenting only that had Dayan realized Syria was collapsing and ready for a cease-fire, he could have just as easily seen this as reinforcing his original position that there was no need to attack.[11]

---

*Allon was not the most objective of Dayan observers: his archives contain a file of materials meant to disgrace Dayan, including accounts of archaeological digs he conducted illegally and details of his divorce.[10]

• • •

THE SECURITY CABINET CONVENED AT NINE ON FRIDAY MORNING. DAYAN ANNOUNCED that he had ordered the seizure of not only the northern part of the Golan, but the entire Golan Heights. He explained what he had just told Eshkol: Syria's willingness to accept a cease-fire had created a new opportunity. He emphasized that Eshkol had given his authorization.

Shapira proposed canceling the operation, saying the arguments against it made by Dayan himself the night before were very persuasive. If the operation ended at once, there would be less bloodshed. He was furious: "I want to know who is responsible for the violation of our decisions." Begin said that there was indeed an "aesthetic flaw" in the fact that Dayan had acted against government decisions, but he offered a precedent from Austria under Empress Maria Theresa: when a soldier committed a disciplinary offense that entailed an act of heroism, he received both a reprimand and a medal.

Eshkol explained his dilemma to the cabinet: although he could not claim to have been asked, he was still in favor of the operation, and did not think it should be stopped now. His position was accepted. Shapira retreated, avoiding a vote on his proposal: "I don't want to seem like the last of the just." Zerah Warhaftig was absent. That morning, before he learned of the order to strike at the Golan, he had headed north hoping to meet his son; on the way he distributed to soldiers copies of the Book of Psalms.

In the evening, Dayan reported to Eshkol that some difficulties had arisen with seizing the Golan, despite his original expectations. The Syrians were fighting boldly and were holding up respectably against the air force; but the IDF would take the Banias area by morning. Yaacov Herzog, something of an Israeli Sir Humphrey, described the rest of the conversation as if it were straight out of an episode of *Yes, Prime Minister*. Of course, said Dayan, it really would be preferable for the IDF to seize the mountain ranges to the south, but that would be impossible if they had to halt their efforts in the morning. Eshkol wondered out loud: "Since we've already begun, perhaps we could go a little farther in the morning?" Dayan quickly agreed: "Why not, if that is what the Prime Minister directs us to do—certainly." Eshkol continued, "We can't have the Syrians walking away with a victory, with Israel defeating all the Arab states but this one." There was still time before the UN Security Council would convene. Meanwhile, Elazar was leading his Northern Command forces. "It was as if," wrote his biographer, "a taut spring was suddenly released and flew out like a wild thing."[12]

"IT WAS A HORRIFYING ASCENT," RECOUNTED HAIM BROM OF YEHIAM, WHO TOOK part in the conquest of Tel Azaziat. "There was a smell of burning, and not just of things. The sense was that it was people too, the smell of people. . . . Anyway, it was something I had never smelled. The people who came later didn't notice it, maybe they just saw the scorched half-tracks, but that smell, it gets into your brain. We saw the bodies of our own guys. . . . It was a brutal battle."[13] Israel Huberman, from Haifa, a soldier in the Golani Brigade, was riding in a half-track when the Syrians shelled it: "Everything became terribly foggy all at once," he recalled later. "I saw fire and smoke coming from the engine. I thought I was alone in the half-track. I jumped out and started running. Suddenly I heard shouts from behind: 'Help! Help!' I turned around and saw that the driver and the gunner, Moshe Drimer, had been hit and were stuck in the driver's compartment. The driver was lying on the wheel and not moving. Drimer was writhing. His face was covered with blood, he was bleeding everywhere. He tried to get out, but the machine gun was in his way." Huberman acted instinctively. He ran back, opened the door, and tried to get Drimer out. "He kept mumbling. I think he was saying, 'Mom, Mom.' I think he had blood in his eyes and couldn't see. There was fire all around us." Huberman learned later that he managed to get Drimer out, but just then a second shell hit the vehicle and ignited the fuel tank. "There was an ocean of flames. I suddenly felt very hot. I was burning up, I caught fire." He ran without knowing where. He was told he looked like a burning torch. An officer ran after him, knocked Huberman to the ground, and started putting the flames out with water. Huberman screamed that there were still people in the half-track. The officer said it was too late, there was nothing to be done.[14]

SINCE BECOMING MINISTER OF DEFENSE, DAYAN HAD PRESENTED PERSUASIVE REASONS F for not capturing the Suez Canal: control of the canal might complicate Israel's relations with the countries that used it, he thought. But he had also argued against conquering the Golan Heights, and the Gaza Strip, and had then reversed himself. Similarly, he suddenly favored the conquest of the canal. Here too, the story is perplexing.

Rabin wrote that Dayan had ordered taking the canal after Nasser declared his acceptance of a cease-fire. It is possible, then, that Dayan had
yet again been seized by a last-minute "now or never" state of mind, and
that he authorized the move in a sort of snatch-and-grab frenzy, at odds
with his own reasoned perspective. He then apparently changed his mind
yet again and ordered that the forces stop some twelve miles short of the
canal. On Friday, Yeshayahu Gavish announced to Rabin that his men
had reached the banks of the canal, and later he commended his soldiers
for arriving "upright, battle victorious, and proud." But Dayan, who had
only recently been willing to force Gavish out and take over his command, threatened to court-martial the general as though he had broken
through to the canal against orders.[15]

A FEW HOURS AFTER THE START OF THE COMBAT IN THE GOLAN, YONINA BEN-OR
obtained the battle issue of the official *Air Force Journal*. On the second
page she found an interview with Major Arieh, a squadron commander.
"This time we feel that we're fighting for our sacred, historical land," he
said. "Each one of us feels a deep sense of connection to our targets. It's a
profound experience to fly over Jericho, Bethlehem, Hebron, and
Ashkelon of the Philistines." Arieh's tone was described as "awestruck."
The major went on to compare the IDF's conquest of Jericho to the biblical victory of Joshua. "We'll do it again," he said, thrilled and unabashedly
emotional. "Maybe even I myself didn't realize the deep feelings buried inside me toward the Jewish people's historical places. Two thousand years
of history have sprung to life before my very eyes." He said the enemy
army was fleeing, "just like in biblical times, after the Jewish victories."

When she read this, Yonina Ben-Or later recalled, she felt she was not
just reading printed words but hearing the speaker's voice. The pilot, Major Arieh, was her husband, an archaeology buff. The *Air Force Journal*
quoted him saying: "I want my children to learn about Eretz Israel not
just theoretically, in school, but in real life. I want them to be able to visit
the places where the Jewish people lived, the places they fought for and
built generations ago. I would like to visit them after the war." Yonina
Ben-Or was beside herself with excitement: "My temples were pounding.
Together we will go there, you, me and the girls," she thought.

At just about the same time, Arieh Ben-Or's plane took a direct hit. The
plane crashed and Ben-Or was killed.

"Aki" Urbach, as he had been called in childhood, was born in Herzliya. His widow later recounted that in October 1948, when he was ten,

his father punished him because he ran out to see the remnants of the plane belonging to Modi Allon, commander of the first fighter squadron in the air force; Allon had crashed at the Herzliya airport. Arieh and Yonina went to elementary school together. She had been born in a Polish village that later became part of the Ukraine. During World War II, she had been sent to a ghetto with her parents, and then to a forced labor camp. She came to Israel at the age of twelve, in 1950. She and Arieh also went to high school together in Tel Aviv. "It was a wonderful school. It wasn't afraid of the word 'Zionism.' It gave us values and taught us to love this country." They married at twenty-two. He was already a fighter pilot, and had taken part in the Sinai Campaign.

He served in the regular air force as a pilot trainer, among other duties. He usually flew the new Mirages, but in early 1967 took command of a Fouga squadron. She was an elementary school teacher. They had two daughters, Arza and Mihal. They lived on the Tel Nof air base, near the runway. At first she would always look out the window when Arieh took off. "My heart would swell with pride and contract with worry and then swell and contract again," she recalled. Later, she stopped looking. "You can't stand at the window for eight years and watch Arieh taking off and landing. At some point you stop. He goes. He takes off. He lands. He comes back." He would say good-bye to his daughters and see them at the end of the day like any father coming home from work, she said, but he often left when the girls were still asleep and returned after they'd gone to bed. It wasn't easy. He was devoted to his job, she to the family. "It was typical of pilots' wives. We live our husbands' lives." Her purpose was to enable him to dedicate himself to the air force. Once or twice a year they would go on a picnic.

Prior to the war, she hardly saw him. One night he came home just before midnight. He woke the girls up and hugged them. Arza was six and a half, Mihal was three. The next day, they thought they had been dreaming. Their mother was worried: "Years spent with a fighter pilot and in family housing on the base makes the wife a semi-expert, too," she said. "The Fouga is not a battle plane. It's slow. Its performance is limited. It's a training plane." Her husband tried to reassure her, adding: "You see, the decision to stay in the air force was so wise. I couldn't forgive myself today if I was outside all of this. I could never forgive myself." She was not reassured.

When the war started, the pilots' families were evacuated from Tel Nof to a military convalescent home in Netanya. Yonina Ben-Or shared a room with another pilot's wife and the two girls. "The atmosphere was electric with anxiety. It started with the announcement that four Fougas had been lost on the first day. Who? Who's gone?" Major Ben-Or led a quartet of planes in an attack on Jordanian tanks east of Jerusalem, for which he received a posthumous commendation from the chief of staff. He just had time to celebrate with his men, and then he was sent to the Golan.

On Thursday evening, her mother and mother-in-law were visiting. "Why don't you eat, Yonina?" Arieh's mother asked. "Why haven't you brushed your hair? You'll go home and Arieh won't recognize you!" She replied that until the business on the Golan Heights was over, she couldn't eat, brush her hair, or get dressed. She simply couldn't. She followed the war on the radio and picked up rumors. On Friday evening, after reading the interview with her husband, the families lit the Sabbath candles and sang some songs. There was a big dinner with pilots' wives from another base. Yonina Ben-Or felt sad and confused. Her husband's comrade, Arnon Livnat, had been killed on the first day of war. His widow, Hava, asked her to come and visit. "I couldn't. I thought, 'How can I talk to her when her husband is gone and mine is alive?' I was very upset. Perhaps I should have gone to see her?"*

She went to bed early, tense. At nine-thirty, someone called for her roommate. Ben-Or was happy: she thought her roommate had gone to speak with her husband on the phone, and asked her to send her love to Arieh. A few minutes later, a soldier came to get her, too. Now she was even happier: here was her own phone call. It was dark. The blackout was still in effect. She had often wondered what it would be like if she was ever notified that Arieh had been killed. How would she react? Would she ever get over it? The actual event was completely different from anything she had imagined. "I went to the other wing of the building, where the phone was. People were walking around the courtyard with flashlights. Someone came over to me, put his arm through mine, and said, 'My name is Dr. Baruh. Your husband has fallen in the course of duty.' I trembled like a leaf. I fought. To not fall down. Not slip. Not collapse. I thought this was beyond bearing. I thought no woman had the strength to bear this."

One of the last times they saw each other, Arieh asked her not to break down if he were killed. She saw that as his will. She went back to her room and did not cry. "I was in a vacuum. The hands on my watch stopped moving. I wasn't there."

---

*At the beginning of the last week of his life, Arieh Ben-Or wrote a condolence letter to Hava Livnat. The letter arrived on Friday, the day he died.

...

THAT NIGHT, YAACOV HERZOG WENT TO SLEEP IN ESHKOL'S TEL AVIV OFFICE. WHEN Yigal Allon came in later, he noticed that Herzog, who was Orthodox, had not turned the lights off, in observance of the Sabbath. Allon turned them off himself and lay down on the floor to sleep. Just before four in the morning, Eshkol and his advisers came in. They decided to continue the fighting in the Golan at least until midday. Herzog and Begin went on a Sabbath walk and talked about the Jewish people. Herzog said they were the only nation in history that had managed to control time: the Christian and Muslim rest days were inspired by the Jewish Sabbath, and that was how the Jews had determined the weekly order in the world, unchanged for some four thousand years. Begin was sad, Herzog wrote in his diary. He felt the Golan campaign should have started on Wednesday or Thursday despite Dayan's objections. Now Syria was urging the UN to arrange a cease-fire, and Israel would not have enough time to take the entire Golan. According to Herzog, Begin also condemned Dayan's behavior in the cabinet meetings.

YONINA BEN-OR WAITED FOR THE GIRLS TO WAKE UP. THEN SHE TOLD THEM, "GIRLS, Daddy flew in his plane to get rid of the Syrians; they broke his plane and his plane fell and Daddy was killed and he's not coming home anymore." The girls refused to believe her. She took them to her parents in Herzliya. She could not bring herself to see Arieh's mother. She asked the family physician to break the news to her.[16]

ESHKOL WENT ON A TOUR OF THE NORTH AND MET WITH DAYAN. HIS IMPRESSION WAS that the IDF was having great difficulty gaining control of the key town of Kuneitra. At this point, the Golan was a race against time. Eban telephoned Eshkol's house to inform him that the UN Security Council had issued a cease-fire resolution, and so the fighting had to stop immediately. Since Eshkol was in the north, his wife took the call. Later Eshkol phoned her, full of enthusiasm about the view from the Golan, the water, the greenery. She gave him Eban's message and Eshkol shouted, "Hello? Hello? I can't hear you. There's something wrong with the line, I can't hear you. Hello?" He repeated this over and over, until she understood that he did not want to hear.[17]

A few hours later, Kuneitra fell. Lior was with Eshkol when he heard the news. "Eshkol was a very sensitive man," he wrote, "but I don't believe I can ever recall such a response: he hugged and kissed the officers next to him like a young man. It wouldn't have taken much for him to start skipping and dancing."

Haim Bar-Lev was among the first to enter Kuneitra. "The town itself was intact, but it looked abandoned," he recalled. "The signs of life there up to that morning were visible in every home." The town reminded him of Beersheba during the War of Independence, except that the desertion of the Golan Heights was more abrupt. But the residents had not left before the war began: Eli Elad, a reporter for *Ha'aretz*, could see long lines of villagers walking east.

Uri Chizik, of Yehiam, found himself in the village of Pik, also deserted. "What made the strongest impression was that the people left their homes just as they were, they took their personal belongings and fled. You could see baby cribs overturned and damaged in the bombing—some were bloodstained. That made me miserable, so much so that even if I could have taken home a gift or some loot—well, I couldn't have taken anything from there."*

Rafi Rubinstein, also from Yehiam, remembered seeing a wounded Syrian soldier on the road. His back was injured and he was still alive, but dying. "We go by with our jeeps and not one of us dares get down," Rubinstein recounted. "Not to kill him, nor to take him for treatment. No one dared do anything. Myself included. He must have been one of the Syrians who'd been hit, maybe in the bombing, who'd managed to make it to the road to ask for help. He was sprawled out with his hands up. It was as if he was asking, with his hands, to be taken somewhere. And we just drove by. I remember we drove around him in the middle of the road, no one went over him, no one dared move him to the side of the road or anything. I can't quite take it in, but it's a fact."

For the first time, Rubinstein could see Israel from high up, from the other side of the border. "I saw our kibbutzim, so beautiful, so lush, and, really—it was beautiful. You see all that farming land and you see what a kibbutz is. And with them, everything's so neglected, poverty, so much poverty, barbed-wire fences and ditches." He was convinced that the view from the Golan Heights had fueled the Syrians' hatred. "It must get to the Arabs. I'm almost certain that was one of the reasons why they kept shooting at us."

---

*Nils Gussing, the representative of the UN secretary general, quoted two estimates of the number of refugees: the Syrians said 110,000, Israel 85,000.

Rubinstein and Uri Chizik reached El-Hama, or Hamat Gader, in Hebrew, in the southern Golan, a complex of hot springs prized for their
healing properties since antiquity. There were the ruins of a Roman theater and a synagogue. Rubinstein found two large bottles of beer at the
site and promptly got drunk. He jumped into a hot spring, Chizik said,
and started swimming and yelling, "I'm Herod, I'm Herod, I'm Herod."[18]

YAACOV HERZOG SPENT THE SABBATH IN PRAYER AND REST, AND WHEN HE RETURNED
to the prime minister's office he found that Dimitri Chuvakhin had come
to inform Eshkol that the USSR was severing diplomatic ties. Eshkol promised the ambassador that Israel did not intend to attack Damascus. Eban
later said that the ambassador wept, either because he was reluctant to
leave Israel or because he feared the welcome he could expect at home.*

Dayan agreed with Odd Bull on a cease-fire that would take effect at
six-thirty that evening. The cabinet reconvened in Tel Aviv. Warhaftig
and Shapira came in from Jerusalem, even though the Sabbath had not
ended. The IDF held positions in the northern and southern Golan.
Dayan wanted a decision as to whether to seize the areas between those
positions. Shapira opposed any continuation of the fighting, and Minister Yosef Sapir asked why the soldiers had to return fire every time they
were shot at. Dayan erupted that ten thousand orders could not stop IDF
soldiers from responding to fire. Eshkol reiterated his position: he really
only wanted to control the northern Golan and the water sources.

In the middle of the discussion, Yigal Yadin came in and announced
that the IDF now controlled the entire Golan, which put an end to all the
talk. Begin asked that his opinion be recorded in the minutes anyway: had
he been given the floor before receiving the news, he would have spoken
against ongoing fighting. The international situation was extremely
tense. Sometimes military considerations took precedence; at other times
political considerations outweighed them, and the General Staff had to
understand this. Dayan said he was surprised at his colleagues: they
should be celebrating the occupation of the Golan Heights. He suggested
having a drink and toasting their victory.

During the meeting a note was handed to Yaacov Herzog: Itamar
Warhaftig, the minister's son, had been taken from the battlefield with a
head wound. Following surgery, he was now out of danger. Zerah Warhaftig

---

*Many years afterward, Chuvakhin explained that he cried only because on his way to Eshkol
he had twisted his ankle and was in pain.[19]

nonetheless remained steadfast in his opposition to the attack on the Syrian front. Years afterward, he wrote that had Israel not attacked Syria, and had Syria not responded, Egypt would have been angry at Syria for not coming to its aid, Arab unity might have crumbled, the Communist world might have maintained diplomatic ties with Israel, and peace with Egypt might have been achieved prior to Anwar el-Sadat's visit to Jerusalem in 1977.[20] Ben-Gurion was also not pleased. In his opinion, Israel should have respected the cease-fire with Syria. "We have no need for the Golan Heights, because we will not remain there," he wrote. But one of Dayan's aides warned Ben-Gurion not to argue with Dayan or else he might resign. He needed encouragement.[21]

Dayan, as was his wont, was thinking of history. He sent Yigal Yadin a note saying, "I think Eshkol started to say something about denying that he authorized the Syrian operation yesterday morning. . . . Perhaps you would be willing to talk to him about it, to prevent any unpleasantness." Yadin confirmed that Eshkol was told about the order only after it had been issued; however, since the operation had not yet begun, he still could have stopped it.[22]

3. EXPULSION: "TEARS OF THE INNOCENT"

On Saturday evening, when the Sabbath was over, fifteen veteran Jerusalem contractors arrived at the Western Wall with bulldozers and other heavy equipment. One of them shouted, "On thy walls, Jerusalem!" His friends stood and prayed, and they wept. They decided to hold a havdalah ceremony, marking the end of the Sabbath. Some soldiers gave them wine for the blessing. When the ceremony was over, they began to destroy two public toilets at the site. By early Sunday morning they were calling themselves the "Kotel detail" and had decided to commemorate the historic occasion annually.[23] Meanwhile, bulldozers had destroyed 135 homes that had stood in front of the wall.

The Mugrabi houses, as they were known, were a slum. While the contractors knocked down the public toilets, an officer on reserve duty went from house to house, ordering the residents to evacuate. He promised they would be given new homes. The people sobbed and wailed, and begged for time to remove their possessions, to which the officer consented. And so, wrote the journalist Uzi Benziman, "with the contractors still busy smashing the toilets, the people struggled to make their way to a gathering point near Zion Gate. They carried personal belongings and household items on their backs." Some refused to leave their homes. The bulldozers approached and the weeping residents departed only after the walls of their houses began to come down. Floodlights lit up the darkened area. One elderly woman was found beneath the ruins of a wall. She was unconscious and clearly dying, although there were no external signs of injury. She was taken out of the rubble in her bed and efforts were made to help her, beneath the floodlights, among the clouds of dust raised by the bulldozers. By the time medical help arrived, the woman had died.

One of those forced out, Farj Abdel Balas, later listed the items in his two rooms: two wooden beds; a Formica wardrobe with mirror; armchairs; a child's bed; a Formica table and chairs; a large heating stove; winter and summer clothes, including a coat and a wool suit; kitchen items, including copper bowls and pots, plates, mugs, glassware, knives, spoons, and forks. In the cellar he had stored rice, sugar, oil, flour, tea, and coffee. He made his living selling tourist souvenirs at the wall. When his house was demolished he also lost camera film, pictures, and wooden crucifixes.[24]

The first person to complain about the public toilets near the wall had probably been David Ben-Gurion. Teddy Kollek promised him they would be removed. The house demolitions were done to create an open area for mass prayers on the upcoming Shavuot holiday. Uzi Narkis authorized the demolitions. In his memoirs, he wrote that the houses had been built originally to limit Jewish visitors' access to the wall. But he knew the operation was problematic, so he consulted neither Rabin nor Dayan. "If I ask for authorization, I'll get a negative response. Or else I won't get any response. Or else they'll ask me to wait. In certain situations, you don't need to involve the upper ranks." He took the responsibility upon himself. Chaim Herzog, soon to become the first military governor of the West Bank, wrote in a similar vein, "Had we waited for the necessary permits, no decision would have been made." Like Rabbi Goren, who demanded that Narkis blow up the mosque, Herzog "understood that a few days later it would be too late."

They naturally approached Mayor Kollek, who summoned an architect and an archaeologist. They toured the area on Friday and drew up plans. Kollek talked to the minister of justice, who responded, "I don't know what the legal status is. Do it quickly and may the God of Israel be with you." Given the legal and international sensitivity involved, the operation was carried out swiftly, under the cover of night, and with sufficient obfuscation to claim that neither the military nor the municipality had demolished the houses, but rather the contractors' association, a private organization. As everyone was aware, the struggle between Jews and

Arabs over control of the wall had been going on for years; in 1929 it had led to the murder of dozens of Jewish residents in Hebron and Jerusalem. Narkis detailed in his memoirs a series of unsuccessful attempts made by Jews starting in the nineteenth century to purchase the wall and its surroundings. "Now we had been given the opportunity to create new facts," he wrote.

"Those who orchestrated the destruction of the neighborhood," wrote Uzi Benziman, "believed that their work was not related purely to security or planning: that night they acted out of a near-mystic sense. In their eyes, they were representatives of the Jewish people who had come to establish sovereignty over their most sacred site. The officers and the contractors considered themselves emissaries, come to renew Jewish statehood as it had been 1,897 years earlier. At that moment they had no interest in the fate of the 135 Arab families who became the victims of these longings."[25]

WHEN YOSEF WEITZ LEFT HIS BOMB SHELTER, HE FOUND THAT THREE OF THE TREES IN his yard had been damaged in the fighting. The large carob and one pine had lost some branches, and the Jerusalem pine was entirely knocked down. Weitz started clearing it away from the other plants. His grandson, Nir, was still in the Sinai. There was no news from him, and Weitz was worried. He read in the paper that Ben-Gurion considered the conquest of Jerusalem the second greatest day of his life; the first was the day he had come to Palestine. Weitz sent him a hurried letter: What about the day independence was proclaimed? Ben-Gurion quickly replied: That was a day of great worry, but his visit to the Kotel had filled him only with joy. "Perhaps that's not the right word for the deep, thrilling experience that filled my whole being with the wonderful, swift victory the IDF has given us," he wrote. "I had just such a profound experience on my first night, after I arrived in Petach Tikva and heard the jackals crying and the donkeys braying, and felt that here I was, in our nation's resurging homeland, no longer exiled in a foreign land."[26]

Everyone was preoccupied with the question of what to do next. Ben-Gurion claimed that the government would not know how to "consolidate the conquest" in Jerusalem and Hebron. In both places, they should establish great centers of Jewish population, he told Haim Moshe Shapira and Menachem Begin, as if forgetting his earlier opposition to the war. The West Bank should not be returned to Hussein, although its annexation would add a million Arabs to Israel, which posed a grave danger.

There was also the problem of the refugees in Gaza. Begin suggested moving them to El Arish and leaving them there. "It is doubtful whether they will want to go," wrote Ben-Gurion. Begin agreed that the West Bank should remain part of Israel. Ben-Gurion tried to recruit Begin and Shapira in a war against Eshkol. Clearly, Eshkol was not adequate for the imminent diplomatic struggle. "From Shapira's response it was obvious that he did not want another battle with Eshkol. Begin did not answer," wrote Ben-Gurion.[27]

Eshkol, meanwhile, was sharing his initial thoughts with Harry McPherson, President Johnson's special envoy in Israel. Perhaps there would be a protectorate in the West Bank, neither Jordanian nor Israeli, under international rule, he suggested. McPherson told Johnson that on the first day of the war he had awoken to the sound of shells falling on Netanya, a mere six miles from the American ambassador's home, where he was staying that night. In that area at least, he wrote to the president, there was a clear need to expand Israel's territory.[28]

As he repaired the damage in his yard, Yosef Weitz waxed nostalgic for the early days of the state: "I argued and worked against the return of the Arabs who had fled," he recalled. Early in the evening of Sunday, June 11, Eshkol phoned to ask Weitz to come to his house. Like everyone else, he wanted to discuss the future of the territories. At the cabinet meeting that same day, he said he was reminded of King Saul, who had set off to search for his father's she-asses and had ended up finding a kingdom.[29]

THE ROADS OF THE WEST BANK WERE FILLED WITH LONG PROCESSIONS OF REFUGEES. "You see here how the war has destroyed the lives of thousands of families, uprooting them from their homes," wrote Minister of Agriculture Gvati in his diary.[30] Many people saw the refugees, and articles about them appeared frequently in the papers. "It was terrible," said Lieutenant Colonel Aharon Shtengl in a military summary of the war. "Two-year-old children, mothers without any water, dreadful screaming all along the road." He was reminded of a verse from a poem by Natan Alterman: "The judgment of swords had no fault / But when shedding of blood is spent / It leaves like a taste of salt / The tears of the innocent."[31]

Ze'ev Schiff described the way the refugees cast off their belongings by the side of the road to lighten their load in the oppressive heat. "Bundles of clothes mark the roads," he wrote, along with suitcases and other items. On the road near Ma'aleh Adumim, someone had discarded a prosthetic leg.[32]

One of Dayan's assistants, Arieh Brown, wrote that Dayan instructed the army to take control of the West Bank without harming citizens, but asserted, "Any citizen who wants to must be allowed to escape."[33] When Dayan heard that the residents of Tul Karem were fleeing, he welcomed the news and instructed that all traffic arterials remain open.[34] Before the bridges over the Jordan River were bombed, Rabin explained to the government that the IDF was leaving them alone so that anyone who wanted to could leave.[35] Shortly before seizing the Old City, Dayan ordered that all its gates be left open. Uzi Narkis explained: "We certainly hoped they would flee, like in 1948. But this time they didn't. We made buses available. Whoever wanted to could go to the Allenby Bridge. At first some left. Then fewer and fewer every day, until they stopped."[36]

On the third day of the war, Wednesday, June 7, IDF forces stopped on the way to Jericho. Uzi Narkis's diary reads, "It turns out there was a decision not to touch Jericho for a few hours, to let the refugees cross to the east bank of the Jordan."[37] The American embassy in Amman heard from UN eyewitnesses that the IDF had bombed refugee camps in the Jericho area housing refugees from 1948. Other sources said the IDF had fired at processions of refugees who had found themselves sharing the road with Iraqi soldiers trying to reach Jerusalem.[38] Moshe Sasson, a senior Foreign Ministry official who toured the region shortly after the war, reported, "The massive refugee camp looks like a ghost town. . . . Empty streets. Shuttered houses. Stores and cafés closed. The health clinic is empty."[39]

According to the U.S. consulate in Jerusalem, 90 percent of the 1948 refugees living in the Jericho area left their homes, a total of approximately fifty thousand people. Shlomo Gazit, the newly appointed coordinator of operations in the territories, estimated that the number of 1948 refugees who fled the Jordan Valley during the 1967 war reached seventy thousand.[40] They had been brought up on horror stories repeated, in part, to justify the original flight during the 1948 war, and which included accounts of massacres, rape, and torture. "We did not encourage them to leave, but they were simply afraid," said the soldier Rafi Rubinstein from Yehiam.[41] The 1948 refugees were described thereafter as "old refugees," while those from 1967 were "new refugees."

The U.S. embassy in Amman reported that Israeli vehicles with loudspeakers were going through West Bank villages, announcing that as long as residents maintained order they would be allowed to stay, and that anyone who wished to leave would receive assistance. A car with loudspeakers went through Bethlehem too, calling on residents to leave.

Daniel Rubinstein, stationed in the city, saw the loudspeakers.[42] The American consulate in Jerusalem reported that some 7,000 of Tul Karem's 25,000 residents had been forced to leave their homes.[43]

Ranan Lurie, a well-known cartoonist, told the journalist Gideon Levy that during his active service as an officer in Anabta village on the West Bank, commercial Israeli buses arrived to find residents waiting on the sidewalks with mattresses. Lurie's direct superior told him: "You have to load them all onto the buses. We're moving them to Jordan." Lurie refused, and someone else did the job instead.[44] Haim Brom, of Yehiam, saw refugees from Kalkilya driving by in trucks "filled to capacity, with babies and women mainly. Because there weren't any men. There were buses too." One soldier threw some of his battle rations to the refugees. "It was dreadful to see. They fell upon them . . . and that really shocked me."[45]

The Kalkilya residents had left their homes because the IDF called upon them to do so. "The people from psychological warfare turned up in the middle of the night with loudspeakers," recounted Colonel Ze'ev Shaham in an official inquiry. "I sent them to the Kalkilya area. . . . That made [the residents] really afraid. They were told all sorts of tall tales. They got up en masse and started leaving town. The men from psychological warfare told them about an Iraqi attack that would hit them there. That helped a lot."[46] Shaham later wrote: "Kalkilya sat there for all those years, breathing down the neck of Kfar Saba, giving it no rest. Many terrorist units had come from there, spreading terror and death. The instructions were clear: evacuate the residents and destroy the place. Part of the city was in fact destroyed." Kalkilya's mayor recalled that soldiers put him in a jeep, gave him a piece of paper with Arabic writing, and told him to instruct the residents to leave town. The UN representative, Nils-Göran Gussing, determined that some 850 of the town's 2,000 houses were demolished. Dayan confirmed the details of the destruction but claimed to have had no prior knowledge of it.[47]

Ezer Weizman attributed the events in Kalkilya to "the unwelcome initiative of a few commanders." Dayan, said Weizman, was furious when he found out about the destruction; he went there himself, with Weizman in tow. "We were greeted by one of the saddest spectacles of war. A city abandoned but not destroyed. An entire city, apart from a few houses with holes made by tank shells, deserted by its residents. All the stores were broken into, most of them looted, and one old man riven with age and desperation wandered around with a glazed look. And a few chickens who had not obeyed the marching orders. And one dumb donkey."[48]

Dayan remembered the Kalkilya refugees camping in some olive groves nearby. "Were Kalkilya not right across from us, with its ruined houses, one might have thought it was a large picnic," he wrote. "I know that had their hopes come true, had the Arabs won the war, they would have destroyed not only our towns and cities, but would have slaughtered us all." According to Dayan, it is possible that the Arabs indeed perceived the destruction of their homes as inevitable, but "what they would have done to us" cannot be a guideline for IDF conduct. Unwilling to tell the Palestinians that he regretted what had happened and was ashamed of it, Dayan said nothing further.[49]

Two villages near Hebron were destroyed—Beit Awa, with some 2,500 residents, and Beit Mirsim, with a population of 500. In both villages, the method was identical: soldiers came early in the morning, located the village *mukhtar*, ordered through him that all weapons be turned in, then instructed the residents to leave. They were allowed to take only food. Almost all the houses in both villages were first blown up, after which residents were allowed to return to the ruins. The *mukhtar* of Beit Awa told the UN representative that the IDF had accused the villagers of assisting Fatah.

Dayan later claimed that the villages were destroyed on the order of an officer who wanted to expel the residents. Narkis himself claimed the credit. Dayan's thoughts on the events led him to historical contemplation: "Every generation and its wars. Every generation and its destructions. But even when gardens are uprooted and people are killed and exiled, the stones remain. They will be gathered from old ruins and, for the umpteenth time, set down, one by one."[50]

On June 25, Dayan reported to the government on the circumstances of the West Bank residents' departure for Jordan.[51] First he read a letter he had sent to the chief of staff, in which he asked who had ordered the demolition of houses in Kalkilya and why. He also wanted to know who had taken young men out of Tul Karem and where they were. Rabin replied that the troops about to occupy Kalkilya had met with resistance and had acted in accordance with the directive to blow up any house from which shots were being fired. Then the orders had changed and they only blew up houses from which fire was being continued. According to Dayan these were "specific actions that might bring about the departure of people" and they ceased on the third day of the war. Other people, Dayan explained, left their homes of their own free will. He numbered those who left at 50,000 from among the 65,000 1948 refugees residing in the Jericho area. Many apparently fled because they feared they would lose their permanent UNRWA aid had they stayed. Many were dependent on money from relatives who worked in Arab oil countries. Some were employees of the Jordanian government—clerks, teachers, hospital and clinic staff, and their families—and feared losing their jobs. Among those who fled were also Jordanian soldiers disguised as civilians.

One participant in the cabinet meeting did not believe Dayan. A note among Yaacov Herzog's papers reads, "Yesterday he explicitly explained that they were keeping up the pressure by doing night searches and all sorts of petty nipping at them, 'so that they'll get the hint.' "[52]

Israel made every effort to emphasize that the majority of those who left did so willingly, and denied having forced people to leave. This version of events was often in the press. According to *Maariv*, the refugees "chose to depart their homes." Ze'ev Schiff maintained, "They are all willing refugees, mostly because of their desire to rejoin their families on the other side."[53] A Foreign Ministry report found that in addition to the destruction of Kalkilya, there was damage to five other villages. The ministry advised Israel's representatives around the world to point out that there were a thousand villages in the West Bank, and if only six of them had been affected, this was a sign that Israel had been careful to prevent pain and suffering among civilians.[54]

During the cabinet meeting discussing the refugees, Dayan expressed satisfaction with the fact that 100,000 had crossed the Jordan. "I hope they all go. If we could achieve the departure of three hundred thousand without pressure, that would be a great blessing. If we could achieve hundreds of thousands from Gaza crossing with UNRWA approval, we would be blessed." He reported that approximately a thousand refugees were leaving every day. Conceding that the situation was "awkward from a public relations point of view," he suggested bringing back the Kalkilya refugees, to which the government consented. They also discussed refugees who had fled the Latrun area; Dayan proposed not bringing them back, and the ministers decided not to decide. A sort of deal had been struck between Dayan and his colleagues: he would agree to the return of the Kalkilya refugees, while they would agree not to readmit those from Latrun.[55]

There were three populated villages in the Latrun area: Imwas, Yalu, and Beit Nuba. Nearby was Dir Ayub, abandoned. The residents were first told to leave their homes and gather in an open area outside the villages. At around nine in the morning, they were instructed over loudspeakers to march toward Ramallah. There were some eight thousand of them.[56] In the general order distributed to Central Command soldiers, Imwas and Yalu were associated with the failure to take the area in 1948 and were described as "terms of disappointment, terms of a long and painful account, which has now been settled to the last cent.

Houses suddenly left. Intact. With their potted geraniums, their grapevines climbing up the balconies. The smell of wood-burning ovens still in the air. Elderly people who have nothing more to lose, slowly straggling along."[57]

Dayan later claimed that the Jordanians had been firing from the Latrun area toward Lod Airport. "The fellahin in the Latrun-area villages were certainly not to blame for this, but for us it was not a question of punishing the guilty, but of doing what was necessary for Israel's security," Dayan wrote."[58] Nils-Göran Gussing reported that Dayan told him some of the village houses had been hit during the fighting, and that he had ordered the rest destroyed because of the area's strategic importance, given its location between Jerusalem and Tel Aviv.[59] One eyewitness, the journalist Amos Kenan, who was present as a soldier, heard the same argument from the company commander in charge of destroying the villages. The commander gave two more reasons: "To punish these nests of murderers" and to prevent the houses from becoming terrorist bases in the future.

Beit Nuba had beautiful stone houses, wrote Kenan, some of them grand. Each house was surrounded by a garden with trees—olives, apricots—vines, and ornamentals, such as cypresses. The plants grew on small mounds, and the trees stood among well-manicured, weeded, and tilled greenery. Kenan and his fellow soldiers' job was to comb the houses and make sure they were empty. They found an injured Egyptian commando officer and a few elderly men and women. At noon the first bulldozer to arrive immediately drove up to a house at the edge of the village. First it uprooted a few cypresses and olive trees; then it demolished the house itself. Within ten minutes, the house was in ruins, including the few items left inside. Then a group of refugees suddenly appeared, village residents. Someone had apparently told them to come back, and a few had even heard on the radio that Israel was not deporting refugees.

Kenan and his fellow soldiers prepared to defend themselves and those among them who spoke Arabic approached the refugees. "There were elderly people there who could barely walk," Kenan wrote. "Mumbling old women, babies in their mothers' arms, small children. The children cried and begged for water. The procession waved white flags." The soldiers told them to go to another village, Beit Sira. "They told us they had been kicked out of every place they went. They had been walking for four days without food or water, and some had died. They asked to come back to the village and said they'd be better off if we killed them." Some had goats, sheep, camels, or donkeys. "A father chafed a few grains of wheat in the palm of his hand and gave them to his four children to eat."

Another procession was visible on the horizon. Kenan described it: "A man walks, on his back a hundred-pound sack of flour. That's how he walks, mile after mile. More old women, more mothers, more babies. They collapsed in exhaustion wherever we told them to sit. Some had a cow or two, a calf. All their worldly possessions. We didn't let them return to the village to get their belongings, because the order was that they were not allowed to see their homes being destroyed." The children cried, and some of the soldiers also wept, wrote Kenan. They couldn't find water to bring the refugees, so they stopped a military vehicle, took out a jerrycan, and distributed that water. They also gave out candy and cigarettes. More soldiers started crying, and a few of them asked the officers why the refugees were being moved around and kicked out of everywhere they went. Some of the officers replied that this was the best thing: "Why worry about a bunch of Arabs?"

More and more groups arrived; there were already hundreds of refugees. They could not understand why they had been told to come back but were not allowed to enter the village. "Their pleading was unbearable," wrote Kenan. "One person asked us why we were destroying the houses—it would be better if we lived in them ourselves." The company commander decided to go to headquarters to find out whether there were instructions on how to handle the refugees, where to send them, and whether there was any possibility of organizing vehicles for the women and children, and some food. He returned saying there were no written orders and that the people must be deported.

"We deported them," wrote Kenan. In the evening, he found out the refugees had been lied to: bulldozers had started demolishing houses in Beit Sira, too, where they had been sent. According to Kenan, "Most of the soldiers were furious and most of the guys did not want to do the job," but no one refused the order. The soldiers stayed there that night to guard the bulldozers, and in the morning they were transferred elsewhere.

"None of us could understand how Jews could do this," Kenan wrote at the end of his report. "Even those who approved of the operation argued that temporary camps could have been set up for the people, a final decision made about where to put them, and then they could have been driven there with their belongings. No one understood why these fellahin could not take their Primus stoves, their blankets, and their supplies." Kenan was forty at the time, a writer with a column in *Yediot Aharonot*, and a formative figure in Israeli culture and the emerging Hebrew language.

Almost twenty years earlier, in 1948, as a Lehi member, he had been wounded in the battle for the Arab village of Dir Yassin, on the outskirts of Jerusalem. That operation had ended with a massacre of civilians and caused thousands of Arabs from all over the country to flee their homes.[60] Kenan concluded his Latrun report: "The chickens and the doves were buried under the ruins. The fields turned desolate before our very eyes, and children walked down the road sobbing." As he saw it, when the next round came, nineteen years later, these children would be the terrorists. "That was how we lost our victory that day," he ended.[61]

At a meeting of officers a few months after the war, Moshe Dayan said that the destruction of the villages had been done with "Zionist intentions," with which he was entirely in agreement "within the complex framework of the unpleasant and unpopular aspects of fulfilling Zionism." But he added that villages should be destroyed "up to a certain limit" only, which in his opinion must not be breached under any circumstances.[62]

According to Israeli estimates, the war produced between 200,000 and 250,000 refugees. More than half left during and immediately after the war, and the rest in the following months. Thousands were housed in tent camps, in conditions described in a special report to President Johnson as "appalling."[63]

LOOTING, BY BOTH SOLDIERS AND CIVILIANS, WAS WIDESPREAD. THEY BROKE INTO houses and shops, stealing furniture, jewelry, electrical appliances, and often even cars. "For a while, most of our Old City friends went about on foot," wrote the American consul in Jerusalem.[64] The looters also robbed Armon Hanatziv. Two days after its seizure, Michael Pragai, a Foreign Ministry official, learned that "an abundance of articles had disappeared" from the site. Food and beverage storehouses had been emptied; communications equipment had been dismantled and removed. Then Pragai heard about a "rampage" in General Odd Bull's private residence and he went to see for himself. The officer who accompanied him said that what was going on there "exceeded any reasonable rules." In response, Pragai wrote, General Uzi Narkis agreed to conduct a "campaign to smooth things out" before Bull returned, to create the impression that fighting, rather than looting, had caused the damage. Meanwhile, Bull inquired about his apartment several times; among other things, he was concerned about a pipe he had left there. Pragai told him it had been damaged in the fighting, and the dismayed general replied graciously that he understood—after all, there had been a war.[65]

Shuka Bar-Dayan's fellow soldiers also did a lot of looting. At first they took souvenirs from the convoys of burned-out Egyptian tanks. "It's as if some people are bewitched and don't know what to take. They see a hand grenade—they take it," wrote Bar-Dayan on the morning of June 8. A few hours later he wrote, "Everyone's looting. They've got a real lust to loot. They're pinching soldiers' backpacks, socks, wallets, and lots of letters with pictures of girlfriends and mothers." He thought this was very human: after all, the Egyptians had forced them into this lethal war. The next day he wrote, "Everyone's under a spell . . . in the evening they throw away what they looted that morning."[66]

Soldiers on other fronts did the same. One Yehiam soldier back from the battle on the Golan recounted, "Our soldiers went in and basically took everything, every dagger, every shiny object. All at once, they fell into some kind of looting frenzy."[67] Civilians who heard similar accounts from soldiers, or even visited the Golan Heights themselves shortly after its capture, described the looting in their letters. "The division of the spoils went like this," wrote one woman. "They asked each soldier how many kids he had, and each one chose a gift for every kid." Her boy got some lovely things, she wrote. An Israeli who wanted to visit Kuneitra found access barred. "The guys in there were doing a good job of grabbing everything they could lay their hands on," he wrote.[68] "Our soldiers," said Haim Brom from Yehiam, "not everyone, but quite a lot of them, treated this property in a humiliating way. They looted, and they not only looted—they smashed, they destroyed. They wanted to be heroes but not in battle."

General Yeshayahu Gavish found it necessary to devote an entire general order to the phenomenon. "There is great temptation in the circumstance that we are a victorious, conquering army. There are many enchanting items inside the stores and the houses. It requires an emotional effort, maturity, intelligence and awareness, as well as self-control to prevent the disgrace of looting." He called upon the stronger soldiers to help their comrades in moments of weakness. "Robbery, plundering, rampaging, and harming peaceful civilians—all these harm and destroy the effort and the goal of maintaining normalcy in the conquered areas. They distract soldiers from their primary mission, which is to fight and strike at the enemy and its positions." Every little break-in could lead to gross rampages and indiscipline, Gavish asserted, and warned that he was determined to punish any instance of rebelliousness, looting, or theft to the full extent of the law.[69] The next day another announcement was distributed among the soldiers, reminding them that under military law, looting was punishable by up to ten years in prison. "Our victory and our accomplishment are dear to us and they are pure. Let us not sully them," said the announcement.[70] Other official documents confirm the gravity of the problem.

A Foreign Ministry official told the U.S. ambassador that General Chaim Herzog had been appointed military governor of the West Bank, partly to put a stop to the wave of looting, as he was known for maintaining discipline among his troops.[71] Herzog was indeed troubled by looting, which he attributed to the reservists who had replaced the paratrooper units.[72] From New York, Abba Eban wrote to Eshkol about the political damage resulting from the news of the deportations and looting. Others voiced similar concerns. The phenomenon worried Eshkol himself.[73] Rabin reported that an investigation had resulted in the recommendation that those responsible for the looting at Armon Hanatziv be reprimanded. A kibbutz newsletter recounted one officer's method: "The commander took a Bible from his pocket and read us the chapter about looting from the Book of Joshua. When he finished, all the soldiers silently put down the things they had taken, collected everything in a pile, poured lighter fluid on it, and burned it."[74]

4. FINAL PARADE: "THESE ARE MY SONS"

On Monday, June 12, Shuka Bar-Dayan spotted the famous entertainers Shaike Ofir, Uri Zohar, and Arik Lavi. He went up to Lavi, introduced himself as a relative of the singer Rema Samsonov, Yehiam Weitz's widow, and asked if he would possibly put in a call to Gili. The newspapers arrived from the previous Friday, informing the troops that the Western Wall would soon be open to visitors. Valencia oranges were brought in, and Bar-Dayan recognized a crate he had packed with his own hands meant for export. He was proud of the fruits of his labor: the oranges looked fresh and firm and the soldiers gobbled them up. A tractor started piling mounds of sand over Egyptian soldiers' bodies: "burying the Egyptian army," Bar-Dayan wrote, "so never again will it rise from its desert grave."

His brigade was now encamped near Bir Gafgafa. The tanks were preparing for the final parade. Shuka wrote a long letter to his wife. Every morning when he woke up and found he was still there, he got a bit of a shock, but it passed after a second. "To hell with everything, the main thing is that you're alive, alive, alive—that you've come out of this thing, of this war, unhurt, without a scratch—that you'll go home to Gili and Yariv," he wrote to her. The thought gave him the strength for another day in the desert. He reminded Gili of something she had said to him that Saturday over lunch in Beersheba: "I don't care if you stay a bit longer, or a lot longer, as long as you're alive, as long as we know you'll come back." And that would happen, he promised, it would. But there were many who would not be going home. "Magnificent young men who sacrificed themselves in the enemy's fires." He knew several of them. He was still constantly kissing his wedding ring, the amulet that had been with him in the most difficult moments. "Kiss Yarivi for me and have Yarivi kiss you," he asked.

He had reached the "guest house," a camp that had been built for Egyptian officers. Even the transistor radio sounded better there. He shaved and showered for the first time, after eight days without water or soap, and changed his underwear. "I started shouting and floating on air like a helicopter." His mustache had grown, his stomach was flat, he felt wonderful. He had a lot of time; he was rereading some paperbacks other soldiers had brought. Everyone kept repeating the same word: "freedom."* "God, I wish the day would come already," he wrote. "A three-hour drive and I'm home." He hoped Gili had received all his letters; he hoped Arik Lavi had called. He told her, for the first time, about his diary: "I wrote it during battle, under fire." He could see the Suez Canal from afar. He had become very friendly with Binyamin, a young soldier of Iraqi origin who had not yet seen his own newborn son. They made tea together. "This war, Gili, was more than a war of independence. The precious blood spilled in the War of Independence pales in comparison to this crimson blood, if one can say that—because this one was crueler and involved terrible weapons of destruction. I'll have a lot of slides from pictures we've been taking, and we'll prepare lectures and go and talk to young people and to adults."[76]

IN AN IDF DISCUSSION OF THE LESSONS OF THE WAR, UZI NARKIS SAID, "WE WERE warned about a terrible enemy. It turned out to be worthless. That's the only lesson." Rabin listed in his memoirs a series of tough battles, but maintained that the IDF could have conquered Cairo and Amman and, without much effort, Damascus too.[77] The military attaché at the British embassy, a Colonel Rogers, thought that Israel had exaggerated in

---

*Two days earlier, Zvi Zur, assistant to the minister of defense, had reported to David Ben-Gurion that the reservists numbered roughly 171,000 and that they would soon begin discharging 140,000 of them.[75]

describing the battles. He wrote that most were not that fierce. The IDF had enjoyed continuous air supremacy and had fought fifth-class forces that had retreated quickly. The IDF excelled at offense, but the British colonel wondered whether it would have fared as well in a defensive war.[78]

Three days after the end of the war, Dayan went before the Knesset Foreign Affairs and Defense Committee and reiterated his claim that Eshkol's government had caused war to break out by exacerbating tensions with Syria. The gamble that Egypt would not interfere had been a mistake, as had the belief that the United States would open the Straits of Tiran and that there had therefore been no need to respond immediately to their closure. Dayan said the air force was ill-equipped, with an insufficient number of planes. Eshkol fumed: "Dayan walks in one minute before the play starts, then he claims the director and the actors were weak, the theater was dirty, and the audience was lousy. What is he thinking?"

Dayan failed to mention that roughly six months earlier he himself had written in *Maariv* that Egypt would not allow Syria to drag it into a war. Nor did he mention his own part in the events that led up to the war, including his claim that one more week of waiting would lead to the country's annihilation. He neglected to mention his warning regarding the danger that the USSR would intervene if Israel seized the Golan.[79] The waiting period left history grappling with a difficult question: an immediate military response to the Straits blockade might have limited the scope of the war, thereby preventing the occupation of the West Bank. Eshkol observed later that had his government acted sooner, there might have been no need for the national unity government.[80]

Approximately 340 Israeli soldiers were killed in the Sinai and roughly 300 in the fighting in the West Bank, including 183 in Jerusalem. Fourteen residents of Israeli Jerusalem were killed, and approximately 500 were wounded. In the Golan Heights, 141 Israelis were killed and some 2,500 wounded. A few later died of their wounds, bringing the total deaths to 800, far below the fearful predictions before the war.[81]

AN ORANGE BLAZE SLOWLY SET AT THE EDGE OF THE DESERT, WROTE SHUKA BAR-Dayan on June 12, and a cool breeze began to blow. People huddled around the jeeps, tanks, and half-tracks, trading stories while they waited for the final parade. They talked about Ehud, the regimental commander, and other men who were killed. A tape recorder played military marches. They waited for the divisional commander. A makeshift stage had been set up on a pilfered vehicle, decorated with a large Star of David and lots of flags—green and black, the armored corps colors, as well as blue and white. There were dozens of tanks and other vehicles, and thousands of soldiers.

Uri Zohar, Arik Lavi, and Shaike Ofir got up to organize a sing-along. The great Chaim Topol was also there. They sang "Nasser Is Waiting for Rabin." The soldiers didn't sing much. Shaike Ofir read out Israel Tal's original directive, written by Amos Oz. The entire division stood at attention. Uri Zohar recited Yizkor, the memorial prayer, for the roughly seventy soldiers of the 7th Division who had fallen in battle.

Yaffa Yarkoni, the legendary wartime singer, sang "Bab El-Wad," a song memorializing the convoys that had broken through to Jerusalem in the War of Independence. "A hand reaches out from the convoys of 1948 to the division fighters near Ismailia," wrote Bar-Dayan. Then the commander's convoy arrived.

Gorodish wore dark glasses, as he always did. "My friends and brothers—I am both humbled and proud to be your commander—you fought like lions—your heroism rivals that of the Hasmoneans—you have written a glorious page in the history of our nation—our hearts are with the families of the fallen soldiers—we fought because there was no other choice—you, my glorious brothers." Bar-Dayan wrote down only fragments.

Haim Hefer read "The Parade of Fallen Soldiers," a story in verse describing a meeting of soldiers in heaven—strong, bronzed men who emerge from downed planes and burned-out tanks and ascend to the angels. Up above, they hear familiar voices crying down below. "They look home to Dad and Mom, to the wives, the children and the siblings / Their faces fall still and they stand awkwardly / Then one of them whispers: 'I'm sorry, but we had to / And we won the battles and now we can rest.'" As they stand with the light on their faces, God comes and passes between them. "And with tears in his eyes, He kisses their wounds / And says in a trembling voice to his white angels, / 'These are my sons, these are the sons.'"

It was moving, Shuka wrote in his diary. He looked around for Arieh and Leon, two young tank commanders who had befriended him before the war, when he, the soldiers' "dad," had given them cigarettes. He found Arieh. They hugged. He asked about Leon. Leon had been killed in Jiradi. Arieh reminded Shuka of the Patton tank, with a soldier in torn clothes lying on top, all splattered with blood. Shuka had not recognized him at the time. It was Leon.

He was devastated, and no longer heard what was being said on stage. He went to sit alone in his truck. But then Yaffa Yarkoni climbed up on the stage again, embraced a twenty-two-year-old soldier, and performed what she had sung twenty years earlier to fighters in the War of Independence, back when the soldier she now hugged was an infant. "Believe me, the day will come / It will be good, I promise you / I will come to hold you / And make you forget everything." The atmosphere was electric. Shuka wrote to Gili, "They began singing their lungs and hearts out in their thousands. I was really trembling with excitement—unbelievable." Then they all sang "Jerusalem of Gold." Shuka was overcome with longing for home, but he knew everything would be fine.[82]

PART IV

THEY THOUGHT THEY HAD WON

Thirty years after he began to work as a journalist in Jerusalem, Gabriel Stern was asked about his hardest moments. "The most difficult thing," he replied, "was writing against our own military operations and denouncing our acts of injustice and vengeance while our dead were still with us and my readers' hearts were bleeding."[1]

CHAPTER 16

A NEW LAND

1. MOURNING: "WHY DID YOU MARRY A PILOT?"

The body of Major Arieh Ben-Or was recovered from the wreckage of his plane a few days after the crash. Many people attended his funeral, at the military cemetery in Herzliya. His body was interred in a wooden casket. Yonina, his widow, did not ask to see it and did not trouble herself with thoughts of what remained of her husband. They were secular people; they did not sit shiva, though numerous visitors paid their respects. Moshe Dayan sent a condolence letter.

It took time for Yonina Ben-Or to come to terms with her husband's death. Hardest of all was the first trip to their apartment in Tel Nof. For her, this was the most concrete encounter with the tragedy—harder than the burial, harder than the memorial service thirty days after his death. She cried the whole way there. "I go into the neighborhood and it's like it used to be: nothing has changed. Children ride bikes. Women shake out rugs. Laundry hangs on the lines. Everything I used to be. And I'm no longer part of it. Because Arieh is gone and I am part of this life only thanks to him." Before the war, they had planned to move to the base at Hatzerim, in the south. Now she decided to move elsewhere. "Life is stronger than we are," she said a few months later. "I go on. I live. I keep busy with the same thousands of trivialities. Shopping, cooking, washing the dishes . . . I do things mechanically. After all, the girls have to go to kindergarten and school. You have to get up. You have to live—because they're living." It was not forgetting, she said. It was repression. Escape. And she was a realistic woman: as soon as the war was over, she sought emotional support from friends. Even strangers seemed to draw close, and she was grateful. But she knew that this time would pass and friends would go on with their lives. Other people were happy; she was not. They were entitled to be happy; they had reason to be. Historians wrote of the country's "huge victory," perhaps adding a statistical note about the "low cost." But for Ben-Or, the cost was not low. "There is a terrible void, and nothing can fill it. An endless struggle to live without Arieh. For the girls."

Mihal, at three, drew a picture for her daddy. She asked when his plane would come back and he would step out of it. "No, Mihal, that's not how it is," her mother had to say. "They've already brought back his plane and your daddy was killed. He was a hero. He drove out the Syrians and they shot his plane down and he was killed." The girl said, "Mommy, you know what? I'll get a really really big gun and I'll go to Daddy and give him the gun and he'll kill all the Arabs and then his plane will come back, because there'll be no more Arabs in his way. Okay, Mommy?" Six-year-old Arza asked, "Mommy, why did you marry a pilot? Why? I'll never marry a pilot. A pilot could get killed in the war, like Daddy. I'll marry a doctor, or a mechanic." And her mother had to explain some things to her as well: "When you love someone, it doesn't really matter what he does. When you love someone, you tie your lives together. And I married your daddy not because he was a hero or because he was a pilot. I just loved him." A few months after Ben-Or's death, his widow told an interviewer from *Maariv* that sometimes she and the girls talked about Arieh as if he were still alive.[2]

THE ISRAELI CULTURE OF MOURNING WAS WELL DEVELOPED BY THIS POINT, WITH ITS ceremonies and symbols, its rhetoric of private and public consolation, and its special rights for those who were left behind. Israel embraced the families of fallen soldiers and, at times, exploited them.

Many Israelis wrote about the casualties of the war in their letters, even when they themselves were not directly affected. For a time, mourning was at the center of Israeli experience. "There is such heartache over the fallen, each one is so precious to us. Thank God everyone in our family came home safe," wrote Rivka Cohen. Edith Ezrachi of Jerusalem wrote to Norwalk, Connecticut, "I feel so sad and depressed about the sacrifice involved that I haven't been able to lift my head and try to understand and accept what has been achieved so miraculously." These were not mere platitudes: grief was a concrete part of the Israeli routine, at least while people daily encountered the names of the dead that appeared in black mourning notices in the newspapers. A significant number of Israelis at least knew someone who knew someone who had lost a relative or a friend or an acquaintance, and even these indirect connections were troubling. "It's terrible when you want to comfort someone and you know you can't and you leave exactly as you came," wrote one kibbutz woman to her daughter in Los Angeles.

Many Israelis, not sure about the proper way to behave, wrote to Hana Bavli, whose etiquette column in *Ha'aretz* performed a public service. Should one greet mourners with the usual "Shalom" when entering and leaving their homes? Was shaking hands in order? Bavli ruled against "Shalom," but approved of shaking hands. One reader wrote that he had gone to visit an acquaintance on business and found the household in mourning over a family friend who had been killed. What should one do in this situation? Bavli advised that at the moment it would be prudent to inquire about the situation before visiting, through mutual friends or relatives. If that was impossible, it was best to simply take the risk and go. Never hesitate to visit or postpone it—precisely because there might have been a tragedy in the household: "There is nothing worse than feeling indifference and loneliness." Other readers wanted to know whether to invite to their daughter's wedding close friends who had lost their son in the war. Bavli asserted, "You must not isolate parents in mourning. A routine invitation is inappropriate here, but you must find a way to share your celebration with them. Perhaps they might like to meet the couple in a more private setting?"[3]

Bereavement renewed old ties and forged new ones. Yitzhak Knafo, a teacher, wrote to his sister, Odette, in France about the death of a distant relative, Max Ben-Ezra. Knafo, who was born in Morocco, had been in Israel for eleven years and had never visited the Ben-Ezras. "I don't know anything about them. I know nothing about poor Max. I don't know whether he was single or married, or if he had children." But the death seemed to bring the family suddenly closer; Knafo grieved, because back in Casablanca, Max used to talk to him about his studies.*

National mourning made the war seem larger, commensurate somehow with both the immense anxiety that had preceded it, and with the magnitude of the victory. The greater the feeling of bereavement, the less Israelis wondered whether their prewar fears had been warranted, and

---

*Max Ben-Ezra, of Dimona, was a draftsman. He was killed in the battle for Gaza, on the second day of the war. He left a wife, two sons, and a little daughter.

whether the perils faced by the country justified the occupation of the captured territories. Death, in the context of war, was often portrayed as a great privilege. A Tel Aviv high school principal wrote to the parents of a graduate killed on duty, "Who would have thought that Amiram was destined at such a young age to attain the greatest honor a man can achieve: to pay with his young life for the nation and the state."

It was customary to say that the soldiers had not been killed in vain, but in a just and inevitable war—in defense of the country, of life itself, and of peace—and that Israel was doing everything to make sure that this would be the last war. The general view was that the soldiers had not gone to war joyously, that they had not fought with hatred, and that in their deaths they had bequeathed their people life. The fallen soldiers were often endowed with the qualities society valued and nurtured: a close bond with the country, its land and landscapes; courage, a willingness to sacrifice, team spirit, levelheadedness, sociability, helpfulness; a deep connection to their parents, the ability to love, a sense of humor, a joy both in work and in recreation, like sports, hiking, photography. The dead were often said to have held political opinions that justified the war, the conquests, and even death itself. "During his brief life, he displayed loyalty and dedication to his friends and a great love of his country," reads the book *In Memoriam*, published by the Ministry of Defense, in a description of one fallen soldier. The passage goes on to quote the young man: "I am still young and I still have time to learn a lot. But first, I owe my time to the army." Another soldier reportedly signed up for medical school, "because the paratroopers need doctors." Of a third, the book said: "In his death while fulfilling his duty on the Shechem–Ramallah road, he proved his love of the country in which he grew up and for which he fought."

The soldier Yehoshua-Mordehai Azriel Diamant, known as Shaia, had apparently asked a comrade in arms to tell his parents not to grieve, because he was glad to have had the privilege of fighting to liberate Jerusalem. Yoel Yinon from Jerusalem wrote to Vardit and Adir Zik in Los Angeles about Shaia's memorial service, a moving and painful event. The men stood up one after another and talked about Shaia as a leader in the national-religious youth movement, Bnei Akiva, and about his training as a tour guide. His sister read from a postcard he had written, which proved that he felt something great was about to happen. One friend described him in his role as a squad leader and a fighter during his final battle. Other friends spoke; a rabbi offered scriptural teaching in Shaia's memory; "and everything everyone said gave such a complete picture that it really brought him to life," Yinon recounted. "And it's always that way," he continued. "When you live with a person you feel all sorts of things about him, but you don't actually say them. Either because you don't really think about them or because you don't like to be so emotional and sentimental. Only when, God forbid, a tragedy happens and the time comes to give a eulogy, you see that all the flowery expressions are not so empty, and that, in fact, you don't have the words to express your feelings." He told the Ziks that the eulogies had been tape-recorded, and they could hear them when they came home from America.[4]

YEHOSHUA BAR-DAYAN WAS RELEASED FROM ACTIVE DUTY AT THE END OF JUNE, BUT before then, he got a forty-eight-hour leave. He told Gili and everyone else about the war, and played at soldiers with Yariv, who put on his father's army beret. Bar-Dayan wrote in his diary that the little boy felt like a real soldier.

"It's disheartening to go back," he wrote afterward. He was still posted at Bir Gafgafa in the Sinai Desert. The repair shops were full of vehicles now, both damaged IDF machines and captured vehicles made in the Soviet Union. Almost three weeks after the war, Bar-Dayan happened on the body of an Egyptian soldier lying under the radiator of an abandoned vehicle. He must have been hoping to find water. The first Israeli visitors began arriving in the Sinai, including women and children; some were bereaved families wanting to see where their loved ones had been killed. On June 29, just before midnight, Bar-Dayan received his discharge notice. Before leaving the desert, he had to hose the mud off the commandeered pickup truck that had been his home for the past forty days. Its owner had already been by to check up on it. On his way north, Bar-Dayan passed through Gaza. Children lined the streets, waving and shouting, "Bread, bread!" Sprinklers were watering the cotton fields as Bar-Dayan drove past his old kibbutz, Erez, which was quite close to the barrier between Israel and the Gaza Strip. "Let's hope it's never closed again," he wrote. The next day he was in Rishon Lezion. As he neared his home, he could see Gili and Yariv on the balcony. Yariv was playing with a new toy tank.*

---

*Bar-Dayan began preparing his diary for publication when he got home. The idea had come to him soon after he began writing, but it was not easy to find a publisher. The writer Moshe Shamir, who worked for the publisher Sifriat Maariv, told him that the diary was not fit for publication because soldiers were not supposed to cry. A modified version was published a year later in *Ha'aretz*, and then in book form.[5]

· · ·

THE BURDEN OF PUBLIC GRIEF SOON MADE WAY FOR THE INTOXICATION OF VICTORY, although at first there was some mingling between the two. "Everyone alternates between tears and laughter," wrote one woman to America, "joy and sorrow are woven together." Many letters reflected a confused sense of time and general disorientation. "It's like we've taken drugs," one said. Scores of Israelis went to see the captured territories. "The whole country is celebrating and taking field trips; all the liberated areas are full of curious Israelis shopping," one wrote to friends in Los Angeles. "The Jews are on the move," wrote Yosef Weitz a few days after the war, as he watched convoys of vehicles filled with day-trippers. "Everything is moving, shifting, in a frenzy."[6]

2. EXCURSIONS: "THIS IS MY JOY IN LIFE"

Israelis came to see the West Bank as the true Eretz Israel, the land of biblical promise, and in the first few weeks after the war they crossed it like adventurous explorers who have landed on a yearned-for continent, long forbidden and beyond reach. They brought their vast curiosity, and in many cases nostalgia and historical romanticism. Many were caught up in religious fervor. The rush to the territories fulfilled a need to break through Israeli insularity, like traveling abroad. Israelis flooded the Arab markets. Many searched for acquaintances from the Mandate era: neighbors, landlords, employees. While some were uncomfortable with their new status as occupiers, many resented the Arabs and approached them with arrogance, gloating, and the possessive authoritarianism of the victor, the essence of which was: We're back.

Soldiers were taken on outings to the territories as a perk. Hen Ronen recounted his first visit to occupied Kalkilya. His parents were from a moshav in the nearby Sharon region. "I knew Kalkilya from my schooldays. Back then, I would go there and be welcomed like a prince. After all, I was my father's son. He was in charge of all the orchards there." He remembered a tombstone the children had liked to see on school trips; it was still there, just like twenty years ago. "I've lived my whole life about three miles from Kalkilya, and now I'm so excited. I know Kalkilya. It was full of all those bastards who used to bother us when we were working in the fields. And there were friends there, too. It would have been interesting to meet some of them. But they're gone. No one was there. I was dying to see one of the little guys I used to fight with, we threw stones at each other. They were gone."*

"We have the most wonderful country, and the more you get to know it, the greater you love it and feel attached to it," wrote Yitzhak Kotler, a soldier, to his girlfriend. "I found places that for me were part of my life's dreams, places I had longed to go to one day; I had never imagined the dream would come true so soon." He remembered the two of them looking out to the West Bank from the Israeli side of the border. They would often point to Nebi Samuel, near Jerusalem, and talk about it. Now he was about to find himself "right on the Nebi," as he wrote, with all of Jerusalem at his feet. "A dream, an absolute dream!" He was amazed by the beautiful palm trees on the beach in Gaza, and the monasteries carved out of cliffs in the Judean Desert. He was drawn to the territories by "an inner pull," perhaps an "emotional need." He wanted to see more and more. "This is my joy in life."[8]

Moshe Dayan marveled at the springtime blossoms that welcomed him on the outskirts of Hebron, and was inspired by Jericho, the "City of Dates." "It is a wonderful city," he wrote. "To really see it, you have to close your eyes." The oldest city in the world sat at the lowest point on earth, he wrote. "Everything around is dry, desolate, white as chalk, but the city is rich with gardens, stories and legends—from Rahab the prostitute in her window, to the Chariot of Israel and its horsemen rising up to the heavens." No conqueror has not crossed it but no war can destroy it, wrote Dayan; Jericho had always been rebuilt. "The Jordan, the sweet water, the fertile valley—they are stronger than any destruction."

Ezer Weizman was often with Dayan. He had the peculiar sense of having woken from a nineteen-year slumber to find himself, when opening his eyes, back again under British rule, with the same narrow roads, the same landmarks and the signs, the same vineyards, watermelon fields, and fragrant orchards. "For someone who grew up under the British, this is not just the land of the Bible," wrote Weizman. "As I traveled the roads of the liberated land of Israel, I kept thinking a British policeman would appear from around the bend on a motorcycle, stop me, and give me a speeding ticket."[9]

---

*Before visiting Kalkilya, Ronen passed through the village of Kibya. White flags flew on every house. He knew the significance of where he was, and felt "the great stain" that had marked the IDF since a force commanded by Ariel Sharon blew up a few dozen of the village houses, killing their inhabitants, in October 1953, in retaliation for the murder of an Israeli woman and her two children in nearby Yehud.[7]

Civilians needed an army permit to visit the territories; in the first days and weeks after the war, there was no document more sought-after. The permits testified to a person's status, to his connections and his part in the victory. One man called his duty commander, the other knew the general's aide; this one talked to the CEO's brother-in-law, and the next got his permit from the head of his yeshiva. David Bartov, an administrator in the court system, wrote to his brother, Haim Israeli, assistant to the minister of defense: "You'll surely understand that the status of a Supreme Court justice, equal to a minister, entitles him to a permanent permit rather than the temporary one that has to be periodically replaced or reissued." He did not explain the urgent need for judges to visit the West Bank; it was simply a matter of entitlement and respect.

Some permits were valid only for visiting specific places in Sinai, the West Bank, or in the Golan Heights. Some limited visits to a few hours, with or without private vehicles, with or without an escort; others were broader. Some were collective: duplicated on mimeograph machines and filled in by hand, or typed. They were white and blue, pink and green, square or rectangle; every so often the permit forms were changed and replaced with others.[10] Many people simply ignored the need for a permit, and found that no one tried to stop them.

The members of Kibbutz Yehiam set off for the West Bank in five yellow buses. "The road is hilly and reminiscent of familiar landscapes," wrote one member, "with one difference: the mountain agriculture here has been cared for wonderfully. There are vineyards, terraces, and fields as far as the eye can see. Everything is neat, cultivated, clean, and pleasing. Here and there, wheat is reaped with sickles or pulled up (mostly by women) by hand." Seeing a grove of pines in Gush Etzion, the tourists called out jokingly, "The Jewish National Fund!" They did not know that the trees had in fact been planted by the JNF in the forties.

Yosef Weitz was also impressed by the quality of Palestinian agronomy, calling it a lovingly cultivated "life support." As he neared Hebron his delight grew: "The more I look closely, the more ashamed and embarrassed I feel comparing 'our' Jerusalem mountains to their Hebron mountains. We, who use steel (large tilling machines), have training, huge budgets, and expensive water, have not achieved anything so flourishing. We are culturally and practically inferior by comparison, and all because they are people who work the land, and that land is their sole livelihood, and we are far from being that."

This was one of the surprises awaiting Israelis who visited the territories, because in "Homeland," as geography classes were called, they were taught that the Arabs neglected their land: they did not repair the stone terraces built by the Hebrews two thousand years ago, and they allowed the earth to erode and expose the rock; their goats destroyed the ancient natural forests; they neglected to weed the streams, so that vegetation clogged them; they stole stones from ancient sites and used them to build houses. Israeli geography books frequently quoted a British official who had concluded that "the Bedouins are not the children of the desert, but rather its creators." A few days after the war, signs appeared in the Occupied Territories, cautioning against harming animal and plant life. The National Parks Authority and the Nature Reserve Authority were asked to include the West Bank and the Gaza Strip in their activities, which included "the improvement of Israel's landscape."

"Visitors were thrilled to see Israelis showing such sensitivity to the landscape, even at the height of a cruel war," wrote historian Meron Benvenisti. Upon returning from a visit to the Banias estuary, Yehuda Yost wrote, "It is a real pleasure to come to such a place weeks after the conquest and see signs warning people not to despoil the environment and to respect the place as a nature preserve." The Syrians, he noted, had done nothing to open the area to visitors. "But this sensitivity," Benvenisti continued, "had another purpose as well: to stake a claim. The landscape is precious to us because it is ours. The test of a proprietary claim is in the extent of our caring. And of course there is the flip side of this approach: neglecting the country, as others have done, is decisive proof that they do not care, and therefore have no right to the land."

Israelis flooded the territories, as if they felt a need to take the land again and again. "Our trip to the conquered territories was fantastic," wrote two Israelis to friends abroad. "It's hard to describe the amazing landscape, particularly the desert and what's been left on the battlefields. It's impossible to take in. Simply a dream, and all this in six days."[11] The heaps of abandoned weapons that the army had not yet cleared away stood like monuments to victory, especially in the Golan Heights. "The entire valley looks like the palm of your hand," wrote one IDF officer. "On one hand there's great concrete slabs (which now stink because of the quantities of urine left by Israeli hikers) and on the other, the farmed fields. And perhaps there's no greater contrast between war and peace than this scene."

Yosef Weitz noted a sense shared by many who visited the Golan: "As we stood next to the Syrian and Russian posts we understood full well how important it is for the Golan to be part of the country, for the security of people in the Hula valley and at Lake Tiberias." However, he thought it unnecessary to hold on to the entire Golan: the outskirts would be sufficient, and Israel might obtain those through a peace agreement. Like Eshkol, he was also entranced by the source of the Banias: "It is important to us that this spring be inside our borders."*

Many Israelis experienced religious exaltation when they visited the territories. In its intensity, this feeling rivaled the existential anxiety that had preceded the war. Yehuda Yost from Jerusalem wrote to Adir Zik that he had been to the Sinai, the West Bank, and the Golan, but nothing could compare with his visit at Rachel's Tomb and the Tomb of the Patriarchs. "All the things you read about in the Bible and in history become real right before your eyes; reading the Bible now has a completely different meaning." Rivka Cohen wrote, after visiting the Tomb of the Patriarchs, "There was such excitement that we had tears in our eyes, and Bina cried hysterically and I could not calm her down." Others described a "strange happiness, like waking up after a faint."[13]

The encounter with the holy places exposed the gap between religious and secular Israelis. Moshe Dayan was not particularly impressed by the ancestral sites. The Tomb of the Patriarchs was "a typical Hebron cave, carved out of the gray rock of the mountainside, with fields of barley below." Yitzhak Kotler, a soldier, admitted, "To be honest, I'm not so excited about having all the holy sites, like the Western Wall, the Tomb of the Patriarchs, or Rachel's Tomb." The Yehiam newsletter described Rachel's Tomb with some scorn: "An officer in the paratroopers wages a hopeless war against Jewish women who insist on suffocating in the crowded, smoky room, long since filled beyond capacity, and he looks helpless in this kind of battle, which he is not used to fighting." Nor were members of Yehiam particularly fond of the Palestinian souvenir sellers. "The way they do business is demanding and aggressive. It's not enough for you to walk away from them. They plant themselves in front of your nose and offer their wares again and again, tug at your sleeve and even curse at pictures of Hussein to please you, anything for business."[14]

Some denounced "the second conquest of the West Bank," as they termed the tourists' eager spending. "The Arabs have quickly learned how to sell *metsiyes* ["bargains" in Yiddish] to the Jews, all for a lira. . . . The scourge of shopping has hit Israelis hard and is giving generous support to people who only yesterday wanted to murder and rob us." Weitz

---

*Ben-Gurion, who had opposed the incursion into the Golan, now had a change of heart. Following a visit with General Elazar, he described the Golan Heights as critical to Israel's security.[12]

described similar scenes in Gaza: "The city is bustling with Jews. The streets are full of them, buying all sorts of haberdashery and fabrics."

Israelis frequently talked of their trips to the West Bank without mentioning the thousands of Palestinian refugees who continued to wander on the roads. "Arab families throng to the bridge with their chattels," wrote Weitz. "We do not linger here. The scene is disheartening." Deputy Minister Arie Lova Eliav wrote, "Like many of my generation, we have developed a blindness of sorts, the skill of not seeing living people, living Arabs: not them, and not their problems." But Eliav felt, in the territories, as if he were twenty years younger: "Something between a Boy Scout and a soldier." Weitz also felt reinvigorated. He still had the sense of being "disconnected from the pulse of life," but his trips in the territories and the discussion over their future seemed to give him new energy. A few ministers, including Yigal Allon, asked for his opinion on proposals they were preparing for the government. He ordered maps and began thinking about the future borders. "It is not at all easy," he wrote. Two days after the war, Weitz could already discern "a huge desire" to hold on to the West Bank and Gaza. That Israel should keep them "seems to be an accepted opinion," he wrote. He quoted *Maariv*, which was aware of what Weitz described as "the question of the million," meaning the one million Arabs living in the territories, but the paper's solution was simple: to counter the million Arabs in the territories, Israel would bring a million Jews from the Diaspora. Weitz found this difficult to accept. He reckoned that together with the Arabs already within the state, there would now be many more than a million Arabs living in Israel, as against fewer than two and a half million Jews. In light of the birthrate, before long half the state's population would be Arab. "There is a glint in their eyes, certainly not from love for us or servility, and the problem distresses me, stifling any joy and certainly any desire to celebrate," he wrote.[15]

Three days after the war, Weitz took a tour of Gush Etzion, south of Jerusalem. His son, Raanan, head of the Jewish Agency's settlement department, organized a bus for some forty people, including JNF and Jewish Agency officials and a few veterans of the four Gush settlements the Jordanians had occupied in the War of Independence. Weitz went as a delegate of Eshkol.

The prime minister had called him unexpectedly the day after the war ended. When Weitz went to see him at home that evening, Eshkol wanted to know whether the Gush could be resettled, explaining that the head of Mafdal, Haim Moshe Shapira, was already pressuring him: three of the original Gush settlements had been religious. Weitz had brought his son to the meeting. Raanan was a former assistant to Eshkol and his successor in the settlement department. Eshkol's appeal to Weitz did not seem to be coincidental. Humiliated by his ousting from the Defense Ministry, disappointed in his party comrades who had not stood by him on the eve of the war, and feeling generally isolated, Eshkol saw the elderly forester, one of his generation, as a partner in the worldview that had guided him for half a century: the State of Israel depended on settlement; Israelis must populate as much territory as possible, with as few Arabs as possible.

Weitz opposed a renewed settlement movement in Gush Etzion. First, he explained, there was the danger that Jewish refugees returning to their old homes would bolster the Arab demand to allow refugees to return. Second, Israel should not establish facts in the West Bank before deciding what it wanted: Annexation of all the territories, along with the million Arabs who lived in them? A realignment of the borders? Gush Etzion might not remain in Israel's possession. The whole situation required some consideration. Eshkol agreed that with respect to the West Bank and Gaza, waiting made sense, but that no delay was possible regarding the future of Jerusalem. Raanan Weitz suggested that the city's boundaries should stretch from Kalandia in the north to Gush Etzion in the south. His father thought this too broad, and Eshkol agreed. Raanan also proposed defining the Gaza Strip as Israeli territory. Eshkol asked what he proposed to do with the Palestinian population. Raanan replied that part of the Sinai should be annexed along with the Gaza Strip, and the population should be transferred there. His father objected to this too: Israel had repeatedly declared that it did not intend to annex Arab territories, and Sinai belonged to Egypt. No part of it should be annexed. Eshkol agreed, saying that for this same reason, Israel should not annex the Golan Heights; they should only ensure that the Golan did not serve as a base for Syrian aggression. "So what do we do now?" he asked. The Weitzes reiterated that a detailed study of the territories and their inhabitants was required. Eshkol agreed and said he would talk to Dayan.

Nineteen years had done nothing to erase the country's geographical integrity from Weitz's mind. To him, the Green Line represented a temporary expedient, which had now been revoked. He came to Gush Etzion like a landowner returning to inspect his property after a relatively brief absence. He had no trouble locating a piece of land that the JNF had been about to purchase in 1947, shortly before the UN partition resolution.

The plan had been to establish "lookouts" in the area, communication outposts meant to help protect settlements. According to Weitz, the transaction was halted because Ben-Gurion had objected to it.

The old residential buildings in the Gush settlements had disappeared. In their place were Palestinian refugee homes, surrounded by little gardens of vines and tomatoes. Weitz surveyed the crops with a professional eye and determined that they were properly cultivated. Most of the current residents had fled to the mountains during the recent fighting. Weitz also found the pine grove planted by the JNF in the forties. One member of his tour group found an Arab guard who had worked for the Jewish residents before 1948. "The meeting was warm, to the point of embracing," wrote Weitz. Then the Israelis sat down to discuss the future in the shade of "the tree": everyone knew the ancient oak that had served as a connecting point of the four settlements.

Avraham Herzfeld, seventy-nine at the time, a labor movement activist and JNF leader who had been instrumental in establishing many settlements in Israel, said that the children of the original Gush settlers should return immediately; some of them were on the tour. Others argued that the West Bank should be held as collateral until there was peace. Raanan Weitz said they should prepare settlement plans and wait for a government decision. The discussion itself made Weitz senior angry: an entirely new situation had developed, and these people were talking about two or three settlements instead of considering the larger problem of the West Bank. He got up and measured the trunk of the oak tree; its circumference was over six feet. "The tree is very old and has seen many changes," he wrote.

Weitz was impressed by Beit Jalla, a flourishing village of stone houses built in magnificent Arab style. The village vineyards gave it a vernal liveliness that he found charming. But the heat was oppressive, he was thirsty, and they all decided to go back to Jerusalem. On the way they passed heavy traffic—tourists and hikers. Weitz assumed, correctly, that the people were rushing to see the territories, in the belief that they would not remain under Israeli control. "In the first week after the war," wrote one of the young men named after the first Yehiam, "we managed to get a permit to travel around the area and we went all over the West Bank, because we were sure that in a very short time it would all be given back." But one woman reported in a letter to the United States that within a few days, someone had changed one of the yellow signs bearing the warning "Caution, Border Ahead" to read "No Border Ahead."[16]

3. PARTITIONS: "BALADNA—BALADKOM"

On Wednesday, June 14, the holiday of Shavuot, access to the Western Wall was opened and roughly a quarter of a million Israelis came. Under heavy security, they crossed Mount Zion in a long line, walking along what was known as the Pope's Road, a joint Israeli-Jordanian venture, built for Pope Paul VI's visit to Jerusalem in 1964. They then crossed the old border, went down alongside the wall, and entered the Old City through the Dung Gate to arrive at the large square in front of the Kotel. The event was both a traditional pilgrimage and victory celebration.

Many of the visitors were devout and wanted to pray, but others came in cars and carried transistor radios, violating the Sabbath and holiday prohibitions. The majority were seeing the Kotel for the first time, especially the younger Israelis and the recent immigrants. Some hoped to revisit the Kotel they had known in the past, before the destruction of the Mugrabi houses, and were disappointed to find the huge empty square. "In the open space that now surrounds it, the wall loses its sorrow and its air of weeping," wrote Weitz. "In my opinion, the Kotel was at its greatest when it was an enclosed area, accessible only through narrow alleyways; its captivity evoked its antiquity, exile, and destruction. Now it sits idly in the open." Someone standing behind Weitz commented, "It is no longer the Kotel, but just a wall." There was a cruel heat wave, and dust rose from the road and the square. The odor of perspiration still mingled, at times, with a strong smell of corpses, reported one paper.

Upon leaving the site, the throngs of visitors reached the open area in front of the Jaffa Gate and had their first glimpse of the Arab city itself. The shops and cafés had been shut by military order, and strips of white fabric hung in the windows. "The children stood on the balconies; men and women looked out through the windows, practically hidden from the passersby," reported Ha'aretz. "Even so, they could hardly avoid the contempt and mockery of the crowd, who only a week ago had been huddled in shelters in fear of the bombardments falling on the city." The day after Shavuot, tens of thousands more came, and by the end of the week there had been almost half a million visitors.[17]

The crowds visiting the Kotel threatened to co-opt the site as a national symbol, expropriating it from religious Jews. A few rabbis protested the desecration of the holiday and the Sabbath. Israel's chief rabbi, Isser Yehuda Unterman, demanded that the Kotel be closed to visitors on the Sabbath. Yosef Weitz, in contrast, disliked the worshipers more than the regular visitors; "most of them are Mizrahi," he noted, who kissed the stones and pushed notes with appeals to God through the cracks—"an act of idolatry." Professor Yeshayahu Leibowitz, the Orthodox scientist and philosopher, wrote a scathing letter to *Ha'aretz* on the matter. He was furious at the way the Western Wall had been turned into a symbol of conquest; he saw this as idol-worshiping. "Here is my proposal," wrote the professor. "The square in front of the Kotel should be revamped as the largest discotheque in the State of Israel, named the Divine Disco. This will satisfy everybody." *Ha'aretz* printed his letter under the title "DisKotel."*

Attempting to integrate the Kotel's dual identity, the editors of *Maariv* declared: "Jerusalem is ours, rooted in the collective soul of the Jewish people and stamped on its consciousness." They were referring to the entire city, not just to the Western Wall.[18]

This view represented a wide and virtually unchallenged consensus. Even Gabriel Stern, a veteran of the Ihud movement, which had supported Jewish-Arab coexistence in one state, was swept up in the excitement. "Is this real, or is the mind playing games?" he wondered. "The scenery was so familiar to me and yet I wandered around in a daze . . . as if I had suddenly seen the other side of the moon." He viewed the renewal of the Kotel as a possible step on the way to binational existence. "May we, the two peoples of this city, this country, be fortunate enough now also to tear down the partitions that still separate our hearts, for the fruits of a new peace," he wrote hopefully. But even he, an avowed and courageous humanist, was unmoved by the destruction of the houses in front of the Kotel: "They had no historical or religious value."[19]

Stern was probably unaware that a ministerial committee was secretly meeting at that very moment to consider the best way to "tear down the partitions"—namely, to annex the Arab city.

The cabinet supported annexation unwaveringly, although a few members were wary of "explosive declarations" that might turn the entire world against Israel and even revive the idea of international rule in the city. There was no way of knowing what might happen in the world, warned Warhaftig. Dean Rusk asked Israel to take no steps toward annexation. Abba Eban wished to postpone the decision until after the annual UN assembly in the fall. The question was whether the eastern part of Jerusalem could be annexed without any kind of declaration. Menachem

---

*A small group calling itself the League for the Prevention of Religious Coercion soon began to barrage government ministers with letters protesting the partition erected along the Kotel square by the Ministry of Religious Affairs to separate men and women. Others demanded to be allowed to follow the Reform movement's prayer traditions at the site.

Begin cautioned against using the word "annexation," suggesting that the city's borders be expanded in "complete silence."

Meanwhile, a ministerial committee was discussing the possible borders of annexation. The goal, wrote General Rehavam Ze'evi to Minister of Justice Shapira, was to turn Jerusalem into a metropolis. Dayan asked Ze'evi to draw up a map of an expanded Jerusalem and then sent it back twice asking that its size be decreased to reduce the number of Arabs within the city boundaries. The approach was secular: Rachel's Tomb in the south was excluded, but a long narrow corridor would lead to the airport in the north.

Begin proposed camouflaging the annexation within a law that would apply to the entire West Bank. The ministers wondered whether it might be possible to proceed without legislation, but Minister of Justice Shapira insisted on Knesset approval. The least dramatic method they came up with was to hide the legislation in three amendments to existing laws. These would be phrased in legalese, implying that they merely addressed administrative issues that applied to the entire country. The word "annexation" did not appear, nor was the legislation listed as a proposed bill on the Knesset agenda. Rather, it was introduced for a first reading immediately before deliberation on it began. Eshkol was intentionally absent. The legislation was passed on to the appropriate committees and sent back for second and third readings and then for a vote, all in the same evening. There was "no commotion and no rejoicing," as Minister Gvati wrote. Almost all the Knesset members voted in favor, including Uri Avneri; only the Communists objected.

The Foreign Ministry instructed its representatives to "minimize" the political and historical significance of East Jerusalem's annexation, depicting the legislation as an administrative step necessary to facilitate water and power supplies, public transportation, and health and education services. Inspired by Begin, the ministry told its staff to use the phrase "municipal integration" and avoid the term "annexation" whenever possible.[20]

TWO DAYS AFTER THE KNESSET APPROVED THE ANNEXATION, FREE MOVEMENT WAS permitted between the two parts of the city. Crowds of Arabs flowed into western Jerusalem, prompting Gabriel Stern to enthuse: *"Baladna—baladkom, wa'baladkom—baladna,"* he wrote in Arabic: "Our town is your town, your town is our town."

The scene during the midday hours of June 29 was described by *Ha'aretz* as a "mutual invasion," a festive discharge of the stress of war, the intoxication of victory, and the shock of defeat. Jews and Arabs mingled in both the eastern part of the city and in the west. Israelis poured into the Arab markets and came back with umbrellas from Japan, American cigarettes, rugs, canned food from Lebanon, pencils made in China. "The crowds in the Old City markets made it almost impossible to walk, and you would have thought there were rationing and starvation in the new Jerusalem," reported one journalist. "People bought things they would never otherwise have bought, believing they were getting good prices (even though they were being taken for a ride)," wrote Avigail and Yoel Yinon to friends in Los Angeles. "They're embarrassed to come home from the Old City unless they have a basketful of rags. It's really sickening."*

The Arabs came to see the traffic lights; there were none in their part of the city. There was also excitement over ice cream bars. Israeli boys were interested in the Jordanian license plates on the Arab cars. The Arabs visited the public parks, and some went to the movies. Many went that same day to see the houses they had lost in 1948. "There's going to be trouble," Gabriel Stern predicted.[21]

The idea of allowing free movement throughout Jerusalem had originated with Moshe Dayan. The necessity seemed to arise from the change in the laws governing the eastern part of the city, but many were fearful and opposed it. "Who knew what smoldering hatreds might flare up?" Teddy Kollek recalled thinking. He thought the city should open up gradually, at first for just an hour or two a day. "Any other way seemed a wild risk," he wrote. He brought Dayan to meet with the minister of the interior, a few IDF officers, and people in the Shabak, the Security Service, on the terrace of the King David Hotel. They all opposed the idea. Dayan put his feet up on the table and insisted on the need for "a new reality."

It happened quickly, as three communiqués published in the press made clear. Mayor Kollek invited Jerusalem residents who owned property in the eastern part of the city to come to the city offices and register their ownership, on forms filled out in duplicate. This was solely for the purpose of a census, he emphasized, but the announcement included a phrase borrowed from scripture: "Blessed be he who sets a boundary for Jerusalem." A local airline, Arkia, offered sightseeing flights over Jerusalem. And the Postal Ministry notified stamp vendors that if they wished to stock large quanti-

---

*A Jerusalem pencil manufacturer soon complained that the market had been flooded with Chinese pencils. "The State of Israel has turned into a bargain basement, with everyone rushing to buy in the Arab stores," protested the Association of Merchants in a letter to Eshkol. "Why are so many Jews running to shop in Gaza?" Eshkol wondered. Dayan responded, "Because they're Jews."

ties of envelopes with the stamp of the new post office in East Jerusalem, they would need to request them in advance.[22]

YOSEF WEITZ AND HIS WIFE DROVE TO THE JEWISH CEMETERY ON THE MOUNT OF Olives. It was not easy to find their son Yehiam's gravestone. The Jordanians had built a hotel and paved a road on the mount, shattering many gravestones in the process. "Utter destruction," wrote Weitz, and there and then he formulated an argument against handing the city over to international rule: the UN observers had witnessed the barbaric desecration of the cemetery and done nothing to prevent it. They were not worthy to protect holy sites.

"Uncertain whether we were treading on Yehiam's grave, we felt no flutter in our hearts," Weitz wrote in his diary. "Twenty-one years have passed. Changes upon changes, until one's heart is paralyzed." But the magnificent view of "the city joined as one" plunged him into contemplation of Jerusalem's past and future. "There is a great longing to restore it to its ancient glory in the Kingdom of Israel, and the struggle before us is vast and difficult." For now, a weight had been lifted: his grandson Nir had telephoned, and he was fine. His unit was encamped six miles from the Suez Canal.[23]

Private Yehoshua Bar-Dayan

Gabriel Stern (*Ricarda Schwerin*)

An Israeli in the White
House: Mathilde Krim with
President Lyndon Johnson

Krim at the president's ranch
(*Johnson Library, Texas*)

The first strike: an Egyptian Air Force base

POWs at Sharm el-Sheikh *(Yaakov Agur)*

Victors: Levi Eshkol, Menachem Begin *(Moshe Milner)*

The taste of victory: the advertisement reads, "Mirage Glory with Every Smoke."

Yitzhak Rabin on the cover of a special edition of *Life-Maariv*: "Israel's Lightning Victory," reads the headline.

Rabbi Shlomo Goren and paratroopers at the Western Wall *(David Rubinger)*

Paratroopers at the Western Wall: "It's the Kotel! The wall of prayer, the wall of tears. We are dreaming . . . " *(David Rubinger)*

Jenin in June
(Arieh Kanfer)

The new refugees:
residents of the
village of Im'us, in
the Latrun area,
on their way to
the West Bank
(Yosef Hochman)

Ada Sereni

Occupation currency
(The Bank of Israel)

Yaacov Herzog and
King Hussein at a
secret meeting in
London (c. 1970)

Eshkol on Dayan, in a note
passed to Yaacov Herzog:
"The ledger is open and the
hand is writing"

Eshkol and Dayan

Jerusalem, 21 June 1967 *(Moshe Freidan)*

CHAPTER 17

VICTORY ALBUMS

1. IMAGES: "WAR BRINGS OUT THE BEST IN PEOPLE"

The evening before free movement began between the eastern and western parts of Jerusalem, some three thousand guests filled the amphitheater at the Hebrew University on Mount Scopus, where honorary doctorates were being awarded to the president and to a few less significant dignitaries, including a major donor to the university. The highlight of the evening was the honorary degree being bestowed on Yitzhak Rabin. His acceptance speech formed a milestone in Israeli political culture.

In the conflict between value systems—between "the two Peoples of Israel"—the university community acted as if it had a monopoly on "Jewish morality." Nathan Rotenstreich, the rector, had led a protest against the air force recruitment slogan "The best join the air force," with the aim of playing down the military's role in shaping society's fundamental values. But Rabin's address presumed a universal recognition of the IDF's moral superiority—almost as if the university had signed a decree of capitulation. Rabin began by saying that he stood before "the teachers of the generation" with "reverence," and went on to explain that he saw the occasion as a "deep recognition of the uniqueness of the IDF, which is nothing less than an expression of the uniqueness of the People of Israel." This was an army like no other, he continued: it pursued missions of peace, to "glorify the strength of the nation culturally and morally." He noted the IDF's role in a number of educational enterprises, such as sending female soldiers to teach in new immigrant communities, but asserted that these were not the reasons for the university's respect for the army, evident in the honor bestowed upon the military. In so doing, the university had "acknowledged the IDF's spiritual and moral advantage in warfare itself." Rabin described the fighters' courage and their dedication to their mission, as well as to one another, as a "human display of brotherhood and comradeship and even idealism." The conquest of the Old City, he said, had stirred the soldiers to "wells of emotion and spiritual elevation."

Acknowledging the value system of the academic elite, but positioning the IDF alongside it, Rabin argued that the army did not share the "joy of victory" felt by "the entire nation." The soldiers' celebrations were mingled with sadness and shock, he said, "and there are even some who do not celebrate at all," because they know the cost of victory. The new honorary doctor of philosophy then proposed a historiosophic explanation: "It is possible that the Jewish people never learned to feel the joy of the conqueror and the victor, and so these events are met with mixed feelings." He added that the terrible price exacted from the enemy had also deeply touched the hearts of many soldiers. Rabin described the soldiers' heroism as "a bravery of spirit." When they fought, "a few against a multitude," they did so with "all the resources of spiritual strength." Even as they watched their friends fall beside them, the military units were fueled by "moral values, spiritual reserves, not by weapons or combat strategies." The slogan "The best join the air force," he explained, referred not merely to the soldiers' technical prowess but to "values of moral goodness, values of human goodness."* Rabin concluded, "This is an army that comes from the people and returns to the people, a people that rises above itself in the hour of need, and that, when tested, can defeat any enemy thanks to its moral, spiritual, and emotional superiority."

Israel's chief education officer, Mordechai Bar-On, who wrote the speech, introduced no ideas that were not already acceptable in Israel. But as the chief of staff stood on Mount Scopus, "in this ancient and splendid site that looks over our eternal capital," he offered not merely self-flattery, but also a basic moral and political declaration: the army was the source of moral values, the war an expression of human greatness. Many people heard Rabin's words as justifying the occupation.

There was a political background to this symbolic and emotionally charged embrace between the academy and the military. According to

*Benyamin Galai wrote in *Maariv*, "No slogan has ever proved so true. Indeed the best, the dedicated, the young and the handsome, join the air force. The elite join the armored corps, the brave the navy, the great the infantry, the all-around excellent the paratroopers, and the slandered the intelligence service."[1]

Rabin, the initiative for awarding this honorary degree had come from Eshkol's adviser Professor Yigal Yadin. Moshe Dayan, a man of letters, an amateur archaeologist, and a world famous decorated hero, might have been a more appropriate candidate and more effective in public relations and fund-raising for the university. But Yadin thought poorly of Dayan the archaeologist; moreover, Dayan represented Rafi, Ben-Gurion's party, and the Rector Rotenstreich had been a major adversary of Ben-Gurion during the Lavon affair. Ben-Gurion did not attend the ceremony, but he heard Rabin's speech on his car radio and sent him a congratulatory letter. Rabin himself wrote, "If there is any reward for the long nights of apprehension, for the terrible sense that you are sending young people to face death, for the heavy burden of responsibility on your shoulders, I have reaped it at the stand at Mount Scopus." His choice of words evoked the familiar Hebrew phrase for the revelation of the Torah to Moses, "the stand at Mount Sinai."

The author Aharon Megged wrote that Rabin had spoken for all the other military commanders, and that no other army in the world spoke in such a voice. "It is the voice of the true Israeli, a race that has sprung from this country, and it is that race, more than anything, that brought about this victory."[2]

A FEW DAYS AFTER THE WAR ENDED, THE CHILDREN'S MAGAZINE *DAVAR LEYELADIM* began a "Helicopter Campaign," in which young readers were asked to send in their pocket money to raise funds for a military helicopter to be used for evacuating wounded soldiers. Students at the Adihu school in Beit Shemesh sent 160 liras, while students at Druyanov in Tel Aviv raised 640. Their letter to the brave IDF soldiers read, "We are very happy for your victory." They hoped the helicopter would be used for peaceful purposes only, and signed the letter "with blessings of victory."

The papers celebrated with a torrent of articles glorifying the IDF. Some of the commanders were depicted as mythical figures, larger than life. "Yitzhak has a phenomenal memory," *Maariv* quoted one General Staff officer speaking of Rabin, and reported that everyone who worked with him joked that if their computers crashed, nothing disastrous would happen because they'd still have Yitzhak Rabin.

"When he sits at his desk, he looks huge," wrote one paper of Shmuel Gorodish. "He walks with a threatening animal spring in his step." Shabtai Teveth compared Gorodish to "a legendary giant," although he was of average height, as Teveth himself noted; Yehoshua Bar-Dayan repeatedly observed that his commander was a short man. Journalists could not conceal their admiration of the commanders they interviewed. "Raful, Raful—worshipped, legendary," wrote one of Rafael Eitan. "I am among those who admire Arik—a rare combination of battle spirit, strength and human feeling," wrote another, of Ariel Sharon. To speak to Sharon, wrote Geula Cohen, was to "interview a living legend . . . a legend in uniform." He "gives you the feeling that he is just an ordinary person, but larger and wiser and handsomer." She marveled at his silver hair, his sturdy shoulders, his chest, his eyes, and his smile. "Warm and innocent and clear like a child's, a smile that pauses briefly as it emerges, like someone who knows that not everything is clear and innocent, but then it reaches you, still warm, still clear, but now a little harder, hinting at the scent of the battlefield." This was not the first time she had interviewed an officer only to hear him talk of faith and spirit, she wrote; she should have been used to it. Sharon had told her he felt no guilt toward the Arabs, and recounted how when he had visited the Kotel he had worn tefillin for the first time since his Bar Mitzvah.[3]

The generals were feted as celebrities, sought-after guests at public and social events, from restaurant openings and fashion shows to galas and cocktail parties. Everyone wanted them at their weddings and Bar Mitzvahs. Their pictures appeared on dishes, mugs, key chains, children's games, watches, and holiday cards. Other celebrities had their pictures taken with them—Leonard Bernstein, Danny Kaye, Sean Connery, Richard Nixon. More and more victory balls were held. IDF officers, among them Mordechai Hod, Ariel Sharon, and other generals, appeared on American television and at fund-raising events in the United States. But when the United Jewish Appeal invited Yitzhak Rabin to speak at a fund-raiser, a protest erupted, as if the occasion were somehow beneath his dignity. In a letter to Eshkol, a sixteen-year-old girl repeated what she had read in an article written by Elie Wiesel. It was one thing to send ministers to events, she explained, "but not our Chief of Staff, the hero of the Six-Day War."

The admiration of the army was also embodied in the popular demand for military decorations. Firefighters, El Al employees, Kol Israel radio staff, yeshiva students, Egged bus drivers, and postal workers—they all wanted decorations. And the country was soon flooded with the coffee-table books known in Hebrew as *albomim*, albums.

They appeared by the dozen, in every size and shape. Some were elaborate two-volume sets with velvet bindings, gold engraving, magnificent photographs, and captions in Hebrew, English, and French. Others were hastily assembled booklets of photographs copied from newspapers. The Ministry of Defense and the IDF issued war albums and helped soldiers publish albums about their units and battles. There were books in black and white, books in color, some with maps, with or without introductions by Levi Eshkol or Moshe Dayan or Yitzhak Rabin, and a few in Yiddish.* Most of the books featured the word "victory" in their titles, but few used the word "war." Those that did referred to "the War of Victory," "the War of Redemption and Peace," or "the War for Peace." The title of a large album issued by the IDF eschewed "war" entirely: *Six Days*.

One might occasionally find a picture of Eshkol, usually wearing khaki, but more often than not the albums celebrated victory without any political context. They never asked whether the war had been inevitable; this was a given. They never mentioned the question of whether to hold on to the Occupied Territories or withdraw. There was virtually no reference to IDF casualties. The widely projected view was that the victory had created an ideal situation. The captions were formulated in quasi-poetic language, replete with meaningful ellipses at the ends of sentences. All the albums reflected varying degrees of fiery patriotism, in the spirit of the era. "The IDF is a better army than the contemporary German military," *Maariv* proudly quoted an American general from one album. They all underscored the historical and religious attachment to the territories, and often they expressed contempt for the enemy armies and condescending mockery of the POWs. "The heat and the thirst spared a significant amount of ammunition," said one album in both Hebrew and English, beneath a picture of Egyptian soldiers' corpses in the Sinai. Another picture in the same album depicted a dead Egyptian soldier with his arms spread out, and the caption "Even in death he raised his hands in surrender."

The albums were extremely popular. Israelis bought them for themselves and gave them as gifts to friends and relatives both at home and abroad.[5] After the albums came the records and plays. The military troupes worked overtime, as if the war were still raging. Soon came the movies, among them a few features, such as *Is Tel Aviv Burning?* The IDF produced its own films, some of which involved reenactments of battles, including the conquest of the Old City; for this purpose they employed air force planes and allegedly also called up reservists.[6]

The media cultivated the image of the civilian volunteer. The Ministry

---

*One publisher, Ohad Zmora, later admitted that he had planned an album even before the war began. He collaborated with Uri Ben-Ari, an employee who was a colonel in the reserves.[4]

of Education portrayed such civilians in a special edition of a publication for new immigrants, written in simplified, vowelized Hebrew. "An eighty-year-old man came to see the town marshal. 'I cannot fight, but I can make coffee for the soldiers,' he said, and went to one of the army camps." Another story told of a moshav member who took all the blankets he could find at home, loaded them on his tractor, and set off. "I'm bringing the blankets to our soldiers on the northern border," he said; "it's cold there at night." And one man with a weak heart drove his car to an IDF camp. "I can't fight; my heart is not worth much. But my car engine works great. Won't you take it?"

Davar wrote, in quasi-biblical style, "A great spirit has touched the entire nation—and it shall be purified." *Yediot Aharonot* quoted a psychologist who claimed that "war brings out the best in people." Dozens of books about the war, in addition to the albums, voiced similar sentiments, and many of them became best sellers.[7] Every Israeli became a strategic expert: "We are blessed by the quality of our people and especially our commanders, whose slogan is not 'Go, go, go,' but rather 'Follow me,'" wrote one woman knowledgeably. Esther Mandelbaum from Tel Aviv wrote, "It is thanks to the IDF that we are alive."[8]

THE HIGH REGARD FOR THE IDF SPILLED OVER TO RENEW THE PRESTIGE OF THE KIBBUT-zim. The kibbutz was rehabilitated, once again acclaimed as an ideal that defined the values and image of the state. This happened primarily because kibbutz members were represented among the war casualties at a rate almost five times higher than their proportion of the population as a whole. Almost a fifth of fallen soldiers came from a kibbutz, although kibbutz residents represented only about 4 percent of the population. Almost every third officer killed in the war was a kibbutz member.

But many kibbutzim were averse to the militaristic revelry, adopting instead a different image of the victor. The Yehiam newsletter announced, "The library has decided not to purchase war albums." At the members' assembly there was a principled debate: "In light of what we have been through, should we allow guns, tanks, and other military toys into the children's houses and playrooms?"[9]

2. *SOLDIERS TALK:* "A HOLY BOOK"

A few weeks after the war, a kibbutz movement official invited Amos Oz, a teacher on Kibbutz Hulda, to his office. Oz had begun to emerge as a major writer. The official also invited Avraham Shapira from Kibbutz Jezreel, who divided his time between agricultural work and editing the literary and intellectual journal *Shdemot*. The two were asked to edit a collection of kibbutz members' war experiences. They knew from the start that any such collection would give voice to a sense of unease, even distress. This would not be a victory album or a volume of heroism, they decided.

They traveled among the kibbutzim, recording hundreds of hours of interviews with people who recounted their experiences in the war and, in some cases, their views on the future of the Occupied Territories. Most of the interviews were conducted in groups. In all, there were thirty conversations with 140 participants, the majority of whom were officers. Only a fraction of the huge quantity of material was transcribed; from the transcripts, Oz and Shapira compiled one of the most important books ever published in Israel.

Soldiers Talk was not immediately released for sale to the general public but was distributed solely among kibbutzim. However, rumors of its existence soon spread, enveloping it in a cloak of mystery, as if it expressed an underground truth to which only a few were privy. The text found its way into the press and eventually the book was issued for sale. Roughly 100,000 copies were sold, an astronomical figure at that time. Only one other book achieved similar success: *Exposed in the Turret*, a blockbuster epic about the heroic war of the armored corps, written by Shabtai Teveth. Like the victory albums, Teveth's book was considered the polar opposite of the refined *Soldiers Talk*, whose subtitle was *Episodes of Listening and Observation*. Haim Gouri thought the book had the power to "mold the soul and consciousness of an entire generation." Golda Meir decreed it "a holy book." She echoed a popular sentiment when she added, "We have been blessed to have such sons as these." The Foreign Ministry incorporated the book into its public relations campaign. It was translated into several languages, including Swedish and Yiddish, and excerpts were dramatized and performed in New York.*

The book surprised many of its readers. Kibbutzniks were considered introverted people who did not disclose their feelings. Even Yitzhak Rabin, in his speech on Mount Scopus, observed that "Sabra youths, particularly soldiers, tend not to be sentimental and are ashamed to reveal their emotions." But *Soldiers Talk* reflected an emotional need to talk about the experience of war and to expose feelings and thoughts. The interview

---

*An abridged English translation was published in 1971 as *The Seventh Day: Soldiers Talk About the Six-Day War* (New York: Scribner's).

participants seemed gentle, peace-loving, awkward, thoughtful, sad, sensitive to human rights, and tormented by questions about the necessity of the war and the cost of victory, just as Rabin had described them.* They were identified by their first names only, which made them seem like close childhood friends of the readers—and of the entire country.

The soldiers recollected how they had gone to war enthusiastically and how they had learned to hate it. They spoke of fear and of how they overcame it, partly because they were afraid of what people on the kibbutz might say about them. They looked back in amazement at the process by which they had become part of the war machine, automatically shooting at human beings. They talked of death, of how they sealed up their feelings and came to hold human life cheap, eventually developing a disregard even for their own lives. They spoke at length about the brotherhood among soldiers and about the difficulty of returning to routine.

Soldiers Talk was received as a complete and authentic document, an Israeli truth-telling worthy of pride. But the raw material collected by the editors paints a different picture. A Ph.D. dissertation written by Alon Gan, at Tel Aviv University, shows that to a great extent the finished book presented a deliberately constructed myth. Some responses were censored, at times at the participants' own request. Parts of the transcripts were altered, in a few cases to the point of distortion, before the book went to press, in order to suit the words to the image of innocent young soldiers, humanists in distress. The approach might also have been part of the general tendency to shed a positive light on the war itself, and thereby on the annexation of some of the territories occupied in its course. The publicly issued version of the book omitted some of the accounts included in the initial version. According to Gan, "extremely graphic" testimony about war crimes was dropped; he mentioned only some of these in his dissertation.

Nahum and Tikva Sarig, of Kibbutz Beit Hashita, and their son Ran and his wife, Ora, refused to allow the editors to identify them by name, and their remarks were not published. Nahum Sarig, a founding member of the Palmah, was one of the most revered commanders in the War of Independence. Ran described the occupation of the West Bank as the completion of a mission his father and his generation had left undone, prompting the "weeping for generations," and in so doing, he seemed to diminish the glory of the founding fathers. Tikva Sarig told of how, when the war broke out, she prayed to her dead parents and asked them to protect her two

---

*Mordechai Bar-On, the author of Rabin's speech, also had a hand in editing *Soldiers Talk*.

sons. Three weeks later, she went back to her mother's grave to thank her for sending everyone home safely. She asked that this account be left out of the book, fearing the kibbutz members would mock her.

One participant, a member of Kibbutz Ein Shemer, asked the editors not to publish his doubts concerning the Zionist idea itself. "I feel increasing despair," he had said, and wondered, "Why not go to Canada?" He went on to explain his despondency: "With us, every ten years . . . every so often, we'll have to have a war. . . . It won't be a safe haven for the Jewish people. . . . I fully admit that I don't want to live in a country destined to fight a war every ten years, and I identify with and understand all the Jews in the world who can give money to it but aren't willing to come and live here themselves."

The editors excluded content they recorded in a conversation with some religiously devout soldiers, students at the Mercaz Harav yeshiva in Jerusalem, known even before the war for its nationalism that included nostalgia for those areas of Palestine under Jordanian control. The yeshiva students seem to have been left out not necessarily because they were religious or because they were insufficiently humanistic, but primarily because they did not share the unease about victory and occupation that played such a central role in the emotional and political world of the kibbutz members. The editors were apparently concerned that the vehement nationalistic messianism the students expressed would overshadow the kibbutzniks' ambivalence.*

One participant talked about his feelings at seeing the bodies of Egyptian soldiers. "And I think at that point, when the price started to seem cheap, that was when we stopped calling out, 'Look, there are two dead lying here,' and instead we said, 'Look, there are two stiffs here.' . . . The price became cheap." These words were omitted, as were statements about the superior quality of the "human material" on the kibbutzim, whose members did not engage in looting, unlike the city boys. The editors also left out remarks attributing greater brutality and lower ethical standards to the Mizrahim than the kibbutzniks. "Some very negative things are revealed," one speaker was quoted as saying, when in fact he said, "Some terribly negative things are revealed. When you see soldiers shooting at defenseless civilians . . . elderly people." The editors attributed to another kibbutznik the following remark: "And there was a kind of unleashing . . . unbelievable, really. . . ." The actual statement

---

*The editors claimed that the religious soldiers' quotes were left out "for technical reasons," but they were not included in later editions either.

was, "Unleashing that really bordered on cruelty . . . I know that one squad commander . . . some guy, around forty, put his hands up—so he shot a round into his stomach. . . . There was a kind of unleashing . . . grenades in all the houses . . . just burning houses for no reason. . . ."

Another statement left out was from a speaker who believed that kibbutz members were not suitable for carrying out acts of occupation: "Maybe the Border Patrol is better . . . maybe the police . . . maybe they do it more quietly." As a rule, remarks that included the word "expulsion" or "evacuation" were omitted. One speaker who talked about the occupation of Gaza was quoted as saying, "There was no law." What he actually said was "We had to take very drastic measures . . . blowing up houses and searching houses . . . and extreme things. . . . There was a situation where human life played no role. You could kill. There was no law."

Another soldier recalled that he and his friends were ordered to kill anyone coming from the eastern bank of the Jordan River. The book editors replaced "to kill" with "to prevent the crossing of." The same order was described elsewhere: "There was an explicit, written order . . . as of today, whoever crosses the Jordan—shoot. Doesn't matter who he is, what he is, how or why." In *Soldiers Talk* the same reference reads, "There was an order not to permit anyone to cross the Jordan except over the bridges. I know that we carried out the spirit of the order, without hurting people." In fact, according to this soldier, his company did not obey the order to kill.

A member of Kibbutz Yifat told of a wounded Syrian soldier his unit found on the road. There was an argument over whether to kill him. Suddenly one of the soldiers held his rifle to the wounded man's head and fired, killing him. In *Soldiers Talk*, the same story ends with the words: "One guy suggested killing him. Of course we wouldn't allow it." A commander quoted in the book recalled his response after the soldiers killed an Arab farmer. "What may have added to the terrible feeling was how impressed I was by the soldiers with me on the ambush, who ended up killing the man." His actual words were "What may have added to the terrible feeling was, maybe, that I was impressed by the great glee of the soldiers on the ambush with me, who ended up killing that *fellah*."

Some of those interviewed spoke of their compulsive desire to see dead bodies. The editors cut a detailed description of soldiers getting out of their vehicle to photograph corpses. The following words were omitted: "I never had a desire to see death, and here it was, this kind of insatiable desire." One man asked himself how he could kill people "just like I kill flies on a screen"; these words were left out.

Most of the interviewees said they felt no hatred for the enemy, that they saw "the Arab" as human. They appeared to be sincerely pained when they talked about hurting civilians. "I think that for me this was a terrible thing," said a young man named Shai in a conversation with Amos Oz. "Children my son's age walking with their hands up. I remember that elderly people or women had to come and beg. It was a terrible feeling, horrible." Oz asked, "If you had been given a direct and personal order to shoot people in a way that seemed contradictory to things you believe in, to humanism, to your education, would you refuse such an order at any cost? Under any condition?" Shai replied, "I would refuse the order at any cost and under any condition."[10]

The editors were careful to avoid distancing the speakers from the national consensus—rather, they did just the opposite, placing them at its forefront and center. The soldiers had wept like everyone else when they heard about the capture of the Old City. The encounter with the "land of the Bible" filled them with a sense of belonging to their people. They spoke about the Holocaust: for the first time they had learned to see it as part of their identity. But some soldiers likened IDF operations against civilians to Nazi acts. "I felt like a member of the Gestapo," said one; this was left out. Others equated themselves with SS men following orders. "Every soldier out there created a 'concentration camp,'" one young man said. House searches, in the soldiers' slang, were *aktziot*, a neologism borrowed from the German word for the Nazi arrests and deportations. All this was omitted.*

Soldiers Talk met a profound need among many Israelis to be not only strong and victorious, but also just. In letters sent abroad, people expressed hope that the war would convince the Arabs to make peace. "We are a people who have suffered so much throughout history—why can't they let us live?" wrote one man from Tel Aviv.[12] They went back to recounting family news in their letters: celebrations and worries, children, illnesses, work, gossip. But much like the depression and anxiety evident prior to the war, "the situation" continued to be part of their daily routine. "Rochelle feels well," wrote Rivka Cohen to her sister in America; "she's already eight months pregnant and feels heavy. Let's hope she gives birth safely. It's a good thing the war is over. We were worried about her giving birth. Now we just hope for peace."[13]

---

*Some of the omissions were probably enforced by military censors. Mordechai Bar-On made his own amendments: one speaker said his friends "behaved like animals," and Bar-On suggested modifying this to read "behaved improperly." But the editors stood their ground and the original statement was published.[11]

3. DELUSIONS: "ONCE IN A THOUSAND YEARS"

A few months after the war, a parapsychological society became active in Tel Aviv. At a meeting just over a year later, the society reported to its 188 members that it had held no fewer than three hundred lectures, almost one a day. The society's books and archives document its emergence throughout the country. Members gave frequent talks on kibbutzim and in private homes, and sometimes in public auditoriums, before crowds of up to a thousand people. Students thronged to hear them, Knesset members and businesspeople took an interest. The society charged entrance fees and speaker honoraria, generating significant income. Everyone talked about the special skills of the society's chairwoman, Margot Klausner: she could talk with the dead.

This cultural heroine, more than anyone else, embodied the great delusions that took hold of Israelis in the aftermath of the war. In frequent coverage, the press approached her with a mixture of skepticism and astonishment, mockery and reverence. The society's archives reveal that she offered Moshe Dayan "information" that reached her from the world of truth, including a warning about a new war that would break out, she said, in the fall of 1969. Dayan sent her at least three polite thank-you notes.

Klausner was in her sixties. She had come to Palestine from Berlin in 1926, and the Habima Theater, which she managed, owed its existence largely to her. She wrote several books, including a few novels, and in 1933 she produced a movie. In 1948, she founded a film studio in Herzliya. Her interest in the occult and the supernatural, which extended to dream interpretation and reincarnation, prompted curiosity among newspaper reporters. In the fall of 1954, two years before the Sinai Campaign, *Ha'aretz* published information Klausner claimed to have received through direct contact with Benjamin Disraeli. She said he had told her that in the next war, Britain and France would support Israel; this, of course, is what happened.

In January 1968, Klausner was involved in the efforts to find an Israeli submarine, the *Dakar*, that had disappeared somewhere in the Mediterranean. The wife of the submarine commander and the father of a crew member came to Klausner and she "summoned" the submarine crew to a séance. She sat with her guests in a darkened room and proceeded to use a Ouija board to describe various technical aspects of the lost submarine. To her listeners, she appeared to be communicating with the vessel itself.

She was later contacted by the father of a soldier from a kibbutz who had been killed in the war. She promised to try and make contact with the son. She was also able to communicate with a well-known Episcopal bishop from California, James Albert Pike, who had gone wandering in the Judean Desert and died there.

A few senior Israeli archaeologists, including representatives from the Israel Museum's antiquities division, accompanied Klausner when she went to search for the treasures of the Second Temple. The official report of the excursion shows clearly that everyone treated the task with the utmost gravity. They worked with maps, and one member of Klausner's society came equipped with a pendulum hanging from a string. During repeated attempts, the pendulum hovered over the maps and kept stopping at the same point, near the walls of the Old City. Everyone set off for Jerusalem, and the pendulum led them to the Temple Mount, where it started to twirl wildly. According to the report, "The vigor of the rotations surprised everyone." And then they knew: this was where the treasures were buried. The participants concluded: "One must assume there is a subterranean tunnel leading from the Temple's foundations to the walls and ending at the Kotel itself, at the point looking over the steps of Zachariah's Tomb. In this tunnel, specifically in the place where it ends at the wall, the treasure we seek is hidden." Klausner made further inquiries and suggested that the place indicated by the pendulum also concealed the Holy Ark. She was not alone in her endeavors: masses of Israelis became passionately addicted to the supernatural, until it seemed the entire country was hearing voices.*

THE PROPOSAL BY GENERAL SHLOMO GOREN, THE CHIEF RABBI OF THE IDF, TO DESTROY the Dome of the Rock had not been publicized, but an idea proposed by David Ben-Gurion was widely discussed. He suggested destroying the Old City walls so that Jerusalem, modern and ancient, would become one city. This was no momentary aberration: Ben-Gurion wrote of this plan in his diary and repeated it often, both publicly and in writing. "The walls have no sanctity and no necessity," he wrote, noting that they had been

---

*Within a few days after the war, people began contributing to a special fund set up to finance the reconstruction of the Second Temple. It then transpired that for years there had been a bank account collecting funds for this purpose. A day laborer from Ramat Gan promised the minister of religious affairs that he would donate a month's income for the reconstruction.[14]

built by an Ottoman sultan. "A united city requires the destruction of the walls." In another letter, he added, "In our days, the IDF is Israel's wall."*

Moshe Dayan opposed demolishing the walls, but he did suggest opening a new gate to symbolize the conquest of the city, to be named the Gate of Return. Eshkol did not want a new gate; it would probably be known as Dayan's Gate. His idea was to build in Jerusalem a replica of the Arch of Titus in Rome, which bears a relief depicting Roman soldiers with their spoils of war, among them the menorah from the Temple. Eshkol wrote an utterly serious letter to Dayan about this. He was undecided as to whether the arch should be erected in West or East Jerusalem, or perhaps on a high hilltop overlooking the city, but he had already thought of the arch's inscription. In contrast to *Judea Capta* ("Judea Captured"), the phrase engraved on an ancient Roman coin, they would write "Judea Liberated." Eshkol wanted to form a planning committee. "The prime minister is certain that such an arch will fill the hearts of Jews everywhere with joy and pride," wrote one of his aides.

"Let us go and build a victory arch for the soldiers of the IDF," proposed an organization of Bulgarian immigrants. The Tel Aviv architect Zvi Hecker proposed an arch thirty stories high. He told critics that the construction of the Eiffel Tower in Paris had also produced heated controversy. A group calling itself the Society in Defense of the Dignity of the Departed of Israel initiated a campaign to locate the remains of people who died in the uprising against the Romans, so that they could be properly buried. The president, the prime minister, and a series of other officials addressed an initiative to add retroactively the name of Chaim Weizmann, the first president, to the Declaration of Independence. Some people suggested turning Armon Hanatziv into the president's official residence, and Teddy Kollek wanted to move the UN headquarters from New York to Jerusalem.[16] This swirl of activity was accompanied by an ongoing debate over the name of the war. The question had come up as early as June 11, in a cabinet meeting, at which Minister of Education Aran had suggested calling it the Israeli War for Survival.

Eshkol's office was flooded with suggestions: "the Peace Campaign"; "the War of Heroism"; "the War of Life"; "the War of Victory"; "Defender of Peace"; "Zion"; "Shai" (from the Hebrew acronym for "Six Days"); "Moshe" (the Hebrew acronym for "War for State Peace"); "the Jerusalem War." The Knesset chairman received many more proposals. Among the

---

*Many people wrote to Ben-Gurion to protest the idea. *Ha'aretz* took issue with it in an editorial called "The Barbarians Are Coming."[15]

ideas sent to *Maariv* was the wry "Rabin-Hod Campaign." The press had begun referring to "the Six-Day War" as soon as the fighting ended, and in late July, Eshkol informed the Ministry of Defense that this was his choice.* There was something businesslike about the name, statistical almost, and yet it also evoked the six days of creation, in the spirit of the messianic euphoria that had spread through the country. In her article on Ariel Sharon, Geula Cohen wrote, "A nation that has such Ariks can not only sleep safely at night, free of fear of enemies, but can achieve wonders and victories—such as in the war of the six days of creation."[17]

Everyone had an opinion about symbols. Some suggested changing the national anthem. Instead of the lyrics "Our hope is not yet lost," one woman offered "Our hope has come to be." Others thought "Hatikva" should simply be replaced by "Jerusalem of Gold."[18]

Shortly after the war, a rumor went around that Naomi Shemer had borrowed the melody for "Jerusalem of Gold" from a Basque lullaby. "I was very angry," wrote Shemer, and demanded that people "stop this nonsense." But a few days before her death, in June 2004, she revealed the truth. In the mid-sixties, she recalled, she used to spend time with Nehama Handel, a singer for whom Shemer wrote many songs. They would laugh, sing, cook, and eat together. "I made her couscous and soup," Shemer wrote in a letter to a friend. "Nothing was ever written down or recorded; I don't think I had a tape recorder back then," she stressed. "I suppose that during one of those meetings, Nehama sang that Basque lullaby for me, and it went in one ear and out the other. When I was writing 'Jerusalem of Gold,' the song must have come to me without my realizing it." But an "invisible hand" guided her to make changes to the original, although she was not conscious of this either, she said. "The transition to a major key in the fourth bar, third sequence . . . and the ending. It turns out that someone seemed to be protecting me and providing me with my eight bars, which give me the rights to my own version of the song. But all this was done, as I said, unwittingly."

Although at the time Shemer denied the claim that she had not composed the music, she knew the truth: "I recalled with a fright that Nehama had indeed sung something like that to me, at the time. I was so panicked that I could only remember the first note." Two decades went by, and then a reporter from *Yediot Aharonot* brought her the original Basque song. But Shemer once again denied any familiarity with it. "I

---

*Menachem Begin was still protesting this in mid-August. He preferred "the War of Redemption."

consider the whole business a regrettable workplace accident, so regrettable that perhaps it is why I became ill," she confessed shortly before her death. "I tell myself that perhaps it was a Marrano tune, so that I was simply restoring it where it belonged."[19]

THE GIDDINESS RELEASED BY VICTORY WAS ALSO EVIDENT AMONG CERTAIN POLICY makers. Yigal Allon continued to promote the idea of independence for the 150,000 Druze living in the south of Syria. In a confidential memorandum to Eshkol, Allon explained that there was generally tension between the Druze leaders and Damascus, and so the Druze might revolt to establish their own sovereign state. "A condition for this, of course, is that they receive political guidance and military assistance from an external actor," Allon continued, and suggested that Israel take this role. "They are known as good fighters," he pointed out, and added that Israeli Druze, particularly those who had served in the IDF, might also constitute an important factor in the project, as would "Jewish officers and agents." A Druze state would be a buffer between Syria, Jordan, and Israel. Jordan would not object. A mutual defense pact between the Druze state and Israel would assure Israel's permanent hold on the Golan. Moreover, a successful Druze uprising could bring about the collapse of the Syrian regime, which would limit the scope of Soviet involvement. Allon therefore suggested setting up a special staff, comprising the Shabak, the IDF, and the Ministry of Foreign Affairs, to plan and implement the idea. He also suggested establishing a ministerial committee made up of Eshkol, Eban, Dayan, Begin, and himself. Eshkol replied that the matter was "being explored and handled."

Isser Harel, the former head of the Mossad and an adviser to Eshkol, wanted to head an operation that would result in the assassination of Nasser. David Horowitz, the governor of the Bank of Israel, suggested that Israel buy the Sinai Peninsula from Egypt. He raised the idea in Washington, D.C., whereupon a British diplomat commented that no doubt Horowitz had the Louisiana and Alaska purchases "fresh in his mind" when he arrived in the United States.* Meanwhile, the Bank of Israel was issuing occupation currency.

---

*The Suez Canal also fired the imagination of many Israelis, some of whom suggested digging alternate routes. One proposed rebuilding the memorial for Ferdinand de Lesseps, the builder of the canal, which the Egyptians had destroyed. [20]

. . .

THIS WAS A PECULIAR UNDERTAKING, TYPICAL OF THE GROTESQUE NATURE OF THE emerging occupation apparatus: improvised, rushed, secretive, wasteful, grounded in government decisions and an endless series of injunctions, ordinances, and regulations. The subject of an occupation currency was first debated as early as the third day of the war. The governor of the Bank of Israel discussed the matter with the acting minister of finance, Ze'ev Sherf. The currency was intended to ensure control of the economy in the territories and prevent them from being flooded with Egyptian, Jordanian, and Syrian currency; it was also probably meant to emphasize the difference between Israel and the territories.

Two graphic artists from Tel Aviv, Gad Rothschild and Zev Lipman, submitted the first samples days after the war. By June 23, they had produced a revised proposal. They tried to stay as close as possible to the existing currency, but were careful not to violate Egyptian, Jordanian, and Syrian copyright. The palm tree the artists incorporated, they explained, appeared repeatedly in the Koran as a symbol of prosperity. The currency was intended to please the population, and so it was also illustrated with camels, ornamental arches that suggested a palace from the Arabian Nights, and other Oriental motifs, as well as an image of David's Tower in Jerusalem. There were different-sized bills, and the bank also began minting coins. The bills bore the words "IDF Command Forces" in Hebrew, Arabic, and English, and they were signed by the commanding officers of the Sinai, the West Bank, and the Golan. A veteran worker at the Bank of Israel, Dov Gnichovski, later talked about the masses of legal opinions and injunctions produced in preparation for the currency issue, one of which was "as long as a book." On July 21, a ministerial committee on economic affairs decided to print two million "Jordanian dinars," one million "Egyptian pounds," and 100,000 "Syrian pounds." It was a large commission, and the government printer in Jerusalem could not fill it in time. The government rushed urgent orders to printers in Holland and Belgium, and flew the bills to Israel with great secrecy.

No one needed this money, and no one wanted it. The hundreds of thousands of Israelis flooding the markets in the territories brought their own currency with them. The Bank of Israel and the Treasury reconsidered and ultimately concluded that "occupation currency" carried unwelcome associations and might be misinterpreted in the international press: someone might even think Israel had planned the occupation in advance.

And so the millions of bills were put away in a basement and the questions of what to do with them and who would cover the printing costs remained. Someone suggested paying for the production expenses by selling a limited quantity to collectors. Bank of Israel officials went to ask the German-born state comptroller, Dr. Yitzhak Ernst Nebenzahl, an Orthodox and honest man. He decreed it would not benefit a country like Israel to make any profitable use of the occupation bills. And so the head of the bank instructed that the bills not be distributed in any way, not even to be displayed in the bank's museum.*

On October 15 a truck left the government printer in Jerusalem with thirty-three sacks full of the occupation currency. They were taken to a plant somewhere on Israel's coastal plain, where the bills were shredded. The mill was unable to destroy them all, however, so most lay forgotten in the bank basement until someone decided to get rid of them, many years later. In a thick file documenting the affair, there is a letter from Gad Rothschild, the graphic artist, asking whether the bank would be kind enough to give him and his partner, Lipman, two or three samples of their design work. "To design an occupation currency bill—that's something a graphic artist gets to do once in a thousand years," he explained. In the margin of the letter, someone wrote that Dr. Nebenzahl would have to be asked about the matter.[21]

---

*The IDF's legal adviser contacted the Bank of Israel with a request from General Uzi Narkis: he wanted to keep some of the bills as souvenirs. It later transpired that Yitzhak Rabin also had a bill in his possession.

CHAPTER 18

THE ENLIGHTENED OCCUPATION

1. GUIDELINES: "THE MASCULINITY OF THE ARAB"

Not far from Jericho was a model farm used to teach agronomy to the children of Palestinian refugees from 1948. Musa Alami, the founder, had been a prominent figure in Palestine. In the 1930s, he had met with David Ben-Gurion several times to discuss the future of Jewish-Arab relations. Ben-Gurion's account of their conversations was published a few months before the Six-Day War. When the war broke out, the elderly Alami was in London. Ben-Gurion, in both phone calls and telegrams, urged him to return: "There is a unique chance to conclude peace between Israel and her neighbors; your presence now is vital." Teddy Kollek thought Ben-Gurion had erred in his judgment, explaining that Alami could not come home by personal invitation while thousands of refugees were prevented from returning. To make things worse, the invitation was published in the press.* Kollek himself eventually met with Alami and proposed that he return to become the leader of the Palestinians. Alami was not enthusiastic, but he asked Kollek to help protect the farm. Kollek promised to use his connections to do so.[1]

The desire to prove to Palestinian Arabs that Israelis were decent and peace-loving was anchored in the foundations of Zionist ideology: from the day they began settling in Palestine, Zionists had insisted they were

---

*When Ben-Gurion finally managed to get hold of Alami on the phone, the line between Sde Boker and London was very bad. Ben-Gurion's account describes the entire history of Israeli-Palestinian relations: "He couldn't hear me, but I could hear him. Then it got better. He could hear me, but I couldn't hear him."

bringing success and prosperity to all the land's inhabitants. Following the Six-Day War, Israelis identified the occupation as another opportunity to prove their good intentions to the Arabs, to the world at large, and, above all, to themselves. They soon began to refer to the "enlightened occupation." The eagerness demonstrated by Teddy Kollek in attempting to win Musa Alami's cooperation also marked the efforts of a Knesset member, Frija Zuaretz, to help a resident of the village of Sebastia, near Nablus.

A few weeks after the IDF occupied Sebastia, Knesset chairman Kadish Luz received a letter in Arabic. The letter was translated and typed for him: "I, Muhammad Abdullah Mukhaimer, from the village of Sebastia, ask for your help in getting treatment at Hadassah Hospital in Jerusalem." The man had been ill for some four years and had found no one who could cure him, and so he was asking for the Knesset chairman's help. He was willing to bear all the expenses, he wrote. "I own ten dunams of land planted with trees and I am willing to transfer their title to the State of Israel after I leave the hospital. I thank the government of Israel for its help to poor people like me and I hope that you will respond to my request soon."

The request necessitated further inquiries. Luz, a seventy-two-year-old originally from Russia, handed the matter over to Zuaretz. A native of Libya who had come to Israel only in 1949, Zuaretz had been elected to the Knesset as a Mafdal delegate while still living in a transit camp, where he was the principal of an elementary school. He had written a few books, including one on Jewish women in Libya. Zuaretz chaired the Knesset's Public Petitions Committee, and the Palestinian from Sebastia was now considered a member of the public entitled to assistance.

"Perhaps you might be able to respond to this man's request, and this will also sanctify the name of Israel," wrote Zuaretz to the director general of the Ministry of Health. The secretary of the Public Petitions Committee sent a polite letter to Mukhaimer, in Hebrew, informing him that his request had been transferred to the Ministry of Health. The director general of the ministry responded nine days later that he "would be happy" to handle the request, but asked for a medical opinion from Mukhaimer's attending physician. The committee forwarded his letter to Mukhaimer.

Two months later, Mukhaimer wrote to the Knesset chairman again, and his letter was once again translated. He explained that he had already written to the chairman and asked to be admitted to an Israeli hospital. He had no one to help him: his two sons worked in Kuwait and he had not received a penny from them since the beginning of the Israeli occupation, because there was no postal service between Sebastia and Kuwait. He asked that they treat him with the utmost mercy and transfer him to an Israeli state hospital, or at least pay his subsistence expenses so that he could eat and drink. Finally, he wished to thank the State of Israel for its compassion toward the disabled.

Summer and fall came and went. The committee secretary attempted to clarify the situation to the honorable Mr. Mukhaimer: he had written explaining that Mr. Mukhaimer must send a medical opinion, but the letter had been returned to the Knesset by the post office, because apparently the address in Sebastia was not accurate. He was therefore sending Mr. Mukhaimer a copy of that previous letter.

The Mukhaimer file grew thicker and thicker, and in mid-December a letter arrived from the manager of the Jerusalem post office to Knesset member Zuaretz, promising that his letter had been delivered to its intended recipient and that he, the manager, regretted that the first letter had not reached Mr. Mukhaimer in the village of Sebastia.

Mr. Mukhaimer was a tireless man. In another letter to the minister of health, he explained that he had been ill for several years, and that he had asked for the medical opinion, but the doctor who came to the village once a week, Dr. Muhammad Kilani, demanded that he pay one dinar, and Mr. Mukhaimer could not pay even a penny. And so he was asking the health minister and the prime minister to treat him with sympathy and mercy and to send him to a hospital in Israel. Again, he was willing to bear all the costs.

The minister of health passed this letter to Knesset member Zuaretz, who recounted the saga in a letter to Haim Israeli, the omnipotent director of the office of the minister of defense, a position he had occupied since back in Ben-Gurion's days. The question, wrote Zuaretz, was whether there was any objection to the man being treated in an Israeli hospital. "We are willing to help if you respond positively." The Ministry of Defense did not try to evade its responsibility. Israeli replied within six days that orders had been given to the military government in the West Bank to arrange for a medical opinion—at its own expense, if necessary—so that Muhammad Abdullah Mukhaimer could be hospitalized. But Israeli also requested clarification: "Who will bear the expenses? Is your willingness to 'help the man' to be interpreted as an ability to cover the hospitalization expenses?"

At this point there was nothing in the file about the applicant's background, nor about the nature of his illness. All that was known to the kind Israelis who so eagerly came to his aid was that he was a Palestinian now under their responsibility, and that he was asking for help. The secretary of the Public Petitions Committee called around; then he called around some more; and after a few days Knesset member Zuaretz was able to report to the director general of the office of the minister of defense that, according to an assistant of Dr. Mani's, from the military government in Jerusalem, hospitalization "will obviously be arranged at the expense of the Ministry of Health."

Summer came again, almost a year had passed since the war. Muhammad Abdullah Mukhaimer wrote again to the Knesset chairman, introducing himself as an old acquaintance. He explained that he could not travel to Nablus to see a doctor because the left side of his body was paralyzed. Here was a first hint at the nature of his illness. He did not have any money for a taxi. There was no one to take care of him and no one to support him. He was asking for hospitalization in Israel because in his country there were no experienced Arab doctors. He needed help before his life came to an end, and he was willing to pay all the expenses.

On June 11, 1968, the first anniversary of the end of the war, Knesset member Zuaretz himself wrote a letter to the honorable Mr. Mukhaimer. The office of the minister of defense had made such and such promises, he explained, and the military government had made such and such assurances, and he, the chairman of the Public Petitions Committee in the Knesset of Israel, wished Mr. Mukhaimer the best of luck. Zuaretz's letter was written in Arabic.

More and more letters and telegrams piled up in the file, including a medical opinion, which found that Mr. Mukhaimer had been paralyzed on his left side for seven years and that both limbs were atrophied, but he did not require hospitalization. An identical opinion was given by Dr. A. Mani, the medical staff officer—the representative of the Ministry of Health in the military government.[2]

THE FOUNDATION OF MARTIAL LAW IN THE TERRITORIES HAD BEEN LAID YEARS BEFORE the war. In December 1963, Chief of Staff Zvi Zur had appointed General Chaim Herzog as military governor of the West Bank in the event that Israel occupied the area.

The army issued several handbooks for future governors, containing a wealth of information about the legal basis and the organizational structure of a military government, as well as a series of guidelines for handling civilian populations. The assumption had been that most of the residents would neither flee nor be deported. The governors were to treat them according to the Geneva Conventions, which was also provided in a Hebrew translation. According to Shlomo Gazit, the coordinator of operations in the territories, the architects of the military government derived some assistance from a book by Gerhard von Glahn, an American expert on international law, but a significant portion of the instructions were rooted in the British Mandate. The future governors also learned from the brief Gaza occupation after the Sinai Campaign. Many members of the military government staff in the territories had previously been part of the martial-law apparatus that had overseen the Arab citizens of Israel.[3]

The military government was ready to begin operations even before the fighting was over, with the publication of proclamations and ordinances that its people brought with them to the Occupied Territories. Order No. 1 declared a curfew, which was aimed at preventing resistance, sabotage, and looting, and it also empowered the military government to implement its initial organization. The governors' handbook defined their preliminary assignments, mostly related to security, the collection of weapons, the clearing of land mines, the arrest of hostile persons on the basis of lists the army had prepared, and the burial of the dead. The governor was to begin operating intelligence units that would gather information about the area, including its topography, roads and streets, squares and parks, post offices and industrial plants, schools, holy places and mosques, museums and libraries, printing houses, cemeteries, and, at least according to one handbook, brothels.

The working assumption was that the IDF would remain in the territories for a prolonged period. The military government's purpose was to restore civilian life to normal as quickly as possible. The handbooks for enlightened occupation expected the governors to display administrative skills, political instincts, and an understanding of Israeli foreign policy considerations. The governor was to be economist, educator, legislator, and judge.

The military government was instructed to create a portrait of the population's character. The handbooks gave basic information: The Arab population is accustomed to hoarding food supplies and will be able to withstand a few days of full curfew if security needs necessitate it. The governor must identify key figures in every area and make an effort to immediately locate potential collaborators. Accordingly, he must enlist the mayor and the local authorities.* Commanders were instructed to prevent acts of lawlessness and cruelty toward the local population, and to

---

*The study materials given to the thirteenth graduating class of the Command and Staff School in 1966–67 specified, among other things, the duties of the Security Service in the occupation apparatus.

punish soldiers who engaged in looting. "Soldiers must absolutely avoid contact with local women, due to the danger of sexually transmitted diseases, which are extremely common in the enemy countries." In an effort to prevent unnecessary bloodshed, the guidebooks explained that "carrying arms is one proof of an Arab man's masculinity and a means of elevating his status."

Within as short a time as possible after occupying a town, it was advisable to conduct a demonstration of armor, artillery, and aircraft, the handbooks stated. These forces were to pass through the center of town several times, making a loud noise as they came from different directions. "Such a display of power should have a significant effect on the inhabitants." There were also to be patrols, searches, and blockades. Some of these were described in the handbooks in great detail. "During the search one must constantly observe the people's responses; these will often serve as a reliable guide for those searching." And further, "Walls and floors are often hiding places. Therefore, searchers must knock on every wall and floor and listen to the sound. A dull echo indicates the possibility of a hiding place." Each group was to include one soldier "with experience in conducting searches," the handbooks said, although it did not indicate where soldiers were to acquire this experience. Either way, soldiers were to bring their personal weapons and be equipped with hand grenades, axes, iron rods, and flashlights. When a party was carrying out a night search, vehicle headlights should be used to illuminate the surrounding area. All this and much more was basic advice for the beginning occupier.

Members of the military government were cautioned against displaying "an unnecessarily hostile attitude." A governor's success in local politics could "reduce alienation and suspicion toward the occupying country and set the background for normal relations." Governors were to make sure local authorities represented "moderate factors among the public," and that the driving consideration for their operations was to be the welfare of the population, while accepting IDF authority. It might be possible to replace members of the local councils. All action must be taken with extreme prudence and after careful consideration. "Hasty appointments may disrupt the authority of local institutions." The governor was to make an effort from the very beginning to take control of the population registry, and perhaps conduct a new census. Before allowing schools to open, the governor must "closely examine the curriculum and the textbooks" and, if necessary, prepare alternative texts on "sensitive topics," as well as "train a staff of supervisors proficient in the language and culture of the occupied territory." The governor was also responsible for disseminating appropriate propaganda. He was instructed to "explain" to the population the shortcomings of the previous regime and convince them that there was no chance of defeating the IDF.

The governor would oversee the economy and was to "continue collecting taxes and conducting other fiscal and monetary activities." He must "plan the adaptation of the agricultural economy to the new market conditions," oversee industry, and ensure a regular supply of consumer goods "at reasonable prices." The governor must initiate public works in order to reduce unemployment. This approach was more desirable than handing out welfare, and would also be "an important tool in calming tempers and reducing incitement." The extent of a governor's success in the realm of social welfare, including the continuation of international welfare organizations' activities, would influence the population's attitude toward him. The military had a strong interest in maintaining proper sanitation and preventing the outbreak of epidemics. When necessary, the governor should ensure the vaccination of residents.

The governor would be in charge of operating religious services and ensuring access to holy sites and mosques. He would have to make arrangements to guarantee "controlled access, including to Jewish holy sites." He would need to ensure postal and communication services, including phone service, "while implementing meticulous censorship." The governor would naturally come into contact with citizens of foreign countries: UN workers, the staff of welfare organizations, clergymen, diplomats, foreign journalists. He must remember that "there is a political interest" in having such people convey a positive impression of IDF operations to their countries and to public opinion.

This was "a wise policy" of rewards and punishments, avoiding military force whenever possible while always ensuring consideration of "the humane principles accepted among civilized nations," the guidebooks asserted. And in summary, "the military governor must learn to find the golden mean between security and political needs, and the need to restore civilian life to normality, in the event that there is a conflict between the two." The restoration of the legal system was said to be "not one of the initial essential matters that the IDF will handle." Courts were allowed to operate, but the governor was permitted to revoke existing laws and enact others.[4]

THE FIRST GOVERNOR OF HEBRON, ZVI OFER, REMEMBERED THAT AT SOME POINT IN HIS studies at the Command and Staff School there was some talk about occupation, but it was negligible. "It is true that there was a brief chapter on military government," he said, "but when that chapter was being discussed, that seemed the right time to run errands and so on, because we didn't view it as important. It was a bit of a fantasy: why would we suddenly be governing towns or territories?" But Ofer also described his principles of occupation as a reflection of his basic decency as an Israeli, and it was important for him to know that the residents respected him for this. "One of the things that impressed the local people happened when a three-year-old girl was injured," he recollected. "My operations commander . . . went to visit her and even brought her some candy. That really impressed them, and the echoes that came back to us after that were very positive and showed us, in fact, in our true colors." It was important to remember, Ofer continued, that this occurred after the local population had been fed all sorts of stories for twenty years, about "how we'd rape them and how we'd murder them and how we'd steal from them."

Ofer saw himself representing a society that was more fair than Palestinian society, and he wanted to impose his values on the latter. When he demanded that hospital doctors make house calls to civilians during curfew, he was told that among Palestinians it was customary for the patient to come to the hospital or clinic to see the doctor, as a matter of respect. "For an Arab doctor to go to some Arab house in the kasbah, to visit a patient? That's beneath him! It would be more convenient for the doctor if the patient died, rather than lower himself to go among the people and examine the patient," said Ofer. He needed someone to help keep records on any infectious diseases in town, as instructed in the occupier's handbook. He asked a doctor who refused to make house calls where he had studied: England. Ofer asked what his specialty was: internal medicine and heart disease. "Is your diploma from a good school?" he asked, and the doctor said it was. Ofer then told him, "From now on your diploma will be good for washing dishes and cleaning out sewage." The governor reminded the doctor that he had sworn an oath to help anyone who needed it, no matter who or what he was. " 'So either you start making house calls and reporting to me, or your diploma will be good for cleaning out latrines,' " he decreed. "And then the doctors started rushing around the houses and the neighborhoods, visiting the *mukhtars,* to get reports on the health situation. Before that, they didn't even think they needed to do it."[5]*

---

*Ofer recounted these events to the journalist Shabtai Teveth. Ofer was killed while pursuing terrorists, and Teveth made him the hero of the "enlightened occupation" myth in his book *The Blessed Curse,* a sequel of sorts to *Exposed in the Turret.*

Shlomo Gazit recounted events described by the governor of Jenin, a reservist named Amnon Bronstein. Because of the war, the villagers in Jenin were cut off from the Jordanian side of the river and would not be able to harvest their crops in time using their traditional methods. And so Bronstein enlisted five combines from Jewish farms in the Jezreel Valley to replace the tractors that used to be brought in from the Jordanian East Bank. Gazit quoted one of the tractor drivers who took part in this project: "I was one of the occupiers. We are not capable of being occupiers. Only a month ago I risked my life here and now I'm coming to help them harvest their crops."

In the first few months of the occupation, Israelis wrote to friends and relatives abroad about visits to the territories, mainly the West Bank, where they could drive for hours without seeing any military personnel or vehicles. The military government emerged from such descriptions as an invisible force. This was the essence of the policy Shlomo Gazit credited to Moshe Dayan: Israel was not imposing itself on the Arab population, but rather granting it maximal freedom to conduct its life, including open communication with the Arab world and freedom of the press.[6] Like some other sensible ideas that Dayan espoused, this one remained on paper.

2. INITIATIVES: "WE FELT LUCKY"

Chaim Herzog claimed that he spent the years prior to the war preparing himself adequately for his duties. "We studied Jordanian events in depth. I made sure we received the daily newspapers from Jordan. The basic idea was to keep the team members up to speed on life in Jordan." Before the war, his brother, the director general of the prime minister's office, who dealt extensively with relations between Israel and the Christian world, cautioned him against bombing the Old City. Chaim Herzog reassured him: he had a detailed map indicating all the Christian holy sites.[7]

But the early stages of the occupation were extremely disorganized. "It would be difficult to exaggerate when describing the chaos," wrote a veteran member of the military government. A colleague added, "Everyone was wandering around in a dream." Herzog set up his headquarters in the Ambassador Hotel, in East Jerusalem, while Uzi Narkis was still based in Binyanei Hauma, the West Jerusalem convention center. Hundreds of reserve officers—some volunteers, some called up for active duty—scurried between the two. They carried handguns and did a lot of talking, but none of them knew what they were doing. They blamed the confusion on Chaim Herzog, whom they perceived as a British-style governor who stood on ceremony. It didn't take long for Dayan to get rid of him. Herzog was replaced by three long-standing members of the National Defense College: Uzi Narkis, Rafael Vardi, and Shlomo Gazit.[8]

The military and civilian presence in the territories rapidly mutated into an endless labyrinth of headquarters, commands, branches, departments, units, wings, bureaus, authorities, administrations, and outposts—a giant warren of countless officers, soldiers, and civil servants. Their work consisted almost entirely of inventing more and more reasons to interfere in the residents' daily lives, which they accomplished by means of laws and regulations and ordinances and injunctions that, like some of the bureaucratic whimsies that ruled Israeli citizens, reflected no clear policy or a calculated strategy but rather, above all, arbitrariness. The mountains of paperwork this system produced document innumerable duplications, conflicts of interest, and confrontations between egos, both personal and institutional, not only between the security system and the government offices, but also among various military sectors, between the military and other security arms, such as the Shabak and the police, within those sectors themselves, and among government ministries. The separate military government systems for Sinai, Gaza, the West Bank, and the Golan Heights created even further duplication.

The organizational chart of the military government staff at the Central Command headquarters included, in July 1967, six groups of job holders and a total of sixty-one government mechanisms and positions, including staff officer of tourism, staff officer of archaeology, and staff officer for insurance. A board of directors general of government ministries, set up to handle civilian matters, comprised thirty-one members, including the director general of the office of Yosef Sapir, a minister without portfolio. This board was one of a multitude of new committees, including one comprising Hebrew University professors, as well as a variety of teams charged with conceptualizing, planning, implementing, and monitoring.[9] The civil servants did their best to keep themselves busy.

The Ministry of Religious Affairs representative prepared a detailed list of dozens of Jewish holy sites, including some graves that required historical glosses because few people had ever heard of their occupants. Atniel Ben Kenaz, for example, was the son-in-law of Caleb Ben Yefuneh, one of the twelve scouts sent into Canaan ahead of the children of Israel. When he conquered Kiryat Sefer, Caleb gave him his daughter, Achsa, as his wife. All this was explained in the report. The ministry's officials also located the tombs of Ruth the Moabite and Yishai, the father of King David, as well as those of Nathan the Prophet and Gad the Seer, from the Book of Samuel. And there were many more yet to be found, noted one military government member in his diary. The Ministry of Tourism representative was asked to put together a restaurant guide for the West Bank.[10]

The need for government officials clearly arose because the military alone could not fill the void left by the Jordanian government. None of the officers had been trained in pest control or knew how to calculate the requisite amount of milk for infants. But the masses of civil servants who poured into the territories did not come simply because the military government needed them. Each government ministry was eager to grab a piece of the massive bounty that had fallen into Israel's hands. The minister of religious affairs protested to Dayan about his interference in matters involving the Tomb of the Patriarchs, an issue that should have been within the ministry's purview. Dayan replied curtly that responsibility for the cave lay with the military rabbinate. He suggested that in the future, instead of protesting and airing his grievances in the press, the minister should speak to him directly, and then he might learn that he was wrong. Countless other quarrels broke out among civilian entities called upon to handle the territories.[11]

As they expanded the scope of their activities, the ministries also grew in importance and enlarged their budgets. Clerks brought to the territories a burst of energy and a visionary sense of adventure—the Zionist enterprise lived again, and safe from the watchful eyes of the state comptroller.*

Shlomo Gazit complained about how difficult it was to find good people to agree to leave their positions in government offices and work in the territories. Many of those who came were not among the most competent, and they had to be lured with power, salaries, and titles that they would probably not have attained on the civilian track. Moreover, it became difficult to get rid of them because they refused to take a step backward. Some wanted to fill positions in the territories because they perceived an opportunity to take advantage of their knowledge of Arabic and get ahead.[13]

The involvement of the military and civil service in people's daily lives

---

*The state comptroller's report on the first year of Israeli control of the territories was so devastating that the IDF managed to block publication. It has remained classified ever since. Besides detailing violations of Palestinian detainees' rights, the report also contained a small tale of corruption: the chief military rabbinate posted charity collection boxes in holy sites like Rachel's Tomb, but soldiers opened the boxes and no proper accounts were kept.[12]

became ever more entrenched. "Military commanders need to be deployed so that factories producing soap, cigarettes, and arak can get back to work," wrote Major Moshe Goldenberg, the administration officer of the military government staff at Central Command headquarters. The representative of the Ministry of Commerce and Trade in the Golan Heights was tasked with compiling a consumer price list that would be posted in every shop and to which shopkeepers and customers would have to adhere. The Ministry of Finance representative in the Golan reported difficulties collecting income tax. "We have not yet been able to find the Syrian law," he wrote, "and so it has been decided to invite a few Arabic-speaking Israeli workers to sort through the heaps and heaps of disorganized information."

Tens of thousands of Golan residents had lost their homes, yet Captain Mihal Cohen, from the Northern Command headquarters, found time to send the minister of defense a detailed report on an investigation into complaints from the Druze village of Bukata: Hassan Yusuf Abu Shahin's mules were grazing unsupervised near the cease-fire line, and they might have crossed into Syria. A complaint lodged by Ali Mukhassan Tarabia about the loss of a mule was also under investigation, as was his claim that the mule had been seen with a resident of Tiberias. A flatbed belonging to Toufik Hassan Ama'ah had been found on one of the kibbutzim. The missing horses of two other residents were located after an extensive search and returned to their owners.* The military government regulated telegrams sent to West Bank residents and arranged for school buses in the Golan. The lifeguards on the Gaza beaches had to come to Tel Aviv to appear before a Ministry of Labor committee. If they passed the Israeli lifeguard tests, they were given certificates.[14]

Many former Jordanian government employees went to work for the Israeli military government, which had to determine their terms of employment and establish a pay scale to calculate wages for guards, messengers, cleaners, cooks, laundresses, gardeners, electricians, sanitation workers, midwives, and social workers. They reviewed the system of measurements and weights, removed a few traffic islands that were slowing down traffic in Al Arish, and replaced license plates. They permitted the distribution of six Hebrew books in the West Bank, as well as *Ha'aretz*. A

---

*The Ministry of Defense tried to sell off fabric and furniture abandoned by Golan residents in warehouses and homes. The staff officer for the Treasury in the Golan was asked to oversee the sale of some other war booty: 539 heads of beef cattle, 730 sheep, 29 goats, 34 donkeys, and 89 horses. Those who owned confiscated cars could reclaim them; the unclaimed cars were sold.

meeting of district physicians in the West Bank discussed a plan to administer polio vaccines.*

The thirty-one delegates to the Board of Directors General discussed sesame and legume crops. Having considered the matter carefully, they concluded, "To create an incentive for farmers in the territories to plant more sesame and legumes, reducing foreign imports, we have resolved to allow freer trade of these products between the territories and Israel, in both directions. The customs rate on imported sesame and chickpeas will be determined by the relevant office."

One file contains a document that begins: "Israel Defense Forces / IDF Forces Command in the West Bank Region / Tobacco Law No. 32 for 1952 / Order No. 31 (10) / By the powers vested in me by the ordinance concerning appointments as per the Laws of Customs and Excise (West Bank Region) (No. 31), 5727-1967, and Article 40 of the Tobacco Law No. 32 for 1952 (herein below), I hereby order . . ." What followed were twenty-two clauses and subclauses regulating the price of cigarettes and tobacco. The order distinguished between products packaged in paper (with or without cellophane wrapping) and in cardboard boxes; with or without a cardboard bottom; with or without a hinged lid. Particular aspects of the packaging were specified in English, for clarification. Included were cigar and pipe tobacco, with or without external packaging. The ordinance was signed by Y. Peleg, to whose name was appended the somewhat mysterious title of "Commissioner."†

SOME TWO WEEKS AFTER THE WAR, A FEW SOLDIERS PATROLLING THE JORDAN RIVER noticed suspicious movement south of Kibbutz Tirat Zvi. According to Michael Shashar, a military government staff member who described the affair in his diary, a few Palestinian farmers were trying to take a crate of tomatoes or cucumbers to the eastern bank of the river, Jordanian territory. The soldiers responded leniently, providing the farmers with appropriate travel permits. The permits confirmed that Muhammad So-and-So was allowed to take a crate of tomatoes to Jordan and return to the West

---

*The Board of Directors General eventually determined that Palestinians could not be hospitalized in Israel except in extraordinary cases. The board noted that there "is no way to supply the residents of the territories medical treatment that meets Israeli standards."

†The government established at least half a dozen ministerial committees to handle territorial affairs, one of which was named the Ministerial Committee for Coordination Between the Ministerial Committee for Internal Affairs and Services and the Ministerial Committee for Economic Affairs in the Matter of Territories Administered by the IDF.

Bank, and were signed by Sergeant Such-and-Such. Headquarters got wind of this, wrote Shashar, and thought it was a good idea. This was the beginning of the "open bridges policy" of movement across the border, which Moshe Dayan would later take credit for, calling it "one of the most revolutionary innovations we instituted."

It was a good year for West Bank farmers, with surpluses of 20,000 tons of tomatoes, 15,000 tons of melons, and some 50,000 tons of watermelons. The problem was where to market the produce. Israel was out of the question because of Israeli growers' objections. A plan to sell the produce to the U.S. Navy command in Naples seemed impractical. A few farmers went to Amnon Bronstein and told him that although the river bridges had been bombed, it was still possible to drive trucks into Jordan. As an experiment, Bronstein allowed three trucks to make a round-trip. The produce reached Jordan and the trucks came back. Bronstein told a few of his colleagues about the exercise; Dan Bawly of the military government later recalled that it was at the home of Ze'ev Shaham, the governor of Samaria. Bawly and Baruh Yekutieli, a senior official at Bank Leumi, were busy formulating economic policy for the West Bank. A prominent Jerusalem attorney was present, Erwin Shimron, who Bawly noted was "in charge of social issues in the West Bank." The governor's agricultural officer, Eitan Israeli, was also there.

It was a lovely evening, Bawly recalled. "We were at the military camp in the Dotan Valley, sitting on a balcony looking west, letting the light breeze touch our bare feet." The governor served delicious food. "We felt lucky to be there, in those jobs, taking part in building this challenging, important enterprise." Knowing Dayan, the men were sure he would authorize the sale of agricultural produce in Jordan only if he believed he himself had come up with the idea. They organized a field trip for Dayan; when he saw the trucks crossing the Jordan River, he gave his approval. From then on, the "open bridges policy" was identified with Dayan's fair and wise approach to Israeli-Palestinian relations. Former minister Mordehai Bentov later claimed that in fact when Dayan learned that trucks were crossing the Jordan River he was "alarmed" and "didn't know what to do." Halting the traffic would have meant calling in "half the IDF" and perhaps even opening fire on the farmers and truckers, which would have led to "extremely grave political complications." Then the decision was made "to grant them free passage." The policy was not the result of "ingenious planning," Bentov wrote, merely a way out of a dilemma.[15]

The open bridges policy made life under occupation easier, and made it easier for Israel to rule. As for the sale of tomatoes and watermelons, the policy might be viewed as proof of the free market's power to overcome political stumbling blocks. But the policy had implications beyond economics, because it effectively opened the door to the movement of people between the territories, including East Jerusalem and the Gaza Strip, and the Arab world. Residents were permitted to come and go and to send funds to students overseas; students were allowed back to the territories for summer visits.[16] These factors gave the occupation a great deal of power, because Israel could close the bridges at any time. The open bridges were also good for Israel's image worldwide. The direct and straightforward contact between the territories and the Arab world nurtured the hope that the occupation would facilitate a "reality of peace," and strengthened the illusion that there was no need to rush to find a political settlement.*

APART FROM THE CONSTANT CONCERN ABOUT SECURITY, NOTHING PREOCCUPIED THE military governors more than the economic situation in the territories. Economic problems were also first on the agenda for the Board of Directors General. The main difficulty was that until the government decided what it wanted to do with the territories, it was impossible to adequately plan their economies. Every decision was supposedly short-term, just until the end of the occupation. In reality, though, the administrators began tying the territories' economies to Israel's almost immediately.

Israeli banks were allowed to open branches in West Bank cities within weeks, and they operated alongside the Arab banks, which were also authorized to reopen for business. Israeli companies began export-import trade with companies from the territories. In mid-December, the supervisor of mining found that the stone industry in the Occupied Territories had managed to largely "take over" the Israeli construction market. Laborers from the territories soon began commuting to work in Israel. The West Bank population could supply a cheap workforce for the Israeli textile and confection industries, wrote one military administrator in his diary as early as July 26. The minister of labor, Yigal Allon, tried to block this trend, as did Minister of Finance Sapir. Arabs from the territories worked for low pay and under exploitative conditions, wrote Allon to

---

*As part of the effort to normalize ties with Jordan, Israel wanted to restore mail service between them. This could have been accomplished through the International Red Cross in Switzerland, but a forum called the Committee for the West Bank wished to impose direct contact with Jordan, and so it decided to throw sacks of mail to the other side of the Jordan River every day and wait for responses.[17]

Dayan. Sapir correctly feared that Palestinian labor would accelerate the economic integration of the territories and Israel, making withdrawal more difficult. This was precisely Dayan's intention, and he proved that Sapir himself had allowed Arabs from the territories to work within Israel.[18] Eshkol decided to make the Israeli lira legal tender in the West Bank, alongside the Jordanian dinar. The government discussed the question of currency frequently, often reversing its prior decisions.*

In early November, the requirement for permits to enter the West Bank and the Golan Heights was lifted. In January 1968, the minister of the interior and the minister of defense decided that residents of the West Bank and the Gaza Strip would receive Israeli identity cards. A week later, the Board of Directors General reported that it had decided in favor of full economic integration of the Golan Heights within the Israeli economy. Customs stations established immediately after the war still operated at transit points between the territories and Israel, but in February 1968 they were shut down.[19]†

3. CONTROL: "WHIP AND CARROT"

On the morning of March 20, 1968, Moshe Dayan took a few hours' leave from his office and went to an excavation site in Azur, near Tel Aviv, where bulldozers were digging up dirt in preparation for new roads. Dayan had come to search for antiquities, illegally. On other occasions, he had found five-thousand-year-old tombstones at this site. He was accompanied by an expert on local archaeology. Spotting a few interesting shards at the top of a mound of earth, he began to climb up it and was almost killed.

The landslide occurred in two stages, he recounted later. The first layer of earth to collapse buried half his body. Then the upper level collapsed and caved in on him. "This is the end," he had time to think, unable to move. Another heap landed on his head. The man who had come with him called for help. A few people who lived nearby brought shovels and

---

*This was a clear step in the creeping annexation. At the request of the Foreign Ministry, the government agreed that if the Israeli lira was declared the sole currency in the West Bank, they would delay publication of the ordinance until after the annual UN General Assembly meeting.
†These decisions were part of a much larger process that later included the decision to encourage Israelis to open factories in the West Bank. If there were any doubts about Israel's reluctance to leave the territories quickly, they were quelled by a secret communication by Shlomo Gazit to the Board of Directors General: certain sites in the Occupied Territories had been earmarked for future nuclear reactors, "if needed."

started digging Dayan out. He had injured two vertebrae, broken some ribs, and torn a vocal cord. He was hospitalized for three weeks. According to Avner Falk, a clinical psychologist who wrote a biography of Dayan, "The correct psychiatric term for what occurred is 'unconscious suicide attempt.'" Dayan's sister, Aviva Geffen, had killed herself some four months earlier.

There is nothing surprising about the desire to put Moshe Dayan on the analyst's couch. He was a difficult man to decipher, and many tried. "Everyone wants to 'understand' him," wrote the journalist Amos Elon, who also wondered, "What in God's name does he want?" Elon had no answer. "Dayan is the mysterious Cyclops of Israeli politics." The black patch over his left eye evoked heroism and sacrifice. But it also aroused a voyeuristic streak: who was not tempted by frightening fantasies about what Dayan looked like without it? There was something almost pornographic about what it might conceal. *Ha'aretz* was explicit: Dayan had sex appeal. The eye patch made him immediately identifiable, and advanced his career. "He would never have gone as far as he did if he'd had two eyes," his rivals claimed.[20]*

Dayan was a lonely man. He found it extremely difficult to forge genuine relationships. He had no friends; his family life was unstable. Driven entirely by impulse, he could commit neither to a woman, nor to a worldview, nor to a party, the law, or the truth, as if he were beyond them all. A wizard of public relations, he sold himself as the embodiment of Israel's mythos: Dayan was associated with all its aspects—love of the homeland, youthfulness, masculinity, the new Hebrew strength, the Bible, David Ben-Gurion, the IDF, and, above all, the war against the Arabs. Born on Kibbutz Degania in 1915, Dayan came of age with the first conflicts in the struggle over the land, against shepherds and farmers and Palestinian neighbors. The Six-Day War positioned him at the center of a cult of admiration. In Dayan, Israelis saw their fate and everything they wished to be. Chaim Herzog likened him to "an emperor returning to Rome after a great military victory." Dayan's biographer Shabtai Teveth wrote: "His one eye glimmered with an enormous lust for life, his other eye was extinguished beneath the black patch, dead. At times he seemed to symbolize Israel itself, in which life and death are close partners, and which draws its courage from its very willingness to die in order to live."

---

*Dayan suffered from severe eye pain his whole life, which often made him impatient and unkind.

Intelligent, cold, and arrogant, hungry for power and with no respect for limits, Dayan seemed the very opposite of the aging political establishment and the entire party system. For this reason he frightened many Israelis too: they believed he wanted to take over the country. Menachem Begin thought Dayan's conduct was reminiscent of a military dictator. But in retrospect, Dayan in fact emerges as a man who recoiled from taking ultimate responsibility. Throughout his life he built himself up under the auspices of stronger figures: David Ben-Gurion, Golda Meir, Menachem Begin. He always took care to obtain permission and support for his decisions, even if after the fact. And so there was never really any danger that he would take over the country. The Six-Day War, however, delivered a stage for his lust for power: he became sole ruler over the territories and their million subjects.

"Dayan was a peculiar Jew," said Rehavam Ze'evi, "One day he wanted to kill all the Arabs, the next day he was the defender of Islam."[21] His capriciousness—doubtless an aspect of his reluctance to commit—makes Dayan's regime in the territories hard to grasp. His policy drew on at least four sources: lessons learned during British rule; the restrictions imposed upon Israeli Arabs by martial law; the Israeli rule of Gaza after the Sinai Campaign; and impressions from his visits to Vietnam.

Like the Arab citizens of Israel, the Arabs of the territories were to become a population that Israel would have to live with on a permanent basis. Unlike the Arab citizens, however, the residents of the territories were not going to become Israelis. They were not required to prove their loyalty to Israel, but simply to obey it. An apt depiction of Dayan's rule in the territories was offered, probably not coincidentally, by the British ambassador to Israel, Michael Hadow. He described Dayan's attitude as "essentially paternalistic," not unlike, say, that of a Pashtun-speaking British colonial administrator in an Indian province. Dayan enjoyed tending to the needs of "his" tribe, wrote Hadow, protecting them from unnecessary interference by other military administrators. But the moment they took so much as a small step beyond the line he had marked in the sand, he would use the stick—"quickly, effectively, and drastically."

When he first went to Saigon, Dayan felt as if he had been there before. Everything looked familiar. Even the soldiers posted behind sandbags at intersections were not new to him, he wrote: this was how towns in Palestine—Jerusalem, Haifa, Jaffa—had looked during British rule. Like the British colonialists—and unlike the French—Dayan had no interest in imposing his nation's culture on the Palestinians. He could not understand why it was important to the Americans that the children of Saigon play baseball, he wrote when he returned from Vietnam. He told the American generals he met that when the IDF had controlled Gaza in 1956, he had assured the mayor that the army would not force open schools or shops. If the residents wanted to go on strike, let them strike. They were only hurting themselves.

Indeed, the most precise expression of the policy in the territories seized during the Six-Day War appears in the minutes of government meetings held after the occupation of Gaza in the Sinai Campaign. Ben-Gurion, not Dayan, was the speaker. Foreshadowing Dayan's position prior to the Six-Day War, Ben-Gurion hesitated to authorize the occupation of Gaza in 1956. When it was captured, he told the government that annexation would be a disaster, because Israel could not absorb 300,000 Arabs. But he feared giving the Gaza Strip back to Egypt, or even turning it over to UN control, in case it turned into a terrorist base. And so he proposed at first doing precisely what Israel eventually did a decade later: taking "temporary de facto control" for an unspecified period. The territories would be bound to Israel through close economic ties, but their inhabitants remained without civil rights. Ben-Gurion had also demanded the "normalization" of life in Gaza, including a renewal of local authority.

The British era, martial law, the first occupation of Gaza, and the trip to Vietnam taught Dayan that it was extremely difficult, if not impossible, to control another people and crush a national uprising. It is in the occupier's interest to create favorable living conditions, but the slightest display of rebellion must be put down with an iron fist. Furthermore, the civilian population must be pressured to take its own steps against rebellious factions. This was the "whip and carrot" method, as Dayan called it—retribution and reward.[22]*

MICHAEL SHASHAR, IN THE MILITARY GOVERNMENT, DESCRIBED THE OPENING OF THE post office in Hebron, in July 1967, as a "carrot." Israeli flags adorned the building, and armed soldiers patrolled nearby roofs. "We convinced ourselves that the atmosphere was festive, but it is doubtful whether the local dignitaries felt that way," Shashar observed. The governor of Hebron,

---

*The phrase merits further consideration. Both the "carrot" and the "whip"—or the stick—are used by people when driving beasts. The phrase belongs to a long line of expressions that reflect common Israeli attitudes toward Arabs; for example, the uproar that followed whenever the Arabs "raised their heads," meaning that they behaved impudently. *The Carrot and the Stick* was also the title of a book by Shlomo Gazit, coordinator of operations in the territories.

Major Israeli, said that opening the first Israeli post office in the West Bank was another stage in the restoration of civil services. He expressed his hope that the people appreciated the steps the military government was taking for their benefit. Colonel Eliezer Amitai, military commander of the Jerusalem region, which included Hebron, said, "Let us make an effort to live together in peace, for the sake of the people who history has determined must live in peace in this region." Shashar commented, "A very diplomatic choice of words from an officer." Amitai spoke in Hebrew, and his speech was translated into Arabic.

The elderly mayor, Sheikh Muhammad Ali Jaabari, welcomed the guests warmly, thanked them for opening the post office, and gave the audience a short history lesson. He had been a young boy when the first post office opened in Hebron, during Turkish rule. He had also opened the British post office. And he had opened the Jordanian post office. It was clear to Shashar that deep down the sheikh believed the Israeli regime would also come and go. Meanwhile, Jaabari called upon the Arab states to permit postal communication with Hebron. Then Amitai gave him the key to the building. The sheikh handed it to the manager—one of his sons—and went inside to send a telegram to President Zalman Shazar. On behalf of the local people, he expressed his gratitude for the IDF soldiers' fine conduct, he wrote. There was a reception, and refreshments were served: fruit and cucumbers. There were not enough chairs for all the guests, so Jaabari asked a few of the town dignitaries to leave so as to make room for the IDF officers.*

The "stick" was brandished in, among other places, Nablus, as part of an effort to force the Palestinians to reopen schools after the war. Dayan had not forgotten the lesson he tried to give the Americans in Vietnam: it hardly mattered whether or not the children of Nablus went to school. But he could not ignore the political resistance implied by keeping the schools closed. Nablus organized a trade strike, too, and, the night before widespread disciplinary action was taken, Border Patrol jeeps were fired on by machine guns, and hand grenades were thrown at them.

The punishment was designed to affect everyone. The intention was

---

*Like many Israelis, Shashar brought with him to Hebron memories of the murder of Jews there in 1929. When he first arrived, he imagined he could see "murder in the eyes" of the inhabitants. Following an Israeli citizen's application to the prime minister, the attorney general examined, and rejected, the possibility of revoking the statute of limitations on the murders in Hebron; the petition was based on the fact that the statute of limitations did not apply to murders of Jews by Nazis.[23]

to hurt their pocketbooks and their dignity. A curfew was imposed on the city, bus service was halted, twenty randomly selected stores were forcibly closed, and the telephone network was shut down. Soldiers were ordered to harass residents with house searches. Various public figures were arrested and humiliated. The movement of goods between Nablus and Jordan was frozen. Benefits were offered to Hebron tradesmen, competitors with Nablus merchants. Within three weeks Nablus surrendered, in a fairly humiliating meeting with Dayan himself. The mayor promised to cooperate.[24]

The collective punishment was reminiscent of British methods, as were other methods the IDF inflicted on residents of the territories, usually in response to acts of rebellion. They included searches, arrests, torture during interrogation, deportation, and, even back then, house demolitions as punishment for acts of sabotage. All these acts were allowed under emergency laws instituted during British rule, and, as under the Mandate, they were often imposed arbitrarily.

In early November, a reporter for *Ha'aretz* described a routine search in the Gaza Strip. Five armed jeeps roared down the dirt roads. An Arab man carrying a large bundle of twigs on his head leaped aside, staring after the convoy. The jeeps sped past, raising a huge cloud of dust as they drove around an abandoned packing house, and stopped noisily in front of a group of shacks. Soldiers in dusty uniforms, armed with machine guns, burst into the shacks, yelling, and ordered the inhabitants outside. As infants cried and chickens screeched, the men were gathered under a palm tree while the women and children waited by a wall of prickly pears. A young private watching them took a banana out of his pocket and proceeded to eat it, "slowly and indifferently," his loaded gun held loosely in one hand.

The frightened residents pleaded with the soldiers, swearing they were innocent and had not violated a single rule. The soldiers were looking for weapons. They searched closets and trunks, tossed aside blankets, pulled back sheets, moved mats, dug through pockets. They found nothing suspicious and went back to their jeeps. Two elderly people accompanied them, blessing them in the name of Allah. The women went inside and started picking up the blankets and mattresses.*

---

*Immediately after the war, a mine had exploded in one of the Gaza refugee camps. The army demanded that the residents turn in the operatives, at which point roughly a hundred PLO members gave themselves up but refused to say which one had laid the mine. They were all deported to the Sinai and "left to their own devices," as an official report stated. The army also blew up eight houses in the camp.[25]

Some of the military government officers were housed in installations called Tegart forts, after Charles Tegart, a British expert on quashing civil uprisings who had been brought to Palestine in the 1930s to suppress the Arab rebellion. Back then, the British paratroopers sent to quell riots in Palestine were known by the Jews as Kalaniot ("Poppies"). Now, Israeli paratroopers in red berets were sent to put down demonstrations in the West Bank. Dayan had been an admirer of Captain Orde Wingate, a disturbed British officer who employed particularly cruel punishments against the Arab population. Israeli officers and Shabak interrogators similarly referred to themselves as "Captain," using the English word, and that was what the Arabs called them. Gazit recollected that "Dayan often mentioned the British captain who would go into an Arab village, not far from where there had been an act of sabotage . . . and with his officer's baton he would point arbitrarily to three houses and they would be demolished then and there." Wingate was a great believer in the effectiveness of house demolitions.*

The house demolitions were partly intended as psychological warfare, which was the special role of the IDF's Unit 640. The idea was to convince people that it was not in their best interest to engage in hostilities, and to encourage them to collaborate with the Israeli regime. The working assumption was that rebellion and terrorism arose from uncertainty: the inhabitants did not know whether Israel would hold on to the territories or leave. They were intensely nationalistic and influenced by hostile propaganda and rumors. To demonstrate Israel's power, the psychological warfare officers proposed holding air shows and paratrooper displays near Gaza and Jericho. They also suggested organizing a tour of Israel for West Bank dignitaries, so that they could behold the country's scientific and technological superiority. Appropriate films and books were to be distributed. They also suggested bringing the dignitaries to visit the Egyptian POWs who had not yet been returned, and showing them the piles of war booty. To convince the population that Israel was there to stay, military psychologists suggested sending Israeli hotel owners to the West Bank to discuss vacation packages with Jericho hotel owners, as well as having wealthy Israelis, including Arabs, go there to talk about buying real estate.[27]

---

*A house Dayan demolished in Ramoun, a village near Ramallah, on the pretext that it was the home of a Palestinian underground member, belonged to an American citizen. The man, Suleiman Mohammed, of Ann Arbor, Michigan, demanded $30,000 in compensation. The American consulate in Jerusalem took up the affair, and the wrangling over his claim went on for years.[26]

• • •

ROUGHLY SIX MONTHS AFTER THE WAR, THE IDF DESTROYED THE SEMI-ABANDONED VIL-lage of Jiftlik, between Nablus and the Damia Bridge. Dayan cited "security and sanitary considerations." The residents, he said, had been transferred "elsewhere" in the West Bank.[28]* The military government prepared a survey on the condition of the nine thousand Latrun refugees, two thousand of whom remained in the West Bank. A few were allowed to work some of the land they had previously farmed. Some moved into houses abandoned by other residents, in Ramallah and the surrounding area. Others were living with relatives, in public buildings, stables and pens, and under trees.[30]

It was not long before the first irregularities occurred. Two Border Patrol policemen murdered two residents, apparently in the wake of a dispute between drivers. The policemen were brought to trial and Israel promised to compensate the victims' families. There were also unpublicized murders. A senior officer in the paratroopers shot dead six suspected Palestinian terrorists, after they surrendered and had been taken prisoner.[31]

SHLOMO GAZIT, THE COORDINATOR OF OPERATIONS IN THE TERRITORIES, PRAISED THE occupation. The IDF was considerate of the Palestinians' needs, going beyond the requirements of international law, he wrote. "With no residual hostility, the Israelis have listened to the desires of the population, offered assistance to solve human and economic problems, repaired houses damaged in the war, and almost immediately consented to the return of various people who abandoned their homes." Considering the challenge of the war and the abysmal hatred projected from every Arab capital, Gazit added, the Israeli response should be viewed as "an amazing metamorphosis."[32]

Moshe Dayan did instruct that Kalkilya residents be allowed to return to their city, and he helped them rebuild their homes. But a few months after the war, he also said that if he had to choose an occupation force from among the nations of the world, he doubted he would choose Israel.[33]

---

*The considerations were aesthetic, too. These prompted the following letter: "The prime minister alerts the minister of agriculture to the presence of ruins that mar the Latrun landscape visible from the Jerusalem–Tel Aviv Highway." Eshkol saw the ruins as a "visual nuisance," the letter continued, and asked the Israel Lands Administration to deal with them.[29]

· · ·

WHILE HE WAS HOSPITALIZED, DAYAN HAD A VISIT FROM HAMDI KANAAN, THE MAYOR of Nablus. A few days later, the mayor came back, with an attorney named Aziz Shehade. Dayan asked about the family reunification program that would permit the return of Palestinians to their homes on the West Bank. When Kanaan told him permits were not being issued quickly enough, Dayan promised that if the matter was not dealt with by the time he got better, "heads will roll." He also warned that if Hussein did not rein in Fatah, the IDF would cross the river and seize Jordanian territory. Kanaan said that as long as the fundamental problem was not solved—referring to the greater Palestinian question—there would be no end to the acts of sabotage.*

Dayan described the Palestinians who came to see him in the hospital as "Arab friends and dignitaries." He was especially touched by a visit from the mayor of Kalkilya, who brought a cluster of oranges complete with their delightful branch and leaves. "From the time our forces destroyed Kalkilya and I personally handled its reconstruction, a personal connection was forged between us, a bond between human beings who, together, care for the needs of the population—their bread, their homes, their jobs and their health," Dayan wrote. "It is a very different bond from the expected administrative relationship between an Arab mayor and a Jewish minister of defense, who rules over him through the power of his soldiers."[35]

This was the voice of the Israeli who wanted more than anything to be loved for his kindness. It was the voice of the master who needs the love of his subjects—who, as Dayan suggested, might even rape them into loving him. "The situation between us is like the complex relationship between a Bedouin man and the young girl he has taken against her wishes," Dayan told the Palestinian poet Fadwa Tukan. "But when their children are born, they will see the man as their father and the woman as their mother. The initial act will mean nothing to them. You, the Palestinians, as a nation, do not want us today, but we will change your attitude by imposing our presence upon you."[36]

Dayan's approach toward both death and land, including his attraction to archaeology, reflected something intensely sensual, almost erotic.

---

*In the next conversation with Dayan, Mayor Kanaan began with various requests, the subject approaching his ruler, the occupied his occupier. He brought up visiting and return permits for students who had been abroad during the war. Dayan said that was a matter for the Ministry of the Interior, but promised to do what he could.[34]

Always tempting death, he described war as rebirth. "Death in war is not the end of warfare, but its pinnacle," he said once, "and since war is a part of life—and sometimes its entirety—death too, when it is the pinnacle of war, is not the cessation of life, but its ultimate expression."[37]

Dayan visited the territories often, and one October night he joined a force setting out to ambush terrorists in the Jordan Valley. He was with a unit of four soldiers, led by a corporal. They noticed a few figures and opened fire. "On the path from the mountains to the Jordan lay the bodies of three young Arabs," wrote Dayan. It started to drizzle. He stayed with the soldiers until morning, but nothing much happened. He soon stopped thinking about the encounter and allowed himself to be lost in reminiscence. He looked up at the clouds drifting in the wind, listened to the sounds of the night: crickets, grasshoppers, mosquitoes, nocturnal birds, dogs barking from afar, snakes rustling in the grass. All these reminded him of his youth in Nahalal. "I liked sleeping outside in the summer and falling asleep in a hallucinatory state with the velvety wind caressing my face." He was no longer a seventeen-year-old boy, but forty years later he was intoxicated by the night with its smells and whispers and the close sky. "The gunshot and the dead Arabs were secondary, external," he wrote. "When I curled up under my coat in the car driving to Jerusalem and dozed off, I took with me the sense of the warm earth, the ceaseless whisper and the calming touch of the wind."[38]

4. EDUCATION: "A FUNDAMENTAL QUESTION"

Near summer's end, the government had to decide whether to recognize the Jordanian and Egyptian school curricula, or supply the schools in the territories with the curricula used in Israeli Arab schools. It was a political question, discussed by a ministerial committee set up to handle internal security. The debate reflected the drama of the "enlightened occupation," including the aggressive competition between various government offices. The decision to prepare a curriculum for the following school year again indicated that there was no intention of withdrawing from the territories in the foreseeable future.

The Ministry of Education naturally took upon itself the education of the approximately 200,000 students in the 900-odd public schools in the West Bank and Gaza. They sent supervisors, dubbed "education officers," to the territories, where they learned that some of the textbooks used in the schools were designed to instill a virulent hatred of Israel.[39] Some of the grammars for elementary schools were based in part on speeches given by Nasser. The ministry distributed samples of the books in Hebrew translation. Under the headline "We Shall Not Forget," one text read, "Zionist gangs stole the precious land of Palestine and banished its people from their homes and property, but the nation of Palestine will not be silent about its loss of rights and its anger will not subside. . . . We shall not forget the land of Palestine and its loss and the day of May 15, 1948, the day our beloved Palestine was stolen." Other textbooks included similar passages.[40]

The options were to disqualify the books and replace them, or to censor only certain passages. At first the ministry was inclined to impose the Israeli curriculum and textbooks on the territories, but the army objected, fearing that the residents would refuse to open the schools. General Uzi Narkis recalled a debate with the minister of education, Zalman Aran. Narkis was accompanied at this meeting by the attorney Erwin Shimron. "Shall we teach our own curricula? Bialik, Tchernichovsky, Sholom Aleichem? The Bible? What shall we do?" asked Narkis. Aran, a seventy-year-old native of the Ukraine, asked the general whether he spoke Russian. When the Jerusalem-born Narkis replied that he did not, Aran asked whether he spoke Yiddish, and Narkis again replied that he did not. "*Oy vey,*" the minister murmured, according to Narkis, and reluctantly resorted to Hebrew. "We did not need this war. It has already brought us trouble and it will bring us worse still." In the absence of any practical solutions from the minister, Narkis decided to appoint his own committee of experts.[41]

Dayan acted as if it were beneath him as a warrior and an enlightened occupier to deal with children's grammar books. But some Ministry of Education officials nonetheless suspected the military was scheming to rob them of their role.

In this particular competition, the Education Ministry seemed to have examined the books more closely, and Aran insisted that books be used only if they were absolutely free from anti-Israeli material. The ministry experts disqualified 49 textbooks, but Dayan ordered Shlomo Gazit to reexamine them, and Gazit reinstated 17. A ministry official appealed the decision and Gazit asked him to prepare a new list, but Aran forbade this.[42] The topic was eventually brought before a ministerial committee, which instructed further examination, with the aim of allowing the original textbooks "to the greatest possible extent." This time only 8 of the 150 schoolbooks in use on the West Bank were disqualified; 47 of these were amended. In the Gaza Strip, on the other hand, only 24 of some 160 books were approved.*

The ministry replaced the disqualified books with texts used by Arab students in Israel, entailing a hugely expensive publishing operation. The approved books were stamped, in Hebrew, "This book is authorized as a textbook by the Military Commander." It was decided that the Ministry of Education would prepare a new curriculum for the following school year.

Schools did not open in time for this new school year. They remained closed for several weeks, in one of the first acts of civil disobedience in the territories. Leaflets addressed to students denounced teachers who went to work as collaborators, "traitors who have stabbed the homeland in the back."[44] Schools in East Jerusalem also remained closed. Unlike the rest of the territories, they were ordered to institute the Arab Israeli curriculum, but the strike left no room for doubt: it would not be easy to split off East Jerusalem from the West Bank.

---

*UNESCO's scrutiny of the textbooks used in UNRWA schools seems to have been even stricter than the Ministry of Education's. Out of 38 books in the West Bank, only 4 were approved; 23 required amendments and 9 were entirely disqualified. In Gaza, UNESCO examined 70 books, authorized 24, required amendments in 35, and disqualified 11.[43]

CHAPTER 19

TEDDY'S PROJECT

1. ANNEXATION: "IT WILL ONLY COME BACK TO HAUNT US"

About two hours after the seizure of the Old City, Teddy Kollek arrived at the headquarters of the military governor, Chaim Herzog, in the Ambassador Hotel. Snipers were still shooting intermittently, and Kollek was exhausted, having barely slept since the beginning of the war. But according to Herzog, the mayor "burst in" to his office and demanded immediate arrangements for distributing milk to the Arab residents.

This alluring tale has taken its place among similar anecdotes in the abundant folklore of Jerusalem, which portrays the occupation of the eastern part of the city as aimed solely at alleviating the everyday problems of the residents, both Jewish and Arab, and improving their quality of life. Kollek himself did much to cultivate this myth. No other person so excelled at presenting the occupation of Jerusalem as a humanitarian, almost religious mission, undertaken for the benefit of all mankind. Israelis, for the most part, were only too happy to concur.

"The name 'Jerusalem' inspires awe throughout the world, and whoever controls Jerusalem takes on a duty of loyalty toward a significant part of humankind," wrote *Ha'aretz* the day after the annexation. "We must fulfill this duty meticulously." The paper accepted an obligation, as if on behalf of the state and the entire Jewish people: "This we promise: Jerusalem under Jewish-Israeli control shall be an exemplary symbol of freedom of religion, of study, of research, of humane behavior toward members of all religions."

Israeli rule combined the covetousness of the occupier with religious fervor: a barely controllable urge impelled them to "establish facts" with extreme haste, before it was too late. At times this was done with an iron fist and even cruelty. But the occupiers were always aware of being in a fishbowl, under the watchful eyes of the entire world. And so they also displayed responsibility, goodwill, and occasional compassion.

The director general of the Interior Ministry determined that everything must be done in accordance with Israeli law. "We don't care what kind of arrangements existed before," he said. But he cautioned against creating "a population of embittered souls" in East Jerusalem, and urged awareness of human needs and public relations.[1] Both these considerations suited Kollek's skills and inclinations.

A year after becoming mayor, Kollek was bored and frustrated. He had no one interesting to work with, he grumbled to Ben-Gurion. Divided Jerusalem was too small for his talents. Kollek was born in Hungary and grew up in a wealthy household in Vienna, where he drank in the cosmopolitan air of the city after World War I: he was a liberal and a pragmatist. In the mid-1930s he settled briefly on Kibbutz Ein Gev, on the shores of Lake Tiberias. Like Shimon Peres and Moshe Dayan, he was a follower and an admirer of Ben-Gurion in his youth, and with these men he found the ability to translate Ben-Gurion's great national vision into practical accomplishments. During World War II, Kollek was involved in Zionist attempts to rescue Jews, even meeting with Adolf Eichmann. After the war he took part in efforts to acquire arms in preparation for the War of Independence, and with the establishment of the state he became a diplomat in Washington.

Kollek had an innate ability to charm and impress people and win their trust. Lively and demanding, he knew how to enjoy a good meal, good wine, and good cigars, in the company of beautiful women and well-known artists, writers, and musicians. His love of the good life and his image as a man of the world gave him a measure of detachment and even alienation from the Israeli establishment with its Eastern European provincialism, its troubling insularity, and its constant grumbling. Kollek made no particular effort to adopt the new Hebrew identity. Bucking the nationalist imperative, he kept his European name and never polished his flawed Hebrew. He thought in Viennese German and American English. Despite his foreignness, and perhaps because of it, the state's parochialism did not bother Kollek: his world was London, Paris, and New York, anywhere he could raise funds. Indeed, Kollek was an unrivaled fund-raiser.

He set up a special foundation for the city, and when members of the municipality demanded a supervisory role, he threatened to dismantle it. His foundation had only one ruler.

A master of public relations, he constantly invented headline-grabbing gimmicks, but was also guided by a basic sense of decency—the generosity of the great—and a paternal sense of humor. Everyone knew him simply as Teddy, and he was well liked. A strong man with blond hair, he was dynamic, spontaneous, impatient, often capricious and impetuous, frequently crude and even insulting. He despised bureaucracy, legal restrictions, paperwork, arguments, and speeches. He projected an authentic quality, and an apolitical trustworthiness.

Kollek was a partner in Ben-Gurion's national dream, but it was the Old Man's enormous power that fascinated him. As the director general of the prime minister's office, he was empowered to shape a new approach to the Zionist enterprise, driven by results. Beyond ideology, beyond politics, beyond ambition and personal intrigue, Kollek tended to view the state as one huge project. He was a workaholic and set himself a single standard for success: to do as much as possible. The occupation of Arab Jerusalem finally turned the city into a project that Kollek found challenging. Mayor of the unified city, he instantly became "Mr. Jerusalem," and his name was known the world over. As he came and went among the rich and famous, he exploited the city's emotional power, just as he had taken advantage of Ben-Gurion's energy, all in the service of improved performance.[2]

A few days after the occupation, Kollek visited his Jordanian counterpart, Rawhi al-Hatib. Al-Hatib offered his own chair to Kollek, who replied politely that he had come as a guest. Coffee was served; the atmosphere was friendly. But within days, al-Hatib was summoned to a local hotel, the Gloria, where an IDF officer recited orders to dismiss him and disperse his city council. The officer wrote the orders in translation on a hotel napkin.

Kollek was soon able to articulate his fundamental approach to Jerusalem's Arabs, and it was not unlike Ben-Gurion's basic attitude toward Israeli Arabs. Like Ben-Gurion, and like many Zionist leaders, Kollek would have been glad to see the city empty of Arabs. Had he been able to, he would have acted to remove them. As a realist, he knew that this was not possible. "There are people who believe that if we harass the Arabs, they will leave," he said. "Well, believe me, the Arabs of East Jerusalem will not leave. They are connected to Jerusalem no less than we are. Nothing we do to harass them will make them leave. If there were such a thing,

I would be willing to purchase it." He went on to explain why the Arabs must not be made second-class citizens: "It will only come back to haunt us."[3] He saw unified Jerusalem as a test of Jews' and Arabs' ability to live together. He assumed that the Jews would remain in the majority and that the Arabs would accept their rule.

The annexation entailed a multitude of complex problems that required legal, administrative, and political resolutions, and often called for improvisation and sensitivity. Would the residents of East Jerusalem be made Israeli citizens, entitled to vote and run for the Knesset? Or would they be mere residents? The answer was not obvious. "We did not grant automatic citizenship to Israeli Arabs," one speaker said at a preliminary meeting on the matter. Israel had to decide whether residents of East Jerusalem had the right to reclaim property in the western part of town lost in 1948—or, more precisely, Israel had to find a legal basis to prevent them from doing so.*

The minister of justice suggested appointing a few Arab representatives to the city council. Kollek objected, fearing they would "make all sorts of statements" against the occupation. He proposed designating the eastern part of the city as a borough, with some sort of "advisory board" composed of local residents.† The government rejected this proposal, so as not to plant "a seed of something else" in the city. Ultimately, none of the Arab candidates would agree to be appointed to the city council.

Countless other difficulties arose. The 70,000 residents of the eastern part of the city, who brought the overall population of Jerusalem to 265,000, had been receiving services—education, welfare, public health, utilities, and registration of births and deaths, for example—from the Jordanian municipality. These were services that Israeli residents received from the Israeli government, and it was unclear who would provide them after the war. Kollek asked about closing stores on the Sabbath: would the municipal bylaw on this matter also apply to Old City merchants?[6]

Kollek took on the management of the occupation with gusto. He ordered the immediate demolition of the ugly cement walls that had

---

*More than a hundred Arabs who owned assets in West Jerusalem quickly sued to get their property back, some retaining Israeli attorneys. The Dajani family demanded the return of its labyrinth of halls on Mount Zion, which housed King David's Mausoleum, but failed in their bid.[4]

†Yehuda Arbel, the head of the Shabak's Jerusalem District, sent Kollek a list of members of the eastern city council, which he said was based on material from three archives. In addition to detailed biographies, the document noted personal attributes, such as "tractable," or "member of a family known as arms dealers." Some of the names were marked "no," meaning they were to be excluded from the city council.[5]

divided the city. His desk was soon piled with development plans whose purpose was to enlarge the Jewish population and isolate the Arabs from the West Bank. New residential neighborhoods were planned, along with rebuilding in the former Jewish Quarter of the Old City.

Kollek's operational eagerness infected his assistants, too. Meron Benvenisti, appointed to supervise East Jerusalem, wrote about the former Jordanian side as the Zionist founders had written about Eretz Israel—as if the city itself had been yearning for the progress that Israel was able to bring. The walls of the Old City were somewhat neglected, even housing Gypsies in the northern parts; footpaths had to be paved for visitors to walk around the city walls; loud neon signs had to be removed, as they marred some of the most beautiful city streets; television antennas had to be banned and the telephone and power lines buried, Benvenisti concluded.

The occupation of East Jerusalem did not mean parity of services. At the end of June, a government committee dealing with Jerusalem affairs decided that East Jerusalem would receive only the services previously provided by the Jordanians, at the same level and with the same scope. The municipality protested. "We cannot operate two levels of service in one city," wrote Benvenisti. Still, the committee instructed government ministries "to make an effort" to provide "as soon as possible" equal services required by law, while other services were to be given "in accordance with the possibilities available to each individual ministry."[7]

Kollek might have been "Mr. Jerusalem," but he nevertheless had to contend with a plethora of authorities and offices also demanding their say. For a moment it even seemed as if the IDF might reoccupy the city. This happened in September.

The annexation of East Jerusalem was supposed to bring it within the regular purview of the government ministries and the municipality, just like any other Israeli city. But the military decreed that the city's political, security, economic, and religious problems could not be addressed separately from those of the West Bank. The line on the map "does not automatically create facts in the field," Uzi Narkis's Central Command headquarters claimed, as if the Knesset's annexation decision had never been made. A working paper produced by the headquarters sought to regulate almost all areas of life in the city. It demanded stricter enforcement of the ban on smoking in the area of the Temple Mount, and the requirement that female visitors dress modestly: no "bare arms and miniskirts" there. The document was decidedly political, asserting that "not even the slightest concession could be made in demonstrating exclusive ownership of the Kotel area." The paper also addressed archaeological plans: "We recommend postponing implementation until next season." Narkis's headquarters also wanted to handle local media, including television, which was not even broadcasting yet. It also felt a responsibility for school curricula.

In different circumstances, the army's interference would have been fairly scandalous, but in Jerusalem "everyone thought they had to stick their big noses in," as Kollek put it. Authorities and offices battled one another boldly, as if every ordinance and regulation was destined to leave its mark for the next two thousand years. Kollek denounced them all. "This government has utterly failed," he declared nine months after the end of the war, and claimed he was living in a "bureaucratic jungle" that was delaying the city's reunification.[8]

Meanwhile, Kollek had initiated a series of colorful festivals and events with the participation of international luminaries. The city was bustling with tourists, a sleeping beauty awakened to daily glorification and burdened with the heavy load of historical significance. Every "first" produced prominent newspaper headlines: Celina Sassoon, a wealthy British philanthropist, was buried on the Mount of Olives, the first burial there in twenty years; Ariel Zvi Ben Yehuda Hacohen was the first child to be circumcised in East Jerusalem.[9]

2. EXPROPRIATIONS: "RESTORING IT TO ITS FORMER GLORY"

Within weeks of the war's end, various Jewish institutions and individuals began asking for permission to return to the Old City. The directors of the Porath Yosef yeshiva told Eshkol that back in 1911, they had "redeemed" a lot opposite the Kotel and built a grandiose "compound." During the War of Independence, the yeshiva had been "under siege," wrote the directors, but had defended the Jewish Quarter "right up to the last minute." The yeshiva had been planning to build a new compound in the western part of the city, but now that Jerusalem had been "liberated," the directors saw a "holy purpose" in reviving the old ruins and "restoring" the site "to its former glory." Countless people and organizations sent similar requests.[10]

The frequent references to "restoring" things "to their former glory," which echoed the essence of the Zionist vision, were not coincidental. Everything was supposed to return to what it had once been; the past became the ideal. Even the bus route to Mount Scopus was ceremoniously reassigned the number 9, with which it had been designated before the city was divided. *Maariv* reported, "Advertising signs in Hebrew have returned to the Old City," as if the area used to be an Israeli shopping mall. Everyone seemed to be in a great hurry to act on the right of return. "Agnon Returns to the Kotel," "Yaakov Alsheikh Returns to the Old City," "Michael Luz Returns to Atarot," the headlines announced.[11]

The Jewish Quarter was to be a part of this return. The first task was to remove the Arab residents, who had settled there starting in 1948, following the expulsion of the Jewish residents. Some eighty Arab families lived in buildings that had formerly served as synagogues. Over the next eighteen months, approximately eight hundred people were removed from the quarter, vacating three hundred rooms. They were given compensation. *Ha'aretz* reassured its readers: "The tenants of the former synagogue were transferred to modern apartments equipped with hot and cold running water, indoor bathrooms, electricity and tended gardens." Many of these apartments, in the village of Silwan, in fact belonged to people who had been absent from their homes on June 15: they were considered "abandoned" and could be legally expropriated and given to others.

Yehuda Tamir, who was in charge of restoring the Jewish Quarter, assumed that only 15 percent of the houses had formerly belonged to Jews. The intent was to house two thousand people, mostly—but not all—Orthodox. Construction had already begun on official residences for the deputy prime minister, and the state comptroller was building a house nearby.

Eshkol was intensely involved in populating "Greater Jerusalem," as the government had decided to call it. The mood in cabinet meetings was impatient. "I'm all too familiar with the Turkish *bukra*—tomorrow. It's been three months already. We have to decide. Go and see what's happening," Eshkol urged his assistants. In September, he approved a plan to settle tens of thousands of Jewish families in Jerusalem. He took part in many discussions about the restoration of Mount Scopus. Soon after the war, the Hebrew University began preparations to renew activities on the site it had been forced to abandon in 1948. The institution was soon flooded with donations and began planning the new Mount Scopus campus, one of the largest construction projects ever undertaken in Israel.[12]

Minister of Justice Shapira and Chief Supreme Court Justice Agranat looked into using the Jordanian courthouse. It was a handsome and impressive building from the outside, and the interior was well laid out, "although in poor taste," Shapira reported. It was a two-story building with five courtrooms on the first floor and two auditoriums and several offices on the second. He suggested adding a third floor for the Supreme Court. Shapira also supported moving the president's residence to East Jerusalem.

Populating the city was a slow process. On the first anniversary of the war, Eshkol reported to the Knesset Foreign Affairs and Defense Committee that construction had begun on seven hundred three- and four-room apartments, but only forty-two Jews had rented existing apartments in East Jerusalem, with government assistance. In the coming months their number would reach eighty, Eshkol promised. Roughly eighty Israeli students were living in Arab hotels.[13]

THE DEMAND TO JUDAIZE THE CITY BECAME A POPULAR SIGNIFIER OF PATRIOTISM. BUT the process required restraint, caution, and intelligence, so as not to anger "the world"—meaning the Vatican, the U.S. State Department, the UN, or, God forbid, the *New York Times*. Israel often tried to mislead "the world." Minister of Justice Shapira once suggested announcing that the Jewish Quarter had not been expropriated but rather evacuated "for survey needs." The world, including the United States, was indeed opposed to the annexation of East Jerusalem. Administration officials said so more than once, and the U.S. consulate made a point of demonstrating its position by occasionally holding separate receptions, some for guests from the west and some for those from the east. The Americans monitored the expropriation of land and houses and sometimes conveyed the protests of Palestinians with American citizenship whose homes had been seized.

One of Eshkol's assistants pointed out to him that pressure from the superpowers and international factors might result in a UN Security Council meeting, and there was no doubt that the council would pass a resolution against the annexation policy. "Since our desire is to develop the eastern part of the city more than to talk about it," the assistant conveyed to other government departments, "the prime minister asks that neighborhoods in the eastern city be handled in a businesslike manner, without drawing too much attention."[14]

The military was supposed to be given a building that had been intended as a school, a plan that did not cast the occupation in a good light. It was decided to wait until the annual UN General Assembly session was over. Eshkol supported postponing the expropriation of the school until after his return from a visit to the United States. He agreed to move the police headquarters into a college building, but maintained that if the minister of police or the minister of defense insisted, he would be willing to authorize the expropriation of a hospital for the purpose. Foreign Minister Eban strongly protested the suggestion. "It is a matter of supreme political sensitivity," he wrote to Eshkol, noting further that "the U.S. ambassador will be visiting me tomorrow." And so the prime minister's office tried to dress up the police headquarters move by issuing the following guidelines: "On the day the expropriation is made public, we must make sure the newspapers print stories about Arab patients in Jewish hospitals in Jerusalem, as well as a story about our offer that the A-Tur hospital use the state hospital currently under construction in the north of the Old City. The offer should be made to the Arabs before the expropriation is made public."

Government clerks formulated similar guidelines before the confiscation of eight hundred acres of land to build the neighborhood that would eventually be called Ramot Eshkol. A third of the land was privately owned by Palestinians. The expropriation required the signature of the minister of finance, and the Ministry of Finance spokesman was assigned to brief the press, as if this were an ordinary land deal devoid of political significance. He too was instructed to avoid the term "expropriation" and replace it with "purchase for public needs." He was also asked to highlight that most of the land belonged to the Jordanian government, while some was owned by Jews. The expropriations excluded properties belonging to churches or to the Waqf, the Muslim religious trust. In any case, the government was following a master plan authorized back in the British Mandate era; there was nothing new here.

The tendency to camouflage these projects often gave them an air of a secret operation. It also restricted appropriate public debate. An expropriation plan to allow for the construction of seven hundred apartments stated: "There will be no announcement until an expropriation order is issued."* In fact, the world quickly understood that Israel saw the permanent occupation of East Jerusalem as a done deal. This was the primary conclusion of Ernesto Thalmann, a special envoy of the UN secretary general to Jerusalem. And so the world made do with insisting that the occupation not involve excessively cruel oppression or violate freedom of religion. These conditions were not very difficult to meet. Teddy Kollek was able to forge good relationships with the Christian patriarchs in the city, and even convinced a few to sell, lease, or otherwise transfer lands they owned to Israeli parties.†

---

*When the government decided to issue a stamp with a picture of the Western Wall, it was careful to instruct that the Israeli flag should not appear on the stamp.[15]

†The minister of religious affairs reported to the prime minister that a few clerics from the Christian denominations, as well as some Muslim leaders, protested the evidence of moral decline, particularly in the Arab nightclubs.

The United States did not take action against the de facto annexation, trying only to downplay it as much as possible. The Americans wanted to moderate the celebrations on the first anniversary of the occupation, and Eshkol instructed the municipality of Jerusalem to hold the festivities indoors. He thought the idea of a parade of Orthodox youth "definitely superfluous." Even before the war was over, Abe Fortas had suggested that Israel be restrained in its response. "Ilan warned against victory trumpets," reported Ambassador Harman, and added that he completely agreed. "It is important that we not appear in international public opinion as victors, but rather maintain our status as self-defenders."[16]

Against this background, Israel was asked to give Armon Hanatziv back to the United Nations. This was one of the many issues charged with symbolism, nationalism, and ego.

Israel held that the 1949 truce agreement had ceased to apply with the Six-Day War, and wished to know why the UN still needed the Armon compound. International law experts labored over the question of who actually owned the building that had served the high commissioners during British rule. British consulate officials took part in the exercise with exceptional glee. Israel was also refusing to give back the area surrounding the building.

Everyone involved treated the matter with the utmost gravity. The United States considered it a nuisance and pressured Israel to put an end to the wrangling. Abba Eban saw it as "central" in the international struggle. During the cabinet debate, Dayan agreed to give back the Armon so as to remove a thorn in the side of Israeli-U.S. relations. Allon asked whether it might be possible to give back just one floor, and Eshkol inquired about housing some Jewish institution or other there.[17]

If Israel returned Armon Hanatziv to the UN, it would be the first piece of occupied territory foregone by the country, and the recipient was considered hostile, especially since Secretary General U Thant had rushed to remove UN forces before the war. "This building is a symbol, and symbols are not insignificant or without gravity: this nation has come a long way on the strength of symbols," wrote protesters against the return of the Armon, who called for a rally. "The building has always stood for foreign and hostile rule," argued one opposition Knesset member, and said he feared its return would presage withdrawal from other occupied areas.[18]

Negotiations with the UN were torturous and exhausting. The struggle ultimately came down to one word that the UN demanded be included in the settlement, despite Israel's objections: "return." Israel prevailed and the word was omitted. The UN accepted 11 out of the 43.6 acres it had owned before the war, as well as permission to operate two transmission facilities outside the area that had been restored to its ownership.[19]*

ISRAEL NEEDED TO DECIDE HOW TO REFER TO JERUSALEM IN ARABIC, FOR EXAMPLE IN Kol Israel radio broadcasts. The choices proposed were "Urshalim" and "Al-Kuds," Arabic for "the Holy One." This was yet another question loaded with symbolism, emotion, and politics. Immediately after the occupation, official Israeli spokesmen began saying "Urshalim." Foreign Minister Eban, who was fluent in several languages, elucidated the origins of the term for Eshkol: it was not Arabic or Hebrew, but rather a New Testament translation of the name "Jerusalem." Israel had used it after the War of Independence to distinguish between "our Jerusalem," as Eban wrote, and "Al-Kuds," Arab Jerusalem. "At that time they sought a short name for the purpose and came up with 'Urshalim,'" Eban recounted. Once Jerusalem was unified, there was no longer any need to differentiate the two parts of the town, and one could simply say "Al-Kuds," which was the name used by the Arabs. Eban told Eshkol that "Urshalim" had no Islamic or Arabist significance. "No Arab uses the name 'Urshalim' (not even Christian Arabs). They all use 'Al-Kuds.'"

Meron Benvenisti claimed that the name Urshalim was completely "fabricated" and provoked "furious ridicule" among Arab residents. And so he initiated a "secret agreement" with the editors of Arabic programming at Kol Israel, instructing them to say "Al-Kuds," which they began to do. He viewed this as a simple gesture that had no real cost and that might mitigate the residents' bitterness and perhaps increase their trust in Israeli radio broadcasts, a step on the way to the desired normalization. Predictably, a controversy ensued. The use of the Arabic name was interpreted by some patriots as undermining Jerusalem's status as an Israeli city: what value was there to the unification if Kol Israel itself did not recognize it? As usual, the dispute moved from the newspapers to the government. Foreign Minister Eban wrote: "In my opinion a return to the name 'Urshalim' will only expose our insecurity about the validity of our position on Jerusalem." Minister Without Portfolio Israel Galili came up with a compromise: "Urshalim Al-Kuds." Postage stamps and

---

*A short while later, at a government meeting, Menachem Begin proposed the phrase "hand over territories" instead of "return territories."[20]

the official weather forecast, however, continued to refer to "Ur-shalim."[21]*

3. RETURN: "A RARE LIGHT AND MANY COLORS"

That summer, Israel perceived the occupation as a remarkable success story, and increasingly Jerusalem was seen as a laboratory of Jewish-Arab coexistence. Israelis flocked to Arab restaurants in East Jerusalem; Palestinian children sold newspapers in the west, and some even came to visit the Israel Museum's Youth Wing. The civil status granted to East Jerusalem residents, and the Arab-Israeli educational system imposed on their children, strengthened the impression that they had become Israeli Arabs. There were virtually no violent incidents at first.

Ambassador Barbour reported to Washington that *Ha'aretz* was conducting a new "crusade" to promote equality and peace between Jews and Arabs in Jerusalem. He quoted articles written by Amos Elon and Amnon Rubinstein, in which they argued that the occupation of East Jerusalem offered opportunities for a historical rapprochement, without Israel having to give up control over the city. This could occur, they said, if Israel approached the Palestinians with generosity. Israel should compensate those who had owned property in the western part of the city; institute widespread use of the Arabic language; find a way to include Arab representatives on the city council; and pay comparable salaries to Jews and Arabs. Many people believed that this was the way things were heading. "It is doubtful whether territories occupied by a foreign army have ever been restored so quickly and so effectively to a peaceful routine," *Ha'aretz* wrote in an editorial.

Just before the first anniversary of the war, an improvised Arab memorial for the unknown soldier appeared near the former Mandelbaum Gate. Aware of the power of symbols, and seizing an opportunity to demonstrate enlightenment, Teddy Kollek permitted an official monument commemorating the Arabs killed in the war—in demonstrative contrast to the desecration of gravestones on the Mount of Olives that had occurred during Jordanian rule.[23]

But coexistence was a false perception, or an optical illusion: Jerusalem was far from achieving "a peaceful routine," not only because the Arabs

---

*The question came to preoccupy the U.S. ambassador, Walworth Barbour, who advised his superiors to stop using the term "Arab Jerusalem." His proposed alternatives included "East Jerusalem" and "the Arab Quarter." The U.S. consul, conversely, suggested using a number of different names, including Al-Kuds, interchangeably.[22]

opposed the occupation but also because most Israelis did not want them there. In a survey, the municipality found that approximately 85 percent of Jewish Jerusalemites believed the occupation of the east would mean an increase in crime and create severe social problems. Seventy-five percent feared that unification of the city would result in mixed marriages between Jews and Arabs. More than half (54 percent) would not agree to send their children to schools with Arab children. They had a poor opinion of Arabs: the primary characteristics they attributed to them were "hypocrisy," "poverty," "cowardice," "primitiveness," and "poor hygiene." Few Jews considered them "peaceful" or "educated." Almost nine out of ten said Jews should be allowed to live in East Jerusalem, but nearly six in ten said Arabs should not be permitted to live in the west. Approximately eight out of ten said Jews should be allowed to work in the east, but seven out of ten said they would not agree to work in an Arab-owned factory. About half said Arabs should be allowed to work in West Jerusalem, while seven out of ten said they would not employ an Arab maid.

Many respondents were afraid the occupation would be a burden on the city's economy. Less than half believed unification would lead to economic improvement, and 42 percent said it would cause unemployment in both parts of town. Roughly half the residents said Arabs from East Jerusalem should not be allowed to vote in municipal elections. The survey also exposed significant differences between Ashkenazis and Mizrahim, the latter expressing greater hostility toward the Arabs.*

The survey's results were overwhelmingly negative. The prime minister was distressed by the findings, and Kollek, agreeing with Eshkol in his concern about the destructive potential of the survey, instructed that all copies be destroyed, with the exception of two, one of which he left with Eshkol himself. Letters written by Jewish Jerusalemites also expressed discomfort at the presence of so many Arabs now walking the city's streets. Edith Ezrachi found it difficult to adjust: she had "come all the way from Allentown to live in a Jewish state," as she wrote.[24]

YEHUDA AMIHAI WROTE A POEM INSPIRED BY A VISIT TO THE OLD CITY ON YOM KIPPUR. Wearing "dark holiday clothes," he stands for a long while in front of an Arab shop near the Damascus Gate. The shop sells "buttons and zippers

---

*Approximately half the residents (52.3 percent) said the restaurants in West Jerusalem were better than the ones in the east: more Mizrahim liked the Israeli restaurants, while more Ashkenazis liked the Arab ones.

and spools of thread," and Amichai sees in them "a rare light and many colors, like an open Ark" in the synagogue. He does not speak with the Arab merchant, but silently tells him that his father also owned a shop that sold thread and buttons. "I explained to him in my heart about all the decades / and the causes and the events, why I am now here / and my father's shop was burned there and he is buried here." In these words, Amichai, a German-born teacher, voiced the sentiments of many Israelis: if only they could "explain" to the Arabs the historical circumstances that had brought them to Palestine, including the Holocaust. By the time Amichai finishes "explaining" himself in his poem, the Yom Kippur prayers are drawing to an end. The Arab lowers the shutters and locks the gate, "and I returned, with all the worshipers, home." East Jerusalem, Amichai implies in this bold line, is not his home.*

Israelis sometimes encountered old Arab acquaintances—friends and even relatives. "Ezra and Shehada renew their friendship," reported one newspaper happily, and *Maariv* discovered Samika Nashashibi in the Old City; she had been born Erika (Esther) Wiener, and was the niece of S. Y. Agnon.[25] The daughters of the well-known Palestinian author Khalil Sakakini, who lived in Ramallah, went to see the house their father had abandoned in 1948 in the Katamon neighborhood of Jerusalem. They also went to the National Library to look for the extensive collection of books Sakakini had left. They never came back to Jerusalem again.

THE FIRST SIGNS OF RESISTANCE APPEARED ON THE STREETS WEEKS AFTER THE WAR, AND at the end of July there was even talk in the government of a "civil uprising." Minister of Justice Shapira warned that guerrilla operations against the occupation would plunge Jerusalem into "the Vietnamese era of its history."[26]

Posters put up in the streets led to a strike in the schools and the shops, as well as one by public transportation workers. Lawyers also went on strike. Protest petitions were sent to foreign consulates and international media; women and students demonstrated. One poster was signed by the "Union of Palestinian Suicides."[27]

The first shopkeepers' strike took the authorities by surprise. Policemen and soldiers walked through the empty Old City market and spray-painted circles with an "X" inside on the shuttered blinds, to frighten the

---

*One Foreign Ministry official suggested quickly taking advantage of "the twilight hour" of the early occupation to confiscate anti-Semitic publications from East Jerusalem bookshops.

merchants. Uzi Narkis issued injunctions ordering some store owners to shut their shops. Michael Shashar described in his diary how Narkis's advisers prepared for a meeting with a delegation from the Arab chamber of commerce, who came to ask for permission to reopen the stores that had been forced to close. They decided that the general would not shake the delegates' hands, and they purposely provided an insufficient number of chairs—let them stand. The Arabs probably regretted coming, as Shashar wrote. The meeting with Narkis recalled the British era, and not by chance: the meeting format, including the arrangement of forcing the Arabs to stand, was an idea proposed by Menachem Begin, a key adversary of the British Mandate.

Narkis, formal to the point of rigidity, asked each delegation member to come up before him and give his name. Then he told them—in Hebrew—that Israel had not responded to the strike with mass arrests or expulsions, nor had it opened detention camps, means that were common during the British Mandate and legally available to Israel. But like the British general Barker, who had recommended that his men "hit the Jews in their pockets" as punishment for insubordination, Narkis threatened the Palestinian merchants that if they continued to strike, "we'll open a couple of supermarkets and sell everything ourselves."[28] Some Arab leaders were in fact deported from Jerusalem to various locations around the country.

On September 19, an explosive device blew up in the former Fast Hotel, which had been a luxury hotel during British rule. The building was damaged during the War of Independence, and when the city was divided it remained on the Israeli side of the border and became a crowded and poverty-stricken residential building. A few tenants were injured in the explosion, and the Chen printing house was completely destroyed. The Chen may have been the real target of the attack, as it produced textbooks for use in West Bank schools.[29]

Police and Shabak investigations resulted in the arrest of two young men who admitted a connection to the operation, but said they had not actually carried it out. They signed confessions but pleaded not guilty in court, claiming they had confessed only after being beaten and tortured. One of them, Abdul Razzak Qutub, a twenty-year-old presser in an Israeli laundry, was the eldest son of a widow who worked to support his nine siblings. He was described as a man of limited intellect, embittered and withdrawn, living on the margins of society, who had gotten mixed up in the affair hoping to earn respect. The second man, Abdul Man'im Jibril, recounted a tragic life story that embodied many elements of the

Israeli-Palestinian conflict. He was born in Jaffa and was six years old in 1948 when his family was exiled. As they fled, his parents either lost him or abandoned him beneath a tree in an orchard. Another Arab family, also fleeing, took him in and raised him in the refugee camp in Jericho. At eighteen he went to Kuwait to make his fortune, enlisted in the Palestinian Liberation Army, reached the rank of sergeant, and shortly before the Six-Day War was transferred to the Jericho area. After his convoy was bombed by the Israeli air force, he managed to walk to Amman, where he joined Fatah. He was sent to Nablus, where he claimed to have received orders from Yasser Arafat.[30]

The trial was held in a military court in Lod, and was open to the press and the public. The two young men were accused of violating the emergency defense regulations that Israel had inherited from the British. The maximum punishment for their crimes was death. They had Israeli defense attorneys, one appointed by the court. The hearings were held in Hebrew and translated into Arabic. Before the main trial, a "preliminary trial" was held, in which the defendants were permitted to claim that they had signed their confessions under duress. One of them was allowed to take off his shirt in the judges' chamber, to show evidence of abuse. The judges, who were military officers, were unconvinced; they accepted the confessions given by the defendants to the police and convicted them. Qutub was sentenced to twenty years in prison, Jibril to twelve. The prosecutor explained that he was not seeking the death penalty because neither of the men had actively participated in laying the explosive device, and the death sentence should be employed only in extraordinary cases. In fact, the government had resolved that prosecutors in military courts could not ask for the death penalty, partly out of fear that international pressure would prevent it from being carried out.[32]*

A few days after the attack on the Fast building, Israel deported Sheikh Abd al-Hamid al-Sa'ih to Jordan. He was the presiding judge of the Islamic religious court in East Jerusalem, and was accused of incitement. Police officers appeared at his house at three-thirty in the morning. They allowed him to get dressed and take a few personal belongings. When he reached the police headquarters, they read him his deportation order. He asked for and received a translated copy, but his request to keep the original Hebrew document, signed by Moshe Dayan, was denied.

---

*Israel's ambassador to Paris suggested not using the word "resistance" to describe the Palestinian rebellion; the word was closely associated in France with the opposition to the Nazi occupation.[31]

The sheikh was not particularly surprised by the deportation, but said it was a pity they had not told him while he was still at home, so that he could have taken some clothes. He asked to go back home to pack a suitcase. A police officer, Nahum Bosmi, whose title was "head of the Special Duties Branch," promised to make sure the suitcase reached him in Jordan. Al-Sa'ih wrote a note to his family and attached fifty-one liras—he wouldn't be needing them in Jordan. Before they left, he asked to pray, and was allowed to do so. A few minutes after seven in the morning he arrived at the Allenby Bridge, named for the British general who had taken Palestine from the Turks exactly fifty years earlier. Al-Sa'ih shook the Israeli police officer's hand and crossed the river.

Bosmi later reconstructed the conversation they had on the way. Bosmi hinted that Al-Sa'ih's family might be joining him, and the sheikh asked what would happen to his property. He then went on to declare that everything had happened because of the annexation, not because of the occupation itself. Israel could have saved itself a lot of trouble if it had solidified its rule in stages instead of annexing East Jerusalem at once, through legislation. He wondered how Israel could ignore resolutions made by the UN—the very same organization whose resolution of November 29, 1947, had brought about the state's establishment.

The sheikh asked to send regards to a police officer, David Chen, who worked on relations with Arabs and Christians, and to David Farhi, an officer of the military government. Once, he recalled, he had given Farhi a compliment: better a smart enemy than a foolish friend. Farhi had replied that this was true, but that they were not enemies. En route to the bridge, Al-Sa'ih and Bosmi passed through Jericho, where the sheikh said he owned a piece of land; he had been hoping to build a winter home there.[33]

Less than three weeks after the sheikh's deportation, a Foreign Ministry official, Danny Mihaeli, went to the Zion cinema in Jerusalem to see *El Dorado*, starring John Wayne. In front of him, in the twenty-fifth row, were two black women. In the middle of the movie, they got up and left the theater. Mihaeli felt around with his feet and found a bag. He sent two kids to bring an usher, who found a time bomb in the bag. The usher ran with it to the police headquarters in the nearby Russian Compound, where the bag was detonated without causing any damage. An explosion in the theater would have been disastrous. The two female terrorists were arrested. They belonged to a small community of Africans who lived not far from the Temple Mount.

The uprising and terrorist activities did not bring down Israeli rule, but they demonstrated that East Jerusalem was under occupation and that its residents were unwilling to live in Israel, even though their legal status gave them various advantages over the residents of the West Bank and Gaza. As the threat of terrorism increased, so did the influence of the Shabak. The head of the Shabak, Yehuda Arbel, whose name was a secret at the time, became a powerful man with great influence on the occupation.[34]

Nine months after the war, military and police forces demolished the home of the Fatah commander in Jerusalem, Kamal Nimri, who was captured and accused of murdering a Druze guard near Abu Ghosh. The streets surrounding his home in the Wadi Joz neighborhood were blocked, the residents told to leave. The two-story house imploded with its contents still inside. A few neighboring houses were also damaged. The authorities had acted legally, but the demolition aroused criticism, partly because it blurred the distinction Israel was hoping to create between the status of Jerusalem and the rest of the West Bank.*

Terrorism soon became routine in Jerusalem. The police warned residents to be alert for suspicious objects. Bags were searched at movie theaters. "Anyone could walk in with a nasty package," warned a municipality official. As he had before the war, Eshkol received plenty of suggestions from citizens who knew exactly how to protect the city from terrorism. Among the ideas were special markings on Arab-owned vehicles; guards at schools; underground repositories outside every cinema, where bombs could be thrown if any were found; and two thousand sniffer dogs. Some citizens, demanding the death penalty for terrorists, were divided only over whether to hang them or shoot them. These were the first intimations of a new frame of mind, which grew increasingly brutal over time.[36]

Shortly before the anniversary of the occupation, the city of Jerusalem granted "honorary citizenship" to Levi Eshkol. His acceptance speech no doubt expressed the sentiments of most Israelis. "The unifying act of liberation" was the key experience of the war, Eshkol said. The unification of the city was "a recognition of its status as the nation's life and heart" and was not subject to any rational considerations—political, military, or economic. Rather, it was the unity of Jerusalem that dictated all other considerations.[37]

---

*The American consul in Jerusalem quoted Teddy Kollek's opinion that Uzi Narkis should be removed from his post following the demolition. Kamal Nimri was an engineer, and the son of a Jewish mother. He came from an educated and highly ideological family.[35]

CHAPTER 20

FACE-TO-FACE WITH ISHMAEL

1. CONDITIONS: "FOR THIS WE WENT TO WAR?"

Roughly three weeks after the war, King Hussein attempted to renew contact with Israel. Communicating through the United States and Britain, he proposed a meeting. Yaacov Herzog called this "a sensational development," and at the prime minister's office they began debating who would meet with the king.[1]

Both before and after the war, Israelis generally regarded King Hussein as an object of ridicule. They were particularly adept at insulting his short stature, and he was widely known as "the little king." Ephraim Kishon gave him the moniker "Hussi," and Herzog, in his diary, called him *yanuka* (Aramaic for "baby" or "child"). But when it transpired that Hussein was willing to talk with Israel, prestige battles followed, prompting Ezer Weizman to describe Hussein as "the playboy of Israeli politics."[2] Eban wanted to go to the meeting. Herzog suggested that Eshkol himself go, but Eshkol said he could not talk with the king without "speaking clearly," and the government did not yet have anything clear to say. In fact, they had absolutely no idea what to say to Hussein.

MOSHE DAYAN TOLD A BBC INTERVIEWER IMMEDIATELY AFTER THE FIGHTING ENDED that Israel was satisfied with the new situation and would not, therefore, initiate any negotiations with Arab states. "We're waiting for the Arabs to pick up the phone and call," he declared.[3] As it turned out, Israel called them. Israel offered a withdrawal from Sinai and the Golan in return for direct negotiations for a peace treaty. A decision to that effect was made as early as eight days after the war, on June 19.

"It was the most dramatic initiative the Israeli government ever took, before or since," wrote Foreign Minister Eban. The move arose from the need for a diplomatic formulation that would be acceptable to the world and primarily to the United States. The decision was kept secret and Israelis knew nothing of it. However, it was conveyed to the Americans. According to Eban, they relayed the proposal to Egypt and Syria, who both rejected the offer to parley; there is no confirmation of this account, however.

Israel thus created the impression that it had offered to return the territories in exchange for peace. Since the Arabs refused to hold talks, there was therefore no peace and Israel would keep the territories.[4] The real story, however, was more complex. Under the proposal, Egypt would not recover all its losses: Israel would hold on to the Gaza Strip. The Foreign Ministry lawyers adeptly explained that as part of Mandate Palestine, Gaza had never rightly belonged to Egypt, but their arguments did nothing to change the fact that Israel was demanding control over hundreds of thousands of Palestinians. Egypt was also required to agree to a demilitarization of the Sinai Peninsula, which giving up a facet of its military sovereignty. Naturally, Israel wanted to ensure freedom of access to the Gulf of Aqaba, but also to the Suez Canal. Israeli planes would be granted free passage in the airspace over the Straits of Tiran.

The agreement offered to Syria was also based on the "international boundary" from the British era. Syria was asked to give up the disputed territory along the border, which had, until the war, been a demilitarized zone. The Syrians would have also had to agree to demilitarization of the Golan Heights and to undertake not to obstruct the flow of water from the Jordan River sources into Israel.

These proposed peace agreements with Egypt and Syria were mutually exclusive, but both countries were required to disregard Jordan: the offers formulated on June 19 included not a single word about the future of the West Bank, or about Jerusalem and its residents. This resulted from the ministers' inability to agree on these issues.

The discussion began in the security cabinet on June 15, and according to one minister it frayed everyone's nerves.[5] In some ways the government found itself in an even more stressful situation than before the war, because there was no immediate danger dictating decisions: everything was possible, it was all in the ministers' hands—a key moment. They were partners to a decision on questions that had been with the

Zionist movement since the beginning: What kind of state would Israel be? How would it live with the Arabs? The argument has not ended, and there were probably no ideas that at that government meeting in June 1967.

The starting point was an Arabic maxim quoted by the minister of police, Eliyahu Sasson: "Whether in victory or in defeat, be a realist, demand only what is feasible and what is possible."* Sasson went on to propose an astonishing plan: unilateral withdrawal without a formal peace agreement. Egypt would not sign a peace treaty with Israel, he maintained, and the demand that it do so only gave it a bargaining chip. Sasson also suggested giving up on peace with Syria.

No one agreed. It was not a question of tactics, said Menachem Begin, but of a moral principle accepted throughout history: when there was a war, one usually wanted it to end in peace. He asked Sasson whether he believed, "based on his knowledge of the East," that Nasser could agree to demilitarize the Sinai and allow freedom of shipping without a peace accord. Begin's own answer was that Nasser would agree to nothing—not peace, not demilitarization, not freedom of the seas. Dayan asserted that as long as there was no peace treaty, Israel would not budge from the territories. This was the general opinion around the table. In another forum, Dayan was far more blunt: the Arabs would not make peace, and so Israel would keep the territories.

The main argument revolved around the future of the West Bank. Zalman Aran said, "I'm telling you plainly that we don't need the West Bank. It will do us more harm than good." He was afraid, of course, of the Palestinians. "To this day, I love Eretz Israel more than the State of Israel," Aran said, but as he considered Israel's future with the West Bank, he was sure that "we will choke on it." He prophesied that the West Bank would be the downfall of the state.

The days of empires were gone, added Minister of Justice Shapira: this was the age of decolonization. There were those who denounced Israel as an agent of colonialism, and if it insisted on ruling the Arabs of the West Bank, their voices would only grow louder. "Every progressive person will say, 'Look, this is why we called these people the torch-bearers of imperialism and colonialism. They want to turn the West Bank, which is popu-

---

*Eliyahu Sasson, originally from Damascus, was sixty-five at the time, and one of the few Arabic-speaking government ministers. A journalist and a secret agent, he had started working for the Zionist movement in the 1920s. As a diplomat and a politician, he was involved in all talks between Israel and Arab rulers.

lated by Arabs, into a colony of the State of Israel.'" It was not merely a question of what people would say, Shapira continued. Annexation of the West Bank would turn Israel into a binational state, and it wouldn't be long before the Jews became a minority. "Then we're finished with the whole Zionist enterprise and we'll be a ghetto here." He had no objection to Israel claiming, "to the outside," that the Jordan River was its future border, but "on the inside," they, the ministers, must know that this could not happen if they wanted the state to survive. "We should be very careful of this," concurred Pinhas Sapir.

As the government was debating the question, David Ben-Gurion published a manifesto on the future of the territories. He declared that Israel was prepared to discuss peace with its neighbors, through direct negotiations. If Egypt agreed to make peace and allow free passage through the Gulf of Aqaba and the Suez Canal, Israel would give back the Sinai. The Gaza Strip would remain with Israel. If Syria agreed to make peace, it would get the Golan back. The IDF would not withdraw from the Jordan River. West Bank residents would be given autonomy. The refugees from Gaza would be resettled in the West Bank "or in some other Arab area." If Jordan made peace with Israel, it would be granted access to the Mediterranean. There would be no negotiations over East Jerusalem. The Jews of Hebron would be allowed to return to their homes.

According to Ben-Gurion, he published his views in response to questions from reporters from several foreign countries, following an inaccurate quote on his position in a Japanese newspaper. But by doing so, he insinuated himself into the government discussion, and cast his great shadow over it. The eventual decision did not in fact stray too much from his position.[6]

The debate, which continued in various forums over several days, raised the binational idea, as well as the division of the country into "cantons," the UN partition plan from 1947, and proposals for transferring the West Bank to joint Israeli-Jordanian rule, or for granting the Palestinians a measure of autonomy. Dayan suggested autonomy. He assumed that two or three years would pass by the time they had to reach a concrete decision. During that time, residents of the territories would be subject to martial law, kept behind a border the Arabs would not be permitted to cross: "Up to here—you. From here on—us." When the moment came, the Palestinians would be allowed self-government but not independence: security and foreign policy would stay under Israeli control. Dayan was not sure any of this was plausible: "If it turns out that there's no possibility of granting self-government, and I have to choose between them belonging to Jordan—with the exception of Jerusalem—or becoming Israeli citizens, I'd prefer that they belong to Jordan."

Yigal Allon held the opposite view: "I support keeping the land intact, with all the Arabs," he argued, but he also suggested another possibility: an independent Arab state in part of the West Bank, surrounded by Israeli territories. Allon was already working on a plan revolving around the annexation of the Golan Heights, the Jordan Valley, and the Gaza Strip. He thought Hebron and Bethlehem could be annexed at the same time. In the rest of the territories he suggested, at first, establishing Palestinian quasi-autonomy, and then he proposed giving them back to Jordan. Allon was hoping to establish a secure border along the Jordan River and expand Israel's territory without greatly enlarging the state's Arab population. Dayan was working out the details of his own plan, which involved setting up military outposts and Jewish communities on the mountaintops, in the heart of the Arab population. This was the primary difference between their two plans.

Ze'ev Sherf, the minister of commerce and industry, commented that the precise boundaries were not all that significant. "We have a problem with terrorism, and the problem exists whether or not the Jordan River is the international border." He believed there was no need to make an immediate decision. Menachem Begin also believed in the power of time. Begin rejected every proposal discussed: a "canton" was a ghetto, and where an Arab ghetto rose, a Jewish ghetto would follow; self-government or autonomy would lead to statehood. "This is the ironclad logic of things," he said. He dismissed outright the idea of handing the West Bank back to Hussein: "We send our sons to war so that there will be yet another Arab state, or so that parts of Eretz Israel will be given to an Arab state, so that we'll create an enclave within Eretz Israel from which they can shoot at Tel Aviv? For this we went to war?" He agreed to give back all of the Sinai, but demanded that the IDF remain in Sharm el-Sheikh. He agreed to make peace with Hussein, as the king of the eastern bank of the Jordan. But he "begged" the government not to hurry. Martial law was working, and it was sufficient to let the United States know that Israel was seeking solutions. The time frame he had in mind was at least seven years, after which they could offer the Palestinians a choice: accept Israeli citizenship or leave the country. He assumed Israel would attract a large number of immigrants in the interim. "This is Greater Israel," concurred Minister Israel Yeshayahu, who sought to impose some of the responsibility on the Jews of the world: "Let the Jewish people exert themselves to make Eretz Israel Jewish, with a decisive Jewish majority."

Eshkol maintained that the Jordan River should be Israel's security border, apparently making a distinction between that and a political border, although he did not specify how he imagined that this would work. He also differentiated Jerusalem from Gaza. "For Jerusalem, we are willing to die; for the Gaza Strip, when we think of the 400,000 Arabs, our hearts are a little bitter," he said, as if Jerusalem were not populated by Arabs, and as if many soldiers had not been killed while seizing the Gaza Strip. But he nonetheless called for annexing them both.[7] As he had before the war, Eshkol spoke at length about the need to consider U.S. demands. He offered a comparison: the governor of Rhodesia thumbed his nose at the British government and treated the black population as he saw fit. Israel could thumb its nose at the United States, but not for long: a few months, perhaps. No more.

Abe Fortas was indeed attempting to influence the government's decision, almost as if he were one of its ministers. He "pleaded" with Israel, through Ambassador Harman, that its decision should not only stress the need for peace but also involve an explicit declaration that it did not intend an occupation. The U.S. ambassador to Israel received a report on the government discussions. The ministers argued over what to tell the Americans. Waiting for the June 19 decision, President Johnson intended to present the U.S. position in a televised address.[8]

Yaacov Herzog's summary of the discussion indicates four alternatives on the matter of Syria and Egypt: peace based on the international border, and on other specific terms; a demand for peace, not specifying any terms (Dayan's proposal); presenting terms with no request for peace (Sasson's proposal); and Minister Moshe Carmel's suggestion, "peace, but with all the territories." With regard to Jordan, there were two outlooks: the Jordan River as the border between Israel and the Hashemite Kingdom; alternatively, setting no final border, because that would put an end to talks with Jordan. The ministers also debated three options for the refugee problem: a plan to settle them in Arab states; the avoidance of any resettlement plan, while investigating the possibility of settling the refugees in the Sinai, the West Bank, or on the eastern bank in Jordan; and finally, tabling the problem for now.

One minister said he feared a war among Jews more than one between Jews and Arabs. So that everyone could support the final decision, they agreed not to mention the West Bank. They were playing chess with themselves, Eshkol observed. And then the telephone rang with Hussein on the line. Minister Aran breathed a sigh of relief: "If there were no Hussein, we would have had to invent him."

In preparation for the meeting with the king, Eshkol wished to consult with Golda Meir as head of his party, and with Menachem Begin. But not with Dayan, whose advice he did not want. It was decided to send Herzog to the meeting with Hussein, as the two had met in the past. Herzog suggested offering Hussein an economic union with Israel and joint control of the West Bank, until a confederation could be established.[9]

2. THE KING: "PEACE WITH DIGNITY"

The first meeting between Hussein and Herzog had taken place in September 1963. By the time of the Six-Day War, they had met four times in London. Another meeting was held with Golda Meir, in Paris. In documents pertaining to the meetings, Hussein is given the code name Charles.

The secret contacts were intended to establish a stable framework for the cooperative relationship between the two countries, while the declared enmity was merely for show. Herzog once passed on a warning to Hussein about a Jordanian air force officer who was plotting against him, and Hussein gave Israel information about an Arab plan to assassinate Moshe Dayan.[10] Both Herzog and Hussein might well have considered the war a personal failure. When they met three weeks after the fighting, they both felt the need to begin by picking up the pieces, exchanging views on the historical and emotional roots of the conflict. Like previous meetings, this one took place at the clinic of Dr. Emmanuel Herbert, Hussein's Jewish doctor, and in his presence. They began at eight-fifteen in the evening on Sunday, July 2. Their conversation lasted an hour and thirty-five minutes. Herzog wrote a fifteen-page summary of the meeting, in English. Had he not disclosed what he really thought about his conversations with the king, one might have believed he was striving for a peace agreement.

HERZOG ARRIVED FIRST. HUSSEIN WAS COMING FROM A VISIT WITH SOME OF HIS SOL-diers who had been wounded in the war and were hospitalized in London. He was accompanied by a British bodyguard, whom he asked to wait outside as if he were going in for a medical check-up. Dr. Herbert took him into one of the examination rooms. Herzog came in next and bowed to the king. There was great drama in the air: Hussein was risking his life by coming to the meeting. Herzog thought he could see the toll of war and defeat on Hussein's face, but he found that more than anger and bitterness, Hussein projected sorrow and resignation.*

Herzog sat down next to the king. He began by saying that their previous meetings had not been for nothing and repeated the "biblical undertaking" he had given the king in the past: this meeting, like previous ones, would remain secret. He conveyed good wishes from Eshkol and Eban and said he was there to ask whether the king had anything to say in the aftermath of the war. Herzog stressed that the conversation was unofficial and that the Israelis were aware of the extreme strain the king was under. They expressed their sorrow for the loss of life on both sides.

With the dignity of a wounded knight, Hussein said that had he been in the Israelis' position, he would have acted as they did. He had known for some years that war was inevitable. The country's difficult political and strategic condition had led him to conclude that Israel would eventually try to solve the problem by force. He had seen the crisis coming. The Arabs had made grave mistakes, and he had warned them repeatedly. He took responsibility for what had happened because he could have done more to emphasize the urgency of his warnings. The Middle East was now at a crossroads, with a choice between a better future and another war. There would soon be an Arab summit, and if no understanding was achieved, each state would consider itself free to act as it saw fit.

As if addressing future historians, Herzog offered a correction. The king was under a misconception: Israel had never planned a war; the war was entirely unnecessary. Its military preparations had been aimed solely at defense. He lectured the king about the strategic aims that had guided the Arab world since 1964; he talked about Syria and about Fatah. In his analysis, it was clearly the Palestinians who had brought about the crisis that ultimately led to war. Had the terrorist attacks continued, Israel inevitably would have had to act to defend itself, but it had not planned a comprehensive attack on Syria, Herzog claimed. He described at considerable length the chain of events that had led to the war, up until the point at which Israel had felt the noose tightening around its neck. Nasser had surprised Israel; they had not expected anything of this sort to occur before 1970.

Israel was not to blame for the war with Jordan. He could give the king his word of honor that there had been no plan to attack his country. As

---

*The U.S. ambassador to Amman, who met with Hussein frequently, reported that the king had developed a profound sense of guilt.[11]

he well knew, Israel had relayed two warnings to him, one through General Odd Bull and another through the Jordanian delegate to the Mixed Armistice Commission, Colonel Daoud. When Herzog mentioned the warning sent through Bull, he wrote, Hussein "smiled wistfully"; upon mention of the second warning, he seemed surprised. At this point Herzog went on to preach about the roots of the Jewish mentality and Zionist ideology, including the commonly held view that the Arab leaders "did not understand" Israel. The persecution of Jews, culminating in the Holocaust, had led them to see any assault on one Jew as an assault on the entire people. Jews could not live their lives quietly in Jerusalem or in Tel Aviv while farmers in the north were being fired on. This was the meaning of the "transcendental unity" of the Jewish people, said Herzog, the son of the late chief rabbi, referring to the traditional saying, "All the people of Israel are responsible one for the other."

Herzog proceeded to explain that the Arabs had also never understood the bond between the Jews and the land of Israel, which was unique in human history and anchored in the spiritual origins of the Jewish people. Instead of trying to understand this phenomenon, the Arabs had looked for rational explanations for the renewal of the Jews in the land of their forefathers, as if they had returned there as mere refugees, as if the Jewish national movement were an artificial construct without roots, and as if the sources of its strength were the wealth and the power of the Western capitals. It was true, Herzog said, that the Nazi persecution of Jews had spurred the Zionist movement, and that the influence of Jews around the world was also an essential element. But beyond these, there had been, and still was, the eternal covenant between the people of Israel and the land of Israel, and with it the sense that as long as the people are severed from their land they are in exile, without shape or realization.

Hussein replied that at the Arab summit in Morocco in 1965, the participants had decided that they would be ready within three years. "Ready for what?" Herzog asked. Hussein paused and then replied, "To talk with you as equals." He must have meant war, Herzog observed, because Hussein went on to explain the Arabs' motivation: within three years, they estimated, Israel might acquire nuclear weapons. The Arab states agreed to act in concert, but it quickly transpired that there was no unity. The supposed unified command turned out to be an empty shell. A few people, Hussein said, took advantage of the Israeli problem to assume leadership. The Fatah operations were in contradiction to the states' decision to wait until they could act in unison.

Hussein said he had tried to the best of his abilities to suppress Fatah, as agreed by the Arab states. The Fatah units that operated from his country received no official support and had acted irresponsibly. He had received warnings from Israel, via the United States and other channels, and had done what he could. Israel had once given him information about a Bedouin terrorist unit, but all his efforts to locate it failed. And then came Samua.

The Samua operation had been a shock to him. Only a few days earlier, he had received a message of thanks from Israel for his efforts to combat Fatah. After Samua, Hussein found himself in a corner. On the one hand, he was being severely criticized by other Arab states for his actions against Fatah. On the other, the Samua operation convinced him that Israel made no distinction between Jordan and Syria. And so he had no choice but to draw his own conclusions. Without saying so explicitly, Hussein seemed to agree with Herzog that the Six-Day War was a result of the Palestinian struggle.

When he visited Nasser, Hussein continued, he learned that the Egyptian president believed Israel was planning to attack Syria. Nasser had no choice but to prepare accordingly, and as an Arab, neither did Hussein. He was certain that there had been no plan to launch a full-scale attack against Israel, he assured Herzog. There was no coordination between Jordan and Egypt; they had no joint plans. Hussein had asked Nasser why he had not sought Hussein's advice before sending forces into the Sinai. Nasser replied that he had not had time; he had had to act quickly, in light of the threats against Syria. He had not meant to take the UN forces out of the picture. Hussein told Herzog that Israel should not have taken Nasser's declarations to heart, and, like Herzog, he proceeded to deliver an analysis of his own people's mentality: "With the Arabs, words don't have the same value as they do for other people. Threats mean nothing." For many years, this had been one of the great failings of the Arabs: they confused words with intentions and acts. For a moment, it seemed as if the events of the past weeks were nothing more than a mutual misunderstanding.

Hussein said he had hoped to be able to restrain his colleagues. He pointed out that Saudi Arabia had sent not a single soldier to Jordan, and only one Iraqi unit had reached the Jordan Valley. But Herzog surely knew all this, he added bitterly. Herzog commented that there were Egyptian commando units in Jordan, and an Egyptian general had been placed in command of some Jordanian forces. To this Hussein made no response.

The warning he had received through Bull had reached him when his warplanes were already in the air, the king said, but added candidly that even had it arrived sooner, it would probably not have done any good. His planes had gone to attack military targets, mainly Israeli air force bases, so as to restore the balance of forces upset by Israel's air attack on Egypt. He also explained that it had been important for him to maintain positions in the Mount Scopus area, because it controlled strategically valuable roads. When Herzog asked about the bombing of Jerusalem, Hussein looked stunned and said it had happened in contravention of his orders. One could not always control all the forces involved, he explained, also bitterly; perhaps one of his men had decided to bomb Jerusalem in response to the bombing of Amman. Herzog assumed he was referring to the bombing of the Amman airfield.

Hussein, also seeming to speak for the history books, listed the factors that had led to Israel's victory: its air force, its intelligence, its ability to shift large forces quickly and effectively. Its power was enormous; his military had felt that keenly. "Such is war," he added contemplatively. He said he would not allow the Arab states to evade their responsibility so easily, and would demand a commission of inquiry into the war's beginnings. Herzog replied magnanimously that the Jordanian army had fought courageously, and told Hussein how the Israelis had felt great fear. That those feelings had shifted to elation was not, he assured Hussein, the result of conquest, but of survival. Herzog sounded as if he were attempting to persuade himself. How could Nasser think that all his behavior would go unanswered? "We had to take his actions and words seriously."

At this point the conversation was halfway over. Herzog and Hussein seemed to have made their points. Hussein was downcast but at ease, Herzog noted, broken but also hopeful, depressed but also somehow liberated. It occurred to Herzog that although he had lost the war and a large part of his kingdom, Hussein had acquired, for the first time, the status of a true Arab leader: his motives were no longer under suspicion in the Arab world, his patriotism not questioned. Defeat had not, it seemed, shaken the core of his personality. The "furtive look" in the king's eyes was now gone.

What was done was done, Herzog told Hussein. The question now was the future. The friendship the two had developed over the years made it impossible for him not to ask: Was Hussein headed toward a new war or to peace?

Hussein responded slowly and firmly in his deep voice. "The extremists," he said, with a hint of sarcasm in his tone, "have one course. I have another. I must say frankly to you, if it is peace, it will have to be peace with dignity." He had for a long time understood the connection between the Jewish people and the land of Israel, he said, although others did not. This was the point that the Arabs found most difficult to accept. The fundamental problem they faced now was how to preserve their Arab identity in the region. "Not only you have rights. We also have rights. Do not push us into a corner. . . . Be careful of our feelings. Treat them with respect and understanding. The region is at a crossroads. I hope we will take a positive course. So much depends upon you."

Herzog offered a gloomy vision of what might happen in the absence of peace, and reminded Hussein that he had not heard officially whether he was willing to enter negotiations. Without that willingness, Herzog could not discuss details of a settlement. He was not authorized to offer Hussein an agreement, but he could share his own private thoughts, he said, and repeated the idea of establishing an economic union between Jordan and Israel, which would lead to a confederation. He said the region could become "the garden of the world," and Hussein lowered his head in contemplation.

Later in the conversation, Herzog showered Hussein with praise, lauded the social institutions in his country, and described his survival skills as evidence that he had been "providentially saved" so that he could make peace. The king, predictably, replied that his personal survival was unimportant, only the future of his people.

Hussein asked for a little more time and promised a response to the question of peace. In Herzog's summary of the meeting, written with the assistance of Dr. Herbert, Israel is depicted as peace-loving, while even this most moderate of Arab leaders, in a secret meeting, face-to-face, emerges as hesitant in this respect. But apart from his personal vision of a confederation, Herzog had brought Hussein no proposal. Noting that the king did not mention the West Bank or Jerusalem, he surmised that Hussein wanted to leave the question open. But Herzog did not explain why Israel had made no offer to return the West Bank and Jerusalem.

In reality, Herzog had not come to Hussein seeking peace. He wanted to negotiate in order to buy time—to delay, at least for a while, the need to withdraw from the West Bank. Herzog had made no secret of his intentions. "Eban and I disagree," he had told Yigal Allon. "While Eban maintains that there is a chance [for a peace agreement with Jordan], I dispute this. I see the importance [of conversations with Hussein] as purely tactical." He made similar statements to Begin: "I view the continued contact with Charles as necessary, although I am certain it will not lead to anything."[12] Meanwhile, Israel was also talking with Palestinian leaders in the West Bank.

3. COLLABORATION: "A GROVELING TYPE"

As soon as the war was over, and in some cases even before fighting had ended on all fronts, Israeli military government officials, army intelligence officers, Shabak and Mossad agents, and senior government officials began approaching Palestinian public figures: mayors; members of the Jordanian parliament; former cabinet ministers; and prominent attorneys, journalists, and businessmen. The Israelis were extremely curious to meet these people, whose names they knew mainly from intelligence reports and from the media. They came as victors, some speaking as masters and occupiers. A few of these initial conversations seemed more like interrogations aimed at updating intelligence files. But Israelis also had a sincere desire to find out whether an independent Palestinian state was feasible in the West Bank and Gaza, thereby putting an end to the conflict over Palestine.

Dozens of such conversations occurred over the following months, producing hundreds of pages of minutes. With the exception of a few secret and amateurish probes conducted in the past, these talks were the first attempt to weave an agreement between Israel and the Palestinians. The Israelis who met with Palestinian leaders included Eshkol, Dayan, and Eban.

THEY BEGAN IN AN ARBITRARY AND IMPROVISED WAY, SUBJECT TO THE GENERAL CHAOS of Chaim Herzog's command. David Kimche, a Mossad employee on leave, was sent to try and restart the radio station in Ramallah. He was accompanied by Dan Bawly, a former *Jerusalem Post* reporter and one of the many reservists still on active duty who now had little to do.* The two ran into someone who knew a senior Palestinian journalist, who said he could take them to the manager of the radio station. The date was probably Saturday, June 10. The fighting on the Golan Heights was not yet over, but the military government in the West Bank had already begun returning civilian life to normal. The man Kimche and Bawly were looking for was not home, but they somehow ended up in the home of Aziz Shehade, a Christian lawyer born in Jaffa, who had represented Jordan in talks with Israel in Lausanne, Switzerland, back in 1949. They talked about the present and the future. Shehade sent them

---

*During the tense period before the war, Kimche and Bawly had decided to co-author a book about the events of those weeks, and after the war they did so.[13]

to see a friend of his, and gave them a memorandum outlining his positions.

When they had met with ten people, Kimche sent a report to the head of army intelligence; the next day he reported conversations with five more Palestinians. He wrote that his interlocutors were stunned by defeat and felt that peace must be achieved. They hoped the Jordanian regime would not return: they wanted independence or autonomy. In their current state of shock, they were prepared to cooperate with Israel, and quick action was therefore called for.

Kimche seems to have introduced himself to these people as someone from "the IDF's political wing." He and Bawly were joined by Aluf Hareven and Yitzhak Oron, who had represented army intelligence and the Mossad in the comprehensive inquiry into the future of the West Bank initiated by Abba Eban after the Samua operation. The document produced by the four men reflects the work of those teams. It also projects the sense that victory had brought with it a chance for peace, and an enormous faith—almost mystical, somewhat naïve and arrogant—in the power of the Mossad to make history. The establishment of a Palestinian state necessitated "magnanimity and boldness," wrote Kimche and his associates, but Palestinian statehood was to be a Mossad operation, a "sting" that required fast action: Palestinian leaders would need to agree to the decision to establish the state within twenty-four hours after Israel approved the plan.

The Palestinian state would be "under IDF patronage," without an army but with a police force. An "Israeli military delegation" would be "credentialed" to the government of Palestine, and the IDF would have a permanent presence in the Jordan Valley and would protect the state of Palestine from external threats. The border between Palestine and Israel would be "based on" the 1947 partition borders, but Israel would annex some territories, including the Latrun corridor. To preserve Palestinian "dignity," Israel would also "give up" a few of its own Arab villages. The state of Palestine would have access to the sea through an Israeli port, and free passage between the West Bank and Gaza. East Jerusalem would remain in Israel, but there would be a Palestinian "submunicipality" in the Old City, and the holy sites would receive "special status." The Palestinian state would establish its capital "at the closest possible point to Jerusalem," which would be part of "greater Jerusalem." Israel would undertake to solve the refugee problem by means of an international fund that would encourage the refugees to leave Gaza and the West Bank and settle in other countries. As a first step toward founding the state, Kimche and his colleagues suggested convening Palestinian public figures in a congress of sorts.* The proposal was dated June 14, but even then, four days after the war, it was not the first: Dayan and Eban had started receiving proposals for a Palestinian state on June 9.[15]

Eshkol did not reject the Kimche proposal outright. In order to hear more Palestinian opinions, he set up a "Special Inter-Office Committee," whose members were Chaim Herzog, now removed from his position as governor of the West Bank; David Kimche; and two Foreign Ministry employees, Shaul Bar-Haim and Moshe Sasson, the son of the minister of police. Yaacov Herzog was appointed as the committee's government liaison, but it was to operate in affiliation with the Secret Service and receive orders from a body called the Select Committee of Heads of Services, meaning the Mossad and the Shabak. They were instructed to address Palestinian leaders "politely, respectfully, but firmly and clearly," with the aim of impressing them. They had to make clear to their interlocutors that their people's future now depended exclusively on the government of Israel. The Palestinians had to be made aware that this was the only communication channel available to them. The talks were supposed to take place without publicity: "Prevent contact between Israeli journalists and these people," read the committee's guidelines.[16]

Equipped with biographical details pulled from various intelligence files, the four split up into two teams and set off on their mission: the Irish-born Herzog and the British-born Kimche spoke English, while Bar-Haim and Sasson spoke Arabic. They were instructed to listen and report, but like everyone else they also wanted to make history. Even before they had done much, they proposed grooming leaders whom they identified as suitable. The grooming would be achieved through "close contact" with the leaders, "under committee supervision." The potential leaders would be divided into groups, each of which would be handled by a groomer to be introduced as a "liaison officer." The grooming was supposed to include "responding to wishes." The proposal echoed attempts made by the Zionist movement, even during British rule, to finance Palestinian parties and newspapers, bribe leaders, and buy collaborators.[17†]

And so Herzog, Kimche, Bar-Haim, and Sasson began to perceive themselves as an apolitical body with the power to intervene in almost all aspects

---

*The four-page proposal was sent to Eshkol, Dayan, Allon, Ezer Weizman, and others. Weizman's assistant, Rehavam Ze'evi, concocted a name for the Palestinian state: "Ishmael."[14]
†Following some interministerial wrangling, it was decided that the Shabak would handle the "grooming," in coordination with the Ministry of Defense and the Foreign Ministry.[18]

of life. They recommended conducting a population census; sending a delegation of dignitaries to Hussein, to demand that he permit the export of produce from the West Bank to Jordan; arranging financial matters in cooperation with banks in Switzerland and London; and publishing a newspaper under the supervision of Gabriel Tzifroni, a veteran of the Hebrew press. They prepared a list of individuals who should be brought in as members of the Jerusalem city council, and advised against allowing any direct contact between residents of the territories and representatives of Israeli political parties. All this was done within five days of the committee's inception.[19]

Most of the Palestinian leaders interviewed by the committee were summoned to the offices of the military government, away from neighbors' prying eyes. They all said they wanted peace with Israel. Some wanted an independent state, while others conditioned any settlement on a treaty between Israel and Jordan. They were not in an easy position: there was no assurance that Israel would remain in the territories, and so they were afraid to commit to a settlement in case they later came to be seen as collaborators and traitors. They also worried that Israel would reach some accord with Hussein behind their backs.

Almost every one of them needed something, in those days of shock after the war: contact with relatives, transit permits, money. "The sheikh's family is in Jordan and he asked for our help bringing them back. This could serve as a means to pressure him," said the background material on Sheikh Mohammed Ali Jaabari, the mayor of Hebron. The Israelis wrote down much of the flattery they heard, apparently with some delight. Palestinian leaders repeatedly expressed their endless wonder at the scope of the victory, repeating again and again how amazed they were that the IDF soldiers did not slaughter civilians or rape women. Jaabari said he had no words adequate to praise the attitude of the commanders and their men. He said he had warned Hussein not to go to war, and declared that if Nasser had a shred of military dignity, he would commit suicide, as Hitler had done.

The Israelis' notes reveal an ambivalent value system in their attitude toward the collaborators: they needed them, they encouraged them, and they scorned them. "He seems like a coward, flattering those stronger than him," they wrote of one man. And of another, "a groveling type, interested in collaborating with the Jews." Of Sheikh Jaabari they wrote, "Greedy and easily bribed. Hated in the West Bank because of his corruption." But these were precisely the people they were looking for: "We understand that he is inclined to look for a positive settlement solution. He will receive our encouragement and full support."[20]

Yet, three weeks after initiating these talks, the four committee members concluded that there was no chance of success. Even the West Bank leaders who were at first inclined to a bilateral settlement with Israel had quickly changed their minds and refused to act without coordination with Hussein. They had also begun to recover from the shock of defeat and occupation. The more they got to know the wonders of the "enlightened occupation," the more the West Bank leaders were emboldened to demonstrate their resistance. "The situation is deteriorating," wrote Sasson, and listed several acts of rebellion: dignitaries from Nablus suggested to Hussein that he not sign a separate peace agreement with Israel; a few clergymen in Jerusalem protested the occupation in a telegram to the UN secretary general; eight of the dozen Arab judges in Jerusalem refused to go back to work; none of the Arab members of the city council would agree to serve on a joint council. "The pride and boastfulness exceed permissible limits," wrote Sasson, and suggested imposing house arrest on a few personages, including Anwar Khatib, who, as governor of Jerusalem, was the most senior Jordanian official remaining in the West Bank. "I suspect that he is the one directing all this activity in the occupied territories," Sasson explained.[21]

The failure of the talks led the committee to conclude that efforts to make peace with Jordan should be stepped up, and that full and exclusive control of the West Bank must be maintained for now, without involving representatives of the local population.

IN THE REPORT THEY SENT TO ESHKOL, THE COMMITTEE MEMBERS DETAILED THE TERMS of a desirable agreement with Jordan. They proposed joint Israeli-Jordanian rule of the West Bank; annexation of the Gaza Strip—"emptied of refugees"—to Israel; and a defense pact between Israel and Jordan that would grant the IDF an "automatic right to enter the East Bank" in the event that circumstances deteriorated, endangering the peace agreement. In the interim, they suggested setting up a special government ministry entrusted with ruling the West Bank.

This was only one of the many fantasies piling up on the prime minister's desk, and it reflected, predictably, a disagreement between doves and hawks. One of the four, Chaim Herzog, agreed to sign the plan only if three reservations were made: the government of Israel must decide that the border was the Jordan River; he agreed with his colleagues that West Bank residents should not be allowed to purchase land in Israel, but thought Israelis should be allowed to purchase land in the West

Bank; and, instead of setting up a government ministry to oversee the West Bank until a peace agreement was reached, he proposed appointing a "high commissioner" along the lines of the Mandate-era commissioners.*

4. CONVERSATIONS: "SORRY WE WON"

Eshkol was fond of Moshe Sasson, whom he nicknamed "Mussa." In November he appointed Sasson to a newly created position as the "Prime Minister's Representative for Political Contacts with Arab Leaders in Jerusalem, the West Bank, and Gaza." The appointment letter was carefully worded, mandating "coordination" among the foreign minister, the minister of defense, the head of the Mossad, the head of the Shabak, and the minister of police, Sasson's father. To prepare Sasson for his new role, Eshkol convened a meeting with Moshe Dayan and a few others. The question was what, in fact, Sasson was supposed to accomplish. Dayan instructed him to try to ensure that West Bank residents would "swallow the annexation pill" of East Jerusalem.

And so Sasson once again went visiting with West Bank leaders. He listened, he talked, he stirred things up here and there, he occasionally agreed to handle complaints about the ills of the occupation, including house demolitions, arrests, and interrogations under torture. The complaints became more numerous as Fatah's terrorist activities increased. Once in a while, Sasson did some favors and "acquiesced to wishes." In the hundreds of pages of notes he made of his conversations, Sasson usually identified Palestinians by their first names, out of either condescension or friendship. He often visited their homes, and they his. He knew all the secrets of Palestinian politics, the rivalries and the intrigues, the schemes and the deceptions, on both sides of the river. He was constantly informed about events in Hussein's court. His notes testify that he enjoyed every minute of his role as part governor, part public commissioner, pulling strings and orchestrating events. He cultivated a complex network of contacts, among whom was the particularly mysterious figure of the Greek Catholic bishop Hilarion Capucci.

In February 1968, Capucci approached Sasson with a proposal. He said it had come from the Vatican, and that King Hussein had also authorized

---

*In mid-July, the ministerial "West Bank Committee" discussed a working paper by Mordehai Gazit of the Foreign Ministry, in which he proposed no fewer than seven possible alternative settlements.[22]

him to suggest it: Israel would withdraw from the Occupied Territories and be replaced by UN forces. The parties would agree in advance to a transition period lasting from six months to a year. During this time, negotiations would be held between the Arab states and Israel, with the aim of reaching permanent peace. If within the stated time they did not achieve peace, Israel would return its forces to the territories upon prior UN authorization. In this case, the inhabitants of the territories would be allowed to take matters into their own hands and sign a separate agreement with Israel. Sasson responded that there were no interim solutions, and advised the bishop not to get carried away by such flimsy initiatives. The two met frequently. Capucci was later caught smuggling a large quantity of explosives in his diplomatic car, but during that initial period he seemed to have been operating as Sasson's covert agent.[23]

Anwar Nusseibeh, of Jerusalem, also met with King Hussein on occasion. Nusseibeh was a Cambridge-educated lawyer and a founding father of the Palestinian national movement, who had served as a judge and a senior minister in the Jordanian government. Sasson introduced him to Eshkol and a few days later he was dispatched to Amman with an urgent message for the king: there must be immediate talks to coordinate positions and curb the activities of Fatah. Nusseibeh came back with an idea he said had come from the king: "Why shouldn't the Israelis allow us to reinstate our civil administration and police? If their army leaves the West Bank, we will agree not to post our own forces there."

Sasson introduced Hikmat al-Masri, of Nablus, to Foreign Minister Eban, who allowed him to tell Hussein—and Nasser himself, if he so wished—that within the framework of a peace treaty, Israel would allow Jordan to fly its flag over the Dome of the Rock on the Temple Mount. Al-Masri went to Egypt, and when he returned he said he had met with Nasser alone. Sasson heard various reports of their conversation. From Capucci, he heard that if Israel announced its willingness to withdraw from all the territories, Nasser would agree to hold direct negotiations. He was not demanding a withdrawal as a precondition for these negotiations, only a statement of intent. According to Capucci, al-Masri had told him he would not pass on directly to Israel the content of the conversation.[24]

With extreme caution and secrecy, Sasson sent Aziz Shehade to see Yahya Hammuda, the chairman of the PLO, to find out whether he would agree to any contact with Israel. Hammuda replied, in writing, that he would agree under "certain conditions," which he did not specify. Dayan was not enthusiastic: "There's no hurry. First we need a chance to destroy Fatah. The way to handle them is to destroy them." Dayan spoke with

Hamdi Kanaan, of Nablus, and with Aziz Shehade. He treated them as popular leaders and asked whether the Palestinians were willing to sign a separate peace agreement with Israel, unrelated to Egypt, Syria, or Jordan. They replied positively and implied that all problems could be solved, with one exception: they could not agree to leaving all of Jerusalem under Israel's exclusive sovereignty. Dayan suggested flying a Muslim flag over the Temple Mount, but the Palestinians said that this was not enough.*

The prospects were not promising to begin with. "Everyone is afraid for themselves," Capucci told Sasson, "afraid to voice their opinion even to their closest friends. Mutual accusations. Quarrels and suspicions. A Tower of Babel."

Sasson was authorized to offer the Palestinians civil autonomy in the West Bank, including autonomy with respect to security and foreign affairs. He was instructed not to discuss Gaza, and to clarify that Israel was not leaving the territories. Dayan had no objection to locating the offices of the autonomous entity in Jerusalem, but Sasson was supposed to impress upon the Palestinians that unified Jerusalem, in its entirety, would remain the sole capital of Israel. "On Jerusalem, there's nothing to talk about," Eshkol asserted.[26]

Eshkol himself met with eight Palestinian leaders, including Anwar Khatib, who had been exiled to Safed a few months earlier and was now allowed to return.† Sasson chose to hold some of the meetings in the home of his father, who lived in the Rehavia neighborhood of Jerusalem, not far from the prime minister's residence. Before the first meeting, Eshkol told Sasson that the last Arab he had met was a laborer who had worked with him in an orchard in Petach Tikva more than half a century ago. He remembered his name: Mustafa. He had probably spoken with other Arabs since then, but he usually viewed them as enemies or, at best, as undesirable foreigners.

Eshkol seemed to assume that when they left their meetings with him, the Palestinians would go home, sit around with their friends, and tell them everything. He therefore recommended to Dayan, Eban, and Sasson

---

*Weeks later, Dayan stated that he would not object to the Palestinians calling Ramallah part of Jerusalem, just as Ramat Gan was in fact part of Tel Aviv. Over the years, the two cities would become one larger metropolitan area anyway, he said.[25]

†The first Arab who came to see Eshkol with Sasson wanted money. His name was Ayub Musalem; he was a Christian from Bethlehem and a former Jordanian minister. In return for a onetime confidential payment of 60,000 liras, he agreed to publish a daily newspaper named *The Brotherhood*. Sasson supported the idea, but thought it might be better to start with a weekly publication and a more neutral name, such as *News, This Morning*, or *The Time*.[27]

that they conduct their conversations with the Palestinians as if they were talking "to the whole world."[28] So he did, repeating again and again: "You want me to say to Hussein, 'Sorry we won the war you started, please forgive us and kindly take the territories back.'" In response to questions about his position on Jerusalem, he said, "I heard that Faisal, the king of Saudi Arabia, said he would not go to the Temple Mount on a road guarded by Jewish policemen. Let him come in a helicopter, or on a flying carpet. Jerusalem will not be divided and it is the capital of Israel. The undivided capital."

When one of his Palestinian interlocutors, Nasser Eddin Nashashibi, asked if Eshkol wished to send Nasser a message, such as an offer of peace, he replied, "Why should I propose solutions? We didn't start the war. Your question makes it seem as if I have to get up and say, 'Please forgive us for not being killed.' I have nothing to say to him. We're staying here, so there will be peace. But maybe you could tell him that I am honestly more sorry than he is for all the many thousands of people killed. I'm sure he does not take that attitude even toward his own people."

Beyond the common slogans, these conversations demonstrated the breadth of the discrepancy between the Zionist movement's aspirations and those of the Palestinian national movement. "The starting point is that this is our only place in the world," Eshkol told one of his Palestinian guests. "In some place, in this place, we have to stop being a minority." Had the Jews not been persecuted in their countries of exile, he said, there might have been a hundred million of them today, and if not for Hitler, thirty million. Now there were thirteen million. "I recall our philosophy when we took our first steps as a movement to return to this land after two thousand years. We believed that we could live in peace here. I know how I view the Arabs. I have been here for fifty years and I worked with Arabs as a laborer, together. And now here we are after the third war. It is clear to me that one of these days we will stop fighting, because there is enough land in the region. But obviously, the point of departure must be your willingness to understand the condition and the history of the Jewish people."

Eshkol's contention that there was enough land "in the region" was not accidental. He proceeded to offer a "regional solution" for the refugees, particularly those who resided in Gaza, which Eshkol described as a "ghetto." His suggestion was to move them to Iraq. Anwar Khatib was horrified. "I never imagined that this was your outlook on the question of the refugees," he said. "After all, you suffered from exile and you know what it is like. The Palestinians today are in exile. I am first and foremost a Palestinian, and then an Arab. My family has been here since before the appearance of Islam. If you want peace, you cannot say, 'Let them go to Iraq.'" He demanded that the refugees be offered a choice between returning to their homes and receiving compensation, and he assured Eshkol that they would not all want to return. Eshkol replied that there was nowhere to return to. "We will not create a Cyprus here," he said in a conversation with Nashashibi, and reiterated his view that Iraq was the place for the refugees. Israel was willing to help finance the project, and would enlist support from the United States and from wealthy Jews.

Khatib, a former Jordanian ambassador to Egypt, told Eshkol about his acquaintance with Nasser and tried to convince him that Nasser had changed his fundamental approach to Israel, as he himself had done. "If I had been asked before the Six-Day War whether I was willing to recognize the Jewish state's right to exist, even just in the area of Tel Aviv, I would have replied no," he said. Now, everything was different. The Arabs recognized the State of Israel, and peace would have to be made. He tried to persuade Eshkol that Israel's demand to expand the state boundaries to security borders was meaningless: "What are secure borders in a time of rockets and other modern tools of warfare?"

MOST PALESTINIANS WERE UNWILLING TO ACCEPT THE OCCUPATION ARRANGEMENTS. They spoke of independence, of Jerusalem, and of the refugees. Aziz Shehade said, "A Palestinian state without Jerusalem is pointless and impossible. It would be better to annex the West Bank to Jerusalem." Eshkol agreed: "That seems to be inevitable. And so we will remain as we are, and will defend ourselves." In another conversation he observed, "I have a nation here too."[29]

Sasson believed everything revolved around Jerusalem. "If we find a formula that the Palestinians can accept on the issue of Jerusalem, the other problems can be solved," he was about to write to Eshkol, but on second thought he shelved the draft of his letter.

Eshkol saw little value in the meetings, and feared contacts with the Palestinians would go too far, to the point where they would harm Hussein. He noted that this was also why the United States objected to a separate settlement between Israel and the Palestinians.* He suspected that the Palestinians did not truly want a settlement with Israel. In a discussion with Dayan, Eban, Sasson, his father, and other senior officials,

---

*The U.S. embassy and the American consulate in Jerusalem closely monitored the meetings with the Palestinians and received updates from both sides.[30]

Eshkol compared the Palestinians to certain Jews in Russia, whom he termed *yishuvniks:* Jews who lived in remote, rural areas, far from the nearest Jewish village. On Yom Kippur such a Jew would come to the village and enter the synagogue, where he would be blessed and honored with a call to the Torah. "In the end it would turn out that what he'd really come to town for was to buy a dress for the shiksa who works for him," said Eshkol.[31]

Sasson continued to "groom leaders" over the next few months, and tried to build up a Palestinian administration under the leadership of Sheikh Jaabari. When he brought Jaabari to his father's home to meet with Eshkol, the sheikh offered Eshkol a deal: he would "demand" that Israel appoint him sole ruler of the West Bank, and Israel would "accept his demand." This proposed conspiracy produced another series of discussions and a large pile of top-secret minutes, but nothing more.

DID ISRAEL MISS ITS CHANCE TO PUT AN END TO THE CONFLICT OVER PALESTINE? PERhaps not. Israel never offered the Palestinians full independence or a compromise they could accept on the matter of Jerusalem. But Dayan may have been right when he said, "Even if we had offered them mountains of gold, they would have been suspicious."[32] Israel did, however, miss an opportunity to solve the refugee problem.

CHAPTER 21

THE BLUNDER

1. PLANS: "A HUNDRED THOUSAND PEOPLE WON'T TURN IRAQ UPSIDE DOWN"

On the afternoon of November 30, Yosef Weitz's telephone rang and one of the prime minister's secretaries asked him to "pop over" to see Eshkol. Weitz asked for a car to "pop over" and pick him up, and by six he was at the prime minister's office. Eshkol led him to a large map on the wall and asked, "Where should the new West Bank border be?" A UN-appointed negotiator was arriving soon, and they had to decide what to tell him.

A few weeks earlier, Weitz had published an article in *Davar* in which he suggested solving the refugee problem by "transferring" them from the Gaza Strip to the West Bank. He suggested giving the West Bank back to Jordan, with certain amendments to the border.[1] "How do we do that?" asked Eshkol. Weitz promised to draw up plans, and the prime minister instructed that he be sent adequate maps.

ESHKOL WAS HAUNTED BY THE VACILLATION AND INDECISION OVER THE FUTURE OF Palestine. He had no idea what should be done, and practically no one to consult with. He wanted to get rid of the refugees but did not know how; he was not even considering the hundreds of thousands of "new refugees," but only the 1948 refugees who were still living in camps, primarily in Gaza. The problem had suddenly risen from oblivion to irk him.* His feelings were apparently shared by the man from whom he had inherited the problem, David Ben-Gurion.

Four days before the war, Ben-Gurion had copied down in his diary some numbers from a nineteen-year-old newspaper article that claimed the estimated number of Palestinian refugees was vastly exaggerated. Even the most thorough probe would find no more than 300,000, the article said, and Ben-Gurion thought that this was information he should keep. He did not explain why he suddenly felt the need to consider the issue, but he probably assumed that the imminent war would once again confront Israel with the Palestinian population. Either way, the number of Arabs who had lost their homes in 1948 was at least twice the figure Ben-Gurion had quoted in his diary, and he surely knew it.†

About six months after the war, Ben-Gurion employed a pseudo-legal argument in an attempt to absolve Israel of any responsibility for the fate of the refugees: "All the refugees left following their leaders' incitement during the British Mandate era and not after Israel was established." This was untrue: Lod and Ramle were captured and most of their inhabitants expelled approximately two months after Israel's declaration of independence, as Ben-Gurion himself had once pointed out in a government debate. At the time, he at first said that they "left," and then conceded that "they were pressured to leave."[4] Additional refugees were deported even later, from the Galilee, the Ashkelon area, and elsewhere.

Israel's heads of state had not concealed their satisfaction. Moshe Sharett described the refugees' "wholesale evacuation" as "more wonderful than the creation of the Jewish state."[5] In 1949 Israel offered to readmit 100,000 refugees as part of a peace settlement, but the plan failed and Israel rescinded the offer. The UN demanded that Israel give the refugees a choice of returning to their homes or receiving compensation. Ben-

---

*Eshkol had already had reason to worry about the Gaza refugees roughly two years before the Six-Day War. The refugees were multiplying, and when their numbers reached half a million, he feared the situation would become explosive. Once, he asked the chief of staff what would happen if the Egyptians simply marched the refugees—women and children in the vanguard—toward the border with Israel. Rabin said they would not do that, and if they did, as soon the IDF killed the first hundred, the rest would go back to Gaza.[2]

†No one knew exactly how many of the 1948 refugees remained in the territories after the flight that took place during the Six-Day War and continued for some time afterward. Furthermore, there were different ways of deciding who was a refugee. According to the Israeli data, there were 122,000 refugees in the West Bank and roughly 234,000 in Gaza. UNWRA cited far higher numbers.[3]

Gurion objected. "Everyone will want to come home and they will destroy us," he said in 1961. This was the fear that dictated Israel's position until the Six-Day War. "We have nothing to give and nothing to concede," Eshkol told Jean-Paul Sartre.

Most Israelis knew little of the refugees' plight. Some saw them after the occupation of the Gaza Strip in the Sinai Campaign, but in the following decade there was little talk of the problem. When Israel entered the territories in the Six-Day War, many people were stunned at what they found, and realized that a solution had to be reached quickly.[6] "We have a moral obligation," wrote Amos Elon in *Ha'aretz* a week after the war, "because the road to Israel's independence was paved on the backs of these people, and they paid, with their bodies, their property, and their future, for the pogroms in the Ukraine and the Nazi gas chambers."[7] These were extraordinary words: until then the received view was that Israel had not expelled the refugees, even that in many cases it had urged them to stay, and was therefore not responsible for their fate. It was later established that roughly half the refugees left their homes and fled out of fear of the war, and half were forcibly deported.[8]

Israel insisted that the UN was inflating the number of refugees in order to enlarge its budgets and the scope of its activity, while the Arab states were preventing the refugees from settling down and were perpetuating their suffering in order to harass Israel.[9] Efforts to convey this message preoccupied the Foreign Ministry for years, but now even some ministry officials were demanding an immediate solution to the refugee problem by means of a quick, comprehensive, unilateral operation, regardless of what was to happen with the territories. "We can start working immediately," wrote one, noting that such a step would strengthen Israel's "moral right" to hold on to the West Bank. Israel's ambassador to Canada, Gershon Avner, tried to prod the government from his offices in Ottawa: Why weren't they setting up at least one factory for refugees and providing affordable housing nearby? he asked. He emphasized the propaganda value of such a step, and suggested allocating funds from the Foreign Ministry's publicity budget. A senior ministry official proposed immediately setting up two agricultural settlements. Ambassador Harman sent Jerusalem similar proposals from Jewish and other organizations.[10] Several Jewish public figures and organizations offered to raise funds for the relief of the refugees. Among them were Lord Rothschild and the World Bank. Eshkol instructed Yaacov Herzog to coordinate the various parties.* Israel's ambassador to Washington reported to the prime minister that the United States expected Israel to initiate a program to resettle the refugees. He tried to convince Eshkol to agree, but Eshkol responded, "Maybe for once we can hear something from you about Jewish refugees instead of Arab refugees?"[12]

Most Israelis did not yet acknowledge that their country bore at least partial responsibility for creating the refugee problem. The almost existential need to believe that Zionism had caused no injustice was deep-seated. When they discussed the refugee problem a few days after the war, the government ministers also found it difficult to overcome this conviction.

They all had their own solutions; Eshkol had two. Haim Moshe Shapira proposed an astonishing plan by which Israel would take in 200,000 Palestinian refugees. This would raise the number of Israeli Arabs to over half a million, some 20 percent of the population, Shapira estimated, but he observed, "That's not so terrible." In order to maintain the Jewish majority, the government would have to encourage immigration, "do something" about the birthrate, and make sure the number of deaths in car accidents dropped.

Allon suggested settling the Gaza refugees in El Arish, in the northern Sinai, as well as on the West Bank. Menachem Begin also thought they should be rehabilitated: the refugee situation was a huge moral and human problem, he said. He supported the idea of settling them in El Arish. The minister of development, Bentov, suggested moving them from Gaza to the West Bank, and this was one of Eshkol's two suggestions. He noted explicitly that instead of setting up new Jewish settlements in the West Bank, it would be better to resettle the refugees of Gaza there. Minister Sasson believed that the refugees were "the root of the conflict" and proposed founding an independent state for the Palestinians, or granting them an autonomous region. Dayan maintained the opposite view: UNRWA was handling the refugees and there was no reason to absolve it of that task.

Minister Ze'ev Sherf, conversely, believed Israel should begin quiet negotiations with foreign countries, with the aim of settling the refugees "overseas." This was also the hope guiding Pinhas Sapir, who described the refugees as explosive; Eshkol, too, supported this view. They toyed

---

*The conductor Erich Leinsdorf, who had so hastily canceled his concert and left Israel before the war, was now quick to call President Johnson and suggest immediate action on behalf of the refugees. The fund started by Rothschild was apparently supposed to finance, among other things, the establishment of a new city for refugees in the West Bank, to be built with plans submitted by the architect Moshe Safdie.[11]

with moving the refugees to Algeria, Morocco, Syria, or Iraq. This was not merely meant to irritate Eshkol's Palestinian guests: he was quite serious. "There has been a population exchange," he said, as Israel had often argued. "We got population from Iraq: we got a hundred thousand Jews. They'll get a hundred thousand Arabs. It's the same language, the same standard of living, there's water and there's land."* Eshkol admitted that the Iraqis might not accept the plan, but he thought the idea was "pure justice." Minister Shapira disagreed: "There is no reason to pull out Arabs who were born here and move them to Iraq." Begin intervened: "In Greece they took out Turks who were born there and that was as part of an agreement." Eshkol quickly responded, "That's exactly what I wanted to say, and I saw the way they were settled." This had occurred some four decades earlier, in 1926. The young Shkolnik (Eshkol) had traveled to Greece to learn about the resettlement of 600,000 Greek refugees from Asia Minor. It was "an enormous and interesting project," he wrote at the time, and he assumed it could be instructive in the context of Jewish settlement in Palestine.†

The refugees in Gaza could no longer return to their homes, Eshkol contended, but "one hundred thousand people won't turn Iraq upside down." One could not say such a population transfer was unjust, he added, and the same applied to the "new refugees" living in Jordan: "First they lived here, now they live in Jordan." A few weeks later, Allon also suggested "encouraging" the refugees to emigrate, but warned his colleagues: "I am not suggesting that we publicly adopt the emigration solution for the Arabs, because it sounds somewhat unpleasant, especially for Jews and Zionists."

Everything came back to the foundations of Zionist ideology. "After all, we did not come in here as an underground movement," said Eshkol. "We declared that Palestine was ours by right." Minister of Health Barzilai disagreed: "But they are residents of Palestine." The prime minister stood his ground: "All the Jews of the world are residents of Israel who were uprooted and expelled, and then found a lifeline in other places." A few ministers tried to argue, but Eshkol silenced them.[15]

The proposed resolution submitted to the cabinet stated that Israel would "demand" of the Arab states that they take in the refugees. To ensure

---

*Eshkol was not the first person to talk of resettling refugees in Iraq: David Ben-Gurion had suggested it at a government meeting over a decade earlier. Shimon Peres thought the refugees should be encouraged to emigrate to the Persian Gulf oil states.[13]
†Eshkol received letters from ordinary citizens demanding that he empty the territories of their inhabitants and reminding him of the population exchange between Turkey and Greece. He responded to one with a polite letter of thanks.[14]

unanimity, they eventually agreed on broader wording: "The establishment of peace in the Middle East, and the cooperation thereby engendered, will open the door to an international and regional settlement to resolve the refugee problem."[16]

BY THE TIME HE CALLED YOSEF WEITZ IN NOVEMBER, ESHKOL'S DESK WAS PILED HIGH with plans and proposals to solve the refugee problem.[17] Weitz's proposal, to settle the refugees in the West Bank, was reinforced by a plan Eshkol received from a small group of academics led by the economist Michael Bruno. Their proposal provided for 40,000 families, some 250,000 people, who would move from Gaza to the West Bank over the course of ten years. The cost per family, including housing, job creation, roads, schools, and hospitals, was between 20,000 and 25,000 liras. The average annual cost would be 200 million liras, or $50 million, at most. The project would create a huge economic upsurge in Israel and on the West Bank, making the net cost far lower, and it would not burden the country's economy, even without taking into account foreign aid.* Raanan Weitz sent Eshkol his own detailed plan. He suggested resettling some refugees near Jericho, and about 50,000 in the El Arish area. His father opposed the idea, and recalled heated arguments with his son.†

2. POSSIBILITIES: "I DON'T KNOW WHAT I WANT"

On December 6 Eshkol convened a lengthy consultation with two professors, Roberto Bacci, the director of the Central Bureau of Statistics, and Aryeh Dvoretzky, a professor of mathematics at the Hebrew University, who were trying to convince him that the Gaza refugees should be moved to the West Bank. The Italian-born Bacci was involved in efforts to raise the birthrate among Jews and reduce it among Israeli Arabs.[20] Dvoretzky was among the scientists who made their skills available to the security establishment; in 1960, he was appointed head of Rafael, the weapons development authority.

The three did not talk much about the human plight of the refugees,

---

*Weeks after Bruno's plan reached Eshkol, his office director wrote to Eban that it was being kept top secret because it demonstrated that there was no economic barrier to settling the refugees in the West Bank—a conclusion that could result in international pressure.[18]

†The idea of settling the Gaza refugees in the northern Sinai was examined at the end of the 1950s, and also turned up in proposals Professor Yuval Ne'eman sent to Dayan before the war was even over, on June 9.[19]

whom they viewed as a problem for Israel. At no point in the conversation did they raise the possibility of absorbing the refugees within Israel or leaving them in Gaza. They began their meeting by studying a map. Bacci gave Eshkol alarming information: a survey had shown that infant mortality in Gaza might decrease. "If we continue to be as compassionate as we are now," he said, infant mortality in the territories might even come to rival that of Israeli Arabs. "This is a shocking situation," he observed. Seeking some reassurance, Eshkol asked whether there was no hope that Westernization would lead Arab girls to have fewer babies. Bacci said yes, but it would take at least fifteen years for that to occur, "unless we are able to assert more control over the Palestinian family unit." Eshkol asked how this could be done, and Bacci replied, "It is a real problem." He told the prime minister that more than half of the territories' inhabitants were under the age of fifteen, which was another "frightening thing." On the other hand, there was reason to hope that those Gaza refugees who moved to the West Bank would go on to emigrate to Jordan or elsewhere. One-third of West Bank families sent one of their children overseas, Bacci explained. Like the Israelis who left the country for good, many Palestinians believed they would return but ended up staying abroad. Bacci and Dvoretzky asked the prime minister for direction.

"Now I'm going to show my cards," said Eshkol. "First, I don't know what I want. Second, I would like to do something." It would be difficult to find any statement that better expressed Eshkol's position on almost everything at any given time. He was not certain whether it was prudent to initiate action for the benefit of the refugees, he said; perhaps it would be better to wait for other countries or large organizations to do so. Or perhaps they should wait until there was a peace treaty. Perhaps there would be a war. Perhaps they should start dismantling one refugee camp on the West Bank, the smallest one, and see how its inhabitants fared. "Regarding the Arabs of Gaza, I would like to hope that they will leave Israel," Eshkol said, as if Gaza were a part of the state. Bacci asked how that could come to pass, and Eshkol replied, "I don't know. I'm looking for people who can find the solution."

Bacci suggested that Eshkol not count on the Arabs of Gaza to emigrate voluntarily. Before the war, many of them had left for Egypt. Now they were stuck. Eshkol asked about Libya: he had been told it was a country of immigrants. But Bacci replied, "You can't expel them. You can only encourage emigration." Still, even Bacci himself did not believe that this was sufficient: "To assume that it will solve the problem—that is a very dangerous illusion."

Eshkol did not give up: he was interested only in the emigration of the camp residents. Bacci reminded him that they were talking about 180,000 people; they could not bring about the emigration of such a large number. "It's thirty thousand households," Eshkol tried, almost pleadingly, but Bacci insisted: "In my opinion we should look for other ways." Eshkol, ever the joker, could not resist: "There is one other way: another six-day war."

The two professors stepped up their efforts to persuade Eshkol that only the West Bank offered a solution. The refugees could be settled in the Jordan Valley, said Dvoretzky, but quickly added, "It's very important that this fact not be disclosed to anyone, because if anyone knew that Israel could resettle twenty-five thousand families and is not doing so, there would be a huge outcry." Dvoretzky proposed, therefore, that the Gaza refugees be moved into houses vacated by the "new refugees," and explained to Eshkol why this was a good idea: the more Gaza refugees occupied the houses of people who had recently left the West Bank, the less chance there was that those people would return. "In addition, you are provoking internal strife among the Palestinians themselves."

Like Michael Bruno and his colleagues, Bacci and Dvoretzky stressed that there was no real basis for the plan to settle the Gaza refugees in El Arish. Besides, said Bacci, an El Arish of refugees could create a "refugeestan" over there, while on the West Bank they would be diluted by the other residents. "If we move even a hundred thousand, and pray that another hundred thousand emigrate, we've achieved a great thing," said the mathematician.

Eshkol was also opposed to the El Arish idea. "I don't know all of the Sinai, but I haven't heard that they've found any water there," he said. In a conversation with IDF generals he said he "felt instinctively" that the El Arish plan would be a disaster for Israel.[21] But he also found it difficult to accept that the right place for the Gaza refugees was in the West Bank. "What a mess," he commented. He looked at the map and said he did not know whether there would be another war, but he did know one thing: Gaza must remain under Israeli control. Bacci said this was "a serious matter," and asked whether the prime minister intended to incorporate the Gaza Arabs into Israel; here was another reason to move them to the West Bank. Eshkol was unconvinced. "I don't like this idea," he said: they might move the refugees to the West Bank and then Hussein might suddenly declare, "Keep the land along with the Arabs, and leave me alone." Bacci offered a contrasting scenario: Israel would move 150,000 Arabs to the West Bank and Hussein would accept them.

"Good for him. He'll have another hundred and fifty thousand Arabs," Bacci said.

Eshkol said that the Ministry of Defense did not think the area would be turned over to Hussein. He did not say "Dayan." Bacci said that even so, the Gaza Strip should be emptied. "Let us assume for a moment that you move a hundred and fifty thousand to the West Bank. If the whole area ever goes back to Jordan, you've tossed the Arabs outside your borders. And that is advisable. If the area remains in our hands, then you'll have less trouble from those in the West Bank than in the Gaza Strip. Because in Gaza they're presented for all the world to see as refugees." Not necessarily, Eshkol replied: "If they stay in the Gaza Strip, we'll pressure them to move somewhere." Bacci was not certain he had understood: "But why would they leave? It's a fantasy." Eshkol repeated his original idea: "I say to them: take a hundred thousand refugees from here to Iraq. Isn't that moral?" Then he argued with his guests over their data. What would the refugees eat on the West Bank? he wanted to know. The professors eventually gave up. Perhaps it was better to wait for the Iraqi government to take in the refugees, Bacci said, and Eshkol responded, honestly: "I don't know where I stand with this whole business."[22]

The proposal to move the refugees to the West Bank ran into resistance from Begin, who had earmarked the area for Jewish settlement. Allon objected to the refugees being moved to the Jordan Valley, which he also intended for Jews. From time to time, the initiative to resettle the refugees served as a focal point for personal quarrels between the ministers, replete with leaks to the press, but it eventually melted away.[23] Dayan was opposed to resettling the refugees on the West Bank, insisting that they belonged with Hussein. Then he added, "I don't mind if they all emigrate." Eshkol attempted to bring this idea to fruition.[24]*

3. ATTEMPTS: "HOW MANY ARABS HAVE YOU DRIVEN OUT SO FAR?"

Eight months after the war, a new position was created in the prime minister's office. Eshkol described the job: Ada Sereni was to "see but not be seen," and her function was to coordinate efforts to encourage Gaza Strip residents to leave the country. Her first meeting with Eshkol was attended by Meir Amit, head of the Mossad, and by Yosef Hermelin, head of the Shabak.[26]

---

*Various experts who examined the resettlement and emigration options also considered whether refugees could be settled on the eastern bank of the Jordan, and found that with adequate development more than a quarter of a million people could be resettled there.[25]

• • •

THE HOPE OF MOVING THE ARABS OF PALESTINE TO OTHER STATES HAD BEEN A CON-stant factor in the Zionist movement. During British rule, Zionist leaders looked into various ways of paying Arabs to move to distant provinces.[27] The Arabs' flight and expulsion during the War of Independence and afterward did not put an end to these schemes. Israel made several attempts to encourage the emigration of Israeli Arabs to Latin America and elsewhere.[28] When the Gaza Strip was occupied in the Sinai Campaign, Levi Eshkol, who was then the minister of finance, allocated half a million dollars to finance the emigration of two hundred families of Palestinian refugees from Gaza, as well as a number of Israeli Arabs, mostly well-off Christians. The project was coordinated by Ezra Danin, one of Zionism's first secret agents.[29]

In 1962, the same Danin came up with an idea known as Operation Worker. The purpose was to encourage Palestinian refugees to emigrate to West Germany, where there was new demand for foreign labor. Roughly eighteen months before the Six-Day War, Israel tried to orchestrate an agreement between Germany and Jordan that would expand the emigration of Palestinian refugees from Jordan to Germany through the German trade unions. Ruth Wolf, the Foreign Ministry official involved in the project, declared, "Perhaps it is necessary to hint to the Germans that they bear a special 'guilt' for the establishment of Israel, because of the Holocaust. Here they have a chance to help resettle refugees whose problem resulted from the creation of the State of Israel."[30]

IN EARLY 1968, A SMALL UNIT OF FIVE PEOPLE BEGAN OPERATING IN GAZA UNDER THE direction of an IDF major. Their job was to encourage the local population to leave. They worked through collaborators who went around the camps promising people money in return for their agreement to go. This was a joint operation of the military government, the Shabak, and the prime minister's adviser on Arab affairs. The Foreign Ministry also tried to promote refugee emigration, and the Ministry of Finance was asked to fund the operation. Eshkol sent Ada Sereni to coordinate the various actors. "She has a special knack for underground work," he explained.[31]

The sixty-two-year-old Sereni was a heroic figure in the Zionist drama. She had been born in Rome to a wealthy and highly respected Jewish family, the Ascarellis, who were originally from Spain. One of the women in the family was a well-known sixteenth-century poet. Sereni's father was a history buff who had a large library at home. He kept flocks of sheep in Sardinia, where he produced Pecorino cheese, most of which ended up garnishing spaghetti made by Italian immigrants in America. His daughter Ada was a short child with a small, sweet face, warm eyes, and a long black braid. As a schoolgirl, she fell in love with a classmate, Enzo Sereni, also from a Jewish aristocratic family. He read a lot and wrote a novel, and when Ada became pregnant they married and went to Palestine. They lived in Rehovot at first, then joined the founders of a new kibbutz, Givat Brenner. Enzo Sereni became an activist for the labor movement. In the early 1930s he traveled to Germany as a delegate of a youth movement, and later the couple went to New York, where they lived in a Zionist commune on Riverside Drive. They had two daughters and a son. Sereni had been a moderate man, but he changed his views during World War II and demanded "transfer" for the Arabs in Palestine. In Palestine, he dealt with issues of defense, security, and secret operations. He eventually joined a unit of paratroopers in the British army, set up to infiltrate enemy territory. He was parachuted into northern Italy, where he disappeared.

After the war, his wife went to search for her husband through the ruins of Europe and, in an adventurous and dangerous operation, she found evidence that he had been murdered in the concentration camp at Dachau. She stayed on in Europe, where she worked for the Briha organization, which helped illegal Jewish immigrants reach Palestine, and assisted in efforts to purchase arms in preparation for the War of Independence. Ben-Gurion asked her to use her connections to acquire aircraft. Not long after her return to Israel, several founding members of Givat Brenner left because of an ideological rift. Sereni joined a kibbutz that was originally called Buchenwald, after the concentration camp, and was now named Netzer Sereni, in her husband's memory.

In July 1954, on the shores of Lake Tiberias near Kibbutz Ma'agan, a state ceremony was held in memory of Sereni and the other paratroopers. There was a large crowd, and Prime Minister Moshe Sharett was in attendance. A small plane flying in an air show for the occasion crashed into the audience only yards from the prime minister. Two of those killed were Daniel Sereni, Enzo and Ada's son, and his wife.

Sereni, an energetic woman with hawkish views, went on to join Nativ, the covert Israeli organization that helped Jews leave the USSR. Nativ sent her to work in Italy.[32] In choosing her in 1967 for the job, Eshkol hoped her contacts in Italy might facilitate the relocation of a large number of refugees from Gaza to Libya.

Sereni's appointment lasted for six months. She believed that within two years, forty thousand families—almost a quarter of a million Palestinians—could be removed to Jordan. She assumed the refugees would agree to leave in return for one thousand liras per family, and so she cited a cost of forty million liras, less than $10 million.[33]

"I want them all to go, even if they go to the moon," Eshkol told her. The operation reminded him of the process of emigration from Jewish villages in Russia to America: "There were a few companies that dealt with transporting people, and they took the shirts off their backs," he recounted. "They led them like sheep, but the Jews went." But even Eshkol, motivated as he was, found it difficult to believe that the campaign would succeed, so he was reluctant to finance it. Thousands of refugees left the Gaza Strip during those months with no encouragement from the military government, and Eshkol hoped this process would continue without any financial investment. He wanted to know all the details, and expressed concern upon learning that many of the people leaving were young men, while the young women were being left behind. "This is a big problem for us. I have four daughters and I know what trouble is. We may have to set up a matchmaking office to give money to whoever takes young girls out of here."

This was not the only idea discussed at the meeting. Eshkol's adviser on Arab affairs, Shmuel Toledano, reported happily that he had a thousand passports from a certain foreign country, which he was distributing to Gaza residents who wished to leave. Meir Amit commented sternly that fake passports should not be used; doing so could endanger all of Israel's covert operations. Toledano, insulted, assured him the passports were genuine. Later, it transpired that they had apparently been bought from the interior minister of a South American country. Nevertheless, skepticism prevailed: a holder of one of these passports might be involved in a car accident, and the police would discover that he didn't even speak the language. And the next day a different interior minister would come along and start asking questions. Eshkol was not enthusiastic either, but Toledano believed his passports could also be utilized to get rid of the Israeli Arabs: "Any Israeli-Arab citizens we can get rid of—that's very important. It turns out hardly any of these people are leaving the country."*

When Sereni began her assignment, Eshkol promised to meet with her weekly, and they did meet frequently. "What's the situation? Is there a

---

*Eshkol had his own thoughts on this point: perhaps if they made the Israeli Arabs join the army, they would all leave, he once mused.

chance? Is there any hope of anything?" he would ask. And sometimes, "How many Arabs have you driven out so far?"[34]

Most of the time they talked about money. Eshkol agreed to increase the number of field agents from five to twenty. He authorized Sereni to send people to Australia and Brazil to look into emigration options there. Sereni and her contact in the army, Shlomo Gazit, told Eshkol about additional needs: the Jordanian officer in charge of refugee crossings at the Allenby Bridge was demanding kickbacks. They also had to bribe a man in Saudi Arabia. Eshkol agreed to allocate funds and authorized an operational budget of over five million liras. But he repeatedly warned Sereni not to give money to Arabs who left the country, because as soon as you gave money to one, the rest would want even more.[35]

Eshkol was right. At first Sereni wanted only five liras per refugee, to pay for travel from Gaza to the West Bank. Eshkol said he did not believe an Arab from Gaza couldn't come up with five liras for cab fare, but he consented. Sereni said they also had to give out flour and sugar and subsistence money to tide people over when they first arrived in Jordan. Then it turned out Jordan would not allow people to bring their belongings with them, and Sereni said the refugees should be compensated for what they had to leave behind. She discussed sending people to South America and to the United States, at a cost of $1,000 per family. When she asked what to do about a man who had $300 to get to America but needed three hundred liras more, Eshkol decreed: "First let the people go who have the means to go." On another occasion he said, "Perhaps we should have stolen their money on their way out of here, like they've always done to Jews around the world." Sereni said there were "enormous difficulties all around the globe." Australia, for example, was willing to take Israelis, but they wanted only Jews, not Arabs; and it was difficult with those Australians, Sereni reported: they wouldn't take bribes.

Gazit backed up Sereni's requests, but the prime minister said he had no money. When he balked at her request for a hundred million liras, she asked if he would give her fifty million. The cost could reach a billion liras, Eshkol said, and she replied that it would not. She wanted only two and a half million. Every so often she went back to the original calculation: "You won't agree to finish off the Gaza Strip affair for forty million liras? That's a very reasonable price!" Eshkol replied, "If you make a contract with me that you'll remove forty thousand people for such and such a price—then maybe. But you can't commit yourself." He was afraid the refugees would end up in such harsh conditions that Israel would have to come to their aid. He also demanded that people getting money from Israel provide receipts, so he could prove how much had been spent.

Gazit tried to convince Eshkol to finance the departure of an entire tribe—one thousand families—from the Jebalia camp. Sereni had already mentioned the plan. The tribal sheikh wanted 200 liras per capita, which amounted to 1.2 million liras. He was also asking for 200,000 liras in return for the orchard and water pump he owned. The prime minister responded like a seasoned salesman: "It would be foolish of us to agree. The price of an orchard in the Gaza Strip, including a water source that's getting saltier all the time, cannot be so high." But he toyed with the idea of purchasing lands and orchards in Gaza and settling Jews there; he would give them stores and barbershops, he said dreamily. It would be just like the old days in Palestine: they would give a loan to an Arab, he would lose the money, and then they would buy up his lands. Sereni wanted to open a mortgage bank, an idea Eshkol did not rule out.

Yaacov Herzog wrote in his notes from one meeting that "Mrs. Sereni claimed there is a general moral problem." It is unclear what he was referring to; perhaps only to the administrative arrangements and the need to work within approved budgets. Either way, Eshkol replied, "I am willing to take upon myself all moral responsibility in this matter. Because I do not know where this business will start and where it will end."

FEW ISRAELIS KNEW OF THE TRANSFER PROJECT. EVERYTHING WAS DONE SECRETLY, AS IF it were something to be ashamed of, but many people in the Gaza Strip knew about the "emigration offices" set up by the military government in the camps. The U.S. embassy reported on the project, even specifying the code names of two of Gazit and Sereni's operatives, "Wolfie" and "Yehuda." The International Red Cross sent a teenaged boy to Sereni's "travel agents" to find out what was on offer. The boy returned with a quote of five hundred liras if he left with his mother and siblings. The father had already gone. Earlier, the American diplomats wrote, Wolfie and Yehuda met with the *mukhtars* and asked them for a list of separated families. Upon departing the country, the emigrants had to leave behind the identification cards they had received from the military government.[36] They also had to sign a form declaring, in Hebrew and Arabic, that they were leaving willingly and understood that they would not be able to return without a special permit. They signed with thumbprints; if they could, they added their names in writing. Men signed for their wives. The form was occasionally modified, as was the custom in the Occupation bureaucracy.[37] Gazit told Eshkol that Dayan wanted to speed up the project: the Jordan bridges might be closed any day.

IN MAY 1968, SERENI REPORTED TO ESHKOL THAT DURING THE FIRST THREE MONTHS OF her work approximately 15,000 people had left Gaza. Gazit estimated around 50,000 had left the Gaza Strip since the war; some of them might have gone to the West Bank. The Central Bureau of Statistics found that in the first six months of 1968, approximately 20,000 people had emigrated from the Gaza Strip.[38] The IDF counted how many people crossed the Jordan bridges, as did the UN and foreign embassies in both Israel and Jordan, but no one could provide an accurate figure. The numbers ranged from 220,000 to 250,000, from Gaza and the West Bank.[39]

It is difficult to estimate how many left as a result of Sereni and Gazit's efforts. Dayan's assistant Zvi Zur told Eshkol about six different studies of why people were leaving the Gaza Strip. Nine out of every ten emigrants were young men, almost half of them single. Eight out of every ten were refugees. Seven out of ten went alone. Most left behind no property; most had relatives in Jordan. They said they were leaving because of unemployment, and because they were no longer receiving the financial support their relatives in Arab states used to send them. Some wanted to reunite with family members, and some went to study.*

Hopes that the refugee problem might be solved by emigration to far-away countries were bolstered from an unexpected direction: the U.S. senator Edward Kennedy supported a plan to disperse 200,000 refugees from Gaza around the world. Between 25,000 and 50,000 of them were supposed to make their new homes in the United States. Another senator, Jacob Javits, initiated a plan to resettle the refugees, and the Israeli consul in New York reported that the Lutheran church had pledged assistance. There was also promising news from Australia after all.[40]

Alongside Gazit and Sereni's "travel agents," the Foreign Ministry, apparently in coordination with the Mossad, did what it could to encourage refugees to emigrate to Brazil and elsewhere in South America. Within weeks after the war, Israeli ambassadors in various foreign countries were asked to respond to a questionnaire about the prospects for immigration.

---

*Gazit explained to Eshkol why many of the refugees hesitated to leave: they were afraid that Israel would seize Amman, and they had had enough in Gaza. Eshkol authorized him to tell them that Israel would not seize Amman.

In August 1967, Eshkol wrote to Eban that conversations with the Brazilian ambassador in Israel had led him to conclude that there was a possibility of removing thousands to that country, "if not tens of thousands." The Foreign Ministry reported to Gazit about the arrival of a Brazilian travel agent who specialized in immigrants.[41]

Israeli diplomats in Washington tried to convince the administration to support the transfer policy. They also established contact with an international organization that worked with refugees and displaced persons, the Intergovernmental Committee for European Migration. The purpose of ICEM, wrote Mordehai Kidron, the Israeli delegate to the UN, was not to absolve Israel of responsibility for the refugees' plight. Rather, the organization, which was founded after World War II to help displaced persons in Europe, was fighting for survival: in the late 1960s, this large organization could no longer justify its existence, and it needed emigrants "as a fish needs water." Nor had the potential host countries suddenly developed a desire to help Israel. They needed skilled labor: Brazil wanted agricultural workers, Australia needed both shepherds and urban laborers, Canada wanted foresters and construction workers. The Israelis suggested starting with a small group of about 150 refugees. When they reached their destination, they would be met by a Mossad representative who would take care of their initial needs. If the project was successful, news would spread by word of mouth and the number of emigrants would grow.

One of the people involved in the attempt to organize the emigration of refugees from Gaza was Charles Jordan, a senior executive at the American Jewish Joint Distribution Committee. Jordan addressed the issue during his final visit to Israel, in August 1967.[42]*

The Foreign Ministry seems to have been functioning during this time as a global travel agency. Discussions revolved around passports, visas, and airplane tickets. There was a proposal to exempt refugees leaving Gaza from the travel tax. The ministry inquired about airline deals, noting that the refugees from Gaza refused to fly El Al. Someone suggested chartering flights, and another said the minister of the interior had to work faster: there was no justification for taking so long to issue the refugees' transit papers.

An argument ensued among the officials, some of whom claimed that

---

*Jordan was involved in covert Israeli activities related to Nativ. In mid-August, he went to Prague and disappeared; his body was later found floating in the Vltava River. He was presumably murdered, but the circumstances of his death remain a mystery.[43]

the test group proposed by ICEM was too small—they could go straight to mass emigration, fifteen hundred or two thousand families, between five thousand and ten thousand people, in two years. On the other hand, ICEM was considered a pro-Zionist organization, and had given Israel $15 million to absorb immigrants in the past. And so they continued to fantasize about a future without Arabs, and to work on ways of making it happen. One Foreign Ministry official, Shlomo Hillel, was so gung-ho about the project that he wanted to present the Arabs with a condition: no peace treaty until the refugees were gone.

As it turned out, most of the refugees did not leave Gaza in return for plane tickets. Mass deportations were more or less impossible, because diplomats and the world press were always watching. But there was a third way. A senior official in the Foreign Ministry, Michael Comay, wrote to Ambassador Harman that the military governor of the Gaza Strip, Mordechai Gur, was pushing people to leave Gaza by eroding their standard of living; he said Gur himself had admitted to this. Not everyone in the military government favored this approach: Dayan believed that although a deterioration of life in the Gaza Strip might bring about the departure of refugees, it might also make things difficult for the military government and damage Israel's reputation.[44] In preparation for the new budget, it was decided that the standard of living in Gaza should be "reasonable" but only "close to that which existed before the occupation." What this meant, according to one document, was that new sources of income would not be created for refugees living in the camps. In that same period, unemployment in Gaza reached 16.6 percent. The government did, however, decide to attract refugees from Gaza to construction and agricultural jobs in the West Bank.[45]

From time to time horror stories spread about initiatives to deport the residents of the Occupied Territories, and on one occasion the Jordanian authorities refused to allow a few hundred refugees to cross a bridge, claiming they had been brought there against their will. In December, the British consulate in Jerusalem confirmed a London *Times* story about some two hundred Bedouins from the Nusseirat tribe who had been forced over the Jordan River. About six months after the war, a discussion in which Dayan took part was summarized: "There is authorization to continue the policy of imposing local curfews, searches, and arrests following every act of terrorism, as one means of encouraging departures."[46]

But the more the war receded into a distant memory, the fewer claims there were of forced deportations, and so it appeared that most Palestinians who left the West Bank and the Gaza Strip were not forced to go. They were not, however, allowed to return. Hundreds tried to slip back in, including women and children. But they were usually sent back, and some were shot dead. The Jordan was not a deep river. In August a few soldiers wrote to Eshkol and told him they were being asked to kill women and children crossing the Jordan. Eshkol sent the complaint to Dayan to investigate. Meanwhile, more rumors spread of women and children being wounded. On September 13, Dayan gave Eshkol a report on the investigation. Minister of Justice Shapira demanded a more detailed report. In the afternoon, the issue was raised in the security cabinet. Yitzhak Rabin told the ministers that under the rules of engagement, soldiers were to open fire on people trying to cross the Jordan at night, unless they identified them as women or children. In daytime, the soldiers were to shout a warning, and if the suspect did not stop, they were to fire shots in the air. In the three months since the war, Rabin said, 146 people had been killed trying to cross the Jordan, including two women and four children. Fourteen had been wounded. Just over a thousand had been arrested and deported back to Jordan. Minister Kol suggested installing lighting. Minister Eban proposed instructing the soldiers to shoot to wound, not to kill.

A report contained in the IDF archives adds details: every night the army positioned fifty ambush parties along the Jordan River. In the three months after the war, there were ninety-five encounters. Some of the detainees were Fatah members, but most were refugees trying to get back home. Two of those wounded were children. According to Israel Lior, Eshkol demanded an end to the killings, but Rabin insisted that the rules of engagement remain unchanged. Dayan added, "It's not that bad." He assumed that by winter there would be fewer refugees trying to get back, and thus fewer casualties. Eshkol asked to be kept informed.[47]

The plight of the refugees was a photogenic subject. Israeli ambassadors overseas wrote to Jerusalem that television broadcasts from the bridges and the tent camps set up by the UN on the eastern side of the river were damning. They reported on pictures of Israeli soldiers firing shots in the air to hurry the refugees over the bridges. Correspondents estimated that the new tent camps housed some eighty thousand refugees from Gaza and the West Bank. Winter was coming, threatening to make their conditions intolerable. "The most terrible impression is made by scenes of fathers with children in their arms, begging our guards to let them go back to their wives and children still on our side," wrote Israel's ambassador in Germany. He added, "We cannot stand up, here or in other countries, to the wave of protest, which we believe will also have political implications." He asked that Israel at least permit family reunifications. The ambassadors were right: the ugly images in the media led many governments, including the United States, to demand that Israel allow the refugees to return.[48]

Attempting to improve its image, the Israeli cabinet agreed to help not only the residents of Kalkilya, but also those of two villages in the Hebron area.* Eshkol gave orders to explain to British prime minister Harold Wilson that the reporters were misconstruing the scenes: the people they were photographing had left their homes willingly. As was the usual custom, he also cited the Holocaust. "No people," he told the vice president of the International Red Cross, "that, like ours, saw six million of its old and young butchered and burnt by the Nazis less than a generation ago, could be unresponsive to any humanitarian interest." He pledged one million liras to the UN to finance tent camps for the "new refugees."[50]

It was not enough, and the ministers knew it. Abba Eban was shocked by scenes he saw on television during a visit to New York, and told Eshkol to immediately arrange for a televised return of refugees. The ministers received a copy of an extremely blunt letter published in the *Times* of London by a member of Parliament, Margaret McKay.[51†] In July, the government gave in and grudgingly decided to allow a few thousand people to return for a limited time. They were carefully selected, with the purpose of preventing the return of 1948 refugees. Ruth Wolf, from the Foreign Ministry, believed, conversely, that it was these refugees who should be preferred, because their economic situation was better thanks to financial support from the UN. "Furthermore, I recommend paying attention to the demographics—not only the number of children, but also the prospects for future births in terms of the women's age," she wrote. Her advice on deterring people who wanted to return: "Make sure there are suitable broadcasts on Kol Israel in Arabic about the insecurity of funds transfers from overseas, and the meticulous searches; also, do not conceal the current economic hardships." The Jordanians caused their own share of difficulties by refusing to allow refugees to sign up for their return on

*The villages, Beit Awa and Beit Mirsim, near Hebron, became a focus of attention by Swedish charitable organizations, perhaps because the Swedish consul in Jerusalem was one of the first to discover their destruction. Israel tried to prevent the Swedes from rebuilding the villages, lest it appear that the refugees needed the beneficent world to protect them from Israel's acts of malice. Dayan suggested telling the Swedish ambassador to worry about Swedish affairs.[49]
†In order to pacify the refugees and improve the ugly impression left on foreign visitors, a Foreign Ministry official suggested setting up toilets and benches in the shade, "so farewells will not have to be made in the middle of the road."[52]

forms bearing the seal of the State of Israel. While the two countries quar-
reled, summer was drawing to an end. Eventually, Israel permitted a larger
number of refugees to return.

This was Operation Refugee, and it was well publicized. The poet Haim
Gouri was among those who went to the Allenby Bridge to watch the
refugees return. "Women wearing black clothes walk by, carrying children
who doze in the sun while flies buzz around them. A porter walks by with
a huge pile of blankets and mattresses on his back. A woman with copper
pots. A young man carrying a suitcase. And again the porters, dragging
household goods and linens, and someone carrying a Singer sewing machine and a Primus stove, a handkerchief wrapped around pitas and
onions. . . . An elderly hajji with a distant look seems to come from ancient pictures of the Palestine that died long ago."[53] The initial intent was
to allow twenty thousand people to return, but by the time the operation
was over only fourteen thousand had managed to do so.[54]

And so Israel missed the great opportunity offered by the victory in
the Six-Day War to heal the malignant wound, as Ezer Weizman called it,
left by the War of Independence. This was the "refugee blunder," Weizman argued many years later, "a painful and damaging blunder, perhaps
no less so than the intelligence and military blunders committed prior to
the Yom Kippur War."[55] It is hard to explain. In the course of less than
two decades, the 600,000 Jews living in Israel at its inception took in
more than a million new immigrants. They built hundreds of new communities, including cities, all within the confines of the Green Line. The
refugees could have been rehabilitated as well.

There were several alternatives, and there were adequate plans to settle
the refugees in Gaza and in the West Bank. Their rehabilitation would not
have required allowing them to return to their homes in Israel. Nor would it
have necessitated a decision on the future of the territories—whether withdrawal or annexation. The millionaires who offered to finance the rehabilitation were only waiting for the call. And it was an undertaking that could
have offered something for everyone: national interest, humanitarian decency, Jewish solidarity, economic and social momentum, and international prestige; Zionist history would have seemed that much more noble.

But Eshkol, Dayan, and the other partners in the blunder believed there
was no reason to hurry. Lacking vision, courage, and compassion, capti-
vated by the hallucinations of victory, they never accepted Israel's role in
the Palestinian tragedy, or perhaps they simply did not have the courage to
admit it; this was probably the main inhibition. And perhaps they truly believed that one day they would succeed in getting rid of them.

CHAPTER 22

HAWKS AND DOVES

1. WORDS I: "A SIN AND A CRIME"

One of the topics discussed at Rabin and Dayan's regular weekly meeting after the war was recorded in the minutes as "events in the occupied territories." In a revised version of the document, the word "occupied" was crossed out and replaced with "liberated." Rabin and Dayan frequently referred to both "occupied territories" and "liberated territories," but the minutes may have reflected the worldviews of different note-takers. While "occupation" was considered negative and temporary, "liberation" was a positive state, worthy of permanence.[1] The military advocate general, Meir Shamgar, who prepared the legal infrastructure for the military government, suggested "administered territories" as a compromise. This artificial construct served official needs adequately, but the press used it with scare quotes at first, as did Moshe Dayan.[2]

These linguistic fluctuations reflected more than mere political disagreement; there was a genuine difficulty in adapting to the situation the war had created. Soldiers serving in the territories on their way home for leave said they were going "to Israel," implying that the territories were in a foreign country and that "Israel" referred exclusively to the state, not "the land"—Eretz Israel. At least one soldier from Yehiam described his return from the West Bank as a return to Eretz Israel.[3]

On June 11, *Yediot Aharonot* published a declaration that declared, "No part of our land that has been liberated shall be returned." *Maariv* described a visit Eshkol made to some wounded soldiers; the story's headline was " 'Do Not Leave!' Called the Wounded." One general order issued by

General Uzi Narkis read, "You did not go to battle in vain. . . . The land is large and whole, my soldiers, because the land is yours."[4] This was the prevalent view in the General Staff.

The IDF generals held that relations between Israel and the Arabs were unchanged: the Arabs had not given up their desire to destroy Israel. The territories improved Israel's strategic position and should therefore not be relinquished, at least as long as there was no peace with Egypt. The General Staff ruled out a separate peace with Hussein and thought it was better to reach a settlement with the Palestinians. They explained their position to Eshkol.

Yitzhak Rabin, soon to become Israel's ambassador to the United States, supported founding a Palestinian state that would be "connected to Israel"—namely, one that would enable Israel to make the Jordan River its security border. Eshkol asked, with little enthusiasm, if the new state would have an army. Rabin said it would have a police force but no army. "Who decides that?" asked Eshkol. "We do," Rabin replied. Eshkol was not convinced, and Rabin admitted, "We're not saying it's an ideal solution. The question is what would be worse."

Haim Bar-Lev, who had replaced Rabin as IDF chief of staff, recognized that the situation might change. Unlike the other generals, he supported a treaty with Hussein. But he also agreed that under the present circumstances, the balance of forces should not be altered. Narkis proposed counting the Israeli-Arab conflict among those world problems that had no solution. Besides recommending that Eshkol maintain the current state of affairs, the generals also thought it possible that the Palestinians would emigrate, flee, or be deported over the years. Gavish pointed out that 400,000 Palestinians had left the West Bank in the past two decades; his colleagues reminded him that this figure included the 200,000 who had left in the most recent war. Gavish said there was no telling what would happen in the next one.

Haim Bar-Lev cautiously said, "There may be a war that we do not want, but it will be imposed upon us, and it will offer another solution of sorts, the way some four hundred thousand Arabs left the territories during this war." The generals assured Eshkol he was under no obligation to grant the inhabitants of the territories citizenship or the right to vote for members of the Knesset.[5]

The generals were speaking not only in response to victory: the continued occupation was supposed to prevent the next threat of annihilation. The anxiety that had gripped so many Israelis before the war now served as an argument against withdrawing from the territories. Two days after the war was over, Narkis was still describing Nasser as an "Egyptian Hitler" and calling him "the Führer of Cairo." He said that the IDF had to remind Nasser "what became of Hitler." Similar sentiments appeared in countless newspaper articles and books. Golda Meir wrote, "We resolved that there would be no return to Hitler's Final Solution; there would be no second Holocaust."[6] A group of prominent writers published a proclamation "for a Greater Israel." They included some of the luminaries of Israeli literature: S. Y. Agnon, Natan Alterman, Uri Zvi Greenberg, Haim Gouri, Moshe Shamir, and Haim Hazaz, among others. As befits people who live by the pen, they invested a great deal of thought in every word, during lengthy discussions held mostly in such well-known Tel Aviv cafés as Herli, Kassit, and Roval.

The opening of the proclamation was misleading—or deceitful. "The IDF victory has positioned the nation and the state in a new era. Greater Eretz Israel is now in the hands of the Jewish people." This was untrue: the territories occupied by the IDF in the Six-Day War did not encompass all of biblical Palestine—and the State of Israel was not "the Jewish people." The announcement went on to position the territories as equal to the state itself: "Just as we have no right to give up the State of Israel, so we are commanded to realize what it has given us: the Land of Israel." The verb "commanded" implied an almost religious obligation, a vow of sorts, and then came the decisive declaration: "We are bound to loyalty to the integrity of our land—to the past and to the future, and no government in Israel has the right to give up this integrity." Here the authors seemed to sever the occupation from political reality, as well as to wrest it from democratically made decisions. The signatories made an effort to position themselves at the center of Zionist ideology. The inhabitants of the territories, they wrote, would enjoy freedom and equality; the Jewish majority in Israel would be preserved thanks to immigration and settlement.

The declaration was also signed by a few former senior officers, academics, and other public figures. Unlike the writers, they were not renowned personalities, but together with them they constituted a pressure group that could not be ignored. This collaboration between figures formerly identified with the left, including various labor movement members such as Natan Alterman, and the left's detractors, among them Uri Zvi Greenberg, showed the extent to which the terms "left" and "right" had lost their original meanings. This same point had been illustrated by the establishment of a national coalition government on the eve of the war.[7]

The primary political distinction was no longer between a socialist "left" and a capitalist "right," but between "doves" and "hawks." The argument between them was conducted, as always, in the Knesset and on the editorial pages, but the central role now assigned to writers and academics deepened the sense that there was no need for an immediate decision, as if the war had mainly raised questions concerning Israeli society's fundamental values.[8]

"I must reformulate the conventions of identity and identification, because there has been a major earthquake, an erosion of words and meanings," wrote Amos Oz. " 'Judaism,' 'Zionism,' 'homeland,' 'national right,' 'peace.' These words are being drawn into new realms and taking on new meanings that we had not previously imagined." The phenomenon was widely prevalent. Many people described the occupation of the territories as part of a "miracle." Levi Eshkol said, "What the army has done up to now is a miracle on top of a miracle."[9]

The feeling was genuine, devoid of political identification, and it gave the victory a religious dimension. "The great miracle that has occurred astonishes us all. We were certain of destruction, and now everything has changed and we are the victors," wrote a Tel Aviv woman to her sister in Boston. "A miracle for the entire people, and a private miracle for almost every person, wherever they are," wrote a woman from Kibbutz Tirat Zvi to friends in Los Angeles. "A great miracle has occurred here," wrote the elderly philosopher Schmuel Hugo Bergman, echoing the traditional description of the Hanukah miracle. "God has saved our little country," he added.[10]

A number of rabbis added their voices. Most of them, including Sephardic chief rabbi Yitzhak Nissim, objected to any territorial withdrawal, and not only from sites holy to Orthodox Jews, such as the Temple Mount and the Western Wall. "No one from Israel, including the government of Israel, has the right to give back an iota of land from the land of Israel which we hold," wrote Nissim, implying that this was primarily a question of faith, not of politics or security.[11]

One of the most vocal and visible advocates of the imperative to hold on to the territories was Shlomo Goren, the chief rabbi of the IDF, and the man identified more than any other with the conviction that the Occupation embodied divine will was Rabbi Zvi Yehuda Kook, from the Mercaz Harav yeshiva in Jerusalem. Equipped with his shofar and military rank, Rabbi Goren traveled the territories sharing with soldiers his belief that the State of Israel existed thanks to an unshakable divine mandate and that the IDF was implementing the prophets' predictions for the end of days.

"The divine spirit, which has never left the Western Wall, now walks before the armies of Israel in a pillar of fire to light our way to victory," he said when he reached the wall with the first of the soldiers. Over the next weeks he blew his shofar all over the country, from Mount Sinai in the south to Mount Hermon in the north. On August 10, Goren came to the Temple Mount and found the gates blocked. He and a group of soldiers began to break the gates down so they could enter and pray, thus reoccupying the compound from the Muslims.

From the moment Moshe Dayan had been wise enough to order the removal of the Israeli flag from the Dome of the Rock, immediately after the occupation, Israel had in fact conceded the Temple Mount to Muslims. The chief rabbinate ruled that Jews were not permitted to go to the mount lest they accidentally desecrate the site where the Temple had stood, which would be a sin. The government decided that Jews who tried to pray there would be told to move to the Kotel square. The ministerial committee in charge of maintaining holy sites asked Dayan to instruct Goren, through Rabin, to stop trying to take control of the Temple Mount, so as to avoid involving the IDF in a religious conflict.

Rabbi Kook was less theatrical than Goren, but he too forbade the division of the land: "It is a sin and a crime to deliver our lands to gentiles." Kook had opposed partition of the land as early as the 1940s, for reasons of both nationalism and theology. He assigned religious significance to the state, which he viewed as a stage in the mystical process from destruction to redemption. The seizure of the territories, in this view, was also sanctified: "This is the determination of divine politics, which no earthly politics can rival." He did not represent all of Orthodox thinking, but he did have a profound influence on a generation of young religious Israelis, and they played a central part in the struggle against withdrawal.[12]

THE POSITION ADVOCATED BY THE MILITARY, THE WRITERS ADVOCATING A GREATER IS-rael, and the rabbis presented itself as an absolute truth. The powerful messianic emotion turned to a sweeping torrent of patriotism and religious fervor, and the voice of the faithful reverberated as the voice of true Zionism. At the Herut party congress in East Jerusalem, convened on the first anniversary of the war, Menachem Begin presented a "declaration of the rights of the Jewish People" formulated as if it were intended to replace the Declaration of Independence.[13]

The doves found such fervor difficult to contend with. Most of them merely cautioned against "annexation."

2. WORDS II: "NOT AT ANY PRICE"

A number of poets and writers came out against annexation of the territories, including Dalia Ravikovitch, Natan Zach, and Yizhar Smilansky.
But when they opposed "annexation," they were in essence mirroring the
government's stance. Some writers who were identified with the labor
movement, such as Amos Oz, made explicit statements in support of
Eshkol, maintaining that there should be no withdrawal without peace.
Only a handful of people endorsed withdrawal from all the territories, including Gaza and East Jerusalem, and their position deviated from the
Zionist consensus to which most doves subscribed.* They argued frequently with one another, and at times it seemed they doubted their own
declarations.[14]

Eshkol spoke often about the future of the territories too. His style was
light-years away from Dayan's: less arrogant, not as blunt, and tormented
with doubts, he tended to think out loud, which often made him sound
hesitant. Dayan never shared the rough drafts of his ideas with anyone; as
a result, he always sounded as if he knew exactly what he wanted, even
though he frequently contradicted himself. In a conversation with a
group of IDF generals, Eshkol left no doubt about what he wanted: a large
country with no Arabs in it. But, as he had often done in the past, he projected a sense that Israel was trapped by historical factors and processes
over which it had no control.[16]

Eshkol's aspirations in fact showed how similar he and Dayan were. The
"Arab issue" was no closer to Dayan's heart than it was to Eshkol's. Both
men believed that Israel should keep East Jerusalem, parts of the West
Bank, Gaza, and a few other points on the map of occupation. Countless
discussions on the future of the territories revolved primarily around what
should be done and said so as to maintain the current situation. Instead of
looking for a solution to the conflict, they administered it. The long-term
effects of occupation on Israel's status as a Jewish and democratic state
troubled Eshkol more than they did Dayan; this was almost the only difference between the two. Everything else was ego and politics.

The tension between the two men was rooted in Eshkol's ouster
from the Defense Ministry, a defeat from which he had never recovered.

---

*Abie Nathan visited the West Bank soon after the war and handed out food and candy to
forty thousand local children. In July, he made another failed attempt to fly to see Nasser. In
December, the Israeli consul in New York reported with some disgust that Nathan was planning to start a seagoing radio station to promote peace.[15]

Associates observed that as time went by, his pain only deepened. He had trouble living with the fact that Dayan was appropriating the glory of victory, while he remained in the shadows.* Attempting to resolve the situation, Israel Lior asked a few colleagues to clarify Dayan's true role in the victory. Rabin, Aharon Yariv, and Dayan's bureau chief, Rafi Efrat, replied with extreme caution that Dayan had contributed significantly to the decision to go to war. His membership in the government had accelerated the decision making. His involvement had inspired confidence and faith: he had helped lift morale.[18] Golda Meir later wrote that she found it difficult to believe that the war would have ended in any other way even if Dayan had not joined the government. If Dayan was such a clear choice for minister of defense, she wondered, why had Ben-Gurion never given him the job?

The rivalry between Dayan and Eshkol affected almost every political and military issue, including the nuclear project and talks with Arabs in the territories, with Jordan and Egypt, and with the United States. In one incident, Dayan gave orders concerning the Dimona project, and only afterward instructed that Eshkol be asked whether he had any objections. For Eshkol and his people, this was reminiscent of the way Dayan had decided to occupy the Golan. Eshkol did not want Dayan to meet with U.S. secretary of defense Robert McNamara, mainly because of how much the latter admired Dayan. President Johnson also wanted to see Dayan, but he told Ambassador Harman he did not know how to do so without offending Eshkol.[19]

Dayan complained that Eshkol treated him "with suspicion and envy," and claimed that every meeting with him caused emotional distress. He thought Eshkol was trying to prevent him from handling the Arab population in the territories. Pinhas Sapir was also interfering, according to Dayan. He believed that neither man was capable of handling the Arabs: "As was true of most of the old-time leaders, their views on the Arabs had evolved not as a result of direct and continuous contact with them, but through debates and exchanges of opinions among themselves. The truth is that the Arab issue was alien to them and not close to their hearts."[20] This was the voice of an Israeli generation that thought in Hebrew

---

*Shortly before Eshkol gave his victory speech in the Knesset, Yaacov Herzog's diplomatic skills were called upon to convince him to acknowledge Moshe Dayan. Grudgingly, Eshkol finally consented to mention "the minister of defense." Herzog then noticed someone else who had been left out of the speech: God. He quickly inserted Him: "And thanks to the Rock of Israel and the redeemer, Israel shall dwell securely." The term "Rock of Israel"—one of the biblical appellations of God—appears in the Declaration of Independence.[17]

and scorned the founding generation, which thought in Yiddish. It also perceived control of the territories as a locus of political power—another good reason not to relinquish them.

Yaacov Herzog observed that Dayan's position changed over time. Immediately after the war, he tended to think about the territories in terms of security. As time went by, his spiritual affinity with them deepened; Herzog once heard him say, "As far as Zionism is concerned, I am a religious Jew." In August, Herzog wrote, "I believe that the minister of defense is gradually beginning to shape the state of things in the West Bank according to his own basic policies. This development results not only from his personality and status, but also from the fact that he brings clear proposals and at the same time shows both firmness and flexibility."[21] Polls asking Israelis about their choice for prime minister showed that between 43 and 47 percent wanted Eshkol, 17 to 19 percent Dayan, 13 to 14 percent Ben-Gurion.[22] None of the cabinet ministers were pressed to explain why they had not prevented the war or the Occupation; the question was only who had done more for the victory. The desire to keep the territories was equated with patriotism. Dayan was criticized, but only because he had not immediately supported the occupation of Gaza, the canal, Jenin, the Old City, and the Golan Heights.* The competition for fame was played out in a number of books about the war, some of which were clearly intended to exalt or embarrass certain ministers and based on information leaked accordingly. One minister complained about the leaks; the IDF decided not to cooperate with writers.[24]

THE MINISTERS SQUABBLED FREQUENTLY OVER THE FUTURE OF THE TERRITORIES. GOVernment discussions mirrored public opinion, and often reached a high pitch. Herzog described a meeting during which Begin stood up in great excitement and began to orate as if he were at a public square. "Will we be the ones to divide the land of Israel for the first time since the destruction [of the Second Temple]?" He added, "I admit I am a sentimentalist. It was sentiment that brought me here." Minister Aran replied that he had also come to Palestine because of a sentiment: the promise of a safe haven for the Jewish people in a Jewish state. "A state with forty percent Arabs is not a Jewish state! It is the ultimate fifth column! The kiss of death in twenty or thirty years." Begin claimed he "dreamed of negotiations for

---

*Most lower-educated Israelis believed that Dayan's was the glory of victory, while the better educated thought Rabin was the true hero.[23]

peace" and spoke of the possibility of an "economic union" with Jordan, but argued, "We must move not one inch from the Jordan." He said this was also a security imperative and demanded that the General Staff be brought before the ministers to answer one question: was there a line to the west of the Jordan that could assure the security of Israel?[25]

AMBASSADOR WALWORTH BARBOUR TRIED TO IMPRESS UPON THE STATE DEPARTMENT how difficult he found it to determine who was a dove and who was a hawk, even in the Knesset. It took him eleven pages to classify the cabinet ministers, and he concluded that approximately half were doves and half were hawks. The ambassador's difficulty resulted primarily from the fact that even the doves were unwilling to give up East Jerusalem Gaza, or other territories. And so their underlying rationale—whether nationalist, religious, or pragmatic—was of no great significance. The ambassador described Eshkol as "a mild hawk."[26]

Immediately following the war, almost six out of ten (Jewish) Israelis believed that some of the Occupied Territories could be given back within the framework of a peace agreement. Only one in three thought all the territories should be annexed. But when asked which territories they thought should be returned, even as part of a peace agreement, nine out of ten replied that the Old City should not be given back; 85 percent said the Golan Heights should not be returned; 73 percent thought the Gaza Strip should not be relinquished; 71 percent said the West Bank should not be given back; and the same number also said that Sharm el-Sheikh should not be returned. A smaller minority, 52 percent, said the Sinai Peninsula should not be given back, either.

The survey indicated a correlation between the respondents' level of education and their opinions: the more highly educated the respondent (which also meant the more Ashkenazi), the more likely he or she was to support dovish positions. Women took more hawkish positions than men: 40 percent of all housewives supported annexation. Other surveys gave varying results, but the trend was identical in all of them: no significant portion of the territories should be returned, even for peace.[27]*

Everyone agreed that Israel should strive for peace, but they also agreed with Yitzhak Rabin when he declared, "Not peace at any price."

---

*Only 14 percent of Jewish Israelis supported a proposal to establish an independent Arab state in the territories, with ties to Israel.

This was the headline *Ha'aretz* had used eight days after the war, above a letter from the poet Yitzhak Shalev; according to the paper, dozens of letters arrived expressing similar sentiments.[28]

Still arguing over the future of the territories, nine out of every ten Israelis believed that the Arab states were not yet ready for true peace, which absolved Israel from having to make any decisions. Letters abroad reflected a sincere hope for peace without withdrawal. "We must take more and more trips to the territories, and observe and enjoy and hope that we will never give them up, that we'll never have to go to war again," wrote one woman; "perhaps the dream of peace will come true." Meanwhile, almost everyone agreed that the current situation was preferable. Returning to the prewar situation would be a "horrifying disaster," said Eshkol.[29]

CHAPTER 23

STARTING OVER

1. ISRAELIS II: "WHAT A WONDERFUL NATION"

Israelis seemed to rediscover themselves after the war; and the country, on the face of things, was changed. "What a wonderful nation we have," one Israeli wrote to relatives in Boston. Abba Eban declared in the Knesset, "In six days of action, a new State of Israel was created." The general sense was that life after the war was better than it had been before. Many people attributed the sudden reversal in circumstances to the victory—and victory, in turn, was associated with the newly occupied territories.*

Everyone now praised the young—a most striking illustration of the reversal in mood. "The papers constantly write about the golden youth from Dizengoff who fought heroically," wrote a Tel Aviv woman to Los Angeles.[2] "We were wrong to denounce our young people, because they exceeded all expectations," wrote one newspaper.†

Six weeks after the war, *Maariv* reported a sharp decrease in unemployment, and several weeks later the government heard the same information from Pinhas Sapir.[4] Within three months after the war, more than four thousand sales contracts for newly built apartments were signed, almost four times as many as in the three months before the war. Over the

---

*As the growing wave of patriotism engulfed Israel, a few *Ha'aretz* readers asked Hana Bavli whether it was permissible to beat their rugs over a balcony flying the Israeli flag. Bavli responded that it was not: the national flag deserved supreme respect. Likewise, laundry should be hung to dry elsewhere.[1]
†The war brought about a change in school curricula: seventh-graders began learning about the territories in an extra hour of civics.[3]

next three months, just under five thousand more contracts were signed.[5] These transactions were incomplete, and were not sufficient to bring the construction industry out of its crisis, but they reflected a dramatic change in the mood of Israelis: for the first time in many months, they had faith in the future of Israel, and much as the recession had been rooted to a great extent in the gloom preceding the war, the economic situation was now affected by the heady feeling of victory.

Pinhas Sapir estimated that the war had cost Israel $1 billion; fortunately, a large portion would be recouped through foreign aid and donations. "Otherwise we'd be lost," Sapir told the government. Various estimates pegged the cost of the Occupation at between $50 million and $150 million a year. Sapir was concerned about the tens of millions Israel was about to spend on Phantom war planes. But the war also generated income. Oil production in the Sinai would bring in several million dollars. Victory brought foreign investors and promised flourishing tourism, including domestic tourism. The need to reequip the army stimulated defense manufacturing. The construction industry recovered, partly as a result of the building surge in Jerusalem. The inhabitants of the territories provided cheap labor and bought Israeli products.[6]

Sapir highlighted a new phenomenon that was becoming more prevalent: many Jews were no longer willing to work in construction and agriculture, because they were finding permanent work in factories. In some industries there began to be a shortage of skilled labor. Eshkol complained to IDF generals that Jewish women no longer wanted to work as maids: Arab women were cheaper and Jewish homes were flooded with them.[7] Many people also objected to Sapir's dovish positions, and clearly viewed the sudden prosperity as a result of the victory. They rediscovered the "good life," and America was once again the role model, as it had been before the recession.

The owner of an appliance store in Tel Aviv told a reporter that many soldiers returning from the war celebrated by buying gifts for their families. The man's next line illuminates the interplay between economics and psychology: "New bonds of affection have been forged, and this is clearly reflected in the increase in food processor sales." The birthrate in 1968 was higher than in the previous year.[8] All this reflected a new faith in Israel's ability to afford its people the good life, and, more important, a life that would improve year by year. Just like in America.

Victory also brought about the beginning of Israeli television programming. The Knesset was asked to approve the establishment of the General Television network for "emergency" needs, with the initial purpose of increasing control over the Arabs in the territories. The first broadcast showed the huge victory parade in Jerusalem. "This is a type of weapon," explained Israel Galili, the minister in charge of the Broadcasting Authority.[9] Most Israelis welcomed the programming enthusiastically: nothing was more American than TV. Television allowed Israelis to feel that they were breaking out of the insularity that had burdened the state before the war. Not only did Israelis control the territories, but also they increasingly felt that they were gaining control of their own daily lives. Telephone service improved; the papers began reporting the computer revolution and the increasing use of the birth control pill.[10]*

2. CHANGES: "PEOPLE GOT SO WORKED UP"

Before the war, most of the unemployed were Mizrahim, and now they were among the first Israelis to benefit and derive some hope from the victory. *Maariv* sent its senior reporter, Dov Goldstein, to revisit Amalia Ben-Harush, the woman from Kiryat Ata who had given birth to her twentieth son on Independence Day. He found five-month-old Israel doing nicely, but the father revealed that few of the promises that had been made before the war had been kept. Eshkol had sent a lovely telegram promising that a gift was on its way. Four months later, it had not arrived. Someone had promised a Frigidaire, but never brought it.

Goldstein's piece ran on the eve of Rosh Hashanah, and when he went back to see the family again ten days later, he could barely squeeze into the apartment because there were so many boxes of clothes, toys, books, and shoes. They had arrived from all over the country, by mail and special delivery—entire truckloads of packages. The neighborhood mail carrier had almost collapsed, Goldstein reported, after delivering hundreds of letters, many registered, some containing checks. Someone sent apples, which the Ben-Harush children had never seen before. And the man who had promised the refrigerator had shown up. A few regional municipal councils wrote and offered to provide the family with housing in their jurisdictions. The father, a public works laborer, needed a job, and received some offers. "People got so worked up, as if they didn't have anything else to worry about," Amalia Ben-Harush commented.[12]

---

*An advertisement for the grand opening of a new café in Tel Aviv, Bambi Milk Shake Bar, promised a bounty of delicacies, including waffles, pancakes, and milkshake specials—not a word was in Hebrew.[11] The official exchange rate was still three liras to the dollar, but in November it was revised to 3.5.

. . .

THE DAY AFTER THE WAR ENDED, *HA'ARETZ* HIGHLIGHTED THE ROLE OF MIZRAHI SOLDIERS in the victory and extolled the IDF's ability to integrate them into the military. "The IDF victories have proved that the numerous soldiers from the later immigrations fought well and integrated without friction within the units, where they encountered veteran Israelis." The paper added that preparations for the war "reinvigorated the IDF as an army in which all strata of the people play their part." Aharon Megged observed that the war had knocked down the barriers "between ethnicities, classes, and parties."[13]

This was not quite accurate. A book of life stories of fallen soldiers, published by the Ministry of Defense, rarely noted the ethnic origin of the deceased, but at least 60 percent were Ashkenazi, 15 percent more than their proportion of the population among their age group. At least 80 percent of officers killed were Ashkenazi.[14] Among recipients of commendations, not even 20 percent were Mizrahi.[15]

Many Israelis, in a manifestation of their prewar prejudices, claimed after the war that Mizrahi soldiers had shown vindictive hatred of the Arabs but had not excelled as fighters.[16] Herut's role in the victory government offered Mizrahim, for the first time, the hope of a true share in determining their own future and that of the entire country. But anxieties about their cultural influence had not disappeared. "The country is becoming more and more Levantine," wrote one Israeli from Holon to friends overseas.[17]

And so the war and the Occupation did not eradicate the gaps between Mizrahim and Ashkenazis. The Mizrahim were to remain disadvantaged for a long time, but the new situation offered an improvement in their relative status—for beneath the Israeli Arabs were now the Palestinians. Many Mizrahim entered managerial positions. They were often fluent in Arabic, and some employed their own Palestinian laborers. The recovery from the economic recession and the presence of the Palestinians also improved the relative welfare of Israeli Arabs. Like many of the Mizrahim, a large part of this population also shifted from menial work in agriculture and construction to skilled jobs, including white-collar posts. But like the Mizrahim, they also remained deprived: at the end of 1968 only 32 percent of Israeli Arabs belonged to the Histadrut health fund.[18]

The new encounter with the population of the territories did raise questions of identity and loyalty among Israeli Arabs, many of whom now rediscovered their Palestinian identity.[20] The war also deepened the identification between many Israeli Jews and Jews in other parts of the world.*

3. IDENTITY: "THIS IS WHAT THE PEOPLE NEED"

A study comparing aspects of Israeli high school students' identity a few years before and after the Six-Day War found notable changes. Following the war, 25 percent more Israeli teenagers declared, "The fact that I am Jewish fulfills a very important role in my life." There was an increase of 50 percent in the number of young people who said that the presence of Jews in Palestine in ancient times justified the establishment of the State of Israel. Twice as many respondents now agreed that "almost all non-Jews are anti-Semites." The study found significant discrepancies among students who defined themselves as religious, traditional, and nonreligious, but also found that the secular now gave more weight to their Jewish identity than they had formerly. Thirty percent more young people said they were more religious than their parents; among those who defined themselves as secular, only 2 percent had made the same statement before the war, while a few years afterward 5 percent did.[21]

AS TENSIONS ESCALATED BEFORE THE WAR, ISRAELI EMBASSIES ABROAD WERE FLOODED with requests from young professionals, mostly Jewish, who wanted to volunteer in Israel. It soon became evident that the supply exceeded the demand, and the Foreign Ministry scaled back its offer to finance flights for volunteers; it would now subsidize only Jews willing to spend at least four months in Israel (doctors would need to commit to a minimum of six weeks). Two days before the war, the volunteers were already becoming a nuisance, and on the third day of the war the embassies were asked to stop the flow: there was no further need for volunteers, Jewish or non-Jewish, doctors or other professionals.

It was not easy to get rid of them. One physician from Boston City Hospital wanted to set up a two-hundred-bed hospital in Israel. He said that he would bring fifty staff members, and that if Israel was not interested he would move his project to an Arab state, on humanitarian grounds. The

---

*Israel agreed to respond to a series of questions on the condition of Israeli Arabs presented by the UN emissary, Nils Gussing; Syria answered similar questions from Gussing about the conditions of its Jewish community.[19]

pressure kept up after the war, and the Foreign Ministry practically begged the volunteers to stop coming. Some ambassadors still tried to obtain authorizations for distinguished volunteers. The ambassador in Germany reported that Günter Grass wanted to bring a group to Israel, and urged the government to view this as a symbolic act of solidarity. From Abidjan, the ambassador reported that the daughter of the president of Ivory Coast had announced a visit; rejection of her offer would be a terrible insult.

More than 22,000 people signed up to volunteer before and during the war, and 7,500 arrived in the six months afterward. "They came on a rescue mission and were sent to pick plums," wrote *Ha'aretz*. Almost five thousand of them did work on kibbutzim, while more than a thousand served in civilian auxiliary corps operated by the army.[22] Although most of the volunteers served no real purpose and complained a lot, the volunteerism fed the atmosphere of elation. Israelis wrote about the phenomenon in their letters, often citing the Jewish awakening as one of the war's accomplishments. "Not only the State of Israel, but the People of Israel has been reborn," declared one Knesset member. "We are moved by the awakening of the Diaspora: we did not see the like even during the War of Independence." He believed this had occurred because Israel had finally managed to present young people with a challenge. Another speaker located this challenge in the sands of the Sinai, the rocks of the Golan, and the walls of Jerusalem—"our stolen land, which the IDF has restored to us." Victory appeared as a return to the early days of the first Zionist pioneers, including a renewal of mass immigration—the only chance to overcome the "demographic problem."

But the idea of settling the territories did not draw the Jews of the world to Israel. Everyone was aware that most of the volunteers would eventually go home. "I read beautiful letters from America, written by young men who had visited here," Eshkol told the generals. "They had a good time, soaked up enough sunshine for decades. Now they have calluses on their hands and stories to tell in America."[23] Eshkol encouraged suggestions of ways to increase immigration, and he received many ideas for boosting the Jewish birthrate. One citizen thought the issue should be handled by the Ministry of Defense. Another suggested giving aid only to families producing babies who could be identified as potential IDF soldiers. The government set up a "Demography Center," directed by Zina Harman, the wife of the ambassador, who had now returned to Israel.

The low birthrate, which had worried Israel even before the war, was now at the center of attention. The "Arab womb" continued to threaten the Zionist existence in Palestine.* However, the number of Jews who immigrated to Israel in 1968, more than thirty thousand, was 40 percent higher than the number who had come in either of the preceding two years.[25†] The new optimism was therefore not unfounded, and it suited the postwar sense of Jewish solidarity. The press and the Knesset often discussed the persecution of the few remaining Jews in Arab states, particularly Egypt, Syria, and Iraq. The Jews of Libya were allowed to leave. As in 1948 and 1956, Israel's interest was once again in conflict with that of Jews in the Arab world, but Israeli newspapers addressed the issue as if there were no difference between Jews and Israelis. Israel tried to help persecuted Jews, acting in concert with the United States and other countries, as well as through international organizations, including the UN and the International Committee of the Red Cross.[27] Activism on behalf of Soviet Jews was also reinvigorated; the new campaign employed the slogan "Let my people go."[28]

Israelis observed the effects of the victory on American Jews, who went through a vast spiritual awakening that was authentic and no less exciting than the one Israelis themselves had experienced, and in many cases even more profound.

Prime Minister Eshkol was inundated with letters of support and checks sent by Jews from the United States and other countries, some of them made out to him personally. The sixty largest totaled $450,000, but many people sent small amounts; one man sent Eshkol his entire life savings of $5,638.‡ A worldwide fund-raising drive held after the war raised some $287 million by the end of September, almost ten times the amount collected the previous year.[29]

"American Jews now understand that Nasser's war is not directed solely against the Jewish state, but against the Jewish people," wrote Elie Wiesel. Leon Uris contributed an essay, "The Third Temple," to one of the first published books of war photographs. In the autobiographical passages of his piece, Uris described the anti-Semitic harassment he had endured as a child in Norfolk, Virginia. His original name, he wrote, was Yerushalmi; his brother Yossi lived in Israel and was among the liberators of the Kotel. Uris explained that the essay belonged to what he saw as a sequel to the Bible, and he referred to it as the Book of Return. It included a short history of the Holocaust. At the end of the essay, God recognizes

---

*Walworth Barbour shared these demographic anxieties, once commenting that even if Israel gave fertility drugs to every woman, it could not outdo the Arab population explosion.[24]
†In 1969, there were forty thousand.[26]
‡Bank regulations required Eshkol to individually endorse every single check.

that the Jews have suffered enough and tells them to build a third Temple and dwell in their own land forever.[30]

James Michener wrote a letter of love and identification with Israel, in which he said he was working hard "to keep attitudes here from returning to an idea of a divided Jerusalem and a divided Palestine."[31] The *Washington Post* published the impressions of the prominent historian Barbara Tuchman after her visit to the recently captured Jerusalem. "It may have been something this nation needs: Proof to itself that submission is a thing of the past, that the ghetto is dead for good."[32]*

An age-old problem soon reemerged from the oblivion. One of the oldest and wealthiest of Jewish leaders, the oil magnate Jacob Blaustein, read that Eshkol had referred to the "Jewish nation." He quickly pulled out a letter he had once received from Ben-Gurion, in which the latter promised that Israel would not interfere in the lives of American Jews and did not pretend to speak for them. Blaustein contacted Ambassador Harman to explain that the term "Jewish nation" undermined his membership in the American nation. The ambassador hoped Blaustein would let the issue drop, but the elderly industrialist persisted. Harman suggested that Eshkol send Blaustein a conciliatory letter to the effect that there were no disagreements between them and the misunderstanding had probably resulted from translation problems. In Jerusalem, they took the matter seriously: Eshkol maintained that the prime minister of Israel could not take back, even by implication, his use of the expression "Jewish nation." He agreed to write to Blaustein that notice had been taken of his comments.[34]

A FEW MONTHS AFTER THE WAR, CHARLES DE GAULLE ISSUED AN EXTREMELY SHARP attack on the government of Israel. He demanded a withdrawal from the territories, an end to the conflict, mutual recognition between Israel and its neighbors, freedom of navigation, a solution to the refugee problem, and international rule in Jerusalem. This was enough to irritate most Israelis, but de Gaulle made matters worse by asserting that the State of Israel had been "implanted" in the Middle East under circumstances whose

---

*A Tucson, Arizona, man named Kenneth Trim argued with David Ben-Gurion over the question of how many Arabs an Israeli soldier equaled. Ben-Gurion thought it was five, but Trim replied that one Israeli soldier was worth twenty Arabs. Another American cabled Ben-Gurion with an idea: the United States would provide Israel with five hundred B-50 bombers; in return, Israel would "lend" it Moshe Dayan for six months, to help the war in Vietnam. "What should I tell him?" Ben-Gurion asked Dayan. A man named Erwin Moskowitz demanded that Israel immediately begin building settlements in the territories.[33]

justice was dubious, and by describing the Israelis as "self-confident and domineering." His words were interpreted as an attack on Jews. "One day, two or three generations from now," wrote Elie Wiesel, "they will mention Charles de Gaulle and say . . . he did a lot for his people, but he was an anti-Semite."[35] On the eve of the war, de Gaulle had demanded that Israel not fire the first shot. When the fighting began, France imposed an embargo on military supplies to Israel, including sales of Mirage planes.

The elderly general had a tendency to put on nationalist and Caesar-like airs, as if he represented a country on an equal international footing with the USSR and the United States. This was preposterous, but many Israelis looked on him with reverence and viewed France as important to Israel. Everyone knew that France had sold Israel the aircraft that won the war, and many people were aware of its role in advancing the Dimona project. So de Gaulle's statements stunned them and for many Israelis deepened their sense that the State of Israel, the Jewish people, and the territories were one.[36]

CHAPTER 24

ABSALOM DAYS

1. PROSPECTS: "KNOW WHAT TO SAY"

One day in October, a military government official left his office in Gaza for the Sinai Desert, in pursuit of a legend. Some Bedouins directed him to a lone palm tree, not far from Rafiah. When he dug beneath the tree, he found that it was growing out of the skeleton of a young man. These were the bones of Absalom Feinberg—or at least, that was what Israel decided to believe. Major Shlomo Ben-Elkana, a veteran police officer, was very familiar with the story of the handsome Zionist spy, who set off to help the British wrest Palestine from the Turks and disappeared in the desert in 1917. On the eve of the Six-Day War, nostalgia for Absalom had been an expression of despair and ennui. Now, the remains of "history's first son of Israel" symbolized the delusions of the Occupation and the settlement of the territories; the old bones seemed to reinforce the founding aphorism of Zionism: *If you will it, it is no legend.* Before Ben-Elkana's discovery, one could still cast doubts on the story passed down by the Bedouins from father to son, according to which the lone palm tree had sprouted from one of the dates in Feinberg's pocket after he was buried in the desert. But now the age of doubt was over: it was no legend.

The tale was intensely political. The underground Nili movement, to which Feinberg had belonged, had acted against the judgment of the Jewish community's leaders, and over the years this "activist" opposition came to serve as a symbol of national courage, patriotism, and the demand for quick action—in stark contrast to the realistic pragmatism and self-restraint that had caused the Eshkol government to delay the beginning of the war.

A few of Absalom Feinberg's relatives demanded that he be reburied beneath the same palm tree in the Sinai. "Absalom dreamed of the great Eretz Israel," said one of them. But other relatives, fearing that the grave would one day remain beyond Israel's borders, demanded a state military funeral at Mount Herzl in Jerusalem. Eshkol was not enthusiastic about this demand, but eventually acquiesced, just as he had agreed to bring Jabotinsky's remains to burial in Israel. *Yediot Aharonot* found that with the burial, the Nili ethos had earned the admiration of an entire people. Thousands attended the funeral; many were in tears, although they did not know whether of sorrow or joy.

Shaul Avigur wrote to Eshkol that the commotion surrounding Feinberg's funeral was excessive and unjustified "from an educational point of view"—by which he meant politically. As the man who had spearheaded efforts to bring Soviet Jews to Israel, Avigur was aware of the end of the country's Ashkenazi majority, and of the decline in the founding elite's status. Israel would soon be a different country, he knew, with different values, and so he cautioned his party against losing its monopoly over national symbols. His fears were warranted: with the establishment of the national unity government on the eve of the war, the labor movement began the countdown to its eventual loss of power, ten years and one war later.[1]

BEFORE THE FIRST ANNIVERSARY OF THE WAR, THE PRIME MINISTER'S OFFICE PUBLISHED another booklet in the series "Know What to Say," which included the following statement: "The fact is that until this day no Arab ruler has shown a willingness to reach a peace treaty with Israel."[2] This was not so: Nasser had offered at least a "nonbelligerency" agreement, and Hussein had offered a peace accord.

In early October 1967, Abba Eban spoke with Robert Anderson, an American friend of Nasser's who had gone to see the Egyptian president before the war in an attempt to prevent it. Eban was now asking Anderson to try to reach a peace agreement with Egypt. Eban would tell him only what he said in public appearances. Still, Anderson went to Egypt again, with the approval of Dean Rusk. President Johnson was also in the picture. Anderson spoke with Nasser and came home with exciting news: Nasser was willing to make peace with Israel, but his terms were far from what Israel was willing to accept. He would not agree to direct negotiations, on which Israel insisted: no Arab leader could hold direct negotiations with Israel and survive, he maintained, so mediation was necessary. Nasser would prefer that the superpowers impose a settlement and said that no Arab government would sign a separate peace with Israel. He demanded withdrawal from all the territories, including Gaza, and a solution to the refugee problem. He would agree to allow Israeli ships through the Suez Canal, although he could not ensure that some fanatic would not open fire on them, he added. He did not rule out, in principle, the demilitarization of certain territories.

White House documents show that Eban backed off from the initiative even before Anderson left for Egypt. The White House assumed that he had been discouraged from pursuing it in Jerusalem. Whatever the reason, Walt Rostow told the president that the endeavor was done: "I do fear the Israelis will overplay their hand, but then I don't live in the Middle East."[3]

TOWARD NOVEMBER, THE UN IN NEW YORK WAS THE CENTER OF A FRENZY OF TRANSATlantic activity. More and more draft proposals changed hands, the crafters of diplomatic language toiled over words and sentences in almost every capital in the world, and finally the diplomats were sent to battle over a single word: "the." The question was whether the Security Council would demand that Israel withdraw from "the territories" or merely from "territories." Two of the official UN languages, Russian and Chinese, do not use definite articles, but everyone was working in English, and they finally agreed on "territories." Only the Spanish-language document, for some reason, referred to "the territories."[4]*

United Nations Security Council Resolution 242, dated November 22, brought a Swedish diplomat to the Middle East. Gunnar Jarring shuttled back and forth, then eventually gave up. Israel had decided that as long as there was no peace, it would "fortify its position" in the territories. Instead of talking about the international border, it was now speaking of "secure and recognized boundaries." The decisions of June 19, which had proclaimed a willingness to withdraw from the Sinai and the Golan Heights in return for peace and demilitarization, had evaporated. For a while it seemed that no one knew what to do, and so no one did a thing. "The is-

---

*Eshkol followed the squabbles, and when he found a draft resolution that asserted that a country was not entitled to annex territories it had occupied in war, he wrote in the margins: "They added this line against us."[5]

sue of policy concerning the territories is so complex that I do not dare summarize it on paper," wrote one of Eshkol's assistants to Ambassador Harman. But as time went by, Israel's grip on the territories tightened.

SEVERAL STATESMEN AND A NUMBER OF PRIVATE INDIVIDUALS, FROM PRESIDENT TITO OF Yugoslavia to the elderly Field Marshal Viscount Montgomery, the hero of El Alamein, made efforts to broker settlements between Israel and Egypt.[6] An American attorney named James Birdsall, who represented a fertilizer company and was a friend of Arthur Krim, saw Nasser a few times, and in December he brought Johnson a personal letter from him, in which Nasser offered a state of nonbelligerency with Israel. The Americans were not enthusiastic about this unusual channel of communication, but Johnson did send Nasser a reply, and this was a step on the way to a renewal of the diplomatic relations that had been cut off because of the war.[7]

In June 1968, the Romanian foreign minister, George Macovescu, also tried to work out an agreement between Israel and Egypt. According to his report, Nasser had reiterated that he sincerely wanted to reach an agreement. However, he felt it could not be done in one leap, but only step by step. He offered Macovescu what he had proposed to Anderson months earlier: an Israeli withdrawal from all the territories, a solution to the refugee problem, Israeli shipping in the Suez Canal, and "nonbelligerency," all in one package based on a predetermined timeline. He added that he did not predicate negotiations on an immediate and unconditional withdrawal from the territories.

Eshkol told the Foreign Affairs and Defense Committee about the initiative, and shared the response he had given his Romanian visitor: Israel wanted a signed peace treaty, to be obtained through direct negotiations. He reiterated that it was unacceptable that the victor in a war forced upon it should have to kneel before the loser and plead with him to take back captured territories in return for verbal declarations. If Nasser felt he was under pressure, well, Eshkol, too, was under pressure: "Decades of pressure, the pressure of an attempt to destroy us, the pressure of the people in Israel and the Jewish people in the Diaspora, of whom we are only the vanguard."

At the end of August, the Arab foreign ministers convened in Khartoum, the capital of Sudan, and agreed upon three negations that were prominently publicized in Israel: no peace with Israel, no recognition of it, no negotiations with it. But at least one Arab leader disregarded his peers: King Hussein.[8]

• • •

ROUGHLY FIVE MONTHS AFTER THEIR PREVIOUS MEETING, YAACOV HERZOG MET WITH
King Hussein again, but this time it was mainly because neither of the two
could find any more excuses to offer the former British politician Julian
Amery. Amery, full of energy and a desire to help, kept on pressing; he did
not know that Herzog and Hussein were old acquaintances. The two were
finally forced to come to his home and pretend they had never met before.* Abba Eban arranged his own meeting with Hussein, through Julian
Amery's good offices. Before leaving, Eban consulted his colleagues in the
party. Golda Meir was afraid the king might say he was willing to sign a
peace treaty with Israel, which would put Israel in the uncomfortable position of having to acquiesce to all his demands. The other party members
were also filled with apprehension and suspicions.[10]†

Eban's meeting with Hussein was held in London and lasted three
hours. For the first time, the king was accompanied by Zaid Rifai, his chief
of the Diwan, as well as by his chief of staff. Eban came with Haim Bar-
Lev. The generals met separately. In response to Eban's question, Hussein
said he did not rule out a separate peace with Israel. He wanted to know
what Israel was offering. Eban replied that this had not yet been decided,
but explained the various viewpoints: some held that the West Bank
should be annexed; some preferred to establish a Palestinian state; and
others wanted peace with Jordan but stipulated various conditions, including "not insignificant border amendments" in the Jordan Valley and
elsewhere, as well as demilitarization of territories; Israel would not give
up control over Arab Jerusalem.

Hussein replied that there was a basis for talks, and proposed holding
them in New York, under the auspices of Gunnar Jarring. A few hours
later, Hussein heard from Cairo that Nasser did not believe the talks
would succeed, but did not object to them. In the interim, Eban asked
Hussein to take action against Fatah. Hussein, in turn, encouraged the
IDF to strike at the Palestinians, as long as they did not harm his own
army. Bar-Lev convinced his counterpart that this was impossible: if the
IDF responded, it would inevitably hit the Jordanian army too.

Hussein was punctilious about maintaining royal etiquette, Eban told

---

*Amery thought he was making history until Hussein made a slip of the tongue, asking Herzog
when he had stopped smoking, at which point Amery realized he had been duped.[9]
†Eshkol once voiced a similar fear: "I'm afraid of the day the Arabs say, 'You want direct negotiations? Fine!' "[11]

his colleagues. "The proper way to address him is 'Your Majesty,'" he recounted with amazement, as if Hussein were not a real king. It was the first meeting of its kind, he said proudly, ignoring the many meetings held with Herzog.

There are several accounts of the meeting. Herzog found that Hussein was more restrained than Rifai, who took more extreme positions. Herzog reported to the government about an argument he had with Rifai about Jerusalem. "There's nothing to be done about it," Herzog said, and his Jordanian counterpart replied, "That's what you think. That's not the way it is." The chief of Diwan maintained that it was not enough to fly a Jordanian flag on the Temple Mount. But he did offer Israel ownership of the Western Wall. He explained that Hussein could make any concession in the West Bank, but on Jerusalem he had to represent the entire Arab world. Herzog responded, "Sir, we stood before the entire world, we fought and we stood strong: do you imagine that we cannot stand up to you?" To which the Jordanian replied, "It will take as long as it takes, but we cannot live without Jerusalem." He told Herzog that participants in a discussion with Nasser had shed tears over the loss of Jerusalem. "Even those who had never visited Jerusalem could not bear the disgrace of losing the city," he said, and added, "If you insist on your position regarding Jerusalem, we will make no progress." Herzog responded in a similar vein. Abba Eban observed, on another occasion, "We have nothing to say, in fact."[12]*

ESHKOL TOLD HIS PARTY, "WE KNOW FROM VARIOUS SOURCES THAT HUSSEIN WOULD like to make peace with us. He would like to reach a settlement, and a settlement for him means nothing other than peace. If we were to offer him peace with honor, he would reach an agreement with us." The difficulty was no longer a fundamental one. "It is easiest to reach a settlement with Hussein," Eshkol added.[14] This was also Yaacov Herzog's view. He told Moshe Dayan that if Mapam controlled the government—that is, if the doves in Israel had a majority—Israel could make peace with Hussein. Herzog, always the diplomat, had a professional view of the matter: "There is an objective gap between the minimum we can agree to and the minimum C[harles] can agree to." Dayan himself surmised that the Arabs

*The CIA director, Richard Helms, reported on the meeting to President Johnson. Over the next months, other Israelis met with Hussein, including Chief of Staff Bar-Lev and Minister Yigal Allon. None offered Hussein an agreement he could accept.[13]

would only be willing to declare a state of nonbelligerency in return for an Israeli withdrawal to the Green Line. And so he concluded: "I am not aware of any plan that we can agree to and that the Arabs will accept."[15]

THE EFFORT ISRAEL INVESTED IN TALKS WITH HUSSEIN WAS INTENDED LARGELY TO CONvince the United States that it was genuinely trying to achieve peace. The fear in Jerusalem was that the Americans might force Israel to withdraw. In October, Johnson met with Eban, and made his view of the war very clear. He regretted that Israel had acted alone rather than heed his advice. He thought at the time that Israel had acted unwisely, and he still thought so.[16] Besides Skyhawk aircraft and other military equipment, the Israelis were hoping the United States would also sell them Phantom fighters, which were at the top of their shopping list. They therefore had to be extremely cautious. Washington was making angry noises, but as the months went by, the United States turned out not to be putting any real pressure on Israel.

2. FRIENDSHIP: "THIS MAKES NO GOOD DAMN SENSE AT ALL!"

In the weeks after the war, Israel had to handle the aftermath of the *Liberty* attack. The Israeli embassy in Washington reported that the White House and the State Department were both encouraging the "wicked insinuation" that had accompanied the affair—namely, the claim that Israel had intentionally attacked the ship. In an off-the-record press briefing, Johnson himself used the term "deliberate attack." *Newsweek* was planning to print an article suggesting that by inflating the affair the president meant to lessen his dependency on pro-Israel public opinion.

The Israeli embassy fought back. Harman and the embassy spokesman, Dan Patir, managed to tone down the *Newsweek* article: a question mark was added to the headline and a sidebar commentary was dropped. But their influence was not limitless, and the following week they were no longer able to halt *Newsweek*'s story.[17] Ephraim Evron believed that Secretary of State Rusk was trying to exploit the incident to create a bridge to Arab states. If he succeeded, the United States would have "free rein" to act on positions that would not be convenient for Israel. But the Israeli diplomat had suggested a means of restraining Johnson: "Alert him to the personal implications if the public finds out that he participated in spreading the story, which borders on blood libel." The embassy staff, Harman reported, were working via Ilan and Harari (Fortas and Ginsburg).

Justice Fortas spoke with the president and the public accusations were dropped, but Fortas said that a lawyer would have trouble defending Israel's denial. Harman believed that Fortas was basing his opinions on information obtained at the White House. Abe Feinberg also reported, on behalf of a source referred to in the embassy telegrams as "Hamlet," that the United States had evidence of an Israeli pilot continuing to attack the ship even after having verified its identity. Harman replied cautiously that there was a difference between accusing one pilot and publicly charging Israel. The ambassador wrote to the foreign minister that Israel was continuing to defend itself against the charges, but that "Menashe," Arthur Goldberg, had suggested to Harman that he be very careful because Johnson was extremely angry. Goldberg also revealed to the ambassador that the Americans had managed to record the Israeli pilots during the attack, and the recordings proved that they knew their target was an American vessel. Goldberg told Harman there was only one way out of the crisis: Israel had to put someone on trial.[18]

THE CHIEF OF STAFF APPOINTED COLONEL RAM RON TO INVESTIGATE THE INCIDENT. Within four days, he produced a report concluding that the *Liberty* had been attacked as a result of a series of errors, each of which seemed reasonable under the circumstances. The ship had been identified in the morning hours, but when the pilots shot at it later they did not realize their target was the same ship. Ron also reprimanded the Americans: "One must emphasize the contributory negligence of the *Liberty* itself, by sailing in that location at a time of war, without notification or identification."[19]

This looked like a cover-up, and Harman immediately demanded another investigation. The appointment of a single investigator for an incident that had caused the deaths of thirty-four people would only arouse anger, he wrote. Colonel Ron was well-known in Washington, he added, and people were aware that he was not an expert on air force or naval matters. There was no chance that the president and the families of those killed would be satisfied with his report. Harman sent Jerusalem a detailed analysis of the report, exposing its defects and contradictions: "Even a superficial analysis of Ron's findings provides a basis to assume that several parties acted negligently and recklessly," he wrote. He particularly criticized Ron's failure to consider the material the Americans had provided to Israel. Ephraim Evron cabled Walt Rostow's response: "This makes no good damn sense at all!"

The affair would not go away. "The issue has become an open wound with the potential to cause severe harm on all levels, including the president, the Pentagon, public opinion, and the intelligence community," cautioned the ambassador. The next day he wrote, "I cannot overstate the explosiveness of this matter." He demanded immediate notice, that same day, that official charges had been brought. "This is the only way to make clear, both to the U.S. government and to the public, that the attack on the ship was not the result of malicious intent or carried out by authorized parties in the IDF."

The recently sanctified IDF agreed only to appoint an investigating judge, Lieutenant Colonel Yeshayahu Yerushalmi. Harman demanded that his investigation lead to indictments for negligence and recklessness. Rabin protested these attempts to dictate the results of an investigation. "Would you or your American counterparts imagine that in the United States the administration would try to influence the work of a Supreme Court justice?" he wrote.

Weeks went by. The ambassador pressed; the military said the investigation would take time. Yerushalmi summarized his findings at the end of July: "There appears to be insufficient evidence justifying charges against any person." He emphasized that the mistakes that had led to the *Liberty* attack were reasonable at a time of war, though it was conceivable that during peace he would have applied an entirely different standard of reasonable conduct. He added that his investigation materials might be helpful for the future.[20]

The Americans were not satisfied. The State Department said the report pointed to "terrible and culpable negligence." Evron himself thought the report indicated recklessness: "I do not think this behavior is appropriate conduct for a well-organized army like ours." But the Foreign Ministry in Jerusalem soon determined that the affair was "almost history," and only the question of compensation remained. Israel employed David Ginsburg's services again, this time as an attorney. A predictably tedious series of negotiations ensued, replete with emotional drama and mutual accusations. The victims' families demanded more money than Israel was willing to pay; the U.S. government demanded its share too. Over the next three years, Israel paid $6,889,957; roughly half the amount went to the victims' families.[21]*

---

*Ambassador Yitzhak Rabin sent Eshkol a detailed account: had the sailors been killed on active duty, the U.S. government would have had to pay their families compensation of $1,054,527. In negotiations with Israel, the families demanded additional compensation for their emotional distress: $1,240,000 for the parents, $540,000 for the wives and children, and $1,540,000 for loss of support and services.[22]

• • •

IN EARLY JANUARY 1968, LEVI ESHKOL CAME TO ASK LYNDON JOHNSON TO SUPPLY ISRAEL with fifty Phantom planes. The preparations for his visit reflected the special nature of relations between Israel and the United States. Ambassador Harman noticed that Johnson was scheduled to host Eshkol for lunch. "We must—particularly for reasons of prestige—seek a dinner invitation," he wrote, and went to look into the matter with President Johnson's adviser on Jewish affairs, Harry McPherson. The adviser told Harman that as a result of a visit from the king of Nepal, Johnson had instructed his staff not to burden him with dinners or excessively long meetings with foreign leaders. "Apparently the Nepalese king's visit was catastrophically boring and tried Johnson's patience to its limits," wrote the ambassador. Harman explained to McPherson that, with all due respect, Israel was no Nepal, and President Johnson's relationship with King Mahendra was not the same as his relationship with Eshkol. Clearly, Johnson himself should be interested in hosting a dinner, so that he could invite the Who's Who of American Jewry.

McPherson agreed, but said he would have to speak with the president himself. Harman also discussed the matter with Arthur Krim, now the treasurer of the Democratic Party, who for his own reasons promised to recommend a dinner. The ambassador believed that everything would work out. But the matter became so complicated that the Israelis resorted to their diplomatic code names, Issahar (Johnson) and Yehuda (Eshkol), and all correspondence was "top secret, eyes only." Issahar wanted to meet Yehuda in a way that would not make trouble for him with the Jewish public in America. Experience had shown that if he held a dinner for Yehuda, he would offend a lot of Jews who were not invited. After the dinner he had hosted for President Zalman Shazar, Issahar had declared he would never again hold a dinner for an Israeli, because he had made so many enemies among those not invited.

Ginsburg offered a possible solution that he had suggested to Johnson: the president would host Eshkol on his ranch in Texas. According to Ginsburg, Issahar was very interested in this way out. The ambassador explained that welcoming Yehuda at the ranch would demonstrate friendship and even intimacy, without the need to invite Jewish dignitaries to a formal dinner, and there was no danger of anyone being offended. Harman recommended that Israel accept the offer. It was clear that a stay on the ranch would be an opportunity for business talk without the constraints of Washington, whereas the original plan offered only a single hour-long conversation.

The next day, the ambassador reported back on his conversation with Ilan (Fortas). Abe Fortas had settled the ranch matter with the president, "in light of the insurmountable difficulties of arranging a dinner in Washington." Fortas had also asked Johnson about the additional twenty-seven Skyhawks Israel had asked for, and Issahar replied that there was no need to wait for Yehuda to request the aircraft officially: they were already in production. When Fortas raised the question of the Phantoms, Issahar said only, "In my entire administration, I am Israel's greatest friend." It was clear that there had not yet been a decision on the matter, Harman reported. Ambassador Arthur Goldberg told Harman that the working paper prepared by the State Department for the president was not "encouraging." Fortas was worried, too. The president was surrounded by advisers who wanted the United States to embark on its own peace initiative. For months, Fortas had been advising the president not to initiate any settlement, but rather to lead the parties to do so themselves. But he felt that Johnson was under increasing pressure to find a solution. Fortas suggested that Eshkol bring a long list of ideas for regional development. He mentioned to the ambassador that the summary statements should be formulated before the conversation with Eshkol.

Israel's representatives in the United States were now finding it more difficult than ever before to control the burgeoning political activism of U.S. Jews. They reported again and again on various public statements that had not been coordinated with them, including vocal demands to annex the territories and excessively enthusiastic support for Johnson's policy in Vietnam.[23] Israel hoped Johnson would be reelected. Eshkol was afraid of a Nelson Rockefeller presidency, and even more wary of Ronald Reagan, another contender for the Republican nomination. "A Johnson defeat would be a thoroughly bad thing for us," he said. But he did not lose heart: "I would still like to hope that, with our help, Johnson will be reelected."[24]*

The atmosphere at the ranch was warm and informal, and Johnson seemed friendly. But the official talks were uneasy. Eshkol wanted to talk about the Phantoms. Johnson, and his secretary of state, repeated over and over again that the planes would not alter reality. They wanted to know "what kind of Israel" Eshkol wanted—or, in other words, what he

---

*Ambassador Barbour offered Israel his own advice: President Johnson would appreciate nothing more, in preparation for Eshkol's visit to his ranch, than the establishment of diplomatic relations between Israel and South Vietnam. This did not happen, but Evron did let Johnson know that in the next few months he would be appearing almost every weekend before Jewish groups, "to help the president." Johnson had not yet announced that he would not be running for office again.[25]

was willing to give up. The United States, Johnson said, would "resist aggression, whether it be Hitler, Nasser, or Israel."* Eshkol could have taken offense, but he wanted the Phantoms. According to his military secretary, the Israelis were not sure the president would consent. Eshkol spared Johnson almost no Israeli cliché: Israel was a small country surrounded by enemies who could destroy it at any moment, and so it would not agree to go back to the prewar conditions or withdraw to the June 4 lines. Israel sought peace. It was not enough for Nasser to talk of nonbelligerency. Israel was fighting for its right to peace. After three wars, it deserved peace. For now, there was no one to talk to. Egypt had forbidden passage of Israeli ships through the Suez Canal, and he, Eshkol, remembered how they used to hang signs up in Russia: "No Jews." The Israelis could not live forever with the feeling that they were pariahs. He also reiterated to Johnson his idea of resettling the Palestinian refugees in Iraq.

Eshkol almost begged, as well: he could not possibly leave without a promise concerning the Phantoms, not only because of public reaction at home, but also because the Arabs would conclude that the United States had abandoned Israel. The commander of the air force, Mordechai Hod, who took part in the talks, said that only by strengthening the Israeli air force could the United States be sure it would not have to send forces in to help Israel. Johnson replied that he had not yet decided to sell the Phantoms to Israel, but agreed that Israeli pilots could come to train on them. The Israelis were very pleased.[27]

THE WORKING PAPERS THE AMERICANS HAD PREPARED FOR THE VISIT DEALT WITH SEVeral topics, including the possibility that Israel had developed, was developing, or would develop a nuclear bomb. The minutes of the conversations between Johnson and Eshkol do not mention the issue. The two met for a short while in private, and over the two-day visit they had plenty of time to talk about the bomb. Over the next few months, the United States tried to predicate the sale of the Phantoms on an Israeli commitment not to make a bomb, but it eventually contented itself with an agreement that the planes would not carry nuclear weapons. The man who conducted the official negotiations on the issue was Israel's new ambassador, Yitzhak Rabin; the details were worked out by Abe Feinberg.†

*Eshkol told Rabin about a pun Johnson had made: "You claim you want peace. In fact you only want a piece of this and a piece of that."[26]
†The draft agreement for the sale of the Phantoms, including restrictions on the use of nuclear arms, is among Feinberg's papers in the Israeli State Archive.[28]

On one of Feinberg's visits to see Eshkol, he brought him the first case of Coca-Cola manufactured in Israel.[29]

Disagreements, mutual suspicion, and reciprocal pressures notwithstanding, the bottom line was that the United States stood by Israel and did not compel it to withdraw from the territories. The American position reinforced the sense that there was no reason to hurry and no need to be content with an agreement to establish nonbelligerency between Israel and Egypt. The United States also did not block Israel from building new settlements in the territories.

3. SETTLEMENTS: "JUST LIKE IN THE UKRAINE!"

Twenty-four hours after the occupation of the Golan Heights, Raanan Weitz met with Haim Gvati, the minister of agriculture, who wrote in his diary, "The prime minister asked to prepare material about the settlement possibilities in the administrated territories." In fact, Weitz himself had called Eshkol on the fourth day of the war to propose sending someone to the Jordanian land registration offices to obtain information on titles, water sources, and development plans. Eshkol had laughed and exclaimed in Yiddish that the meshuggener was still meshuggener, but he did not object to obtaining the information.

This initiative embodied the essence of the Zionist entity—the vision, the yearning: a new movement was on the horizon, a second beginning, a late youth. "The Jewish plowman shall follow the swordsman," wrote Yehiel Admoni, one of Raanan Weitz's men—just the way it used to be, in Mandate days, the early days of Zionism.[30]

Yigal Allon accompanied Eshkol when he toured the Jordan Valley just after the war. Every few miles the prime minister ordered the jeep convoy to stop and jumped out to look at a brook or examine the quality of the earth. Someone would dig a small hole and show Eshkol the color of the soil. Eshkol would feel it and smell it and taste it; he wanted to know whether there was salt in the earth, Allon recalled: "He was the land man." When he looked out at the expanses of the Golan Heights on his first tour there, Eshkol was overwhelmed. "Just like in the Ukraine!" he exclaimed delightedly.[31]

THE GOVERNMENT'S DECISION TO FARM THE LANDS OF THE GOLAN HEIGHTS WAS MADE only at the end of August, but on June 30, Rafi Ben-Yehuda, of Kibbutz Neot Mordehai, took a few friends to the Golan to look for a suitable spot for a settlement. Some kibbutz movement people had discussed this option even during the war. Ben-Yehuda's diary evokes the first days of Zionist settlement. On his list of things to "get hold of," dated July 4, were "food, mattresses, weapons, licenses, water tank, cigarettes, hammer, pliers, pipe wrench." All the settlement preparations were coordinated with the government and authorized by it. One of the kibbutz members, Dan Laner, was a senior officer in the Northern Command, and was able to contact General David Elazar. The kibbutz people also had open communication lines with Yigal Allon. A few days later, Ben-Yehuda and his friends appeared before the Upper Galilee Regional Council and explained that they were going to the Golan "to start collecting cattle, sheep, horses and donkeys"—booty—as well as to harvest crops still in the fields. They might have to go into tourism or open a concession stand at first. The council approved a budget of 10,000 liras and allocated the kibbutzniks a jeep. The next day, Raanan Weitz proposed budgeting another forty thousand liras. Minister of Labor Allon gave them funds he took from the budget for public works for the unemployed.

After examining two possible sites, on July 17 the group decided to settle in the abandoned military camp of Aleika, and called themselves Kibbutz Golan. The name was later changed to Merom Golan, and they ultimately moved to Kunetra. Everything else is folklore: the first generator, the first snowfall, the fleas, the first wedding. On the first anniversary of the Six-Day War, the kibbutz had 169 members, including a few dozen volunteers from overseas.[32]

The government resolution on settling Golan lands was classified top secret. A note in the margin reads: "This resolution was not included in the minutes of the government meeting because of its confidential nature, and it is preserved in the government secretariat." The secrecy was necessary because the United States was opposed to settlements. But more outposts were soon set up in the Golan. One of them, whose name was not yet finalized and which was identified only as "the Banias outpost," prompted someone in the prime minister's office to author the following blessing: "This land is ours. We have learned to understand that land is bought with three things: tears, blood, and sweat. We have shed our tears. We have spilled our blood. Today we have begun pouring our sweat, to betroth this land to us forever. . . . It is ours and we shall not leave it." In order to establish this particular outpost, the army destroyed the village of Banias; "it was probably a pretty little town," commented an American embassy staffer who toured its ruins in September, when only a mosque and a church remained standing. In the next few months, another hundred or so abandoned villages in the Golan Heights were systematically destroyed.[33]

ROUGHLY THREE MONTHS LATER, A TOP SECRET—AND QUITE EMBARRASSING—LEGAL opinion by the foreign minister's legal counsel stated that civilian settlement in the "administrated territories" contravened international law. The counsel, Theodor Meron, was unequivocal: according to Article 49 of the Fourth Geneva Convention of 1949, an occupying country shall not deport or transfer parts of its own civilian population into the territory it occupies. Meron quoted an authoritative interpretation of the clause, which reinforced his opinion that Israel could not settle its citizens in the territories. He concluded that settlements should be implemented by the army, in camps that were—at least in appearance—temporary. Military camps could not be set up just anywhere, and ownership titles had to be respected. These restrictions, the opinion went on, applied first of all to the Golan Heights, which undoubtedly constituted an occupied territory.*

According to Israel, the final status of the West Bank had never been determined, and its annexation to the Hashemite Kingdom had not been carried out legally. And hence Israel claimed that the West Bank was not an occupied territory, which meant that it was not prevented from settling its citizens there. Meron did not refute this argument, but noted that it was disputed by the international community. Furthermore, Meron noted with embarrassment, Israel itself had recognized the status of the West Bank as an occupied territory by publishing military decrees declaring explicitly that it would respect the Geneva Conventions.[35]

The publicity surrounding the Golan settlements made Ambassador Harman's job difficult; the situation was "absolutely catastrophic," as he put it. Eshkol replied that he understood, but there was nothing to be done—the Israeli public had its own moods and needs.[36] But at the ambassador's request, and upon the advice of Theodor Meron, the settlements were at first depicted as military outposts, and at some point the settlers were even required to wear army uniforms. "The fact that these outposts exist is widely known, among governments and political parties as well, but we must avoid repeatedly giving journalists cause to dwell on the matter," cautioned Minister Israel Galili, a prominent hawk who was

---

*Meron also determined, however, that there was no legal argument to prevent Israel from moving Palestinian refugees from Gaza to settle in the West Bank.[34]

in charge of propaganda. The quasi-covert operation brought to mind the semi-underground settlements during British rule. In January 1968, there were five settlements in the Golan, comprising some 450 residents.[37]

AT THE END OF SEPTEMBER, JUST BEFORE ROSH HASHANAH, A FEW DOZEN YOUNG PEOPLE set out to reestablish Kfar Etzion, south of Jerusalem. Some of them were the children of the original "Gush" settlers who had been killed or taken hostage in 1948. In the intervening two decades, they had kept in touch, hoping to return one day. One of their main supporters in the government was Yigal Allon. "I never forgave Ben-Gurion for preventing us from taking the Gush, which would have been very easy to do," Allon once said. They organized quickly and coordinated efforts with the Orthodox ministers in the government. They also met with Eshkol, who supported them. This settlement, too, was initially described as a military outpost, but the celebrations accompanying its establishment were widely covered in the press.[38] The settlers set out from Jerusalem in a long convoy of vehicles, led by one of the armored buses that used to go to the Gush in 1948. Some of the government ministers took part in the ceremony, and the newspapers devoted supportive editorials to the operation.

It was not as foreign occupiers that they were settling on the land of Gush Etzion, wrote *Maariv*, but rather "as children coming again to their borders." The Arab occupation of the Gush during the War of Independence was described as "a holocaust." *Ha'aretz* also depicted the settlement as a return home. This was, of course, a problematic claim, because Israel was denying the rights of the Arab refugees to return to their homes. However, even the Foreign Ministry's legal counsel decided, albeit in fairly weak language, that it might be possible to find a legal justification for the settlement of Gush Etzion.[39]

One man stood out in his objection: Yosef Weitz, a founding father of the original Gush. He was unsympathetic to "the hysterical cries" of writers, journalists, and activists in support of the hasty settlement of the West Bank. In contrast to the "tempestuous days" of the Zionist struggle, he wrote, there was no longer any need to seize every possible spot. He feared that settlement in Gush Etzion would hurt the prospects for peace. He thought this move constituted a provocation of the few friends Israel had left, including the United States, and that it would strengthen Israel's enemies to the point of damaging the unity of Jerusalem. Nor were there many young people wanting to go to new settlements, wrote Weitz. He believed that the few who did want to go should be sent to the Galilee, where Jewish ownership of the land, although currently inhabited by Arabs, was undisputed—"Not by Isaiah and not by Jeremiah and not by the goyim."[40]

AMONG THE ATTENDEES AT THE KFAR ETZION CEREMONY WAS A RABBI IN HIS THIRTIES named Moshe Levinger. He wanted to join the Gush settlers, but was apparently prevented from doing so because his American-born wife did not want to live there. A few months later, Levinger settled in Hebron. In the history of Israeli settlement in the territories there has been no greater fanatic. Levinger came from Jerusalem. His father, a physician, had immigrated from Munich, where he had belonged to the ultra-Orthodox national youth movement, Ezra. Most of the German Jews who settled in Israel were not ultra-Orthodox, and the few who were found it difficult to integrate into the Eastern European ultra-Orthodox communities, which eschewed their comparatively modern way of life.

"The greatest madwoman of the family was the aunt," wrote the journalist Nahum Barnea. This aunt, well-known in Jerusalem, used to roam the city streets followed by a trail of children, enigmatically mumbling, "Bond with one, bond with one." Her brother, Avraham Halevy Frankel, was considered a mathematical genius. Moshe Levinger studied at the Mercaz Harav yeshiva in Jerusalem, known for its nationalistic fanaticism, and one of his teachers was Rabbi Zvi Yehuda Kook. When he finished his military service, Levinger lived for a few years on a religious kibbutz, where he worked as a shepherd and a rabbi. When the Six-Day War broke out, he was serving as the rabbi of a moshav near Petach Tikva. He was not drafted. Immediately after the war, he went to Hebron, where he experienced an awakening of "tempestuous spirits," as he later said, and was forever altered. A wrinkled-looking man, he had eleven children. *Newsweek* once wrote of him that had he lived during antiquity he would have been seen as a prophet; Barnea called him "a dervish."[41]

HEBRON WAS CONSIDERED A HOLY CITY; THE MASSACRE OF JEWS THERE IN 1929 WAS imprinted on national memory along with the great pogroms of Eastern Europe. The messianic fervor that characterized the Hebron settlers was more powerful than the awakening that led people to settle in East Jerusalem: while Jerusalem had already been annexed, the future of Hebron was still unclear.

Knesset member Shmuel Tamir, an attorney, wrote to Eshkol on behalf of Rabbi Yehezkel Sarna, a survivor of the 1929 massacre, who had founded the Hebron yeshiva in Jerusalem and now wanted to renew its activity in the occupied ancient city. The prime minister invited the elderly rabbi to see him. They spoke for three or four hours, Eshkol later told members of the General Staff. He thought the rabbi would ask for a particular building, but Sarna said, "I want you to clear out the whole street for me." Eshkol thought he might have misunderstood, but Sarna explained that as soon as the war began, Israel "should have slaughtered the Arabs of Hebron one by one." In May 1968, the government decided to renew settlement activities in Hebron.[42]

Eshkol was contacted by other yeshivas that wanted to operate in Hebron, and by Levinger's group, which asked Yigal Allon to help coordinate plans to hold a Passover seder in a local hotel, the Park. Allon gave his approval, provided that the military governor agreed, and on condition that they stay not in the city but only nearby. Levinger and his people moved into the hotel, celebrated Passover—and refused to leave. Allon asked Eshkol to allow them to remain, at least until the government could decide what to do with them. Eshkol agreed. "I have to say that I did not have to push very hard," Allon recounted. The minister of labor himself provided Levinger and his group with money that came, once again, from the public works budget.

Allon went one step further: he spoke with one of the Gush Etzion settler leaders, Hanan Porat, and asked him to send arms to the hotel dwellers—a few submachine guns, handguns, and some hand grenades. He feared for their safety, and also believed he should create a link between Gush Etzion and the Park hotel, "just in case, God forbid, there should be fighting," as he later revealed in an interview that was supposed to remain classified for many years. He promised Porat he would ensure "military cover" for the operation, and indeed, upon returning to Jerusalem he went to see Israel Lior and asked him to report on the matter to Dayan.

Allon later said, "I am certain that the Gush Etzion people to this day think I made some non-kosher deal with them, that I illegally transferred weapons to the Park hotel. It is true that I took upon myself an authority I did not formally have, but as a minister, and as a general in reserve duty, I thought I could not leave the area without promising something."[43]

The Jewish presence in Hebron aroused tensions in the city. Mayor Jaabari complained to Eshkol, and the settlers were moved to a military camp, where they continued to make trouble for the army. The military threatened to expel them from Hebron, but they apologized and were allowed to stay.[44]

. . .

A SHORT WHILE AFTER THE FOUNDING OF THE GUSH ETZION SETTLEMENT, ESHKOL MET for a long talk with leaders of the Greater Israel Movement, including the writers Moshe Shamir and Haim Hazaz and the poet Uri Zvi Greenberg. At moments the meeting was tense, but most of the time Eshkol tried to convince his guests that he and they did not disagree in principle: he was also in favor of settlements in the territories; he was just as patriotic, and knew there was no occupation without settlements, but unlike them, he had larger responsibility and had to consider political constraints.

Ha'aretz predicted a future for the Israeli settlers in Hebron, with diamond-polishing workshops, a kosher restaurant or even a hotel, a print shop, a souvenir factory, and so forth.[45] But settlement in Hebron also produced the first cracks in national unity. A few academics published a statement headed, "Security and Peace, Yes; Annexation, No!" All of them were well-known, and they gave the dovish protests an institutional respectability they had lacked.*

About six months after the war there were ten Israeli settlements in the territories, including two in Sinai, and more than eight hundred settlers.[47] On November 12, the security cabinet accepted Allon's proposal and decided that maps would no longer be marked with the Green Line, but rather with the cease-fire lines—the occupation borders of the Six-Day War. The new boundaries would be drawn in purple.[48]

4. MILESTONES: "IT'S NICE TO BE IN POWER"

Press coverage of daily life in the territories during the year following the war painted a rosy picture for Israelis. "Today Hebron is a quiet, obedient city," *Ha'aretz* reported. According to *Maariv*, "The Khan Younis district is ruled with ease." A reporter who visited Gaza provided the headline, "We Are Happy in the Refugee Camps." From Jenin, reports came that the locals preferred to get their bread and medical care from Israel. "In Kalkilya they worship Dayan," announced *Yediot Aharonot*, and the news from the Golan was also good.† Bank Leumi published an Arabic phrasebook, from

---

*Among the dozen protesters were the historian Saul Friedlander and the writer A. B. Yehoshua.[46]

†The U.S. ambassador reported on Shabak successes in the territories, noting that the deputy head of the intelligence branch, David Carmon, was "nearly ecstatic" over operations to expose terrorists, which he called "simply fantastic."[49]

which Israeli visitors to the West Bank could learn how to say "Please," "Thank you," "Hello," "How are you?," and "Sorry."[50]

"It's nice to be in power," Moshe Dayan observed, saying all there was to say. He felt that ruling the territories gave Israel "a great opportunity to shape and determine ways of life with the Arabs." To illustrate, he spoke of the Tomb of the Patriarchs in Hebron, a holy site for both Jews and Muslims. There was no chance that the Arabs would willingly allow Jews to pray there, and so "we imposed our presence there by force of power. We assumed a partnership, and we also refused to take off our shoes when entering a site that is holy to us." But when the mufti asked that Jewish visiting hours be reduced during Ramadan, Israel complied. "It's a matter of courtesy," Dayan explained. "If your neighbor is in mourning and asks you not to play dance music for a week—it is natural that you would honor his request."

In December 1967, Dayan explained to the government that there was no chance of peace. Consequently, he proposed unilaterally instituting arrangements as if there were peace. What he meant was the "enlightened occupation," including free passage between the West Bank and the Arab world. Summarizing the situation one year after the war, Dayan stated, "The current reality in the territories—that is my plan. The plan is being implemented in actual fact. What exists today must remain as a permanent arrangement in the West Bank." Earlier, Dayan had proposed revoking the withdrawal decision of June 19, 1967.[51]

Dayan now began taking an interest in the writings of Arthur Rupin, one of the originators of the binational idea, which called for full equality between Jews and Arabs in one state. Dayan also thought Jews and Arabs could live together—but, in contrast to the tenets of the binational movement, he assumed the Jews would retain control. For the time being he was satisfied: Israel might even continue to rule the Palestinians for fifty years, he commented.[52]

Edith Ezrachi of Jerusalem told her relatives that she and her family often went hiking in the territories and did not encounter a single soldier for hours. But she knew this seeming absence was illusory. In the year following the war, there were 687 acts of terror and border incidents, approximately two a day. One hundred seventy-five Israelis were killed, including thirty civilians—nearly one every other day—and more than five hundred were injured, eighty-five of them civilians.[53] In the last week of September, terrorists entered the moshav of Ometz, in the center of Israel, and murdered three-year-old Yosef Salomon. A few days later, the Movement for the Annexation of the Liberated Territories published a statement quoting a poem by Bialik: "Satan has not created the vengeance for the blood of a small child." Could this murder have been prevented, and could the next one be prevented? asked the authors of the statement. Their own response: "The government is capable of preventing murder if it simply declares that we are staying in the West Bank, and immediately begins settling it with Jews."[54]

On October 21, the Egyptians attacked an Israeli destroyer, the *Eilat*. Forty-seven crew members were killed. The IDF responded by bombing the refineries in the city of Suez.[55]

THE IDF KNEW HOW TO CONTEND WITH THE EGYPTIANS, BUT THE REAL CHALLENGE was Fatah, whose presence only grew after the war. The army once again demanded authorization to take large-scale action against terrorist bases. This time it did not want to act against Syria but against Jordan. Yaacov Herzog later commented that the situation reminded him of the days preceding the war.

On March 18, 1968, a school bus from Herzliya drove over a land mine near Be'er Orah, some twelve miles north of Eilat. A doctor and one of the adults chaperoning the trip were killed, and dozens of children were injured. In response, the IDF launched an attack on Karame, a village in Jordan.

The Karame operation, a near repeat of the failed operation in Samua eighteen months earlier, caused the deaths of thirty Israeli soldiers. Dozens of Jordanians and Palestinians were killed. Many of the terrorists managed to escape, including Yasser Arafat. The Palestinians described the battle as a defeat for Israel and built it into a national myth. Eban quoted the U.S. ambassador as predicting that in twenty years' time a historian would cite the Karame operation as the beginning of Israel's end. A furious Menachem Begin retorted that a foreign representative prophesying the destruction of Israel should not be quoted in a government meeting. Abe Feinberg sent a reassuring message: he had been with President Johnson when news of the operation arrived. Although Johnson said Israel was making trouble for him, his tone was not especially sharp. The Palestinians stepped up their activities; they soon began hijacking planes.[56]

"We have once again returned to the nights of Fatah—like before the Six-Day War," wrote a woman from Ein Hanatziv to her children in Los Angeles. "They are so dark, the skies, and especially the stars, very distant, and when you walk alone in the early hours of the night, which are the most dangerous, you feel a terrible loneliness." A week earlier, her husband had been called up for guard duty, and she was alone, surrounded by a grove of trees that cast a heavy shadow on her home, and it was awful.

Edith Ezrachi wrote to Connecticut about her constant worry: Where would this end? Most observers believed the Vietnam War would end, but that was not the case here: "I can't see the Arabs changing their line of hatred and murder."[57] On June 6, the anniversary of the war's start, Ezrachi sent her relatives one of the saddest letters she had ever written. She had just learned that Robert Kennedy had been assassinated. "One just wants to weep and scream and bang one's fist," she wrote, "for him, for his wife, his kids, for the world." And again the "little state of Israel" was involved, she wrote, because the assassin was a "former Palestinian Jew-hater, the father living not so far from here."[58]

IN THE SPRING OF 1968, DAVID BEN-GURION STILL MAINTAINED THAT IF HE HAD TO choose between a small Israel with peace, and a Greater Israel without peace, he would prefer the former. But as time went by, he, too, became more sure that peace was unattainable, which led him to support not only enlargement of the Jewish population in Jerusalem, Hebron, and Gush Etzion, but also "anywhere it is possible in the West Bank." He repeatedly denied having opposed the war, claiming that from the moment Nasser had announced the closing of the Straits he had supported the operation. "No one heard from me that we should hunker down, because such a nonsensical idea never even occurred to me," he wrote.[59] On Independence Day, Ben-Gurion agreed to attend the greatest military parade in Israel's history, which passed by the walls of the Old City with tanks and captured vehicles and an air show, but he refused to sit on the dignitaries' dais next to Eshkol. They assigned him a seat among the tourists; Teddy Kollek left the dais and sat next to him.[60]

The Six-Day War brought new vigor to the prewar compulsion to reexamine the state's ideological identity. Countless journalists wanted Ben-Gurion to speak about the foundations of Zionism. "What is our historical right?" he was asked by two young reporters from Kol Israel. They were two years old when the state was established, Ben-Gurion noted with astonishment, and proceeded to offer them a basic lesson: Eretz Israel belonged exclusively to the Jewish people. The Arabs also had rights in the country, but it was not theirs.* But in a moment of candor he

---

*Ben-Gurion amused himself with the notion that the Palestinians were descendants of the ancient Hebrews who had converted to Islam.[61]

wrote that, in fact, he did not know the meaning of the term "Zionism."
"Once, in my youth, I believed that I knew, but over time I learned that I
do not know, and I also doubt whether the word even has any significance." If he were in his twenties again, having read all the books he had
read in his life, he would go and study biology, particularly the structure
of the brain, he wrote to the editor of a student newspaper.

As he often did, Ben-Gurion expressed a feeling that many Israelis
could relate to: as time went by, they longed to escape the situation the
war had created—but they did not know how. Most of them did not want
to go back to the reality that had prevailed before the war, but more and
more of them began fearing that Israel's rule over the residents of Gaza
and the West Bank was not helping the country but harming it. On the
face of things, everything was temporary, it would stay as it was just until
a solution could be found, but between one war and the next, 1967 began
to emerge as its own "weeping for generations," with its own troublesome
permanency; everything that would happen from now on occurred in its
shadow.

YOSEF WEITZ, WHO HAD GIVEN THE ZIONIST MOVEMENT ONE OF ITS FIRST HEROES, WAS
not optimistic. In his view, the occupation that had saved Israel from destruction was now threatening to destroy it as a Jewish and democratic
state. Everything would have been simpler had Israel not conquered East
Jerusalem, the West Bank, and Gaza, or if it had immediately set about
resettling the refugees. But perhaps everything would have also been simpler if Israel had taken advantage of the war to expel all the Arabs, including the residents of East Jerusalem; Weitz was among those who were
capable of defending such a step, as he did his whole life. When he suggested concentrating the Gaza refugees in the West Bank and giving it
back to Jordan, he did not do so wholeheartedly: he would be sorry to
give up the West Bank. Everything might have been simpler had they
taken his advice—but he did not suggest giving up control of East
Jerusalem, not even for peace.

In the summer, Weitz went to the Rockefeller Museum, a picturesque
castle built during British rule, whose grand opening in 1938 was canceled when one of the guests, the British archaeologist James Leslie
Starkey, was murdered by Palestinian terrorists on his way to the ceremony. Several of the IDF soldiers who had captured Jerusalem had been
wounded near the museum. Weitz wanted to measure the age of an old
pine tree in the courtyard; the drill only went in to a depth of seven

inches, which meant there were 104 rings. Weitz calculated the tree to be between 250 and 260 years old. He spent the next few weeks researching its history, paying a special visit to the National Library, where he found "a spirit of tranquility" and a pure human setting. He eventually wrote on the history of the tree, entitled "Perfect Old Age." He dedicated the article to the IDF in gratitude for its liberation of Jerusalem.

IN HIS OWN OLD AGE, YOSEF WEITZ CONTINUED TO FOLLOW THE NEWS, AND HIS DIARY notes the first large-scale terrorist attacks. When he had time, he worked in his garden. As he was planting dahlias one day, his wife, Ruhama, came out and spoke three words: "Eshkol is gone." It was February 26, 1969. "I was stunned," wrote Weitz. "Shall I eulogize him, though I always predicted he would eulogize me?" He pondered the passage of time, how the Angel of Death had freed Eshkol from his torments as prime minister, and how insignificant life was.[62] He lived for almost four more years and died shortly before the next war.

NOTES

LIST OF ARCHIVES

INTRODUCTION: HEROES

1. Biographical notes, CZA, A246/579; Yosef Weitz, *My Diary* (in Hebrew) (Tel Aviv: Masada, 1973), vol. VI, p. 160; "Yehiam," a biographical essay probably written by his father (1956), CZA, A246/795; Raanan Weitz, *The Scent of Acacia* (in Hebrew) (Jerusalem: Keter, 1997), p. 82ff.; Shraga Kadari, ed., *Beit HaKerem Is Forty* (in Hebrew) (unnamed publisher, 1966); *Jubilee Book of the High School Affiliated with the Hebrew University in Jerusalem* (in Hebrew) (jubilee book, unnamed editor, unnamed publisher, 1987); Yehuda Slotzki, ed., *History Book of the Hagana* (in Hebrew) (Tel Aviv: Am Oved, 1973), vol. III, part II, p. 880ff.

2. *Davar*, 19 June 1946, p. 1, CZA, A246/797 [press clippings file]; Rina Gal and Chava Yalon, eds., *Kibbutz Yehiam Jubilee Book* (in Hebrew), 1997, p. 34; Weitz diary, 24 June, 19 July, 30 July 1946, CZA, A246/795; "Yehiam," a biographical essay probably written by his father (1956), CZA, A246/795.

3. CZA, A246/797 [press clippings file]; Tom Segev, *One Palestine, Complete: Jews and Arabs Under the British Mandate* (in Hebrew) (Jerusalem: Keter, 1999), p. 211ff.; Yehiam Weitz, *Letters* (in Hebrew) (Tel Aviv: Am Oved, 1948); Shlomo Halevi: "Inside One Sabra," *Ha'aretz*, 24 Sept. 1948, p. 3; *HaMishmar*, 6 June 1947, CZA, A246/797 [press clippings file]; Reuven Avinoam, ed., *Parchments of Fire* (in Hebrew) (Tel Aviv: Ministry of Defense, 1952).

4. CZA, A246/793.

5. Letters to the author and in response to questions.

6. *Ha'aretz*, 14 Dec. 1947, p. 2.

7. Tom Segev, *1949: The First Israelis* (in Hebrew) (Jerusalem: Domino, 1984), p. 43ff.; Uzi Benziman and Atalla Mansour, *Sub-Letters: Israeli Arabs, Their Status, and the Policy Toward Them* (in Hebrew) (Jerusalem: Keter, 1992), p. 54ff.; Benny Morris, *Errata: Jews and Arabs in the Land of Israel, 1936–1956* (in Hebrew) (Tel Aviv: Am Oved, 2000), p. 117ff.

8. Mordechai Bar-On, "Status Quo Before—or After?: Interpretive Comments on Israel's Security Policy, 1949–1958" (in Hebrew) in *Studies on the Establishment of Israel* (1995), vol. 5, p. 65ff.; Mordechai Bar-On, "Security-Mindedness and Its Critics, 1949–1967" (in Hebrew) in *The Challenge of Sovereignty, Creation and Contemplation in the First Decade of the State,* ed. Mordechai Bar-On (Jerusalem: Yad Ben-Zvi, 1999), p. 62ff.; Arieh Naor, *Greater Israel—Belief and Policy* (in Hebrew) (Haifa: Haifa University; Tel Aviv: Zmora-Bitan, 2001).

9. Amos Elon, *The Israelis: Founders and Sons* (in Hebrew) (Tel Aviv: Adam, 1981), p. 27.

10. Yehiam Kapman in letter to the author, 24 May 2004.

11. Central Bureau of Statistics, *Statistical Abstract of Israel, No. 19,* 1968 (in Hebrew), p. 453; see also: *Ha'aretz,* 23 March 1967, p. 9.

12. *Ha'aretz,* 24 July 1967, p. 8 (announcement).

13. Efraim Ilin, *I, the Undersigned* (in Hebrew) (Tel Aviv: Sifriyat Maariv, 1985), p. 215ff.; Arieh Avnery, *Sapir* (in Hebrew) (Tel Aviv: Peleg, 1976), p. 142ff.; ISA, P-9/907 (Pinhas Sapir, "Autocars").

14. Zohar, Kenan, and Tomarkin to Eshkol and auxiliary documents, 18 April 1965, YEA, copy owned by author.

15. Yoram Rosler, ed., *Abie Nathan* (in Hebrew) (Tel Aviv: Sifriyat Poalim, 1998), p. 32.

16. Ibid., p. 40.

17. Ezer Weizman and Dov Goldstein, *The Sky Is Yours, the Land Is Yours* (in Hebrew) (Tel Aviv: Sifriyat Maariv, 1975), p. 218; "Ness" platform, *Ha'aretz,* 29 Oct. 1965, p. 23.

18. National Elections Supervisor, results of the elections for the Sixth Knesset and local authorities, 2 Nov. 1965, Central Bureau of Statistics, special publication series, vol. I, no. 216, p. 73.

19. Bunche to Nathan, 30 Dec. 1966, ISA, HZ-1/3835; Rosler, ed., *Abie Nathan,* p. 66.

20. Amos Oz, *Elsewhere, Perhaps* (in Hebrew) (Jerusalem: Keter, 1991), p. 107.

21. "Sign the Peace Petitions," *Ha'aretz,* 11 Feb. 1966, p. 13; 16 Feb. 1966, p. 6; 28 Feb. 1966, p. 6; Rosler, ed., *Abie Nathan,* p. 66.

22. *Maariv,* 1 March 1966, p. 3.

23. Shapira in the Knesset, 8 March 1966, *Knesset Minutes,* vol. 45, p. 856. Al-Ahram based on *Ha'aretz,* 2 March 1966, p. 1.

24. *Ha'aretz,* 1 March 1966, p. 1; *Maariv,* 1 March 1966, p. 2; *Yediot Aharonot,* 1 March 1966, p. 2; ("7 Days" supplement), 3 March 1966, p. 8; 4 March 1966, p. 9; Rosler, ed., *Abie Nathan,* p. 78; Central Bureau of Statistics, *Statistical Abstract of Israel, No. 18,* 1967 (in Hebrew), p. 20.

25. Eshkol in the government, 16 May 1967, estate of Yaacov Herzog, with the kind permission of his daughter.

26. *Yediot Aharonot,* 25 Nov. 1966, p. 8.

27. *Ha'aretz,* 23 Dec. 1966, p. 3. Reuven Bareket at Mapai secretariat, 1 June 1967, LPA, 24-1967-3-5.

28. *Maariv* (Saturday), 4 March 1966, p. 1.

29. Gvati diary, 26 May 1967, p. 129, YTA, Unit 15, Container 12, File 02; Ibid., 25 May 1967, May 26, 1967, YTA, Unit 15, Container 12, File 02; Ibid., 23 May 1967, p. 125, YTA, Unit 15, Container 12, File 02; Ibid., 2 June 1967, p. 140, YTA, Unit 15, Container 12, File 02.

30. Eshkol and Rabin in cabinet meeting, 26 May 1967, estate of Yaacov Herzog, with the kind permission of his daughter; Gvati diary, 26 May 1967, p. 129, YTA, Unit 15, Container 12, File 02.

31. Letter to Vardit and Adir Zik, 28 May 1967, with the kind permission of Zik.

32. Rostow to President, 31 May 1967, FRUS, vol. XIX, p. 202.

33. Gvati diary, 5 June 1967, p. 142, YTA, Unit 15, Container 12, File 02.

34. *Yediot Aharonot,* 6 June 1967, p. 1.

35. *Complete Jokes of Eshkol* (in Hebrew) (unnamed author, unnamed publisher, 1966), p. 23; Michael Shashar, *The Seventh-Day War: Diary of the Military Governance in Judah and Samaria, June–December 1967* (in Hebrew) (Tel Aviv: Sifriyat Poalim, 1977), p. 225.

36. Moshe Dayan, *Vietnam Diary* (in Hebrew) (Tel Aviv: Dvir, 1977), p. 111.

37. *Israel: Annual Review for 1967,* p. 5, PRO, FCO 17/468, 104038.

PART I: BETWEEN RISHON LEZION AND MANHATTAN

CHAPTER 1: SUSSITA DAYS

1. Bar-Dayan diary, 18 May 1967, with his kind permission. Yehoshua Bar-Dayan's war diary is usually quoted from the original manuscript. See also: Moshe Admon and Yehoshua Bar-Dayan, *A Soldier's Diary* (in Hebrew) (Tel Aviv: Othpaz, 1968); *Ha'aretz* (supplement), 10 May 1968, p. 14ff.; 17 May 1968, p. 14ff.; 24 May 1968, p. 26ff.
2. Central Bureau of Statistics, *Statistical Abstract of Israel, No. 18,* 1967 (in Hebrew), p. 26; *No. 19,* 1968, p. 31, 46.
3. P. Ginur, "Twenty Years of Israeli Economy," *Economic Quarterly* (in Hebrew), 16: 57–58, Aug. 1968, p. 16ff.; A. Halperin, "The Recession and the Recovery in the Economy," *Economic Quarterly* (in Hebrew), 14: 56, Feb. 1968, p. 287ff.
4. *Maariv,* 9 Oct. 1966, p. 19 (Beit Shemesh and Kiryat Eliezer); *Ha'aretz,* 28 March 1966, p. 1 (Ramat Gan); 9 Feb. 1966, p. 10 (Arad); *Maariv,* 19 Oct. 1966, p. 12 (*Beit HaTefutzoth,* Museum); *Yediot Aharonot,* 30 Aug. 1966, p. 1 (the Knesset); see also: Susan Hattis-Rolef, "The Knesset House on Givat Ram, Planning and Construction," *Kathedra* (in Hebrew), no. 96, July 2000, p. 131ff.; *Kathedra,* no. 105, Sept. 2002, p. 171ff.; *Maariv,* 9 Jan. 1966, p. 8 (Beit Shemesh); *Maariv,* 13 Jan. 1966, p. 15; *Ha'aretz,* 25 Feb. 1966, p. 3; 22 Jan. 1967, p. 8 (Haifa); 5 July 1966, p. 5 (Faculty); *Maariv,* 19 Sept. 1966, p. 1 (satellite); *Ha'aretz,* 25 Aug. 1966, p. 22 (space); *Yediot Aharonot,* 17 March 1967, p. 1 (matriculation); *Ha'aretz,* 20 Dec. 1966, p. 1 (basketball); 4 April 1966, p. 3 (Bentov).
5. Letters from Rishon Lezion, 1966–67, given to the author anonymously and same hereinafter.
6. Letter to Adir Zik, 29 Aug. 1966, with his kind permission.
7. Ibid.; Central Bureau of Statistics, *Statistical Abstract of Israel, No. 20,* 1969 (in Hebrew), p. 162 (income), 174.
8. Ilin advertisement, *Maariv,* 17 May 1967, p. 11; *Ha'aretz,* 22 July 1966, p. 4; Mercedes advertisement, *Ha'aretz,* 14 Feb. 1966, p. 9; BMW advertisement, *Ha'aretz,* 3 April 1966, p. 2; Volvo advertisement, *Ha'aretz,* 18 April 1966, p. 12; Vauxhall advertisement, *Ha'aretz,* 2 Feb. 1966, p. 2; Dodge and Chevrolet advertisements, *Ha'aretz,* 3 April 1966, p. 2.
9. Central Bureau of Statistics, *Statistical Abstract of Israel, No. 20,* 1969 (in Hebrew), p. 162; *Yediot Aharonot,* 7 Jan. 1966, p. 7; Minister of Post in the Knesset, 7 Feb. 1967, *Knesset Minutes,* vol. 48 (in Hebrew), pp. 1175, 1309; Central Bureau of Statistics, *Statistical Abstract of Israel, No. 19,* 1968 (in Hebrew), p. 431; *Ha'aretz,* 4 July 1966, p. 9 (Bavli); see also: *Yediot Aharonot,* 10 Jan. 1966, p. 8.
10. *Ha'aretz,* 8 Feb. 1967, p. 3; 9 Feb. 1967, p. 2; 12 Feb. 1967, p. 2 (oil); 2 Jan. 1967, p. 9; 28 Feb. 1967, p. 2; 20 March 1967, p. 2 (milk).
11. Ibid., 12 Sept. 1966, p. 12.
12. Ibid., 12 March 1967, p. 11.
13. Central Bureau of Statistics, *Statistical Abstract of Israel, No. 18,* 1967 (in Hebrew), p. 95; *Ha'aretz,* 22 June 1966, p. 4; 8 Jan. 1967, p. 5; 22 June 1966, p. 4; *Yediot Aharonot,* 3 March 1967, p. 15.
14. *Ha'aretz,* 12 Aug. 1966, p. 12; *Maariv,* 24 Jan. 1966, p. 10.
15. Moshe Shamir, *The Border* (in Hebrew) (Tel Aviv: Sifriyat Poalim, 1966); *Ha'aretz,* 3 June 1966, p. 2 ("too small"); letters to the editor, *Ha'aretz,* 4 July 1967, p. 2; David Hacohen and Abba Eban in the Knesset, 11 Jan. 1967, *Knesset Minutes,* vol. 47 (in Hebrew), p. 849 (visas); *Ha'aretz,* 30 Jan. 1966, p. 6 (takeoffs), p. 7; *Maariv,* 17 June 1966, p. 1; 5 Aug. 1966, p. 1 (Shazar); ISA, GL-7/4618 (travel tax).
16. Yisrael Galili in the Knesset, 15 Feb. 1967, *Knesset Minutes,* vol. 48 (in Hebrew), p. 1309; 29 March 1967, *Knesset Minutes,* vol. 48 (in Hebrew), p. 1877; Central Bureau of Statistics, *Statistical Abstract of Israel, No. 20,* 1969 (in Hebrew), p. 173; *Ha'aretz,* 4 Jan. 1966, p. 2; 5 Jan. 1966, p. 12; announcements, *Ha'aretz,* 6 Jan. 1966, p. 11; *Maariv,* 7 Jan. 1966, p. 11.
17. *Report of the Educational Television Council* (in Hebrew), 1962; *Report of the General Television Committee* (in Hebrew), 1965; ISA, GL-1/4604.
18. *Maariv,* 7 Jan. 1966, p. 9; *Ha'aretz,* 4 Jan. 1966, p. 5.
19. *Ha'aretz,* 25 March 1966, p. 8.
20. Ibid., 27 March 1966, p. 2.
21. Ibid., 7 Sept. 1967, p. 2 ("common sense"); Bodinger to Eshkol, 9 Oct. 1966, YEA.

22. *Yediot Aharonot* ("7 Days" supplement), 27 Jan. 1967, p. 6 (Godick); *Ha'aretz,* 27 March 1967, p. 2.

23. *Ha'aretz,* 8 July 1966, p. 12 (Cinerama); Central Bureau of Statistics, *Statistical Abstract of Israel, No. 19,* 1968 (in Hebrew), p. 552; *Maariv,* 16 May 1966, p. 16; *Ha'aretz,* 7 Jan. 1966, p. 2 (censorship); 21 Oct. 1966, p. 9; *Yediot Aharonot* ("7 Days" supplement), 19 May 1967, p. 10 (Gashash); *Ha'aretz,* 1 Dec. 1966, p. 4 (Ben-Amotz); *Maariv,* 19 Oct. 1966, p. 12 (Wimpy); *Ha'aretz,* 22 March 1966, p. 10 (Pam Pam); 2 Feb. 1966, p. 11 (wine).

24. Eran to Eshkol, 12 May 1968, ISA, G-2/561 (20); *Ha'aretz,* 12 June 1966, p. 2; 1 Aug. 1966, p. 6; 2 Sept. 1966, p. 3; 6 Feb. 1966, p. 4; *Maariv,* 14 Sept. 1966, p. 18; *Misholim,* the student newspaper at the Arlozorov Beit Hinuch school in Jerusalem, Chanukah 5724 (1954), JMA, container 3127; see also: *Maariv,* 14 Sept. 1966, p. 18; Central Bureau of Statistics, *Statistical Abstract of Israel, No. 19,* 1968 (in Hebrew), p. 534; Zion Rabi, "Demographic Development in Israel, 1948–1966," *Economic Quarterly* (in Hebrew), 14: 56, Feb. 1968, p. 318.

25. Letters from Israelis to overseas, copies in possession of the author.

26. Ami Gluska, *Eshkol, Give the Order!* (in Hebrew) (Tel Aviv: Ministry of Defense, 2004), p. 149; Meir Amit, *Head to Head: A Personal Look at Great Events and Secret Affairs* (in Hebrew) (Tel Aviv: Hed Arzi, 1999), p. 179ff.; Herzog diary, 9 Aug. 1966, 18 Aug. 1966, ISA, A-16/4510.

27. Carl von Horn, *Soldiering for Peace* (London: Cassel, 1966), p. 104.

28. Central Bureau of Statistics, *Statistical Abstract of Israel, No. 19,* 1968 (in Hebrew), p. 543ff.

29. D. Teneh, "Building and Populating Apartments in 1967," *Economic Quarterly* (in Hebrew), 16: 57–58, Aug. 1968, p. 157ff.; Zion Rabi, "Demographic Development in Israel, 1948–1966," *Economic Quarterly* (in Hebrew), 14: 57–58, Aug. 1968, p. 53; *Ha'aretz,* 24 Aug. 1966, p. 10; Ministry of Housing advertisements, *Yediot Aharonot,* 22 April 1966, p. 10; Breshkev advertisements, *Maariv,* 15 Aug. 1966, p. 8.

30. *Yediot Aharonot,* 2 April 1967, p. 1; *Ha'aretz,* 4 April 1967, p. 5 (dollar rate); Pan Loan advertisement, *Maariv,* 25 Nov. 1966, p. 9; see also: Neveh Ram advertisement, *Yediot Aharonot* ("7 Days" supplement), 21 Oct. 1966, p. 8; Africa Israel Investments advertisement, *Ha'aretz,* 3 April 1966, p. 2; lottery results, *Ha'aretz,* 5 Aug. 1966, p. 6.

31. Rimon advertisement, *Ha'aretz,* 26 April 1966, p. 1; see also: Keret advertisement, *Ha'aretz,* 5 June 1966, p. 1; Ascot advertisement, *Maariv,* 7 Jan. 1966, p. 10; *Maariv,* 15 Feb. 1966, p. 2 (cigarettes).

32. Yosef Goldstein, *Ahad Ha'am* (in Hebrew) (Jerusalem: Keter, 1992), p. 264ff.

33. Bar-Dayan in response to the author's question.

34. *Ha'aretz,* 6 Feb. 1966, p. 4 (quality of life); A. Halperin, "Recession and Recovery in the Economy," *Economic Quarterly* (in Hebrew) 14: 56, Feb. 1968, p. 287ff.

35. Eshkol speech, *Maariv,* 22 Feb. 1966, p. 3; Yemima Rosenthal, Arnon Lemfrom, and Hagai Tzoref, eds., *Levi Eshkol, the Third Prime Minister* (in Hebrew) (Jerusalem: Israel State Archives, 2002), p. 498ff.; Sapir in the Knesset, 14 Feb. 1966, *Knesset Minutes,* vol. 44 (in Hebrew), p. 604ff.; see also: review of the Minister of Finance in the government, *Ha'aretz,* 26 July 1966, p. 10; Dan Patenkin, "Thoughts on the Budget," *Maariv,* 24 Feb. 1966, p. 4; see also: *Maariv* (business), 22 Nov. 1983; *Ha'aretz,* 5 July 1966, p. 8 ("concessions").

36. Barbour to Washington, 19 Jan. 1967, USNA, Box 2236, File POL 12; Hadow to Brown, 24 Jan. 1967, PRO, FCO 17/468, 104038; unsigned memo, 16 March, 1967, LBJL, NSF, Country File, Israeli Aid, Box 5/67; "Israel's Economic Squeeze," *New York Times,* 24 March 1967, p. 30; Miriam Biham and Ephraim Kleiman, "The Price of Recession," *Banking Quarterly* (in Hebrew), 8: 29–32, 1968–1969, p. 31ff.; Nahum Gross, "The Israeli Economy" (in Hebrew) in *The Second Decade,* eds. Zvi Tzimrat and Chana Yablonka (Jerusalem: Yad Ben-Zvi, 2000), p. 29ff.; *Ha'aretz,* 4 Feb. 1966, p. 3 (quality of life); Lev Greenberg, *The Histadruth Above Everything* (in Hebrew) (Jerusalem: Nevo, 1933), p. 130.

37. *Ha'aretz,* 10 June 1966, p. 9 (restaurants); 16 March 1966, p. 13.

38. Letter to Adir Zik, 24 July 1966, with his kind permission; *Ha'aretz,* 16 Aug. 1966, p. 9 (apartments); letter to Chaim Haskal, 3 March 1967, with his kind permission; *Ha'aretz,* 30 March 1966, p. 2 (university); 7 April 1966, p. 5 (theater); *LaMerchav,* 8 July 1966, p. 4 (museum); *Ha'aretz,* 22 July 1967, p. 4 (villas); 23 March 1967, p. 9 (vehicle); 14 April 1967, p. 9 (Hilton); *Maariv,* 2 Sept. 1966, p. 8 (engineer); *Ha'aretz,* 21 April

1967, p. 2 (sighing); A. Halperin, "Recession and Recovery in the Economy," *Economic Quarterly* (in Hebrew) 14: 56, Feb. 1968, p. 291; *Davar,* 17 June 1966, p. 2 (ill wind).

39. Pinhas Sapir in the Knesset, 13 June 1966 and others, *Knesset Minutes,* vol. 46 (in Hebrew), pp. 1701, 2189; Moshe Carmel in the Knesset, 8 June 1966, *Knesset Minutes,* vol. 46 (in Hebrew), p. 2407; see also: *Knesset Minutes,* vol. 47 (in Hebrew), p. 370ff.

40. *Maariv,* 27 Jan. 1967, p. 5; Government Minutes, 12 Feb. 1967, with the kind permission of Yossi Goldstein.

41. Yosef Almogi and Yochanan Bader in the Knesset, 3 May 1967, *Knesset Minutes,* vol. 49 (in Hebrew), p. 2217; *Yediot Aharonot,* 2 Nov. 1967, p. 11; *Maariv,* 28 Dec. 1967, p. 15; Esther Raziel-Naor in the Knesset, 3 May 1967, *Knesset Minutes,* vol. 49 (in Hebrew), p. 2220; Aharon Kidan to Anat Levin, 10 May 1967; Karavan to Minister of Transportation, 14 April 1967, ISA, G-9/6356; see also: *Maariv,* 28 Dec. 1967, p. 15.

42. *Ha'aretz,* 10 June 1966, p. 9 (restaurant); 1 April 1966, pp. 1, 4 (Sapir); 31 May 1966, p. 1 (airplane); 24 Jan. 1967, p. 2 (embassy).

43. Letters to Adir Zik, 26 March 1967; 3 Aug. 1966, with his kind permission.

CHAPTER 2: OTHER PEOPLE

1. Draft of a survey on the Musrara neighborhood, JMA, container 2472, street gangs file.

2. Yochanan Peres, *Ethnic Relations in Israel* (in Hebrew) (Tel Aviv: Sifriyat Poalim, 1977), pp. 45, 115; Zion Rabi, "Demographic Development in Israel, 1948–1966," *Economic Quarterly* (in Hebrew) vol. 15, 57–58, June 1971, p. 43ff.; Central Bureau of Statistics, *Statistical Abstract of Israel, No. 18,* 1967 (in Hebrew), p. 42.

3. *Yediot Aharonot,* 21 Oct. 1966, p. 9.

4. Peres, *Ethnic Relations in Israel,* pp. 106, 112; Central Bureau of Statistics, *Statistical Abstract of Israel, No. 20,* 1969 (in Hebrew), pp. 162, 175, 178; see also: *Ot,* year I, book 2, 1967, p. 62ff.

5. Tom Segev, *The Seventh Million: Israelis and the Holocaust* (in Hebrew) (Jerusalem: Keter, 1992), p. 230ff.

6. Draft of a survey on the Musrara neighborhood, JMA, container 2472, street gangs file; see also: ibid., Haim Degan to Y. Gil, 15 Feb. 1966; S. N. Eisenstadt in an interview, *Maariv,* 11 Feb. 1966, p. 13.

7. Marziano to Municipal Engineer, 7 Nov. 1967; Suissa to Amidar, 19 Jan. 1967; Sela to Ministry of Health, 17 April 1967, JMA, container 1121, Morasha file; report of the Association for Morasha, 23 April 1967, JMA, container 4918; Peres, *Ethnic Relations in Israel,* p. 115ff.; Zalman Aran in the Knesset, 17 July 1967, *Knesset Minutes,* vol. 49 (in Hebrew), p. 2600; Rabi, "Demographic Development in Israel, 1948–1966," 15: 57–58, June 1971, p. 43ff.; Aran to Eshkol, 6 Aug. 1967, ISA, G-1/6301, file 5; Aran to Eshkol, 12 May 1968, ISA, G-2/561 (20); see also: Eshkol in the Knesset, 20 March 1967, *Knesset Minutes,* vol. 48 (in Hebrew), p. 1756.

8. Shakedi to Galili, 23 Oct. 1966, JMA, container 1954 (riots); Amnon Ramon, "Doctors Living Among Doctors: The Rehavia Neighborhood in Jerusalem," Yad Ben-Zvi; report from the meeting of the Council on Working with Street Gangs, 5 Dec. 1966, JMA, container 2472, street gangs file; *Ha'aretz,* 2 April 1967, p. 2; 3 April 1967, p. 4; 24 April 1967, p. 8.

9. *Yediot Aharonot,* 14 March 1966, p. 10 (Ofer); Sami Shalom Shitrit, *The Mizrahi Struggle in Israel, 1948–2003* (in Hebrew) (Tel Aviv: Am Oved, 2004), p. 99ff.; A. Cohen, "Problems of Development Towns and Urban Housing Projects," *Economic Quarterly,* 49–50, June 1966, p. 117ff.; see also: *Ha'aretz,* 6 May 1966, p. 11.

10. Yossi Goldstein, *Eshkol* (in Hebrew) (Jerusalem: Keter, 2003), p. 719; see also: Yigal Allon in the Knesset, 9 May 1966, *Knesset Minutes,* vol. 45 (in Hebrew), p. 1335; Eshkol in ministerial consultation, 7 April 1966, ISA, A-9/7922; see also: *Ha'aretz,* 20 Jan. 1967, p. 3.

11. *Maariv,* 4 May 1966, p. 11; 30 Nov. 1966, p. 9; ("Days and Nights" supplement), 23 Dec. 1966, p. 4; 19 May 1967, p. 6; *Yediot Aharonot* ("7 Days" supplement), 21 Oct. 1966, p. 8; see also: *Maariv* ("Days and Nights" supplement), 19 Aug. 1966, p. 18; *Ha'aretz,* 13 Feb. 1967, p. 4; *Maariv,* 9 Jan. 1967, p. 9; *Ha'aretz,* 30 Dec. 1966, p. 9.

12. Consultation on Economic Affairs, 7 April 1966, ISA, A-9/7922; Yosef Weitz, *My Diary* (in Hebrew) (Tel Aviv: Masada, 1973), vol. VI, p. 156; Sapir at Mapai secretariat, 6 April 1967, PSA, KSMA, folder 16; see also: Allon in the Knesset, 9 May 1966, *Knesset Minutes,* vol. 45 (in Hebrew), p. 1335; Allon and Eshkol in the Knesset, 20 March 1967,

Knesset Minutes, vol. 48 (in Hebrew), p. 1752; Government Minutes, 15 Oct. 1967; Lev Greenberg, "The Israeli Labor Movement in Crisis, 1957–1970: The Political Economy of the Ties Between Mapai, the Histadrut, and the State" (in Hebrew) (diss., Tel Aviv University, 1991), p. 340ff.

13. Arieh Avneri, *Sapir* (in Hebrew) (Tel Aviv: Peleg, 1976).

14. Sapir at the Mapai secretariat, 6 April 1967, PSA, KSMA, folder 16; *Maariv* ("Days and Nights" supplement), 24 Feb. 1967, p. 8.

15. Weitz, *My Diary,* vol. VI, pp. 7, 62ff., 224, 227, 495.

16. Eshkol in the Knesset, 8 Nov. 1966, *Knesset Minutes,* vol. 47 (in Hebrew), p. 242; *Maariv,* 8 Jan. 1967, p. 9; *Ha'aretz,* 13 Feb. 1967, p. 4; Government Minutes, 5 Feb. 1967, with the kind permission of Yossi Goldstein; *Maariv,* 15 March 1967, p. 2; discussion summary, 11 July 1965, ISA, A-3/7928.

17. *Ha'aretz,* 24 Nov. 1966, p. 14 (landfills); *Maariv,* 14 Jan. 1966, p. 9 (Mechasia); *Maariv,* 6 March 1966, p. 18 (Shefer); 27 Nov. 1966, p. 18 (Or Akiba); *Ha'aretz,* 13 Jan. 1967, p. 9 (Yerucham); *Maariv* ("Days and Nights" supplement), 3 March 1966, p. 11 (Ma'alot); 23 Oct. 1966, p. 10 (Zanoach and Kfar Truman); *Ha'aretz,* 3 Feb. 1967, p. 9 (Ramleh); *Maariv,* 25 Dec. 1966, p. 9 (Carmiel); *Ha'aretz,* 23 Aug. 1966, p. 9 (Yokneam); *Maariv,* 22 Nov. 1966, p. 5; *Yediot Aharonot,* 20 May 1966, p. 8 (Kiryat Shmoneh); see also: *Ha'aretz,* 1 April 1966, p. 9; 6 Jan. 1967, p. 9 (Beit She'an).

18. Raffi Man, *Inconceivable* (in Hebrew) (Tel Aviv: Hed Arzi, 1998), p. 38; *Maariv,* 18 Nov. 1966, p. 6; Arieh Ben-Eliezer in the Knesset, 19 Dec. 1966, *Knesset Minutes,* vol. 47 (in Hebrew), p. 583; *Ha'aretz,* 16 Jan. 1967, p. 2; Peres, *Ethnic Relations in Israel,* p. 124.

19. Ben-Gurion diary, 7 March 1966, BGA; *Ha'aretz,* 6 May 1966, p. 9 (Lazimi); *Ha'aretz,* 2 May 1966, p. 1; *Yediot Aharonot,* 2 May 1966, p. 3; 3 May 1966, p. 5 (Ashdod); *Maariv,* 2 May 1966, p. 15 (other places); *Ha'aretz,* 13 Jan. 1967, p. 9 (Yerucham); *Yediot Aharonot,* 28 Sept. 1966, p. 15 (Kiryat Shmoneh); *Maariv,* 1 Nov. 1966, p. 9 ("Who Imagined?"); *Ha'aretz* (supplement), 6 Jan. 1967, p. 5 (Tel Aviv); Dale to Department of State, 24 Jan. 1967, and Barbour to Department of State, 7 April 1967, USNA, Box 2224, File POL 2; see also: Ephraim Ben Haim, "The Ethnic Gap" (in Hebrew), *Ot,* Winter 1967, p. 62ff.

20. Weitz, *My Diary,* vol. VI, p. 192; *Yediot Aharonot,* 20 Dec. 1966, p. 4.

21. Tom Segev, *One Palestine, Complete: Jews and Arabs Under the British Mandate* (in Hebrew), p. 128ff.; Segev, *The Seventh Million,* p. 109.

22. Zvi Tzameret, *On a Narrow Bridge: Education in Israel During the First Years of the State* (in Hebrew) (Beersheba: Ben-Gurion University, 1997).

23. *Maariv,* 14 Sept. 1966, p. 16 (Hazaz); Tom Segev, *1949: The First Israelis* (in Hebrew) (Jerusalem: Domino, 1984), p. 105ff.; Peres, *Ethnic Relations in Israel,* p. 83ff.; see also: Ilana Shelach, "Inter-Ethnic Marriage Patterns in Israel During 1952–1958" (in Hebrew) in *Israeli Society, 1967–1973,* eds. Reuven Kahana and Simcha Koppstein (Jerusalem: Hebrew University, 1974), p. 333ff.; *Maariv,* 2 Sept. 1966, p. 11; Belha Noy, *First Children: Memories from School During the State's Early Years* (in Hebrew) (Tel Aviv: Sifriyat Poalim, 1996), p. 174ff.; *Ha'aretz,* 6 Feb. 1967, p. 2.

24. Mizrahi ethnicities, general, ISA, 6397/10-C.

25. Peres, *Ethnic Relations in Israel,* p. 125ff.

26. Nitzan to Tzabari, 2 July 1965, ISA, 6397/9-C; ISA, 6397/10-C; Herzog diary, 25 Sept. 1966, ISA, 4510/16-A.

27. *Maariv,* 7 Jan. 1966, p. 23 (Sasson); *Ha'aretz,* 17 Feb. 1966, p. 3 (Eshkol); 1 Jan. 1967, pp. 2, 7 (Yeshayahu).

28. Dale to Department of State, 24 Jan. 1967, USNA, Box 2224, File POL 2.

29. *Yediot Aharonot,* 21 Oct. 1966, p. 9; *Maariv,* 28 Jan. 1966; Ben-Gurion to Mansur, 6 June 1967, BGA.

30. *Maariv,* 1 April 1966, p. 8; *Ha'aretz,* 2 Sept. 1966, p. 9; 4 Sept. 1966, p. 8; *National Investigative Committee in the Matter of the Disappearance of Children of Yemenite Immigrants During 1948–1954* (in Hebrew) (Jerusalem: Government Printer, 2001), appendix to report, part I, p. 335.

31. *Report of the National Investigative Committee in the Matter of the Disappearance of Children of Yemenite Immigrants During 1948–1954* (in Hebrew) (Jerusalem: Government Printer, 2001).

32. Ben-Gurion to Ben-Harush, 21 May 1967, BGA; *Ha'aretz,* 23 May 1967, p. 4; ISA, 6402/24-C (child allowance); Rabi, "Demographic Development in Israel, 1948–1966," June 1971, p. 43ff.; *Maariv,* 19 May 1967, p. 10; *Ha'aretz,* 21 May 1967, p. 8.

33. *Maariv* ("Days and Nights" supplement), 6 Jan. 1967, p. 21; Gvati diary, 17 July 1967, p. 182, YTA, Unit 15, Container 12, File 02.
34. Tom Segev, *Elvis in Jerusalem* (New York: Metropolitan, 2002), p. 62; Segev, *1949*, p. 170; *Maariv*, 14 Sept. 1966, p. 16.
35. *Maariv* (special supplement on the occasion of David Ben-Gurion's eightieth birthday), 28 Sept. 1966, p. 11; Alon Gan, "The Discourse That Died?: 'Discourse Culture' as an Attempt to Define a Special Identity for the Second Generation on the Kibbutzim" (in Hebrew) (diss., Tel Aviv University, 2002), p. 45; see also: Uziel and Avneri in the Knesset, 28 Dec. 1966, *Knesset Minutes*, vol. 44 (in Hebrew), p. 262.
36. *Ha'aretz*, 15 July 1966, p. 2.
37. Ibid., 11 March 1966, p. 3.
38. Ibid., 25 Aug. 1966, p. 2.
39. Ibid., 27 July 1966, p. 2; *Davar*, 19 Aug. 1966, p. 15.
40. Reudor Manor, series of interviews with Avraham Harman, Hebrew University, Institute for International Relations, second meeting, 16 July 1974, p. 6ff., quoted with the kind permission of David Harman.
41. Ben Yaakov to Harman, 21 Aug. 1966, ISA, 3979/4-HZ.
42. Central Bureau of Statistics, *Statistical Abstract of Israel, No. 18*, 1967 (in Hebrew), p. 42; Jewish Agency, *21 Years of Immigration and Absorption*, p. 4ff., ISA, 3497/16-C.
43. Yaakov Shabtai, "The Spotted Tiger" (in Hebrew) (Tel Aviv: HaKibbutz HaMeuchad, 1985), p. 27; *Yediot Aharonot* ("7 Days" supplement), 21 Oct. 1966, p. 8; see also: *Maariv* ("Days and Nights" supplement), 19 Aug. 1966, p. 18; Andre Chouraqui, "From Wadi Salib to Ashdod," *Today*, 6 May 1966, p. 3; Zvi Loker to Ministry of Foreign Affairs, 26 Jan. 1966; Israeli Consul in Brussels to Ministry of Foreign Affairs, 16 Feb. 1966, ISA, 4042/24-HZ.
44. *Maariv*, 2 Sept. 1966, p. 3; Amos Oz, *A Tale of Love and Darkness* (in Hebrew) (Jerusalem: Keter, 2002), p. 543.
45. Atallah Mansour, *In a New Light* (in Hebrew) (Tel Aviv: Karni, 1966); see also: Fauzi Al-Asmar, *Being Arab in Israel* (in Hebrew) (Jerusalem: Shachak, 1975), p. 124ff.; *Maariv*, 21 March 1968, p. 13.
46. Zeev Sternhell, *Nation Building or Society Mending* (in Hebrew) (Tel Aviv: Am Oved, 1986); Eyal Kafkafi, *Lavon: Anti-Messiah* (in Hebrew) (Tel Aviv: Am Oved, 1998), p. 102.
47. Central Bureau of Statistics, *Statistical Abstract of Israel, No. 18*, 1967 (in Hebrew), pp. 20, 39; Yair Baumel, "The Israeli Establishment's Attitude Toward Arabs in Israel: Policy, Principles and Actions: The Second Decade, 1958–1968" (in Hebrew) (diss., Haifa University, 2002), p. 15ff.
48. Hillel Cohen, *Good Arabs: The Israeli Security Services and the Israeli Arabs* (in Hebrew) (Jerusalem: Keter, 2006); Sarah Ozacky-Lazar, "Martial Law as a Mechanism of Control over the Arab Citizens: First Decade, 1948–1958," *The New East*, vol. 43, p. 103ff.; Baumel, "The Israeli Establishment's Attitude Toward Arabs in Israel," p. 272ff.; Ben-Gurion in the Knesset, 16 Jan. 1960, *Knesset Minutes*, vol. 3 (in Hebrew), p. 536.; Aharon Shay, "The Fate of the Abandoned Arab Villages in Israel Before and After the Six-Day War," *Kathedra*, no. 105, Sept. 2003, p. 151ff.; Eshkol with Toledano, 8 Feb. 1966, ISA, 7924/1-A.
49. Baumel, "The Israeli Establishment's Attitude Toward Arabs in Israel," abstract, p. 7ff.; Eitan to Ya'ari, 1 Feb. 1967, YYA, 90.77.1, Container 841 (Mapam).
50. *Ha'aretz*, 18 Feb. 1966, p. 3; 20 Feb. 1966, p. 12; 21 Feb. 1966, p. 4.
51. Gvati diary, 21 April 1967, p. 104, YTA, Unit 15, Container 12, File 02; *My Name Is Ahmed*, film, Jerusalem Cinematheque—Israel Film Archive; newspaper clippings collection, Cinematheque library, Jerusalem; see also: *Maariv* ("Days and Nights" supplement), 30 Sept. 1966, p. 19; *Ha'aretz*, 17 Jan. 1967, p. 8; 17 Feb. 1967, p. 3.
52. Toledano to Director General of Ministry of Foreign Affairs, 2 April 1967, and confidential memorandum, unidentified author, Jan. 1967, ISA, 4032/HZ-2; *Ha'aretz* (supplement), 24 March 1967, p. 5; Eshkol in the Knesset, 19 July 1966, *Knesset Minutes*, vol. 46 (in Hebrew), p. 2204; response draft, 7 July 1966, ISA, 6404/24-C; *Ha'aretz*, 20 July 1966, p. 14; 17 Aug. 1966, p. 2; 7 April 1967, p. 9.
53. *Maariv*, 5 Jan. 1966, p. 3; 6 Jan. 1966, p. 5; *Yediot Aharonot* ("7 Days" supplement), 29 July 1966, p. 1.
54. Ben Ami in ministerial committee on population dispersion, 18 Feb. 1963; Baumel, "The Israeli Establishment's Attitude Toward Arabs in Israel," p. 280.
55. The Chief of Staff with the Minister of Defense, 31 March 1967, IDFA, 118/117/70; *Ha'aretz*, 8 Feb. 1967, p. 12; 21 Feb. 1967, p. 2.

56. *Maariv,* 3 July 1966, p. 10 (Mohar); *Ha'aretz* (supplement), 7 Jan. 1966, p. 12 (medicine); 12 April 1966, p. 9; 8 May 1967, p. 8 (foreigners); Uri Kesari, "The Jewish Dignity of Mizrahi the Gambler," *Ha'aretz,* 10 Sept. 1966, p. 3; Gideon Telpaz, "Diaspora," *Ha'aretz,* 24 June 1966, p. 10.

57. Gideon Telpaz, "Diaspora."

58. Yitzhak Rafael in the Knesset, 19 July 1966, *Knesset Minutes,* vol. 46 (in Hebrew), p. 2204ff.; Rafael, Stern, and Avneri in the Knesset, 19 July 1966, *Knesset Minutes,* vol. 46 (in Hebrew), p. 2207ff.; Vilner in the Knesset, 5 April 1967, *Knesset Minutes,* vol. 48 (in Hebrew), p. 2028ff.

59. ISA, 6402/24-C (birthrate encouragement); Ben-Gurion to leaders of Efrat society, 4 May 1967, BGA; see also: Ben-Gurion diary, 18 May 1967, BGA; Uzi Benziman and Atallah Mansour, *Sub-Letters: Israeli Arabs, Their Status, and the Policy Toward Them* (in Hebrew) (Jerusalem: Keter, 1992), p. 51 (conversion to Judaism); Bachi to Eshkol, 21 July 1966, ISA, 6401/2-C; Government Minutes, 9 April 1967, with the kind permission of Yossi Goldstein.

60. Weitz to Danin, 4 Aug. 1966, CZA, A 246/696; debate on policy toward Jordan, 26 Dec. 1966, ISA, 4094/10-HZ.

61. Baumel, "The Israeli Establishment's Attitude Toward Arabs in Israel," p. 181.

62. Yair Baumel, "Martial Law and Its Revocation Process, 1958–1966," *The New East* (in Hebrew), vol. 43, 2002, p. 132ff.

63. Eshkol with Harel, 15 Feb. 1966, ISA, 7921/1-A.

64. Eshkol in the Knesset, 8 Nov. 1966, *Knesset Minutes,* vol. 47 (in Hebrew), p. 228; "Revocation of Martial Law—Questions and Answers," undated, YEA, copy in possession of the author; Goldstein, *Eshkol,* p. 470; Eshkol with Golda Meir, 9 July 1963, ISA, 7921/1-A; Baumel, "The Israeli Establishment's Attitude Toward Arabs in Israel," p. 194ff.; Toledano to Eshkol, 9 April 1967, ISA, 6405/2-C; see also: weekly meeting, 21 April 1967, IDFA, 118/117/70.

65. *Yehiam Newsletter,* 335/17, 4 Oct. 1967, p. 2ff.

66. Weitz, *My Diary,* vol. VI, p. 285.

67. *Yehiam Newsletter,* 312/4, 1 Dec. 1966, p. 18ff.; 109/1, 14 Sept. 1966, p. 2.

68. Central Bureau of Statistics, *Statistical Abstract of Israel, No. 18,* 1967 (in Hebrew), p. 29.

69. Gan, "The Discourse That Died?" p. 14.

70. *Yehiam Newsletter,* 315/7, 27 Jan. 1966, p. 25; Gan, "The Discourse That Died?" p. 9ff.

71. *Davar,* 25 Feb. 1966, p. 3.

72. *Yehiam Newsletter,* 313/5, 25 Dec. 1966, p. 4.

73. Hazan in the Knesset, 10 March 1949, *Knesset Minutes,* vol. 1 (in Hebrew), p. 125.

74. Gan, "The Discourse That Died?" p. 47ff.

75. *Yediot Aharonot* ("7 Days" supplement), 24 Sept. 1966, p. 3.

76. *Maariv,* 3 Jan. 1966, p. 7; 10 April 1966, p. 14; *Yediot Aharonot,* 2 Sept. 1966, p. 7; *Yediot Aharonot* ("7 Days" supplement), 24 Sept. 1966, p. 3; *Yediot Aharonot,* 2 Nov. 1966, p. 7.

77. Segev, *The Seventh Million,* p. 230ff.; *Yehiam Newsletter,* 318/10, 7 April 1967, p. 8.

78. *Yediot Aharonot* ("7 Days" supplement), 24 Sept. 1966, p. 3.

79. *Yehiam Newsletter,* 335/17, 4 Oct. 1967, p. 32.

80. Gan, "The Discourse That Died?" p. 35ff.

81. *Yehiam Newsletter,* 335/17, 4 Oct. 1967, p. 20; 313/5, 25 Dec. 1966, p. 2; 312/4, 1 Dec. 1966, p. 9; 109/1, 14 Sept. 1966, p. 18; 310/2, 20 Oct. 1966, p. 5 (wedding gifts); 319/11, 5 May 1967, p. 28 (compensation, insurance); 109/1, 14 Sept. 1966, p. 14; 315/7, 27 Jan. 1967, p. 11; 312/4, 1 Dec. 1966, p. 5; 310/2, 20 Oct. 1966, p. 3; 312/4, 1 Dec. 1966, p. 6; Gan, "The Discourse That Died?" p. 35ff.

82. Noy, *First Children,* p. 188ff.; *Ha'aretz,* 3 Aug. 1966, p. 2; *Yediot Aharonot,* 20 May 1966, p. 8.

83. *Maariv,* 28 Sept. 1966, p. 7; Weitz, *My Diary,* vol. 6, p. 211.

84. Noy, *First Children,* p. 185ff.; *Yehiam Newsletter,* 319/11, 5 May 1967, p. 1.

85. Gan, "The Discourse That Died?" p. 30; *Yehiam Newsletter,* 319/11, 5 May 1967, p. 25; 314/6, 6 Jan. 1967, p. 14 The Jewish Agency, *17 Years of Absorption,* ISA, 6377/18-C.

86. Yehuda Amir, "Kibbutz Members in the IDF," *Megamot,* vol. 16, no. 2–3, Aug. 1967, p. 250ff.

87. *Yehiam Newsletter,* 313/5, 25 Dec. 1966, p. 8ff.; *Ha'aretz,* 16 Oct. 1966, p. 2; *Yediot Aharonot,* 18 Nov. 1966, p. 13; *Ha'aretz,* 30 Oct. 1966, p. 12 (Amidror).

88. *Yediot Aharonot,* 4 Nov. 1966, p. 10; see also: *LaMerhav,* 11 Nov. 1966, p. 2; *Al HaMishmar,* 11 Nov. 1966, p. 3; *Yediot Aharonot,* 18 Nov. 1966, p. 13.

89. Yemima Rosenthal, Arnon Lemfrum, and Hagai Tzoref, eds., *Levi Eshkol, the Third Prime Minister* (Jerusalem: State Archives, 2002), pp. 396, 462.
90. *Nitzotz*, 15 [March] 1967; *Yediot Aharonot*, 7 March 1967, p. 2; Ben-Gurion diary, 27 Feb. 1966.
91. Shabtai Teveth, *The Season of Fleecing* (in Hebrew) (Tel Aviv: Ish Dor, 1992); Kafkafi, *Lavon*.
92. National Elections Supervisor, *The Results of the Election for the Sixth Knesset and the Local Authorities*, Central Bureau of Statistics, Special Publications no. 216, p. 73; Central Bureau of Statistics, *Statistical Abstract of Israel, No. 19*, 1968 (in Hebrew), p. 583ff.; data on the Knesset Web site.
93. *Ha'aretz*, 10 March 1967, p. 2.
94. Rosenthal et al., eds., *Levi Eshkol*, pp. 147, 75, 109; Goldstein, *Eshkol*; Reudor Manor, "Images and Decision-Making on the Subject of Borders in Israeli Foreign Policy, 1973–1948" (diss., Hebrew University, 1980), p. 109.
95. *Time*, 9 June 1967, p. 21; Eitan Haber, *Today War Will Break Out* (in Hebrew) (Tel Aviv: Idanim, 1987), p. 48; *Ha'aretz*, 4 Jan. 1967, p. 2.
96. Haber, *Today War Will Break Out*, p. 39; Gvati diary, 8 Jan., 13 Jan., 5 March, and others, 1967, YTA, Unit 15, Container 12, File 02.
97. Barbour to Department of State, USNA, Box 2226, Pol 12; *Ha'aretz*, 18 March 1966, p. 2; *Maariv*, 10 June 1966, p. 6; *Ha'aretz*, 14 Oct. 1966, p. 3; 4 March 1966, p. 9.
98. *Maariv*, 2 Sept. 1966, p. 3 (Amisragas); 25 Dec. 1966, p. 9; *Ha'aretz*, 14 Sept. 1966, p. 41; *Maariv*, 17 June 1966, p. 6; *Ha'aretz*, 14 Oct., 1966, p. 3; 4 March 1966, p. 9.
99. *Ha'aretz*, 19 Sept. 1966, p. 2.
100. Ben-Gurion to Sharon, 20 Feb. 1967; see also: Ben-Gurion to Hod, 8 April 1967; Ben-Gurion diary, 24 Nov. 1958; correspondence file 1082; Ben-Gurion to Frisch, 4 May 1967; Ben-Gurion to Todd, 26 Jan. 1967; Ben-Gurion to Blumberg, 29 Jan. 1967; Ben-Gurion diary, 23 Oct. 1966, BGA.
101. *Ha'aretz*, 3 Oct. 1966, p. 1; Ben-Gurion to Ya'ari, 11 Feb. 1967, BGA; Ben-Gurion diary, 10 Sept. 1966; 27 Feb. 1967, BGA; Ben-Gurion to Meir, 29 Sept. 1967, BGA; Ben-Gurion to Avigur, 7 Jan. 1967, BGA; see also: *New Look*, 26 May 1966, p. 7; Goldstein, *Eshkol*, p. 525; Ben-Gurion to Hacohen, 12 Oct. 1967, BGA; *Ha'aretz*, 17 Feb. 1966, p. 2; Haver, *Today War Will Break Out*, p. 44.
102. Ben-Gurion to Avigur, 7 Jan. 1967; Ben-Gurion to Menachem Zichroni, 30 Jan. 1967; Ben-Gurion diary, 25 and 28 Nov. 1966; 26 Jan. 1967; 27 Oct. 1966; Ben-Gurion to Bar-Av, 31 Jan. 1967; Ben-Gurion to Karoy, 6 June 1967—all BGA.
103. Meir Amit, *Head to Head: A Personal Look at Great Events and Secret Affairs* (in Hebrew) (Tel Aviv: Hed Arzi, 1999), p. 149; Ian Black and Benny Morris, *Israel's Secret Wars* (London: Hamish Hamilton, 1991), p. 202ff.; Shlomo Aronson, *Israel's Nuclear Programme: The Six Day War and Its Ramifications* (London: King's College, 1999); David Golomb in answer to the author's question; see also: Golomb to Ben-Gurion (undated) and letter to *Ha'aretz*, ISA, 7231/1-A.
104. Eshkol in the government, 12 Feb. 1967 and others, ISA, 6339/52-C; *Ha'aretz*, 21 Feb. 1967, p. 2; 3 April 1967, p. 2; and others; Uri Avneri in the Knesset, 7 March 1967, *Knesset Minutes*, vol. 48 (in Hebrew), p. 1599; no-confidence votes, 20 March 1967, *Knesset Minutes*, vol. 48 (in Hebrew), p. 1746ff.
105. Shazar to Ben-Gurion, 23 Feb. 1967, ISA; see also: Dayan and Eshkol in the Knesset, 20 March 1967, *Knesset Minutes*, vol. 48 (in Hebrew), p. 1746ff.; BGA ISA, 4042/28 1-HZ.
106. Herzog diary, 2 and 9 Aug. 1966; 17 and 25 Sept. 1966, ISA, 4510/16-A.
107. *Maariv*, 6 Jan. 1967, p. 10.
108. Ben-Gurion to Rachel Mishal, 19 Jan. 1967, BGA; Ben-Gurion to Alexander Pili, 26 Jan. 1967, BGA.
109. *Maariv*, 17 Feb. 1967, p. 6.
110. Yehiam Weitz, *From Underground Fighter to Political Party: The Founding of the Herut Movement, 1947–1949* (in Hebrew) (Beersheba: Ben-Gurion University, 2002); *Ha'aretz*, 28 June 1966, p. 2; 11 Sept. 1966, p. 2; Ben-Gurion to Haim Gouri, 15 May 1963, BGA; *Maariv*, 10 July 1966, p. 12; 24 Feb. 1967, p. 12; Ben-Gurion to Ari Mordechai, 27 Nov. 1962, ISA, 6380/7-C; *Ha'aretz*, 18 July 1966, p. 10.
111. *Maariv*, 27 June 1966, p. 2; 29 June 1966, p. 2; *Ha'aretz*, 29 June 1966, p. 3; *Maariv*, 3 July 1966, p. 3.
112. *Ha'aretz*, 10 Sept. 1966, p. 9; 8 Jan. 1967, p. 2.

113. Letter to Adir Zik, 23 March 1967, with his kind permission; *Maariv,* 30 Jan. 1966, p. 5.
114. Letter to New York, 15 Jan. 1967, copy in possession of the author; *Ha'aretz,* 19 Aug. 1966, p. 3; Ofra Nevo-Eshkol, *Humorous Eshkol* (in Hebrew) (Tel Aviv: Yediot Aharonot, 1968), pp. 11, 127; Rosenthal et al., eds., *Levi Eshkol,* p. 512.
115. Ronny Stauber, *A Lesson for a Generation: Holocaust and Heroism in Public Thought in Israel During the Fifties* (in Hebrew) (Jerusalem: Yad Ben-Zvi, 2000), p. 137.
116. Ben-Gurion to S. Perldman, 8 Feb. 1967, BGA.
117. *Ha'aretz,* 24 April 1966, p. 4; 28 April 1966, p. 2.
118. *Maariv,* 21 Feb. 1966, p. 10; 1 April 1966, p. 1.
119. *Yehiam Newsletter,* 315/7, 27 Jan. 1967, p. 1.
120. *Ha'aretz,* 7 July 1977, p. 2; 13 July 1966, p. 2.
121. Ibid., 10 Feb. 1966, p. 2; Simon to Uzai, 16 Feb. 1966, ISA, 6399/26-C; *Maariv,* 16 Feb. 1966, p. 2.
122. *Ha'aretz,* 23 Jan. 1966, p. 2; see also: *Ha'aretz,* 17 Feb. 1966, p. 2.
123. Ibid., 31 July 1966, p. 4.
124. Ibid., 3 Jan. 2002, p. 10 (Omer); *Maariv,* 20 April 1967, p. 3 (Yehezkel); *Ha'aretz,* 3 Jan. 1966, p. 2 (Kook).
125. Oz Almog, *The Sabra: The Creation of the New Jew* (Berkeley: University of California Press, 2000), p. 73ff.; *Ha'aretz,* 11 Aug. 1966, p. 2 (Shazar); Gan, "The Discourse That Died?" pp. 108 (Sarig), 14 (Katznelson).
126. *Ha'aretz,* 5 April 1967, p. 2.
127. Inquiry on the question of Jewish awareness, 16 Feb. 1966, ISA, 12973/10-GL.
128. *Ha'aretz,* 11 July 1966, p. 11.
129. Ibid., 21 April 1966, p. 6; *Yediot Aharonot,* 10 Aug. 1966, p. 1; 3 Jan. 1967, p. 1; *Maariv,* 3 April 1966, p. 1; *Yediot Aharonot,* 7 Jan. 1966, p. 2 (Fagin).
130. Amos Oz, *Elsewhere, Perhaps* (in Hebrew) (Jerusalem: Keter, 1991), p. 267.
131. "Nativ" activities, 12 Jan. 1967, ISA, 7938/6-A; Shmorak to Ministry of Foreign Affairs, 3 Nov. 1966, ISA, 4051/2-HZ ("Emanuel"); Dinstein to Bar, 5 Feb. 1968; Netzer to Adi Yaffe, 14 Feb. 1968, ISA, 7938/6-A; Reudor Manor, series of interviews with Avraham Harman, Hebrew University, Institute for International Relations, meeting 21, 31 Aug. 1976, p. 1ff., with the kind permission of David Harman; see also: *Ha'aretz,* 1 April 1966, p. 3; Arieh Loba Eliav, *Rings of Testimony* (in Hebrew) (Tel Aviv: Am Oved, 1983), vol. II, p. 165ff.
132. Eshkol to Avriel, 13 Feb. 1966; Eban to Ministry of Foreign Affairs, 21 Sept. 1967; 4064/13-HZ.
133. *Maariv,* 15 Aug. 1966, p. 8.
134. *Ha'aretz,* 9 Jan. 1967, p. 1.
135. Ibid., 18 May 1967, p. 11 (Kahana); Yitzhak Rafael, on the question of autopsies, ISA, 3979/4-HZ; posters of the Public Committee for the Protection of Human Dignity, ISA, 6399/20-C; see also: *Ha'aretz,* 19 April 1967, p. 8.
136. Levi and Gross in the Knesset, 13 March 1967, *Knesset Minutes,* vol. 48 (in Hebrew), p. 1663ff.; Yadid and Barzilai in the Knesset, 3 July 1967, *Knesset Minutes,* vol. 49 (in Hebrew), p. 2447; Laurence and others in the Knesset, 23 March 1967, *Knesset Minutes,* vol. 48, p. 1831ff.; Yael Zerubavel, *Recovered Roots: Collective Memory and the Making of Israeli National Tradition* (Chicago: University of Chicago Press, 1995); see also: ISA, 6399/20-C; *Yediot Aharonot,* 3 May 1967, p. 3; *Ha'aretz,* 4 May 1967, p. 1; *Maariv,* 9 May 1967, p. 3 (doctors).
137. Man to Cohen, 17 May 1966, ISA, 3979/3-HZ; Jacobson to Man, 8 May 1967, ISA, 6399/18-C; Zohar to Jerusalem, 11 and 12 July 1966, ISA, 3779/3-HZ.
138. Arnon to Jerusalem, 26 April 1966, ISA, 3979/4-HZ; New York Consulate to Jerusalem, 17 March 1967, ISA, 3979/7-HZ; New York Consulate to Jerusalem, 20 Sept. 1966, ISA, 3979/4-HZ; Harman to Argov, 28 Oct. 1966; Zohar to Ministry of Foreign Affairs, 5 Oct. 1966, ISA, 3979/5-HZ; Harman to Bitan, 10 April 1967; Remez to Jerusalem, 5 April 1967, ISA, 3979/7-HZ.
139. Livneh to Eshkol, 12 Feb. 1967, ISA, 6360/25-C.
140. Central Bureau of Statistics, *Statistical Abstract of Israel, No. 18,* 1967 (in Hebrew), p. 21; Jewish Agency, *21 Years of Immigration and Absorption,* p. 4ff., ISA, 3497/16-C; *Ha'aretz,* 14 Sept. 1966, p. 11; *Maariv,* 8 Nov. 1966, p. 9; Etta Zablocki Bick, "Ethnic Linkages and Foreign Policy: A Study of the Linkage Role of American

Jews in Relations Between the United States and Israel, 1956–1968" (diss., CUNY, 1983).

141. Livneh to Eshkol, 12 Feb. 1967, ISA, 6360/25-C; *Ha'aretz,* 28 June 1966, p. 2 ("holding out hands"); 29 April 1966, p. 13 (Tammuz); 28 July 1966, p. 2; see also: *Ha'aretz,* 5 Aug. 1966, p. 2 (Livneh).

142. Rosen to Marmour, 27 July 1966, ISA, 3979/3-HZ; ISA, 4006/13-HZ (Britain); *Ha'aretz,* 28 July 1966, p. 2 ("spiritual life"); see also: *Ha'aretz,* 5 Aug. 1966, p. 2; Israel consul in Los Angeles to Israel consul in New York, 28 Dec. 1966, ISA, 3979/9-HZ; Arnon to Ministry of Foreign Affairs, 17 Nov. 1966, ISA, 3979/5-HZ (reforms).

143. *Ha'aretz,* 24 April 1967, p. 3 (Wiesel); *Maariv,* 8 Nov. 1966, p. 9 (Pushkin); Harman to Eban, 5 July 1966, ISA, 7938/6-A.

144. Reudor Manor, series of interviews with Avraham Harman, Hebrew University, Institute for International Relations, meeting 20, 23 Aug. 1976, p. 13ff., with the kind permission of David Harman.

145. Eshkol in the Knesset, 20 March 1967, *Knesset Minutes,* vol. 48 (in Hebrew), p. 1752; ISA, 4006/1-HZ; see also: 3979/5-HZ.

146. Charles S. Leibman, "Diaspora Influence on Israel: The Ben-Gurion–Blaustein 'Exchange' and Its Aftermath," *Jewish Social Studies,* vol. XXXVI, 1974, p. 271ff.; Blaustein-Rusk conversation, 17 Oct. 1966; Harman to Bitan, 4 Nov. 1966; Harman to Bitan, 15 Nov. 1966, ISA, 3977/10-HZ; Evron to Gazit, 2 Jan. 1967, 4096/2-HZ; see also: Reudor Manor, series of interviews with Avraham Harman, Hebrew University, Institute for International Relationships, Meeting 20, 23 Aug. 1976, p. 13ff., with the kind permission of David Harman.

147. Reudor Manor, series of interviews with Avraham Harman, Hebrew University, Institute for International Relationships, 1974–1979, with the kind permission of David Harman.

148. Evron to Bitan, 2 March 1967, ISA, 3979/7-HZ; T. H. Baker, interview with Harry McPherson, no. 3, 16 Jan. 1969, p. 24, LBJL, Oral Histories.

149. Reudor Manor, series of interviews with Avraham Harman, Hebrew University, Institute for International Relationships, meeting 20, 23 Aug. 1976, p. 7; meeting 18, 3 May 1976, p. 4, with the kind permission of David Harman.

150. *Maariv,* 17 April 1966, p. 20; *Yediot Aharonot,* 22 April 1966, p. 7; *Ha'aretz* (supplement), 22 April 1966, p. 29.

151. Arnold Forster, *Square One: The Memoirs of a True Freedom Fighter's Life-Long Struggle Against Anti-Semitism, Domestic and Foreign* (New York: Donald I. Fine, 1988), p. 259ff.; Yuval Elitzur, *From Shachrit to Maariv: Chapters of Life in Journalism* (in Hebrew), certificate (undated), p. 172ff.; Reudor Manor, series of interviews with Avraham Harman, Hebrew University, Institute for International Relationships, meeting 26, 19 Dec. 1977, p. 10, with the kind permission of David Harman; see also: Harman to Bitan (undated), ISA, 3977/22-HZ.

152. Richard D. McKinzie, Oral History, interview with Abraham Feinberg, Harry S. Truman Library, ISA, 1885/P-3.

153. Robert Dallek, *Lone Star Rising: Lyndon Johnson and His Times, 1908–1960* (New York: Oxford University Press, 1991), p. 512.

154. Valenti to President, March 31, 1965, LBJL, WHCF, Name File, Box F47; Michael Beschloss, ed., *Reaching for Glory: Lyndon Johnson's Secret White House Tapes, 1964–1965* (New York: Simon and Schuster, 2001), pp. 21–23, 188ff.; see also: *Money* (in Hebrew), 29 Nov. 2001, p. 10ff.

155. Rostow to President, 8 March 1967, LBJL, NSF, Country File Israel, Israeli Aid 5/67 Box 145; see also: Yaffe to Bitan, 19 Feb. 1967; Evron to Bitan, 17 March 1967, ISA, 7938/A-10; Rostow to President, 13 Feb. 1967, LBJL, NSF, Country File Israel, vol. VI; Feinberg Good Words, LBJL, NSF Files of Walt W. Rostow, Box 12.

156. Beschloss, ed., *Reaching for Glory,* p. 188.

157. Evron to Bitan, 31 March 1967, ISA, 3979/7-HZ; Israeli Consul to Ministry of Foreign Affairs, 13 June 1967, ISA, 3979/9-HZ; Hartman to Eshkol, 19 Feb. and 20 July 1967, ISA, 7231/1-A; see also: *Ha'aretz,* 23 Sept. 1966, p. 13; Abba Eban, *Life Stories* (Tel Aviv: Sifriyat Maariv, 1978), vol. II, p. 351.

158. Rostow to President, 13 Dec. 1966, FRUS, vol. XVIII, Doc. No. 369.

159. Interview with Ginsburg, Johnson Archives, quoted with his kind permission; also, Ginsburg in response to questions from the author and Yoav Karni.

160. Harman to Bitan, 9 June 1966, ISA, 3979/3-HZ.
161. Avner Cohen, *Israel and the Bomb* (in Hebrew) (Tel Aviv: Schocken, 2000), p. 102; Michael Karpin, *The Bomb in the Basement: How Israel Went Nuclear and What That Means for the World* (New York: Simon and Schuster, 2006), p. 129ff.
162. Evron to Bitan, 17 March 1967; Harman to Bitan, 17 March 1967; Evron to Bitan, 20 April 1967; Ginsburg and Feinberg with Eshkol, 28 April 1967; American Jewry and Israel, ISA, 7938/10-A; Rostow to President, 20 April 1967, LBJL, NSF Country File, Israel, Container 140–41, Doc. No. 98a; see also: Zachi Shalom, *From Dimona to Washington: The Fight for Developing Israel's Nuclear Option, 1960–1968* (in Hebrew) (Beersheba: Ben-Gurion University, 2004).
163. Harman to Bitan, 21 April 1967, ISA, 7938/10-A.
164. Bitan to Harman, 30 April 1967, ISA, 7938/10-A; interview with Ginsburg, Johnson Library, with his kind permission; American Jewry and Israel, ISA, 7938/10-A.
165. Meyer Weisgal, *So Far* (London: Weidenfeld and Nicolson, 1971), pp. 122ff., 313ff.; Mathilde Krim, in response to the author's questions.
166. Michael L. Gillette, interview with Arthur B. Krim, no. I, p. 4 (party); no. VI, p. 6 (Meir); no. IV, p. 34 (services); no. II, p. 13 (Feinberg); no. II, p. 14 (Eshkol); no. II, p. 6 (Harvard); no. IV, p. 6 (roots)—all LBJL, Oral Histories; President Lyndon B. Johnson's Daily Diary, 26 May 1967ff., LBJL, WHCF, Box 11; Mathilde Krim, in response to the author's questions.
167. Avidar to Ministry of Foreign Affairs, 6 Jan. 1967, ISA, 3979/6-HZ; Fortas speech, BGA, File 1064; Ben-Gurion to Fortas, 5 Feb. 1967, BGA; Laura Kalman, *Abe Fortas: A Biography* (New Haven, Ct.: Yale University Press, 1990), p. 36.
168. Reudor Manor, series of interviews with Avraham Harman, Hebrew University, Institute for International Relationships, meeting 20, 23 Aug. 1976, p. 10, with the kind permission of David Harman; Harman to Ministry of Foreign Affairs, 28 May 1967, ISA, 7919/1-A; Richard B. Parker, ed., *The Six-Day War: A Retrospective* (Gainesville: University Press of Florida, 1966), p. 225.
169. Michael L. Gillette, interview with Arthur B. Krim, no. IV, 9 Nov. 1982, p. 34, LBJL, Oral Histories; Bruce Allen Murphy, *Fortas: The Rise and the Ruin of a Supreme Court Justice* (New York: William Morrow, 1988), p. 450; Harman to Bitan, 25 Oct. 1966, ISA, 3977/20-HZ.
170. *New York Times,* 31 Dec. 1963, p. 16.
171. Lady Bird Johnson, *A White House Diary* (New York: Holt, Rinehart and Winston, 1970), p. 28.
172. Louis Stanislaus Gomolak, "Prologue: LBJ's Foreign-Affairs Background, 1908–1948" (diss., University of Texas, 1989); Dallek, *Lone Star Rising,* pp. 169ff.
173. LBJL, Reference File, LBJ and the Jews.
174. T. H. Baker, interview with Harry C. McPherson Jr., no. III, 16 Jan. 1969, p. 24; Michael L. Gillette, interview with Harry C. McPherson Jr., no. VII, 9 Sept. 1985, LBJL, Oral Histories; Beschloss, ed., *Reaching for Glory,* p. 396; Mathilde Krim, in response to the author's questions.
175. Uzi Peled, "The Israelis and the Vietnam War," *International Problems* (in Hebrew), VI: 1–2 (13), May 1968, p. 41ff.; *Ha'aretz,* 30 May 1966, p. 15; Barbour to Department of State, 24 March 1967; Wilson to Department of State, 12 April 1967, USNA, Box 2228; minutes of Mapai's political committee, 28 June and 24 July 1966, ISA, 7922/90A; Rostow to President, 20 April 1967, LBJL, NSF, Country File, Israel, vol. VI; see also: Director General of Ministry of Foreign Affairs to Asia Department Director, 29 March 1967, ISA, 3977/22-HZ; lunch with Vietnamese delegation, 26 Dec. 1966, ISA, 3977/20-HZ; *Ha'aretz,* 23 March 1966, p. 2 (relations).
176. Harman to Bitan, 9 June 1966, ISA, 3979/3-HZ; Arnon to Ministry of Foreign Affairs, 22 Sept. 1966, ISA, 3979/4-HZ; Evron to Ministry of Foreign Affairs, 8 Sept. 1966, ISA, 3979/4-HZ; Bick, "Ethnic Linkages and Foreign Policy," p. 209ff.; Judith A. Klinghofer, *Vietnam, Jews and the Middle East: Unintended Consequences* (New York: St. Martin's Press, 1999); Ariel to Ministry of Foreign Affairs, 28 Sept. 1966; Arnon to Ministry of Foreign Affairs, 3 Oct. 1966; Frintz to Arnon, 26 Sept. 1966, ISA, 3979/5-HZ.
177. Michael L. Gillette, interview with Morris Abram, no. II, May 3, 1984, LBJL, Oral Histories; Ariel to Ministry of Foreign Affairs, 21 Sept. 1966, ISA, 3979/4-HZ.
178. Arnon to Ministry of Foreign Affairs, 20 Sept. 1966, ISA, 3979/4-HZ.

179. Prinz to Arnon, 26 Sept. 1966, ISA, 3979/5-HZ; Israel Consul in New York to Ministry of Foreign Affairs, 2 Jan. 1967; Argov to Israel Consul, 15 Jan. 1967, ISA, 3979/6-HZ.

180. *Yediot Aharonot,* 11 Sept. 1966, p. 1; *Maariv,* 23 Nov. 1966, p. 3; *Jerusalem Post,* 18 Sept. 1966, pp. 1–2; Evron to Ministry of Foreign Affairs, 11 Sept. 1966, ISA, 3979/4-HZ; Arnon to Ministry of Foreign Affairs, 26 Oct. 1966, ISA, 3979/5-HZ.

181. *Maariv,* 24 June 1966, p. 10; Eban in the Knesset, 15 June 1966, *Knesset Minutes,* vol. 46 (in Hebrew), p. 1775; Ministry of Foreign Affairs to Israeli Embassy in Paris, 22 June 1966; Bitan to Harman, 12 June 1966; Eban to Harman, 13 June 1966, ISA, HZ-31/4023; Herzog diary, 1 Oct. 1966, ISA, 4510/16-A; *Ha'aretz,* 9 June 1966, p. 2; Feinberg to Rostow, June 16, 1966, LBJL, Confidential Name File DEL Box 145 FE; Moshe Dayan, *Vietnam Diary* (in Hebrew) (Tel Aviv: Dvir, 1977), p. 29.

182. Livneh to Eshkol, 12 Feb. 1967, ISA, 6380/25-C.

183. *Ha'aretz,* 9 Jan. 1966, p. 12.

184. Ibid., 2 Jan. 1966, p. 11.

185. *Yediot Aharonot,* 13–17 March 1966; *Ha'aretz,* 9 Nov. 1966–6 Jan. 1967; *Maariv,* 9 Dec. 1966–6 Jan. 1967; *Davar,* 27–31 Oct. 1966.

186. *Yediot Aharonot,* 10 April 1966, p. 17 (Ashkelon); *Maariv,* 2 May 1966, p. 14 (Ashdod); 15 Jan. 1967, p. 10 (agent).

187. Jewish Agency, *21 Years of Immigration and Absorption* (in Hebrew), p. xxx, ISA, 3497/16-C; Arnon to Ministry of Foreign Affairs, 27 Oct. 1966, ISA, 3818/5-HZ; see also: *Ha'aretz,* 4 Jan. 1966, p. 2.

188. Reuven Lamdani, "Emigration from Israel" (in Hebrew) in *The Israeli Economy: Growing Pains,* ed. Yoram Ben-Porat (Tel Aviv: Am Oved, 1989), p. 181; Jewish Agency, *21 Years of Immigration and Absorption* (in Hebrew), p. 4ff., ISA, 3497/16-C; see also: Zvi Sovel, *Journey from the Promised Land* (in Hebrew) (Tel Aviv: Am Oved, 1986); Israeli Immigration and Emigration, 26 April 1968, USNA, Box 2228, File, POL 23-9; *LaMerhav,* 31 Oct. 1966, p. 2 (Gouri).

189. Israeli Consul to Ministry of Foreign Affairs, 3 May 1967, ISA, 3818/5-HZ; *Yediot Aharonot,* 13 Dec. 1966, p. 1; ISA, 3818/5-HZ (diplomats' reports); Weitz, *My Diary,* vol. 6, p. 203.

190. *LaMerhav,* 30 Feb. 1967, p. 4.

191. Zigel to Shragai, 2 Nov. 1966, ISA, 4601/10-GL; Paul Ritterband, "Out of Zion: The Non-Returning Israeli Student" (diss., Columbia University, 1968); see also: *Ha'aretz,* 9 Nov. 1966, p. 2; 13 Dec. 1966, p. 2; Barzilai in the Knesset, 20 March 1967, *Knesset Minutes,* vol. 48 (in Hebrew), p. 1768; see also: *Ha'aretz,* 19 July 1966, p. 5; government decision, 2 Feb. 1967, ISA, 10136/2-C.

192. Shimoni to Ministry of Foreign Affairs, 10 Feb. 1966, ISA, 3818/5-HZ; *Yediot Aharonot,* 17 June 1966, p. 8; *Maariv,* 27 Dec. 1967, p. 1 (Vietnam).

193. Tamir in the Knesset, 1 June 1966, *Knesset Minutes,* vol. 45 (in Hebrew), p. 1593; Ben-Eliezer in the Knesset, 20 March 1967, *Knesset Minutes,* vol. 48 (in Hebrew), p. 1745; Eshkol in the Knesset, 20 March 1967, *Knesset Minutes,* vol. 48 (in Hebrew), p. 1745.

194. *Davar,* 4 March 1966, p. 3 (Shamir); 18 March 1986, p. 3 (Gutthelf); 22 April 1966, p. 4 (Yagol); 12 Aug. 1966, p. 3 (Shachar); 14 Sept. 1966, p. 9 (Gutthelf); 5 May 1967, p. 3 (Gutthelf); 12 May 1967, p. 3 (Ya'ari); *LaMerhav,* 17 Feb. 1967, p. 2 (Hagor); see also: Yonah Hadari, *A Messiah Riding a Tank* (in Hebrew) (Jerusalem: Hartman Institute, 2002), p. 386ff. (Hofshi, readers write); *Davar,* 8 April 1966, p. 3 (desertion); *Ha'aretz,* 25 Oct. 2002, p. 2; 25 Oct. 1966, p. 2 (Aran); 29 Dec. 1966 (Sapir); *Yediot Aharonot,* 2 Dec. 1966, p. 5 (Gouri).

195. *Davar,* 29 March 1966, p. 3 (parents); 11 Nov. 1966, p. 3 (soldier); 4 Nov. 1966, p. 3 (fate); 11 Nov. 1966, p. 3 (beast).

196. *LaMerhav,* 21 June 1966, p. 2 (Bartov); *Maariv,* 21 Oct. 1966, p. 3 (Schnitzer); *Davar,* 27 Jan. 1967, p. 4 (Livneh); *Yediot Aharonot,* 17 March 1966, p. 5 (Germany).

197. *Ha'aretz,* 29 Dec. 1966, p. 2 (Sapir); see also: 13 Dec. 1966, p. 2 (abroad); 2 Nov. 1967, p. 2 (America).

198. Ibid., 20 Jan. 1967, p. 3 (interest); *Maariv,* 9 Jan. 1967, p. 9 (soldiers); 2 Sept. 1966, p. 8; see also: *Ha'aretz,* 16 Dec. 1966, p. 2; 17 Jan. 1967, p. 2; Naomi Niv to Eshkol, 16 Oct. 1966, ISA, 6378/16-C.

199. *Ha'aretz,* 15 July 1966, p. 9; 16 Dec. 1966, p. 2; *Maariv,* 21 Aug. 1966, p. 14; *Yediot Aharonot* (Shabbat supplement), 17 June 1966, p. 1; see also: Eban to Eshkol and appendix, 21 Nov. 1966, ISA, 6378/16-C.

200. Letters to Penina Axelrod, 23 Dec. 1966–3 Aug. 1967, with her kind permission; letters to Ruthi and Haim Haskel, 15 April 1967–3 Feb. 1968, with their kind permission.

201. *Maariv*, 21 Oct. 1966, p. 3 (Schnitzer); *Yediot Aharonot*, 2 Dec. 1966, p. 4; *Ha'aretz*, 6 Jan. 1967, p. 2.

202. *Ha'aretz*, 28 Jan. 1966, p. 2; 10 March 1966, p. 4 (who is to blame); *Maariv*, 15 Nov. 1966, p. 9; 18 Nov. 1966, p. 8 (Cohen); *Davar*, 27 Jan. 1967, p. 3 (Gotthelf); Hadari, *Messiah Riding a Tank*, p. 385 (save); *Knesset Minutes*, 27 Dec. 1965–3 Jan. 1966, vol. 44, p. 226ff.

203. Yariv Ben Aharon, *HaKrav* (in Hebrew) (Tel Aviv: Am Oved, 1966), p. 179; see also: Gan, "The Discourse That Died?", p. 15; Hadari, *Messiah Riding a Tank*, p. 387 (how have we reached).

204. Yedlin in the Knesset, 27 Dec. 1965, *Knesset Minutes*, vol. 44 (in Hebrew) p. 227; *LaMerhav*, 17 Feb. 1967, p. 2.

205. *Ha'aretz*, 28 Sept. 1966, p. 9; see also: *Maariv*, 26 Sept. 1966, p. 14.

206. Hadari, *Messiah Riding a Tank*, p. 386.

207. *Ha'aretz*, 28 Sept. 1966, p. 9 (Teveth); 6 May 1966, p. 2 (Rubinstein).

208. Ibid., 28 Sept. 1966, p. 9; *Davar*, 18 March 1966, p. 33.

209. *Yediot Aharonot* ("7 Days" supplement), 2 Dec. 1966, p. 9; *Davar*, 22 April 1966, p. 4; 5 May 1967, p. 3; see also: *Maariv* ("Days and Nights" supplement), 12 Aug. 1966, p. 4; 20 Jan. 1966, p. 20; 23 Jan. 1966, p. 15.

210. Aloni in the Knesset, 28 Dec. 1965, *Knesset Minutes*, vol. 44 (in Hebrew), p. 252.

211. *Ha'aretz*, 5 Jan. 1966, p. 2; 19 Jan. 1966, p. 4; 6 May 1966, p. 2 (Rubinstein); 6 Jan. 1967, p. 2; 9 Nov. 1966, p. 2 (Teveth); *Maariv*, 2 Sept. 1966, p. 14 (Ben-Yehuda); 20 Sept. 1966, p. 13 (Ben-Gurion).

212. *Yehiam Newsletter*, 310/2, 20 Oct. 1966, p. 19; 313/5, 25 Dec. 1966, p. 4; see also: Gan, "The Discourse That Died?" p. 2; *Ha'aretz*, 28 Sept. 1966, p. 9 (Bnei Akiva); Haim Adler and Reuven Reuven, "A Social Portrait of the Youth" (in Hebrew) in *Education in Israel*, ed. Haim Ormian (Jerusalem: Ministry of Education and Culture, 1973), p. 195ff.; *Ha'aretz*, 6 June 1966, p. 4; Hadari, *Messiah Riding a Tank*, p. 398 (Kolberg); *Ha'aretz*, 29 Dec. 1966, p. 2 (desperation); 16 Jan. 1967, p. 2; see also: Moshe Shamir, *Nathan Alterman: The Poet as Leader* (in Hebrew) (Tel Aviv: Dvir, 1988), p. 11.

213. *Yediot Aharonot*, 28 Jan. 1966, p. 10 ("How Did They Manage to Destroy"); *Ha'aretz*, 2 Feb. 1966, p. 2 ("The Seed of Destruction"); *Maariv*, 12 May 1955, p. 14 ("The Dream and Its Meaning"); 17 June 1966, p. 2 ("The Crisis"); 14 Sept. 1966, p. 6 ("Death of a Vision"); 7 Oct. 1966, p. 5 ("Vision and Failure"); *Ha'aretz*, 24 April 1967, p. 3 ("Israel Is Not a Challenge"); *Maariv*, 12 May 1967, p. 3 ("Long Live the Future Country").

214. *Maariv*, 17 June 1966, p. 3 ("crisis"); *Ha'aretz*, 3 Feb. 1966, p. 2 ("demoralization"); see also: 29 April 1966, p. 13 ("bitterness"); *HaTzofeh*, 30 Dec. 1966, p. 3 ("distress"); *Yediot Aharonot*, 30 Dec. 1966, p. 5 ("Indifference and Desperation"); *Davar*, 17 June 1966, p. 2 ("Ill Wind"); *Ha'aretz*, 2 Feb. 1966, p. 2 ("Fundamental Weakening"); *Davar*, 19 June 1967, p. 6 ("Suffocation and Despair").

215. *Maariv*, 14 Sept. 1966, p. 3; 12 May 1967, p. 3 (Schnitzer); *Ha'aretz*, 7 Oct. 1966, p. 3 (Teveth); Amos Oz, "Tired Man," *Davar*, 10 April 1966, p. 5; see also: Hadari, *Messiah Riding a Tank*, p. 46ff.; Pinchas Sadeh, *On Man's Condition* (in Hebrew) (Tel Aviv: Am Oved, 1967), p. 243; see also: *Ha'aretz*, 4 March 1966, p. 10; 4 April 1966, p. 18 (Kurtzweil); 23 Sept. 1966, p. 9 (Talmon); 10 Oct. 1966, p. 8 (Shalmon).

216. Hadari, *Messiah Riding a Tank*, p. 402ff.; see also: *Yediot Aharonot*, 2 Dec. 1966, p. 5.

217. *Yediot Aharonot* ("7 Days" supplement), 13 Jan. 1967, p. 7; *Ha'aretz*, 21 Jan. 1966, p. 3; Gan, "The Discourse That Died?" p. 152.

218. Herzog diary, 7 Oct. 1966, ISA, 4510/16-A; see also: Gvati diary, 2 Jan. 1967, YTA Unit 15, Container 12, File 02.

PART II: BETWEEN ISRAEL AND PALESTINE

CHAPTER 3: MAPS AND DREAMS

1. *Maariv*, 28 Jan. 1966, p. 8; see also: *Yediot Aharonot*, 24 April 1966, p. 10.

2. Sabotage Activities in Israel, 10 March 1967, USNA, Box 2228, POL 23, 1/1/67; The Palestine Liberation Organization (no date), PRO, FCO 370/285, 104038; Fatah incidents (no date), UNA, S-312, Box 26, File 5; summary of acts of sabotage, 7 April 1967–9 May 1967, YEA, copy in possession of the author; see also: Infiltration and Acts of Sabotage 1966–1968, ISA, A-5/7936.

3. *Maariv,* 14 Jan. 1965, p. 1; *Yediot Aharonot,* 14 Jan. 1965, p. 1.
4. *Yediot Aharonot,* 31 Oct. 1966, p. 3; Ami Gluska, *Eshkol, Give the Order!* (in Hebrew) (Tel Aviv: Ministry of Defense, 2004), p. 421.
5. *Yediot Aharonot,* 2 May 1966, p. 10.
6. Security survey (undated, probably 22 Nov. 1966), ISA, A-7/7935; Joint Research Department Memorandum, 15 Nov. 1966, PRO, FCO 370/285, 104038; The Palestine Liberation Organization (undated), PRO, FCO 17/5, 104038; Intelligence Memorandum, 2 Dec. 1966, FRUS, vol. XVIII, Doc. No. 356.
7. *Yediot Aharonot,* 31 Oct. 1966, p. 3; Idith Zertal, *Death and the Nation: History, Memory, Politics* (in Hebrew) (Tel Aviv: Dvir, 2002), p. 147ff.; *Maariv,* 20 March 1967, p. 14.
8. The Palestinian Liberation Army, ISA, HZ-9/4096; *Yediot Aharonot* (Shabbat supplement), 24 June 1966, p. 1; *Ha'aretz,* 2 Dec. 1966, p. 2. *Maariv,* 3 Aug. 1966, p. 6 (Shukeiri); *Ha'aretz,* 29 Sept. 1967, p. 6; see also: Ehud Yaari, *Fatah* (Tel Aviv: Levin Epstein, 1970).
9. *Maariv,* 11 May 1967, p. 9 (public opinion); Oron in debate, 14 Dec. 1966, ISA, HZ-13/4092 ("Palestinian Zionism").
10. Eshkol and Yosef Sapir in the Knesset, 17 Oct. 1966, *Knesset Minutes,* vol. 47, pp. 4, 7.
11. Yehoshafat Harkabi, *The Palestinians: From Slumber to Awakening* (in Hebrew) (Jerusalem: Magnes, 1979), p. 59ff.; security survey (undated, probably 22 Nov. 1966), ISA, A-7/7935.
12. Eban with Katzenbach, 12 Dec. 1966, ISA, HZ-20/3977; *Yediot Aharonot* (Shabbat supplement), 12 May 1967, p. 1; *Ha'aretz,* 10 March 1967, p. 9 ("fieldsmen"); Yosef Serlin in the Knesset, 17 May 1966, *Knesset Minutes,* vol. 45, p. 1439; see also: *Ha'aretz,* 6 Aug. 1966, p. 2; 4 April 1967, p. 2.
13. UNA, Summaries of Complaints, 7 Oct. 1966, S-312, Box 26, File 3; *Ha'aretz,* 9 Oct. 1966, p. 1; Eitan Haber, *Today War Will Break Out* (in Hebrew) (Jerusalem: Idanim, 1987), p. 104.
14. Herzog diary, 8 Oct. 1966, ISA, A-16/4510; *Ha'aretz,* 9 Oct. 1966, p. 2; *Hayom,* 9 Oct. 1966, p. 1; *Yediot Aharonot,* 9 Oct. 1966, p. 3; *Maariv,* 6 Nov. 1966, p. 3.
15. *Maariv,* 10 Oct. 1966, p. 3; *Ha'aretz,* 10 Oct. 1966, p. 2.
16. *Maariv,* 9 Oct. 1966, p. 1 (*Sunday Times*); 11 Sept. 1966, p. 9; *Ha'aretz,* 28 Oct. 1966, p. 3 (campaign details); Moshe Dayan, *Diary of the Sinai Campaign* (in Hebrew) (Tel Aviv: Am HaSefer, 1965); *Maariv,* 28 Oct. 1966, p. 3; (Shabbat supplement) p. 1 (depression); 28 Oct. 1966 ("Days and Nights" supplement), p. 6 (Rommel); *Ha'aretz,* 28 Oct. 1966, p. 3ff. (disappointment); *Maariv,* 14 Feb. 1966, p. 11; David Ben-Gurion, *Meetings with Arab Leaders* (in Hebrew) (Tel Aviv: Am Oved, 1967).
17. *Ha'aretz,* 30 Oct. 1966, p. 1 (announcement); *Yediot Aharonot,* 31 Oct. 1966, p. 1 ("tomorrow we will reach"); Government surveys, ISA, C-15/6381; *Yediot Aharonot,* 4 Nov. 1966, p. 4; 25 Oct. 1966, p. 3 (restrain).
18. Gluska, *Eshkol, Give the Order!* p. 161; Eban to Israeli Ambassadors, 14 Nov. 1966, ISA, HZ-6/4030, A-7/7935; *Ha'aretz,* 13 Nov. 1966, p. 2 (get used to); *Maariv,* 13 Nov. 1966, p. 2 ("avenge").
19. Golda Meir with Dean Rusk, 13 Oct. 1965; Rafael Efrat to Haim Israeli, 14 April 1965; undated diary entries, Adi Yaffe, ISA, A-7/7935; Bitan at State Department, 29 Nov. 1966, ISA, HZ-20/3977; Harman to Foreign Ministry, 14 Nov. 1966, ISA, HZ-6/4030; see also: Samir Mutawi, *Jordan in the 1967 War* (Cambridge: Cambridge University Press, 1987), p. 76ff.
20. Report by the Chief of Staff, UNSTO, November 1966, UNA, See S-0/67-0014, Box 14, File 6; Evron to Foreign Ministry, 14 Nov. 1966, ISA, HZ-6/4030; security survey, undated, ISA, A-7/7935; Avraham Ayalon: "Operation 'Shredder,'" *Ma'arachot* (in Hebrew), 261–262, March-April 1978, p. 27ff.; Haber, *Today War Will Break Out,* p. 105ff.; see also: *Yediot Aharonot,* 13 Nov. 1966, p. 1 (three issues); 14 Nov. 1966, p. 1.
21. *Ha'aretz,* 14 Nov. 1966, p. 2; see also: *Ha'aretz,* 18 Nov. 1966, p. 2 (poll); *Yediot Aharonot,* 13 Nov. 1966, p. 2 ("urges"); *Maariv,* 14 Nov. 1966, p. 8 ("lack of choice").
22. *Ha'aretz,* 14 Nov. 1966, p. 2; see also: *Ha'aretz,* 18 Nov. 1966, p. 2; *Yediot Aharonot,* 25 Nov. 1966, p. 8.
23. Yemima Rosenthal, Arnon Lemfrum, and Hagai Tzoref, eds., *Levi Eshkol: The Third Prime Minister* (in Hebrew) (Jerusalem: Israel State Archive, 2002), p. 520; Government Minutes, 13 Nov. 1966, Security cabinet meeting, 13 Nov. 1966, government meeting, 20 Nov. 1966, with the kind permission of Yossi Goldstein; Gluska, *Eshkol, Give the Order!* p. 162.

24. Eban to Israeli ambassadors, 14 Nov. 1966, ISA, HZ-6/4030; Aviad Yaffe records, undated, ISA, A-7/7935; Eban with U Thant, 9 Dec. 1966, UNA, S-512-0131; Israeli Embassy in the United States to Foreign Ministry, 15 Nov. 1966; Harman to Foreign Ministry, 16 Nov. 1966, ISA, HZ-6/4030.

25. Politico-Military Contingency Planning for the Arab-Israeli Dispute, May 1966, USNA, Box 19, Memos to the President, Folder 1 of 2; Komer to President, 16 No. 1966, FRUS, vol. XVIII, Doc. No. 336; Adi Yaffe records, 21 Nov. 1966, ISA, A-7/7935.

26. Rosenthal et al., eds., *Levi Eshkol*, p. 520; Israel consul in New York to Foreign Ministry, 29 Nov. 1966, ISA, A-7/7935; Arnon to Foreign Ministry, 7 Dec. 1966, ISA, HZ-5/3979; Eban with officials in Washington, 12 Dec. 1966, ISA, HZ-2/3987; *Ha'aretz*, 11 Jan. 1967, p. 2; Eban with Katzenbach, 12 Dec. 1966, ISA, HZ-20/3977; Ofra Nevo-Eshkol, *Humorous Eshkol* (Jerusalem: Idanim, 1988), p. 150.

27. Reudor Manor, series of interviews with Avraham Harman, Hebrew University, Institute for International Relations, meeting 7, p. 7ff.; meeting 12, p. 6, with the kind permission of David Harman; *Ha'aretz*, 28 Nov. 1966, p. 2; see also: *Ha'aretz*, 25 Nov. 1966, p. 2; 27 Nov. 1966, p. 2; 9 Dec. 1966, p. 3; Yaacov Herzog estate, with the kind permission of his daughter.

28. Davies to Secretary, 8 Feb. 1967, USNA, Box 2228, POL 23, 1/1/67; *Maariv*, 2 Dec. 1966, p. 1; 30 Dec. 1966, p. 2.

29. M. Werner to Eshkol, 28 Nov. 1966 (electric fence); Salim David to Eshkol, 24 Jan. 1967 (death penalty); Boch to Eshkol, 13 March 1967 (diagrams); A. Waxman to Eshkol (undated) (bag checks); Weitzman to Eshkol, 10 May 1967 (Israeli Arabs); Mizrahi to Eshkol, 14 Nov. 1966; Avivi to Eshkol, 28 Nov. 1966; anonymous to Eshkol, 15 Jan. 1967—all YEA, copies in possession of the author; see also: *Ha'aretz*, 14 Oct. 1966, p. 3.

30. General Staff meeting, 23 Jan. 1967, IDFA, 205/117/70; Department of State to Embassy in Israel, 15 Nov. 1966, FRUS, vol. XVIII, Doc. No. 335; Eshkol at editors' board, 18 May 1967, ISA, A-4/7920 (terrorist); Gluska, *Eshkol, Give the Order!* pp. 166ff., 125ff., 41 (Dayan), 148, 186, 195 ("Jews"); Nevo-Eshkol, *Humorous Eshkol*, p. 57 (Prussians).

31. David N. Myers, *Re-Inventing the Jewish Past* (New York: Oxford University Press, 1995), p. 109ff.; Baer to Eshkol, 23 Nov. 1966, ISA, G-17/6301; Yossi Heller, *From Peace Treaty to Unification: Yehuda Leib Magnes and the Struggle for a Bi-National State* (in Hebrew) (Jerusalem: Magnes, 2003); *LaMerhav*, 24 April 1967, p. 16 (Bar-Hillel); *Ner: Journal of Public Issues and Jewish-Arab Relations* (in Hebrew), 15th Year, 1965, books 6–8, p. 5 (Shereshevski); Schmuel Hugo Bergman, *Tagebücher, Briefe 1948–1975: Jüdischer Verlag bei Atheneum, Königstein*, TS 1985, vol. II, p. 497, 395 (21 Dec. 1961); Mordechai Bar-On, "Status Quo Before or After? Commentary on Israel's Security Policy, 1949–1958," *Studies in the Establishment of Israel* (in Hebrew), vol. 5, 1995, p. 65ff.; see also: Bar-On, "Security-Mindedness and Its Critics, 1949–1967" (in Hebrew) in *The Challenge of Sovereignty, Creation, and Thought in the First Decade of the State*, ed. Mordechai Bar-On (Jerusalem: Yad Ben-Zvi, 1999), p. 66ff.

32. The Israeli Communist Party, *Fifteenth Congress* (in Hebrew), 1965, p. 21ff.; Yaari to Aliza Dror, 7 May 1967, YYA; "Between War and Peace," *New Outlook*, vol. 8, no. 3 (70) April–May 1965, p. 4ff.; Amnon Zichroni, *1 Against 119: Uri Avneri in the Knesset* (in Hebrew) (Tel Aviv: Daf Hadash, 1969), p. 204; *HaOlam HaZeh*, no. 1513 (Jan. 1967), p. 12; Israel Bar, *Israeli Security Yesterday, Today, and Tomorrow* (in Hebrew) (Tel Aviv: Amikam, 1966), p. 411; *Ha'aretz*, 12 Aug. 1966, p. 2; 12 Aug. 1966, p. 2 (Baer).

33. Alek Epstein, "For Freedom's Sake: The Public Struggles of Jerusalem Professors After the Establishment of the State," *Kathedra*, no. 106, Dec. 2002, p. 139ff.; Gvati diary, 5 March 1967, p. 78, YTA, Unit 15, Container 12, File 02.

34. Eshkol to Baer, 11 Jan. 1967, ISA, G-17/6301; see also: Zertal, *Death and the Nation*, p. 181ff.

35. Galon to Eshkol, 8 Dec. 1966, Ben-Yohanan to Galon, 12 Dec. 1966, YEA, copy in possession of the author.

36. *Maariv*, 24 April 1966, p. 5 (Rabin); Yitzhak Kotler to his girlfriend, 3 March 1967, in *Parchments of Fire*, Zvi Haber, ed., vol. 5, book I (in Hebrew) (Tel Aviv: Ministry of Defense, 1981), p. 336.

37. *Ha'aretz*, 26 April 1966, p. 1; *Yediot Aharonot*, 26 April 1966, p. 4.

38. *Maariv*, 26 April 1966, p. 4 (parade); *Ha'aretz*, 8 July 1966, p. 8; see also: USDAO Tel Aviv to RUEPJS/DIA, 21 June 1967, USNA, Box 1796, File 6/12/67.

39. *Yediot Aharonot*, 13 Jan. 1967, p. 5 (Tel Katzir); *Ha'aretz*, 12 May 1967, p. 10 (myths); Poochoo, *I'm a Coward, I Am* (in Hebrew) (Tel Aviv: Masada, 1966); see also: *Ha'aretz*, 13 June 1966, p. 10; Ze'ev Schiff and Eitan Haber, *Lexicon of Israel Security* (in Hebrew) (Tel Aviv: Zmora Bitan Modan, 1976), p. 109 (Gadna); *Davar Le-Yeladim*, 10 Jan. 1967, p. 415 (Gadna); 17 Jan. 1967, p. 447 (boarding school); 17 Jan. 1967, p. 486 (comics); see also: 23 May 1967; *Maariv LaNoar*, 9 May 1967; Children to Ben-Gurion, undated, BGA.

40. K. J. McIntire, "Israel and the Israelis in 1967," p. 5, PRO, FCO 17/576, 104225.

41. General Staff discussion, 13 March 1967, IDFA, 205/117/70.

42. *Maariv*, 12 May 1967, p. 11.

43. *Yediot Aharonot* ("7 Days" supplement), 7 Oct. 1966, p. 14 (Vered); *Maariv*, 20 Feb. 1966, p. 10; see also: *Maariv*, 25 Feb. 1966, p. 10 (Sharon).

44. *Maariv*, 29 April 1966, p. 10; *Yediot Aharonot*, 29 April 1966, p. 5.

45. *Maariv*, 25 Feb. 1966, p. 10.

46. Mordechai Bar-On, "Security-Mindedness and Its Critics, 1949–1967" (in Hebrew) in *The Challenge of Sovereignty, Creation, and Thought in the First Decade of the State*, ed. Mordechai Bar-On (Jerusalem: Yad Ben-Zvi, 1999), p. 92.

47. *Ha'aretz*, 12 July 1966, p. 8; 24 July 1966, p. 2; 21 Aug. 1966, p. 2; *Maariv*, 5 May 1966, p. 7.

48. Herzog diary, 12 Sept. 1966, ISA, A-16/4510; *Ha'aretz*, 21 Feb. 1966, p. 1; 9 May 1966, p. 1; Eshkol in the Knesset, 18 May 1966, *Knesset Minutes*, vol. 45, p. 1469; *Ha'aretz*, 28 Jan. 1966, p. 2; Avner Cohen, *Israel and the Bomb* (in Hebrew) (Tel Aviv: Schocken, 1998); Eshkol with Eban and others, 28 Feb. 1966, ISA, A-2/794.

49. Foreign Affairs and Defense Committee meeting, 8 Feb. 1966, ISA, A-1/7924.

50. *Ha'aretz*, 10 Jan. 1966, p. 1; 23 Jan. 1966, p. 1; *Yediot Aharonot*, 23 Jan. 1966, p. 1; 28 Jan. 1966, p. 1; *Maariv*, 27 Jan. 1966, p. 1; *Yediot Aharonot*, 3 March 1966, p. 1; *Maariv*, 18 April 1966, p. 1; *Ha'aretz*, 19 April 1966, p. 1; *Maariv*, 22 April 1966, p. 11; *Yediot Aharonot* (Shabbat supplement), 22 April 1966, p. 1.

51. Yuval Neeman, "Israel in the Age of Nuclear Arms," *Nativ*, no. 5, Sept. 1995, p. 35ff.; Cohen, *Israel and the Bomb*, p. 353; Karpin, *The Bomb in the Basement*.

52. Tom Segev, *The Seventh Million: Israelis and the Holocaust* (in Hebrew) (Jerusalem: Keter, 1992), p. 347; Cohen, *Israel and the Bomb*, p. 28ff.; *Yediot Aharonot*, 13 April 1966, p. 2.

53. *Ha'aretz*, 21 April 1966, p. 2 (ego); Baer, *Israeli Security Yesterday, Today, and Tomorrow*, pp. 262, 310; *Maariv*, 15 April 1966, p. 3; 5 May 1966, p. 2.

54. Zeev Zur in the Foreign Affairs and Defense Committee, 8 Feb. 1966, ISA, A-1/792.

55. Cohen, *Israel and the Bomb*, p. 195.

56. Herzog diary, 18 Aug. 1966, ISA, A-16/4510.

57. Katzenbach to President, 1 May 1967, LBJL, NSF, Country File, Israel, Aid, 5/67, Box 145; Zachi Shalom, *Between Dimona and Washington: The Struggle over Developing Israel's Nuclear Option, 1960–1968* (in Hebrew) (Beersheba: Ben-Gurion University, 2004); Herzog diary, 12 Sept. 1966, ISA, A-16/4510 (Argentina).

58. *Yediot Aharonot*, 14 Sept. 1966, p. 18; *Maariv*, 2 Nov. 1966, p. 4; Uri Zvi Greenberg in the Knesset, 9 March 1949, *Knesset Minutes*, vol. 1, p. 107.

59. Amnon Ramon, *Divided Jerusalem: The Municipal Line, 1948–1967, Guided Walks* (in Hebrew) (Jerusalem: Yad Ben-Zvi, 1987); Moti Golani, *Zion in Zionism: The Zionist Policy on the Question of Jerusalem, 1937–1949* (in Hebrew) (Tel Aviv: Ministry of Defense, 1992); Tom Segev, *1949: The First Israelis* (in Hebrew) (Jerusalem: Domino, 1984), p. 52ff.; Amos Elon, *Jerusalem: An Obsession* (in Hebrew) (Jerusalem: Domino, 1991).

60. Central Bureau of Statistics, *Statistical Abstract of Israel, No. 19*, 1968 (in Hebrew), p. 30; David Kroyanker, *Architecture in Jerusalem: Modern Construction Outside the Walls, 1948–1990* (in Hebrew) (Jerusalem: Keter, 1991), p. 158ff.

61. *Yediot Aharonot*, 5 Aug. 1966, p. 6 (sewage); *Ha'aretz*, 15 Jan. 1967, p. 8 (HaMekasher); 6 May 1966, p. 11 (Scharf); *Maariv*, 14 Oct. 1966, p. 7 (Ofakim).

62. *Yediot Aharonot*, 9 Oct. 1966, p. 5 (Tanus house); *Maariv*, 11 March 1966, p. 10 (Eshkol); ("Days and Nights" supplement), 13 Jan. 1967, p. 3 (stolen sites); *Yediot Aharonot*, 5 April 1967, p. 1 (Alborak); Raphael Israeli, *Jerusalem Divided: The Armistice Regime, 1947–1967* (London: Routledge, 2002) (tourists); Israeli delegation to the Israel-Jordan cease-fire committee, summary report on the special committee, 30 Nov. 1965, and Lieutenant Colonel Y. Bieverman, 30 Nov. 1965, with the kind permission of Meron Benvenisti.

63. Zippora Gilad, ed., *Complete Palestine: Goodbye to a Dream?* (in Hebrew) (Kibbutz Beit Hashita, 1999), p. 25; Leah R. (7th grade A): "If Only I Saw the Old City," *Misholim*, the student newspaper of Beit Hinuch named after Arlozorov, Jerusalem, Chanukah 1954, p. 28, JMA, Container 3127; Yisrael Segal, *One of Us Two* (in Hebrew) (Jerusalem: Keter, 1995), p. 45.

64. Mordechai Gilat, *Mount Scopus* (in Hebrew) (Tel Aviv: Masada, 1969); Carmit Guy, *Bar-Lev* (in Hebrew) (Tel Aviv: Am Oved, 1998), p. 137; Odd Bull, *War and Peace in the Middle East* (London: Leo Cooper, 1973), p. 59ff.; Gvati diary, 11 June 1967, YTA, Unit 15, Container 12, File 02; Ball to Bunche, August 22–23, 1966, UNA, SE, S-0512-0113 SG. Code Cables—Jerusalem, Unnumbered, 1966; UNA DAG-1/5.2.2.0:2; Office of the Secretary-General S-0512-0113.

65. Special UNGA, June 1967, USNA, Box 18, vol. III, Folder 1; Bernard Wasserstein, *Divided Jerusalem: The Struggle for the Holy City* (London: Profile Books, 2001), pp. 203, 195ff. (international status); ISA, HZ-19/4032 (reporters); Sapir in the Knesset, 15 June 1966, *Knesset Minutes*, vol. 46 (in Hebrew), p. 1773; Kollek to Eban, 3 Feb. 1967; 1 March 1967, JMA, Container 1346; Sapir to Director of the Prime Minister's Office, 20 Dec. 1966; Yaffe to Baram, 26 Dec. 1966; Shapira to Eshkol, 18 Jan. 1967, ISA, C-1/6303; see also: ibid., proposed legislation for Jerusalem; Foreign Ministry response, ISA, HZ-14/4033; Uzai to cabinet, 27 Nov. 1966, ISA, C-1/6303 (displays); *Maariv* ("Days and Nights" supplement), 19 May 1967, p. 3 (capital for three days); Kollek to Eshkol, 5 Dec. 1966, ISA, C-1/6303.

66. The author served as Kollek's office manager between 1977 and 1979; Teddy Kollek, *One Jerusalem* (in Hebrew) (Tel Aviv: Maariv, 1979), p. 200 (Dietrich); *Yediot Aharonot*, 21 Oct. 1966, p. 10; *Ha'aretz*, 14 Oct. 1966, p. 9; 16 Oct. 1966, p. 8; 17 Oct. 1966, p. 8 (Benziman); *LaMerhav*, 19 Jan. 1967, p. 4; 5 May 1967, p. 5; *HaTzofeh*, 18 May 1966; Ben-Yaakov to Kollek, 13 Sept. 1966, ISA, HZ-14/4032 (shtetl); *Maariv*, 27 June 1966, p. 2; *Bat Kol*, 20 Dec. 1966, p. 2; *Jerusalem: Scenes from the Eternal City* (in Hebrew) (Jerusalem: Universitas, 1958), pp. 7, 14 (Agron); *Davar*, 14 April 1967, p. 2 (memorial).

67. Allon to Ben-Gurion, 24 March, 1949, BGA; Anita Shapira, *Yigal Allon: The Springtime of His Universe* (in Hebrew) (Tel Aviv: HaKibbutz HaMeuchad, 2004), p. 426; Allon in an interview with Reudor Manor, Institute for International Relations, Hebrew University, ISA, A-19/5001, meeting 2, p. 11; see also: Mordechai Gazit, "Ben-Gurion's 1949 Proposal to Incorporate the Gaza Strip with Israel," *Studies in Zionism*, vol. 8, no. 2 (1987), p. 223ff.; Ezer Weizman, *For You the Sky, for You the Land* (in Hebrew) (Tel Aviv: Sifriyat Maariv, 1975), p. 285.

68. Reudor Manor, "Images and Decision-Making on the Subject of Borders in Israeli Foreign Policy, 1948–1973" (in Hebrew) (diss., Hebrew University, 1980); Bar-On, "Status Quo Before or After?" p. 65ff.

69. Analysis of possible developments in the Jordanian situation, 9 May 1963, ISA, HZ-10/4094; Shlomo Gazit, *The Carrot and the Stick: Israeli Governance in Judah and Samaria* (in Hebrew) (Tel Aviv: Zmora-Bitan, 1985), p. 23; Gluska, *Eshkol, Give the Order!* p. 258; ("grabs"), 3 June 1967, and Operation "Mozart," 5 June 1967, IDFA, 1176/192/74; Uzi Narkis, summary report on the Six-Day War, IDFA, 1/901/67, p. 75 ("sentimental value"); Avraham Tamir, *Peace-Loving Soldier* (in Hebrew) (Jerusalem: Idanim, 1967), p. 317; *Ha'aretz*, 6 Nov. 1998, p. 6 ("Bnei Or").

70. Lieutenant Colonel Bieverman, 30 Nov. 1965, with the kind permission of Meron Benvenisti (Latrun); Haber, *Today War Will Break Out*, p. 118 (Eshkol); Uzi Narkis, summary report on the Six-Day War, IDFA, 1/901/67, p. 75; see also: Tamir, *Peace-Loving Soldier*, p. 317; *Ha'aretz*, 6 Nov. 1998, p. 6 (target); Gluska, *Eshkol, Give the Order!* p. 50ff.; Government Minutes, 9 July 1957, ISA (Litani); Eshkol with Golda Meir, 9 June 1963, ISA, A-1/7921 ("Switzerland").

71. Meron Benvenisti, *The Slingshot and the Stick: Territories, Jews, and Arabs* (in Hebrew) (Jerusalem: Keter, 1988), pp. 58ff.; see also: Yoram Bar-Gil, *Homeland and Geography in One Hundred Years of Zionist Education* (in Hebrew) (Tel Aviv: Am Oved, 1993); Zippora Gilad, ed., *Greater Israel: Separation from a Dream?* (in Hebrew) (Kibbutz Beit Hashita, 1999), pp. 13, 17, 29, 37; Arieh Naor, *Greater Israel: Faith and Policy* (in Hebrew) (Haifa: Haifa University, 2001), p. 104ff. (Tabenkin).

72. *Ha'aretz*, 15 July 1966, p. 11 (Thirty-five); see also: 19 Sept. 1966, p. 10; 14 May 1967, p. 2 (race); Nathan Shacham and Shmuel Katz, *Journey Through Eretz Yisrael* (in Hebrew) (Tel Aviv: Levin Epstein, 1966); *Yehiam Newsletter*, 317/9, 17 March 1967, p. 6;

Amos Oz, *Resting Place* (in Hebrew) (Jerusalem: Keter, undated), p. 155; *Yediot Aharonot,* 24 April 1966, p. 10 (Mei Ami); Shimon Rimon, *I Am "Kushi"* (in Hebrew) (Jerusalem: Idanim, 1978), p. 35; *Unto Rock: Five Who Were Lost* (in Hebrew) (Tel Aviv: HaKibbutz HaMeuchad, 1966); see also: government meeting, 7 April 1957, ISA.

73. *Maariv,* 16 Aug. 1963, p. 6; Bar-Gil, *Homeland and Geography in One Hundred Years of Zionist Education,* p. 133ff.

74. *Israel from Dan to Eilat* (Head Education Officer, 1958–1959); *Israel: Talking Maps,* prepared and printed by the Measurements Department, Ministry of Labor, illustrated by Friedl Stern (Tel Aviv: Leon Printing, 1958) (no page numbers); Segal, *One of the Two of Us,* p. 22 (Radio Ramallah).

75. Naor, *Greater Israel,* pp. 116ff., 77; *Ha'aretz,* 25 May 2004, p. h/1 (poets).

76. Naor, *Greater Israel,* pp. 80ff., 116ff., 98ff.; Begin in the Knesset, 15 Jan. 1957, *Knesset Minutes,* vol. 21, p. 750; 13 March 1957, *Knesset Minutes,* vol. 22, p. 1346; *Yediot Aharonot,* 14 Feb. 1967, p. 19 (Ben-Gurion); *Mabat Chadash,* 19 April 1967, p. 9.

77. *Ha'aretz,* 25 March 1966, p. 2; see also: 24 June 1966, p. 3; Begin in the Knesset, 16 March 1966, *Knesset Minutes,* vol. 45, p. 1010; *Maariv,* 26 Sept. 1966, p. 14; *Ha'aretz,* 30 March 1966, p. 2; 31 March 1966, p. 2; Naor, *Greater Israel,* p. 100 (Kook).

78. *Yediot Aharonot,* 11 Nov. 1966, p. 6ff.; see also: *Yediot Aharonot,* 16 March 1962, p. 1; Ben-Gurion to David Shnir, 15 May 1967, BGA; *Maariv,* 14 May 1967, p. 9ff.; *Ha'aretz,* 17 May 1967, p. 4 (Yadin); Avi Shlaim, "Interview with Yitzhak Rabin" in *Studies in the Establishment of Israel* (in Hebrew), vol. 8, 1998, p. 683; *Ha'aretz,* 14 May 1967, p. 9; 19 May 1967, p. 2; 22 May 1967, p. 2.

79. *Yediot Aharonot,* 25 Nov. 1966, p. 2; *Ha'aretz,* 19 Dec. 1966, p. 1; *Maariv,* 23 Dec. 1966; 29 Dec. 1966, p. 9 (Allon); 22 Dec. 1966, p. 3 (Dayan); 23 Dec. 1966, p. 1 (Eshkol); see also: *Maariv,* 13 Jan. 1966, p. 16.

80. Sasson review, 13 Dec. 1966, ISA, A-7/7935; *Yediot Aharonot,* 25 Nov. 1966, p. 2; *Maariv,* 12 Jan. 1967, p. 6.

81. Ben-Gurion diary, 3 May 1963, BGA.

82. Discussion in the Prime Minister's office, 28 Dec. 1966, ISA, A-7/7935.

83. Platform for policy toward Jordan, 23 Dec. 1966, ISA, HZ-9/4094.

84. Discussion summary, 22 Dec. 1966, ISA, HZ-9/4094.

85. Gazit at the National Defense College, 13 Oct. 1966, ISA, HZ-10/4094.

86. Ibid., Peled to the Chief of Staff, 12 Dec. 1966, with the kind permission of Elad Peled.

87. Gazit to Eban, 4 Jan. 1967 and appendices, ISA, HZ-13/4092.

88. Rosenthal et al., eds., *Levi Eshkol,* p. 522; Gluska, *Eshkol, Give the Order!* p. 165ff.

89. Meir Amit, *Head to Head: A Personal Look at Great Events and Mysterious Affairs* (in Hebrew) (Tel Aviv: Hed Arzi, 1999), p. 204ff.

90. Discussion summaries, ISA, HZ-19/4091; Egypt-Israel, discussion platform, 31 June 1966, and summary of the Egypt question, 31 March 1966, with the kind permission of Elad Peled.

91. Meeting at Meir Amit's home, 27 Nov. 1966, ISA, HZ-19/4091; *Ha'aretz* (supplement), 18 March 1966, p. 13; see also: *Maariv,* 25 Oct. 1967, p. 1.

CHAPTER 4: THE SYRIAN SYNDROME

1. *Maariv,* 1 April 1966, p. 5; *Ha'aretz,* 19 July 1966, p. 2; 14 Oct. 1966.

2. *Ha'aretz,* 19 July 1966, p. 2; 19 Aug. 1966, p. 2; Moshe Shemesh, "The Arab Fight Against Israel over Water, 1959–1967," *Studies in the Establishment of Israel* (in Hebrew), vol. 7, 1997, p. 103ff.; Eitan Haber, *Today War Will Break Out* (in Hebrew) (Jerusalem: Idanim, 1987), p. 99; *Maariv,* 4 Oct. 1967, p. 9; see also: Yemima Rosenthal, Arnon Lemfrum, and Hagai Tzoref, eds., *Levi Eshkol: The Third Prime Minister* (in Hebrew) (Jerusalem: Israel State Archive, 2002), p. 475; Ami Gluska, *Eshkol, Give the Order!* (in Hebrew) (Tel Aviv: Ministry of Defense, 2004), p. 110; Avi Shlaim, "Interview with Yitzhak Rabin, *Studies in the Establishment of Israel* (in Hebrew), vol. 8, 1998, p. 680; *Ha'aretz,* 19 Aug. 1966, p. 2 (legumes).

3. Eyal Zisser, "Between Israel and Syria: The Six-Day War and After," *Studies in the Establishment of Israel* (in Hebrew), vol. 8, 1998, p. 219ff.; *Yediot Aharonot* (holiday supplement), 27 April 1997, p. 2ff.; see also: *Ha'aretz,* 18 May 1997, p. 2; Bull to Bunche, 12 Aug. 1966, UNA, S-312, Box 29, File 6; Gluska, *Eshkol, Give the Order!* p. 178ff.

4. Herzog diary, 11 Aug. 1966, ISA, A-16/4510; Intelligence Branch for IDF attachés, 24 July 1966, ISA, HZ-11/4069; M. Michaeli to Israel Embassies, 18 Dec. 1966, ISA,

A-5/7936; see also: discussion at Prime Minister's office, 28 Dec. 1966, ISA, A-7/7935.

5. *Maariv,* 19 Oct. 1966, p. 8 (Agnon); see also: 5 Dec. 1966, p. 1; 6 Dec. 1966, p. 1; *Ha'aretz,* 18 Oct. 1966, p. 2.

6. Herzog diary, 15 Aug. 1966, ISA, A-16/4510; *Maariv,* 16 Aug. 1966, p. 3; Eitan Haber, *Today War Will Break Out* (in Hebrew) (Jerusalem: Idanim, 1987), p. 110ff.; Gluska, *Eshkol, Give the Order!* p. 148ff.; Odd Bull, *War and Peace in the Middle East: The Experiences and Views of a UN Observer* (London: Leo Cooper, 1973), p. 96ff.

7. Haber, *Today War Will Break Out,* pp. 96, 139.

8. Gluska, *Eshkol, Give the Order!* p. 115ff.

9. *Ha'aretz,* 16 Aug. 1966, p. 2; *Maariv,* 16 Aug. 1966, p. 8; Haber, *Today War Will Break Out,* p. 147.

10. *Bamahane,* 18 Sept. 1966, p. 8; *Ha'aretz,* 12 and 19 Sept. 1966; Gluska, *Eshkol, Give the Order!* p. 158; Herzog diary, 14, 17, 18, and 30 Sept. and 2 Oct. 1966, ISA, A-16/4510; *Maariv,* 11 Sept. 1966, p. 1; 19 Sept. 1966, p. 28; Sept. 1966, pp. 2–3; *Ha'aretz,* 25 Sept. 1966, p. 2; Yoram Peri, *Between Battles and Ballots* (Cambridge: Cambridge University Press, 1983), p. 160.

11. Eshkol in the Knesset, 17 Oct. 1966, *Knesset Minutes,* vol. 47, p. 4; 17 Jan. 1967, *Knesset Minutes,* vol. 47, p. 916; *Ha'aretz,* 8 Feb. 1967, p. 1; see also: *Maariv,* 11 Oct. 1966, p. 2; 9 Jan. 1967, p. 2; *Maariv,* 15 Jan. 1966, p. 8 (other choice).

12. Eshkol at the Foreign Affairs and Defense Committee, 17 Jan. 1967, ISA, C-15/6301; *Ha'aretz,* 15 Jan. 1967, pp. 2, 1; see also: *Maariv,* 15 Jan. 1967, p. 2; *Yediot Aharonot,* 15 Jan. 1967, p. 3.

13. *Yediot Aharonot,* 20 Jan. 1967, p. 7; 15 Jan. 1967, p. 3 ("take control"); *Ha'aretz,* 15 Jan. 1967, pp. 2, 1 (response); Carmon at General Staff meeting, 30 Jan. 1967, IDFA, 205/117/70.

14. Gluska, *Eshkol, Give the Order!* p. 107.

15. Ibid., p. 175ff.

16. General Staff meeting, 16 Jan. 1967, IDFA, 205/117/70.

17. Walid Khalidi, ed., *All That Remains: The Palestinian Villages Occupied and Depopulated by Israel in 1948* (Washington, D.C.: Institute for Palestine Studies, 1992), p. 445ff.

18. Rabin at General Staff meeting, 16 Jan. 1967, IDFA, 205/117/70.

19. The Department of State to the Embassy in Israel, 17 Jan. 1967, FRUS, vol. XVIII, Document No. 382.

20. Harman to Eban, 8 Oct. 1966, ISA, HZ-2 /3987; Russian notice to Israel, 9 Nov. 1966, ISA, C-2/6382; see also: ISA, HZ-27/4048; *Maariv,* 3 June 1966, p. 27 (Chuvakhin); Avramov with Sneh, 8 July 1966, ISA, C-4/6399; memo, 12 Oct. 1966, ISA, A-7/7228; *Maariv,* 13 Oct. 1966, p. 10; see also: Russian notice to Israel, 9 Nov. 1966, ISA, C-2/6382.

21. Eshkol at the Knesset, 17 May 1966, *Knesset Minutes,* vol. 45, p. 1441; see also: 17 Oct. 1966, *Knesset Minutes,* vol. 47, p. 5; 17 Jan. 1967, *Knesset Minutes,* vol. 47, p. 916; Shlomo Argov to Foreign Ministry, 26 Dec. 1966, ISA, HZ-20/3977; Warnings: *Maariv,* 11 Oct. 1966, p. 2; 9 Jan. 1967, p. 2; *Ha'aretz,* 12 Jan. 1967, p. 1; 16 Jan. 1967, p. 1; 17 Jan. 1967, p. 1 (Eban); Rostow to President, 16 Jan. 1967, FRUS, vol. XVIII, Doc. No. 380; Yariv in discussion with Eshkol, 28 Dec. 1966, ISA, A-7/7935.

22. General Staff meeting, 23 Jan. 1967, IDFA, 205/117/1970.

23. *Ha'aretz,* 11 Nov. 1966, p. 3; 10 March 1967, p. 9.

24. Rabin at General Staff meeting, 8 Feb. 1967, IDFA, 205/117/1970.

25. Matityahu Mayzel, *The Battle over the Golan: June 1967* (in Hebrew) (Ma'arachot, 2001), p. 93ff.

26. Gluska, *Eshkol, Give the Order!* p. 186.

27. Fatah Incidents Summaries, Feb. 1965–May 1967, UNA, S-312, Box 26, File 5; see also: *Israel Annual Review for 1967,* PRO, FCO 17/468, 104038; Tel Katzir and HaOn members to Eshkol, 14 Feb. 1967, YEA, copy in possession of author; Chief of Staff meeting with Minister of Defense, 31 March 1967, IDFA, 118/117/70; Eban to Eshkol, 4 April 1967, ISA, 6301/15-C; *Ha'aretz,* 4 April 1967, p. 2; Shofman in the Knesset, 5 April 1967, *Knesset Minutes,* vol. 48, p. 2039; *Maariv,* 9 April 1967, p. 3 (Spector); *Ha'aretz,* 9 April 1967, p. 1; 12 April 1967, p. 12 (Keshet); *Maariv, Yediot Aharonot,* 9 April 1967, p. 1ff.; see also: *Maariv,* 16 Aug. 1966, p. 8; *Maariv* ("Days and Nights" supplement), 14 April 1967, p. 4 (Gadot); *Yediot Aharonot,* 10 May 1967, p. 5 (ledger); *Maariv,* 9 April 1967, p. 1ff.; *Yediot Aharonot,* 9 April 1967, p. 1ff.; see also: *Maariv,* 16 Aug. 1966, p. 8;

Ha'aretz, 14 April 1967, p. 3 (Schiff); *Maariv*, 19 April 1967, p. 3; 30 April 1967, p. 3 (Eshkol); Gluska, *Eshkol, Give the Order!* p. 192; Haber, *Today War Will Break Out*, p. 141ff.; Ezer Weizman, *For You the Sky, for You the Land* (in Hebrew) (Tel Aviv: Sifriyat-Maariv, 1975), p. 254.

28. *Ha'aretz*, 24 March 1967, p. 10; 31 March 1967, p. 10.

29. Gilan to Sartre, 30 March 1967; Eshkol in the government, 12 Feb. 1967, ISA, 6339/52-C; Kol in the government, 19 March 1967, ISA, 6381/C-15; Barbour to Department of State, 7 April 1967, USNA, Box 2228, File 1/1/67.

30. *Ha'aretz*, 30 March 1967, pp. 1–2.

31. *Maariv*, 22 May 1967, p. 15.

32. Philatelic Service, 19th Independence Day Stamps (copy in possession of the author); Government Decisions, 23 Jan. 1967, ISA, 10136/C-2.

33. *Yediot Aharonot*, 2 May 1967, p. 1; Yossi Goldstein, *Eshkol* (in Hebrew) (Jerusalem: Keter, 2003), p. 537.

34. *Ha'aretz*, 10 May 1967, p. 1; 14 May 1967, p. 1; *Davar*, 31 May 1967, p. 1; see also: Foreign Ministry to Prime Minister's Office, 22 Feb. 1967, ISA, 7935/8-A.

35. *Maariv*, 14 May 1967, p. 12; *LaMerhav*, 14 May 1967, p. 1; Gluska, *Eshkol, Give the Order!* p. 213; *Ha'aretz*, 10 May 1967, p. 1.

36. *Yediot Aharonot* (Shabbat supplement), 12 May 1967, p. 1; *Yediot Aharonot*, 14 May 1967, p. 2; *Maariv*, 12 May 1967, p. 1.

37. Director General of the Ministry of Foreign Affairs with Chuvakhin, 13 May 1967, ISA, 4048/27-HZ.

38. Rostow to Johnson, 15 May 1967, FRUS, vol. XIX, p. 4f; Saunders to Rostow, 16 May 1967, LBJL, National Security File, Box 7.

39. *Yediot Aharonot*, 14 May 1967, pp. 1–3; *Ha'aretz*, 14 May 1967, p. 1 (Eshkol); Eshkol in the Knesset, 17 Oct. 1966, *Knesset Minutes*, vol. 47, p. 3; *Ha'aretz*, 23 Dec. 1966, p. 1.

40. Abba Eban, *Life Episodes* (in Hebrew) (Tel Aviv: Sifriyat Maariv, 1978), vol. II, p. 314.

41. Rostow to Johnston, 29 April 1967, FRUS, vol. XVIII, Doc. No. 413; *HaOlam HaZeh*, no. 1549, p. 9; Ben-Gurion diary, 19 April 1966, BGA; Eshkol and others in the Knesset, 16 Feb. 1966, *Knesset Minutes*, vol. 44, p. 645ff.; *Ha'aretz*, 21 April 1966, p.1.

42. *Ha'aretz*, 22 April 1966, p. 2; 1 March 1966, p. 9 (Ben-Gurion); Michael Bar Zohar, *Zaphenath Paneah: The Life and Times of a Jewish Prince* (in Hebrew) (Tel Aviv: Yediot Aharonot, 2003), p. 234 (Hussein); Levavi to Eshkol, 25 Sept. 1966, ISA, 7935/7-A; see also: *Maariv*, 12 May 1967, p. 3; Haber, *Today War Will Break Out*, p. 188; *Ha'aretz*, 21 April 1967, p. 8 (Rabin).

43. Government Minutes, 11 Dec. 1966, with the kind permission of Yossi Goldstein; *HaOlam HaZeh*, no. 1549, p. 9; *Yediot Aharonot*, 28 April 1967, p. 2; Eshkol to Rosenblum, 30 April 1967, ISA, 6339/9-C; Ben-Gurion to Yehuda Ilan, 28 March 1967, BGA.

44. Memorandum of Conversation, 26 Jan. 1967; Barbour to Rusk, 13 May 1967; Memo, 26 April 1967, Saunders to Rostow, 6 May 1967, LBJL; Smythe to Davies, 25 March 1967, USNA, Box 2228, File 1/1/67; NSF Central File Israel, vol. VI, Memos [1.f2], Doc. 93; Rusk to Embassy in Israel, 22 Aug. 1967, FRUS, vol. XVIII, Doc. No. 317.

45. *Ha'aretz*, 24 April 1967, p. 1; see also: *Maariv*, 28 April 1967, p. 1.

46. Rostow to Johnson, 29 April 1967, FRUS, vol. XVIII, Doc. No. 413.

47. *Maariv*, 14 May 1967, p. 2 (settlements); *Yediot Aharonot*, 16 May 1967, p. 5 (Malagasy); Haber, *Today War Will Break Out*, p. 145; *Ha'aretz*, 18 May 1967, p. 7; *Maariv*, 19 May 1967, p. 12 (Alterman); Bull to Bunche, 17 May 1967; UNA, UNSTO-Israel, Oct. '63–'67, Series 312, Box 29, File 5, ACC.79/58; U Thant, *View from the UN* (New York: Doubleday, 1978), p. 218; *Yediot Aharonot*, 16 May 1967, p. 5 ("Parade"); Ben-Gurion diary, 15 May 1967, BGA.

48. Meir Ezri, *Independence Day and Its Development in Israel* (Council of Progressive Rabbis in Israel, 1994); see also: *Ha'aretz*, 26 April 1966, p. 2; *Maariv*, 18 May 1967, p. 15 (flag); 16 May 1967, p. 6 (quiz); Ben-Gurion diary, 15 May 1967, BGA; Eban, *Life Episodes*, vol. II, p. 311.

49. *Maariv*, 12 May 1967, p. 6; *Mabat Chadash*, 19 April 1967, p. 9; see also: Ben-Gurion to Ben Erev, 4 May 1967, BGA; Ben-Gurion to Shmuel Goldnick, 14 May 1967, BGA.

50. *Ha'aretz*, 15 May 1967, p. 4; Yonah Hadari, *Messiah Riding a Tank* (in Hebrew) (Jerusalem: Hartman Institute, 2002), p. 47; see also: Dan Miron, *If There Will Be No Jerusalem: Hebrew Literature in a Cultural-Political Context* (in Hebrew) (Tel Aviv: HaKibbutz HaMeuchad, 1987), p. 175ff.

PART III: THE FORTY DAYS OF PRIVATE YEHOSHUA BAR-DAYAN

CHAPTER 5: THREE WEEKS TO WAR: WHAT DOES NASSER WANT?

1. Bar-Dayan diary, 21 May 1967, with his kind permission.
2. Eshkol at Mapai secretariat, 1 June 1967, LPA 2246790; Yeshayahu Gavish, interview, *50 Years War,* Israel, Disk 1, MECA.
3. Government meeting, 16 May 1967, Yaacov Herzog estate, with the kind permission of his daughter; Herzog diary, 16–17 May 1967, ISA, A-3/4513; Gvati, 16 and 17 May 1967, YTA, Unit 15, Container 12, File 02; Ami Gluska, *Eshkol, Give the Order!* (in Hebrew) (Tel Aviv: Ministry of Defense, 2004), p. 222; Eitan Haber, *Today War Will Break Out* (in Hebrew) (Tel Aviv: Yediot Aharonot, 1987), p. 148; Yitzhak Rabin, *Service Book* (in Hebrew) (Tel Aviv: Sifriyat Maariv, 1979), vol. 1, p. 134; Uri Bar Joseph, "The Forgotten Crisis on the Road to the 1967 War," *Journal of Contemporary History,* vol. 30, no. 3 (July 1996), p. 547ff.; *Yediot Aharonot,* 16 May 1967, p. 1; *Maariv,* 16 May 1967, p. 8; *Ha'aretz,* 17 May 1967, p. 1.
4. U Thant, *View from the UN* (New York: Doubleday, 1978), p. 197ff.; see also: unedited versions of the book *The Withdrawal of the United Nations Emergency Force (UNEF),* UNA, SG, S-0512-0417, New York, UN Office of Public Information, 1967; Memorandum for the Secretary, 29 May 1967, USNA, Box 1792, File 5-1-69; see also: ISA, HZ-2/4085.
5. Reudor Manor, series of interviews with Avraham Harman, Hebrew University, the Institute for International Relations, meeting 8, 14 April 1975, p. 6ff., quoted with the kind permission of David Harman; government meeting, 21 May 1967, Yaacov Herzog estate, with the kind permission of his daughter.
6. Secretary-General with Ambassador Rafael, 18 May 1967, UNA, Series 370, Box 43, File 5; Rostow with Harman, 20 May 1967, USNA, Box 7, Daily Chron., May 3–10; government meeting, 21 May 1967, Yaacov Herzog estate, with the kind permission of his daughter.
7. *Ha'aretz,* 22 May 1967, p. 2; Shoshana Ofrecht to Ben-Gurion, 2 June 1967, BGA; Avnery in the Knesset, 22 May 1967, *Knesset Minutes,* vol. 49, p. 2243.
8. Rabin with Eshkol, 15 May 1967; Rabin at the Knesset Foreign Affairs and Defense Committee, 17 May 1967, discussion brief in possession of the author; see also: Rabin, *Service Book,* vol. I, p. 135ff.; Yariv in discussion group, 29 May 1967, IDFA, 1176/192/74; Haber, *Today War Will Break Out,* p. 155.
9. Dayan and others at Foreign Affairs and Defense Committee, 17 May 1967, discussion brief in possession of the author; Moshe Dayan, *Milestones* (in Hebrew) (Jerusalem: Idanim, 1982), vol. 1, p. 356; Rabin, *Service Book,* vol. I, p. 137; Gluska, *Eshkol, Give the Order!* p. 227; see also: *Maariv,* 11 Nov. 1966, p. 5; 28 Nov. 1966, p. 7; *Yediot Aharonot,* 12 Dec. 1966, p. 1; *Ha'aretz,* 24 June 1966, p. 2.
10. Government meetings, 17 and 21 May 1967, Yaacov Herzog estate, with the kind permission of his daughter; Politico-Military Contingency Planning for the Arab-Israeli Dispute, May 1966, USNA, Box 19, Memos to the President, Folder 1 of 2; see also: Yariv in discussion groups, 29 May 1967, IDFA, 1176/192/74; Gluska, *Eshkol, Give the Order!* pp. 220ff.
11. Moshe Zak, *Hussein Makes Peace* (in Hebrew) (Ramat-Gan: Bar-Ilan University, 1994), p. 104; Sasson in security cabinet, 21 May 1967, discussion brief in possession of the author; see also: Rabin, *Service Book,* vol. I, p. 136; Rusk to Embassies, 20 May 1967; Burns to Department of State, 21 May 1967, USNA, Box 1788, File 5/20/67; Herzog diary, 15 May 1967, Eban at Government meeting, 21 May 1967, Yaacov Herzog estate, with kind permission of his daughter; ISA, A-3/4512.
12. Richard B. Parker, *The Six-Day War: A Retrospective* (Gainesville: University Press of Florida, 1996), p. 50ff.; see also: Avraham Ben-Zur, *Soviet Factors and the Six-Day War* (in Hebrew) (Tel Aviv: Sifriyat Poalim, 1975); Yosef Govrin, *Israel-USSR Relations Since Their Renewal in 1953 to Their Discontinuation in 1967* (in Hebrew) (Jerusalem: Magnes, 1990), p. 235ff.; *Yediot Aharonot* (Independence Day supplement), 30 April 1968, p. 3.
13. Brezhnev at the Central Board, 20 June 1967, Bundesarchiv, DY/3537; Isabella Ginor, "The Cold War's Cover-Up: How and Why the USSR Instigated the 1967 War," *Middle East Review of International Affairs,* vol. 7, no. 3, September 2003; government meeting, 21 May 1967, Yaacov Herzog estate, with the kind permission of his daughter; Barbour to Department of State, 22 May 1967, USNA, Box 2226, POL. 15-1; Memorandum of

Conversation, 23 May 1967, USNA, Box 1788, File 5-23-67; *Yediot Aharonot,* 17 May 1967, p. 2; *Maariv,* 25 May 1967, p. 8; *Ha'aretz,* 26 May 1967, p. 1.

14. Eshkol and others in the Foreign Affairs and Defense Committee, 17 May 1967, discussion brief in possession of the author; Galili in the government, 21 May 1967, Yaacov Herzog estate, with the kind permission of his daughter; Barbour to Department of State, 21 May 1967, USNA, Box 2226, POL 15-1.

15. *Ha'aretz,* 17 May 1967, p. 4; 18 May 1967, p. 6 (Yadin); *Yediot Aharonot,* 19 May 1967, p. 2 (Ben-Gurion); *Maariv,* 17 May 1967, p. 3 (Malhi); *Yediot Aharonot* ("7 Days" supplement), 19 May 1967, p. 10 (Gashash); *Ha'aretz,* 18 May 1967, p. 11 (autopsies); 17 May 1967, p. 5 (Leinsdorf).

16. *Ha'aretz,* 19 May 1967, p. 2 (eruption); *Maariv,* 19 May 1967, p. 1 (nerves); *Yediot Aharonot,* 19 May 1967, p. 1; 16 May 1967, p. 6 (war; Sinai).

17. Ben-Gurion diary, 17 and 23 May 1967, BGA.

18. Discussion briefs in possession of the author; see also: Gluska, *Eshkol, Give the Order!* pp. 221, 226, 228, 253.

19. Bar-Dayan diary, 19 May 1967, with his kind permission; Dayan, *Milestones,* vol. 1, p. 191; Bar-Dayan in response to the author's questions.

20. Yariv at the General Staff, 28 May 1967, IDFA, 1176/192/74; see also: Aharon Yariv, *Cautious Estimation* (in Hebrew) (Tel Aviv: Ministry of Defense, 1998), p. 157ff.; Gluska, *Eshkol, Give the Order!* p. 252ff.; Eshkol with Rabin, 20 May 1967, discussion brief in possession of the author; Rabin, *Service Book,* vol. I, p. 138ff.

21. Bar-Dayan diary, 21 May 1967; Bar-Dayan to his wife, 21 and 22 May 1967, with his kind permission.

22. *Ha'aretz,* 21 May 1967, p. 2; Security Cabinet and Government meeting, 21 May 1967, Yaacov Herzog estate, with the kind permission of his daughter; Rusk to U.S. Embassies, 18 May 1967, FRUS, vol. XIX, Doc. 15; Gvati diary, 21 May 1967, YTA, Unit 15, Container 12, File 02.

23. *Ha'aretz,* 14 May 1967, p. 10; *Maariv,* 22 May 1967, p. 3; Ben-Gurion diary, 21 May 1967, BGA.

24. Rabin, *Service Book,* vol. I, p. 148ff.; Dayan, *Milestones,* vol. 2, p. 399; Abba Eban, *Life Episodes* (in Hebrew) (Tel Aviv: Sifriyat Maariv, 1979), vol. 2, p. 329; Haber, *Today War Will Break Out,* p. 173ff.; Ben-Gurion diary, 21 and 22 May 1967, BGA; see also: H. to Ben-Gurion, 21 and 22 May 1967, BGA; Michael Bar-Zohar, *Ben-Gurion* (in Hebrew) (Tel Aviv: Am Oved, 1977), vol. 3, p. 1588.

25. Bar-Dayan diary, 22 May 1967, with his kind permission.

26. Bar-Dayan to his wife, 23 May 1967, with his kind permission.

27. Consultation at Northern Command Post, 23 May 1967, Yaacov Herzog estate, with the kind permission of his daughter; Rabin, *Service Book,* vol. I, p. 150; Eshkol at the Foreign Affairs and Defense Committee, 22 May 1967, discussion brief in possession of the author; see also: Haber, *Today War Will Break Out,* p. 164ff.

28. Security cabinet, 23 May 1967, Yaacov Herzog estate, with the kind permission of his daughter.

29. Rabin, *Service Book,* vol. I, p. 157.

30. *Ha'aretz,* 24 May 1967, p. 1; Eshkol and others with Begin and others, 23 May 1967, discussion brief in possession of the author; see also: Dayan, *Milestones,* vol. 2, p. 400.

31. Rabin, *Service Book,* vol. I, p. 158; Ezer Weizman, *For You the Sky, for You the Land* (in Hebrew) (Tel Aviv: Sifriyat Maariv, 1975), p. 259; see also: *Ha'aretz,* 22 April 1974, p. 1.

32. General Staff discussion group, Operations 241030, 24 May 1967, IDFA, 1176/192/74; Weizman with Eshkol, 24 May 1967, discussion brief, copy in possession of the author; Eshkol with IDF generals, 24 May 1967, discussion brief in possession of the author; Haber, *Today War Will Break Out,* p. 176.

33. History Department, the alertness period, 24 May 1967, IDFA, 1176/192/74; Weizman, *For You the Sky, for You the Land,* p. 259; Bar-Dayan diary, 24 May 1967, with his kind permission; Gluska, *Eshkol, Give the Order!* p. 281.

34. Bar-Dayan to his wife, 24 May 1967, with his kind permission; *Maariv,* 23 May 1967, pp. 1, 9; *Ha'aretz,* 24 May 1967, p. 2; 26 May 1967, pp. 3, 7.

35. History Department, the alertness period, 24 May 1967, IDFA, 1176/192/74.

36. Moshe Admon and Yehoshua Bar-Dayan, *Diary of a Soldier* (in Hebrew) (Tel Aviv: Othpaz, 1968), p. 15.

CHAPTER 6: ELEVEN DAYS TO WAR: NOA'S FATHER IS WAITING

1. Bar-Dayan to his wife, 25 May 1967; Bar-Dayan diary, 25 May 1967, with his kind permission.
2. *Yediot Aharonot*, 23 May 1967, pp. 1, 8; *Maariv*, 28 April 1967, p. 4; 29 May 1967, p. 3; *Ha'aretz*, 29 May 1967, p. 6; Yosef Weitz, *My Diary* (in Hebrew) (Tel Aviv: Masada, 1973), vol. 6, p. 245.
3. Halevi to Ben-Gurion, 18 May 1967; Bermes to Ben-Gurion, 31 May 1967; "Anonymous soldiers" to Ben-Gurion, 31 May 1967; Ben-Asher to Eshkol, 23 May 1967; Sedewitz to Shazar and to Eshkol, 30 May 1967; Aloni to Dayan, 31 May 1967; Gotleib to Ben-Gurion, 28 May 1967; Okon to Ben-Gurion, 30 May 1967, BGA; citizen to Knesset Chairman, 26 May 1967, ISA, C-5/594.
4. Ben-Gurion diary, 26 May 1967, BGA.
5. Yitzhak Rabin, *Service Book* (in Hebrew) (Tel Aviv: Sifriyat Maariv, 1979), vol. I, p. 150; Ben-Gurion diary, 21 and 26 May 1967, BGA; Ami Gluska, *The Conflict Between the General Staff and the Eshkol Government in "The Waiting Period," May–June 1967* (in Hebrew) (Jerusalem: The Davis Institute for International Relations, 2001), p. 6.
6. Ben-Gurion diary, 21 and 25 May 1967, BGA; Peres at Rafi secretariat, 25 May 1967, LPA, 24-1967-3-5; Begin at "Herut" party, 30 May 1967, JIA, 2/2/10/2; Begin with Eshkol, 24 May 1967, discussion brief in possession of the author; Yossi Goldstein, *Eshkol* (in Hebrew) (Jerusalem: Keter, 2003), p. 551.
7. Hazan to Yaari, 26 Feb. 1982, YEA (7) 95-23.7; Ben-Gurion diary, 24 and 25 May 1967, BGA; Ben-Gurion to Avigur, 25 May 1967, BGA; Avigur and Meir at the Ma'arach political committee, 25 May 1967, discussion briefs in possession of the author.
8. Bar-Dayan to his wife, 26 May 1967, with his kind permission.
9. *Maariv*, 24 and 26 May 1967, p. 1; Dayan, *Milestones*, vol. 2, p. 414; Arieh Dissentchik, *Tchik* (in Hebrew) (Tel Aviv: Sifriyat Maariv, undated), p. 157; see also: *Maariv*, 31 May 1967, p. 8; *Yediot Aharonot*, 23 May 1967, p. 2; *Ha'aretz*, 25 May 1967, p. 2.
10. Mordechai Gur, *The Temple Mount Is Ours* (in Hebrew) (Tel Aviv: Ministry of Defense, 1984), p. 35.
11. Hadden in response to the author's questions; Meir Amit, *Head to Head: A Personal Look at Great Events and Secret Affairs* (in Hebrew) (Tel Aviv: Hed-Arzi, 1999), p. 235.
12. Katzenbach to Johnson, 1 May 1967, LBJL, NSF, Country File, Israel, Box 145, Israeli Aid, 5/67.
13. Politico-Military Contingency Planning for the Arab-Israeli Dispute, May 1966, USNA, Box 19, Memos to the President, Folder 1 of 2.
14. Rostow to Johnson, 15 May 1967, FRUS, vol. XIX, p. 4f.
15. Rostow to President, 23 May 1967, LBJL, NSF, Box 145, Country File Israel, Israeli Aid, 5/67.
16. Harman to Eban, 22 May 1967, ISA, A-2/7919.
17. Evron to Bitan, 22 May 1967, ISA, A-2/7919.
18. Bitan to Israeli Embassy in Washington, 21 May 1967, ISA, A-3/7920.
19. Reudor Manor, series of interviews with Avraham Harman, Hebrew University, Institute for International Relations, meeting 9, 10 July 1975, p. 7ff., with the kind permission of David Harman; Abba Eban, *Personal Witness: Israel Through My Eyes* (New York: G. P. Putnam's Sons, 1992), p. 382ff.
20. Evron to Bitan, 22 May 1967; Bitan to Harman, 23 May 1967; Argov to Israeli Embassy in Washington, 24 May 1967, ISA, A-2/7919; Rusk to U.S. Embassy in Tel Aviv, 26 May 1967, USNA, Box 1789, File 5/27/67.
21. Evron to Bitan, 20 May 1967, ISA, A-3/7920.
22. Eban to Harman, 20 May 1967, ISA, A-3/7920.
23. Memorandum for the President, 21 May 1967, USNA, Box 15.
24. Reudor Manor, series of interviews with Avraham Harman, Hebrew University, Institute for International Relations, meeting 9, 10 July 1975, p. 17, with the kind permission of David Harman; see also: Abba Eban, *Life Episodes* (in Hebrew) (Tel Aviv: Sifriyat Maariv, 1979), vol. 2, p. 349.
25. Rusk to President, 26 May 1967, LBJL, NSF-NSC History, Middle East Crisis 1967, Box 17, Doc. 219.
26. Eshkol with Rabin and others, 25 May 1967, discussion brief in possession of the author; Eshkol and Avigur at the Ma'arach political committee, 25 May 1967, discussion brief in possession of the author; Rabin, *Service Book*, vol. I, p. 161.

27. Eshkol at the Southern Command; Eshkol with Rabin and others, 25 May 1967, discussion briefs in possession of the author.
28. Eban, *Personal Witness*, p. 382ff.
29. Consultation, 25 May 1967, ISA, A-3/4512.
30. Yemima Rosenthal, Arnon Lemfrum, and Hagai Tzoref, eds., *Levi Eshkol: The Third Prime Minister* (in Hebrew) (Jerusalem: Israel State Archive, 2002), p. 538.
31. Eban to Eshkol, undated, ISA, HZ-30/5979; Rusk to U.S. Embassy in Tel Aviv, 26 May 1967, USNA, Box 1789, File 5/27/67; Rusk to President, 26 May 1967, USNA, Central Files, Box 15, Memos to the President; Rusk to U.S. Embassy in Cairo, 26 May 1967, USNA, Central Files, POL ISR, Box 1788, File 26/5/67.
32. Rostow to Johnson, 25 May 1967, LBJL, Box 17, Middle East Crisis, vol. II, tab 31–42, memo no. 6.
33. Eban, *Life Episodes,* vol. 2, p. 345; Eban, *Personal Witness,* p. 382ff.
34. Reudor Manor, series of interviews with Avraham Harman, Hebrew University, Institute for International Relations, meeting 9, 10 July 1975, p. 4ff., with the kind permission of David Harman.
35. Ibid., meeting 10, 22 July 1975, p. 3ff., with the kind permission of David Harman.
36. Rosenthal et al., eds., *Levi Eshkol,* p. 538; Intelligence assessments, 25 May 1967, 8:00 P.M., IDFA, 1176/192/74.
37. *Maariv,* 4 Oct. 1967, p. 10.
38. Government meeting, 26 May 1967, ISA, A-3/4513.
39. Herzog diary, 30 May 1967, ISA, A-3/4513.
40. Moshe Shemesh, *From the Naqba to the Naqsa: The Arab-Israeli Conflict and the Palestinian National Problem, 1957–1967: Nasser's Path to the Six-Day War* (in Hebrew) (Sde Boker: Ben-Gurion Institute, 2004), p. 606ff.; Ami Gluska, *Eshkol, Give the Order!* (in Hebrew) (Tel Aviv: Ministry of Defense, 2004), p. 283ff.
41. Bar-Dayan diary, 25 May 1967, with his kind permission.
42. Amit with Hadden, 25 May 1967, minutes provided by Meir Amit, copy in possession of the author; see also: Amit, *Head to Head,* p. 235.
43. Bar-Dayan diary, 26 May 1967, with his kind permission; see also: Gur, *The Temple Mount Is Ours,* p. 29.
44. History Department, the readiness period, 25 May 1967, IDFA, 1176/192/74.
45. Ben-Gurion diary, 26 May 1967, BGA.
46. Bar-Dayan diary, 26 May 1967, with his kind permission.

CHAPTER 7: TEN DAYS TO WAR: WHAT DOES AMERICA WANT?

1. Ami Gluska, *The Conflict Between the General Staff and the Eshkol Government in the "Waiting Period," May-June 1967* (Jerusalem: The Davis Institute for International Relations, 2001), p. 15.
2. Security cabinet, 26 May 1967, Yaacov Herzog estate, with the kind permission of his daughter; Eshkol with Rabin and Weizman, 26 May 1967, discussion brief in possession of the author; Eitan Haber, *Today War Will Break Out* (in Hebrew) (Jerusalem: Idanim, 1987), p. 186
3. Harman to Foreign Ministry, 26 May 1967, ISA, HZ-30/5973.
4. Evron to Levavi, 26 May 1967, ISA, A-3/7919; President's Daily Diary, 26 May 1967, LBJL, Box 11; William B. Quandt, "Lyndon Johnson and the 1967 War: What Color Was the Light?" *Middle East Journal,* Spring 1992, vol. 46, no. 2, p. 221.
5. Ginsburg to Rostow, Rostow to President, 26 May 1967, LBJL, NSF Middle East Crisis, May 12–June 19, 1967, Box 17.
6. Memorandum of Conversation, 26 May 1967, USNA, Box 15, Memos to the President.
7. Geva to Chief of Staff, 26 May 1967, ISA, A-3/7920; see also: U.S. Forces for an Arab-Israeli Crisis, USNA, Box 18, vol. I, Folder 1 of 2.
8. Abba Eban, *Personal Witness: Israel Through My Eyes* (New York: G. P. Putnam's Sons, 1992), p. 394.
9. Memorandum of Conversation, 26 May 1967, USNA, Box 15, Memos to the President; Notes of a Meeting with President Lyndon B. Johnson and Foreign Minister Abba Eban at the White House, 26 May 1967, ISA, A-3/4511; Zachi Shalom, "Foreign Minister Abba Eban's Meeting with President Lyndon Johnson on the Eve of the Six-Day War," *Yahadut Zemanenu,* vols. 11–12, 1989, p. 301ff.; Abba Eban, *Life Episodes* (in Hebrew) (Tel Aviv: Sifriyat Maariv, 1979), vol. II, p. 347.

10. Eban, *Life Episodes* (in Hebrew) (Tel Aviv: Sifriyat Maariv, 1979), vol. II, p. 356; Reudor Manor, series of interviews with Avraham Harman, Hebrew University, Institute for International Relations, meeting 9, 10 July 1975, p. 5, with the kind permission of David Harman.

11. President's Daily Diary, 26 May 1967, LBJL, Box 11.

12. LBJL, OH, John P. Roche, no. I, p. 68.

13. Eshkol at the Ma'arach political committee, 27 May 1967, discussion brief in possession of the author; Haber, *Today War Will Break Out*, p. 191; Eban, *Life Episodes*, vol. II, p. 363; Miriam Eshkol, Interview, *50 Years War*, Israel Disk 1, MECA.

14. *Ha'aretz*, 5 June 1992, p. B/5; Government meeting, 26 May 1967, Yaacov Herzog estate, with the kind permission of his daughter; see also: Eban, *Life Episodes*, vol. II, p. 319ff.

15. Moshe Dayan, *Milestones* (in Hebrew) (Jerusalem: Idanim, 1982), vol. II, p. 405; see also: Uri Milstein and Dov Doron, *The Shaked Commando Unit: Interdiction and Regular Security in IDF History* (in Hebrew) (Tel Aviv: Yediot Aharonot, 1994).

16. Dayan, *Milestones*, vol. II, p. 512.

17. Eshkol et al. at the Ma'arach political committee, 27 May 1967, discussion brief in possession of the author; Yitzhak Rabin, *Service Book* (in Hebrew) (Tel Aviv: Sifriyat Maariv, 1979), vol. I, p. 168; Yossi Goldstein, *Eshkol* (in Hebrew) (Jerusalem: Keter, 2003), p. 555.

18. Ben-Gurion diary, 27 May 1967, BGA.

19. Ibid.; Dayan, *Milestones*, vol. II, p. 413.

20. Bar-Dayan diary, 27 May 1967, with his kind permission.

21. Ben-Gurion diary, 27 May 1967, BGA; Shlomo Nakdimon, *Toward Zero Hour* (in Hebrew) (Tel Aviv: Ramdor, 1968), p. 114.

22. Eshkol at the Ma'arach political committee, 25 May 1967, discussion brief in possession of the author.

23. Barbour to Rusk, 2 June 1967, USNA, Box 2226, POL 15-1; Hadow to Morris, 2 June 1967, PRO, 17/465.

24. Herzog diary, 4 Sept. 1967, Yaacov Herzog estate, with the kind permission of his daughter; Ami Gluska, *Eshkol, Give the Order!* (in Hebrew) (Tel Aviv: Ministry of Defense, 2004), p. 522.

25. S. Daniel, ed., *Minister Shapira* (in Hebrew) (Jerusalem: Yad Shapira, 1980), p. 252ff.

26. Security cabinet, 27 May 1967, discussion brief in possession of the author; Gluska, *Eshkol, Give the Order!* p. 315ff.

27. Ben-Gurion diary, 27 May 1967, BGA; *Ha'aretz*, 28 May 1967, p. 2; *Koteret Rashit*, 3 Oct. 1984, p. 26ff.

28. Bar-Dayan diary, 27 May 1967, with his kind permission.

29. Chief of Staff discussion group, 27 May 1967, IDFA, 1176/192/74.

30. Security cabinet, 27 May 1967, discussion brief in possession of the author; Gvati diary, 27 May 1967, YTA, Unit 15, Container 12, File 12.

CHAPTER 8: NINE DAYS TO WAR: A TERRIBLE SITUATION

1. Yosef Weitz, *My Diary* (in Hebrew) (Tel Aviv: Masada, 1973), vol. 6, p. 246.

2. Riki Ben-Ari to Adir Zik, 7 June 1967, with his kind permission.

3. *Ha'aretz*, 24 May 1967, p. 6; 25 May 1967, p. 6 (Leinsdorf); Chief of Staff discussion group, 29 May 1967, IDFA, 1176/192/74 (Eilat); Deputy Chief of Staff planning group, 3 June 1967, IDFA, 1176/192/74; Moshe Dayan, *Milestones* (in Hebrew) (Jerusalem: Idanim, 1982), vol. 2, p. 424.

4. Yeshurun Keshet, *In Besieged Jerusalem: Diaries from the Home Front* (in Hebrew) (Jerusalem: Reuven Mass, 1973), p. 203; *Yediot Aharonot*, 1 June 1967, p. 4; see also: Weitz, *My Diary* (Tel Aviv: Masada, 1973), vol. 6, p. 245; Edith Ezrachi, letters, 26 May, 6 and 8 June 1967, with the kind permission of her son; see also: *Ha'aretz*, 24 May 1967, p. 6; *Maariv*, 25 May 1967, p. 3; *Yediot Aharonot*, 1 June 1967, p. 4; Gvati diary, 25 May 1967, YTA, Unit 15, Container 12, File 02.

5. Civil Defense instructions, KYA, Container 29, File 246; see also: Alon Gan, "The Discourse That Died?: 'Discourse Culture' as an Attempt to Define a Special Identity for the Second Generation on the Kibbutzim" (in Hebrew) (diss., Tel Aviv University, 2002), p. 66ff.

6. Bar-Dayan diary, 31 May 1967; Bar-Dayan to his wife, 29 and 31 May 1967, with his kind permission; Arieh Goldberg to Sara'leh, 1 June 1967; Yoav Haruvi to Chaya'leh,

30 May 1967; Reuven Avinoam, ed., *Parchments of Fire* (in Hebrew) (Tel Aviv: Ministry of Defense, 1970), pp. 302, 359; see also p. 323.

7. *Maariv*, 22 May 1967, p. 18 ("secret weapon"); 24 May 1967, p. 11; 22 May 1967, p. 7 (shoemaker); 1 June 1967, p. 7 (elderly couple); *Ha'aretz*, 25 May 1967, p. 6 (Helena Rubinstein).

8. Letters to Penina Axelrod, 23 to 28 May 1967, with her kind permission; Shapira to Bnei Akiva members, 2 June 1967; letter to Adir Zik, 1 June 1967; Paschors to their daughter, 24 May and 3 June 1967, with the kind permission of Adir Zik; *Yediot Aharonot* (Sabbath supplement), 2 June 1967, p. 4 (blood donations).

9. Letters to Penina Axelrod, 28 and 30 May 1967, with her kind permission.

10. Letters from Rishon Lezion, 22 May–4 June 1967.

11. Riki Ben-Ari to Adir Zik, 7 June 1967, with his kind permission; Weitz, *My Diary*, vol. 6, p. 245; Keshet, *In Besieged Jerusalem*, p. 203; see also: *Ha'aretz*, 24 May 1967, p. 6; *Maariv*, 25 May 1967, p. 3; *Yediot Aharonot*, 1 June 1967, p. 4.

12. Edith Ezrachi, 1 June 1967, with the kind permission of her son; *Yediot Aharonot*, 5 June 1967, p. 7, ISA, HZ-6/4090; Avner (Walter) Bar-On, *The Untold Stories: The Diary of the Head Censor* (in Hebrew) (Jerusalem: Idanim, 1981), p. 195ff.; Ben-Gurion diary, 21 May 1967, BGA.

13. *Ha'aretz*, 22 May 1967, p. 6 (denial); Keshet, *In Besieged Jerusalem*, p. 200; Tekoah to Gussing, 27 August 1967, Conditions of Arabs in Israel and of Jews in Arab States, UNA, DAG-1/2.3, Box 136, File 1065 (Annex); See also: Shlomo Gazit, *The Carrot and the Stick: Military Governance in Judea and Samaria* (in Hebrew) (Tel Aviv: Zmora-Bitan, 1985), p. 34ff.

14. Lior with Harmelin, 19 May 1967, discussion brief in possession of the author; Renewal of Military Supervision over the Minorities Population, 26 May 1967, IDFA, 76/117/70; Fausi Al-Asmar, *To Be an Arab in Israel* (in Hebrew) (Jerusalem: Shachak, 1975), p. 126; Monthly security report, 7 July 1967, IDFA, 76/117/70.

15. Lochamei HaGetaot, *Update Sheet for Enlisted Soldiers*, no. 5, 3 June 1967, with the kind permission of Zvika Dror; See also: Yair Baumel, "The Israeli Establishment's Attitude Toward Arabs in Israel: Policy, Principles, and Actions: The Second Decade, 1958–1968" (in Hebrew) (diss., Haifa University, 2002), p. 196; *Ha'aretz*, 25 May 1967, p. 6.

16. *Ha'aretz*, 22 May 1967, p. 3; *Ha'Olam Hazeh*, 25 May 1967, p. 8.

17. Zichroni to Eshkol, 28 May 1967, ISA, C-15/6301.

18. Edith Ezrachi, 1 June 1967, with the kind permission of Ilan Ezrachi, copy in possession of the author.

19. Tom Segev, *The Seventh Million: Israelis and the Holocaust* (in Hebrew) (Jerusalem: Keter, 1991).

20. Meeting protocol, youth who traveled to Poland, 25 Aug. 1966, ISA, GL-12/12976.

21. Horowitz to Weisblatt, 29 March 1967, ISA, GL-12/12973.

22. Ofer Feniger, *The World Was Within Me* (in Hebrew) (Tel Aviv: Levin Epstein, 1972), p. 53.

23. Herzog diary, 9 Aug. 1966, ISA, A-16/4510.

24. Livneh to Eshkol (undated, apparently 29 May 1967), ISA, A-1/7231.

25. *Ha'aretz*, 22 May 1967, p. 2; 29 May 1967, p. 2; 31 May 1966, p. 2; 5 June 1967, p. 2.

26. Herzog diary, 1 June 1967, with the kind permission of his daughter; *Maariv*, 25 May 1967, p. 8; 26 May 1967, p. 1; 2 June 1967, p. 2; 4 June 1967, p. 3; *Yediot Aharonot*, 23 May 1967, p. 2; 26 May 1967, p. 2.

27. *Ha'aretz*, 30 May 1967, p. 2.

28. Bentov to Eshkol, 1 June 1967, ISA, C-1/6301; Foreign Ministry to Israeli Embassy, 2 June 1967, ISA, HZ-6/6444; see also: Idith Zertal, *Death and the Nation: History, Memory, Politics* (in Hebrew) (Tel Aviv: Dvir, 2002), p. 171ff.

29. *Yediot Aharonot*, 5 June 1967, p. 6.

30. *Yediot Aharonot*, 19 June 1967, p. 12.

31. Ami Gluska, *Eshkol, Give the Order!* (in Hebrew) (Tel Aviv: Ministry of Defense, 2004), p. 318.

32. Avinoam, ed., *Parchments of Fire*, p. 328.

33. Lochamei HaGetaot, *Newsletter for Enlisted Soldiers* (in Hebrew), no. 5, 5 June 1967, no. 3 (undated), with the kind permission of Zvika Dror.

34. Naomi Shukri to Vardit Zik, 28 May 1967, with the kind permission of Adir Zik; see also: Shlomit Levi and Eliyhu Katz, "Public Opinion and the Mood in the Six-Day

War" (in Hebrew), in *Six Days—Thirty Years: New Perspectives on the Six-Day War*, ed. Asher Sashar (Tel Aviv: Am Oved, 1999), p. 246.

35. Gluska, *Eshkol, Give the Order!* p. 252; Ami Gluska, *The Conflict Between the General Staff and the Eshkol Government During the "Waiting Period,": May–June 1967* (in Hebrew) (Jerusalem: Davis Institute, 2001), p. 6; Israel Erlich (former head of Chevra Kaddisha), in response to the author's question; *Ha'aretz* (supplement), 25 Aug. 1967, p. 5ff.

36. Rostow to Goldberg, May 26, 1967; Rusk to U.S. Embassy in Israel, May 20, 1967, USNA, Box 1788, File 5/2/67.

37. Goldberg to President, May 26, 1967, LBJL, White House Central Files, Box 66.

38. Sisco to Rusk, May 30, 1967, USNA, Box 1789, File 5/30/67; Prospect for a political settlement, June 2, 1967, USNA, Box 18, Vol. I, Folder 1 of 2.

39. "The Voice of Thunder from All the Fronts" (album produced by R.T.A.), in possession of the author; letter to Penina Axelrod, 18 June 1966, with her kind permission; Haim Hefer and Marcel Yanko, *Fraternity of Soldiers* (in Hebrew) (Tel Aviv: Amikam, 1968) (no page numbers); *Ha'aretz*, 4 June 1967, p. 5.

CHAPTER 9: ONE WEEK TO WAR: THE GENERALS' REVOLT

1. Bar-Dayan diary, 28 May 1967, with his kind permission.
2. AHA, P/0/03.
3. Bar-Dayan to his wife, 28 May 1967, with his kind permission.
4. Bar-Dayan diary, 28 May 1967, with his kind permission; Bar-Dayan to his wife, 28 May 1967, with his kind permission; Rostow to President, 27 May 1967, LBJL, NSF Middle East Crisis, May 12–June 19, 1967, Box 17; Evron to Foreign Ministry, 27 May 1967, ISA, A-1/7919.
5. Johnson to Eshkol, 27 May 1967, FRUS, vol. XIX, p. 163.
6. Mapai Secretariat, 1 June 1967, LPA, 2246790.
7. Government decision, 28 May 1967, Yaacov Herzog estate, with the kind permission of his daughter; Gvati diary, 28 May 1967, YTA, Unit 15, Container 12, File 02; Ami Gluska, *Eshkol, Give the Order!* (in Hebrew) (Tel Aviv: Ministry of Defense, 2004), p. 321ff.
8. Yossi Goldstein, *Eshkol* (in Hebrew) (Jerusalem: Keter, 2003), p. 557.
9. Miriam Eshkol, Interview, *50 Years War*, Israel Disk 1, MECA.
10. Herzog diary, 4 Sept. 1967, with the kind permission of his daughter; Eitan Haber, *Today War Will Break Out* (in Hebrew) (Jerusalem: Idanim, 1987), p. 194; Yeshayahu Gavish, Ariel Sharon, Interviews, *50 Years War*, Israel Disk 1, MECA.
11. Bar-Dayan diary, 28 May 1967, with his kind permission.
12. Allon in an interview with Reudor Manor, ISA, A-19/5001, meeting 1, p. 21.
13. Eshkol at the General Staff, 29 May 1967, IDFA, 1176/192/74; Haber, *Today War Will Break Out*, p. 194ff.; Goldstein, *Eshkol*, p. 558.
14. Ariel Sharon, Interview, *50 Years War*, Israel Disk 1, MECA.
15. Haber, *Today War Will Break Out*, p. 199.
16. General Staff discussion group, 28 May 1967, IDFA, 1176/192/74.
17. Bar-Dayan diary, 29 and 30 May, 1967; Bar-Dayan to his wife, 30 May 1967, with his kind permission.
18. Bar-Dayan diary, 31 May 1967, with his kind permission.
19. Haim Herzog, *The Great Days* (in Hebrew) (Tel Aviv: Sifriyat Maariv, 1967), p. 15; see also: Shlomit Levi and Eliyhu Katz, "Public Opinion and the Mood in the Six-Day War" (in Hebrew), in *Six Days—Thirty Years: New Perspectives on the Six-Day War*, ed. Asher Sashar (Tel Aviv: Am Oved, 1999), p. 252.
20. Moshe Admon and Yehoshua Bar-Dayan, *Diary of a Soldier* (in Hebrew) (Tel Aviv: Othpaz, 1968), p. 24.
21. Bar-Dayan diary, 30 May 1967, with his kind permission.
22. Gvati diary, 30 May 1967, YTA, Unit 15, Container 12, File 02.
23. Moshe Dayan, *Milestones* (in Hebrew) (Jerusalem: Idanim, 1982), vol. II, p. 412.
24. Ezer Weizman, *For You the Sky, for You the Land* (in Hebrew) (Tel Aviv: Sifriyat Maariv, 1975), p. 261; Horev in Chief of Staff discussion group, 29 May 1967, IDFA, 1176/192/74.
25. Operational discussion group, 30 May 1967 (morning session); Operational discussion group, 30 May 1967 (afternoon session); Deputy Chief of Staff discussion group, 1 June 1967; Plan presentation discussion group, 31 May 1967; Chief of Staff discussion group, 31 June 1967; "Whip" orders, 1 June 1967, IDFA, 1176/192/74.

26. Mordechai Gur, *The Temple Mount Is Ours!* (in Hebrew) (Tel Aviv: Ministry of Defense, 1984), p. 43.
27. "The Significance of a Freeze in the Situation for 2–3 Weeks," 31 May 1967, IDFA, 1176/192/74.
28. President's Daily Log, May 19, 1967, LBJL, Box 11.
29. Ibid., May 27, 1967, LBJL, Box 11.
30. Ibid.
31. Rostow to President, 26 May 1967, LBJL, NSF Middle East Crisis May 12–June 19, 1967, Box 17; see also: Anderson to President, 2 June 1967, USNA, Box 1792, File 6/1/67; Richard B. Parker, *The Politics of Miscalculation in the Middle East* (Bloomington: Indiana University Press, 1993), p. 55ff.
32. Evron to Foreign Ministry, 27 May 1967, ISA, A-2/7919.
33. Harman to Foreign Ministry, 28 May 1967, ISA, A-1/7919.
34. Evron to Foreign Ministry, 31 May 1967, ISA, A-2/7919.
35. Evron to Foreign Ministry, 29 May 1967, ISA, A-2/7919.
36. Eshkol to Johnson, 30 May 1967, FRUS, vol. XI, p. 187ff.; Editorial Note, p. 196; Evron to Foreign Ministry, 31 May 1967, ISA, A-2/7919.
37. Rostow to President, 31 May 1967, LBJL, White House Central Files, Box 67.
38. Comparison of the Eshkol letter and the President's conversation with Eban (undated), USNA, Box 19, Memos to the President, Folder 2 of 2; Harman to Bitan, 28 May 1967; Foreign Ministry to Israeli Embassy, 28 May 1967, ISA, A-2/7919; Rusk to U.S. Embassy in Israel, 28 May 1967, USNA, Box 1789, File 6/25/67.
39. Moyers to Johnson, 24 May 1967, LBJL, ND 19 CO 1-6, Box 193; Wattenberg to President, 31 May 1967, LBJL, White House Central Files, Box 67.
40. LBJL, NSD EX ND, Box 194, 19/CO 1-6, 6/22/67.
41. Cohen to President, 31 May 1967, LBJL, ND 19/CO, Box 193.
42. Sue Sacks to the Maizlish Family, 30 May 1967, AJA, SC 5520.
43. U.S. Consulate in Jerusalem to Department of State, 1 June 1967, USNA, Box 1790.

Chapter 10: Five Days to War: The Ouster

1. *Ha'aretz*, 26 May 1967, pp. 1, 2.
2. Ibid., 28 May 1967, p. 2.
3. *Maariv*, 28 May 1967, p. 1; 26 May 1967, p. 4.
4. *Ha'aretz*, 29 May 1967, p. 2.
5. *Maariv*, 29 May 1967, p. 8.
6. Ibid., 22 Sept. 1968, p. 11.
7. *Yediot Aharonot*, 1 June 1967, p. 8.
8. Yadin Diary, 30 May 1967, ISA, P-16/1403.
9. *Ha'aretz*, 30 May 1967, p. 1; Ami Gluska, *The Conflict Between the General Staff and the Eshkol Government During the "Waiting Period," May–June 1967* (in Hebrew) (Jerusalem: Davis Institute, 2001), p. 35; see also: Tom Segev, *1949; The First Israelis* (in Hebrew) (Jerusalem: Domino, 1984), p. 246.
10. Eshkol in the Knesset, 29 May 1967, *Knesset Minutes* (in Hebrew), vol. 49, p. 2283ff.
11. Ben-Gurion diary, 31 May 1967, BGA.
12. Herzog diary, 30 May 1967, ISA, A-3/4512.
13. Gvati diary, 29 May 1967, YTA, Unit 15, Container 12, File 02; Aran with Ma'arach ministers, 31 May 1967, discussion brief in possession of the author.
14. Galili with Ma'arach ministers, 31 May 1967, discussion brief in possession of the author.
15. General Staff discussion group, 29 May 1967, IDFA, 1176/192/74; Eitan Haber, *Today War Will Break Out* (in Hebrew) (Jerusalem: Idanim, 1987), p. 200.
16. Ami Gluska, *Eshkol, Give the Order!* (in Hebrew) (Tel Aviv: Ministry of Defense, 2004), p. 369.
17. Allon in an interview with Reudor Manor, ISA, A-19/6001, first meeting, p. 15ff.; Hanoch Bartov, *Dado, 48 Years and 20 Days* (in Hebrew) (Tel Aviv: Dvir, 2002), p. 143.
18. Eshkol with Ma'arach ministers (morning session), 31 May 1967, discussion brief in possession of the author; Carmit Guy, *Bar-Lev* (in Hebrew) (Tel Aviv: Am Oved, 1998), p. 129; Ezer Weizman, *For You the Sky, for You the Land* (in Hebrew) (Tel Aviv: Sifriyat Maariv, 1975), p. 263.
19. Meir Amit, *Head to Head: A Personal Look at Great Events and Secret Affairs* (in Hebrew) (Tel Aviv: Hed-Arzi, 1999), p. 237.
20. Mati Golan, *Peres* (in Hebrew) (Tel Aviv: Schocken, 1982).

21. Yitzhak Rabin, *Service Book* (in Hebrew) (Tel Aviv: Sifriyat Maariv, 1979), vol. I, p. 166; Government meeting, 31 May 1967, Yaacov Herzog estate, with the kind permission of his daughter.

22. Peres in discussion with opposition members, 23 May 1967, discussion brief in possession of the author; Ben-Gurion diary, 25 May 1967, BGA.

23. *Maariv,* 31 May 1967, p. 2; Moshe Dayan, *Milestones* (in Hebrew) (Jerusalem: Idanim, 1982), vol. II, p. 415; Kishon in response to the author's questions; see also: *Yediot Aharonot,* 1 June 1967, p. 1.

24. Bar-Dayan diary, 1 June 1967, with his kind permission.

25. Meir with Ma'arach ministers (morning session), 31 May 1967, discussion brief in possession of the author; see also: Meir at Mapai secretariat, 1 June 1967, LPA, 2246790.

26. Dayan, *Milestones,* vol. II, p. 420; see also: *Maariv,* 22 Sept. 1968, p. 11.

27. Rachel Tzabari at Mapai secretariat, 1 June 1967, LPA, 2246790; Anita Shapira, *Yigal Allon: The Springtime of His Universe* (in Hebrew) (Tel Aviv: HaKibbutz HaMeuchad, 2004).

28. Allon in an interview with Reudor Manor, ISA, A-19/5001, first meeting, p. 23.

29. Ibid., pp. 17, 34; see also: Yigal Allon, *A Screen of Sand* (in Hebrew) (Tel Aviv: HaKibbutz HaMeuchad, 1959), p. 61.

30. Eshkol at Ma'arach party, 30 May 1967, discussion brief in possession of the author.

31. Ben-Gurion diary, 30 May 1967, BGA.

32. Gvati diary, 31 May 1967, Unit 15, Container 12, File 02.

33. *Ha'aretz,* 30 May 1967, p. 1; Weizman, *For You the Sky, for You the Land,* p. 262.

34. Allon in an interview with Reudor Manor, ISA, A-19/5001, first meeting, p. 25.

35. Peres at Rafi secretariat, 1 June 1967, LPA, 24-1967-3-5.

36. Discussion brief, copy in possession of the author; see also: Mapai secretariat, 31 May 1967, LPA, 2246790; Haber, *Today War Will Break Out,* p. 200ff.

37. Gvati diary, 31 May 1967, YTA, Unit 15, Container 12, File 02.

38. Government meeting, 31 May 1967, Yaacov Herzog estate, with the kind permission of his daughter; see also: Zerach Warhaftig, *Fifty-One Years* (in Hebrew) (Tel Aviv: Yad Shapira, 1998), p. 185.

39. Mapai secretariat, 1 June 1967, LPA, 2246790.

40. Yadin diary, 24 May, 1 and 2 June 1967, ISA, P-16/1403.

41. Weizman, *For You the Sky, for You the Land,* p. 262ff.; Haber, *Today War Will Break Out,* p. 199; Herzog diary, 12 Sept. 1967, with the kind permission of his daughter.

42. Minutes summaries, copies in possession of the author.

43. Mapai secretariat, 1 June 1967 (evening session), LPA, 2246790.

44. Peres and Almogi at Rafi secretariat, 1 June 1967, LPA, 24-1967-3-5.

45. Shimon Peres: "The Wisdom of Compromise," *Yediot Aharonot* ("7 Days" supplement), 9 March 1979, p. 16.

46. Ben-Gurion diary, 2 June 1967, BGA; see also: Herzog diary, 1 June 1967, ISA, A-3/4512.

47. Herzog diary, 1 June 1967, ISA, A-3/4512; Dayan, *Milestones,* vol. II, p. 421.

48. Yemima Rosenthal, Arnon Lemfrum, and Hagai Tzoref, eds., *Levi Eshkol, the Third Prime Minister* (in Hebrew) (Jerusalem: Israel State Archive, 2002), p. 550.

49. Yadin diary, 2 June 1967, ISA, P-16/1403; Eshkol to Dayan, 4 June 1967, Yaacov Herzog estate, with the kind permission of his daughter.

50. *Yediot Aharonot,* 4 June 1967, p. 2.

51. Ibid., 2 June 1967, p. 1.

52. Bar-Dayan to his wife, 2 June 1967, with his kind permission.

CHAPTER 11: THREE DAYS TO WAR: THE DECISION

1. Eitan Haber, *Today War Will Break Out* (in Hebrew) (Jerusalem: Idanim, 1987), p. 204ff.

2. Kashti to Sapir, 29 May 1967, ISA, A-4/7920.

3. Special meeting of the General Staff with the security cabinet, 2 June 1967, IDFA, 3/46/80; Moshe Dayan, *Milestones* (in Hebrew) (Jerusalem: Idanim, 1982), vol. II, p. 421; Herzog diary, 4 Sept. 1967, with the kind permission of his daughter. See also Yemima Rosenthal, ed., *Yitzhak Rabin: Selected Documents* (Jerusalem: Israel State Archive, 2006), vol. 1; Yossi Goldstein, *Rabin: A Biography* (Tel Aviv: Schocken, 2006).

4. Abba Eban, *Life Episodes* (in Hebrew) (Tel Aviv: Sifriyat Maariv, 1979), vol. II, p. 380; Abba Eban, *Personal Witness: Israel Through My Eyes* (New York: G. P. Putnam's Sons, 1992), p. 405; Eban to Quandt, 26 July 1990, courtesy of William B. Quandt; Yitzhak

Rabin, *Service Book* (in Hebrew) (Tel Aviv: Sifriyat Maariv, 1979), vol. I, p. 179; Evron to Foreign Ministry, 1 June 1967; Harman to Foreign Ministry, 2 June 1967, ISA, A-2/7919.

5. Amit to Mossad, 2 June 1967, estate of Yaacov Herzog, with the kind permission of his daughter.

6. Dayan, *Milestones*, vol. II, p. 422; Haber, *Today War Will Break Out*, p. 212; Shimon Peres, *Battling for Peace* (London: Weidenfeld and Nicolson, 1995), p. 166ff.

7. Peres, *Battling for Peace*, p. 166ff.

8. Dayan, *Milestones*, vol. II, p. 423.

9. Yariv at Chief of Staff discussion group, 29 May 1967, IDFA, 1176/192/74; Defense and Military Attaché's Office, Dispatch No. 1, 13 Dec. 1967, PRO, FCO 17/S26/104157.

10. Plan presentation to the Chief of Staff, 2 June 1967, IDFA, 1176/192/74.

11. Ben-Gurion diary, 2 June 1967, BGA.

12. Bar-Dayan diary, 3 June 1967, with his kind permission.

13. Haber, *Today War Will Break Out*, p. 215; Dayan, *Milestones*, vol. II, p. 424.

14. Amit with Eshkol and others, 3–4 June 1967, ISA, A-3/4512.

15. Mossad representative in Washington to Mossad head, 8 June 1967, Yaacov Herzog estate, with the kind permission of his daughter.

16. Reudor Manor, series of interviews with Avraham Harman, Hebrew University, Institute for International Relations, meeting 10, 22 July 1975, p. 11, with the kind permission of David Harman.

17. Amit report, 4 June 1967, with his kind permission; Meir Amit, *Head to Head: A Personal Look at Great Events and Secret Affairs* (in Hebrew) (Tel Aviv: Hed-Arzi, 1999), p. 237ff.; Amit in response to the author's questions; see also: Richard Helms, *A Look over My Shoulder: A Life in the Central Intelligence Agency* (New York: Random House, 2003), p. 273ff.

18. Amit, *Head to Head*, p. 242; Hadden to the author, 2 Jan. 2004; Reudor Manor, series of interviews with Avraham Harman, Hebrew University, Institute for International Relations, meeting 11, 29 July 1975, p. 1ff., with the kind permission of David Harman; Ami Gluska, *Eshkol, Give the Order!* (in Hebrew) (Tel Aviv: Ministry of Defense, 2004), p. 382 (gas masks); see also: William B. Quandt, "Lyndon Johnson and the 1967 War: What Color Was the Light?" *Middle East Journal*, Spring 1992, vol. 46, no. 2, p. 198ff.

19. Battle to Rusk, 3 June 1967, USNA, Box 2226, POL 16; Reudor Manor, series of interviews with Avraham Harman, Hebrew University, Institute for International Relations, meeting 9, 10 July 1975, p. 13ff., with the kind permission of David Harman; Herzog diary, 15 Aug. 1967, ISA, A-3/4511.

20. Rusk to U.S. Embassy in Israel, 3 June 1967, USNA, Box 1790, File 3/6/67; Haber, *Today War Will Break Out*, p. 217.

21. Reudor Manor, series of interviews with Avraham Harman, Hebrew University, Institute for International Relations, meeting 9, 10 July 1975, p. 13ff., with the kind permission of David Harman; Harman with Eshkol and others, 3–4 June 1967, ISA, A-3/4512.

22. Amit with Eshkol and others, 3–4 June 1967, ISA, A-3/4512.

23. Richard B. Parker, *The Politics of Miscalculation in the Middle East* (Bloomington: Indiana University Press, 1993); Richard B. Parker, *The Six-Day War* (Gainesville: University Press of Florida, 1996); Avi Shlaim, *The Iron Wall: Israel and the Arab World* (New York: Norton, 2000), p. 218ff.; Benny Morris, *Victims: The History of the Zionist-Arab Conflict, 1881–2001* (in Hebrew) (Tel Aviv: Am Oved, 2003), p. 286ff.; Michael Oren, *Six Days of War: The Battle That Changed the Face of the Middle East* (in Hebrew) (Tel Aviv: Dvir, 2004).

24. Bar-Dayan diary, 4 June 1967, with his kind permission.

25. Government meetings, 4 June 1967, Yaacov Herzog estate, with the kind permission of his daughter; Gvati diary, 4 June 1967, YTA, Unit 15, Container 12, File 02.

26. Allon in an interview with Reudor Manor, ISA, A-19/5001, second meeting, p. 9ff.

27. Gila Bar-Dayan to her husband, 4 June 1967, with their kind permission.

CHAPTER 12: DAY ONE

1. Michael Oren, *Six Days of War: The Battle That Changed the Face of the Middle East* (in Hebrew) (Tel Aviv: Dvir, 2004), p. 221ff.; Tamar Brosh, ed., *A Speech for Every Occasion* (in Hebrew) (Tel Aviv: Yediot Aharonot, 1993), p. 133; Oz to the author, 13 Dec. 2003.

2. Ben-Gurion diary, 5 June 1967, BGA.

3. Ezrachi on 8 June 1967, with the kind permission of her son; Yosef Weitz, *My Diary* (in Hebrew), vol. 6 (Tel Aviv: Masada, 1973), p. 246; Kollek to Eshkol, 7 June 1967, ISA, C-1/6301; see also: *Ha'aretz*, 6 June 1967, p. 3; 7 June 1967, p. 2.

4. Shabtai Tevet, *Exposed in the Turret* (in Hebrew) (Tel Aviv: Schocken, 1968), p. 170; Reuven Avinoam, *Remembrance* (in Hebrew) (Tel Aviv: Ministry of Defense, 1971).

5. Foreign Ministry to Israeli Embassy in Washington, 5 June 1967, ISA, HZ-6/6444; Odd Bull, *War and Peace in the Middle East* (London: Leo Cooper, 1973), p. 108; Yossi Goldstein, *Eshkol* (in Hebrew) (Jerusalem: Keter, 2003), p. 731; Rusk to Burns, 5 June 1967, USNA, Box 1791, File 6/9/67.

6. Hadow to Brown, 6 July 1967, PRO, FCO 17/526/104157; see also: Hadow to Morris, 22 June 1967, PRO, FCO 17/504.

7. Ezrachi on 8 June 1967, with the kind permission of her son; Weitz, *My Diary*, vol. 6, p. 246; Kollek to Eshkol, 7 June 1967, ISA, C-1/6301; see also: *Ha'aretz*, 6 June 1967, p. 3; 7 June 1967, p. 2.

8. Weitz, *My Diary*, vol. 6, p. 246; Ezrachi on 8 June 1967, with the kind permission of her son.

9. Letters to Penina Axelrod, 12 and 18 June 1967, with her kind permission; letter to Adir Zik, 6 June 1967, with his kind permission.

10. Avner (Walter) Bar-On, *The Untold Stories: Diary of the Head Censor* (in Hebrew) (Jerusalem: Idanim, 1981), p. 231ff.; Moshe Dayan, *Milestones* (in Hebrew) (Jerusalem: Idanim, 1982), vol. II, p. 436; "The Voice of Thunder from All Fronts" (record produced by R.T.A.); Hagai Pinsker and Yigal Lussin, *The Six-Day War: Kol Israel and Galei Tzahal at War*, CBS Record; Ezer Weizman, *For You the Sky, for You the Land* (in Hebrew) (Tel Aviv: Sifriyat Maariv, 1975), p. 269; Ben-Gurion diary, 5 June 1967, BGA; Dayan on the radio, 5 June 1967, ISA, C-17/6270; Gvati diary, 5 June 1967, YTA, Unit 15, Container 12, File 02; *Maariv*, 5 June 1967 (Third Edition), p. 1; Yehuda Ariel, *The Six-Day War* (in Hebrew) (Jerusalem: Ministry of Education and Culture, 1999), p. 17; McPherson to Johnson, 11 June 1967, LBJL, Office files of Harry McPherson, Box 42.

11. U.S. Consulate in Jerusalem to Department of State, 5 June 1967 (Three cables), USNA, Box 1792, POL 27, 6/5/67; Dayan, *Milestones*, vol. II, p. 437ff.

12. Eitan Haber, *Today War Will Break Out* (in Hebrew) (Jerusalem: Idanim, 1987), p. 228.

13. Moshe Zack, *Hussein Makes Peace* (in Hebrew) (Ramat-Gan: Bar-Ilan University, 1994), p. 57ff.; Avi Shlaim, "His Royal Shyness: King Hussein and Israel," *The New York Review of Books*, July 15, 1999, p. 14ff.; Rostow to President, 12 Dec. 1966, FRUS, vol. XVIII, Doc. 364; Herzog to Remez, 23 Nov. 1966, Herzog estate, with the kind permission of his daughter.

14. Operation discussion group, 25 May 1967; Chief of Staff discussion group, 27 May 1967, IDFA, 1176/192/74; Haber, *Today War Will Break Out*, p. 228.

15. *Ha'aretz*, 6 June 1967, p. 3; 7 June 1967, pp. 2, 6.

16. Weizman, *For You the Sky, for You the Land*, p. 270.

17. Dayan, *Milestones*, vol. II, p. 436; Bar-On, *The Untold Stories*, p. 228.

18. Bull, *War and Peace in the Middle East*, p. 115; Narkis in internal discussion on the history of the Six-Day War, IDFA, 1/901/67; U.S. Consul, Jerusalem to Department of State, 5 June 1967, Box 1796; 14 Aug. 1967, Box 1799.

19. Merle Miller, *Lyndon: An Oral Biography* (New York: G. P. Putnam's Sons, 1980), p. 480.

20. Memorandum for the Record (Rostow Recollections), 17 Nov. 1968, FRUS, vol. XIX, pp. 290; President's Daily Diary, June 5, 1967, LBJL, Box 11; Lyndon Baines Johnson, *The Vantage Point: Perspectives on the Presidency, 1963–1969* (New York: Holt, Rinehart and Winston, 1971), p. 296.

21. Mathilde Krim, in response to the author's questions. Rostow to Johnson, 6 June 1967, LBJL, NSF-NSC Middle East Crisis, Box 18, Document 39; see also: Penina Lahav, *Israel in Law: Shimon Agranat and the Zionist Century* (Tel Aviv: Am Oved, 1999); Raphael to Levavi, 6 June 1967, estate of Yaacov Herzog, with the kind permission of his daughter.

22. Bar-Dayan diary, 5 June 1967, with his kind permission.

23. Weitz, *My Diary*, vol. 6, p. 246.

24. Gvati diary, 5 June 1967, YTA, Unit 15, Container 12, File 02.

25. Bar-Dayan diary, 5 and 6 June 1967, with his kind permission; Ben-Gurion diary, 6 June 1967, BGA.

CHAPTER 13: DAY TWO

1. Bar-Dayan diary, 6 June 1967, with his kind permission; Amatzia Baram, ed., *The Armored Commando Unit* (in Hebrew) (Chaverim, 1969), p. 95.

2. "Priorities: The Rest of the War," estate of Yaacov Herzog, with the kind permission of his daughter; Moshe Dayan, *Milestones* (in Hebrew) (Jerusalem: Idanim, 1982), vol. II, p. 440.

3. U.S. Consulate in Jerusalem to Department of State, 6 June 1967, USNA, Box 1793, File 6/6/67.

4. Government meeting, 6 June 1967, Yaacov Herzog estate, with the kind permission of his daughter.

5. Eshkol in the Knesset Foreign Affairs and Defense Committee, 7 June 1967, ISA, A-4/7920.

6. Abba Eban, *Life Episodes* (in Hebrew) (Tel Aviv: Sifriyat Maariv, 1979), vol. 2, p. 407.

7. Allon in an interview with Reudor Manor, fourth meeting, 28 May 1967, p. 20; Uzi Benziman, *Jerusalem: Unwalled City* (in Hebrew) (Tel Aviv: Schocken, 1973), p. 20.

8. Bar-Dayan diary, 6 June 1967, with his kind permission.

9. McPherson to Johnson, 11 June 1967, LBJL, Office Files of Harry McPherson, Middle East Box 42.

10. Bar-Dayan diary, 6 June 1967, with his kind permission; Reuven Avinoam, ed., *Remembrance* (in Hebrew) (Tel Aviv: Ministry of Defense, 1971), p. 24; *The Fifty-One Commendations* (in Hebrew) (Tel Aviv: Ministry of Defense, undated), p. 67; Shabtai Teveth, *Exposed in the Turret* (in Hebrew) (Tel Aviv: Schocken 1968), p. 164ff.

11. Benny Morris, *Victims: The History of the Zionist-Arab Conflict, 1881–2001* (in Hebrew) (Tel Aviv: Am Oved, 2003), p. 217.

12. *Maariv,* 7 June 1967, p. 2.

13. Summary Report of the Six-Day War, Introduction—the General's Review, p. 2, IDFA, 3/901/67; The Command Diary of Uzi Narkis, Ruth Bondi et al., eds., *Not by the Sword Alone: The Wonderful Story of the Heroism of the Nation of Israel and Its Victory in the Six-Day War* (in Hebrew) (Tel Aviv: Levin-Epstein, undated), p. 189.

14. Ezer Weizman, *For You the Sky, for You the Land* (in Hebrew) (Tel Aviv: Sifriyat Maariv, 1975), p. 282ff.

15. General Order, 28 May 1967; mobilization order—Central Command newsletter, 5 June 1967, JMA, Container 1699; see also: Uzi Narkis, *A Soldier of Jerusalem* (in Hebrew) (Tel Aviv: Ministry of Defense, 1991).

16. *Call to Battle,* General Order No. 5, 6 June 1967, AHA, PP/12/OR/012/313; Six-Day War Summary Report, Introduction—General's review, p. 4, IDFA, 3/901/67; "The Command Diary of Uzi Narkis," p. 185; Mordechai Gur, *The Temple Mount Is Ours!* (Tel Aviv: Ministry of Defense, 1984), p. 13; see also: Uzi Narkis, *50 Years War,* Israel Disk 1, MECA; Arieh Brown, *Personal Seal: Moshe Dayan in the Six-Day War and Afterward* (in Hebrew) (Tel Aviv: Yediot Aharonot, 1997), p. 64.

17. The Command Diary of Uzi Narkis, p. 189; see also: Dayan, *Milestones,* vol. II, p. 441.

18. Rusk to Barbour, 6 June 1967, USNA, Box 10 and Box 1793; Barbour to Rusk, 6 June 1967, Box 1792 POL 27, 6/5/67; Burns to Rusk, 6 June 1967, Box 1793, File 6/6/67; Eitan to Foreign Ministry; Remez to Foreign Ministry; Bitan to Harman, 6 June 1967, ISA, A-4/7920; Bitan memorandum, 6 June 1967, estate of Yaacov Herzog, with the kind permission of his daughter; Brown, *Personal Seal,* p. 62.

19. Ronen testimony, KYA, Container 29, File 249.

20. Bar-Dayan diary, 6 June 1967, with his kind permission.

21. Yosef Weitz, *My Diary* (in Hebrew) (Tel Aviv: Masada, 1973), vol. 6, p. 246ff.

22. Ruth Geffen-Dotan diary, 6 June 1967, Ruth Bondi et al., eds., *Not on the Sword Alone: The Wonderful Story of the Heroism of the Nation of Israel and Its Victory in the Six-Day War* (in Hebrew) (Tel Aviv: Levin-Epstein, undated), p. 278.

23. Letter to Adir Zik, 6 June 1967, with his kind permission.

24. Eitan Haber, *Today War Will Break Out* (in Hebrew) (Jerusalem: Idanim, 1987), p. 231.

25. *Ha'aretz,* 6 June 1967, p. 2; *Maariv,* 6 June 1967, p. 4.

26. Haber, *Today War Will Break Out,* p. 232; Dayan, *Milestones,* vol. II, p. 442; Ben-Gurion diary, 6 June 1967, BGA.

27. Dayan, *Milestones,* vol. II, p. 437.

28. Ibid., p. 433.

29. Ronen testimony, KYA, Container 29, File 249.

30. Israel Segal, *One of the Two of Us* (in Hebrew) (Jerusalem: Keter, 1995), p. 22; see also: Amram Gabai testimony, ODI, File 1 (226), p. 33.

31. Mosowitz testimony, KYA, Container 29, File 249.

32. Security cabinet meeting, 6 June 1967, Yaacov Herzog estate, with the kind permission of his daughter; discussion brief in possession of the author; Yemima Rosenthal, Arnon Lemfrum, and Hagai Tzoref, eds., *Levi Eshkol, the Third Prime Minister* (in Hebrew) (Jerusalem: Israel State Archive, 2002), p. 557.

33. Ben-Gurion diary, 6 June 1967, BGA.

34. Barbour to Rusk (three cables); Rostow to Embassies; Rusk to Harriman; Rusk to U.S. Embassy in Italy; USDO in Israel to Department of Defense, all 5 June 1967, USNA, Box 1792, POL 27, 6/5/67; McPherson to Johnson, 11 June 1967, LBJL, Office Files of Harry McPherson, Middle East, Box 42; Memorandum for the Record, 5 June 1967 (Rostow Recollections), LBJL, NSF, NSC, History, Box 18, Document 72.

35. Burns to Rusk, 5 June 1967; U.S. Embassy in Egypt to Department of State, 6 June 1967, USNA, Box 1792, POL 27, 6/5/67; see also Rusk to Ambassadors, 7 June 1967, USNA, Box 1793, File 8/6/67; Loper to Rostow, 7 June 1967; Cooper to Rostow, 7 June 1967, Box 18, vol. I, Folder 1 of 2; Cooper to Rostow, 8 June 1967, Box 18, vol. I, Folder 2 of 2; Rusk to Burns, 7 June 1967, POL ISR, Box 1794, File 6/10/67.

36. Yosef Argaman, *It Was Top Secret: 30 Intelligence and Security Affairs in Israel* (in Hebrew) (Tel Aviv: Ministry of Defense, 2002), p. 234; Dayan, *Milestones*, vol. II, p. 460.

37. Rusk to Barbour; Meekr to Rusk, both 6 June 1967, USNA, Box 1792, POL 27, File 6/6/67; see also: Harold M. Saunders, *The Middle East Crisis*, LBJL, NSF-NSC History, Middle East Crisis, Box 17, Doc. No. 2.

38. Lyndon Baines Johnson, *The Vantage Point: Perspectives of the Presidency, 1963–1969* (New York: Holt, Rinehart and Winston, 1971), p. 299; see also: Califano to Johnson, 5 June 1967, LBJL, ND 19CO 1-6, Box 193; Memorandum for the secretary, 5 June 1967, USNA, Box 1789, File 5/30/67; Hackler to Christian, 5 June 1967, LBJL, ND 19 CO 1-6, Box 193.

39. Califano to Johnson, 5 June 1967, USNA, Box 15, Memos to the President.

40. Califano to Johnson, 5 June 1967, LBJL, ND 19 CO 1-6, Box 193.

41. Roche to President, 6 June 1967, LBJL, WHCF, Box 67.

42. LBJL Oral History Interviews, John P. Roche, I, P. 64.

43. President's Daily Diary, 5 June 1967, LBJL, Box 11.

44. Robert Dallek, *Lone Star Rising: Lyndon Johnson and His Times, 1908–1960* (New York: Oxford University Press, 1991), p. 429.

45. Donnelley to Secretary, 7 June 1967, LBJL, ND 19, CO, 1-6, Box 193.

46. Dayan, *Milestones*, vol. II, p. 442.

47. General Order No. 2, 6 June 1967, AHA, P/200/9.

CHAPTER 14: DAY THREE

1. Bar-Dayan diary, 7 June 1967, with his kind permission.

2. Arieh Brown, *Personal Seal: Moshe Dayan in the Six-Day War and Afterward* (in Hebrew) (Tel Aviv: Yediot Aharonot, 1997), p. 68.

3. Mordechai Gur, *The Temple Mount Is Ours!* (in Hebrew) (Tel Aviv: Ministry of Defense, 1984), p. 16.

4. Ibid., p. 318.

5. Mosowitz testimony, KYA, Container 29, File 249.

6. Uzi Narkis, Interview, *50 Years War*, Israel Disk 1, MECA; Carmit Guy, *Bar-Lev* (in Hebrew) (Tel Aviv: Am Oved, 1998), p. 138; *The Six-Day War, Kol Israel and Galei Tzahal Reporters at War* (CBS record).

7. Mosowitz testimony, KYA, Container 29, File 249.

8. Moshe Dayan, *Milestones* (in Hebrew) (Jerusalem: Idanim, 1982), vol. II, p. 443.

9. Yemima Rosenthal, Arnon Lemfrum, and Hagai Tzoref, eds., *Levi Eshkol, the Third Prime Minister* (in Hebrew) (Jerusalem: Israel State Archive, 2002), p. 566; Ofra Nevo-Eshkol, *Humorous Eshkol* (in Hebrew) (Jerusalem: Idanim, 1988), p. 1561; see also: Eshkol with the Movement for Greater Israel, 12 Nov. 1967, ISA, A-7/7920.

10. Security cabinet, 7 June 1967, Yaacov Herzog estate, with the kind permission of his daughter; Eshkol at the security cabinet, at the Foreign Affairs and Defense Committee, and at the political committee, 7 June 1967, discussion briefs in possession of the author.

11. *Maariv* (weekend supplement), 10 April 1997, p. 44.

12. Uzi Narkis, Interview, *50 Year War*, Israel Disk 1, MECA; Nadav Shragai, *The Disputed Mountain: The Fight for the Temple Mount* (in Hebrew) (Jerusalem: Keter, 1995), p. 22.

13. *Ha'aretz,* 8 June 1967, p. 1; *Maariv,* 8 June 1967, p. 3.
14. Eitan Haber, *Today War Will Break Out* (in Hebrew) (Jerusalem: Idanim, 1987), p. 234.
15. Ezer Weizman, *For You the Sky, for You the Land* (in Hebrew) (Tel Aviv: Sifriyat Maariv, 1975), p. 289.
16. Yashayahu Gavish, Interview, *50 Years War,* Israel Disk 1, MECA; General Order No. 4 (Southern Command), 4 June 1967, AHA, P/200/19.
17. Weizman, *For You the Sky, for You the Land,* p. 290.
18. Dayan, *Milestones,* vol. II, p. 487; Herzog diary, 10 June 1967, ISA, A-3/4512; see also: Yitzhak Rabin, *Service Book* (in Hebrew) (Tel Aviv: Sifriyat Maariv, 1979), vol. I, p. 196; "Whip" Operation, Operational Command No. 2, 4 June 1967, IDFA, 1176/192/74.
19. Ronen testimony, KYA, Container 29, File 249.
20. Chizik testimony, KYA, Container 29, File 249.
21. Bar-Dayan diary, 11 June 1967, with his kind permission.
22. Bar-Dayan diary, 10 June 1967, with his kind permission.
23. IDF Spokesman to Shlomo Hillel, 2 March 1968, ISA, HZ-44/4090.
24. Chizik testimony, KYA, Container 29, File 249.
25. Uri Milstein and Dov Doron, *Shaked Commando Unit: Interdiction and Continuous Security in the IDF History* (in Hebrew) (Tel Aviv: Yediot Aharonot, 1994), p. 149ff.
26. *Yediot Aharonot,* 17 Aug. 1995, p. 3; see also: *Washington Post,* 17 Aug. 1995, p. A30.
27. Yaakov Rabinowitz, *Kobi* (in Hebrew) (Tel Aviv: HaKibbutz HaMeuchad, 1981), p. 23; Alon Gan, "The Discourse That Died? 'Discourse Culture' as an Attempt to Define a Special Identity for the Second Generation on the Kibbutzim" (in Hebrew) (diss., Tel Aviv University, 2002), p. 73ff.
28. Ga'aton members to Yaari, 14 June 1967, Yaari to Ga'aton members, 26 June 1967, YYA 95-21.7 (2).
29. Dayan in the Knesset, 21 June 1967, *Knesset Minutes,* vol. 49, p. 2384ff.; Dayan, *Milestones,* vol. II, p. 461; Rabin, *Service Book,* vol. I, p. 196; "Whip" Operation, Operational Command No. 2, 4 June 1967, IDFA, 1176/192/74; see also: Command and Staff School (13th Class, 1966–67), *Taking Over Occupied Territories* (Abstract); IDF Operations Branch/Training Department, *Taking Over Occupied Territories* (1960); *Military Authorities in Occupied Territories* (1961), Yaacov Herzog estate, with the kind permission of his daughter.
30. Yehoshua Bar-Dayan to his wife, 7 June 1967, with his kind permission.
31. Bar-Dayan diary, 7 June 1967, with his kind permission.
32. Yadin diary, 9 June 1967, ISA, P-16/1403.
33. Chen Ronen testimony, KYA, Container 29, File 249; see also: Yisrael Harel, ed., *Lions' Gate: The Battle for Jerusalem in the Experience of the Paratrooper Fighters* (in Hebrew) (Tel Aviv: Ministry of Defense, 1977).
34. Remez and Eitan to Foreign Ministry (separate telegrams), 7 June 1967, ISA, A-4/7920; Remez to Levavi and Amit, 7 June 1967, Yaacov Herzog estate, with the kind permission of his daughter; see also: Burns to Rusk, 7 June 1967 (two messages), USNA, Box 1793, File 6/7/67.
35. Uzi Narkis, interview, *50 Years War,* Israel, Disk 1, MECA; *Ha'aretz,* 31 Dec. 1997, p. B/3.
36. Ben-Gurion diary, 8 and 12 June 1967, BGA; Weizman, *For You the Sky, for You the Land,* p. 289.
37. Yeshurun Keshet, *In Besieged Jerusalem: Diaries from the Home Front* (in Hebrew) (Jerusalem: Reuven Mass, 1973), p. 226; Moshe Shamir, *Natan Alterman: The Poet as Leader* (in Hebrew) (Tel Aviv: Dvir, 1988), p. 105.
38. *Maariv,* 7 June 1967, p. 2.
39. Ibid., 8 June 1967, p. 3; 7 June 1967, p. 8; 11 June 1967, p. 5; Mosowitz testimony, KYA, Container 29, File 249.
40. *Battle Call,* General Order No. 5, 9 June 1967, AHA, PP/15/012/313; General Order no. 7 and 8 June 1967, JMA, Container 8034.
41. *Davar,* 8 June 1967, p. 1; *Maariv,* 7 June 1967, p. 2.
42. *Battle Call,* General Orders Nos. 5 and 7, 6 and 8 June 1967, AHA, PP/13-14/012/313.
43. *Ha'aretz,* 7 June 1967, p. 2; *Maariv* (weekend), 9 June 1967, p. 1 (miracle); 8 June 1967, p. 3 (dreamers); *Yediot Aharonot,* 6 June 1967 (4 o'clock edition), p. 1; 7 June 1967, p. 2; see also: Harel, ed., *Lions' Gate.*
44. Letter to Penina Axelrod, 18 June 1967, with her kind permission.
45. Letter to Adir Zik, 7 June 1967, with his kind permission.

46. Letters to Penina Axelrod, 8, 16, and 18 June 1967, with her kind permission.

47. Letter to Penina Axelrod, 8 June 1967, with her kind permission.

48. Rosenthal et al., eds., *Levi Eshkol*, p. 563; Harman to Eshkol, 9 June 1967, and to Foreign Ministry, 8 June 1967, ISA, A-9/7919.

49. President's Daily Log, 5 and 7 June 1967, LBJL, Box 11; see also: Califano to Johnson, 7 June 1967, LBJL, NSF-NSC, History of the Middle East Crisis, Box 18, vol. 3, Doc. No. 47a.

50. Califano to Johnson, 7 June 1967, LBJL, WHCF, Box 67.

51. Levinson and Wattenberg to Johnson, 5 and 7 June 1967, LBJL, WHCF, Box 67.

52. Donnelly to Secretary, 8 June 1967, LBJL, ND 19 CO 1-6, Box 193; see also: Harry McPherson: "The White House, American Jews, and the Six-Day War" (in Hebrew) in *Six Days: Thirty Years: A New Look at the Six-Day War,* ed. Asher Sashar (Tel Aviv: Am Oved, 1999), p. 3ff.

53. Ariel to Foreign Ministry, 13 June 1967, ISA, HZ-9/3979.

CHAPTER 15: THE FINAL DAYS

1. Bar-Dayan to his wife, 8 and 9 June 1967, with his kind permission.

2. Bar-Dayan diary, 8 June 1967, with his kind permission.

3. Barbour to Rusk, 8 June 1967, USNA, Box 1783, File 8/6/67.

4. A. Jay Cristol, *The Liberty Incident: The 1967 Israeli Attack on the U.S. Spy Ship* (Washington, D.C.: Brassey's, 2002).

5. Robert Dallek, *Flawed Giant: Lyndon Johnson and His Times, 1961–1973* (New York: Oxford University Press, 1988), p. 430; Richard Helms, *A Look Over My Shoulder: A Life in the Central Intelligence Agency* (New York: Random House, 2003), p. 301; Dean Rusk, *As I Saw It* (New York: W. W. Norton, 1990), p. 388.

6. Security Cabinet, 7 June 1967, Yaacov Herzog estate, with the kind permission of his daughter; Rostow to Johnson, 13 June 1967, LBJL, NSF-NSC, History, Box 18, Documents No. 8-8a; LBJL, Oral Histories, Paul C. Warnke, interview no. 3, p. 14; see also: Yitzhak Rabin, *Service Book* (in Hebrew) (Tel Aviv: Sifriyat Maariv, 1979), vol. I, p. 196ff.

7. *Ha'aretz,* 8 June 1967, p. 2; *Daf,* 8 June 1967, p. 1.

8. Security cabinet, 8 June 1967, Yaacov Herzog estate, with the kind permission of his daughter; Matityahu Meizel, *The Battle for the Golan, June 1967* (in Hebrew) (Tel Aviv: Ministry of Defense, 2001), p. 241ff.; Hanoch Bartov, *Dado: 48 Years and 20 Days* (in Hebrew) (Tel Aviv: Dvir, 2002), p. 141ff.; *Yediot Aharonot* ("7 Days" supplement), 30 May 1997, p. 16ff.; Zerach Warhaftig, *Fifty-One Years* (in Hebrew) (Yad Shapira, 1998), p. 187ff.; Eitan Haber, *Today War Will Break Out* (in Hebrew) (Jerusalem: Idanim, 1987), p. 247; Yigal Allon in an interview with Reudor Manor, first meeting, p. 15, ISA, A-19/5001; *Land of Golan* (in Hebrew), 9 May 1985, p. 32ff.; Moshe Dayan, *Milestones* (in Hebrew) (Jerusalem: Idanim, 1982), vol. II, p. 473ff.; Rabin, *Service Book,* vol. I, p. 200.

9. Haber, *Today War Will Break Out,* p. 251.

10. Carmit Guy, *Bar-Lev* (in Hebrew) (Tel Aviv: Am Oved, 1998), p. 143; Yigal Allon in an interview with Reudor Manor, first meeting, p. 15, ISA, A-19/5001; YTA, Unit 15, Series C, Container 3, File 2.

11. Rabin, *Service Book,* vol. I, p. 200; Herzog diary, 11 June 1967, ISA, A-3/4511; Meizel, *The Battle for the Golan, June 1967,* p. 271.

12. Security Cabinet, 9 June 1967, Yaacov Herzog estate, with the kind permission of his daughter; Herzog diary, 11 June 1967, ISA, A-3/4511; Bartov, *Dado,* p. 153.

13. Brom testimony, KYA, Container 29, File 249.

14. *The Fifty-One Commendations* (in Hebrew) (Tel Aviv: Ministry of Defense, undated), p. 169ff.

15. Dayan, *Milestones,* vol. II, pp. 443, 471; Rabin, *Service Book,* vol. I, p. 196; Arieh Brown, *Personal Seal: Moshe Dayan in the Six-Day War and Afterward* (in Hebrew) (Tel Aviv: Yediot Aharonot, 1997), pp. 67, 77, 79ff.; General Order No. 5 (Southern Command), 9 June 1967, AHA P/200/19; Yeshayahu Gavish, interview, *50 Years War,* Israel Disk 1, MECA.

16. *Maariv,* 13 Oct. 1967, p. 11; *Air Force Journal,* 8 June 1967, Battle Issue no. 2, p. 2; Reuven Avinoam, *Remembrance* (Tel Aviv: Ministry of Defense, 1971), p. 49; Aviezer Golan and Ami Shamir, *The Book of Heroism* (in Hebrew) (Tel Aviv: Journalists Society, 1968), p. 25; Yonina Ben-Or in response to the author's questions; Herzog diary, 9 and 10 June 1967, ISA, A-3/4512.

17. Miriam Eshkol, interview, *50 Years War*, Israel Disk 1, MECA.
18. Haber, *Today War Will Break Out*, p. 258; Guy, *Bar-Lev*, p. 143; *Ha'aretz*, 12 Sept. 1967, p. 4; Chizik testimony, KYA, Container 29, File 249; Report to the Secretary General, 24 Aug. 1967, S-0321-0002, Box 1, File 1; Rubinstein and Chizik testimonies, KYA, Container 29, File 249.
19. *Ha'aretz*, 5 June 1992, p. 5B.
20. Warhaftig, *Fifty-One Years*, p. 196 ff.; Herzog diary, 9 and 10 June 1967, ISA, A-3/4512.
21. Ben-Gurion diary, 9 June 1967, BGA.
22. Yadin diary, 9 June 1967; Dayan to Yadin, 10 June 1967; undated page, ISA, P-16/1403.
23. Remembrance Album, 1968, with the kind permission of Avraham Kushner.
24. Zlicha to Israel Land Administration, 4 Feb. 1968, Benvenisti to Katzenelbogen, 8 Sept. 1968, JMA, Container 5994, Mograbi and Jewish Quarter file.
25. Uzi Narkis, *Soldier of Jerusalem* (in Hebrew) (Tel Aviv: Ministry of Defense, 1991), p. 333ff.; Chaim Herzog, *Way of Life* (in Hebrew) (Tel Aviv: Yediot Aharonot, 1997), p. 223; Shlomo Gazit, *The Carrot and the Stick: Military Governance in Judea and Samaria* (in Hebrew) (Tel Aviv: Zmora-Bitan, 1985), p. 53; Uzi Benziman, *Jerusalem: Unwalled City* (in Hebrew) (Tel Aviv: Schocken, 1973), p. 37ff.; see also: Meron Benvenisti, *Opposite the Closed Wall: Divided and United Jerusalem* (in Hebrew) (Weidenfeld and Nicolson, 1973), p. 137.
26. Ben-Gurion to Weitz, 12 June 1967, BGA.
27. Ben-Gurion diary, 8 June 1967, BGA.
28. McPherson to Johnson, 11 June 1967, LBJL, McPherson Office Files, Box 42.
29. Yosef Weitz, *My Diary* (in Hebrew) (Tel Aviv: Masada, 1973), vol. 6, p. 247ff.; Government meeting, 11 June 1967, Yaacov Herzog estate, with the kind permission of his daughter.
30. Gvati diary, 20 June 1967, YTA, Unit 15, Container 12, File 02.
31. Report summary of the Six-Day War, Part II, Paragraph 4, Appendix 14, p. 107, IDFA, 901/67/3; Natan Alterman, *"Bederekh Noh-Amon": Poems of the Ten Plagues of Egypt, Old Poems* (in Hebrew) (Tel Aviv: HaKibbutz HaMeuchad, 1972), p. 231, English translation: *Nathan Alterman: Selected Poems*, trans. Robert Friend (Tel Aviv: HaKibbutz HaMeuchad, 1978); see also: Rubinstein testimony, KYA, Container 29, File 249.
32. *Ha'aretz*, 19 June 1967, p. 2.
33. Brown, *Personal Seal*, p. 66.
34. Ibid., p. 68.
35. Security cabinet, 7 July 1967, Yaacov Herzog estate, with the kind permission of his daughter.
36. Dayan, *Milestones*, vol. II, p. 444; Yosef Argaman, *It Was Top Secret: 30 Intelligence and Security Affairs in Israel* (in Hebrew) (Tel Aviv: Ministry of Defense, 2002), p. 246; see also: Gazit, *The Carrot and the Stick*, p. 57.
37. Ruth Bondi et al, eds., *Not on the Sword Alone: The Wonderful Story of the Heroism of the Nation of Israel and Its Victory in the Six-Day War* (in Hebrew) (Tel Aviv: Levin-Epstein, undated), p. 190.
38. Burns to Rusk, 10 June 1967, USNA, Box 1794, File 6/10/67.
39. Sasson report, 12 July 1967, with his kind permission.
40. Wilson to Rusk, 24 June 1967, USNA, Box 1796, File 6/24/67; Gazit, *The Carrot and the Stick*, p. 57.
41. Ronen and Rubinstein testimonies, KYA, Container 29, File 249.
42. U.S. Embassy in Jordan to Department of State, 9 June 1967, USNA, Box 1793, File 6/9/67; Daniel Rubinstein in response to the author's questions.
43. Campbell to Department of State, 29 February 1968, USNA, Box 2224, File POL 2.
44. *Ha'aretz* (supplement), 5 June 1998, p. 14ff.; see also: *Kol HaIr*, 8 Nov. 1991, p. 19; 15 Nov. 1991, p. 23; Herzog, *Way of Life*, p. 222.
45. Brom testimony, KYA, Container 29, File 249.
46. Six-Day War Summary Report, Part I, Paragraph 2, p. 60, IDFA, 3/901/67.
47. Amos Etinger, *My Land, You Weep and Laugh* (in Hebrew) (Tel Aviv: Yediot Aharonot, 1991), p. 269; Note for the record, 29 June 1967, in Nils G. Gussing, Report to the UN Secretary General, 24 August 1967, UNA, S-0321-0002, Box 2, File 1; Evan M. Wilson, *Jerusalem: Key to Peace* (Washington, D.C.: Middle East Institute, 1970), p. 112; Dayan, *Milestones*, vol. II, p. 496.

48. Ezer Weizman, *For You the Sky, for You the Land* (in Hebrew) (Tel Aviv: Sifriyat Maariv, 1975), p. 297ff.
49. Dayan, *Milestones,* vol. II, p. 496.
50. G. P. Cassels, Note for the Record, 8 July 1967; J. Cambray, Notes for the Record, 11 August 1967, UNA, S-0321-0002, Box 1, File 7; Lewen to Moberley, 24 August 1967, PRO, FCO 17/212; Hall to Department of State, 23 August 1967, USNA, Box 1800; Dayan, *Milestones,* vol. II, p. 497; Reuven Pedhatzur, *The Victory of Embarrassment: The Eshkol Government's Policy in the Territories After the Six-Day War* (in Hebrew) (Tel Aviv: Bitan, 1996), p. 265.
51. Government meeting, 25 June 1967, Yaacov Herzog estate, with the kind permission of his daughter; see also: ISA, C-3/10136.
52. Yaacov Herzog estate, with the kind permission of his daughter; British Embassy in Jordan to Foreign Office, 13 June 1967, PRO, FCO, 17/214.
53. Harman to Rostow, 29 June 1967, USNA, Box 1796; *Maariv,* 13 June 1967, p. 11; *Ha'aretz,* 19 June 1967, p. 2; see also: *Ha'aretz,* 12 June 1967, p. 4.
54. Notes on Gussing report, 18 Oct. 1967, ISA, HZ-4/4096.
55. Government meeting, 25 June 1967, Yaacov Herzog estate, with the kind permission of his daughter.
56. Note for the Record, July 1, 1967, in Nils G. Gussing, Report to the UN Secretary General, August 24, 1967, UNA, S-0321-0002, Box 2, File 1.
57. *Battle Call,* General Order No. 6, 7 June 1967, AHA PP/13/012/313.
58. Dayan, *Milestones,* vol. II, p. 496.
59. Report to the Secretary General, 24 August 1967, S-0321-0002, Box 1, File 1.
60. *Koteret Rashit,* 26 Dec. 1984, p. 29ff.
61. Report on the destruction of villages and expulsion of refugees (undated), ISA, C-5/3497; see also: *Ha'aretz,* 18 July 1997, p. 4 (Uri Avneri to Editor).
62. Brown, *Personal Seal,* p. 153ff.
63. Ibid., p. 151; Gazit, *The Carrot and the Stick,* pp. 58, 60; Herzog with Eshkol, 6 Dec. 1967, ISA, A-2/7921; Black to Johnson, February 14, 1968, FRUS, vol. XX, Doc. No. 80.
64. Note by Mr. Bakerjian, 30 June 1967, UNA, S-0321-0002, Box 2, File 2; U.S. Consulate in Jerusalem to Department of State, 7 and 9 June 1967, USNA, Box 1793, File 6/9/67; Campbell to Jim, 12 June 1967, PRO, FCO 17/212/104225; Wilson, *Jerusalem: Key to Peace,* p. 111; see also: *Ha'aretz,* 8 Nov. 1967, p. 2.
65. Memorandum, 9 and 16 June 1967, ISA, HZ-14/4096; Haber, *Today War Will Break Out,* p. 269.
66. Bar-Dayan diary, 8–9 June 1967, with his kind permission.
67. Adam Laslow testimony, KYA, Container 29, File 249.
68. Letters to Adir Zik, 18 June, 14 and 28 July 1967 with his kind permission.
69. General Order No. 3 (Southern Command), 7 June 1967, AHA, P/200/19.
70. "Handling booty and prohibition against looting and arms," 8 June 1967, AHA, P/0/11.
71. Gazit to Chiram, 5 May 1968; Knesset Finance Committee discussion on the State Comptroller's report, IDFA, 80/2845/97.
72. Barbour to Rusk, 11 June 1967, USNA, Box 1794, File 11/6/67; see also: Ben-Horin to Director-General, 4 July 1967, HZ-9/4089.
73. Gazit, *The Carrot and the Stick,* p. 53; see also: Michael Shashar, *The Seventh-Day War: Diary of the Military Governance in Judea and Samaria, June–December 1967* (in Hebrew) (Tel Aviv: Sifriyat Poalim, 1977), pp. 43, 50; Haber, *Today War Will Break Out,* p. 266; Dayan, *Milestones,* vol. II, p. 458; Eban to Eshkol, 29 June 1967, ISA, A-10/7938; Yaish to Foreign Ministry, 2 Aug. 1967, ISA, HZ-6/4088.
74. Rabin with Eshkol, 31 July 1967, IDFA, 118/117/70; see also: Arkin to Division Commander, 24 June 1967, IDFA, 66/117/70. Brom testimony, KYA, Container 29, File 249; Bondi et al, eds., *Not on the Sword Alone,* p. 320.
75. Ben-Gurion diary, 9 June 1967, BGA.
76. Bar-Dayan diary, 12 June 1967, with his kind permission.
77. Central Command, the Six-Day War, Part I, Paragraph 2, p. 134, IDFA, 1/901/67; Rabin, *Service Book,* vol. I, p. 203.
78. Hadow to Brown, Dec. 28, 1967, PRO, FCO 17/526/104157.
79. Dayan, *Milestones,* vol. II, p. 482; *Maariv,* 23 Dec. 1966, p. 5; Brown, *Personal Seal,* p. 110; Haber, *Today War Will Break Out,* p. 273.

80. Herzog diary, recorded at the end of Aug. 1969, Yaacov Herzog estate, with the kind permission of his daughter.

81. Ze'ev Schiff and Eitan Haber, *Lexicon of Israeli Security* (in Hebrew) (Tel Aviv: Zmora Bitan Modan, 1976), p. 15; see also: Benny Morris, *Victims: The History of the Zionist-Arab Conflict, 1881–2001* (in Hebrew) (Tel Aviv: Am Oved, 2003), p. 309; Benvenisti, *Opposite the Closed Wall*, p. 119.

82. Bar-Dayan diary, 10 and 12 June 1967; Bar-Dayan to his wife, 12 and 13 June 1967, with his kind permission.

PART IV: THEY THOUGHT THEY HAD WON

1. Gabriel Stern, "On Mussa the Redhead's Balcony" (in Hebrew), *Al HaMishmar*, 1986.

CHAPTER 16: A NEW LAND

2. *Maariv*, 13 Oct. 1967, p. 11; Air Force Newsletter, 8 June 1967, General Order no. 2, p. 2; Reuven Avinoam, *In Memoriam* (in Hebrew) (Tel Aviv: Ministry of Defense, 1971), p. 49; Aviezer Golan and Ami Shamir, *The Book of Heroism* (in Hebrew) (Tel Aviv: Society of Journalists, 1968), p. 25; Yonina Ben-Or in response to the author's questions.

3. Letter to Penina Axelrod, 19 June 1967, with her kind permission; Edith Ezrachi, 14 and 22 June 1967, with the kind permission of her son; letter to Adir Zik, 18 June 1967, with his kind permission; *Ha'aretz*, 21 June 1967, p. 11; 2 July 1967, p. 10.

4. Letter from 21 June 1967, with the kind permission of Asher Knafo; Avinoam, *In Memoriam*, p. 60 (Ben-Ezra); p. 276 (Amiram); p. 325 (Krock); p. 157 (Tal); p. 169 (Yair); p. 209 (Lecks); p. 214 (Magen); p. 102 (Diamant); *Dear Families: Letters, Envelopes and Stamps for Memorial Day* (in Hebrew) (Tel Aviv: Ministry of Defense, 1999); see also: Ilana Shamir, *Lest It Be as If They Never Lived* (in Hebrew) (The Unit for Commemorating Soldiers in the Ministry of Defense and the National Memoriam Press, Ministry of Defense, 2003); letter to Adir Zik, 5 July 1967, with his kind permission.

5. Bar-Dayan diary, 18–29 June 1967, with his kind permission; Bar-Dayan in response to the author's questions.

6. Letters to Penina Axelrod, 8 and 19 June 1967, with her kind permission ("narcotics"); letter to Adir Zik, 3 Aug. 1967, with his kind permission; Yosef Weitz, *My Diary* (in Hebrew) (Tel Aviv: Masada, 1973), vol. VI, p. 262.

7. Ronen testimony, KYA, Container 29, File 249.

8. Zvi Tzabar, ed., *Scrolls of Fire* (in Hebrew) (Tel Aviv: Ministry of Defense, 1971), vol. V, book I, p. 338ff.

9. Moshe Dayan, *Milestones* (in Hebrew) (Jerusalem: Idanim, 1982), vol II, p. 451; Ezer Weizman, *For You the Sky, for You the Land* (in Hebrew) (Tel Aviv: Sifriyat Maariv, 1975), p. 296.

10. Bartov to Israeli, 24 Sept. 1967, IDFA, 66/117/1970; Permits to enter the territories, ISA, 4091/HZ-10.

11. *Yehiam Newsletter* (in Hebrew) 32/113, 12 July 1967, p. 6ff.; Meron Benvenisti, *The Slingshot and the Stick: Territories, Jews, and Arabs* (in Hebrew) (Jerusalem: Keter, 1988), p. 145; Yehuda Yost to Adir Zik, 29 July 1967, with his kind permission; Dayan to Yanai, 20 June 1967, Chaim Herzog estate, with the kind permission of his son; Dayan to Yaffe, 28 June 1967, ISA, 6301/C-1 (file no. 2); Weitz, *My Diary*, vol. VI, p. 250ff.

12. Letter to Adir Zik, 17 July 1967, with his kind permission; Michael Shashar, *The Seventh-Day War: The Diary of the Military Government in Judea and Samaria (June–December 1967)* (in Hebrew) (Tel Aviv: Sifriyat Poalim, 1997), p. 186; Weitz, *My Diary*, vol. VI, p. 257; Ben-Gurion diary, 9 June 1967, BGA; Ben-Gurion to Benyamin Nahari, 17 July 1967; Ben-Gurion diary, 27 Aug. 1967; Ben-Gurion to Zvi Ben-Erev, 30 Aug. 1967; Ben-Gurion to Tebenkin, 18 Dec. 1967, BGA.

13. Yehuda Yost to Adir Zik, 29 July 1967, with his kind permission; letter to Penina Axelrod, 25 July 1967, with her kind permission; Yonah Hadari, *Messiah Riding a Tank* (in Hebrew) (Jerusalem: Hartman Institute, 2002), p. 95.

14. Dayan, *Milestones*, vol. II, p. 454; Tzabar, ed., *Scrolls of Fire*, vol. V, book I, p. 338; *Yehiam Newsletter* (in Hebrew) 32/113, 12 July 1967, p. 6ff.; see also: *Yehiam Newsletter* (in Hebrew) 190/1, 14 Sept. 1967, p. 7ff.; Weitz, *My Diary*, vol. VI, p. 252.

15. Letters to Adir Zik, 22 July 1967, with his kind permission; Weitz, *My Diary*, vol. VI, p. 267 (Gaza); p. 255 (refugees); p. 247 (birthrate); p. 252 ("eyes glimmer"); *Maariv*, 26

June 1967, p. 3; Arie Lova Eliav, *Rings of Testimony* (in Hebrew) (Tel Aviv: Am Oved, 1983), p. 287; *Maariv,* 12 June 1967, p. 3.

16. Weitz, *My Diary,* vol. VI, pp. 249ff. and 262; Yehiam Frior to the author; letter to Adir Zik, 12 July 1967, with his kind permission (border).

17. Weitz, *My Diary,* vol. VI, p. 254; *Ha'aretz,* 15 June 1967, p. 1; 18 June 1967, p. 6; *Hayom,* 15 June 1967, p. 1.

18. Rosenberger to Shazar, 3 July 1967; meeting summary, 5 July 1967; Sephardic Community Board to Eshkol, 11 July 1967, ISA, 6399/C-25; Weitz, *My Diary,* vol. VI, p. 266; *Ha'aretz,* 21 July 1967, p. 2 (Leibowitz); see also: *Maariv,* 25 Aug. 1967, p. 10; *Davar,* 12 Sept. 1967, p. 3; Arnon to Eshkol, 30 Aug. 1967, ISA 6303/C-3; Eshkolot to Shapira, 2 Nov. 1967; Eshkolot to Eshkol, 10 Nov. 1967, ISA 5712/C-3; *Maariv* (Saturday), 9 June 1967, p. 1 (two identities).

19. *Al HaMishmar,* 9 and 16 June 1967, p. 9.

20. Government meeting, 11 and 15 June 1967, Yaacov Herzog estate, with the kind permission of his daughter; see also: government meeting, 11 and 18 June 1967, ISA, 8164/A-6; 25 June 1967, ISA, 8164/A-10; 26 June 1967, ISA, 8164/A-11; Herzog diary, 17 June 1967, ISA, 4511/A-3; Gvati diary, 11 June 1967, YTA, Unit 15, Container 12, File 02; Rusk to U.S. Embassy in Israel, 17 June 1967, USNA, Box 1795, File 6/16/67; see also: Eban to Eshkol, 29 June 1967, ISA, 7920/A-8; Ze'evi to Shapira, 22 June 1967, ISA, 4089/HZ-14; Michael Shashar, *Conversations with Rehavam Ze'evi* (in Hebrew) (Tel Aviv: Yediot Aharonot, 2001), p. 208ff.; Reuven Pedhatzur, *The Victory of Shame: The State of Israel in the Territories After the Six-Day War* (in Hebrew) (Tel Aviv: Yad Tabenkin, 1966), p. 117ff.; Municipalities Ordinance Amendment Law, 27 June 1967, *Knesset Minutes* (in Hebrew), vol. 49, p. 2421; *Ha'aretz,* 28 June 1967, p. 1; Shlomo Gazit, *The Carrot and the Stick: Military Government in Judea and Samaria* (in Hebrew) (Tel Aviv: Zmora-Bitan, 1985), p. 223ff.; Tkoa to Israeli Embassies, 26 June 1967, ISA, 7020/A-8; see also: Harman to Foreign Ministry, 29 June 1967, ISA, 4089/HZ-14.

21. *Maariv,* 8 Oct. 1967, p. 1; Shiffman to Eshkol, 5 July 1967, ISA, 6301/C-1; Eshkol, Dayan, and others in consultation, 3 July 1968, ISA, 7921/A-5; *Al HaMishmar,* 30 June 1967, p. 1; *Ha'aretz,* 30 June 1967, p. 1; *Maariv,* 2 July 1967, p. 3; letter to Adir Zik, 6 July 1967, with his kind permission.

22. Teddy Kollek, *One Jerusalem* (in Hebrew) (Tel Aviv: Sifriyat Maariv, 1979), p. 215; Dayan, *Milestones,* vol. II, p. 494; Uzi Benziman, *Jerusalem: Unwalled City* (in Hebrew) (Tel Aviv: Schocken, 1973), p. 60; *Al HaMishmar,* 30 June 1967, p. 10; *Yediot Aharonot,* 18 June 1967, p. 5.

23. Weitz, *My Diary,* vol. VI, pp. 259, 253.

CHAPTER 17: VICTORY ALBUMS

1. *Maariv,* 16 July 1967, p. 10.

2. Mordechai Bar-On, "The Testimony of the Man Behind the Speech" (in Hebrew) in *The Second Decade,* eds. Zvi Tzameret and Chana Yablonka (Jerusalem: Yad Ben-Zvi, 2000), p. 405ff.; Tamar Brosh, *A Speech for Every Occasion* (in Hebrew) (Tel Aviv: Yediot Aharonot, 1993), p. 60ff.; Yonah Hadari, *Messiah Riding a Tank* (in Hebrew) (Jerusalem: Hartman Institute, 2002), p. 96ff.; Ben-Gurion to Rabin, 28 June 1967, BGA; Yitzhak Rabin, *Service Book* (in Hebrew) (Tel Aviv: Sifriyat Maariv, 1979), vol. I, p. 207; *LaMerhav,* 11 June 1967, p. 2 (Megged).

3. *Davar Le-Yeladim,* 20 June 1967, p. 1160 (helicopter); *Maariv,* 13 June 1967, p. 16 (Rabin); *Maariv,* 23 June 1967, p. 19 (Gorodish, Sharon et al.); 15 Dec. 1967, p. 17; Shabtai Teveth, *Exposed in the Turret* (in Hebrew) (Tel Aviv: Schocken, 1968), pp. 152, 100; see also: Alon Gan, "The Discourse That Died? 'Discourse Culture' as an Attempt to Define a Special Identity for the Second Generation on the Kibbutzim" (in Hebrew) (diss., Tel Aviv University, 2002), p. 77ff.

4. *Ha'aretz,* 4 Aug. 1967, p. 11; Goldstein to Eshkol, 30 Aug. 1967, ISA, 6303/C-6; Avishai to Eshkol, 5 Dec. 1967, ISA, 6304/C-18; ISA, 6304/C-12 (war medals); *Maariv,* 10 Nov. 1967, p. 24 (Zmora).

5. *Maariv,* 15 June 1967, p. 6 ("better than the German army"); *From Kunetra to the Canal* (in Hebrew) (no identified publisher, date, or page numbers); Gan, "The Discourse That Died?" p. 73ff.; see also: Avner (Walter) Bar-On, *The Untold Stories: The Diary of the Head Censor* (in Hebrew) (Jerusalem: Idanim, 1981), p. 210.

6. *Ha'aretz,* 20 July 1967, p. 12 (spectacle); 4 Aug. 1967, p. 9 (show); 21 Aug. 1967, p. 5; 24 Aug. 1967, p. 2 (reserve); see also: the Chief of Staff with the Minister of Defense,

25 Aug. 1967, IDFA, 118/117/70; *Ha'aretz,* 8 Nov. 1967, p. 4 ("Tel Aviv Burning"); 11 Dec. 1967, p. 4 ("Three Hours in June").

7. "Six Days" (special edition of *LaMatchil*), AHA, P/200/17 (volunteers); *Davar,* 23 June 1967, p. 3 ("great spirit"); *Yediot Aharonot* (Shabbat supplement), 21 July 1967, p. 5; best sellers: Shmuel Segev (in Hebrew), *Red Sheet: The Six-Day War* (in Hebrew) (Tel Aviv: Tversky, 1967); Eli Landau, *Jerusalem Forever* (Tel Aviv: Sifriyat Maariv, 1967).

8. Letter to Penina Axelrod, 18 June 1967, with her kind permission; letter to Ruth Haskal, 26 June 1967, with the kind permission of Haskal.

9. *Yehiam Newsletter* (in Hebrew), 334/16, 22 Sept. 1967, pp. 2, 20; see also *Ha'aretz,* 5 April 1968, p. 3.

10. Avraham Shapira, ed., *Soldiers Talk: Episodes of Listening and Observation* (in Hebrew) (1970), p. 119ff.

11. Ibid.; Gan, "The Discourse That Died?" p. 84ff.; Hadari, *Messiah Riding a Tank,* p. 96ff.

12. Letter to Chaim Haskal, 12 June 1967, with his kind permission.

13. Letter to Penina Axelrod, 19 June 1967, with her kind permission.

14. Margot Klausner archives, CZA, A493/47; see also: *Ha'aretz,* 16 Oct. 1998, p. 12; 31 March 1966, p. 4 (Klausner); *Yediot Aharonot,* 30 Oct. 1967, p. 7; 31 Oct. 1967, p. 7; 1 Nov. 1967, p. 7 (others); *HaTzofeh,* 12 June 1967, p. 4; Ben-Sasson to Warhaftig, 27 June 1967, ISA, 12251/GL-13 (Temple).

15. Ben-Gurion diary, 19 June 1967, BGA; *Ha'aretz,* 20 June 1967, p. 2; Ben-Gurion to Yosef Levi, 17 July 1967; Ben-Gurion to Shoshana Zehavi, 17 July 1967, BGA; *Ha'aretz,* 21 June 1967, p. 2.

16. *HaTzofeh,* 24 July 1967, p. 4 (uprising fallen); Herzog diary, 3 Oct. 1967, ISA, 4511/A-3 (proclamation); *Ha'aretz,* 19 June 1967, p. 45; *Yediot Aharonot,* 15 June 1967, p. 3 (Armon Hanatziv); *Ha'aretz,* 6 July 1967, p. 3 (Kollek); *Maariv,* 21 June 1967, p. 12; Chief of Staff meetings with the Minister of Defense, 2 Oct. 1967, IDFA, 118/117/70; Eshkol to Dayan, 2 Oct. 1967, ISA, 7231/A-2; Yaffe to Ben-Ami, 15 Oct. 1967, ISA, 6301/C-1 (Eshkol); *Maariv,* 21 June 1967, p. 12; *Ha'aretz* (supplement), 16 July 1967, p. 14ff. (Heker).

17. Aran in government meeting, 11 June 1967, ISA, 8164/A-6; ISA, 6302/C-7; ISA, 594/T-5 (proposals); *Maariv,* 12 June 1967, p. 6; see also: 15 June 1967, p. 6 ("Rabin Hod"); 16 June 1967, p. 12; *Ha'aretz,* 19 June 1967, p. 2 ("The Six Days"); Zvi Zur announcement, 24 July 1967, IDFA, 66/117/70; *Maariv,* 11 Aug. 1967, p. 14; see also: *Ha'aretz,* 14 July 1967, p. 3 (Begin); *Maariv,* 15 Dec. 1967, p. 17 (Cohen).

18. Nativ to Eshkol, 23 Aug. 1967, ISA, 6301/C-1.

19. Shemer to Aldema, 12 June 2004, with his kind permission; see also: *Yediot Aharonot,* 14 April 2000, p. 30ff.

20. Allon to Eshkol, 20 Aug. 1967; Eshkol to Allon, 23 Aug. 1967, ISA, 6405/C-2 (Druze); Herzog diary, 16 June 1967, ISA, 4511/A-3 (Harel); Urwick to Morris, 7 July 1967, PRO, FCO 17/11 (Alaska); ISA, 6303/C-8 (Suez).

21. Shamgar to Rabin, 12 July 1967 (with bill photographs), IDFA, 66/117/70; ordinance on issuing military Dinar, 9 July 1967, AHA, W/K/01; Gvati diary, 29 June 1967, YTA, Unit 15, Container 12, File 02; Government Decision 685, 23 July 1967, ISA, 10136/C-4; Bank of Israel documents, with the kind permission of the bank, copies in possession of the author; *Yediot Aharonot* ("7 Days" supplement), 14 May 1976, p. 16ff.; Chaim Nirel, ed., *Uzi Narkis: Pages Left on the Table* (in Hebrew) (Tel Aviv: Sifriya Tzionit, 2000), p. 203ff.

CHAPTER 18: THE ENLIGHTENED OCCUPATION

1. Ben-Gurion diary, 17 June 1967; 29 Nov. 1967, BGA; Teddy Kollek, *One Jerusalem* (in Hebrew) (Tel Aviv: Sifriyat Maariv, 1979), p. 222ff.; Foreign Ministry to London Embassy, 14 July 1967, ISA, 4088/HZ-9; Bruce to Secretary of State, 3 Jan. 1968, USNA, Box 1831; Lewen to Moberly, 7 Dec. 1967, PRO, FCO 17/212/104255.

2. ISA, 594/C-16.

3. Zur to Herzog, 24 Nov. 1963, Chaim Herzog estate, with the kind permission of his son; Chaim Herzog, *Way of Life* (in Hebrew) (Tel Aviv: Yediot Aharonot, 1997), p. 210; Michael Shashar, *The Seventh-Day War: The Diary of the Military Government in Judea and Samaria (June-December 1967)* (in Hebrew) (Tel Aviv: Sifriyat Poalim, 1997), p. 67; Yehuda Harel, *The Six-Day War: From the Journal of a Religious Journalist* (in Hebrew) (Jerusalem: Ministry of Education, 1999), p. 29; Shlomo Gazit, *The Carrot and the Stick:*

Military Government in Judea and Samaria (in Hebrew) (Tel Aviv: Zmora-Bitan, 1985), pp. 19, 25.

4. Command and Staff School (Class 13, 1966–67), *Taking Control of Occupied Territories* (abstract, in Hebrew); IDF Operations Branch/Training Department, *Taking Control of Occupied Territories* (in Hebrew) (1960); *Military Powers in an Occupied Territory* (1961), Chaim Herzog estate, with the kind permission of his son.

5. Zvi Tzabar, ed., *Scrolls of Fire* (in Hebrew) (Tel Aviv: Ministry of Defense, 1981), vol. V, book I, p. 476; Shabtai Teveth, *The Blessed Curse* (in Hebrew) (Tel Aviv: Schocken, 1969).

6. Field security guidelines, 9 July 1967, ISA, 4095/HZ-7; Dayan in the government, 18 June 1967, ISA, 8164/A-7; Gazit, *The Carrot and the Stick*, pp. 56 (tractors), 42.

7. Herzog, *Way of Life*, p. 210; Michael Bar Zohar, *Zaphenath Paneah: The Life and Times of a Jewish Prince* (in Hebrew) (Tel Aviv: Yediot Aharonot, 2003), p. 13.

8. Gazit, *The Carrot and the Stick*, pp. 46, 52; Dan Bavli, *Dreams and Missed Opportunities, 1967–1973* (in Hebrew) (Tel Aviv: Carmel, 2002), p. 159.

9. Distribution chart, ISA, 4095/HZ-7; see also: "The Structure of the Civilian Branch of the Military Government in the West Bank," July 25 1967, ISA, 4095/HZ-6; Board of Director Generals minutes, 18 Sept. 1967, IDFA, 70/117/70; see also: "Operating the Military Government in the West Bank," 10 June 1967, Chaim Herzog estate, with the kind permission of his son; "Military Government, Structure and Authorities," 17 Sept. 1967, IDFA, 70/117/70; Committees: ISA, 7921/A-2.

10. Military Government Staff, 12 July 1967, ISA, 4095/HZ-7; "Survey of the Jewish Holy Sites in the West Bank," July 1967, ISA, 4095/HZ-6; Sashar, *The Seventh-Day War*, p. 109.

11. Warhaftig to Dayan, 2 Aug. 1967; Dayan to Warhaftig, 3 Aug. 1967, ISA, 6301/C-1; other quarrels: Eisenstadt and Patenkin to Eshkol, 13 July 1967, ISA, 6301/C-1.

12. Summary of restricted committee meeting, 4 Jan. 1968, ISA, 4608/GL-1; Notes to the State Comptroller's Report, 5 Feb. 1968, ISA, 4608/GL-1.

13. Gazit, *The Carrot and the Stick*, pp. 76, 78; Shmuel Hacham to Eshkol, 6 July 1967; Ron Sayag to Eshkol, 18 July 1967, ISA, 6301/C-1 (File 4).

14. Central Command Staff meeting summary, 4 July 1967, ISA, 4095/HZ-6 (soap); Weekly Government Report, Golan Heights, 13 Sept. 1967, IDFA, 70/117/70 (prices); Staff Officer for the Treasury to the Deputy Chief of Staff, 1 Jan. 1968, ISA, 4608/GL-1 (income tax); Cohen to Minister of Defense office, 14 June 1968, 7921/A-5 (complaints); "Determining the Fate of Goods Left in Warehouses in the Golan," 18 Jan. 1968, Staff Officer for the General Accountant, 1 Feb. 1968, ISA, 4680/GL-1; Rabin with Eshkol, 29 Sept. 1967, IDFA, 118/117/70; Military Government Staff meeting, 223 June 1967, Chaim Herzog estate, with the kind permission of his son; Director Generals Committee minutes, 18 Sept. 1967, IDFA, 70/117/70 (telegrams); Weekly Government Report for Gaza Strip, 19 Sept. 1967, IDFA, 70/117/70 (lifeguards); additional government ordinances, ISA, 6301/C-14; Report on the Civil Administrations' activities, 23 July 1967, ISA, 4095/HZ-6.

15. Shashar, *The Seventh Day War*, p. 97; Moshe Dayan, *Milestones* (in Hebrew) (Jerusalem: Idanim, 1982), vol. II, p. 503; Bawly, *Dreams and Missed Opportunities*, p. 162ff.; Arieh Brown, *Personal Seal: Moshe Dayan in the Six-Day War and Afterward* (in Hebrew) (Tel Aviv: Yediot Aharonot, 1997), p. 170ff.; Mordechai Bentov, *Time Will Tell: Memories from the Decision Period* (in Hebrew) (Tel Aviv: Sifriyat Poalim, 1984), p. 158; Teveth, *The Curse of the Blessing*, p. 167ff.

16. Board of Directors General, 16 Dec. 1967, ISA, 4608/GL-2 (support); Gazit, *The Carrot and the Stick*, p. 218 (summer visits).

17. The Committee for the West Bank, 19 July 1967, with the kind permission of Moshe Sasson.

18. Mining Supervisor to Deputy Minister of Defense, 19 Dec. 1967, ISA, 4608/GL-1; Shashar, *The Seventh Day War*, p. 114; Allon to Dayan, 13 Sept. 1967, ISA, 7921/A-3; Gazit, *The Carrot and the Stick*, p. 349ff.

19. Herzog diary, 31 July 1697, ISA, 4511/A-3; government decisions, 10, 23, and 31 July 1967 (lira); Government decision no. 42, 5 Nov. 1967 (UN); government decision no. 41, 5 Nov. 1967 (revocation), ISA, 10136/C-5; limited committee, 2 Jan. 1968; Hivner to deputy director generals, 7 Jan. 1968 (certificate); Board of Directors General, 14 Jan. 1968 (integration); Board of Directors General, 12 Feb. 1968, ISA, 4608/GL-1; see also: guidelines for preparing the budget of the civil administration

in the territories, 5 Nov. 1967, ISA, 8122/GL-6; Hiram to ministerial committee, 3 Oct. 1967 (traffic arrangements), ISA, 6301-C-9 (customs); encouraging Israeli factories in the territories, 17 Oct. 1968; Gazit at the Board of Directors General, 2 Dec. 1968, ISA, 4608/GL-2 (reactors); see also: Report on the Military Government's activities, 23 July 1967, ISA, 4095/HZ-6; weekly activity report, 19 Sept. 1967, ISA, 4095/HZ-4.

20. Avner Falk, *Moshe Dayan, the Man and the Legend: A Psychoanalytical Biography* (in Hebrew) (Tel Aviv: Sifriyat Maariv, 1985), p. 263; *Ha'aretz*, 7 July 1967, p. 3; *HaOlam HaZeh*, 4 Oct. 1967, p. 10.

21. Herzog, *Way of Life*, p. 223; Shabtai Teveth, *Exposed in the Turret* (in Hebrew) (Tel Aviv: Schocken, 1968), p. 307; Herzog diary, 12 June 1967, ISA, 4511/A-3; Gazit, *The Carrot and the Stick*, p. 83ff.; Michael Shashar, *Conversations with Rehavam Ze'evi* (in Hebrew) (Tel Aviv: Yediot Aharonot, 2001), p. 124.

22. Hadow to Moore, 13 Sept. 1967, PRO, FCO 17/506; Moshe Dayan, *Vietnam Diary* (in Hebrew) (Tel Aviv: Dvir, 1977), pp. 68, 111, 138; see also: Gazit, *The Carrot and the Stick*, pp. 39, 48; Ben-Gurion in the government, 25 Nov. and 23 Dec. 1956, ISA; Brown, *Personal Seal*, p. 64.

23. Shashar, *The Seventh-Day War*, p. 84ff.; Ben Menachem to Eshkol, 7 Nov. 1967; Terlo opinion, 27 Dec. 1967, ISA, 6301/C-1.

24. Gershoni and Gazit to the Chief of Staff Office, taking steps against Nablus, 20 and 21 Sept. 1967, IDFA, 70/117/70; Gazit, *The Carrot and the Stick*, p. 307ff.; see also: *West Bank Affairs*, 16 Nov. 1967, PRO, FCO 17/212/104225.

25. *Ha'aretz*, 3 Nov. 1967, p. 3; memorandum, 15 June 1967, ISA, 4088/HZ-10.

26. Dayan, *Milestones*, vol. I, p. 38ff.; weekly military government report for Gaza Strip, 13 and 20 Sept. 1967; weekly activity report for the occupied territories, 22 Sept. 1967; acts of sabotage in and from within the West Bank, 25 Sept. 1967, IDFA, 70/117/70; biweekly military government report for Gaza Strip, 26 Dec. 1967, IDFA, 75/117/70; Gazit, *The Carrot and the Stick*, pp. 185, 273, 276ff., 293, 297ff.; USNA, Box 271 (Sofronian).

27. Psychological Warfare, 5 Sept. 1967, ISA, Unit 429/10/L-79; *Kol HaIr*, 4 June 1999, p. 84ff.; Gazit, *The Carrot and the Stick*, p. 133.

28. Avneri and Dayan in the Knesset, 20 Dec. 1967, *Knesset Minutes* (in Hebrew), vol. 50, p. 488; see also: Hillel to Israeli embassies, 23 Nov. 1967.

29. Gilboa to Levi, 21 Nov. 1967, YEA, copy in possession of the author; see also: Avneri and Dayan in the Knesset, 1 Aug. 1967, *Knesset Minutes* (in Hebrew), vol. 49, p. 2814.

30. Vardi report, undated (probably Sept. 1967), ISA, 4096/HZ-4; see also: U.S. Consulate in Jerusalem, Department of State, 30 Aug. 1967, USNA, Box 1800.

31. Ibrahim Tawasha to Eshkol, 21 Oct. 1967; Pado to Yaffe, 17 Nov. 1967, ISA, 6405/C-2; Shashar, *The Seventh-Day War*, p. 208; *Ha'aretz*, 12 Oct. 1967, pp. 1, 2; Avneri to Kol, 20 Aug. 1968, LSA 3497/C-1.

32. Gazit, *The Carrot and the Stick*, p. 61; see also: "Two Years of Military Government: Data on the Activities of the Civil Administration on Judea and Samaria, in the Gaza Strip, and in Northern Sinai 1967–1969" (in Hebrew), internal report, May 1969, Chaim Herzog estate, with the kind permission of his son.

33. *BaMachaneh*, 4 Oct. 1967, p. 13; see also: Benor to Kantrowitz, 7 Jan. 1968, ISA, 4601/GL-11.

34. Hamdi Kanaan with Dayan, 31 Aug. 1968; Hamdi Kanaan and Aziz Shehade with Dayan, 21 April 1968, with the kind permission of Moshe Sasson.

35. Dayan, *Milestones*, vol. II, p. 534.

36. Shlomo Gazit, *Suddenly Trapped: 30 Years of Israeli Policy in the Territories* (in Hebrew) (Tel Aviv: Zmora-Bitan, 1999), p. 218.

37. Shabtai Teveth, *Moshe Dayan* (in Hebrew) (Tel Aviv: Schocken, 1971), p. 600ff.

38. Dayan, *Milestones*, vol. II, p. 537.

39. "Two Years of Military Government" (in Hebrew), internal report, May 1969, pp. 5, 31, estate of Chaim Herzog, with the kind permission of his son; meeting of education supervisors in the administered territories, 11 Sept. 1967, ISA, 5603/C-4.

40. Ministry of Education and Culture, Slanderous Writings in Textbooks (in Hebrew), p. 2, ISA, 5603/C-4; Chava Lazarus-Yaffe, "Guidelines for Researching Arab Textbooks" (in Hebrew), *The New East*, vol. 17, book 3–4 (67–68), 1967, p. 207ff.

41. Yosef Argeman, *It Was Top Secret: 30 Intelligence and Security Affairs in Israel* (in Hebrew) (Tel Aviv: Ministry of Defense, 2002), p. 253ff.

42. Gadish to Aran, 3 Sept. 1967, ISA, 5603/C-4.
43. "Two Years of Military Government," pp. 6, 31; see also: Gadish to Aran, 1 Nov. 1967, 1 Dec. 1967, ISA, 5603/C-4; notes on the State Comptroller's Report, 5 Feb. 1968, ISA, 4608/GL-1.
44. Uzai to Aran, 9 Aug. 1967, ISA, 5603/C-4; ministerial meeting, 17 Sept. 1967, Yaacov Herzog estate, with the kind permission of his daughter; protest posters, ISA, 5603/C-4; see also: Farhi to Narkis, 19 Sept. 1967, IDFA, 70/117/70; Lewen to Moberly, 21 Sept. 1967, PRO, FCO 17/212/104225.

Chapter 19: Teddy's Project

1. Chaim Herzog, *Way of Life* (in Hebrew) (Tel Aviv: Yediot Aharonot, 1997), p. 219; *Ha'aretz*, 28 June 1967, p. 2; Board of Directors General, 26 June 1967; Ministerial Committee on Jerusalem, 21 June 1967, with the kind permission of Meron Benvenisti.
2. Ben-Gurion diary, 6 July 1966, BGA; Kollek at City Council, 16 April 1967, JMA, Container 2295, File No. 5; Teddy Kollek, *One Jerusalem* (in Hebrew) (Tel Aviv: Sifriyat Maariv, 1979); ISA, 6397/C-2; Naomi Shepherd, *Teddy Kollek, Mayor of Jerusalem* (New York: Harper Collins, 1988).
3. Uzi Benziman, *Jerusalem: Unwalled City* (in Hebrew) (Tel Aviv: Schocken, 1973), p. 61ff.; Kollek at the Israeli Management Center, 19 Feb. 1968, Chaim Herzog estate, with the kind permission of his son.
4. ISA, 5688/C-1; *Yediot Aharonot*, 1 Aug. 1967, p. 4.
5. Arbel to Kollek, 21 July 1967, with the kind permission of Meron Benvenisti, copy in possession of the author; Old Jerusalem City Council members (undated), JMA, Container 1331, Six-Day War file.
6. Ministerial Committee on Jerusalem, 21 June 1967; Board of Directors General, 26 June 1967, quoted with the kind permission of Meron Benvenisti, copy in possession of the author; see also: proposal to reorganize the municipal administration in the liberated municipal territory, 28 June 1967, ISA, (2)6303/C-1; Minister of Justice to Minister of Finance, 3 Jan. 1968, ISA, 4601/CL-11 (property); Kollek to Eshkol, 27 Nov. 1967, ISA, 6306/C-1 (pensions for municipal workers); Shapira to Eshkol, 28 June 1967, ISA, 6301/C-1 (municipality assets); Minister of Justice to Prime Minister, 14 March 1968 (absentee assets); 14 March 1968 (citizenship), YEA, copies in possession of the author.
7. Yonatan Shlonsky, ed., *Jerusalem Master-Plan 1968* (in Hebrew) (Jerusalem: Jerusalem Municipality, 1972), p. 29; *Ha'aretz*, 21 July 1967, p. 16 (Benvenisti); Kukia to Director Generals, 18 July 1967, ISA, 5688/C-1.
8. Central Command Headquarters, East Jerusalem Discussion Platform, 11 Sept. 1967; Problems of handling East Jerusalem, 15 Sept. 1967, IDFA, 70/117/70; Kollek at the Israeli Management Center, 19 Feb. 1968, Chaim Herzog estate, with the kind permission of his son.
9. *Al HaMishmar*, 12 Nov. 1967, p. 3; *Ha'aretz*, 15 Nov. 1967, p. 5.
10. Porath Yosef to Eshkol, 27 June 1967, ISA, 6302/C-1; The Yeshiva by the *Kotel* to Eshkol, 3 Sept. 1967; Histadrut HaNoar HaOved VeHaLomed to Tamir, 16 Oct. 1967, YEA, copy in possession of the author.
11. *Ha'aretz*, 27 Nov. 1967, p. 1 (bus route 9); *Maariv*, 3 July 1967, p. 3 (advertising); *Maariv*, 26 June 1967, p. 2 (Agnon); 7 July 1967, p. 6 (Al-Sheikh); *Maariv* (Days and Nights), 16 June 1967, p. 19 (Luz); see also: *Maariv*, 16 June 1967, p. 19 (Hebron); *Maariv* (Days and Nights), 21 July 1967, p. 13 (Gush Etzion); 25 Sept. 1967, p. 11 (Golan Mountains).
12. *Ha'aretz*, 28 June 1967, p. 10 (evacuation); The Jewish Quarter, Activity Report, 23 Dec. 1968, ISA, 7920/A-8; Tamir to Yaffe, 30 Aug. 1967, YEA, copy in possession of the author; see also: ISA, 12252/CL-1; Uzai to Prime Minister, 16 Aug. 1967, ISA, 6030/C-1 ("Greater Jerusalem"); Eshkol at the Ministerial Committee for Jerusalem Affairs, 25 Sept. 1967 ("Bukra"); Plan to settle tens of thousands of families in Jerusalem, 5 Sept. 1967, ISA, 7920/A-8.
13. Sapir to Shapira, 5 July 1967, Shapira to Sapir, 29 June 1967, ISA, 6303/C-1; Ministerial Committee on Jerusalem Affairs, 25 Sept. 1967; Eshkol at Foreign Affairs and Defense Committee, 25 June 1967, ISA, 7920/A-8.
14. Tamir to Yaffe, 30 Aug. 1967, YEA (survey), copy in possession of the author; Argov to Yaish, 15 Oct. 1967, ISA, 4096/HZ-4 ("the world"); Barbour to Department of State, 26 Jan. 1968; Campbell to Department of State, 6 June, 20 June 1968, USNA, Box 2252; Yaffe to Kollek and others, 29 Feb. 1968, ISA, 7920/A-8 ("no advertising").

15. Government decision, 12 Dec. 1967, Uzai to District Commissioner, 28 Dec. 1967, Eban to government secretariat, 3 Dec. 1967; ISA, 6303/C-3; Yaffe to Tamir, 3 Jan. 1968, ISA, 7238/A-8 (school); Eban to Eshkol, 22 Jan. 1968, YEA; Amnon to Adi, 19 Dec. 1967, ISA, 6301/C-1; see also: ISA, 7920/A-8 (hospital); Yaffe to Tamir, 3 Jan. 1968, ISA, 7232/A-8 (A-Tur); purchasing territories in East Jerusalem, 11 Jan. 1968, JMA, Container 1331, Six-Day War (treasury); Ministerial Committee on Jerusalem Affairs, 27 Dec. 1967, ISA, 6303/C-3 (no advertising); Symbols and Ceremonies Committee, 18 June 1967, ISA, 10136/C-3 (stamp).

16. Thalmann Mission, UNA, DAG 1/2.3, Box 1347, File 1066; Box 138, File 1076-1087; Eshkol in Foreign Affairs and Defense Committee, 2 July 1968, ISA, 7921/A-6; Warhaftig to Eshkol, 12 Aug. 1967, YEA, copy in possession of the author; Rabin to Foreign Ministry, 5 May 1968, Eshkol in the government, 5 May 1968, ISA, 7921/A-6; Harman to Foreign Ministry, 9 June 1967, ISA, 7919/A-2.

17. Government meeting, 25 June 1967, ISA, 8164/A-19; Herzog diary, 14 June 1967, ISA, 4511/A-3.

18. Open letter to government ministers, 24 July 1967, ISA, (4) 6301/C-1; Eliezer Shostak and Yaakov Shimshon Shapira in the Knesset, 18 July 1967, *Knesset Minutes* (in Hebrew), vol. 49, p. 2643ff.

19. Eban to Israel delegation to the UN, 19 and 22 June 1967; Tekoa to Rosen, 8 Sept. 1967; ISA, 4086/HZ-1; Moberly to Aspin, 27 July 1967, PRO, FO 961/25 UNA DAG 1/2.3, Box 134, File 1041; Ben-Zur to Kollek, 16 July 1971, with the kind permission of Meron Benvenisti.

20. Government meeting, 11 and 18 June 1967, ISA, 8164/A-6.

21. Eban to Eshkol, 23 Aug. 1967, ISA, 6342/C-1; Galili to Eshkol, 25 Sept. 1967; Galili to Government Secretariat, 1 Oct. 1967, ISA, 6306/C-1; Meron Benvenisti, *The Slingshot and the Stick: Territories, Jews and Arabs* (in Hebrew) (Jerusalem: Keter, 1988), p. 136ff.

22. Barbour to Department of State, 22 March 1968; Campbell to Department of State, 3 April 1967, USNA, Box 2228, File POL 18.

23. Barbour to Department of State, 7 July 1967, USNA, Box 2228, File POL 18; *Ha'aretz*, 3 July 1967, p. 2; 4 July 1967, p. 2; Meron Benvenisti, *Opposite the Closed Wall: Divided and Unified Jerusalem* (in Hebrew) (Jerusalem: Weidenfeld and Nicolson, 1973), p. 283ff.; see also: *Ha'aretz*, 5 June 1968, p. 7.

24. The Jewish Population's Attitude Toward the Arab Population, and Kollek to Eshkol, 11 March 1968, ISA, 7920/A-8; Ezrachi in letter, 14 Aug. 1967, with the kind permission of her son.

25. Yehuda Amichai, *Songs of Jerusalem* (Tel Aviv: Schocken, 1987), p. 52; English translation by Stephen Mitchell, from *Poems of Jerusalem and Love Poems* (New York: Sheep Meadow Press, 1992), p. 45; Bar-Chaim to Director General, 14 July 1967, ISA, 4088/HZ-9; *Al HaMishmar*, 23 June 1967, p. 7; *Maariv*, 19 Dec. 1967, p. 3; see also: *Ha'aretz*, 23 June 1967, p. 9.

26. Hala Sakakini, *Jerusalem and I: A Personal Record* (Amman: [no publisher], 1987), p. 1ff.; see also: *Maariv*, 13 Sept. 1967, p. 20; 27 Sept. 1967, p. 17; Shapira in the government, 11 June 1967, ISA, 8164/A-6.

27. Government decision 692, 27 July 1967, with the kind permission of the government secretariat, copy in possession of the author; uprising posters (Hebrew), ISA, 4095/HZ-5; Central Command Headquarters, 17 Sept. 1967, IDFA, 70/117/70; uprising posters (English), Campbell to Department of State, 3 Oct. 1967, USNA, Box 2228, POL 23.

28. Begin in the government, 29 July 1967, Yaacov Herzog estate, with the kind permission of his daughter; Michael Shashar, *The Seventh-Day War: The Diary of the Military Government in Judea and Samaria (June-December 1967)* (in Hebrew) (Tel Aviv: Sifriyat Poalim, 1977), p. 149.

29. Lewen to Moberly, 21 Sept. 1967, PRO, FCO 17/212/104225.

30. *Ha'aretz*, 29 Sept. 1967, p. 6; see also: Ehud Yaari, *Fatah* (in Hebrew) (Tel Aviv: Levin Epstein, 1970).

31. Eitan to Foreign Ministry, 1 Aug. 1967, ISA, 4088/HZ-6.

32. Trial protocol, copy in possession of the author; see also: *BaMachaneh*, 1 July 1969, p. 12; Shlomo Gazit, *The Carrot and the Stick: Military Government in Judea and Samaria* (in Hebrew) (Tel Aviv: Zmora-Bitan, 1985), p. 298; see also: *Ha'aretz*, 16 Oct. 1967, p. 2; government decision no. 22, 29 Oct. 1967, IDFA, 70/117/70.

33. Bosmi report, 25 Sept. 1967, IDFA, 70/117/70.

34. *Ha'aretz*, 9 Oct. 1967, p. 1; 11 Oct. 1967, p. 6; 25 Oct. 1967, p. 14; Sarah Ozacky-Lazar, *Yehuda* (in Hebrew) (privately published memorial book, 1989).

35. Campbell to Rusk, 26 March 1967, USNA, Box 2252, POL 28; Benvenisti, *Opposite the Closed Wall*, p. 268ff.

36. Mayor and deputies, 10 Oct. 1967, JMA, Container 1331; student survey, Yael High School, Bat-Yam, Oct. 1967, ISA, (7) 6303/C-1 (marking cars); Masuda Shalem to Eshkol, 10 Oct. 1967, ISA, (7) 6301/C-1 (school guards); Shimkin to Eshkol, 18 Oct. 1967, ISA, (8) 6301/C-1 (repository); Naftali to Eshkol, 9 Oct. 1967, ISA, (9) 6301/C-1 (hanging); Hacham to Eshkol, 11 Dec. 1967, ISA, (10) 6301/C-1 (shooting); Greisman to Eshkol, 10 Dec. 1967, ISA, (10) 6301/C-1 (dogs); *Ha'aretz*, 13 Oct. 1967, p. 3; see also: Moshe Dayan in the Knesset, 15 Nov. 1967, *Knesset Minutes* (in Hebrew), vol. 50, p. 162.

37. Eshkol at honorary citizenship ceremony, 26 May 1967, ISA, 7920/A-8.

CHAPTER 20: FACE-TO-FACE WITH ISHMAEL

1. Sandstorm documentation, 20 July, 22 July, 25 July, 7 Aug. 1967, LBJL, NSF Country File, Middle East, Box 113; Rusk to U.S. Embassy in Jordan, 23 July 1967, USNA, Box 1792; Remez to Foreign Ministry, 14 June 1967, Yaacov Herzog estate, with the kind permission of his daughter; Herzog diary, 15 June and 19 July 1967, ISA, 4511/A-3.

2. Ephraim Kishon and Dosh, *Sorry We Won* (in Hebrew) (Tel Aviv: Sifriyat Maariv, 1967) (no page numbers); Herzog Diary, 29 Aug. 1968, ISA, 4511/A-4; Ezer Weizman, *For You the Sky, for You the Land* (in Hebrew) (Tel Aviv: Sifriyat Maariv, 1975), p. 270.

3. *Maariv*, 13 June 1967, p. 1.

4. Abba Eban, *Life Episodes* (in Hebrew) (Tel Aviv: Sifriyat Maariv, 1978), vol. II, p. 430; Prime Minister's Office, Publicity Center, *Know What to Reply* (in Hebrew), Book One, Aug. 1967, p. 16; Book Four, June 1968, p. 3; Avi Shlaim, *The Iron Wall: Israel and the Arab World* (in Hebrew) (New York: Norton, 2000), p. 254.

5. Gvati diary, 19 June 1967, YTA, Unit 15, Container 12, File 02.

6. Ben-Gurion announcements, 18 June 1967, BGA, File 1087.

7. Government meetings, 18 June 1967, ISA, 8164/A-6; 19 June 1967, ISA, 8164/A-8 and ISA, 8164/A-9; Security Cabinet, government meetings, 15–19 June 1967, Yaacov Herzog estate, with the kind permission of his daughter; see also: *Davar*, 2 June 1987, p. 13; 5 June 1987, p. 19; Dayan in the Labor Party, 18 June 1968, YTA, Unit 15—Allon, Container 3, File 2; Dayan with Eshkol et al., 29 May 1968, ISA, 7921/A-4; Eshkol in the government, 19 June 1968, 7921/A-6; see also: Yemima Rosenthal, Arnon Lemfrum, and Hagai Tzoref, Eds., *Levi Eshkol, the Third Prime Minister* (in Hebrew) (Jerusalem: Israel State Archive, 2002), p. 580; Reuven Pedhatzur, *The Victory of Shame: The Eshkol Government Policy in the Territories After the Six-Day War* (in Hebrew) (Tel Aviv: Bitan, 1996), pp. 43ff., 124ff.

8. Harman to Eshkol, 9 June 1967; Harman to Foreign Ministry, 8 Jun. 1967, ISA, 7919/A-9; 21 June 1967, ISA, 7938/A-10; Barbour to Rusk, 16 June 1967, USNA, Box 1795; FRUS, vol. XIX, pp. 483ff.

9. Herzog diary, 18 June 1967 (government discussion); 14 and 19 July 1967 (before Hussein); ISA, 4511/A-3; Moshe Dayan, *Milestones* (in Hebrew) (Jerusalem: Idanim, 1982), vol. II, p. 490ff.; resolution drafts, notes exchanges, and meeting summaries; 15–18 June 1967; government meeting, 15 June 1967 (Aran), Yaacov Herzog estate, with the kind permission of his daughter.

10. Michael Bar Zohar, *Zaphenath Paneah: The Life and Times of a Jewish Prince* (in Hebrew) (Tel Aviv: Yediot Aharonot, 2003), p. 234; U.S. Embassy in Jordan to Department of State, 18 Jan. 1968, FRUS, vol. XX, Doc. No. 50.

11. U.S. Embassy in Jordan to Department of State, 9 Jan. 1968, FRUS, vol. XX, Doc. No. 42.

12. Summary of Herzog meeting with Hussein, 2 July 1967, Yaacov Herzog estate, with the kind permission of his daughter; Herzog diary, 29 Aug. 1967, ISA, 4511/A-4; see also: Bar Zohar, *Zaphenath Paneah*, p. 284; Moshe Zak, *Hussein Makes Peace* (in Hebrew) (Ramat-Gan: Bar-Ilan University, 1996); Avi Shlaim, "His Royal Shyness: King Hussein and Israel," *New York Review of Books*, 15 July 1999, p. 14ff.

13. David Kimche and Dan Bawly, *Firestorm* (in Hebrew) (Tel Aviv: Sifriyat Maariv, 1968); Dan Bawly, *Dreams and Missed Opportunities, 1967–1973* (in Hebrew) (Tel Aviv: Carmel, 2002), p. 120.

14. Bawly, *Dreams and Missed Opportunities*, p. 133.

15. Kimche to head of Intelligence Branch, 12 and 13 June 1967; Proposal to Resolve the Palestinian Problem, with the kind permission of Moshe Sasson; Bawly, *Dreams and*

Missed Opportunities, p. 146; Hillel to Eban, 12 June 1967, ISA, 4088/HZ-10; Danin, Palmon, and Yekutieli Memorandum, 12 June 1967, ISA, 4096/HZ-14; see also: Hillel to Eban, 15 June 1967, ISA, 4088/HZ-10.

16. Memorandum, Committee of Heads of Services, 30 June 1967, with the kind permission of Moshe Sasson; see also: Moshe Sasson: *With No Round Table* (in Hebrew) (Tel Aviv: Sifriyat Maariv, 2004).

17. Tom Segev, *One Palestine, Complete: Jews and Arabs Under the British Mandate* (in Hebrew) (Jerusalem: Keter, 1999), p. 222ff.; Hillel Cohen, *The Shadow Army: Palestinian Collaborators in Service of Zionism* (in Hebrew) (Jerusalem: Ivrit, 2004).

18. Meeting of the Committee for the West Bank, 19 July 1967, with the kind permission of Moshe Sasson.

19. Memorandum, the Committee of Four, 5 July 1967, with the kind permission of Moshe Sasson.

20. The Political Leadership on the West Bank, 18 June 1967; conversation with Jaabari, 7 July 1967, with the kind permission of Moshe Sasson.

21. Sasson to Eban, end of July 1967, with the kind permission of Moshe Sasson; summary of impressions from conversations with West Bank dignitaries, 6–18 July 1967, Chaim Herzog estate, with the kind permission of his son; activity among Palestinians, undated, ISA, 7921/A-6.

22. The Inter-Office Ministerial Committee to Eshkol, 20 July 1967, ISA, 4088/HZ-6; The Committee of Heads of Services to Eshkol, 27 July 1967, with the kind permission of Moshe Sasson.

23. Sasson with Capucci, 28 Feb. 1968, with the kind permission of Moshe Sasson; see also: Farhi to Narkis, 24 Sept. 1967, ISA, 4095/HZ-14.

24. Nusseibeh with Eshkol, 6 Feb. 1968; Nusseibeh with Sasson, 11 Feb. 1968; Sasson with Capucci, 13 May 1968, with the kind permission of Sasson.

25. Dayan in meeting of ministers, 29 May 1968, ISA, 7291/A-4.

26. Sasson with Aziz Shehade, 18 March 1968; discussion with the Minister of Defense, 6 April 1968; Hamdi Kanaan with Dayan, 31 Aug. 1968; Hamdi Kanaan and Aziz Shehade with Dayan, 21 April 1968; Sasson with Capucci, 13 May 1968; report and guidelines from the Prime Minister, 9 April 1968, with the kind permission of Moshe Sasson.

27. Sasson to Eshkol, 24 Jan. 1968; discussion brief, 11 Feb. 1968; Eshkol with Ayub Musalem, 5 Feb. 1968; Eshkol with Jaabari, 12 Aug. 1968, with the kind permission of Moshe Sasson; see also: meeting on the West Bank Arabs, 6 Dec. 1967, ISA, 7921/A-3; Herzog to Dayan, 7 July 1967, Chaim Herzog estate, with the kind permission of his son.

28. Eshkol in consultation with ministers, 21 May 1968, ISA, 7921/A-4.

29. Eshkol with Aziz Shehade, 5 Feb. 1968; Anwar Nusseibeh, 6 Feb. 1968; Hikmat al-Masri and with Walid el-Shak'a, 26 Feb. 1968; Taisir Kanaan, 24 April 1968; Anwar Khatib, 25 April 1968; Nasser a-Din Nashashibi, 27 May 1968, with the kind permission of Moshe Sasson.

30. U.S. Embassy in Israel to Department of State, 13 June 1967, USNA, Box 1794; Feb. 20, 1968, Box 2227; U.S. Consulate in Jerusalem, 17 June 1967, Box 1795; 30 Aug. 1967 and 12 Sept. 1967, Box 1800; 5 Dec. 1967, Box 2224; 20 May 1968 and 12 June 1968, Box 2228.

31. Sasson to Eshkol (draft), 8 May 1967, with the kind permission of Moshe Sasson; consultation on the Arabs in the territories, 21 May 1968, ISA, 7921/A-4.

32. Consultation on the Arab problem, 3 July 1968, ISA, 7921/A-5; see also: Shlomo Gazit, *Suddenly Trapped: 30 Years of Israeli Policy in the Territories* (in Hebrew) (Tel Aviv: Zmora-Bitan, 1999), p. 182ff.; consultation on the Arabs in the territories, 21 May 1968, ISA, 7921/A-4.

CHAPTER 21: THE BLUNDER

1. *Davar,* 29 Sept. 1967, p. 3.

2. Weekly meeting, 4 June 1965, ISA, 7925/A-8.

3. Population Census 1967, Central Bureau of Statistics, *Israel Annual Yearbook* (in Hebrew), no. 18, 1967, p. 593; Bacci and Dvoretzky with Eshkol, 6 Dec. 1967, ISA, 7921/A-3.

4. Ben-Gurion diary, 1 June 1967; Ben-Gurion Diary, 14 Dec. 1967, BGA; discussion with Ben-Gurion, 23 June 1961, ISA, 7936/A-6; see also: David Ben-Gurion, *The Newly Emerging State of Israel* (in Hebrew) (Tel Aviv: Am Oved, 1969), vol. II, p. 845.

5. Shertok to Goldman, 14 June 1948, Yehoshua Freundlich, ed., *Documents on the Foreign Policy of Israel* (in Hebrew) (Jerusalem: Israel State Archive, 1981), vol. I, p. 163; Yemima Rosenthal, Arnon Lemfrum, and Hagai Tzoref, eds., *Levi Eshkol, the Third Prime Minister* (in Hebrew) (Jerusalem: Israel State Archive, 2002), p. 250.

6. Levontin to Eshkol, 12 June 1967, ISA, 5603/C-4; Katz to Eshkol, 15 June 1967, ISA, 6301/C-1; see also: ISA, 6301/C-1 (4); Yesha to Ben-Gurion, 8 June 1967, BGA; Winshel to Ben-Gurion, 25 June 1967; Arthur Katz to Ben-Gurion, 19 June 1967; Goertz to Allon, 15 June 1967, YTA, Unit 15, Series B, Container 16, File 6; *Ha'aretz*, 2 April 1967, p. 1 (Eshkol with Sartre); Shlomo Gazit, *The Palestinian Refugee Problem* (in Hebrew) (Tel Aviv: Tel Aviv University, 1994); Dan Bawly, *Dreams and Missed Opportunities, 1967–1973* (in Hebrew) (Tel Aviv: Carmel, 2002), p. 104ff.

7. *Ha'aretz*, 18 June 1967, p. 2; see also: 21 June 1967, p. 2; *Maariv*, 15 Sept. 1967, p. 13; 17 Sept. 1967, p. 9; *Yediot Aharonot*, 16 July 1967, p. 8.

8. Ben-Gurion diary, 1 June 1967; 14 Dec. 1967, BGA; discussion with Ben-Gurion, 23 June 1961, ISA, 7936/A-6; see also: Ben-Gurion, *The Newly Emerging State of Israel*, vol. II, p. 845; Elisha Efrat, *Geography of Occupation* (in Hebrew) (Tel Aviv: Carmel, 2002), p. 139; Benny Morris, *The Birth of the Palestinian Refugee Problem, 1947–1949* (in Hebrew) (Tel Aviv: Am Oved, 1987).

9. Devorah Kaplan, *The Truth on the Arab Refugee Problem* (in Hebrew) (Jerusalem: Meod, 1956); see also: Lord Sieff of Primton to Chancellor, June 13, 1967, PRO, T 217/950/104225.

10. Yehiel Ilsar to Director General, 18 June 1967, ISA, 4088/HZ-7; Avner to Ben-Horin, 8 Aug. 1967, ISA, 4088/HZ-7; see also: Shacham to Yaffe, 27 June 1967, ISA, 6301/C-1; Hillel to Eban, 6 Sept. 1967, ISA, 7931/A-2; Bernstein to Harman, 21 June 1967, ISA, 3979/HZ-9.

11. Kintner to Johnson, 12 June 1967, LBJL, ND 19, CO 1-6, Box 193; Remez to Foreign Ministry, 12 July 1967, ISA, 4089/HZ-2; Remez to Herzog, 13 Dec. 1967, ISA, 4092/HZ-5; see also: ISA, 7234/A-9; see also: Sapir to Foreign Ministry, 25 Sept. 1967, ISA, 3979/HZ-9; Safdie to Bentov, 10 Jan. 1968; Bentov to Eshkol, 24 Jan. 1968; Eban to Bentov, 4 Feb. 1968, YEA, copies in possession of the author; see also: ISA, 7234 /A-9; 721/A-2.

12. Herzog diary, 7 Sept. 1967, ISA, 4511/A-3; Yaffe to Suzy Eban, 6 Feb. and 3 June 1968 (Rothschild); Tzippori to Yaffe, 28 March 1968; Ben-David and Gnichovski to Taub, 5 March 1968 (World Bank), all YEA, copies in possession of the author; Reudor Manor, series of interviews with Avraham Harman, Hebrew University, Institute for International Relations, meeting 4, 14 Aug. 1974, p. 15, with the kind permission of David Harman.

13. Ben-Gurion in the government, 23 Dec. 1956, ISA minutes; *Ha'aretz*, 9 Nov. 1967, p. 2 (Peres).

14. Knab to Eshkol, 11 June 1967, Eshkol to Knab, 27 June 1967, ISA, 6301/C-1; Yagar to Yaffe, 1 Aug. 1967, ISA, 6303/C-1.

15. Government meeting, 15 June 1967, Yaacov Herzog estate, with the kind permission of his daughter; Allon in government meeting, 30 July 1967, minutes in possession of the author; see also: Yigal Allon, *Striving for Peace* (in Hebrew) (Tel Aviv: HaKibbutz HaMeuchad, 1989); Rosenthal et al., eds., *Levi Eshkol*, pp. 56, 581ff.; see also: Sasson to Eshkol, 15 June 1967, with the kind permission of Moshe Sasson.

16. Government resolution, 19 June 1967, ISA, 7921/A-2; government meeting, 19 June 1967, Yaacov Herzog estate, with the kind permission of his daughter; see also: *Davar*, 2 June 1987, p. 13.

17. Arnon to Sapir, 25 June 1967, ISA, 4601/CL-11; Gvati to Shilo, 30 June 1967, ISA, 6301/C-1; Eshkol to Bacci, 20 July 1967, review of the social problems in the occupied territories, 20 Sept. 1967, YEA, copy in possession of the author; see also: Government Secretariat to Prime Minister, 8 Aug. 1967; Hillel to Eban, 8 Sept. 1967, ISA, 7921/A-2; Eban to Bentov, 4 Feb. 1968, YEA, copy in possession of the author; Komei to Harman, 22 Nov. 1967, ISA, 4092/HZ-5; outline for policy on the refugee question, 8 Sept. 1967, ISA, 4092/HZ-5.

18. Development of the administrated territories, investigation of alternatives, ISA, 7921/A-3; Wiener to Eshkol, 28 Nov. 1967, ISA, 7921/A-3; Plan to Settle 50,000 Refugees in Al Arish Area, CZA, A186/66; see also: ISA, 7234/A-8; Yosef Weitz, *My Diary* (in Hebrew) (Tel Aviv: Masada, 1973), vol. VI, p. 191ff.; Yaffe to Eban, 18 Oct. 1967, ISA, 7921/A-3.

19. Yaffe to government ministers, 27 Sept. 1967, ISA, 7921/A-3; Reuven Pedhatzur, *The Victory of Shame: The Eshkol Government Policy in the Territories After the Six-Day War* (in Hebrew) (Tel Aviv: Bitan, 1996), p. 40.
20. Bacci to Herzog, 18 June 1967, ISA, 6301/C-1.
21. Meeting with the Prime Minister, 5 Dec. 1967, ISA, 7921/A-3.
22. Eshkol with Bacci and Dvoretzky, 6 Dec. 1967, ISA, 7921/A-3; see also: Hillel to Eban, 12 June 1967, ISA, 4088/HZ-10; Sasson to Eshkol, 19 July 1967, ISA, 7231/A-1; Eshkol with Dvoretzky, 20 March 1968, ISA, 7921/A-4; Rosenthal et al., eds., *Levi Eshkol*, p. 582.
23. Allon to Eshkol, 10 Sept. 1967, ISA, 6301/C-14; Yigal Allon in interview with Reudor Manor, fourth meeting, p. 1, ISA, 5001/A-19; see also: *Davar*, 2 June 1987, p. 13; *Yediot Aharonot*, 2 July 1967, p. 3; Shmuel Tamir in the Knesset, 6 Dec. 1967, *Knesset Minutes* (in Hebrew), vol. 50, p. 342; Herzog diary, 10 Sept. 1967, ISA, 4511/A-3.
24. Dayan in consultation with ministers, 3 July 1968, ISA, 7921/A-5; Dayan at ministerial committee on the West Bank, 24 Dec. 1967, ISA, 7921/A-3; Dayan in government meeting, 18 Feb. 1968, discussion brief in possession of the author; Dayan in government meeting, 17 Oct. 1967, Yaacov Herzog estate, with the kind permission of his daughter; Herzog diary, 25 June 1967, ISA, 4511/A-3; Raanan Weitz, *The Great Plow and the Planning Map: A Look at the History of Settlement in the State of Israel* (in Hebrew) (Jerusalem: Weitz Estate, 2003), p. 94ff.
25. The Potential for Settling and Development in the Eastern Bank, YEA; Project for Settling 10,000 Families in East Jordan, ISA, 7921/A-4.
26. Meeting on the Work of Ada Sereni, 19 Feb. 1967, ISA, 7921/A-4.
27. Nur Masalha, *Expulsion of the Palestinians: The Concept of "Transfer" in Zionist Political Thought, 1882–1948* (Washington, D.C.: Institute for Palestine Studies, 1992); Tom Segev, *One Palestine, Complete: Jews and Arabs Under the British Mandate* (in Hebrew) (Jerusalem: Keter, 1999), p. 328ff.
28. Tom Segev, *1949: The First Israelis* (in Hebrew) (Jerusalem: Domino, 1984), p. 68.
29. Danin to Weitz, 25 Nov. 1956, CZA, A246.
30. Operation Worker, ISA, 4095/HZ-16.
31. Eshkol with Sereni and others; Eshkol with Dvoretzky, 20 March 1968, ISA, 7921/A-4; see also: Eshkol in the Foreign Affairs and Security Committee, 11 July 1967, ISA, 7921/A-6.
32. Ruth Bondi, *The Emissary: The Life and Death of Enzo Sereni* (in Hebrew) (Tel Aviv: Am Oved, 1973); Ben-Gurion to Sereni, 29 Feb. 1948; Sereni to Ben-Gurion (1958), BGA, correspondence; Hagar Sereni-Confino in response to the author's questions.
33. Eshkol with Dvoretzky, 20 March 1967; Eshkol with Sereni, 27 March 1967, ISA, 7921/A-4.
34. Eshkol with Sereni, Toledano et al., 19 Feb. 1968, ISA, 7921/A-4; Eshkol with heads of the Movement for Greater Israel, 12 Nov. 1967, ISA, 7920/A-7; Eshkol with Sereni, 27 March 1967, ISA, 7921/A-4 ("how many?").
35. Prime Minister's Office Director to Prime Minister's Office Deputy Director, 2 April 1968, ISA, 7921/A-4; see also: Yaffe to Agmon, 30 May 1968, YEA, copy in possession of the author.
36. U.S. Embassy in Lebanon to Department of State, and U.S. Consulate in Jerusalem to Department of State, 25 July 1968; U.S. Embassy in Israel to Department of State, 2 Aug. 1968, USNA, Box 3049, REF ARAB 1/1/68; Arieh Brown, *Personal Seal: Moshe Dayan in the Six-Day War and Afterward* (in Hebrew) (Tel Aviv: Yediot Aharonot, 1997), p. 154.
37. Greenberg to Gazit, 27 Oct. 1967, declaration draft, ISA, 4095/HZ-4.
38. Eshkol with Sereni, Gazit, Herzog, and others, 19 Feb., 20 March, 27 March, 13 May 1968, ISA, 7921/A-4; see also: *Maariv* (weekend), 13 Aug. 2004, p. 19; Statistical Abstract of the Occupied Territories, ISA, 4608/CL-2.
39. Summary of the number of people crossing from the West Bank to the East Bank, 11 July 1967, IDFA, 66/117/70; see also: Civil Administration Activity Report, 23 July 1967, ISA, 4095/HZ-6; Sweeny Report, 12 Sept. 1967, PRO, FO 961/26/104107; Refugee Statistics, Symms to Department of State, 3 Jan. 1968, USNA, Box 3049, REF ARAB, 1/1/68; Barbour to Rusk, 26 March 1968, USNA, Box 3056; Crawford to Moberly, 26 June 1968, PRO, FCO 17/217/104107; Emigration from the West Bank (Including East Jerusalem), 28 Aug. 1970, with the kind permission of Moshe Sasson.
40. Study on Emigrants Movement; August 1968, ISA, 7921/A-4; Kennedy to Sisco, 10 Aug. 1967, USNA, Box 3048, File REF ARAB 8/1/67; Arnon to Hillel, 14 Nov. 1967, ISA,

7921/A-4; Ben-Haim to Foreign Ministry, Jan. 1968, ISA, 4092/HZ-5; Battle to Rusk, 13 Feb. 1968, USNA, Box 3049.

41. Avner to Rivlin, 24 July 1967, ISA, 4088/HZ-6; Eshkol to Eban, 23 Aug. 1967, ISA, 7921/A-2; Hillel to Gazit, 3 Oct. 1967, ISA, 4096/HZ-4; see also: Yagar to Yaffe, 1 Aug. 1967, ISA, 6303/C-1.

42. Kahan to Minister of Justice Office, 4 Dec. 1967, 5602/C-4; Kidrom to Komei, 11 July 1967, ISA, 4089/HZ-2; Kidrom to Hillel, 1 Nov. 1967, ISA, 4092/HZ-5; Outline of Policy on the Refugee Question, 8 Sept. 1967, ISA, 4092/HZ-5; Komei to Director General, 2 July 1967, with the kind permission of Moshe Sasson; Foreign Ministry to Consulate in New York, 18 June 1967, ISA, 4088/HZ-7.

43. Hillel to Embassy in Washington, 29 Oct. 1967; discussion with Petra representatives; discussion with ICEM representatives, 29 Oct. 1967; Hillel to Eban, 30 Oct. 1967, ISA, 4091/HZ-11; see also: Maariv (weekend), 13 Aug. 2004, p. 18ff.; ISA, 385/HZ-18; 7499/C-26 (Jordan).

44. Hillel to Comey, 3 Dec. 1967, ISA, 4092/HZ-5; The Problems in the Gaza Strip, 21 Jan. 1968, IDFA, 128/2845/97; Brown, Personal Seal, p. 166ff.

45. Hiram to Directors General, 11 Dec. 1967, ISA, 8122/CL-6; Government resolution, 2 July 1967, ISA, 23 July 1967, ISA, 10136/C-4; 5 Nov. 1967, ISA, 10136/C-5.

46. Lewen to Moberly, 14 Dec. 1967, PRO, FCO 17/212/104225; Lapp to Chase, 8 July 1967, MECA, Jerusalem and the East Mission, GB 165-0161, Box 73, File 2; Campbell to Rusk, 29 July 1968; Barbour to Rusk, 1 Aug. 1968, USNA, Box 3049, REF ARAB 1/1/68; The Problems in the Gaza Strip, 21 Jan. 1968, IDFA, 128/2845/97; Government Announcement, 29 June 1967, ISA, 6309/C-3; Yaffe to Levavi, 28 June 1967, 7921/A-2.

47. Herzog diary, 13 Sept. 1967, with the kind permission of his daughter; Infiltration from the East Bank to the West, IDFA, 70/117/70; see also: Fauzi al-Asmar, To Be an Arab in Israel (in Hebrew) (Jerusalem: Shachak, 1975), p. 144; Ross to Komei, 21 Aug. 1967, ISA, 3982/HZ-17; Eitan Haber, Today War Will Break Out (in Hebrew) (Jerusalem: Idanim, 1987), p. 291ff.

48. Ben-Natan to Foreign Ministry, 25 June 1967; Rafael to Foreign Ministry, 26 June 1967, ISA, 4089/HZ-2; Comey to Foreign Ministry, 23 June 1967; Harman to Foreign Ministry, 23 and 26 June 1967; Remez to Foreign Ministry, 26 June 1967, ISA, 4088/HZ-10; Foreign Ministry to Narkis, 18 June 1967, ISA, 4097/HZ-8; Sapir to Foreign Ministry, 27 June 1967, ISA, 7921/A-2; Tkoa to Israeli Embassy in the U.S., 1 Aug. 1967, ISA, 4088/HZ-6; Comey to Eban, 4 Aug. 1967, YEA, copy in possession of the author.

49. Yaffe to Levavi, 28 June 1967, 7921/A-2 (Wilson); Ben-Horin to Director General, 1 Sept. 1967, ISA, 4088/HZ-7; Government decision, 10 Sept. 1967, ISA, 6304/C-9 (Beit Awa and Beit Mirsim); Foreign Ministry to Israel Embassy in Stockholm, 27 June 1967, ISA, 4088/HZ-10; Aspin to Moberly, 3 Aug. 1967 and Moberly to Brenchley, 5 Sept. 1967, PRO, FCO 17/212/40225.

50. Government resolution, 10 Sept. 1967, ISA, 6304/C-9 (Kalkila); Eshkol in the government, 8 Oct. 1967, ISA, 7921/A-6; see also: Government resolution, ISA, 6405/A-2 (aid to Jericho refugees); Eshkol with Vice President of the Red Cross, 22 Oct. 1967, ISA, 6303/C-5; Ha'aretz, 30 March 1967, p. 1; Hillel to Rafael, 16 Dec. 1967, ISA, 4088/HZ-2.

51. Eban to Eshkol, 12 July 1967, ISA, 7921/A-2; ISA, 6303/C-5; see also: The Times (London), 27 Sept. 1967, p. 9.

52. Wolf to Comey, 15 Aug. 1967, ISA, 4088/HZ-7.

53. Lamerhav, 1 Sept. 1967, p. 2; Maariv, 20 Aug. 1967, p. 3; Michael Shashar, The Seventh-Day War: The Diary of the Military Government in Judea and Samaria (June-December 1967) (in Hebrew) (Tel Aviv: Sifriyat Poalim, 1997), pp. 101, 148ff.

54. Government resolution, 2 July 1967; 6, 13, and 27 Aug. 1967; 5 and 10 Sept. 1967, with the kind permission of the Government Secretariat; Meeting summary, 4 July 1967, ISA, 6304/C-11; Tkoa to Dayan, 23 July 1967, ISA, 6301/C-1; Comey to Eshkol, 28 Dec. 1967, ISA, 4092/HZ-5; Tkoa to Raviv, 11 Aug. 1967, ISA, 4088/HZ-7; Hillel to Ganur (undated), ISA, 4088/HZ-5; Wolf to Comey, 15 Aug. 1967, ISA, 4088/HZ-7; Hughes to Rusk, 19 July 1967, USNA, Box 3048, File REF 7/1/67; Barbour to Department of State, 27 Nov. 1967, USNA, Box 3049, REF ARAB 10/1/67; Arab Refugees, 30 Nov. 1967, PRO, FCO 17/217/104107.

55. Ezer Weizman, For You the Sky, for You the Land (in Hebrew) (Tel Aviv: Sifriyat Maariv, 1975), p. 297.

CHAPTER 22: HAWKS AND DOVES

1. Rabin with Dayan, 21 July 1967 (erasure); see also: Weekly Activity Report on the Liberated Territories, 9/67; Rabin with Dayan, 28 and 31 July 1967, 12 Sept. 1967 ("occupied"); Rabin with Dayan, 2 and 10 Oct. 1967 ("liberated"), IDFA, 118/117/70; see also: Dayan in the government, 18 June 1967, ISA, 8164/A-7.
2. Shlomo Gazit, *Suddenly Trapped: 30 Years of Israeli Policy in the Territories* (in Hebrew) (Tel Aviv: Zmora-Bitan, 1999), p. 23; *Maariv,* 29 Sept. 1967, p. 21.
3. Brom and Ronen testimonies, KYA, Container 29, File 249; Military Government Report on the West Bank, 19 Sept. 1967, IDFA, 70/117/70; Rabin with Dayan, discussion brief, 31 July 1967, 118/117/70.
4. *Yediot Aharonot,* 11 June 1967, p. 9; see also: *Ha'aretz,* 27 July 1967, p. 2; *Davar,* 10 Nov. 1967, p. 4; *Maariv,* 16 June 1967, p. 17 ("do not leave"); General Order No. 9 (Central Command), 13 June 1967, AHA, PP16.
5. Meeting with the Prime Minister, 5 Dec. 1967, ISA, 7921/A-3.
6. General Order No. 9 (Central Command), 13 June 1967, AHA, PP16; Golda Meir, *My Life* (in Hebrew) (Tel Aviv: Sifriyat Maariv, 1975), p. 263; see also: *Maariv* (Sabbath), 16 June 1967, p. 1; Shabtai Teveth, *Exposed in the Turret* (in Hebrew) (Tel Aviv: Schocken, 1968), p. 41; Ben-Gurion to Ben Menachem, 7 June 1976, BGA; Yaakov Yadgar, *Our Story: The National Narrative in Israeli Press* (in Hebrew) (Haifa: Haifa University, 2004), p. 40ff.
7. *Maariv,* 22 Sept. 1967, p. 24; Moshe Shamir, *Natan Alterman: Poet as Leader* (in Hebrew) (Tel Aviv: Dvir, 1988), p. 159ff.; Dan Miron, *Touching the Essence* (in Hebrew) (Tel Aviv: Zmora-Bitan, 1991), p. 339ff.; see also: Yitzhak Tabenkin, *The Six-Day Lesson: The Settlement of an Undivided Palestine* (in Hebrew) (Tel Aviv: HaKibbutz HaMeuchad, 1971).
8. Begin to Herzog, 26 Dec. 1967, Yaacov Herzog estate, with the kind permission of his daughter; *Ha'aretz,* 10 Nov. 1967, p. 3; *LaMerhav,* 17 Nov. 1967, p. 2.
9. *Davar,* 10 Nov. 1967, p. 4 (Oz); Rosenthal et al., eds., *Levi Eshkol,* p. 569.
10. Letter to Penina Axelrod, 12 June 1967, with her kind permission; letter to Adir Zik, 3 Aug. 1967, with his kind permission; Schmuel Hugo Bergman, "Sanctification of God," *Shdemot,* issue 27, fall 1968, p. 7.
11. *Yediot Aharonot,* 9 Oct. 1967, p. 4; see also: *Ha'aretz,* 21 Sept. 1967, p. 11; *Maariv,* 25 Aug. 1967, p. 10; see also: Arieh Naor, *Greater Israel: Faith and Policy* (in Hebrew) (Haifa: Haifa University, Zmora-Bitan, 2001), p. 123ff.
12. ISA, 4096/HZ-5; ministerial committee decision, 16 Aug. 1967, 12252/GL-1; *Ha'aretz,* 15 Aug. 1967, p. 10; 21 Sept. 1967, p. 11; Aviad Ravitzky, *The Revealed End and the Jewish State: Messianism, Zionism, and Religious Radicalism in Israel* (in Hebrew) (Tel Aviv: Ofakim, 1993), p. 182; Naor, *Greater Israel,* p. 43ff.; see also: Nadav Shragai, *The Mount of Dispute: The Struggle for the Temple Mount, Jews and Muslims, Religion and Politics* (in Hebrew) (Jerusalem: Keter, 1995).
13. *Hayom,* 27 May 1968, p. 1; see also: Naor, *Greater Israel,* p. 158.
14. Eshkol with writers and professors, 18 Nov. 1967, ISA, 6303/C-4; *Ha'aretz,* 29 June 1967, p. 10 (Ravikovitch); 30 June 1967, p. 10 (Zach); 8 Sept. 1967, p. 10 (Orpaz); 8 Dec. 1967, p. 3 (Smilansky); see also: *Ha'aretz,* 17 Dec. 1967, p. 2 (responses); 25 Dec. 1967, p. 11; 15 Dec. 1967, p. 8 ("Security and Peace Yes—Annexation No").
15. *Yediot Aharonot,* 22 July 1967, p. 1 (Abie); Arnon to Jerusalem, 4 Dec. 1967, ISA, 3835/HZ-1; Yoram Rosler, ed., *Abie Nathan* (in Hebrew) (Tel Aviv: Sifriyat Poalim, 1998), p. 105ff; see also *Ha'aretz,* 22 Sept. 1967, p. 8 (Matzpen); 28 Sept. 1967, p. 7 (refugees).
16. Meeting with Prime Minister, 5 Dec. 1967, ISA, 7921/A-3.
17. Eshkol in the Knesset, 12 June 1967, *Knesset Minutes* (in Hebrew), vol. 49, p. 2331; Herzog diary, 12 June 1967, ISA, 4511/A-3.
18. Herzog diary, 21 Aug. 1967, ISA, 4511/A-3; Eitan Haber, *Today War Will Break Out* (in Hebrew) (Jerusalem: Idanim, 1987), p. 261; Yadin diary, 8 June 1967, ISA, 1403/P-16.
19. Herzog diary, 15 June 1967, with the kind permission of his daughter; Johnson with Harman, 7 Feb. 1968, FRUS, vol. XX, Doc. No. 73.
20. Moshe Dayan, *Milestones* (in Hebrew) (Jerusalem: Idanim, 1982), vol. II, p. 493.
21. Herzog diary, 11 July 1968, ISA, 4511/A-4; 14 Aug. 1967, with the kind permission of his daughter.
22. *Ha'aretz,* 23 July 1967, p. 7; 13 Oct. 1967, p. 2; see also: Barbour to Department of State, 21 Aug. 1968, USNA, Box 2227, File POL 15-1.
23. Shlomit Levi and Elihu Katz, "Public Opinion and the Mood in the Six-Day War" (in

Hebrew) in *Six Days: Thirty Years: A New Look at the Six-Day War*, ed. Asher Sashar (Tel Aviv: Am Oved, 1999), p. 253.

24. Meir, *My Life*, p. 264ff.; see also: *Ha'aretz*, 18 June 1967, p. 3; Kol to Eshkol, 6 Sept. 1967, ISA, 6301/C-1; Rabin with Dayan, 15 Dec. 1967, IDFA, 118/117/70.

25. Government meeting, 14 Dec. 1967, Yaacov Herzog estate, with the kind permission of his daughter.

26. Barbour to Department of State, 1 May 1968, USNA, Box 2227, File POL 15-1.

27. Naomi Kies, "The Effect of Public Policy on Public Opinion: Israel, 1967–1974," *State, Government and International Relations* (in Hebrew), issue 8, Sept. 1975, p. 36; *Ha'aretz*, 18 July 1967, p. 1.

28. Eshkol with Rabin, 24 May 1968, ISA, 7934/A-4; *Ha'aretz*, 19 June 1967, p. 12; see also: Prime Minister's Office announcement, 28 Nov. 1967, ISA, 6303/C-4; *Davar*, 7 June 1967, p. 2; *Maariv*, 11 June 1967, p. 1.

29. Letter to Adir Zik, 8 Oct. 1967, with his kind permission; Eshkol in government meeting, 31 Dec. 1967, Yaacov Herzog estate, with the kind permission of his daughter.

CHAPTER 23: STARTING OVER

1. *Ha'aretz*, 21 June 1967, p. 11.

2. Letter to Chaim Haskal, 16 July 1967, with his kind permission; Eban in the Knesset, 31 July 1967, *Knesset Minutes* (in Hebrew), vol. 49, p. 2761; letter to Vardit and Adir Zik, 7 June 1967, with his kind permission.

3. Ministry of Education Notice, 6 Sept. 1967, ISA, 13173/CL-2.

4. *Maariv*, 17 Aug. 1967, p. 3; Sapir in the government, 15 Jan. 1968 (minutes); Lev Louis Greenberg, "The Israeli Labor Movement in Crisis, 1957–1970: The Political Economy of the Ties Between Mapai, the Histadrut, and the State" (in Hebrew) (diss., Tel Aviv University, 1991), appendix.

5. D. Teneh, "Building and Populating Apartments in 1967," *Economics Quarterly* (in Hebrew), vol. 16, Book 57–58, Aug. 1968, p. 162ff.

6. Sapir in the government, 15 Jan. 1968 (minutes); Greenberg, "The Israeli Labor Movement in Crisis," appendix; A. Halperin, "Recession and Recovery in the Economy," *Economics Quarterly* (in Hebrew), vol. 14, Book 56, Feb. 1968, p. 293ff.; Kol to Eshkol, 12 Sept. 1967 (oil and other resources in Sinai), YEA, copy in possession of the author; The Second Arab-Israeli War, 1967, the Economic Aftermath, 30 October 1967, PRO, FCO 17/568/104225.

7. *Maariv*, 17 Aug. 1967, p. 3; Sapir in the government, 15 Jan. 1968 (minutes); Greenberg, "The Israeli Labor Movement in Crisis," appendix; meeting with Prime Minister, 5 Dec. 1967, ISA, 7921/A-3; *Ha'aretz*, 3 Oct. 1967, p. 11; Central Bureau of Statistics, *Israel Yearbook* (in Hebrew), no. 20, 1969, p. 42.

8. *Ha'aretz*, 3 Oct. 1967, p. 11; Central Bureau of Statistics, *Israel Yearbook* (in Hebrew), no. 20, 1969, p. 42.

9. Galili in the Knesset, 13 Nov. 1967, *Knesset Minutes* (in Hebrew), vol. 50, p. 125; see also: *Yediot Aharonot*, 25 Aug. 1967, p. 5; see also: Galili to Sapir, 31 Oct. 1967, ISA, 4604/CL-1.

10. *Ha'aretz*, 3 Sept. 1967, pp. 9–10 (computers); *Maariv*, 21 Nov. 1967 (pill); *Ha'aretz*, 25 Dec. 1967, p. 8 (phones).

11. *Ha'aretz*, 4 Sept. 1967, p. 4.

12. *Maariv* (Days and Nights), 4 Oct. 1967, p. 8; 18 Oct. 1967, p. 11.

13. *Ha'aretz*, 11 June 1967, p. 2; *LaMerhav*, 11 June 1967, p. 2.

14. Central Bureau of Statistics, *Israel Yearbook* (in Hebrew), no. 18, 1967, p. 40; Reuven Avinoam, ed., *In Memoriam: The Lives and Deaths of the Casualties in the Wars of Israel from the Beginning of the Six-Day War until the General Memorial Day 5729* (in Hebrew) (Tel Aviv: Ministry of Defense, 1971).

15. Aviezer Golan and Ami Shamir, *The Book of Heroism, June 1967* (in Hebrew) (The Journalists Society and the World Alliance of Bergen-Belsen Survivors, 1968).

16. Laslau and Brom testimonies, KYA, Container 29, File 249; see also: Alon Gan, "The Discourse That Died? 'Discourse Culture' as an Attempt to Define a Special Identity for the Second Generation on the Kibbutzim" (in Hebrew) (diss., Tel Aviv University, 2002), p. 120.

17. Letter to Adir Zik, 27 July 1967, with his kind permission.

18. Yair Beumel, "The Israeli Establishment's Attitude Toward Israeli Arabs: Policy, Princi-

ples and Actions: The Second Decade, 1958–1968" (in Hebrew) (diss., Haifa University, 2002), pp. BB, AA.

19. Conditions of Arabs in Israel and of Jews in Arab States, UNA, DAG-1/2.3, Box 246, File 1065.

20. David Grossman, *Present Absentees* (in Hebrew) (Tel Aviv: HaKibbutz HaMeuchad, 1992).

21. Simon N. Herman, *Jewish Identity,: A Social Psychological Perspective* (Jerusalem: HaSifriya HaTzionit, 1979).

22. ISA, 4092/HZ-6; see also: 4089/HZ-8 (distinguished); Eshkol in the Knesset, 22 Jan. 1968, *Knesset Minutes* (in Hebrew), vol. 50, p. 771; Dovkin to Eshkol, 26 July 1967, ISA, 6301/C-1 (4); *Ha'aretz*, 4 Aug. 1967, p. 3; see also: *Al HaMishmar*, 30 Nov. 1970, p. 4.

23. Shneor Zalman Avramov and Akiva Govrin in the Knesset, 5 July 1967, *Knesset Minutes* (in Hebrew), vol. 49, p. 2509ff.; meeting with Prime Minister, 5 Dec. 1967, ISA, 7921/A-3.

24. Herzog diary, 7 Sept. 1967, ISA, 4511/A-3.

25. Jewish Agency, *21 Years of Immigration and Absorption* (in Hebrew), p. 4ff.; ISA, 3497/C-16.

26. *21 Years of Immigration and Absorption,* 1969, ISA 6303/a-6

27. *Maariv,* 25 June 1967, p. 2; 16 Oct. 1967, p. 11; *Knesset Minutes* (in Hebrew), vol. 50, p. 344ff., 6 Dec. 1967; Eban to Security Cabinet, 23 Aug. 1967, YTA, Unit 15, Container 54, File 4; ISA, 4095/HZ-12; 4096/HZ-13; 4095/HZ-17; Conditions of Arabs in Israel and of Jews in Arab States, UNA, DAG-1/2.3, Box 136, File 1065; U Thant with Rafael and others, 24 Aug, 1967, UNA, SG (Middle East Crisis), 13/12/01/NH; Goldberg to U Thant, 19 Jan. and 7 May, 1968, UNA, SG, S-0311-004, Box 4, File 14.

28. *Yediot Aharonot,* 28 Nov. 1967, p. 2; *Knesset Minutes* (in Hebrew), vol. 50, p. 236ff., 27 Nov. 1967.

29. Financial Affairs, ISA, 6303/C-6; see also: government meeting, 18 June 1967, ISA, 8164/A-7.

30. *Yediot Aharonot,* 2 June 1967, p. 6; *Ha'aretz,* 14 July 1967, p. 3; 16 July 1967, p. 8; Leon Uris, "The Third Temple," in William Stevenson, *Strike Zion* (New York: Bantam Books, 1967), p. 119ff.

31. Letter to friends in Israel (undated), ISA, 6301/C-1; see also: Eli Lederhendler, ed., *The Six-Day War and World Jewry* (Bethesda: University Press of Maryland, 2000).

32. *The Washington Post,* 9 July 1967, p. B1.

33. Ben-Gurion to Trim, 6 June 1967; Trim to Ben-Gurion, 19 July 1967, BGA; Ben-Gurion to Dayan, 15 June 1967, BGA, see also: *Yediot Aharonot,* 13 Aug. 1967, p. 7; Erwin Moskowitz to Ben-Gurion, 8 Oct. 1967, BGA.

34. Harman to Herzog, 29 Sept. 1967, and Yaffe to Harman, 13 Oct. 1967, ISA, 6380/C-25.

35. *Yediot Aharonot,* 6 Dec. 1967, p. 9; David Ben-Gurion, *The Newly Emerging State of Israel* (in Hebrew) (Tel Aviv: Am Oved, 1969), p. 837ff.

36. *Yediot Aharonot,* 28 Nov. 1967, p. 2.

CHAPTER 24: ABSALOM DAYS

1. Kol to Eshkol, 7 Nov. 1967 and more, ISA, 6380/C-4; Avigur to Eshkol, 13 Dec. 1967, ISA, 6303/C-1; see also: *Davar,* 16 Feb. 1968, p. 4; *Yediot Aharonot,* 2 Nov. 1967, p. 4; 15 Nov. 1967, p. 3; 30 Nov. 1967, p. 3; *Maariv* (Days and Nights), 13 Nov. 1967, p. 16; *Maariv,* 17 Nov. 1967, p. 2ff.; 29 Nov. 1967, p. 17; *Ha'aretz,* 16 Nov. 1967, p. 1; 30 Nov. 1967, p. 2.

2. Prime Minister's Office, Propaganda Center, *Know What to Reply* (in Hebrew), Fourth Book, June 1968, p. 3.

3. Report on Telephone Conversation, 4 Oct. 1967; Anderson with Eban, McPherson to Rostow, and Rostow to Johnson, 10 Oct. 1967; Rostow to Johnson, 31 Oct. 1967, LBJL, NSF Country File, Middle East, Box 113; Rusk to Johnson, 6 Oct. 1967, FRUS, vol. XIX, p. 877ff.

4. Sydney D. Bailey, *The Making of Resolution 242* (Dordrecht: Martinus Hijhoff, 1985).

5. Eshkol and others in the Knesset, 13 Nov. 1967, *Knesset Minutes* (in Hebrew), vol. 50, p. 120ff.; see also: Yaffe to Harman, 4 Dec. 1967, ISA, 7921/A-3; Galili to Eshkol, 30 Oct. 1967, ISA, 7231/A-1; resolution draft, 17 Nov. 1967, ISA, 7934/A-4.

6. Tito Proposal, 5 Sept. 1967, USNA, Box 1800; Remez to Lurie, 1 Nov. 1967, ISA, 4510/A-16.

7. Rostow to Johnson, 26 May 1967, FRUS, vol. XIX, p. 146; Krim to Rostow, 10 Nov. 1966, and Birdsall to Krim, 2 Nov. 1966, LBJL, Gen Co 303 1/1/68, Box 75; Nasser to

Johnson etc., 9 Dec. 1967, LBJL, NSF Special Head of State, Box 55; Birdsall to Johnson, 28 June 1968, 19 July 1968, etc., LBJL, GEN ND 19/CO 1-6, Box 198.

8. Eshkol in the Foreign Affairs and Security Committee, 25 June 1968, ISA, 7921/A-6; U.S. Interest Section to Department of State, 11 Sept. 1967, FRUS, vol. XIX, Doc. No. 434.

9. Herzog to Eshkol, 21 Nov. 1967; Two Meetings with Charles, on the morning of 19 Nov. and on the morning of 20 Nov. 1967; "Special section on Charles, dictated on 3 Nov. 1967," all in Yaacov Herzog estate, with the kind permission of his daughter.

10. Discussion in the Ma'arach political committee, 14 March 1968; 20 April 1968, discussion briefs in possession of the author.

11. Eshkol at the Foreign Affairs and Defense Committee, 12 May 1968, ISA, 7921/A-6; see also: Eshkol with General Staff, 5 Dec. 1967, 7921/A-3.

12. Purposes of the meeting, 25 April 1968; Eban in the political committee, 19 May 1968, ISA, 7934/A-4; Herzog in the security cabinet, 8 May 1968 and other reports; Eban in the government, 10 Dec. 1967, Yaacov Herzog estate, with the kind permission of his daughter.

13. Helms to Johnson, 8 June 1968, FRUS, vol. XX, Doc. 187; Michael Bar Zohar, *Zaphenath Paneah: The Life and Times of a Jewish Prince* (in Hebrew) (Tel Aviv: Yediot Aharonot, 2003), p. 288.

14. Eshkol in the political committee, 3 June 1968, ISA, 7921/A-13.

15. Herzog diary, 29 Aug. 1968, ISA, 4511/A-4; Bar Zohar, *Zaphenath Paneah*, p. 284; see also: Eban on Goldberg meeting with Hussein, 4 Nov. 1967, ISA, 4510/A-16; Dayan in the Labor Party in the Knesset, 18 June 1968, YTA, Unit 15, Series C, Container 3, File 2.

16. Memorandum of Conversation, 24 Oct. 1967, FRUS, vol. XIX, Doc. No. 488.

17. Evron, Harman, and Patir to Foreign Ministry, 11 June 1967, ISA, 4079/HZ-26; *Newsweek,* 19 June 1967, pp. 10, 13; 26 June 1967, p. 9; Rusk to Barbour, 16 June 1967, FRUS, vol. XIX, p. 439.

18. Harman to Foreign Ministry, 12, 13, and 16 June 1967, ISA, 4079/HZ-26.

19. Ron to Rabin, 16 June 1967, ISA, 4079/HZ-26.

20. Harman to Foreign Ministry, 13, 16, 18, 19, 20, and 28 June 1967; Rabin to Harman, 29 June 1967, ISA, 4079/HZ-26; see also: FRUS, vol. XIX, p. 360ff.

21. Evron to Foreign Ministry, 30 Aug. 1967, ISA, 4079/HZ-26; Payment of U.S. Liberty Claims, USNA, PO/ISR/Box 271, PS 8-4; see also: Evron to Foreign Ministry, 8 March 1968, ISA, 4079/HZ-3.

22. Rabin to Foreign Ministry, 8 March 1968, ISA, 7938/A-11; see also: ISA, 4079/HZ-27.

23. Harman to Yaffe, 13 Dec. 1967; Harman to Foreign Ministry, 20 and 21 Dec. 1967, ISA, 7232/A-7; Arnon to Eitan, 10 Aug. 1967; Ariel to Foreign Ministry, 18 Sept. 1967, ISA, 3979/HZ-9; Evron to Foreign Ministry, 14 Aug. 1967, ISA, 3980/HZ-2.

24. Eshkol with the Movement for Greater Israel, 12 Nov. 1967, ISA, 7920/A-7.

25. Bitan to Israeli Embassy, 29 Nov. 1967, ISA, 7938/A-11; McPherson to President, 31 Oct. 1967, FRUS, vol. XIX, p. 962.

26. Eshkol with Rabin, 24 May 1968, ISA, 7938/A-11.

27. Eshkol with Johnson, 7–8 Jan. 1967, FRUS, vol. XX, Doc. Nos. 39, 40, 41; Eitan Haber, *Today War Will Break Out* (in Hebrew) (Jerusalem: Idanim, 1987), p. 305ff.

28. Rostow to Johnson, 5 Jan. 1968, FRUS, vol. XX, Doc. No. 33; ISA, 188/P-8; Avner Cohen, *Israel and the Bomb* (in Hebrew) (Tel Aviv: Schocken, 2000), p. 380ff.

29. Evron to Foreign Ministry, 15 March 1968; Yaffe to Rabin, 31 March 1968, ISA, 7938/A-11.

30. Gvati diary, 12 June 1967, YTA, Unit 15, Container 12, File 02; Raanan Weitz, *The Great Plow and the Planning Map: A Look at the History of Settlement in the State of Israel* (in Hebrew) (author's estate, 2003), p. 91; Yechiel Admoni, *A Decade of Judgment: Settlement over the Green Line, 1967–1977* (in Hebrew) (Tel Aviv: HaKibbutz HaMeuchad, 1992), pp. 11, 18ff.

31. Yigal Allon in an interview with Reudor Manor, sixth meeting, p. 18, ISA, 5001/A-19.

32. Government resolution, 27 Aug. 1967, ISA, 7920/A-7; Alei Golan (Ben-Yehuda Diary) (in Hebrew), issue no. 32, 17 July 1968; Yigal Allon in an interview with Reudor Manor, sixth meeting, p. 18, ISA, 5001/A-19; Admoni, *A Decade of Judgment,* p. 23ff.; see also: *Ha'aretz,* 4 July 1967, p. 11 (animals and abandoned fields).

33. Uzai to Eshkol, 29 Aug. 1967, ISA, 7920/A-7; see also: government resolution 866, 1 Oct. 1967, with the kind permission of the government secretariat; Prime Minister's Blessing, 23 Oct. 1967, ISA, 7920/A-6; Barbour to Department of State, 13 Sept. 1967,

USNA, Box 1800, File POL 27; Aharon Shai, "The Fate of the Abandoned Arab Villages in the State of Israel on the Eve of the Six-Day War and Afterward" (in Hebrew), *Katedra*, no. 105, Tishrei 5763, p. 168ff.

34. Yaffe to Shapira, 27 Sept. 1967, ISA, 7921/A-3.
35. Meron to Yaffe, 18 Sept. 1967, ISA, 7921/A-3.
36. Harman to Foreign Ministry, 25 Sept. 1967; Foreign Ministry to Harman, 26 Sept. 1967, ISA, 7938/A-10.
37. Galili to Eshkol, 25 Aug. 1968, YEA; *Maariv*, 24 Oct. 1967, p. 13 (Mapam); strongholds in the administered territories, 27 Jan. 1968, ISA, 7920/A-7; see also: Yehuda Harel to Sapir, 25 March 1968, ISA, 4602/CL-1.
38. Yigal Allon in an interview with Reudor Manor, seventh meeting, p. 3, ISA, 5001/A-19; Eshkol with the Gush Etzion people, 22 Sept. 1967, ISA, 7920/A-7; see also: Gush Etzion Children Society to Eshkol, 17 Aug. 1967, ISA, 6301/C-1 (6); Hazani to Eshkol, 29 Sept. 1967, YEA, copy in possession of the author; Admoni, *A Decade of Judgment*, p. 51ff.; Dale to Atherton, 29 Sept. 1967, USNA, Box 3049, REF 9/1/67.
39. *Maariv*, 27 Sept. 1967, p. 9; 20 Oct. 1967, p. 11; *Ha'aretz*, 29 Sept. 1967, p. 2; 2 Oct. 1967, p. 8; Meron to Yaffe, 18 Sept. 1967, ISA, 7921/A-3.
40. Weitz to Eshkol, 29 Sept. 1967, YEA, copy in possession of the author.
41. *Koteret Rashit*, 16 May 1984, p. 13.
42. Tamir to Eshkol, 18 Oct. 1967, ISA, 6301/C-1; meeting with Prime Minister, 5 Dec. 1967, ISA, 7921/A-3; government resolution, 12 May 1968, ISA, 4602/C-1.
43. Yigal Allon in an interview with Reudor Manor, sixth meeting, p. 18, ISA, 5001/A-19; see also: Gazit to Franko, 26 Feb. 1968; Hillel Dan to Prime Minister's office, 26 Feb. 1968; Agmon to Prime Minister's office director, 13 March 1968; Yaffe to Shragai, 3 June 1968—all YEA, copy in possession of the author.
44. Jaabari to Eshkol, 7 May 1968, YEA, copy in possession of the author; Hebron settlers to Dayan, 21 Aug. 1968; Dayan to Eshkol, 22 Aug. 1968, YEA, copy in possession of the author.
45. Eshkol with the Greater Israel Movement, 12 Nov. 1967, ISA, 7920/A-7; *Ha'aretz*, 21 May 1968, p. 2.
46. Statement of Opinion, 12 May 1968, YEA, copy in possession of the author.
47. Strongholds in the administered territories, 27 Jan. 1968, ISA, 7920/A-7; see also: Akiva Eldar and Idith Zertal, *Lords of the Land: The Settlers and the State of Israel, 1967–2004* (in Hebrew) (Tel Aviv: Dvir, 2004); Gershom Gorenberg, *Accidental Empire: Israel and the Birth of the Settlements, 1967–1977* (New York: Times Books, 2006).
48. Minister of Labor proposal, 3 Nov. 1967, ISA, 6253/C-11; see also: Elisha Efrat, *A Geography of the Occupation* (in Hebrew) (Tel Aviv: Carmel, 2002).
49. Barbour to Department of State, 13 Sept. 1967, USNA, Box 1800, File POL 27; see also: Hall to Department of State, 30 Aug. 1967, USNA, Box 1800.
50. *Ha'aretz*, 14 Aug. 1967, p. 2.
51. Dayan in government meeting, 26 Dec. 1967; resolution proposal, 31 Dec. 1967, Yaacov Herzog estate, with the kind permission of his daughter; Dayan in the Labor Party, 18 June 1968, YTA, Unit 15.
52. Moshe Dayan, *New Map Different Relations* (in Hebrew) (Tel Aviv: Sifriyat Maariv, 1969), p. 19ff.; Dayan in the Ma'arach political committee, 3 June 1968, discussion brief in possession of the author.
53. IDF Spokesman data, IDFA, 290/581/75; see also: Dayan in the Knesset, 24 Jan. 1968, *Knesset Minutes* (in Hebrew), vol. 50, p. 803.
54. *Maariv*, 25 Sept. 1967, p. 1; *Ha'aretz*, 8 Oct. 1967, p. 4.
55. *Ha'aretz*, 22 Oct. 1967, p. 1; condolence letters, ISA, 6304/C-5; Eshkol at the editors committee, 24 Oct. 1967, ISA, 7920/A-8; Eshkol in the Foreign Affairs and Defense Committee, 29 Nov. 1967, ISA, 7921/A-6.
56. Yaacov Herzog estate, with the kind permission of his daughter; Eshkol in the government meeting, 31 March 1968, ISA, 7921/A-6; Ze'ev Schiff and Eitan Haber, *Lexicon of Israeli Security* (in Hebrew) (Tel Aviv: Zmora-Bitan, Modan, 1976), pp. 39, 143, 277; Haber, *Today War Will Break Out*, p. 338ff.; see also: *Ha'aretz* (supplement), 6 Feb. 1998, p. 15ff.
57. Letter to Adir Zik, 8 Oct. 1967, with his kind permission; Edith Ezrachi, 2 April 1967; 9 April 1968, with the kind permission of her son.

58. Edith Ezrachi to the Duvinskis, 6 June 1968, with the kind permission of her son.
59. *Nitzotz*, 28 April 1968, p. 2 (prefer small); Ben-Gurion to Dov Golan, 1 Oct. 1967; to Sarah Ozen, 23 Oct. 1967 (anywhere); to Tebenkin, 3 Sept. 1967; to Selfter, 2 Oct. 1967, to Tebenkin, 24 Oct. 1967 (denies), BGA.
60. Amos Elon, *The Israelis: Founders and Builders* (in Hebrew) (Tel Aviv: Adam, 1981), p. 21.
61. Ben-Gurion diary, 25 Nov. 1967 (not their country); Ben-Gurion to Ben-Meir, 16 Dec. 1967 (doubts), to Ilan Cohen, 1 Nov. 1967 (biology); to Zvi Zehavi, 23 Oct. 1967 (converted), BGA.
62. Yosef Weitz, *My Diary* (in Hebrew), vol. VI (Tel Aviv: Masada, 1973), pp. 261, 266ff. (tree), 382 (Eshkol).

ACKNOWLEDGMENTS

This book is the outcome of five years of research and writing that led me to some twenty-five historical archives in Israel, the United States, and England. I thank all of the archives, which are named in the endnotes. The great drama that occurred in Israel in 1967 yielded numerous books and studies that were of help to me, and I owe thanks to their authors. I also made use of the daily newspapers, in particular *Ha'aretz*, *Yediot Aharonot*, and *Maariv*. Together they form a sort of collective diary of the Israelis who read them.

Alongside the thousands of archival documents I reviewed, there is extensive documentation that is not yet available for research and may never be. It is therefore difficult to answer some of the central questions. In order to correctly assess the events of 1967 one needs to know, for example, whether Israel already possessed nuclear weapons; if so, which of the government ministers knew about it; and how, if at all, this affected their decision to go to war. The material that could answer these questions is likely being kept in an archive somewhere; there is some material in the hands of researchers and journalists, but its publication is forbidden by court orders, among other factors. It is very difficult to understand the apparatus of Israel's occupation of the Palestinian territories without examining the Shabak archives, but they too are sealed and may never be opened. An accurate picture of the country's foreign relations would require a review of Mossad documents; their archives are also sealed. The IDF allows access only to a small portion of its archived material. The Israel State Archives also contain classified files, including the minutes of government meetings and some Knesset committees. The same is true of other archives, including some in the United States and England. Israel has adopted a fairly liberal policy toward declassification of official documents, but its decisions are often shaped by arbitrariness and obduracy. Hence the need to climb up into attics and down into basements of people's homes, which often reveal treasures.

This book is also based to a great extent on unarchived material of inestimable value. Shira Herzog granted me access to the estate of her father, Yaacov Herzog, the director general of the prime minister's office. He documented dozens of government meetings and left records of his conversations with King Hussein. Knesset member Yitzhak Herzog made papers available from the estate of his father, Chaim Herzog, the first military governor of the West Bank. Meir Amit, former head of the Mossad, gave me a copy of the report on his covert trip to Washington on the eve of the war, among other documents. Ambassador Moshe Sasson provided transcripts of his conversations with dozens of Palestinian leaders. David Harman, the son of Ambassador Avraham Harman, allowed me to quote from extended interviews recorded with his father. I also received extremely valuable material from Meron Benvenisti, former deputy mayor of Jerusalem, and from Elad Peled, commander of the National Defense College. A small part of the material, including extracts of government meetings and other discussions, was provided anonymously. I am grateful for the generosity and helpfulness of so many people, without whom I could not have written this book.

In the United States I spoke with John Hadden, who was the CIA station chief in Israel. Dr. Mathilde Krim, who knew President Johnson, granted me two interviews at her home in Manhattan. Yoav Karni spoke at my request with David Ginsburg, an attorney in Washington, D.C.

I received further documentary material, oral information, and useful advice from Gil Aldema, Dan Almagor, Rahel Barkai, Nahum Barnea, Avner Cohen, Hillel Cohen, Zvika Dror, Israel Ehrlich, Yuval Elizur, Charles Enderlin, Yitzhak Gal-Nur, Yossi Goldstein, David Golomb, Yehuda Harel, Michael Karpin, Amos Kenan, Ephraim Kishon, Avraham Kushnir, Yehuda Litani, Sarah Ossetzky-Lazar, Danny Rubinstein, Avri Sela, Anat Seltzer, Hagar Sereni-Konfino, Avraham (Pachi) Shapira, and Gil Shiva. A dozen people named after Yehiam Weitz were kind enough to respond to questions both in writing and verbally. I thank them all.

I spent many hours in the kitchen of Miriam Eshkol, Prime Minister Levi Eshkol's widow; I enjoyed her company and gained weight from her excellent cheesecake. Her memory, wisdom, and historical analyses taught me more than many documents ever could. I also visited Yonina Ben-Or, the widow of Arieh Ben-Or, the pilot who was killed on the Golan Heights; I deeply appreciate her willingness to share her story with me.

Profound and special gratitude is due to Yehoshua Bar-Dayan, who allowed me to use his war diary, an extraordinarily powerful document; his voice is the voice of man at war.

A series of people, mainly in the United States, responded to my request and dug through old chests to fish out personal letters they had received in 1967 from friends and relatives in Israel. Much of what I know about the lives of Israelis that year, what they thought and felt, I gleaned from these letters, close to five hundred of them. I acknowledge with sorrow Adir Zik, who died after entrusting me with thick bundles of correspondence he received during his studies in Los Angeles. I owe thanks to Ilan Ezrachi, who allowed me to quote from his mother's letters; to Asher Knafo from Ashdod; to Ruth and Haim Haskal and to Penina Axelrod from Boston, as well as to Anat Perlmuter-Shabo from Jerusalem. Some of the people who gave me their letters asked to remain unnamed, and I thank them too.

I was blessed with wise and kind research assistants. Omri Kaplan-Feuereisen assisted me during the first stages of my work, Avner Inbar during the second half, and Ilan Moradi in between. I thank them for their diligence, precision, patience, and friendship. Avi Katzman edited the Hebrew manuscript with his usual meticulousness, knowledge, and wisdom, and rescued me from several pitfalls. I acknowledge gratefully Deborah Harris, my agent and friend. I also owe thanks to the people at *Ha'aretz* for their patience and support.

Most of the years when I worked on this book were years of terror and oppression, both extremely cruel. Again and again my work was interrupted by the wail of ambulance sirens, rushing to the scene of a terrorist attack, followed by dreadful news. Sitting at my computer, near a window looking out toward the Old City and the Dead Sea, I followed the progress of the ugly cement security wall as it crawled along the hilltops, dividing Jerusalem in the spirit of Moshe Dayan's words, spoken as early as June 15, 1967: "Up to here—you. From here on—us." It was not easy to work against this backdrop, and I often had the sense that I was writing about the year that had sparked all this misery. But just as often, I thought about Gabriel Stern, a journalist and a relentless optimist, who believed in goodness until the end of his days, despite everything. After my father was killed in the 1948 War of Independence, Gabriel Stern was like a father to me; this book commemorates him. I dedicate it to Itai Abera, who is as precious to me as a son. In many respects I wrote this book for him and for his generation, in the hope that they will not live through another war.

INDEX

ABOUT THE AUTHOR

Tom Segev is a columnist for *Ha'aretz*, Israel's leading newspaper, and the author of three now-classic works on the history of Israel—*1949: The First Israelis*; *The Seventh Million: The Israelis and the Holocaust*; and *One Palestine, Complete: Jews and Arabs Under the British Mandate*, which was a *New York Times* Editors' Choice for 2000. He lives in Jerusalem.